Mary Gilmore's life spanned almost a century of Australian history. She lived for ninety-seven years and this selection of her letters covers a period of almost seventy years, encompassing the social, political and literary scene of the period when Australia was changing from colony to nation.

The letters contain perceptive judgements of indigenous literary talent as it was emerging; they contain reflections on the pioneer past as she herself had experienced it and reflections on the contemporary political and social environment. Sometimes they express her anger at injustice and deprivation wherever it occurred—in the treatment of the Aborigines, the returned soldiers, women, children, old people, the sick. As she said, 'There was no hunted one with whom I did not run'. Above all, the letters reflect her immense patriotism and love for her country, her enormous hopes for its future; and they give, often unintentionally, fascinating glimpses of events in which she participated—for example, the New Australia venture in Paraguay—events which are now part of our established history.

Louis Kahan's drawing of Mary Gilmore is reproduced on the jacket with permission from the artist and Meanjin.

LETTERS OF MARY GILMORE

LETTERS OF MARY GILMORE

selected and edited by

W. H. WILDE and T. INGLIS MOORE

MELBOURNE UNIVERSITY PRESS

1980

First published 1980
Typeset by The Dova Type Shop, Melbourne

Wilke and Company Limited, Clayton, Victoria for
Melbourne University Press, Carlton, Victoria 3053
U.S.A. and Canada: International Scholarly Book Services, Inc.,
Box 555, Forest Grove, Oregon 97116
Great Britain, Europe, the Middle East, Africa and the Caribbean:
International Book Distributors Ltd (Prentice-Hall International)
66 Wood Lane End, Hemel Hempstead,
Hertfordshire HP2 4RG, England

This book is copyright. Apart from any fair dealing for the
purposes of private study, research, criticism or review, as
permitted under the Copyright Act, no part may be reproduced
by any process without written permission. Enquiries should
be made to the publisher.

© in this collection William H. Wilde and Pacita Alexander 1980
© in the letters The Public Trustee in and for the State of New South Wales 1962

National Library of Australia Cataloguing-in-Publication data
Gilmore, Dame Mary Jean, 1865-1962.
   Letters of Mary Gilmore.
   Index
   ISBN 0 522 84201 1
   1. Gilmore, Dame Mary Jean, 1865-1962. 2. Poets,
Australian—Correspondence. I. Wilde, William
Henry, joint ed. II. Moore, Tom Inglis, 1901-1978,
joint ed. III. Title.
A821'.2

Contents

Preface	ix
Foreword	xv
A Biographical Note	xxi
Abbreviations	xxix
THE LETTERS	1
A Note on Style	2
Appendix: People, Publications, Places and Events mentioned in the Letters	373
Index	403

Illustrations

Mary as a little girl	facing	34
'Billy' Lane, the 'New Australia' leader, in 1894		34
Mary in 1899		34
Will and Mary with their son		34
The *Royal Tar* at Port Adelaide		35
A typical street in 'New Australia', Paraguay		35
A. G. Stephens		66
Dowell O'Reilly		66
Vance Palmer		66
A. H. Chisholm		66
Mary in 1927		67
R. D. FitzGerald		67
Nettie and Vance Palmer with their family		67
George Robertson		130
Hugh McCrae		130
H. M. Green		130
Frank Dalby Davison and his family		130
John K. Ewers		131
Dr George Mackaness		131
Lionel Lindsay		131
Tom Inglis Moore		131
Miles Franklin		162
Mary E. Fullerton		162
R. G. Howarth		162

Colin Simpson	162
The *Australian Battle Cry*	163
No Foe shall gather our Harvest	226
The sheep dog memorial at Wagga Wagga	227
Kenneth Slessor	258
Roland Robinson	258
Nan McDonald	258
Douglas Stewart	258
On the way to her 90th birthday party with Namatjira	259
Mary's flat at Kings Cross	322
At work in the flat	322
Judith Wright with her daughter Meredith	323
Katharine Susannah Prichard	323
Dame Mary at home	323
Drinking Yerba Maté South American style	354
Mary as the May Queen in 1961	355

Acknowledgements for the use of photographs are due as follows: to Pacita Alexander for Vance Palmer, and the sheep dog memorial; to the Australian Information Service for Miles Franklin; to John Fairfax Limited for Dame Mary at home, drinking Yerba Maté, and as the May Queen; to George Ferguson for George Robertson; to the Mitchell Library, Sydney, for Mary as a little girl and Mary in 1899; to the National Library of Australia for 'Billy' Lane, A. G. Stephens, Dowell O'Reilly, A. H. Chisholm, Mary in 1927, R. D. FitzGerald, Nettie and Vance Palmer, Hugh McCrae, H. M. Green, Frank Dalby Davison, John K. Ewers, Dr George Mackaness, Lionel Lindsay, Tom Inglis Moore, Mary E. Fullerton, R. G. Howarth, Colin Simpson, the *Australian Battle Cry*, *No Foe shall gather our Harvest*, Kenneth Slessor, Roland Robinson, Nan McDonald, Douglas Stewart, Mary with Namatjira, Mary at work in her flat, and Katharine Susannah Prichard; to News Limited, Sydney, for Mary's flat; to Ross Scott for the 'New Australia' street; and to Judith Wright for the photograph of herself with her daughter.

Preface

In 1968 Tom Inglis Moore and I met together over lunch to discuss the possibility of collaborating on the monumental task of gathering together the correspondence of Dame Mary Gilmore and writing her biography. We were both well aware of Dame Mary's passion for writing letters and we felt sure that in those letters, whether deliberately aired for specific purposes in national newspapers and journals, or directed at men and women, like herself, prominent in Australian life, or, yet again, intended only for the personal interest of family and friends, there must lie a great deal of information about Dame Mary herself. As a preliminary step, then, towards the biography, we set out to collect and study as many of her letters as possible. We placed notices in newspapers seeking out her letters, we canvassed likely correspondents by personal enquiries, we searched the manuscript collections of many Australian libraries, and happily for us, many of her correspondents, having heard of the project by one means or another, sought *us* out, sending (usually apprehensively and by registered post) their treasured letters in ones and twos and even boxes full. As the weeks went by and the score of letters mounted to one, two and five and six hundred, we bowed to the inevitable, temporarily put aside plans for the biography and set out to publish first a selection of her correspondence. It would, we felt, be a relatively simple and speedy project and would clear the way for the *magnum opus* itself.

Now—a decade after that first blithe burst of optimism and with the volume finally ready for publication—Tom Inglis Moore is dead and the memory of Dame Mary herself is less sharp and emphatic than it was when the project was conceived. The intervening years have been beset with the many problems that body and soul (and delvers into the lives of the Great) are customarily heir to. Legal problems have arisen and been solved in their traditional slow-motion fashion; other interests (rose gardens, daffodil exhibitions, study leave, other books to be written) have demanded their share of attention; bouts of illness have come, and unhappily have not always gone; the natural difficulties of collaboration and even doubts about the project itself have added further complications. But with the death of my collaborator in July 1978, I felt an added sense of responsibility to complete the task as quickly as possible.

This book, which, quite properly, is dedicated to the place of Mary Gilmore in the Australian social and literary scene is not, I feel, the occasion to pay extended tribute to Tom Inglis Moore. He has his own place in the history of Australian writing and it is as secure as that of Dame Mary herself. His own pen has left behind many memorials to his creative and critical talent and he needs no additional memorials from me. But I find it especially fitting that the final critical analysis that he made at the end of a long and distinguished career should have had Mary Gilmore as its subject. As all students and lovers of Australian literature will know, it was a subject upon which he had written brilliantly and perceptively on many other occasions. The Foreword to this book, then, will be especially valuable and significant because it is Tom Inglis Moore's final word on a subject that was always close to his heart.

With a work such as this, stretching back over a decade, there are dangers that one could, at this last moment, have inadvertently forgotten some of the many people who have had a part in its making. If that has happened, on behalf of us both I offer my regrets and absolve Tom from blame. Three men, above all others, deserve special mention. Douglas Stewart, eminent man of letters and long-time friend of both Tom and Dame Mary, played a significant part in almost every stage of this book—in its conception, its planning and especially in the final stages of its development when he passed judgement on its worth and gave me advice on its publication. Very much a part also of the genesis of the book were George Ferguson (Mary's greatly esteemed G.F. or G.R. II.), grandson of George Robertson, the pioneer co-founder of Angus & Robertson, and Robert D. FitzGerald, the poet, whose admiration for Mary's poetry was matched, as so many of these letters show, by her early-expressed and continuing delight in his.

The Public Trustee of New South Wales, guardian of Mary's estate, and in recent times Mr B. E. Porter of the Public Trust Office, have been most helpful and courteous in solving the problems that have arisen over publication and they continue to offer assistance and advice in the biography which I am now undertaking alone. Dame Mary's grandson, William Wallace Gilmore, has graciously given his approval for the publication of the letters. In that respect I am sure he is correctly interpreting the wishes of his illustrious grandmother.

The Trustees of the Mitchell Library, and especially the Mitchell Librarian, Miss Suzanne Mourot, have actively supported and encouraged the project, allowing access to the Gilmore collection. Other Australian libraries, such as the La Trobe Library of Victoria, the National Library in Canberra and the Bridges Memorial Library at Duntroon, have always provided ready assistance by granting access to their collections and our indebtedness to them is freely acknowledged. To the many correspondents of Dame Mary who have provided us with letters we extend our thanks. They are far too numerous to name here individually but they are recognized in appropriate places throughout the volume.

Ann-Mari Jordens, Research Assistant in the Department of Language and Literature, has been indefatigable in her efforts to assist with the volume, and in the annotations to the letters and the Appendix her contribution has been a major one. She has also been largely responsible for tracking down and securing many of the interesting photographs which illustrate the selection and in the months while I was overseas on study leave she assisted with the editorial queries that a volume such as this inevitably occasions. The Editors are indeed grateful to her for her enthusiastic help. Patricia Middleton, Secretary of the Department of Language and Literature, and the last in a long line of people who have typed fair copies from Mary's rather difficult handwriting, has been a great help in these final weeks of putting the volume together for publication. Before her, Pamela Finn also assisted in the task of typing much of the manuscript.

I know that Peace Inglis Moore and Pacita Alexander (daughter of Peace and Tom) will be especially pleased to see the appearance of these letters, because of their linking again of Dame Mary with the Moore family, and I am particularly grateful to Pacita for her consideration for the project in the difficult days after her father's death. I believe that Mercy, Tom's sister-in-law and Pacita's aunt, should share in these acknowledgements. In the years of editing the selection I have often been the recipient of her unfailing cheerfulness and kindness, not to mention innumerable afternoon teas.

My thanks go as always to my own family; to my wife Ena (whose Paterson-Murray ancestry coincidentally has distant cross-ties with Dame Mary's Cameron background), to Ross and Lee, Margaret and Terry, who have all been blithely confident of the ultimate appearance of this book. Their faith and encouragement have often helped to bolster my own fading hopes.

Finally the gratitude of both of us goes to Dame Mary herself, that indomitable old lady who inspired in us the desire to provide Australians of today and tomorrow with tangible testimony of her boundless wisdom, idealism, humanity and generosity of spirit. There was a time when those qualities of hers would have gone unchallenged. Unfortunately, in recent years, there have been attempts by lesser souls to diminish Dame Mary's reputation and prestige. They have discovered 'unpardonable' (in their eyes) errors of fact in some of the many backward glances that she cast over the events of a life that spanned almost a century. They attribute these errors to an overwhelming vanity, to an irrational obsession by an old lady to be at the centre of the events she recounts. Having dismissed her as an unreliable historical witness they have gone on to question her personal achievements, achievements which saw her accepted as a national figure, even in her own lifetime.

Her denigrators have failed to understand that Mary Gilmore did not wish to be, never aspired to be, an historian in the exact and even desiccated sense of that word. Her role was primarily to gather, document, and then disseminate, the fast-fading body of early Australian folk lore, the disappearing social and cultural heritage of the pioneer days. She encouraged others to gather and store as she was doing; her reminiscences sparked others into action and the store grew. She was responsible for the introduction of Local History days in many schools throughout the land, and children by the hundreds came to those Local History days to recount tales that had been long stored in the memories of parents, grandparents and back as far as pioneer ancestors, first settlers in this land.

Not all those tales were based on factual personal reminiscences but it would be wrong for us to discredit them, to wipe them from our folk legends, because of that. It is the event itself, not the identity of the person describing it, that is paramount. The little girl who gazed with awe upon the row of Chinese swinging from the trees at Lambing Flat was certainly not the young Mary Cameron. But that scarcely matters at all. There *was* a little girl (there must have been many) who, sitting in a spring cart as it passed along the Lambing Flat road, would have had that scene indelibly imprinted on her receptive young mind. But (and Mary knew it well enough even if her modern critics do not) it is the Lambing Flat massacre that is important for us to recall—it is the event itself that is woven into our social and historical fabric, and not the small spectator, whoever she might have been. Mary's Lambing Flat anecdote and Edward Dyson's 'The Golden Shanty' are of the same ilk—and they ought to be considered as such, no more. It is the same with so many of her other snippets of personal reminiscence—the strikes of the 1890s, the birth of Australian trade unionism, the socialist venture to Paraguay, the struggles for justice for the Aboriginals and soldier settlers, the campaign for old age pensions, maternity allowances and child endowment. Perhaps the young schoolteacher, Mary Cameron, was not co-opted to the first executive of the Australian Workers Union, perhaps it was not she whose knuckles whitened as she voted in that critical decision to take strike action (and then again perhaps it was) but her story of those events brought to her readers and listeners an increased awareness of the early socialist struggles in this country. Perhaps the ardent young socialist, Mary Cameron, did not personally save the 'New Australia' venture by persuading wealthy Sydney supporters to pay the bills which allowed the *Royal Tar* to sail for Paraguay (and then again perhaps she did) but her account brings that strange Utopian venture led by William Lane into a living focus for readers to share and understand. In all the events she recalls she did of course play some role, possibly as much even as she claims, but it is the situation, the event, that absorbs her and her intention is that it should absorb her reader and her listener as utterly as it did her, as utterly as it would have absorbed any alive, vital young man or woman of the day. Nor must we lose sight of Mary Gilmore as the social propagandist, propagandist for the causes and issues that permeated her life and work, causes and issues that have, often because of her voice, come to be built into the fabric of Australian society. These causes and issues— egalitarianism, feminism, the Aboriginals, the welfare of the underprivileged, patriotism—she has presented with the verve and immediacy of one who has herself played a leading role in the struggles down the years. This role nobody can gainsay—the pages of the *Worker* over almost a quarter of a century bear witness to her efforts—and it is ungenerous of those who attempt to dim the greatness of her memory with their carping criticism. It is a fault of which she herself would certainly not have been guilty.

W. H. Wilde
Duntroon

Foreword

When Hugh McCrae was asked in 1943 who was then the most outstanding personality in Australian literature he had no hesitation in replying: 'The answer is Mary Gilmore, of course (strictly as a personality)'.

First and foremost, then, these letters of Dame Mary have been selected as her own revelation of those personal qualities and wide-ranging interests that made her so outstanding. They form a fascinating record of a remarkable woman, many-sided: a passionate idealist who fought to remedy social injustices and worked indefatigably to better our society; a crusader for many causes, great and small, including the welfare and culture of the Aboriginals; the one of our major poets with the widest international fame through translation of her poems into seven foreign languages; a deep lover of her country and advocate of its traditions—a great Australian. Along with her varied achievements, the letters indicate why the governments of the Commonwealth and New South Wales combined to give her a State funeral as a national figure, an Australian legend in her own lifetime.

This selection has been made from hundreds of letters written over sixty-six years, spanning the centuries, from the first one written when she was thirty-one to Henry Lawson from Cosme Colony, Paraguay, in 1896 to the final one sent to Robert D. FitzGerald from her Kings Cross flat in 1962, some five months before her death at the age of ninety-seven.

Since Dame Mary was such a prolific letter writer during an exceptionally long life it is likely that letters still remain to be gleaned, but the harvest reaped proved adequate enough for us to provide a comprehensive selection. There are some unfortunate gaps in the letters that were available to us. There are, for example, no letters from Mary's girlhood or from the years when she was teaching in the Riverina and at Silverton, near Broken Hill. One distinct break occurs between the early years of World War I (1915) and 1922 when the letters resume from Goulburn. We have no satisfactory explanation for this gap. Perhaps her biography, when completed, will provide the answer.

We have enlisted both literary and general history to provide an aid to readers by means of explanatory annotations. Many references in the letters, especially the earlier ones, to persons and events, together with the names of correspondents, would be unknown to readers of the present generation. Such information, we trust, will act as a guide to the letters and give a fuller understanding and appreciation of them.

After considering what would be the best form of arranging the letters, whether by grouping them by individual correspondents or by subject matter, or by giving them in a straightforward chronological order, we decided to adopt the latter arrangement. This could not only be effective because Dame Mary almost invariably dated her letters, but also because it is the form which shows most clearly the development of her personality, her ideas, feelings, and attitudes. Moreover, it adds an enriching dimension of narrative to the selection, since it becomes the unfolding of Dame Mary's career and inmost life.

In making this selection we worked on three principles: that the letters chosen should have some biographical, historical, or literary value or interest. The first principle enjoyed the advantage, we felt, that Dame Mary revealed herself more intimately and unconsciously in her letters than in the other two main sources of biographical material, her books and her diaries. Her published poetry and prose were written directly for a reading public, whilst the gargantuan diaries were designed for preservation in the Mitchell Library with an eye to future readers, the present restriction of access to them being only temporary. The letters, on the other hand, were spontaneous outpourings of her thoughts and emotions. Addressed only to her correspondents, they were purely personal. She probably never dreamed they would ever reach a wider public.

They display the unusual scope of her many and widely divergent interests—domestic, social, political, and literary. They range from her simple devotion to her husband and child to her pleasure in the recognition of her as 'the Grand Old Lady of Labour'; from seeking a memorial to dogs to entertaining a fellow Dame, Sybil Thorndike, in her 'Claremont' flat; from descriptions of Paraguay to acute reflections on Australian literature; from comments on Chaucer and Balzac to her encouragement of young writers. Some letters to children are given here since she wrote: 'To see the growing up of these young things is the discovery of new continents and the development of new worlds'. Indeed, when manuscripts poured into her she read them conscientiously at the sacrifice of her own work. 'I am devoured still by other people's affairs', she wrote to Nettie Palmer. 'I swore I would not read another MS. this morning, and just now is gone a working man and his novel is written in an exercise book—script. Oaths seem to be of no use to me. But I do so want to get at my own work; I do not grow younger.'

Of special interest is the way the letters disclose the complexity of Dame Mary's character, with its all too human paradoxes and contradictions coupled with those basic strengths noted by McCrae of 'courage, truth and wisdom, tempered with kindliness and grace'. Yet elsewhere he described her as 'A cross between Doctor Johnson and the Jackdaw of Rheims; stubborn, curiously informed'. In some ways she was a baffling mixture. She was a devotee of peace who wrote a national battle-cry and 'No Foe Shall Gather Our Harvest', which may be termed a battle hymn. She was a socialist and radical who was critical of churches and believed that Christianity was impracticable under capitalism, yet she also wrote: 'The religious is an integral part of me. Not only integral but essential', and a number of her poems are religious, even mystical, in spirit. She sang the praise of our past and stressed the need for Australians to record their history and cherish their traditions, but she lived and worked actively in the present. She kept up to the times remarkably, yet retained some of the proprieties in which she was reared a century ago, so that she was shocked at certain passages in *Coonardoo*, much as she admired its author Katharine Susannah Prichard. A sturdy democrat with a love of humble folk and equality, she could yet write: 'As long as I can follow a cause or worship a leader, I am still alive'. A sharp critic of many established institutions, she nevertheless had a special reverence for the British monarchy. Not only did she write two coronation anthems for the crowning of King Edward VIII, but she also took great pride in being made a Dame of the Order of the British Empire, as I know from personal experience since my wife and I were with her as her guests at her investiture at the Sydney Government House.

Her letters are also fascinating in the way they express her rich development both as a personality and as a writer. From the early simple affections of a devoted wife and mother she moved into a wider world, greater sophistication, and literary maturity. From the simplicity of her humanitarian sympathies, with their warm compassion, she advanced to a more complex humanist philosophy. From some earlier intolerances she progressed to a mellow tolerance and a deeper understanding of people and events. It is a far cry, indeed, from Labour's follower of the White Australia Policy, influenced also no doubt by the racism of William Lane, who thought it was against her principles to have a cup of coffee in Mockbell's cafe, to the champion of the

Aboriginals and the internationalist who crusaded for world peace and welcomed visitors from different nations to her Darlinghurst flat.

In her letters to A. G. Stephens we see her troubled by the inner conflict between her conscience ordering her to concentrate on her domestic duties to husband and child and the vital impulse demanding her fulfilment as a writer. These and other earlier letters are mainly emotional, and their expression often bears the tentative mark of the amateur. In dramatic contrast is the assurance she enjoyed later as a journalist, poet, and literary critic, when the emotions are reinforced by a keen intellect and the prose flows with professional ease. She has developed a mastery of her medium. Her mature comments on fellow writers are usually generous appreciations; if they run to extravagance at times they also abound in illuminating insights. Her judgement too is sound as she singles out for praise such poets as Neilson, McCrae and Judith Wright or such prose writers as Lawson, Palmer and Miles Franklin. She discerns the high merits of 'E' (Mary Fullerton) in poems still unpublished. Her swans are not inflated geese but indubitable swans, as actual as those wild swans of the Murrumbidgee she sang so superbly.

Frequently her letters show a singular facet of her complexity in the opposition between her pride and her humility. Like all of us, she cherished her own characteristic vanities. She was proud of her work for social reforms, her political speeches for Labour, and such 'firsts' as being the first woman on a trade union executive, the first here to write a coronation anthem and a national battle-cry. She delighted, quite naturally, in various recognitions of her, from streets and school houses being named after her to the Mary Gilmore Award created by trade unions in her honour, the national celebrations of her birthday, and the Dobell portrait of her. On the other hand, she was sincerely modest about her finest achievement—her poetry. There was a true humility in her constant depreciation of herself as a poet. Thus she wrote to FitzGerald: 'May I, who wrote little things in little words and in simple form, pay homage to the bigger thing in you?' In a letter to me she insisted on calling herself not a poet but just 'a verse-writer', and she entitled her important 1948 collection simply *Selected Verse*. Yet her stance was against all the evidence. At home such fellow poets as Douglas Stewart, FitzGerald and Judith Wright paid her poetry homage, placing it on the top shelf. McCrae hailed her as 'the voice of our country, authentic and infallible.—Our greatest national poet'. Abroad, English and American critics paid her tribute, she was honoured in China and Russia, and a Rumanian anthology placed her in translation among the great women poets of all times.

Since she had such an abiding passion for our past, it was only natural that her letters also have their own historical value, often presenting sidelights on 'old days: old ways' in their recollections, from descriptions of life in Cosme Colony and among the Aboriginals to details of past figures and events. In particular, there is valuable literary history, such as Dame Mary's account of the founding of the Sydney Fellowship of Writers and her character sketches of authors; for example, her portrait of Vance Palmer and Bernard O'Dowd, whom she found alike in some respects but 'where the one speaks in a small still voice the other shouts: comes trampling out of the forest, hair in his eyes shouting his discoveries'.

Many instances of the vitality and vividness seen in this brief quotation could be given, since they are characteristic of Dame Mary's style in her letters. For she is a stylist, an artist in prose as well as in poetry. Even her occasional letters carry the virtues of simplicity, directness and naturalness. As in Henry Lawson's stories, they are often so effective in expressing their subject matter that their artistry remains undiscerned. It is the art concealing art. At other times there is an emotional exuberance that reminds one of the letters of another celebrated woman akin to Dame Mary in the strength of both her character and her feelings—Queen Victoria. The effusive Queen, however, had to resort to italics and exclamation marks whereas Dame Mary had the innate gifts of imagery and variation.

Indeed, one factor which makes her letters so interesting is the variety of her style as she adapts it to the subject, the correspondent, or her own mood. It is lively and colloquial when she tells McCrae: 'No, I wasn't cutting bread and butter when your letter arrived. I was making toast. I said "Darlingest" nineteen times and the toast burned'. She admonishes FitzGerald with a homely metaphor: 'So, Bob, don't put off your own recollections. Tie up the dog, no matter on how short the chain'. In another letter to him she begins: 'I have been going down hill so fast that the old exuberance of letters is itself failing' and ends with a touch of self-mocking humour: 'Here endeth (the last kick of the dying fowl?)'. Writing to Nettie Palmer, after praising the depth of Vance's observation, she comments in acutely analytical prose on the contrasting thinness of Australian writing in general: 'It has been all on the surface—or too much on the surface, and broken only by the emotions of the appetites. The perceptions of the poet, which are the reciprocal between nature and self, have been too much absent. We have lived *on* nature and not *in* her'. Again, her style grows eloquent when she tells of her feeling that in his verse 'Hardy comes nearer to being God than any writer I know. His work however small is that of a Titan—is titanic. Struggle and strain and with it an implacable must and an equally implacable pity that suffers in all it makes'.

R. D. FitzGerald, in a notable appreciation of Dame Mary (*Meanjin*, no. 4, 1960), found her poetry distinguished by 'the swift illuminating phrase, the mark of the gift of sudden insight', and her work as a whole by 'the unifying principle of her creativeness: the spiritual stir'. These comments apply no less equally to her letters, where the prose is often that of the poet, rich in comparisons and imagery, the tokens of her creative imagination. Thus she sees Mozart as 'the Shaw Neilson of Music'. Telling McCrae how the Hurstville Council had renamed a road 'Dame Mary Gilmore Road', she exclaims gaily: 'There's fame for you, my lad! I feel the horses' hoofs trotting on my back as I think of it'. To J. K. Moir she confesses: 'I am a very tired old woman. The seas are beating hard on the base of the lighthouse'. Touched by her publisher remembering her 89th birthday by a gift of flowers, she tells him: 'At the end of life these things are like a warm hearth to sit by'. When Alec Chisholm in a letter mentions a movement to destroy the wild swans, she replies indignantly: 'To talk of having them proclaimed for destruction is like wanting to put out the stars of the Southern Cross'. We feel 'the spiritual stir' noted by FitzGerald as she expresses to him her exaltation upon rereading his powerful epic *Between Two Tides*: 'I felt like Moses must have felt when he came down from Sinai after talking with God'.

Stars and swans, Mozart and the titanic Hardy, Moses talking with God, the hoofs of horses trotting, the warm hearth, and the beating seas: these are some of the evocative symbols, characteristically far-ranging, lighting up Dame Mary's letters. 'Poetry', she writes, 'is any word when vision is behind it', and her prose is often striking because of this visionary quality. Her letters express the plenitude of her vision as well as the uniqueness of her personality. They offer a highly original contribution to our creative literature, and a memorable addition to our national history by one of its makers.

T. Inglis Moore

A Biographical Note

Mary Gilmore's life (1865-1962) spanned virtually the whole of the second and most vital century of Australia's history. She was born into a country still largely dominated by colonialism; she grew to young womanhood witnessing and contributing to the first lusty stirrings of nationalism; in the ensuing length of years granted to her she grew to be a national figure, insistently urging Australia forward into a position of independence and growing prestige in the eyes of the world.

Mary Jean Cameron was born on 16 August 1865 at Cotta Walla near Goulburn, the first daughter and eldest child of Donal (Donald) Cameron and Mary Beattie. Of her Scottish ancestry, on her father's side, she was enormously proud, and she lost no opportunity in her life to express her delight in being part of the great Cameron Clan. From both pioneer families, who at that time owned the adjoining properties 'Roslyn' and 'Merryvale', she gained strength of character, resourcefulness, and a sympathy for the weak and needy which was to be so marked in her later life.

Donal Cameron arrived in Australia in 1839 as a young child, accompanying his immigrant parents from Argyllshire in Scotland. He was a versatile man when it came to earning a living—being property manager, building contractor and outback wanderer, travelling wherever opportunity led. He passed on to his daughter his own knowledge and love of the Australian landscape and his generous compassion for all its inhabitants, white and black, animal and human. Until she commenced her formal schooling at about the age of ten years she accompanied her father on many of his travels. In reminiscences of later years when the mind of an old woman allowed itself quite a degree of imaginative licence she liked to recount stories of those childhood exploits. She recalled actually living for a brief period with a tribe of Aboriginals on the banks of the Murrumbidgee. From those early years and from her father, who believed that the Aboriginal myths and legends ought to be considered important in our culture, Dame Mary acquired her intense desire to conserve as full a store as possible of Aboriginal history and lore. In a letter to Stephen Murray-Smith of *Overland* in August 1959, she summarized her early education thus,

> I went to school in Wagga Wagga for about two years from 1875 to 1877 ... my real education was the home study of lessons set by my father and mother in earlier years—father teaching me my letters when about five and when about eight or nine he gave me arithmetic generally. I owe my Latin, Algebra, Euclid and History to him ... my mother set and heard me my book lessons: spelling, syntax, geography, reading and writing.

From the age of twelve she became an assistant to the teacher in small schools around Cootamundra, Albury and Wagga. At sixteen she claimed to have gained the highest pass in New South Wales in the pupil-teacher entrance examination. She was already writing verse and had contributed to Wagga and Albury newspapers under the phonetic combination of her initials, Emjaycee. For two years (1888-89) she taught in the mining town of Silverton near Broken Hill and her close association with the militant working-class community there led to her active support for the newly-emerged political Labor movement. She returned to Sydney in 1890, teaching first at Neutral Bay and later at Stanmore. In the city she joined wholeheartedly in the developing radicalism of the day, supporting the turbulent maritime and shearers' strikes and lending her weight to the newly-established Australian Workers Union. In Sydney she also became acquainted with two of the three men, who, she said, 'most shaped my mind and life': William Lane, the founder of 'New Australia' in Paraguay; John Farrell, brewer, journalist, balladist and political commentator; and A. G. Stephens, editor of the *Bulletin*'s 'Red Page' and later of the *Bookfellow*. Her friendship with Henry Lawson also began in those years, and Mary always believed that she gave valuable guidance to him in that formative stage of his literary career. In her words: 'He wanted to write Revolution. I begged him to write Australia'.

Her enthusiastic support helped William Lane to launch the *Royal Tar* on 16 July 1893, on its voyage to establish a socialist utopia in Paraguay. In 1896, equipped with a few basic schoolteaching aids and with enough white hailstone muslin for a wedding dress, Mary answered Lane's appeal to come and teach the children of the Cosme settlement, which was formed after the initial colony, 'New Australia', had failed to prosper. Mary was a tower of strength. She taught the children, organized and administered a library for the adults and edited the daily paper, *Cosme Evening Notes*. It came as something of a surprise to those who regarded Mary as a dedicated feminist that in May 1897 she was married at Cosme. Her husband was her fellow-colonist William Gilmore. Will was a happy-go-lucky shearer from Western Victoria, and one of the few eligible bachelors in the Cosme community. The story of Mary's courtship, rather tartly told by one of the other disappointed young ladies of the colony, was that while Will lay incapacitated as a result of an accident Mary spent many hours reading to him and he fell under the spell of her lovely voice. In May 1897 the muslin was transformed into a wedding dress, a ring was fashioned by cutting the centre out of a shilling, and Mary Cameron became Mary Gilmore. Their only child, William Dysart Cameron Gilmore, was born on 21 August 1898. The Cosme settlement slowly disintegrated and along with numerous others the Gilmores made plans to return to Australia. The family was separated while Will worked to raise their passage money. The letters written by Mary to her absent husband reveal the deep bond of affection that existed between them at this stage. Later she joined Will in Patagonia. Her lively pen tells of those hectic days—of shearing in the Argentine, of a thirty-one day voyage in a decrepit little boat down the South American coast, of governessing to the 'most awful girl that ever lived', of being caught between the two contending sides in a civil war, of being at the mercy of local bandidos ('I slept every night with an axe, two or three carving knives, and a siren whistle under my pillow'), of giving more than a passing thought to the possibility of annexing Patagonia for Great Britain. Finally, in 1902, they returned to Australia by way of England and after a brief stay in Mary's familiar Sydney environment, where she renewed her contact with the literary and journalistic world, they settled down to an isolated farming existence on the Gilmore property at Strathdownie near Casterton in Western Victoria. Visiting Strathdownie today is a pleasant experience. There are green and fertile farms, comfortable farmhouses with all the modern amenities, good roads which give swift access to the world at large. Near by is the thriving western town of Casterton with its wide streets and its courteously-curious, history-conscious citizens. But it is easy to visualize it all as it must have been in 1902. Low, stunted scrub, barely existing in a deprived sandy soil, would have covered much of the area, pressing in gloomily upon the scattered straggling farms. The few tracks, picked out by the odd horsemen or waggons, would have run through the scrub to isolated farmhouses and then to nowhere. The world of men and affairs would have seemed a universe away. Mary, Will, and Billy lived first at the homestead 'Burnside' with the old people but Mary found little to enthuse about in her new life. She spoke of the 'want of educated conversation or discussion'. Later the newcomers moved out of the larger house into a slab hut on the property. Mary made paste and papered the walls with newspapers to keep out the wind. Will was away fencing and shearing and was home only at weekends. Hilda Lane, the daughter of John Lane (William's brother), and herself born at Cosme, recalls Mary's tormented existence in those years.

> I shall never forget how she described the loneliness there. Her husband was away working in the bush. In the evening she would put her arms around the trunk of an old gum tree, still warm from the heat of the day. Her hands would feel that warmth, the only response in that desolate place to her loneliness and isolation.

From Casterton, where she later moved to facilitate Billy's schooling, Mary maintained, largely through A. G. Stephens of the *Bulletin*, a firm contact with the literary world, verse and prose items of hers appearing from time to time in the *Bulletin*, the *Worker*, and other papers. In October 1903 A. G. Stephens devoted an article in the *Bulletin* 'Red Page' to her life and poetry. In 1908 she became, on the insistence of Hector Lamond, the editor of the *Worker*, the guiding force behind the Women's Page of that newspaper. She edited the Women's Page for twenty-three years and it became a forum where she aired her numerous grievances and fought for her legion of causes. Some of her more noteworthy campaigns in those pages were for equal status for women, pensions for the old and the disabled, improved health services for children and expectant or nursing mothers, maternity allowances and child endowment. In 1910 her first volume of poems, *Marri'd and Other Verses*, was published by George Robertson of Melbourne. It contained poems written at Cosme and Casterton, most of them simple but eloquent little lyrics centred on the joys, hopes and disappointments of life's daily round.

In 1912 Will Gilmore joined his brother on the land in Queensland and Mary settled in Sydney on the staff of the *Worker*. After Billy completed his education in Sydney he joined his father and it was only on infrequent occasions and for brief periods that the family was to be reunited. Mary was then forty-seven, but her life's work was really only beginning. Although she longed to give her time to her poetry most of her energy went into writing for the *Worker*. She concerned herself with a wide range of social and economic problems. Some of her campaigns—the responsibility of the community for the young and the old, the sick and the helpless; the moral obligation of the government and the people to improve the conditions of the Aboriginals; the need to preserve the history of the early days of Australia—were carried on over many years. Other battles against passing individual injustices and inhumanities lasted only as long as it took her to print a furious comment in her *Worker* page or to pen a blistering letter for publication in another newspaper. As always she placed herself on the side of the working man, supporting the Labor Party and joining with insistent voice in that Party's demands for social and economic change.

The war of 1914-18 aroused her repugnance and horror. Her reaction to it is amply conveyed in her second collection of poems, *The Passionate Heart*, published by Angus and Robertson in Sydney in 1918. *The Passionate Heart* was dedicated to 'The Fellowing Men', the comrades in arms, who were in Mary's eyes the only worthy ornament in the sordid gallery of war. Many of the poems in this volume tell of the loss and heartache of war as seen through the grieving eyes of womanhood. They reflect also the general disenchantment with war that followed the Allied victory in 1918. The royalties from *The Passionate Heart* she refused to keep. 'I gave them to the blind soldiers. I would have felt like eating blood had I kept them.'

In 1922 her first book of prose, a collection of essays entitled *Hound of the Road*, was published. They are, in the main, little vignettes of the odd, the humorous and the pathetic, scraps from both the factual and the imaginative past, and they give a preview of her later, more substantial, prose writings. In 1925 there came a third volume of poems, mostly ballad-like in form and content, which she called *The Tilted Cart*. On the book's cover there is a sketch of an old hawker's cart, tilted forward, resting on its shafts in the shade of a large gum tree, while near by two old-timers are boiling the billy and obviously reminiscing on times and events long past. The poems were accompanied by copious notes which are witness to Mary's obsession to record, and to encourage others to record, the rapidly disappearing details of early outback life.

In 1930 Mary Gilmore retired from the *Worker* but her life became busier and more energetic than ever before. The demands upon her were endless and the generous gift of her time and advice to young aspiring writers was legend. In 1930 her most significant book of verse, *The Wild Swan*, was published. Published when she was sixty-five years old, *The Wild Swan* embodied all her favourite themes (Nature, the Aboriginals, commitment to Life, Love) in verse of greater craftsmanship than she had previously exhibited. Early in 1931 there followed a volume of poems, chiefly of a religious nature, entitled *The Rue Tree*. The next year, 1932, saw the publication of a further volume, *Under the Wilgas*, which emphasized Aboriginal themes to a greater extent than any of her former collections. Her reminiscences took shape in two volumes of prose anecdotes and commentaries which appeared in successive years, *Old Days: Old Ways A Book of Recollections* (1934) and *More Recollections* (1935). In her role as raconteur it was Dame Mary's object, as she wrote in the foreword to the second collection, to capture for posterity the pioneering days through which she herself had lived; to present 'Australia as she was when she was most Australian'. In 1937 so widespread was the acclaim for her throughout Australia that she was named as a Dame of the British Empire. Her letters at this time reveal her joy in the flood of congratulations which poured into her Kings Cross flat. Then in her seventies, she was still publishing. The prophetically entitled *Battlefields* appeared in 1939 just before World War II began. *Battlefields* is plentifully spiced with radical themes—'There was no hunted one/ With whom I did not run'—but, like Bernard O'Dowd, she also took up fondly the idea of the growth of a truly Australian character.

World War II reawakened the agonies she had told of in *The Passionate Heart* but in this crisis it was her patriotism that was paramount. Perched in her Kings Cross flat at 99 Darlinghurst Road she occupied, during the years of World War II, a ring-side seat at the spectacle of Australia's largest city caught up in the agony of the distant but ever-menacing conflict. The euphoria of the first months of the 'phony' war gave way to the German blitzkrieg of 1940, to Dunkirk, to defeat in Greece, Crete and the Middle East and then to the threat of Japan. In the darkest moments of the war came her defiant 'No Foe Shall Gather Our Harvest' and the bitter 'Singapore' in which she blamed the loss of that fortress, not on the embattled soldiers, but on the self-interest of politicians and profiteers. One enthusiastic and patriotic window-dresser in Murdoch's department store (then diagonally opposite the Sydney Town Hall—now Waltons) displayed an enlarged framed version of 'No Foe Shall Gather Our Harvest' in that store's largest window where it stood as an exhortation to passers-by through the following difficult weeks. Mary herself sent a copy of 'Singapore' to Prime Minister John Curtin defiantly declaring that he must see it 'even though I go to gaol for it'.

1945 was a year of double personal tragedy—both her son and her husband died in Queensland, and the news when it reached her, was a stunning blow. Her refuge from grief was, as always, in her own writing, her tutelage of young writers, her social crusades, her garnering of Australian history, and her active political support of the Labor Party. In 1952 came her association with the Communist newspaper, *Tribune*, an action which some people judged as misguided. It was her zeal as a pacifist that led Mary to offer to write for the Communist newspaper, for she was attempting to protest against the Commonwealth Government's opposition to the Youth Carnival for Peace and Friendship. Nor was Mary one to lose an opportunity for public contact, and her *Tribune* column, 'Arrows', allowed her to make her customary valuable comment on contemporary incidents and situations.

Although approaching her ninetieth year, and hampered by the frustrating physical infirmities of old age (yet with a mind as incisive as ever) she witnessed with great jubilation the publication of what was to be her final volume of poems, *Fourteen Men* (1954). She inscribed this last volume, in some ways the one she loved best, with the words:

> Here at this last I can come home
> And lay me down with a quiet mind;
> For the work is done that I had to do—
> A sheaf that my hand must bind.

It contains some memorable verses, especially 'Nationality' and 'The Pear Tree'.

The Australasian Book Society commissioned William Dobell to do her portrait, to be exhibited on her ninety-second birthday in August 1957. Dobell's reaction was: 'I found her a splendid person with a tremendous vitality and dignity which I wanted to get into paint'. The portrait stirred considerable controversy. Some believed it did her little justice. Mary defended it strongly and became more than a little proud of Dobell's representation of her. Physical vanity had never counted for very much with her and she was delighted that the artist had captured something of her Cameron ancestry.

Dame Mary Gilmore was now truly a national figure. Her final years were made memorable by a wealth of public adulation. Her birthdays were celebrated like feast-days; streets were named after her; scholarships were awarded in her name; she led May Day processions as the May Queen. When she died quietly on a summer morning in December 1962, less than three years short of her century span, the long chapter of Australian life and literature to which she had made such a remarkable contribution came to an end. Kylie Tennant, writing in *Westerly* after Mary's death, summed up her position thus: 'She was a Myth—in a land where myths are needed—and she was the right kind of myth—she joined believers together'. It is my belief that future generations of Australians will continue to cherish the 'myth' of Mary Gilmore, for she symbolizes so admirably that spirit of vision, enterprise and indomitability which was vital to the establishment and development of this nation.

W. H. Wilde

Abbreviations

F.A.W.   Fellowship of Australian Writers
R.A.H.S. Royal Australian Historical Society
S.M.H.   *Sydney Morning Herald*

Note: Imperial measures have been retained throughout. Approximate metric equivalents are as follows:

1 inch	= 2.5 cm
1 foot	= 30.5 cm
1 mile	= 1.61 km
1 acre	= 0.405 ha
1 penny (d)	= .833 cents
1 shilling (s)	= 10 cents
1 pound (£)	= $2
1 hundredweight	= 50.8 kg

The Letters

A Note on Style

Many of the letters contain references to people, publications, places and events, some of which will be unfamiliar to present-day readers. Where we have felt that an explanation is required of particular references in a letter, we have given the appropriate annotations in footnotes to that letter. Sometimes we have directed the reader's attention to sources where further information is available. In the interests of space and economy, however, we have resisted the temptation to explain each and every reference contained in the letters. Readers should also consult the Appendix at the back of the book for brief details of people, publications, places and events mentioned in the letters. Where these details are felt by some readers to be inadequate we plead the same exigencies of space and economy. The purpose of the Appendix is to *identify* the people, publications, places and events, not to supply full information about them. Such full information is, we believe, usually readily available from other sources.

Again in the interests of space we have usually abridged the address at the head of each letter (2 Claremont, 99 Darlinghurst Road, Kings Cross) to Kings Cross, and omitted the signing off to each letter (Yours, Mary Gilmore). Where the address or the ending is, in our opinion, of special significance, indicating where Mary was at the time of writing or her relationship to the person written to, we have included the details.

As Mary was usually in a hurry when writing, she tended to underline only parts of words. As the editors could find no apparent reason for her variation in underlining, they have decided to standardize this feature of her letters by underlining the whole word. The underlining has been indicated by italic type.

To Henry Lawson

La Colonie 'Cosme',[1]
Paraguay, South America
via NZ and Monte Video

Dear Harry,[2]   5 August 1896

I've got such a lot to say to you that I write on a postcard in order to say something. I am glad about your book[3] but I haven't seen

---

[1] On 16 July 1893 the *Royal Tar* sailed from Sydney to establish in Paraguay the settlement of New Australia, William Lane's dream of a socialist Utopia. When the original settlement broke up in discord (May 1894) Lane and a number of loyal followers established a second settlement, Cosme. In response to Lane's plea to come to Cosme to teach the children, Mary Gilmore (then Mary Cameron), who had been a driving force behind the initial effort to get the *Royal Tar* on its way, joined the settlement in 1896. She taught school, wrote much of the colony's daily paper, *Cosme Evening Notes,* and busied herself in the day-to-day activities. In May 1897 she married one of the original New Australia settlers, a shearer from Victoria, William Alexander Gilmore. A son, Billy, Mary's only child, was born 21 August 1898. A full account of the New Australia and Cosme ventures can be found in Gavin Souter's *A Peculiar People; the Australians in Paraguay,* 1968. For Mary's own account see the following letters to her husband, the letter to W. A. Woods, 11 June 1903, and the letter to Julian Ashton, June 1939.

[2] The accuracy of Mary's many claims about the closeness of her relationship with Henry Lawson and her influence on the development of his literary talent is difficult to establish. That there was a close personal relationship is verified by Colin Roderick who makes the following comment on p. 436 of his collection of Henry Lawson letters:

> In 1896 Lawson had one letter from her that has survived [no doubt this letter of 5 August 1896], in which she urged him to come to Cosme: the comment in his footnote to this letter suggests that she was still much in his mind.

The postscript of Mary's letter conveys the same impression. For further information on Henry Lawson and Mary see the letter to the Secretary, Henry Lawson Memorial and Literary Society, 29 August 1928. Volume 41 of the Mary Gilmore collection in the Mitchell Library also contains a long account entitled 'Henry Lawson and I'. Some of Mary's statements are included in the notes to letters 29 August 1928 and 5 June 1926.

[3] *In the Days When the World Was Wide and Other Verses,* 1896.

anything approaching a criticism of it, no one having sent me any papers. As for you, I believe you forgot me—but I know you didn't—only you might have sent me a copy of the book. Send me one anyway. How is it going? . . . I'd give a lot to see you here. The place teems with copy, the life makes it. I wish to Heaven I could write it up. I could cry when I see how it goes to waste. We are all original, everyone of us but as life becomes easier it will grow more commonplace and none but a see-er (?) can write of us as we are now.

Communism as we have it is alright, Harry, and we are getting on—slowly, of course, but in a year or two what now is, will have gone, drowned by prosperity. And the country—it is a constant wonder to me, so beautiful, so rich in bird (life) and plants. And the history!—and the stories of the war. If you were only here, Henry. Don't let someone else snap your chances. Come while the field is new—as a visitor I mean, though I'd like you to come for good only I don't think you would. I am satisfied with life anyway and I wish everyone found life as good as I do. Come if you can, dear old friend. You know I wouldn't ask you if I didn't think it worth it—even from your standpoint.

M. J. Cameron

p.s. I didn't get married.

To William Gilmore

Dear Will,

Cosme
20 October 1899

I am beginning to look for the coming of another letter though it is only a fortnight since you last wrote. I often dread your feeling sorry you left the Colony.[1] Don't for my sake, darling. We can't be much poorer than we were here, you surely won't have to work harder. I think it would be heart breaking if you had to work harder. It was always so heavy for you, always the big lifting and the wet Monte [forest]. Surely it will never be as bad as that again. We can hardly

---

[1] In August 1899 the Gilmore family resigned from Cosme and Will left the settlement to work at various jobs (e.g. shearing in Argentina and on a ranch in Patagonia) to raise their passage money back to Australia. Mary stayed in Cosme until May 1900, when she moved to nearby Villarrica (Villa Rica) into the small dilapidated cottage where her son Billy had been born in 1898. The following letters, dated from 20 October 1899 to 25 February 1900, are a selection from a much larger number of letters, written almost daily by Mary to her husband during their separation. They bring to light interesting facets of life in the experimental colony and reveal Mary's deep affection for her husband at this time. By the end of 1899 William Lane's venture was in ruins and Lane was on his way back to Australia in search of work to pay the colony's accumulated debts. A full account of the New Australia and Cosme ventures can be found in Gavin Souter, *A Peculiar People: the Australians in Paraguay*, 1968.

go to a more trying climate than this, and hardly worse moral surroundings, bad children for the boy to grow up with, a constant straining to individualism, the native girl outside, and the cana [rum] almost for the asking. When we get settled again we will bring the boy up with the idea of community life even if there are only ourselves. If we could get my brother Charlie to join us there would be a start already. Charlie is so good and gentle and of high moral tendency. I have such plans and such ideas looking ahead to what we will have. Probably two slab rooms with a bark roof and an earth floor, but I look forward as I never looked forward here except just at the very first. What can one do in a climate that uses all one's energy and makes life work a burden? We won't like the cold of course, we'll be pinched and doleful, and cold rain will be awful, but we'll eat hearty, and sit by the fire o'nights and talk and think about the people over here gone to bed early to get away from the mosquitos, or staying up late because it is too sweltering hot to sleep. And we'll look at our red-faced boy and think of the yellow-faced children on the Colony, growing more and more like the native under the strain of fever and heat. They talk about what the natives were before the war. All the women were not killed off by the war, and the old women are as much the type as old men—and what old women they are! One looks at the women of a place and knows what the men either are or were.

I wonder if you are warm enough. I do hope you are not stinting yourself in the way of necessary clothes. And dear Will remember to take care of yourself. Your blood is not thick enough yet to stand very much and you must be careful not to run unnecessary risk. I want Billy to grow up under your care as much as under mine—most mine while he is little, most yours when he is bigger. I want him to take you for his example—to grow up like his father. Perhaps he will be our only child and you must take care of yourself for his sake as well as for mine and your own. It is cold tonight and I think I will hurry off to bed. Goodnight, dearest, and keep your heart up. I think I am a bit stronger than I was. I hope I may continue so. And yet again goodnight.

To William Gilmore

Cosme
1 November 1899

Dear Will,

I have had a lazy day today being tired out after a bad night and several days of fever. I feel a bit done, somehow, and it is hard work to frame a sentence. What a blessing it will be to get into a cooler or rather drier climate. I think this climate would give a dry stick fever if it didn't rot out beforehand . . .

Do you know I have an idea in regard to Communalism etc. It is that Communism is only necessary for the material end, not for the moral, the moral side being absolutely an individual matter. For instance no man can monopolize or take from another man's character, Truth, Honesty, Courage, etc. as each of these only exist in any man so far as he has them. Hence there can be no Collectivism or Communism in them or of them that will develop them, therefore Communism can only really relate to things that may be either held in common and which are usually monopolized by a few to the hurt of the many—i.e. material things. Of course the making easier of the material side of things lessens the temptation to do ill, and this, good enough in itself, is really all that it can do.

To William Gilmore

Dear Will,

Cosme
2 November 1899

I do wish you could see the boy grow day by day as I do. He is learning so much. He actually runs away from me now and looks back and laughs. He knows where I usually sit to feed him and stands there and waits as I get his food ready. He is beginning to know such a lot of things—the moment I put him in the back door he runs to the front door without even waiting to see if the gate is being shut, and as I have to run to be there before him he runs faster and laughs.

I am giving him a whole egg a day now in his morning food. I only feed him the three times a day and he gets nothing from 4.30 till breakfast next morning which is between 7 and 8 a.m. so he goes a good long spell. I am quite satisfied that this is a good plan to pursue as he is the only child fed this way and the only one free from breakings out. The McLeods and Titilahs have not had clean skins for over a year, and Artie McLeod and Leon Delugar have great sores behind their ears that look as if the ear were coming off. Beyond a minute heat blister or two Billy has never had a spot or scab. I am not a very handsome or a very robust mother, but I think I have clean blood to match with yours. I think we ought to have real clean healthy children, for we both have clean healthy blood and no gross appetites, while you have form and physique—enough to make up for my lack of both.

To William Gilmore

Dear Will,

Cosme
8 December 1899

I feel that if I don't get a letter tomorrow I shall go nearly out of my mind with anxiety. Why ever don't you write, dear? This suspense is awful. You don't understand how I am—and have always been—haunted by the dread of losing you. When you used to work in the Monte I used to strain my eyes looking for you if you were only five minutes late, and now I have not heard from you since Oct 22nd, nearly two months. Think how you felt when you got no letters, and I so much more excitable than you. But there I will say no more or it will seem as if I am scolding you. I don't suppose, if anything happened to you I would die or go mad—though I could easily enough go mad if I chose to allow myself. I would probably make an idol of the boy but life would be a living death and the spring would never bloom again for me.

Billy is better again. As C. Ray has just mowed a track to the well, I called to Billy 'Come, till I put you in your cot' (so that I could write without alarms) and when I went to take him the young rascal turned and ran for his life. He is alternately bawling with temper and calling 'Dad day'. He is really trying to talk. Of course without any idea of regular or acquired words.

Haidee Rae has been pretty bad with fever the last few days. I still have it. I wish to Heaven we were together again, however poor, for I don't suppose we would starve. People are very kind, do anything I ask, but I feel terribly anxious about you. I suppose not being very strong I feel more acutely or things affect me more.

To William Gilmore

Dear Will,

Cosme
12 December 1899

If you could only see the boy. It is all 'the boy' isn't it? This afternoon as it was too hot to stay in the house I put the rocking chair in the shade at the back for Billy, and your old chair for myself. It looked so homely to see the two chairs and I pictured you in one and me in the other talking, while we watched the little man. His fever seems better today, mine is a bit worse. Billy's favourite attitude in the rocking chair is with his feet on the seat, and his little hinder part up against the back—half sitting, and he literally makes the chair jump. He gets it jammed against the table and against the book shelf and against the partition time after time. It is splendid exercise.

Dave Stevenson called last evening with a book. He told me a Dane came out with him who knew that Regro to Santa Cruz country and spoke of it as being thoroughly suited to English people, so I am hoping the cold will not be as real as I had feared. He also told me that, if one could wait the chance, Houlder Bros. now and then sent boats with horses and mules to S. Africa and thence on to Australia, that they gladly took passengers, that one travelled second cabin instead of steerage, that the fare to Australia from Buenos Aires was only about £20 each. That would be considerably cheaper and much more comfortable than steerage to England and steerage out to Australia—still I would dearly like to see England if we could with perhaps a chance of a walking tour through France and Italy—we could travel with a wheelbarrow or some such thing, and beg our way etc. etc. all for experience.

As the S. African war is causing all the colonies and the Argentine to be drained of their horses and mules as well as wheat and beef (for the war promises more than at first is seen, there being over 70,000 British troops there now) boats will make that trip pretty often. When you come again to Buenos Aires you might call and see Houlder Bros. agent. I believe they are always only too anxious to get passengers.

Another plan would be if, like Bob Miller, you could get on second in charge of cattle and I go as passenger to England. Your passage would be saved and I would not have to go steerage, as cattle boats have no steerage. I think that would be best after all if we could manage it. You see you know as much of cattle as Bob Miller did. Of course he was exceptionally lucky as he got his billet without delay. We could not depend on doing quite so well.

To William Gilmore

My own dear Will,

Cosme
15 December 1899

I am wondering wherever I will send this letter as I have no address beyond Sta. Cruz, Patagonia,[1] and that is so vague. I think I will send a few lines there though, on the off chance of your getting them, and hold this over till I hear from you.

Billy is circus riding in the rocking chair, and is better than he was; the fever seeming to have almost left him again. Six or eight men

---

[1] William Gilmore was working as a shearer in Patagonia. He returned to Villarrica (Villa Rica) early the following year (1900) and in November took his family to Rio Gallegos in southern Patagonia where he worked on a ranch fifty miles from Rio Gallegos. Mary taught English in Rio Gallegos. They went to England early in 1902 and left for Australia on 30 April 1902 in the *Karlsruhe*.

are away with two teams of 16 and 14 bullocks, to try to bring the engine[1] in. They don't expect to get it all the six miles, but near enough to leave it till after Christmas. Isn't it awful? And it only weighs about five tons all told.

Billy wants me to watch him all the time the young rascal. Fancy his growing—what shall I say 'conceit?' and yet it is not conceit, dear little fellow. If you could only see him.

I often wonder if the thought of me gives you such joy as the thought of you gives me, yet I think it can't because I am not as good and as gentle—as great dispositioned as you, and then I think perhaps it does because you love me, dear. I often think of the words 'Blessed art thou among women'. If all women were as blessed as I am how happy all life would be—but then there is only one Will in the world.

People here say I mean to be a writer and that is why we resigned. They know nothing about it. I wouldn't be a writer in case I should let the love of it grow into my life and perhaps owe to it what I only want to owe to you—or that it might set up another aim or tie in which you would not be the centre.

Children—if we have more than the boy, we will love together, and I love to think we will have more little ones coming and growing up as we watch them and help them and teach them to look toward a broader and a greater understanding of life than we can reach—we the stepping stones whereby they shall rise higher.

Dear little Billy—he is in bed now—went to sleep without his usual call to 'Dad-day' or his game of 'Bew pape'. He was so tired, dear lamb.

To William Gilmore

Cosme
17 December 1899

Dear Husband,

I don't often use the name do I? Chiefly I think because it expresses all things between us, and I cannot use it lightly and easily. He who holds my life, to whom I have given up my will, with whom I stand before God to bring forth life and cherish it and prove what I am in its being worthy or unworthy.

I have had quite a feast today. Mrs. Dick got a fowl and invited me over to dinner and tea, and just about dinner time Jim came over with a big fish and I got a bit of that for tomorrow's breakfast. I gave

---

[1] Probably the fourteen-horsepower engine bought by Cosme through a loan from the Banco Agricola. See Gavin Souter, *A Peculiar People; the Australians in Paraguay*, 1968.

Mrs. Dick that pair of khakee trousers of yours as a quid pro quo (a this for that). She had told me she was nearly out of her mind for trousers for William as he had only a ragged rotten old pair for working and his one pair of good. She has to wash the boys' working clothes on Sunday for their wear the following week and they wear them all the week. You can imagine a week's sweat and dirt in one pair of trousers and one shirt . . . I believe I hear the engine[1] in the distance, three months coming three miles! and only five tons. What price getting produce to market!

Seven hours and half a day on Saturday this summer, I wouldn't mind betting next year sees six hours and half a day Saturday. No one has worked over time for a long while. No one goes to attend horses till the work horn goes. I doubt if the anticipated cane growing will be done by colony labour in short hours, long smokehos (no one hurries to time) and easy stroke at work. The idea of Communism is practically dead and the well doing financially of the Colony is the one thing. 'What will pay best?' is the idea . . . Certainly the colony gives nothing to balance its snakes, its fever, its jaundice, and its generally infernal climate. The health of the children shows what a great thing fresh air and plenty of exercise is, for they keep the health fairly average, but they can't do all.

Do you know, dear, what the young imp did today? No less than climbed through the front room window to the back table, and sat among the crockery washing his face in the three legged pot. Did it three or four times. There will soon be no place but the ridge pole on which to keep things out of his way. He also discovered how to get up on the bed. He climbs on a box under the back window, reaches over till he touches the bed, and the rest is easy. Missing him a second this morning I espied his head above the edge of the wash tub where he was seated flat on the washing. He rocks the rocking chair till he backs up against the partition when he climbs up till he can reach the fiddle bag, or till he gets near enough to the table to reach over and upset all things his hands can touch, or the darling just sits or stands rocking gently singing his sweet little songs, and one is divided between the desire to cuddle him up and kiss him, and the desire to keep quiet and listen.

The engine arrived this afternoon, after great work and great excitement. They have been since Friday morning (yesterday included) bringing it six miles or less. I believe before they had moved many feet on Friday they got into a bog that took five hours to get out of, even the men went down up to the knees.

---

[1] See note to previous letter, 15 December 1899.

To William Gilmore

Dearest,

Cosme
23 January 1900

I stopped before I began with the run of some verses in my mind—something like this only it does not quite get it. They are not worth anything except that they are full of the thought of you.

> Home to my own,
> Where the hearth fire burns,
> Home to my own
> My heart ever turns;
> Home to my own
> To come not away
> Home to my own
> At the end of the day.
>
> 'Home is no home, how fair it may be
> Home is no home, apart, love, from thee.'

Billy is asleep. He makes a lot of Mrs. Dick who spends half her time here. She says there never was his equal in the wide world—and of course there isn't. He slept badly last night—too hot. Tonight is worse after a very hot day ... Dear dear husband you don't know how I weary for you, and how sad I feel that you cannot see the boy as I do, the darling.

To William Gilmore

Dearest,

Cosme
25 February 1900

Somehow I feel so sad and done tonight. Billy lay in my arms awhile ago looking so sick and small and miserable that I almost cried and my heart aches for him. What he wants is chicken broth and because he runs about and the Colony is so poor I can't ask for it for him, and he turns against his food and only takes it when hunger forces him to it, all the time craving for variety and saying 'Ta' for what he can't get. I counted twelve dead matches on my table this morning—a match for every time I had to light the lamp, and there were times when I left the lamp alight to avoid striking matches so often.

Mrs. J. Lane[1] is in to see the Doctor, Harry Baker went from V.R. to Pinders[2] where he still is, I hear. A pig killed yesterday, one a fortnight ago—the best pork ever killed on the Colony. Mrs. Davey sent

---

[1] The wife of John Lane, brother of William Lane, leader of the settlement.
[2] Mary means John Pindar.

me up a nice big sweet damper today—the only one in the Colony who ever remembers to do such a thing. I will remember all these things when I get a few cents to spare.

A very heavy rain storm this afternoon, drops came in all over, but soon ceased. Dear darling Will, longing is no word for what I feel and feel more acutely as the time draws near when you expected to travel back to B. Aires. I wonder daily and hourly when I shall hear from you. Sometimes I feel nearly broken-hearted with anxiety which Billy's fever and mine do not lessen or make easier to bear. But some day we will sit together by our own fireside, the heartache all gone.

Do you know I have come to the conclusion that Communism is a failure—is not attainable, real Communism that is, and enforced Communism is worse than none. I think that all co-operation with equal sharing is the truest and most possible—gives most good with fewest ill-results. And now to go to bed, Billy is waiting in the rocking chair with fast ebbing patience.

To W. A. Woods

'Burnside'[1]
Strathdownie E.
via Casterton Vic.
11 June 1903

Amigo,[2]

What sort of auto. notes do you want? Bald facts, or nice little items that will 'frill', or both 'em?

---

[1] The Gilmores arrived back in Australia in 1902. After a few months in Sydney they went to Will's parents' farm at Strathdownie near Casterton in western Victoria. For details of the period see, *inter alia*, W. H. Wilde, 'Mary Gilmore—The Hidden Years', *Meanjin Quarterly*, 4 (1973), 425-32. Will was forced to travel far to look for work and was often away for long periods, as the following letter (reproduced exactly as written) indicates:

Wee Waa
Dear Mary, 26.1.1903

Your letter of the 18 to hand I sent a wire to you yesterday. I have been at work four days 8 shillings per day I am having my food with Mr. Copeland and Mr. Oakes Mr. Copeland is the is the [sic] head manager Oakes is time keeper we have a cook to cook for us we get our bread from the town wich is only two miles off and each one paying his share of the food every pay day which is very two weeks it is aful hard to get meat here and everything is such a price that it will caust us a lot to live here as far as I know the work here will last about three mounths. I do not know if I will be able to get more work when this is done or not. I do not know how half the people out here manage to live there are hundreds of men out of work and the store keepers will not give credit unless they are sure of getting payed. I went into one of the stores the other day and I saw such a lot of orders being made up of tined meat and cheese and such like thir is no such a thing as vegetables in the place. I am getting on very well as ganger the men are local men which is better for me than if I had the Sydney crowd to deal with. The work is the deepening of a creek to run water from the river out through the dry part. My work has been the clearing the timber out of the creek and along the banks so that it can be plowed.

I had a post card from Wallace about Mr. Rundle and he said Mr. Rundle had not made

Anyhow here goes for a sort of personal—but you know what sort I am, so why can't you fix it up?

I was born near Goulburn, N.S.W. Mother N.S.W. native of N. of Ireland parentage, highly strung, nervous, bright woman, without either fads or superstitions. I was born when she was barely twenty. Father; fine looking man of splendid physique, talent for the mechanical, *very* Highland. When he was about forty he met his equal at scratch pulling; I have an idea he and the other man sat and pulled all night without advantage on either side. My father never pulled again. He was too proud to risk a beating. He had all the Highland superstitions,— though he always *said* he didn't believe in 'em. I have them too, and I always say I don't believe in them, nor do I intellectually, but in the bedrock of my soul the belief is there.

In my young days I was considered a prodigy of learning because I could write a fine angular hand and read a newspaper article at the age of seven. One of my earliest recollections is as a child of three sitting on my maternal grandfather's knee and spelling out of the old Family Bible 'In the Beginning was the Word'.

My mother's people were Wesleyans of the rigid Presbyterian kind. Indeed it was simply accident that called my grandfather anything so mild as Wesleyan. No weekly newspaper was read inside his doors on Sundays, and no wicked secular music was ever heard inside his gates. One of my uncles learned in secret to play two hymn tunes on that instrument of evil—the fiddle. As a surprise, he played them to his father, but the old man never spoke, indeed except from the setness of his look one would not think he heard. Yet he was one of the best men I ever knew. He had the sense of contract, which means so much, and is so sure an indication of character. He served the Lord even in his smallest actions, but he held his head on a level with the throne. My father was something the same in his 'face to face with God' attitude, but he was more of the 'The Sabbath is the Lord's and

---

up his minde what he was going to do with his station. I do not [think] ther will be much change.

Dear old Mary I am feeling very depressed and downhearted. I try to shake the feeling off but I don't seeme to get on everything looks so black ahead for us that it is hard to keep ones heart up and then again you are such a parte of my life that I feel utterly lost without you. I miss your kind loveing simpthy and your gentle words and encouragement more than I can tell. But you must not take any notice of this dear do not let it worry you I expect I will feel more cheerful later on even the being able to write about it seems to me a releife. I think it would be better for you to go on to Vic. As you are so far on your way indeed Dear I think the change into the cooler climate would do you good after all your hard work up there and I could send you some money to Strathdownie. If I do not get into permenant work after this I may go over by boat to Strathdownie for a while. I did not pay Miss Rian but I will find out how much it is send it to her how is billy does he stand the heat. I do miss the little fellow life seems very different without you and him dear Your loveing
Will

² Walter Alan Woods.

Let Him not encroach'—on the other days. (If this isn't autobiog., it is at least the springs of my beginnings.)

I went to school in Wagga in due time and found that I had constantly to explain myself to my fellow pupils. 'You use such long words' they used to say. I was surprised; I had no intention of using out-of-the-way language. I was a voracious reader, and spoke like a book. At this school (I was ten) I was put into a low class because I could not add up, but in six months I was in third class, and considered an exceedingly quick child. In third class we had composition and I recollect almost invariably my slate was kept to show round to the teachers. I did not think of it myself. The other girls drew my attention to the fact. When I was eight or nine I would sit for hours writing 'letters' on a slate; no one ever read them—not even myself, and as quickly as one was written it was cleaned off and another begun. At the little Brucedale (near Wagga) school I used to spend all my dinner hour at this, eating my lunch as I wrote. Then I went to school in Wagga. I was ten, and we, my brother and I, had a three-mile walk. I was a thin, tall, delicate child, and the hours of school took so much from my vitality that many and many a time I walked home with the calves of my legs pushing to the front in a state of nervous terror at the imaginary *something* that might be behind. In the morning there were no terrors, only in the evening. I was a child that constantly craved the affection of its nearest, or the signs of it, and because I would not sue I got, or fancied I got, least of it. It is the child that leaps on your lap and kisses you that gets the kiss, not the one that sits in the corner and longs for it, yet the first probably only kisses for love of kissing.

After Wagga School I went to Downside School a few miles away. Here I was a bad girl. The poor old pedagogue for pedagogue he was, used to keep me in and go to his dinner. I used to climb out the window and over the fence, have my dinner and be back again before he remembered me. At the inspection held here the report read 'So and So'; 'One pupil excellent'—which was *ME* no less, though I didn't know it till years after. Fifteen years later I found the widow of my old master in Sydney. She did not know me; I told her who I was. She flung her arms round me—'Ah!' she cried, 'When I saw those wicked eyes I felt there was something I ought to remember'. She told me Mr.— had talked about me up to the day of his death, that he had always been so proud of me, &c., &c. You know there is something in that kind of thing which makes you feel so much. At the time you didn't think of anything, didn't know you deserved anything, and afterwards when you *know* you were different someway from the general run, you find the recognition was there all the time—unknown and unthought of. And, here, the poor old man was dead and I could not tell him how his kindness touched me.

After that I went to school in Cootamundra and later at Bungowannah, near Albury—a small country school among farms, where I had a bed made up in the school quite away from the house, because there was no spare room for me in the residence, where I used to lie awake in the moonlight nights trembling and cold with nervous fear, listening to the cry of the morepork in the hills, and the melancholy wail of the curlew in the flats, while my heart used to nearly burst with fright at the rustle of a mouse among the papers in the empty grate. I left here so thin and nervous I was kept at home for some time before I went to school again. Then I was sent to a good kind uncle—teacher at Yerong Creek, who took such pains with me that, when at sixteen I went up for examination as Pupil Teacher, I was said to have passed highest of all that year's candidates. I was given my choice of appointment in Sydney or any of half a dozen country towns. I chose Wagga as being near my own people, and because I had gone to school there. I was only a gawky country girl dressed in a home made frock when I entered the school to begin work, and when I went eagerly up to an old school-fellow (she wore a watch and her skirt was weighted down with pennies instead of shot, and who afterwards married a clergyman and wore glasses) she coldly gave me the tips of her fingers and turned away to another girl whose dress had six pearl buttons where mine had one. But deep inside the chill that came over me was the germ of a hot feeling of hate and determination to some day make her repent of her snub. Perhaps I did, perhaps I didn't, but when for months she came to me to help her with her hardest sums, unravel the difficulties of her analysis, and give her the punctuation in the punctuation lessons, when indeed she, who previous to my coming had been the bright one, looked up to me as the bright one, then I was satisfied. My pride was soothed, I had had my revenge—and she never knew. No one who ever injured me to a deep hurting can say I ever injured them. Indeed I sometimes feel I hate so hard I *have* to be kind. Well the mistress of the Girls' School at Wagga was Miss Everitt who for so long was Principal of the Hurlstone Training College. A girl from the University told me years afterwards in Sydney that Miss Everitt had told her I was the brightest Pupil Teacher she had ever had. After Miss Everitt left Wagga for Hurlstone other Mistresses used to tell me that my 'prose order' was more poetical than the poetry to *be* prose ordered. At this time I devoured Carlyle and Victor Hugo, and one or two Headmasters used to make fun of me by asking if various compositions were Carlyle or Miss Cameron. Also at the time I used to often read novels till midnight and then study till daylight. I *couldn't help* reading—I read everything, Jack Harkaways, Proctor's Astronom. works, Jevons's Logic, Family Heralds, Gordon's Poems, Kendall, The Koran, fragments of newspaper stories, even if only a few inches long—anything and everything I could get. And at this time I got my best reports as a teacher. It often seems strange to me how it should be so. But I expect it was sheer hard work and an unconscious vitality. I fell into such a condition of anaemia, that I was told that, unless I had a change, I would not live three months. Yet I never thought of either leaving school or of going home. Later, my landlady told my mother she often feared to call me to breakfast lest she should find me dead. Fortunately my mother came to live in town. She fed me up and pulled me round, but I doubt if I ever really got over the strain of that time.

I have so often been told that I have a strong personal influence over people that I begin to believe it especially as, when I look back over my life at school and as Pupil Teacher, I remember that I was either 'leader' or 'ringleader' (amongst my own particular factions or schools)—according to whether I was good or bad. I resigned my pupil teachership and took a small school in order to speedily go up for examination as a classified teacher and to avoid the training school, of which somehow I had a dread. As soon as possible I sat for examination. Feeling sure of III C. and hoping for III. B. to my surprise I came out with III A. Then I went as Assistant to Silverton in the palmy days of Broken Hill. I had 2 years and three months there when I was appointed to Neutral Bay as Assistant, and three years from the previous examination I went up for Class II (this being the earliest opportunity) hoping for II B. I got II A. I was even more astonished over this than over the III A. and to make sure there was no mistake I wrote for the marks I had been awarded in each subject. They convinced me I had gone through alright. Then I went to Stanmore; was there about five years and when I left the streets were lined with weeping children. I left for South America a few days later ... William Lane once said in some surprise, like a man who is convinced against preconceived conviction—'You reason like a man! I have never met any woman who could reason. I speak of pure reason, reason going logically from point to point—indeed I have met few men who can reason like you.' Also 'You have the gift of intuitive perception in an unusually high degree. No matter how one talks to you, you can follow, and though you may not understand *exactly* as the other mind sees, yet there is always perception of the actual behind the seeming and you can always follow.' Another time he told me he never met anyone who knew English as I did—i.e. the language—I wish I knew it now.

Mrs Lane used to say 'I never saw anyone so quick and impulsive over big things, and so deliberate over little things as you'—but that is a question of issues, and in magnitudes for and against are easily decided on.

One of the kindliest things I remember was when I wrote 'The crows kep' flyin' up, boys'—Henry Lawson came up to me in the little old New Aust. Office 'I must congratulate you' he said kindly. I looked at him—'I saw those verses of yours about Larry Petrie' he said in answer to my look, then after a pause he added 'You have beaten me on my own ground, I haven't seen anything better.' It was so kind and so unexpected, and I never forgot it. And you, if you recollect, have often said you never saw anyone 'so doubtful of the worth of your own work' &c.—Farrell has often spoken kindly of my work, but he is too true a friend to ever say it was any better than he thought it, only, when I shewed him those love verses I wrote in December and January he said in a sort of an understanding, half-puzzled surprise 'I didn't think you had it in you!'—and that pleased me more than any compliment, for the only John is too kind a man to overpraise—later he wrote in rather flattering terms of stuff I had sent him for criticism, but the 'I didn't think you had it in you' pleased me most. My mother once repeated to me a saying of an old cousin whom I had visited—'Of all the cousins who come to stay with me, she is the only one who never talks ill of others. She will talk of books, or what she sees or reads, but I have never heard a word of scandal from her.' That also sank in as a pleasant thing to remember. I didn't talk scandal simply because I never thought of it, and later when I did think of it the remembrance of old Cousin Annie kept me from it. So grows the seed of a kindly word.

A woman with a tongue remarked to another that she would rather fall out with the whole neighbourhood than with me, meaning she was afraid of me—yet I never quarrelled with a woman in my life; I only feel that my back gets too stiffly straight to allow of anything but the most dignified and accurate speech, and if that is not possible, there is nothing to be said. I *couldn't* quarrel, the words wouldn't come; a sort of dumb feeling takes possession of me when anything like that approaches me. On the other hand, if anything caused me to think I ought to go out and preach at street corners, nothing would stop me. Duty—or contract—must be obeyed—it is the one thing that lifts man above the brute.

Suppose I get me sister to call on Mr Stevens?[1] She could take some photos and tell him lots of things—for instance how I cried 'Go to ruin! Go to ruin, then' because she would persist (as a little girl) in talking to the servant as an equal. She reminded me of it only recently.

As to South America: I had a lot of fever on the Colony; also people said I worked too hard. I was married there, and my child was born in the neighbouring town. The nurse—an ex-colonist—was drunk from

[1] A. G. Stephens. See note to letter, 22 June 1903.

before his birth till a week after and I did not write to the Colony for help because I did not care to expose her thinking no one but I knew she drank. Only for the kindness of a chance visitor, Mrs J. Pinder,[1] I would have died, and only for the nurse's little girl of eight, I would have often gone all day (while in bed) without food. A month before my child was born, I went into Villa Rica. Imagine, me, a delicate woman, who had been a weakly baby and a frail child, a woman whose heart was so weak my Sydney Doctor had said that I must always be careful—imagine me starting from home with my husband at four a.m. in a spring cart and two horses, and an hour later having to get out and wade through water often over my knees, wading thus, with an occasional 'lift' in the cart where the water and mud were not too deep for the horses to struggle through with my additional weight, till about 11 a.m. when we came out on a plain where the keen June wind cut like a knife. I didn't dare ride then for fear of a chill, and I had to walk on to keep up the circulation till we reached the Railway Station just as the one o'clock train was heard to whistle in the distance. We had just time to change a note and get my ticket. I got into the train wet, cold and alone, for we did not feel justified in spending money on a ticket (1s. 8d.) for my husband. And there I travelled in a filthy third class carriage full of natives, of whose language I was quite ignorant—all smoking, men and women alike, with baskets of meat here and there on the floor—game-cocks perched on the backs of the seats, and young pigs in bags among our feet. I got into Villa Rica about six o'clock. God knows how I escaped fatal harm; yet somehow I got through alright. Vitality I suppose. I have been told more than once that I would have been dead only for my will.

When my child was two weeks old I returned to the Colony, and when he was sixteen days old I was at the wash-tub—this because I knew every woman in the Colony had as much work to do as ever she could manage without mine being added. I remember the longing I had when my child was born to send a wire to my husband, but I was afraid of the expense—it would have seemed like taking bread out of the children's mouths, and I only sent a letter. But I never think of that telegram without a feeling of sadness. I was away and the baby was come, and I had to wait for the chance of the mail being sent for from the Colony for my husband to know.

I remember how we made a cot for the child. Will split the timber—lapacho, a hardwood and a heavy—with maul and wedges, then he trimmed down the splintered sides with an adze, after which he split the pieces with an old saw. He was weeks over the work—the wood was so hard—then with a plane and a spoke shave he smoothed all the surfaces. It was a bit out of plumb in some of its legs, but it would

[1] John Pindar's wife.

take a beautiful polish. The idea of the polish was a joy to us, but we had neither the time nor the material to polish with, so the joy never had a foundation in fact. And though the cot was finished I never put the boy to bed in it except by day. It seemed so cold-hearted to put him away in the night—and we thought he might feel lonely—'besides,' his father said, 'he is such a little fellow'—We made also a what-not—but it was sawn out with a cross-cut; I was the architect, Will was the Executive; it was a thing of beauty, actually had a bead on its front edges, and wouldn't go skew-wise if stood away from the wall. In fact, it could on occasion stand alone; but we kept it nailed to the wall for security and safety's sake.

Some time after we severed our connection with the Colony (Cosme) and while Will was in Patagonia, I went into Villa Rica to live, renting the same little house where my baby was born. The evenings were pleasant, for it was May, and I used to sit in the verandah at sundown and even till nearly dusk. After a week of this my landlord and his six daughters came one evening to see me and remonstrate. 'It wasn't safe' they gave me to understand; 'there were bandidos about'. 'And would I go indoors before sundown and fasten up the house'. And he hauled in the trunk of a small orange tree to add to the security of my door. The door, I may mention, opened in the middle, had a bolt top and bottom, and a double lock in the middle. He fastened the bolts, double locked the door, and then jammed the sapling against the middle of it. One of the daughters, to make things more secure, brought in a long board; this was propped in against the upper part of the door. Some weeks afterwards, finding the door rattle in a high wind, I examined the hinges. There were no screws in them, only nails, old rusty nails, about two to each hinge. I smiled. The thing was so like Paraguay. After that I ceased to barricade the door in the middle and did it at the sides—not that it mattered much, except as a precaution against it being blown in. To this house used poor Larry Petrie to come after his seventeen hours duty at the Railway Station. 'Larry, Larry, you foolish fellow' I used to say—'Why don't you go to bed instead of coming up here?' 'Bed!' he would reply 'How can I sleep? The carpenters work beside me and the lampmen are in and out all the time, and so it's a case of get drunk, or come and talk to you', and he would stay and talk till his nerves quietened and then tramp wearily back to his little lamp-room for an hour's sleep. Twice he prevented a collision; once he saved a train from fire, and died at last with his ribs through his lungs, his life given for that of the Station-master's child.

Will came up to Villa Rica from Patagonia, intending we should all go down as soon as the summer came. We went from Villa Rica to Sapucay (the Railway works) and lived there two or three months.

Then to Buenos Aires for a few more months. Here Will went shearing in the Argentine—such an experience! In November nearly three years ago we left for Gallegos, in South Patagonia. From Gallegos the Falklands lie east 300 miles, so you may guess how cold it was. Magellan's Strait is two days' ride south. On the way south an epidemic of measles broke out; my little son took the complaint, inflammation of the lungs set in. There was no milk, water ran short; it was thick and purple, we were on a waterless coast in an old ship whose engines might blow up any time, whose condenser only condensed enough for the first class, and used to break out in leaks every second day. The Doctor suffered from melancholia and loss of memory; he was kindness itself, and used invariably to pray over my little one, but he dared not trust himself to do anything else beyond take his temperature. When I would beg of him 'Doctor, is there *anything* can be done?' he would say 'We can only wait, we can only pray'—and sometimes 'He is too weak for anyone to do anything'—we were 31 days on a voyage that should only have taken six or seven. The Pacific boats do it in two-and-a-half. *Yet* Billy lived.

In Patagonia I was for a time governess to, I think the most awful girl that ever lived. She was 16; looked 18, and called herself fourteen. She knew everything ever known, and what I told her one day, told me back in a day or two as entirely her own. Among the items of her own peculiar knowledge was that 'she knew the woman who made *all* the lace for Queen Victoria's wedding.' Her mother was a nice woman; her father a big man with a thin nose, a high voice, and a character and reputation to match. After three months' governessing I went from the Estancia to live in Gallegos. Here I was advised to take up English teaching. I demurred on the grounds that I could not speak Spanish. 'Oh, but you are such a good English scholar' was the reply, 'you should do well at it'. It seemed a queer reply and a queer reason for success, but there was a lot in it; so I took a house and began teaching. My first pupil was Don Vicente Cane, of the Bank of Argentina, nephew to a gentleman whose name I forget, but who was one time Plenipoa, for Argentina in London. A fine scholar and a brilliant writer. Don Vicente lent me his uncle's translation of Henry V. which was *really* Shakespeare in another language. The first month of teaching was dreadful. I felt such a fraud, for I hadn't the use of twenty words of the language, though with dictionary I could read fairly well. As the lesson hour came round my knees used to shake with apprehension lest Don Vicente wouldn't come, and my stomach grow sick in dread of the lesson should he come. Whichever way it was it was awful. Yet in a week Senor Cane brought me other pupils, and the Deputy Governor sent me more. Indeed, in a little while I had to take a more convenient house and had as many pupils as I could manage. And they were so kind, all of them. I got on splendidly with my Spanish, and they were kind enough to say they did well with the English—and indeed, after awhile, I think they did for I tried hard enough. Moreover they all expressed their sorrow and disappointment when I told them I was leaving.

Half the lessons I gave at my own house, the rest at the houses of pupils, and many and many a day the wind blew my little boy off his feet as we hurried along to a lesson, or dashed me against a telegraph post or a fence. The wind is incessant. Except in the dead of winter when all is frozen it never ceases. I have been half an hour going 100 yards, and holding on to fences all the way, and I have seen men—who wear no skirts—have to put their hands to the ground to maintain their balance. My little boy I couldn't leave at home as he was too young, and a servant was out of the question. Only soldiers' wives were available, and they would only stay till they had pilfered all they wanted, in addition to which none of them could cook, and all were dirty and immoral.

During the time I was in Gallegos war was threatened between Argentina and Chile. The disputed territory was only 60 miles away. It was a time of great excitement. Soldiers drilled daily back and front of my house beginning at 2 a.m.—the days were long and there was little darkness at night; the pigeons were taken out and trained, and the wildest rumours prevailed. Chilenos were openly arrested in the streets and locked up, and I was frankly told that unless we had our passports Will would be imprisoned. He was away and I was alone—away fifty miles off at Estancia Condor initiating machine shearing at the Station. There was no direct mail to him, and if I wanted to telephone or telegraph I would have to do so via Chile, as the lines ran to and from Punta Arenas, and when Chile chose that we should get news of the progress of negotiations she opened the lines, when she didn't choose she closed them. We had no Consul, but the English officials in the Chilean English Bank swore to defend the bank and the English women with their lives. There were a few robberies and I slept every night with an axe, two or three carving knives, and a siren whistle under my pillow, some of my pupils impressing upon me never to open my door at night should a knock come till I knew who was outside and indeed I was thought to be a phenomenal woman to live alone and not be afraid and indeed I wasn't afraid, but I was mightily excited, and terribly anxious for the future. We had weeks of this, every few days bringing news of mobilization of troops first on one side and then on the other. Our hope was that negotiations would go on till snow fell in the Andes, when the passes—there were only two—would be closed, and in the meantime we might get a man-of-war from the Falklands. Remember we were living amongst people only semi-civilized, and among whom three parts were of Indian extraction. I never kept a revolver in the town, though I had one offered me. It is an awful thing to kill a man, and down there unless you kill it is useless shooting, and I wouldn't dare to kill. My husband, too, was considered mad because he did not carry a knife, not even when over the machines at Condor, where he had all nationalities under him and not one but was armed. For many reasons I liked living in Patagonia, but the cold was too severe, not the degree of cold, but the cold combined with the wind. The wind gets in everywhere. I have been three days (on the edge of the Pampa) trying to get the irons hot enough to iron, and burning English coal all the time; and water dropped on the floor in my kitchen froze at once. In the poorer houses the breath formed frost on the blankets, and I have had ice one-eighth of an inch thick day and night on the inside of my bedroom window. As I sat governessing on the Estancia my breath formed frost flowers on the schoolroom window and the thermom. stood at 32 degrees and a shade under. This with a kerosine heater in the room.

After fourteen months of Patagonia we left for B. Aires and in March 1902 left B.A. for Australia via England. On the way over we fell in with a cold spell shortly after leaving Rio. It was perishing; whooping-cough and bronchitis broke out. Billy got bronchitis; the Doctor said it was whooping cough and made me have him on deck, result pleurisy and pneumonia. At the same time Will got whooping cough. I was weak after being in the B.A. Hospital with an illness caused by the cold of Patagonia and had to nurse single-handed. The cold was intense, with rain, fog and sleet as we neared England. Two or three times every night I had to go from one end of the ship to the other for hot water, feeling my way over the wet dark slippery deck. The marvel is I didn't go overboard in the Bay of Biscay. A few hours before reaching Liverpool Billy passed the crisis. 'He will live—with care' the Doctor said. We came into Liverpool in a drizzling rain and biting wind—too late to draw up to the landing stage, and so had to go off in a tender. Wrapping Billy so that we could keep the air from him I took him out of bed and got a passenger to carry him from the ship to the tender as his father was too weak to hold him. The Doctor came and looked at him. Then he turned to another passenger saying 'He hasn't the ghost of a chance'. The passenger said something. 'He won't live', reiterated the Doctor. Yet he did and I knew he would. Coming to Liverpool I had written to my brother, Mr J. A. Cameron, to Hy. Lawson and another friend. My brother who was then in London did not get my letter. Lawson got his and wrote for us to come from Liverpool to London as soon as we could saying 'Bed's made, and cot's ready for the little fellow. Come at once, am simply mad for the sight of an Australian face.' Three weeks later we came to London staying ten days. Leaving London we took in marble at, I think Genoa. At Suez we ran on a sandbank and the propellor was broken. It was partly fixed at Aden, but another blade dropping, the divers were set to work at Colombo. From Colombo we crossed the Equator, speed dropping to about seven knots when we turned and went back. Permission to land under the ordinary circumstances being refused to the third-class passengers, we went to Bombay to dry dock. The night we left Colombo the tail of a cyclone struck us. The marble shifted. We had been told we would only take two and half days to Bombay. We were six. As the wind and the sea went down the rolling of the ship grew heavier and more alarming, indeed some of the passengers tied themselves in order not to be thrown from their seats. Over and over the vessel hung no one knowing which way she would go. One of the chief officers said, 'I believe that had she gone over not a soul would have been saved,' and another speaking to me of the propellor said that in over twenty years he had never seen one in such a condition, and the marvel was that any of us were left alive. On the return to Colombo Henry Lawson joined his family and we found that the first and second class passengers had gone on by a ship of the same line. Arriving in Sydney the first hand to grasp mine as we landed was John Farrell's and then Charlie White of the Bathurst Free Press. Since which it has been a case of going round renewing old friendships . . .

    I don't think I'm mercenary, and I recollect that when I was leaving the Ed. Dept. the Bill cutting off the Superannuation was about to be passed, I was advised to apply for 12 months' leave instead of immediately resigning, so that I could claim my refund under the about-to-become-law Act, resigning after I got the money. It is a usual thing I believe from Judges down, that kind of thing, but it doesn't and didn't seem to me honest and I resigned right away—eight years ago come next November.

    A girl I met in Sydney—an ex-pupil—told me that owing to my encouragement as a child (in composition) she kept on writing and is now writing a novel; a couple of others kept on writing verse for the same reason. I hope they may be successful and I can certainly say I have always encouraged where I could, both child and adult. And more than one child came to me abjectly untruthful and left me with a pride in himself that kept him from lying.

    I write much about Billy and little about Will. But motherhood is the thing that is of the world and for the world, that says 'This have I done and this do I give', but wifehood is the little world apart where none may come in—and so I only write of the outside things. But of Will Lane said: 'He is the best man I ever knew', and Henry Lawson said 'The best mate; the best mate I ever had. No man ever had a better.' And so let me end. Yours faithfully,

To A. G. Stephens

'Burnside'
Strathdownie E.
via Casterton, Vic.
22 June 1903

Dear Mr. Stevens,[1]

Could you give me the address of Jessie Mackay? And does she write for the 'Bulletin'?

I had a note from Mr. Woods a couple of weeks ago, in which he said you wanted some notes on my life for an article in the Red Page. I have to thank you for notice of my work, on different occasions already past, and I thank you for the proposed article also. The notes[2] I am unable to send this week as I have only odds and ends of time in between cooking sweeping washing & mending—Indeed the stuff I write has simply to be—to use the language of the locality—'chucked' together, and what won't shape in the process of 'chucking' has simply to be chopped off. Hence the singleness of idea, the lack of extension and the want of figure, & the recurrence of form & sameness of rhyme. Another thing, I feel greatly the want of educated conversation or discussion. The people among whom I live have all the individuality and robustness of the country, and in my own household, or rather my father-in-law's—of large and strong brain power, bitter humour & sharp shrewd tongue, but lingual and thought education is lacking. This, not so much for the making & waking of idea, as for readiness of use in language.

However much we may think in, & read thinking language, the habitual use of the language of the smaller, the lesser & the merely everyday of the material, leads in composition to the use of the common daily forms of speech to the exclusion of the others, especially where thought is rapid, and writing must be quick. If the idea to be expressed can be absolutely and wholly expressed in the simple, so best, but in ideas there are flying birds as well as domestic fowl, and that is where one feels the want of habit in the higher and more acutely expressive forms of language.

Of course it all doesn't matter very much, for the little I write isn't going to revolutionize the world or add anything appreciable to thought, but still if one gives a thing one wants to give of one's best—which reminds me that as a girl at school I had written in all my books

---

[1] For some years Mary mistakenly believed that A. G. Stephens spelt his name 'Stevens'. A selection of Mary's verse, some biographical details, and critical commentary by Stephens appeared in the Red Page (instituted in 1896 by Stephens to feature contemporary Australian literature) on 3 October 1903. For Mary's ecstatic reaction see the letter of that date.

[2] Mary had already replied to W. A. Woods with the notes required by A. G. Stephens. See previous letter, 11 June 1903.

'That which thy hand findeth etc'[1]—and my ideal of happiness was to wear a brooch with the word 'Thorough' on it. This by the way. As far as my writing is concerned, I do not think it is of sufficient worth to justify me in neglecting the homely work I took upon myself in marrying in order to devote time to it. There is no excuse for breach of contract—except a greater & I haven't that excuse.

Henry Lawson once told me that I 'beat him on his own ground'[2] and Farrell (I have known both for nearly twenty years) told me once of some stuff 'I honestly didn't think you had it in you',[3] but that doesn't mean genius and genius is the only thing that has a right to break away from that which binds ordinary man which includes Yours faithfully,

M. Gilmore.

To A. G. Stephens

'Burnside'
Strathdownie E.
via Casterton, Vic.
2 August 1903

Dear Mr Stevens,

I would have written earlier, but I was house moving. There's nothing very exciting in housemoving, though it has its 'spassums', as when your only china teapot gets smashed and the jam dish comes out from among the sheets minus the jam (we only moved about 100 yds, and didn't pack), but it's all over now and the cat takes her milk in peace under the dresser. Yours faithfully,

M. Gilmore

To A. G. Stephens

'Windy Hill'
Strathdownie E.
via Casterton, Vic.
19 September 1903

Dear Mr. Stevens,[4]

Mr. Woods writes me 'Had a letter from Mr. Stevens. Article on your stuff in type, may appear any time. He says you're splendid—but uneven, which is no news to you'.

[1] 'Whatsoever thy hand findeth to do, do it with thy might'. Ecclesiastes, ix, 10.
[2] A reference to her ballad 'The crows kep 'flyin' up, boys'.
[3] In response to some love poems Mary had shown him.
[4] See note to letter, 22 June 1903.

I am not foolish enough to suppose you said splendid, but for the 'uneven', I am thankful, for I am looking to you for real hard criticism—for teaching, for training. What is good in one's work can stand, but what is poor wants to come out. As a matter of fact I owe much to you in the matter of style—supposing I have what might be called style—for grace of style has an infinite charm, and your writing has always had that attraction for me, from the first time I read them to the present.

As to these verses of mine, you might well say uneven, for you have the whole 'bilin', good, bad and indifferent. I don't know that any of them are worth much, except perhaps a few of the later ones, but on that point I am open to conviction—at least I am anxious to be open to conviction—and will let the matter go.

In relation to some of these later ones, John Farrell said they were 'distinctive', which was very nice, but I felt as if I had come into a kingdom when he looked at me doubtfully and doubtingly and said 'I didn't think you had it in you'. I asked Woods what he thought was 'distinctive' about them but he was horrid, for he wrote back and said he thought their 'daringness' and he further added 'a woman can handle what a man's clumsy fingers daren't touch', which is perhaps true— Stevenson says something the same, and yet there is Richard Feverel.[1] As to the daringness, if that is the predominant note, then I am disappointed indeed. The merely daring has no charms for me. To express one's beliefs sweetly and wholesomely is one thing, to express one's non beliefs of the natural in any way whatever is another. I have no patience with 'the intoxication of her scented hair' kind of thing, and the being who only feels life under such a stimulus is a perversion. The spring comes round and the birds sing, and in their own vitality is their stimulus and in that is purity and sweetness. One takes delight in the eye, in the colour, the shape, the expression, yet one would hardly like to look upon the bared nerve, the blood vessels or the brain at the back of it. So it is with other things, and one doesn't talk of them. But—yes, one doesn't talk of them, and in the unsaid and the half said lies most understanding.

To come back. If I thought these things were only daring, or have the effect of the only daring, I would burn the whole lot and never write another line, but I can't feel that, I feel so little like that kind of thing, and my beliefs are so strong in the sweetness, and the holiness of life—how can I look at my little son and feel otherwise?—that it seems to me they must be the voicing of these. I am most anxious to know how they struck you: that is, is the impression they give, of the clean and healthy, or of the morbid and unwholesome, of the fresh air and

---

[1] George Meredith's novel, *The Ordeal of Richard Feverel*, 1859.

the sky of heaven, or of the hot-house and the scent pot. I enclose a couple of slips—if the 'Bulletin' will have them—and again thanking you. I am Yours faithfully

M. Gilmore

To A. G. Stephens

'Hilltop'
Strathdownie E.
via Casterton, Vic.
27 September 1903

Dear Mr. Stevens,

I am glad you do not feel obliged to reply to my letters, as I should feel in that case that I was trespassing on your time—& I know you are a busy man—& that there was obtrusion, intrusion, & all the other ugly things one doesn't want to be. One doesn't feel 'in the way' under such circumstances—though perhaps one is.

An hour ago I had an article in my mind, brain-written as hard as thought could go, but the pig and the fowls had to be fed, & now it is all gone but this:— Or I will put it in a separate slip—if you think it worth toning down, cutting out and shaping for the 'Bulletin' will you kindly let me know. I enclose envelope and stamp for its return. Uneven? . . . The pulse is the barometer of the brain & when I'm tired, wh. so easily happens I haven't the brain of an owl. Foolish but well-meaning friends are always urging upon me the writing of a book. How could I write a book! As I said recently to Mr. Farrell 'I only write in flashes & what isn't done on the moment isn't worth putting in the rubbish bin'. Besides even if my brain were equal to the ascertaining of style, tone and thought necessary I haven't the physique—not to write & be what is it! 'Captain . . . & Cook of the Nancy Bell'.[1] By the time a woman has washed & baked, ironed & scrubbed, swept & cleaned & dusted, cooked three meals a day, darned & stitched and made one's own & one's child's clothes by hand & has the reputation of being one who keeps the corners clean, there isn't much time for writing—let alone vitality—and besides—I've said it all before—I didn't contract when I married, to be a writer, I contracted to be a wife & mother & the honour in and of and by one's own home & household is greater than that of all the outside world. If one could write a book

[1] An allusion to 'The Yarn of the Nancy Bell', one of W. S. Gilbert's *The Bab Ballads* in which the ship's cook, as the sole survivor of the shipwrecked crew who had eaten each other, declares:

'Oh, I am the cook and the captain bold,
And the mate of the Nancy brig,
And the bosun tight and the midshipmite,
And the crew of the captain's gig.

that would be great for all ages, one might do it & feel one had acted as one should. But the book that I would write wouldn't do that—though the me that looks at me with two blue eyes & asks 'Isn't it a pity people's teeth wear out when God doesn't give them any more after they're gone', may do what I sometimes think I could do if I were just a bit bigger all round. There are many pages for me to write yet in this living book in my hands, & it is better to write them well & faithfully than to waste my time trying to be the brilliant woman I not only am not, but never would be. Besides, as to books, there's such an infernal gathering of the pretty middling that I don't see why I should add to it. That is why I wrote—some years ago, to stay the publication of verse stuff: the stuff wasn't good enough. Although I wrote it, & allowed it to be submitted I would have been ashamed of it as a publication to the end of my days. I would like to write a volume, but I don't want it to contain what I would characterize as rubbish if another person wrote it. Personality doesn't mean excellence—even if the person be one's self. One writes because the impulse is in one, but in these hard times at any rate one doesn't publish so; & one collects keeps & hands round for perusal & criticism what one would rather die than see printed as a book—at least I think so, for I feel so.

To write as Henley[1] in that one small thing 'Out of the Pit' is it. (It is always a source of shame to me that I cannot quote, though I have a good ear memory for words, I have no eye memory). I mean the one in which he says 'I am the Captain of my Soul, I am the Master of my fate' is to be immortal. To me it seems that the man who wrote that has everything, & that the question of or no for hereafter was a matter of indifference to him as he had it if there were one, & he had it just the same even if there weren't one. To put it in the only word that occurs to me as expressing nearly what I mean, he is of the *undamnable*, which somehow brings me back to my ideal that it is better to write four lines perfectly than a thousand pretty well even if they be gilt edged & in the best morocco, & the others on the back of a grocery label.

About Henley (to change the subject) I saw yesterday an article on Plagiarism, one often sees such, & the calling everything similarly

---

[1] William Ernest Henley is especially remembered for his poem 'Invictus' with its ringing lines, beginning

'Out of the night that covers me
Black as the pit from pole to pole

and ending

'It matters not how strait the gate,
How charged with punishments the scroll,
I am the master of my fate:
I am the captain of my soul'.

Mary's memory of the poem (and of Gilbert's ballad) is not quite exact.

thought or similarly expressed as plagiarism seems so unjust. When I read it I was red hot enough to write on the plagiarism of the man in the street. You meet ten people & nine of them will say it is a fine day, or a wet day as the case may be. But where is the plagiarism? The common perception of a fact in any plane whatever & its expression in the most suitable words is no plagiarism. It seems to me that plagiarism lies not in similarity of the word or of the thought but in the adoption of tone. No two human beings tone alike but all of a nationality speak alike & being educated by the same minds & books, think more or less alike. But I'm expressing very badly. Man's thought is greater than language. Language only expresses that which is common to all, that in wh. all are (for purposes of expression & understanding) equal—roughly speaking equal. One man's thought on a subject is greater—has more nuances more melody more—I haven't got the word—yet he only has the same words the other man has. Just now I wanted a word, should I coin one to express, who would understand it? Which comes back to — to be understood the thought behind the word must be common—i.e. held in common. Thought grows with knowledge & knowledge with thought, & with thought & knowledge, language. The big brain sees biggest & in time the smaller sees what the other saw—though the other is far ahead again. Of his own spontaneity he perceives, & expresses. Is it plagiarism because it was seen & expressed before?

To A. G. Stephens

'Hilltop'
Strathdownie E.
via Casterton, Vic.
3 October 1903

Dear Mr. Stevens,

The enclosed letter written last week is practically an answer to yours received yesterday & I have little to add to it save this that I trust entirely to your judgment in the matter of publication. My opinion of my work is not particularly high, but such as it is I have honestly tried to make it the best of its kind that I could, my idea being that if your work is only third class let it be really third class & not third class calling itself second or fourth calling itself third. If the thing can certainly be made to pay its way it will be a load off my mind, for if it did not I should always feel I owed it to the Bulletin Co. to make up the deficit, & as we are fixed I might as well try to make ropes of sea sand, as try to do that. You are kind enough—kind because it is thoughtful for another, & because it is encouragement—to speak of 'avenues to better work'. Please not to either expect or hope more from me than you already have—have as to kind, quality &c. I write to you as I have written before to Woods & Farrell half explanatorily half argumentatively as to why I never look upon myself as a possible writer, & it is not all to let you know just how I feel, it is as much to argue the matter out with myself. I do feel at times as if I could write, & at such times the feeling is that even if there were much that was second rate as regards the standard of what I would aim to be yet some would be good & all that I would wish it to be. I haven't physique to be two things even if the day had hours enough to allow it, & if I give way to writing & to dreams of writing the temptation to more & more to the neglect of other things manifestly more right to do, the desire will grow, & with desire freedom of capacity in exercises. With practice one increases in power of expression & with growth of power comes better work, & with better work greater love for it till one is given over body and soul to the work—at least that is how it would be with me. Under the circumstances of my life it is better I should be a good house-keeper & home-keeper & maker. If I can.

You must see something in my verses that you have given them so much thought & me so much space. Every time I think of that 'whole page'[1] it seems as if something within me, the real entity, cried out 'My God! how terrible!' & yet you can also believe me that I feel I could go down on my knees for joy. And I know that when the paper comes I will hide it away unopened in the farthest corner of the house & go about my work as if it weren't there until I feel as if I have a grip on myself strong enough to keep from suffocation as I open the wrapper. People always say 'you take things so quietly & so calmly', which shows how little one human being is fit to judge of another!

I wish you could see this place just now. The heaths are lovely with flowers, just wildernesses of blossom & bird, & here at the old house that tilts forward towards the hill because it suffers from age & whiteants & the drift of sand & soakage, the old house with the rabbit skins round the chimney & the mossroses under the windows, there is a lilac bush that makes me forget life & only remember existence, for life is struggle & existence rest. Ten feet high & the shape of a ball & blossom all over it. Plum trees, apple, pear, quince, thirty years old trees that haven't been pruned for the last six or ten years, white & pink & brown & green & the grass like a web of matter green on the old mould beneath. And if you could only sit by the side of our fireplace at night & hear the old man, my husband's father, talk of the early days of the Wimmera & settlement in the stringy bark when the blacks were here, the old man who sold one farm & never stopped till he had drunk the last farthing of the money, & sold another

[1] The Red Page of this date was devoted by A. G. Stephens to Mary's life and poetry.

& stayed in bed till the last bottle bought with that was gone, the old one-eyed man of over 70 who will take his gun & his dogs & go out after foxes all day, & when put out his shoulder (his horse falling) a couple of months ago & refusing a sling spent the afternoon out shooting & tramping round. Or if you could sit in this windy little kitchen-sitting room of ours where the wind whistles up through the cracks in the floor, & under the window & by the door & each side of the fire place, a room thick with tobacco smoke when my husband's half brother comes across the river & talks 'old mares', & fighting fires & floods, & fox hunts & days & nights fowling in the swamps, stuff that one could call 'lore'.

Do you know, sometimes when I look back over so much that seems to me wonderful & so impressed with the seal of reality & the reality of life I wonder whether I have been more than other people or whether it is that imagination runs away with common sense. I would give anything—except duty—to possess the power of putting things as I hear them but I don't seem to have that faculty. I can write *about* them, but I can't write *them*. Lawson or Davis would find stuff down here for the next forty years—& all history—real living, authentic & passing away with every year that goes.

And, now, I won't bother you again for a long time.

Can I thank you? And yet perhaps best thanks are in the fact that I write so freely to you—& then disclose stuff that after writing I was too faint-hearted to send...

[It is difficult to assign this extract to a particular letter. The Editors have decided to include it here.]

... Country life is a sweet & a peaceful thing, but there are times when the strenuous soul cries out for something more than peace & quiet & stillness. If it's a man he goes out & chops trees down, or gets tipsy at the nearest public house which is usually called a hotel. If it's a woman she scrubs the floor, but the soul swears all the time. I had a letter from my brother Jack in London t'other day & at the reading of it my heart leaped as did Elizabeth's child at the voice of Mary; just to be there & amongst it all! And here I am, all the exciting things behind & nothing before, or nearly nothing for there is the old goose to set. Last month was most exciting for the cow calved, the sow littered & the terrier had puppies—& one thinks of the girl in Peg Woffington.[1]

It isn't all nonsense, for it means milk & butter, & bacon & the foxes kept off; & milk & butter & bacon & the foxes kept off mean health & strength, if they don't mean money, & I remember that my little son is getting fat & strong & freckled across the nose, & I am

---

[1] An early novel (1853) by the English novelist Charles Reade.

satisfied. You must excuse me in that I write without repression to you for there is no one here to speak to. There is a brown hillside opposite me as I write with patches of rock breaking through & flashes of green where grass has ousted the fern, & if I were to speak of it to anyone here they would say 'Yes. There's plenty of fern. It means poor ground'—& so it does, but that isn't all.

To A. G. Stephens

'Hilltop'
Strathdownie E.
via Casterton, Vic.
11 May 1904

Dear Mr Stevens,

I write to offer you the thanks of a deeply grateful heart. For a long time I have been afraid that I had some hered—no not hereditary, that wd. be blaming my ancestry & I'm too scotch to admit the ghost of a shadow there—anyhow, some inexcusable lack, some criminal incapacity, some utterly unpardonable want of perception, because I could not regard Ian Maclaren as I do—say Meredith. And here, in the last 'Bulletin' you class him with Marie Corelli! Whoroo! the world sings in tune again.

I don't know, but his work seemed somehow thin to me. Pretty—the frame of a man, perhaps, but the bones of a child.

Curious, the desire to be individual & the satisfaction in being liked—the 'stand still', 'go forward' of humanity, of development—I suppose.

To A. G. Stephens,

'Hilltop'
Strathdownie E.
via Casterton, Vic.
20 March 1905

My dear Mr Stevens,

One wd. almost be led to think you were asking a favour, instead of conferring one.

When I received your letter I was a moving body with a horizon plainly marked out on all sides by one insistent & persistent interrogation—'where *did* I pack that wretched thing?'

I wrote you I had a poor opinion of my own verse, & straightaway copied out *nine slips*.

Since then I have 'tidied up' in the new premises, & now that I can move round without falling over flat irons & wash-tubs. I have reduced the nine slips to two—or three. For this reason: you picked what you regarded best for the 'Red Page' some time ago, & since then I have written but little verse. In any case with so many bigger & better than I you won't want much of *mine*. As to the 'Bulletin' matter why of course that goes without saying, but I thank you for your courtesy all the same. Also, the Lord is merciful in that we can now let Sladen go—to pot.—'To pot', that shd. make a fine leading to many open-& closed-gates—I suppose after all history always circles round the stomach, & the maenad is the eternal. Well never mind. I nearly died yesterday (weak heart; re-action after getting a tooth out) & it struck me then during the spasmodic moments of what was less than thought that the chief feeling was *un* thought—indifference—a sense of end or rest, non-anticipation (perhaps that most of all) & that according to the orthodox I should have seen tongues of flame & hell-fire generally or heard the invisible choir. Just as I was giving up the struggle I thought of Billy lonely without me & his father away near Ararat &—here I am today. Anyhow I pray pretty hard I never may have to take an anaesthetic for I guess the *power* to live is pretty nearly the *will* to live—at least with some people.

To A. G. Stephens

Jackson Street
Casterton, Vic.
Dear Mr Stevens,   29 January 1907

The more your magazine[1] comes, the more I am sorry for the 'Bulletin'—& I couldn't say more than that if I enlarged for a week—and unless the 'taste' of the 'Lone Hand'[2] is different (from that of the present 'Bulletin') I am afraid it won't mend matters. The 'B' will cease even as a tradition to represent Letters (in Australia), be no more than a mere weekly. 'The Bookfellow' is wider & bigger & if possible more individual than the 'Red Page' and Bulletin, but the loss of the latter-as-it-was leaves a sore spot where we call the heart.

Thanks for your 'Postman'[3] compliment, even as a sarcasm it is nice to be joined to the great & the noted. As to the photo. I'll have to get one taken. Then I will send it on—if sufficiently flattering that is.

[1] The *Bookfellow* was revived by Stephens in 1907 soon after he left the *Bulletin*..
[2] The *Lone Hand*.
[3] 'The Postman' was a column of the *Bookfellow*. On 24 January 1907 the column began 'M. G. (Casterton). If you keep on writing letters like that we'll dub you the Sévigné of this bad writing age.'

By the way we have *two* papers here, one a liberal but not too grammatical, the other the 'News' (to wh. your press copy goes) a most awful conservative semi-salvation army paper. The 'Free Press' has a greater circulation than the other & *I* (observe that modest 'I') write the magazine notices for it. The 'News' objects to me because I write for the 'Press' & differ in *Politics*—& this is how it uses the Bookfellow to get at me—the *wretches*!

My 'Bookfellow' file (I'd sooner lose the Bible than it) I have taken down to the leading Bookseller's & left it there for the public to see it & subscribe if they have any sense at all, & I have extracted from the Kaleski articles for the 'Free Press', as the public may be struck by the information in them if not by the writing. I told Mr. James (the Bookseller mentioned) to write direct to you re subs, if any come in. (He lends me books & magazines, consequently if there is any commission I wd. like to see it go to him.) I don't expect a rush, as 'Steele Rudd's'[1] & Nat Gould are high water mark here. However, if any subs. do come in from this part you can thank Harry James.

I can't write today. All the ancestry in me is holding out its ear in anticipation of tomorrow—Highland gathering, bagpipes & sunburnt noses. I don't think you duly appreciate the pipes. Perhaps you esteem the phonograph & the gramophone? There is one in every little shop in the next street & the only expression that fits is one I wouldn't dream of using. But wouldn't I like to. It has only equal & that is an axe and plenty of room to smash. You see there are no trams here & no traffic to deaden the sound. It's easily seen there were no gramophones in Bible times or the other place.

P.P.S. Some days later—

The last 'Bookfellow' to hand—one doesn't know how to feel comfortably thankful enough for an *Australian* periodical wh. is not newspaperish, and is literature. You have been good to Steele Rudd's whenever it came out, but the thought of Harper's (say) coming with it must have had an effect like the dry-eyed weeping of a woman. That isn't very clear—but no matter.

What wouldn't I give to write like Jessie Mackay. (The line of Ross's 'And this the moonlight that she wandered in'[2] is worth everything I ever put together.) And you want to publish *me* when you have those. My Heavens! These have touch but what have *I*? These have originality & strength & delicacy combined though the delicacy is less than the strength & the strength less than the originality. The originality may not be extraordinarily great but it is there in all three qualities. As for me I feel like wiping the slate.

[1] *Steele Rudd's Magazine*.
[2] From the poem 'Love's Treasure-House' by D. M. Ross published in the *Bookfellow*, 24 January 1907.

'Billy' Lane, the 'New Australia' leader, in 1894

Mary as a little girl

Mary in 1899

Will and Mary with their son

The Royal Tar *at Port Adelaide*

A typical street in 'New Australia', Paraguay

I suppose it is a matter of temperament. I can compare myself with Roderic Quinn & Dorothy McCrae but not with—ever so far behind—Hugh McCrae or Mabel Forrest. And for Jessie Mackay I go down crumpled up & collapsed in the dust at once.

M.G.

You know, since the Bookfellow has been coming I have done a lot of hard—no—real thinking. The two aren't one nor the same.

There are writers whose work merely feeds the mind—just feed and no more. There are others who awaken and stimulate. One doesn't so much take their thought as go from a standpoint given, otherwhere and otherhow. One goes because of them into lands justly one's own yet which but for them would never have been entered. And the Bookfellow man is of the latter. Probably as far as we in Australia are concerned he is the latter. Personally the gates open and I walk out after I have been reading your own especial work.

* * *

It has seemed to me that what I want most of all is knowledge. And in this I typify Australia. In all things Knowledge is the one great thing wanted. If I had your knowledge I would write as I can never hope to do even in the margins, and now that I am older and no longer young I begin to understand why people thought me clever. I always used to laugh. I had a half contemptuous feeling to those who said so, a 'wotcher givin' us attitude of mind, for I always knew how little I knew and (here is the pity) never dreamed how much I might know. I remember years ago, too, Brereton (J. Le Gay) urging on Lawson to read—Read with a capital R. Lawson demurred—and I foolish that I was—saw his way of thinking and agreed with him. He said 'If I read I will write what other men say and in the style of other men. I will lose myself. I copy so easily' (he used to beg me be careful how I talked with him lest he 'should steal my ideas'. Poor Lawson!) I saw his honesty, and in those days honesty had but one side. (Now it is different.) For if a man have style he may temporarily lose it in another man, but if it be real it will rise out of folds of that enveloping other and be itself, only better understood and if worth anything better finished. If the string will fray with knowledge, it will fray without. And if it be true without knowledge there will come a time when the practised hand of the knowledged will keep it up to standard in spite of itself. See what I mean? And—would to God that I had knowledge!

* * *

And here you see is how the Bookfellow sends me out into fields that after all are mine own and yet in which I would never have walked—at least not just so—but for it. And in this I have written my congratulations informal though the manner be.

M.G.

To A. G. Stephens

Jackson Street
Casterton
14 February 1907
Dear Mr. Stevens, (St Valentine's day!)

You are more than kind but I hope you don't think I am altogether the bird with a wounded wing. I was really more amused over the poor old 'News'[1] than anything else—The 'News' had a sad history and is a sad household ...

I tried to get a photo taken for you. I took a photo to the photog. and asked to be taken 'Like that' (pose). He took me the other way and I came out with a face like a camel's upper lip. I objected, pointed out I had bared the lofty forehead wanting only a glimpse not a whole landscape view of it. He retorted with frightful emphasis *'Mrs. Gilmore! If you want a pretty picture I can't do it. I can only take likenesses.'* Since then I am looking out for a snap-shotter. There is only one photographer here. He pitches his camera low, and makes his subjects (in a double sense) look down to it. They wilt at his least word, and photographically speaking Casterton is an exceedingly long faced town.

Do you know Miss C. Hay Thomson (lately Melb.) now in London? I had a letter yesterday from her, dated Glasgow, wanting a photo and biog notes as she is doing a Strand article on 'Women Poets of the South'.[2] (It sounds fine and large!) I never saw more beautiful (but not over clear) handwriting in any woman—Beauty—meaning strength and character rather than line though line is included. She writes from Glasgow and says she is making a Magazine Connection. That the illustrated article is the kind always asked for (the Camera takes the place of brains I suppose in most of them—the magazines I mean, not the writers) that interest in Australia now dividends are paying is looking up, and that as an Australian she wants to push Australia as far as she can. A nice, unaffected unboastful letter, though I am afraid my last sentence doesn't carry out that. It is the fault of my wording. I do not know her at all. Do you? Yours very faithfully,

To A. G. Stephens

Jackson St
Casterton
Dear Mr. Stevens, 17 March 1907

I seem to strike auspicious or at all events more or less romantic dates.

---

[1] The *Casterton News*, edited at the time by E. F. Hughes.
[2] The *Strand Magazine* (London) 1, 1 (Jan. 1891).

This time it is genial 17th. I am sending you a photograph. 'Tis the best I can do. The likeness isn't bad because the pose is easy, but the workmanship isn't exactly that of a past master. However the photo as a whole is better than the other one was. It is an outdoor photo & the artist had a belief in the immorality of 'frill' and retouching in relation to portraits. 'Did he retouch at all?' I put the question with due timidity. 'Oh no! retouching spoiled a likeness'. He was plainly shocked and hurt. I pursued the subject no further. So if you will study the photo I send, you will find that there is a mole on the lip & a scratch on the bridge of the nose—the end just appears. Also, wind blew gales that wisped out the new growing hair, wh. the young man was too modest to suggest should be put back—unless he thought the wisps 'natural' & therefore essential to a good likeness. People tell me at first glance it is good. Then they immediately say 'It has a tired dull expression that isn't a bit like you'. The bush photographer takes the same views of retouching that your friend 'Rus'[1] (Bookfellow 14.3.07) takes. 'Rus' retouched his photo, a lovely likeness wh. brought home to all us who ever saw a Kelpie all his dear, quiet, wise, shy, timid, shrinking, faithful little ways. He made him so real I nearly cried over him—I who saw 'Moss' as a girl & knew Wollongong & Humbug Creek—who saw King tell Moss to cut out a fowl from a group & put it in the dining-room—who owned a Kelpie long years ago and then this man 'Rus' comes along—Wd. you mind if I said 'My Oath!'

Well, I think those articles of Kaleski's were worthy to stand with 'The Englishman'.[2] Ah! but you were most subtly fine in that. Its the sort of thing to learn off by heart & carry about as a Thomas a Kempis.[3] I think if I had written that I wd. never have written another line for fear of spoiling the effect—indeed I wd. have been so busy building a four sided altar to it & worshipping at its shrine thought of writing again wd. never have intruded.

Re the paragraphs I sent in & the deformities acquiesced in by religious fathers—It is a big subject. It has been in my mind often in the last four years to suggest it to you as a subject. The cruelty of it all has been so great & the sincerity so real. And though ignorance has been the shut door, the lock has been that sincerity, and, while the suffering has been so unjustly put & held upon the innocent, there is something sublime in the faith of the father (& mother—but I can't

---

[1] 'Rus' was a correspondent to the *Bookfellow*, 14 March 1907, who criticized Robert Kaleski's article on Kelpies (*Bookfellow*, 21 February 1907). Bushmen believe that Kelpie dogs spring from a cross between a dingo and a collie made by an old shepherd at Humbug Creek, Condobolin. Kaleski argued that the Kelpie was the product of mating a fox and a black collie in Scotland. Two dogs of this descent, 'Moss' and 'Kelpie' owned by E. W. King of Wollongong Station near Forbes, produced the first Australian Kelpies.

[2] 'The Englishman', Editorial by Stephens in the *Bookfellow*, 28 February 1907.

[3] A German prior (1390-1471), author of *The Imitation of Christ*, a religious classic.

believe mothers were unrebellious) wh. made him able to view practically without pain, the continual yet wholly curable suffering of his child.

I can so well realize & feel for both. (This is partly because I was not the pretty daughter, my sister was and it made so much difference between us, because of this I suffered continually.) The second father I quoted was my father, & I am my father's daughter. I have the broad easy mind of the free thinker with the prejudices of Calvin.[1] I keep off the rocks of Calvin as much as possible, yet all my altars are built there.

Here again though this doesn't belong. My father's sister allows her boys to play cards. *In the kitchen*. (Her 'boys' are nearly fifty I forgot to mention). She is absolutely certain if we were able to look quickly enough under the table we wd. see the odd foot. While they play cards in the kitchen she sits in the parlour holding fast to her soul. She *does not enter* the kitchen till the cards are put away. She is nearly six feet tall, broad in proportion & about 50 (her years number 75 or thereabout but that is nothing). Her husband (an engineer in years & years gone by) told me himself about the danger of giving a lock of your hair to anyone. *He* knew a girl in Scotland (of course!) and a redcoat came along (*English, of course*) & made love to her. He asked for a lock of her hair. She was going to give it to him, but her friends fearing witchcraft persuaded her not to. So instead she cut a lock of a cow's tail attached to a hide hanging on a fence & gave him that. He never knew the difference. And *then* the girl found out! He left and wd. you believe it? The hide followed him! At that point I laughed—like a 19th century fool!—I couldn't help it. But when I saw the old people's faces! Yes, the hide followed him, *not* stolen as I had flippantly suggested but flopflopflopping along the ground. I wish the tale had stopped there—but it didn't. It went along to running water (of course!) & (I'm not quite sure but I think) the hide came back & next day was found upon the fence. But the story was true he knew it for a fact. And to think that these old people all dying out & no one gathering up their tales. It is cruel. But at Goulburn there is a wealth all going to waste—it makes me want to cry...

My father's brother (dead now) never saw a phonograph. He was 6ft 3½" as an old man of 60 had a 16 inch calf & could put on a woman's boot or wear a woman's glove. A blow from his hand wd. nearly kill a man. His uncle (my grand uncle) known as the 'gentle Allan' because

---

[1] John Calvin (1509-64). Mary Gilmore was brought up as a Presbyterian, rented a pew in St Stephen's Presbyterian Church in Macquarie Street, Sydney, and in her Will left a legacy of £100 to St Stephen's trustees, the interest on which was to provide pew space for strangers. Mary's funeral service was held at St Stephen's in December 1962.

of his gentle ways & because he never had a man flogged, could turn a charging bullock over on his back with his hands.

As a rule I don't believe in the claims of 'blood' but when I get looking back & writing this sort of thing I don't know what *does* count if blood *doesn't*.

But if only someone with an eye (& a heart as well as an eye) would get among the people left of the old emigrant Scotch families. The beliefs, the legends, the histories, the ghosts, the 'h'ants' and 'h'anted houses', the feuds & fights—and talking of fights: my one sole doubt regarding my boy is awa'—he has a fight nearly every day! & his halo now is a pair of black eyes, or rather was a few weeks ago.

Shall I make a paragraph on that? I will though it may not be 'big' enough either as paragraph or as text. Yours faithfully & very bronchitical

To A. G. Stephens

Jackson Street
Casterton
4 April 1907

My Dear Mr Stevens,

Before reading farther please note: (1) I am a person of humble mind, (2) I'm quite aware you are able to do without suggestions—*even* from people of humble mind.

Still sometimes the mind is tired, & a suggestion has its value. If you will look on the other side of this you will see the genesis (& generations) of a single line. It struck me. What about the reduction of say four long central lines to a quatrain of 'so many words'. To 'chuck out' much and still remain?—aye! there's the bloomin' rub.

I see the 'Free Press' (local) has noticed the last 'Bookfellow' (the Ed. is doing his own notices just now) with Billy's & my photo. I was sorry to send you that photo.[1] The work was so far from good enough for the magazine. But there was no choice in the matter—and it must have taken a good big stretch of kindliness on your part to use it. For after all in magazines the picture is of more consequence than the likeness. Yours faithfully,

[1] The photo is in the *Bookfellow*, 28 March 1907, p. 5.

To A. G. Stephens

My dear Mr Stevens,

Casterton
26 June 1907

I wonder wd. you care to reprint 'The Road to Appin'? I forget 'Worker' appearance, but it was soon after I wrote the verse.

And in regard to 'Orientation' if you shd. say 'for God's sake woman! don't try to be humorous' I shan't be offended. Average humour isn't one of my achievements—or failings. As for *unaverage*—it doesn't always bear description—even with a large and tolerant mind.

To A. G. Stephens

My dear Mr Stevens,

Jackson St
Casterton
3 January 1909

I have felt like writing ever since before you left the Red Page to moon along with a candle in a candle stick for illumination—wh. perhaps isn't fair to the other man as his want of personality & vitality may be due to newness to the niche—But I haven't had anything to say except that the preliminary note as to your ad. in the Bulletin set me reading that paper backwards as well as forwards in order to find it with a result that consisted of ejaculation 'coloured & plain'.

You mention a circular sent. I haven't received it, but will be very glad to see it when it does come & if I can write anything I think good enough I shall be only too pleased to submit it. But I write so little! It is so much a matter of health with me. As soon as I feel a little well & strong I feel like writing, but I have such an infernal sense of duty to my house as a possession & myself as a housekeeper the vitality goes out in washing & ironing & scrubbing arrears, unless thought buzz so hard it becomes 'possession' & can't & won't be set aside. Woman is conventional? and conventional because of ages of subjectivity! So is it the Free Kirk[1] spirit that obstinately works for salvation in spite of non-election. I have an idea the Free Kirk reckons itself the equal of the Almighty any time. On what basis? The basis of indestructibility? Probably. I doubt—even as a Free Kirker—It isn't so much what *is* in, as what we *take in* makes us big. The student has all the facets of the diamond, only his peculiar lustre is a man's own.

[1] The Free Church of Scotland, formed as a breakaway from the established Church of Scotland in 1843; joined by the Reformed Presbyterian Church in 1876; in 1900 united with the United Presbyterian Church as the United Free Church of Scotland; united with the established Church in 1930.

I remember years ago—to illustrate a little further what I mean—I was considered to have a good voice, to have the making of a singer if trained. And, whenever I heard a good a really good singer, I always felt 'I too could do that'—almost 'can'. But an ordinary singer left me unstirred.—That is to say 'Had I knowledge' etc. etc. I think that is one reason why we have so few marksmen among Australian writers. The capacity is there but it is never filled to its capability. There is lustre but most else is lacking.

We are so new too. A young man 'at home' meets & compares himself with those who succeed. He measures himself in close quarters with them. He has history & he has achievement. 'Jones', he says, 'went to school with me. Jones is only an ordinary fellow after all. I too can do as Jones' & he writes out of his ordinary manself the extraordinary book that equals Jones's extraordinary book written out of his ordinary manself. We here, look on the writer as something half divine. It hurts us to be told that Jones studied up his subject in libraries & anywhere he could. We like to think of the book as created out of nothing but unseen potential that is within. To say that we too should read up in order to write is like throwing mud on the standard. The standard must stand high even if nothing result. To suggest study to us is to condemn our inspiration—to say our inspiration is not all sufficient—and to us inspiration seems the only right—the only reason, the one thing needing no apology—as a writer that whatever you write will be of consequence more because of yourself & in proportion to the A.G.S.'[1]ness of that writing than for any other reason. Is it for a page in the magazine or how? In any case you pay me a compliment wh. I am only too pleased to have paid even though I do think it beyond my deserts, & I will be very glad for you to carry out your idea.

Did you know I have a garden—or rather had till the sun burned it up—& grew my own potatoes & peas & beans? Also hatched chickens with varying success but much growth of knowledge as to nature. Nature is a wonderful thing! Curious how we persist in calling the little known & the lately acquired wonderful. If we pour out a cup of water & watch it run here & there & develop heads according to lines of depression—the point of least resistance — we don't call that 'wonderful'! And yet in what way & in what department, almost in what particular, is nature different? Just a cup of water spilled out & going where it can. What is development? A *pushing* forward by something within? or a propulsion or rather a falling forward because the 'withouts' allow it? Is there an up or a down in development? If enough water runs into the pool it will begin to go back the way it came—But second glance shews that won't hold water.

[1] A. G. Stephens.

By the way about the anthology. What do you want? Copies of what has been printed or to use what you have? It just struck me I wasn't clear on that point.

To W. A. Woods

Amigo,

Henty Street
Casterton, Vic.
30 November 1909

What about the 'Daily Post', and are you going back to 'the Worker' if the Clipper-Post amalgamation takes place? Or are you going to have charge of the Melb. office or what?

I sent my M.S.[1] to Bernard O'Dowd who said lots of nice things about it. He took it to Geo. Robertson & Co. who said they'd print at their own risk and allow me 10 p.c. in first thou. copies sold (at 2/6) and 15 p.c. on all over that. I wired acceptance as they are said to be a good firm to deal with—a square dealing firm—and am waiting now for the agreement. The book is proposed for Feb. or March. I feel greatly pleased.

Whatever struck the N.S.W. Government? And did you see the 'Age' leader of 29.11.08—'The mine owners refused. On the top of this came the strike of the N.S.W. Rwy. Dept. in refusing to haul the miners' coal. It wd. be difficult to conceive of two actions wh. more clearly put the employers in the wrong and create a feeling that the miners are being oppressed by wealth syndicates in the 1st place, and by a State Govt. in league with those syndicates.' Beautiful! even if Age'. Billy in bed—bronchial catarrh, I had it last week. Pity we can't exchange our bloomin' chests. People tell me my 'Worker'[2] work is much improved. *I* feel its lost its first spontaneous bloom. But perhaps it needed that. It seems to go through. I get letters all the time God Blessing it and me, so that is nice. How are you and yours. Have one eye on the pen and one out the door looking for Will. As usual. Faithfully,

M. Gilmore.

[1] In 1909 the Melbourne publisher George Robertson sought O'Dowd's opinion of Mary's poetry before publishing her first volume *Marri'd and Other Verses*, 1910. O'Dowd wrote to Nettie Palmer (12 September 1909) that he was 'simply enraptured with their lyric magic'. See W. H. Wilde, *Three Radicals*, 1969, in the Australian Writers and their Work series.

[2] Mary's Women's Page in the *Worker* which she began in January 1908 and continued until February 1931. The title of the page varied over the years.

To W. A. Woods

Henty Street
Casterton, Vic.
15 January 1910

Amigo,

Is Ethel earning enough to pay her board? Or help keep herself, because if not I have a spare room and she cd. stay here awhile till you get things straightened up a bit. I expect to go to town about the 26th (excursion time) (so she couldn't come till I returned)—though I am afraid the proofs[1] will hardly be ready for me so soon, as the matter is only just selected and gone to the printer. All verse and A. G. Stephens writes me so good and kindly, about it. If he can say a good word all the other critics will follow. Thanks for the 'Thamyris'[2] book. I had already selected from it—for the 'Worker' page.[3] I will write him a line. Why doesn't Alf. go to Queensland? That's the country for the young and strong. Will's brother went there 15 years ago with bare hands. Now he has an overdraft of £10,000 or £15,000. His wool turns in over £1,000 a year. And he has a wife and four or five small children.

Am expecting Will every moment and have to keep an eye on the door the stove and the paper at once. Both Will and Billy A1.

M. Gilmore

I'd advise 'the Worker' first and foremost. Lamond[4] wants someone and the paper wants a man who won't run wide. I reckon *that's* more important than brains (no exception to *your* brains) and later there will be the Daily and branches etc. etc. Adios.

M.G.

To Edward Tregear

Henty Street
Casterton, Vic.
25 November 1910

Dear Mr. Tregear,

Your letter just arrived, I wish I might send it on to Bernard O'Dowd! I write just as you say you do. You know how you sit sometimes (or

---

[1] Proofs of Mary's book of poems, *Marri'd and Other Verses*, 1910.
[2] In Greek legend a Thracian singer. He boasted he could surpass the Muses, and, for his presumption, was deprived of his sight and the power of singing.
[3] In 1908 Mary began the Women's Page, a feature that she conducted in the *Worker* for over twenty years. See W. H. Wilde, *Three Radicals*, 1969.
[4] Hector Lamond (1865-1947). In June 1911, largely at Lamond's instigation, Mary left Casterton to join the staff of the *Worker* in Sydney. Will Gilmore joined his brother Samuel in Queensland and after Billy completed his secondary education in Sydney he joined his father on the land in Queensland. The family was seldom reunited in later years.

are busy indeed) your mind in a somewhat detached condition, yet working rapidly—or intensely. A butterfly comes flit flitting in at the door. He was a stranger, a foreigner to all your thought, yet at once filling all your attention. That is how I usually find my work come. Generally in my verse the last line is the only one that flashes into the mind (the climax line) the one clearly defined point in a whole, inchoate, yet shaped and unseen, yet perceived. The whole is built from that central idea sometimes without need to alter a word though sometimes a line baffles for years—even a word.

I remember once—or did I tell you?—forgetting a song for a year or two as though for many years (you know the feeling I am sure). I suddenly remembered not the song, but that there was that song and that I had had it and memory had lost all trace of it—only remembering that there was in the brain a place that had held that special thing and no other. For a week the mind tried to get some clue as to style, words, air, name—anything. Then a final cadence came and from that the air was worked out bit by bit and the name (I think) came. But the words were in another world.

One day the remembrance of vowelling at the end of a cadence came, and yet not so active as remembrance—more like recognition. The sound of a hollow 'a' or 'o'. It doesn't matter wh. now. No consonant. But by passivity of mind and unconsciously listening as it were, as the knocks in spirit rapping came up through the wood and the silence, so through the table of mind came the consonant. That day I got three words, I think next day that line. In a little while, by the study of 'impressions' the whole verse all but one word (or line) wh.wd. not come. The whole thing as it were by mental processes of silences or listenings and eliminations came. So with my verse. There is little choosing of suitable words; but there is decided stress of elimination. The mind goes 'take this!' but 'not that, not that!' and like a man with his eyes on his work, the hand reaches out in the darkness and takes the tool that it knows is just there without seeing. The same with matter for the 'Worker'.[1] The thing just comes all in one and at once the whole vision; and it is only a question of moulding the putty fast enough. Goodness only knows what sort of stuff I wrote! I rarely remember even the physical outline of it. Sometimes when in dead earnest the pen goes down, only by 'elimination' and 'building' cd. I tell what I had written. For a few seconds of course (the last point always filling the whole mind to the exclusion of the previous) then memory (natural) re-asserts, or asserts, itself. But I never know 24 hrs. after posting what anything in each week's budget is—unless I make a special note at the time for that purpose. The same with letters. That is letters that

---

[1] Mary's Women's Page in the *Worker*, which she edited for twenty-three years.

are me. They are written as the blood circulates without much sense of anything save the need for expression—i.e. impulsion. Even in spite of erasures and corrections they go on into form without sense of effort. The one trouble is that the pen is never as fast as the vision behind it.

That is why—the whole of this—my verse is as A. G. S.[1] says, a series of 'little flutters'. It comes all in one like a whirlwind and if you don't box your whirlwind in the time—well, you gain nothing by pursuing it! Of course the spiritualists say I write under 'influence'. However, my own impression is that it is all a question of nervous energy—nerves, temperature, (bodily) and balance or the want of it. Some people, like some places, are subject to whirlwinds, and some again are solar radiators, some are just plain bog. My work, too, as you say of yours, often seems as if—'where got I that!' Once I had the pleasure of coming on a piece I had written when about fifteen; and, having not the faintest idea I ever put it together when I got it again eight or nine or more years later, read it as a stranger. I had it some time being greatly struck by the clarity of thought and consonance with my own ideas in it. 'Here's a fine thing!' I thought tremendously pleased with it. (Egotism because it was in accord etc!) Then a something of a hint of a tone or a flavour or a savor struck me, and I suddenly saw myself sitting on a bedside a couple of hundred miles—more!—away vainly trying to understand a book that repelled me and wh. yet I cd. not grasp (I think now it was a metaphysical from the French). It was a sort of revelation of the mental and psychological processes of a man who was unorthodox on every point. All I remember of it is the size, print, smell, and the frequently used word 'libertine' and a name, I think, was St. Leger. Books were scarce up country in those days, and understood or not understood all books were dear to me—even a treatise on 'Villa Fronts and elevations' 'for the use of Builders'. Then my little air castle collapsed and I was only aware of the hitherto quite unseen faults of the verse. The experience was quite curious and interested me very much. I had, now I am on the subject, another strange thing happen. I was waiting for a tram in King Street Sydney twenty years ago (I was about 25) and some train of thought absorbing me I became oblivious to time and place when suddenly I was impelled (without sense of impulsion though) to raise my eyes and look all alive into the eyes of another woman across the road. The feeling was they were my own eyes, and that my own eyes were the eyes of a dog. I have no idea who the other woman was, but something in my look startled her in the same electric way her look startled me. It was one of the vivid moments of existence and while quite easily

---

[1] A. G. Stephens.

explainable on rational lines, is also the full perception of O'Dowd's 'I know that I am also you, what you are! That all are we'[1] and 'the half and the half are whole' even if it means that her eyes were mine and my eyes were a dog's eyes. It is all one after all.

As to death. Death is nothing. I have no fear of death in one way. In another I have a passionate rage and anger against it. Why shd. it come to me who love work? who love life? And as for the ways of going to death, I hate them too. There is here an old, wonderful woman of 86 suffering torture of body—one of the kind women, the women who haven't an idle bone in their bodies, the women who did men's work and worked two men's hours to keep home together and feed their children, women of grit and pluck and courage—and she suffers because she was just that kind of woman. Of course I know why she suffers (neuritis)—it is because she won't give in, she won't give up the fight. But somehow it doesn't seem fair. Another life? Perhaps. It may be. It may not be. If there is, the ravelled may be straightened. If not—one still feels the words of Turgenev (A. G. S. once quoted to me and at me for encouragement) 'Fight on; and, damn it all!'

To sum up. In regard to after death, for the most part I neither affirm nor deny. There is no argument in the mental plane that means proof to me that there is a future, yet point to the cast off feather of a sparrow, the broken leaf of a plant, and I know that what made these can also make futures. All the logic, all the argument, all the possibilities of all the ages are bound up in fragments such as these.

And Man, dear, to use the kindly Irish phrase, don't ever apologize again for saying things or asking things, or thinking things when you write. We aren't dealing with fences, we are dealing with the things behind all fences, above all fences, and the field is yours as much as mine.

As to whether my verses are 'me'—it depends on what one hears them say for one thing and what they find in me when they know me for another. The only thing I know is that they are the sincere cry of my heart in the better and truer ones, and of the mood in the lesser ones. They weren't written with pens, but with every cell that had sense of being in whatever is actual in what is really me. I suppose it was telepathy as I had been all week promising myself I'd write you a 'real' letter (the last one was tired) but yours came first. Yours faithfully,

M. Gilmore.

---

[1] Mary gives a rather free rendering of lines from Bernard O'Dowd's poem 'Bacchus' from his *Dominions of the Boundary*, 1907. The lines should read:
> And we are you, and you are we,
> And all are All—and One.

To Dowell O'Reilly

135 Bondi Rd
Bondi
17 October 1912

My dear Mr. O'Reilly,

I haven't written because I haven't known what to write.

I have shown the verses to several women, Rosamond Benham among the number and they—*even she*—with one exception have taken it as referring to intellectual & go-out-in-the-world life only.

But surely such a bitter cry means something more than that!

If it doesn't mean things beyond the power of expression by ordinary words, then, to me, it has very little meaning. I mean in such case the cry is too sore for the cause.

Of course you don't know what is in it yourself. You set out—judging by your post card—to say a certain thing, but the net always holds more than intention or the intended.

And your explanation only gives me your idea of it, and I don't quite know that I've got that, either all, or even as you mean it.

Perhaps in time I shall spell out the emotional feeling into words, when I might be able to tell you something, but I couldn't just now. And you must not wish to be 'saved' from your friends who say etc., etc. & at last have to thank them.

You talk about 'two' of me & fearing to offend the lesser. Do you suppose I wd. be wandering round the world with a pen in my hand if there were any choice in the matter! There may be a choice next year if sheep are watering at The Lone Star Spring on Springbank[1] between Cloncurry & Richmond . . .

To go back to the verses. You cannot mean it as a song triumphant! Surely!

To me it is a cry of pain not even modified by an *intellectual recognition* that defeat is triumph. It is the parallel, to me, of child birth, the shuddering body remembering its pain even though the child lies in its arms.

To Dowell O'Reilly

135 Bondi Rd
Bondi
22 October 1912

Dear Mr. O'Reilly,

Your card just to hand. I'm not going to say anything, argue anything,

---

[1] The Queensland property being worked by Will Gilmore.

think anything, or do anything. You & Mrs. Griffiths[1] can talk it out. I happen to have trouble with my heart again—a little hot weather & an extra flight of stairs & the old inflammation starts newer than ever. Are there any stairs at Mockbells?[2] And where is Angel Place?[3] And can I ask Dr. Rosamond Benham to come, too? Her husband's name is Taylor, but she prefers to remain Benham. Does that promise an interesting time for you? And will next Friday do?

By the way I can't afford not to say this:— Mrs. Griffiths, Dr. Benham & I are three women of some mental capacity. The first two never abated one fraction of their mental activity because of their motherhood. I gave everything up for the child. He was nearly or quite six years old before I allowed myself to write more than letters for fear of in some way robbing him by neglect or want of interest. If I had had a dozen children it wd. have been the same.

Yet my boy is no stronger, better, finer or more intelligent than Mrs. Griffiths' children. He may be better balanced than Dr. Benham's, but the difference of parentage accounts for that visibly. Dr. Benham is the more mother-caring, Mrs. Griffiths the more feminine, as women. John Lane coming back to Australia said to a connection who had never seen me 'A nice woman, but mad over the baby'. How does all that work out?

To Dowell O'Reilly

135 Bondi Rd
Bondi
24 October 1912

Dear Mr. O'Reilly,

We will be at Angel Place 4.30 Friday. I want to take Dr. Benham to the Lone Hand[4] office earlier in the day, & as a rule I go to my own office Friday for the good golden reason known to us all.

For goodness' sake don't *you* go treating me as an invalid because I can't run up & down stairs like other people! I can manage one flight of stairs without much trouble. It is when there are two the game begins.

And between trying to hide symptoms (for though I love sympathy I hate to display symptoms or have them noticed) & trying to control the disorganized rhythms, I sometimes seem to be the very thing I least want to appear.

[1] Probably Annette Agnes Griffiths, daughter of Joseph Scarffe Willis of 'Graycliff', Vaucluse, but the identity is hard to establish.
[2] One of several coffee shops operated by K. Mockbell (Mocha Coffee Co.) in various parts of Sydney.
[3] Angel Place is a small street off Pitt Street on the Circular Quay side of Martin Place, Sydney.
[4] The *Lone Hand* magazine.

I don't worry over it—I never did any more than over the lungs. Neither of them have killed me yet—the latter thanks to Paraguay wh. healed the lungs till I went to Victoria, when that old trouble started again. However it seems better again.

Considering that I have been nearly drowned & only found by accident; burned (& shut the door on myself in a stable as a little child) & only discovered again by accident; have been met by a maniac (with a gun,) who had been trying to murder his wife; bitten (as far as evidence showed) by a snake; been next door to a shipwreck, twice; had prayers for the dying over me as a consumptive; given 'three months longer' with my heart—I don't think I have done badly, have I! I don't think I wd. have got through if I had worried over such things, for I've had one or the other along with me always.

I'm torn between the doubt of whether Mockbell's is a proper place for a good white Australian[1] to go to, & the desire to taste real coffee again. Wh. shall I give up, the principles or the coffee? Alas! I know not.

The Hon. Henry Willis, M.L.A.   *135 Bondi Rd*
Speaker   *Bondi*
N.S.W. Legislative Assembly   *22 April 1913*

Dear Sir,
I see by the 'Sun' of today that you are to speak at Newcastle on 'The New Australia, Where Socialism Failed'. As one who went through the experience of four years in Cosme (the second colony) and came away with a firmer belief than ever in the possibility of Socialism and of its value as a protector to women and children especially, I shd like to tell you a little about our life there and the grounds for my belief—some day when it is convenient to you. Yours faithfully,
                         Mary (Mrs. W. A.) Gilmore.

I might say the Colony did not fail because of its socialism, but for the same reasons that break up settlement anywhere—accentuated by our poverty. We could not have lived three months, as a colony, *but* for socialism.

I gave a file (last year) of the New Australia Journal and the Cosme Monthly to the C'wealth Library.

I have still a broken file, here, wh. some day I will give to the Mitchell Library.
                                                   M.G.

---

[1] Mary's doubt about the coffee shop being 'a proper place for a good white Australian to go to' is an example of the widely accepted racial attitudes of the day.

To Dowell O'Reilly

214 Glebe Rd
Glebe Pt
11 April 1914

Dear Mr. O'Reilly,

Receipt for your chk. of £1.1.0 enclosed. You may meet Mr. Stephens[1] on the train as they are not at Hornsby as he thought, but 3 mins. from Waitara & near most of their friends, Connie[2] tells me.

If anyone tells you any stories of family troubles (I've heard several & found them no more true of the family mentioned than any other family) don't believe them. A man who will sing the baby asleep for his wife—.

One tale I heard as true described a 'small very fair' woman, as being a pathetic figure of a wife who needed sympathy. As the wife in question is darker than any of her children!—

Another tale was based on the malicious gossip of a dismissed housekeeper; that too, I found to be untrue—or, at most, what'ld be said of every man not a model of patience.

I am just *sick* of hearing people chew over the hasty speech of X. Y. or Z. Carrying it round, patting it into effective shape, & passing it on instead of telling the kinder things & letting the other die on the breath. There isn't one of us who doesn't some time or other in a moment of inattention, of expansion, of anything, say something critical or otherwise that'ld be a cause of soreness if told back. There's too much telling back, & too little telling forward goes on! And if you'll look up to heavens say just as I have, 'Damn telling Back!' I'll be the gratefullest.

Mary Gilmore.

And a P.S. of a sort:—

Re 'just missed'—Keats 'just missed' his own time, Chatterton 'just missed', Thompson 'just missed'—Must have! Because the work was *just the same* in their own time *as in the time* when it was discovered to be genius. Nothing was either put into it or added to it—except the passage of years & the growth of a more generous appreciation. Don't let us have to write in future years 'With a little more generosity & understanding on the part of his contemporaries—' 'Just missed' is like that other saying 'a burnt out volcano' which was the 'fashionable' tag a while ago. When Bertram Stevens, among others, said it to me I laughed. 'Have you been reading Stephens, lately?' I asked. He hadn't. A few weeks later he read an article—on Melba. 'Any falling off there?'

[1] A. G. Stephens.
[2] The daughter of A. G. Stephens, later Mrs Constance Robertson.

I asked. *'No'* he answered emphatically, 'there *isn't!'* & he has never said anything about a burnt out volcano to me since. One or two others whom I put to the test of proof the same.

Do you know the impression I get about Stephens' adverse critics— those I meet? The largeness of their own attainments & the smallness of anyone else's. And those who are more or less friendly seem to me to be afraid to say generously what they think of his work for fear of what the next person may say — an 'afraid-to-stand-on-their-own-feet' kind of thing. Maybe it's the Bulletin hatred of Stephens & their necessity to get work from the Bulletin is the cause. But whatever the cause the thing is distinctly *there*. I've met it over & over again.

To Dowell O'Reilly

214 Glebe Rd
Glebe Pt
30 April 1914
(After tomorrow Havilah, Ocean St, Woollahra)

Dear Mr. O'Reilly,

Useful & not useful. Mr. Stephens[1] intends, I take it, to compel himself to do what he really has it in him to do.

You will perhaps be surprised to know that I consider him as having, naturally, a voice full of flexibility & modulation. It is overlaid with the masking of habit of speech, constriction of vocal chords from nervousness, & possibly catarrh. Now & then the *real* voice utters itself. I have heard it once or twice unconsciously uttered when his mind was for a moment emptied of the present & the external.

If by learning to trust himself, he can go so far as to let his voice speak itself, it will be a revelation to many. It is precisely because of its unusual capacity for expression, that it hardens so easily the armour of the more than ordinarily expressive & sensitive.

Also when one knows that he worked all Sunday night, & Monday & had only an hour or two's sleep Tuesday morning, finished the Adam Lindsay Gordon M.S. only at 3 p.m. Tuesday, had no tea, & corrected proofs till the moment he left for the hall! It is little wonder he hardly did himself justice!

Not for publication—it was Connie[2] told me.

When I think of the curious things I have heard about that man, & the things that I know personally & through things Connie tells me, I wonder what sort of a world I am in! Partly his own fault—he tells

---

[1] A. G. Stephens.
[2] A. G. Stephens' daughter, Constance Robertson.

nothing & the malicious have their fling uncontradicted. And because he chooses not to speak I am almost afraid to say anything for fear of trespass.

The pride in and affection for her father in Connie is simply delightful: such a loyal, brave, loving heart. 'Faithfully yrs' is one of my names for her. And Jack[1]—the father in boyhood, & writing things that even the father thinks good.

And about A.G.S.—I think nine times out of ten, what is simply a high note of mocking fun is taken for earnest. About the 'nation'—we've sparred in that subject. Another instance I saw a letter he proposed sending someone. Met in the spirit written, it wd. have meant friendly laughter, & a reply in like manner. Met in any other way or as a serious composition (as it easily might have been) it was egotism pure & simple. Yet I knew it wasn't egotism. It came from the high pulse of an exuberant vitality (Is there or isn't there an 'h' in that word? !**!?) Sort of thing R. L. Stevenson did constantly but with a wise eye to effect & consequently really & truly egotistic.

I knew Mr. Stephens so well before I met him (& he was one of the few instances in wh. the greeting did not cause alteration in preconceived & foreheld ideas & impression), and I always feel that but for his kindness in sending me books, & the Bookfellow, & an occasional letter of cheer, that I wd. have completely broken down when I was in the bush. The Bookfellow used to come like light into a prison; he always said (when he wrote) the word that gave me strength. It wasn't till years later that I met him, & I always feel that no gratitude & no good word I cd. ever give him cd. make up for what he did for me. He was a friend when I most needed one. He was a friend in the best way; & one who asked nothing. So you see—Yours sincerely & with the good wish

Mary Gilmore

To A. G. Stephens

Lammermuir
96 Glenmore Rd
Paddington
1 November 1915

Dear Mr Stephens,

My sister asked me to remind you of her letter from Justine Kong Sing wh. I sent you for paragraph use. I forgot when you were here, & remembered now.

---

[1] J. G. Stephens, son of A. G. Stephens.

I was—and am—vexed that you went without even the offer of refreshment. Don't know what I was thinking of!

Did you read Bernhardi's article in today's Sunday Times? And did you hear that the publication of Greece bidding the allies remove their soldiers from her territory had foundation, and the contradiction none? I am sending the Sunday Times, & will be glad if you will re-post it by Wed. to Billy for whose benefit it is blue pencilled. If the Russians are asking £90.000.000 loan from America & offering *nine per cent*!?! The leader in the Sunday Times is such a contrast to everything it has written in that place in the past, that something out of the common either in knowledge or common sense must have struck it, & instead of a straw on the wind it looks like a whole hay stack. It also looks as if the whole world wd. have to go in for socialism in order to pay its taxes—It can hardly contemplate one half of its population living on pensions while the other half provides them! For I suppose the pensioners can hardly be taxed to provide their pensions! Antwerp, Gallipoli & now it looks like Salonika to complete the trio. I have an idea the next place the Australians will fight in—& for—is Egypt—for the supremacy there in the Suez. And I admire Botha as you do but with a different glass. In his great speech after driving out the Germans I noticed only one reference to 'the Empire'—toward the close. The *usual* sort of reference. My idea is that Botha is a man of longer vision than others; & that he sees a united S.A. free & independent; but needing the prop of a name to get there. He knows that had Germany won, such a dream wd. have been farther off realization. At present S.Af. is roughly a two party people. Boer & British. The entrance of a third party wd. give the power to the third who wd. use either of the others to *his own* ends.

(Observe the value of an education in politics! Me, of course, not Botha.)

The authors' paper with profits to the authors is 'off' so G.R.[1] told me; & Louis Stone was very savage in the last Bulletin . . . And for an end something I have long wanted to ask. If by any chance I shd. die more suddenly than I either expect or intend to, I want you to take charge of my books & papers & other odds & ends & keep them for Billy. Some of them have a little value some have not, & till Billy is older he wouldn't know one from the other. And I must say I don't like the thought that unauthorized people shd. have the handling of things—not even my sister; the things that matter to me are meaningless to her, & vice versa. I can *make* her see things I see, but directly I let go she drops & they are the other side of the hill out of vision and uninteresting.

[1] George Robertson, one of the co-founders of the publishing house, Angus & Robertson.

Of course I haven't any idea of dying—though I hope when it comes it will be quick & sudden & no one at the funeral. Everyone tells me I look a lot better for being ill-rested. I suppose I do get tired. I think I will go up to Binalong when I feel fit to travel & stay with old friends of my sister's, who will keep me in bed & feed me on cream. They have a farm-station, & live in the town. Yet I hate the thought of being out of Sydney. I have been so long away.

M.G.

To Percival Serle

The Hotel Imperial
Goulburn
Dear Mr Serle, 22 September 1922

I have had a very much occupied and preoccupied time since your letter came and am only now able to attend to it. How much this has been so is shown by the fact that I am late in replying to any inquiry concerning J. Shaw Neilson.[1]

I class Neilson with Lawson in value to Australia. Lawson was first of his kind, Neilson is first of his, and one as distinguished in his way as the other. I have been broken-hearted over Neilson. He is of that generous temperament which always sets himself and his gift aside for the needs of others. When it isn't his family he is helping he is withdrawing from possible help (as you mention) for fear of the needs of others and often much better able to care for themselves than he. They have only themselves to care for, he has his gift as well, and added to that such a defective eyesight that stress and physical fatigue must make it the more inefficient. It was I who made him acquainted with O'Dowd, giving him Mrs O'Dowd's address some years ago when I found he was going to Melbourne about his eyes. I also gave him the then address of Dr Frank Newman, eye specialist, and a friend of mine. Dr Newman wrote me that Neilson's eyes presented a most difficult condition which left very little margin for help in glasses. This

---

[1] Mary had been in contact with John Shaw Neilson for many years prior to this letter to Percival Serle. They were corresponding as early as 1912. In response to a letter of praise from Mary, Neilson wrote (20 October 1912) the following rather illuminating and somewhat startling words:

> I really did not think anyone would be so affected with my verse. I know that you are a woman of a keen imagination. I daresay you can feel things that I cannot feel at all. I may be the means of suggesting to you something that I cannot understand myself. Verse never moves me that much but good prose will bring tears yet . . . I never had much sense about verse till I was 30—and since then I have made such horrible blunders that I have felt like giving it up altogether at times. It is a great business for making money is it not? That's the reason I stick to it perhaps.

is important to remember for a man like Neilson is not like one younger whom the years give room for latent helpful development.

If this has not been told to Neilson do not mention it. But get someone to find you Dr Frank Newman's address (Newman the big jeweller is a brother, but any eye specialist can give it) and get a letter from him about Neilson's sight to strengthen the case for appeal.

Better to help Neilson now, than, as with Lawson, to strew bouquets over his grave, and praise him in death who should have been cared for in life. I cannot tell you how I have grieved over Neilson. His gift is of beauty, and the hand that holds the pen is calloused by the spade; the mind that should sing is broken in bodily fatigue. The cruelty of the position has never lost its sharpness either in my heart or in my forward-looking mind. There is but one Neilson as there was but one Lawson, and Australia should feel shamed to the dust that he has been so much neglected. No man's fancy can weave, no man's mind play, when he aches in the exhaustion of bodily fatigue. And our country is shorn of what he can give in every day in which *he* is shorn of the leisure in which to germinate and give what is in him to give. And if any word of mine can help to get him an allowance you have it with all my heart, for I am grateful to you in the matter as if it were a thing personal to me, myself. Yours sincerely

To A. H. Chisholm

The Hotel Imperial
Goulburn
Dear Mr. Chisholm, 8 July 1923

Are you one of the Goulburn Chisholms, do you belong to the immortal Jane, or are you merely one of the outer barbarians? Anyhow, thank you for your note. About photographs, I have none of New Australia.[1] You can see some illustrations of *Cosme*, which is *not* New Australia, at the Mitchell Library. I gave the Municipal Library a file which has information if not views in it. It is not a complete file. I gave a better one to the Fisher[2] and the best to the Commonwealth Parliamentary Library, in Melbourne. Do not on any account confuse Cosme and New Australia. We (Cosme) were known in Paraguay as the Saints, New Australia as the Sinners. If you look up the Daily Tel. of about twenty years ago (when John Farrell was there,) you will see five or six cols. of my stuff there which the editor rudely headed 'Mary Jane Gilmore'—and really and truly I *am* Mrs. Gilmore!!—presumably to

---
[1] See note to letter, 5 August 1896.
[2] Fisher Library, University of Sydney.

show what he thought of them there Socialists! As for me I was too cruelly sensitive to even tell him I was Jean and not Jane. Not that it matters much except that Jean is not Sassenach.

It was a wonderful experience, that of Colonia Cosme (I was not in New Australia, though my husband was—before we were married of course). I went there a theoretical socialist and came away a confirmed one as a result of experience for five and a half years or thereabouts. No question about the value of Community life; and how it is to be maintained except as under socialism I have yet to be told, as society seems to always need some kind of cement, religion, law, or compulsion by force, to keep it together . . .

To A. H. Chisholm

The Hotel Imperial
Goulburn
Balm, Mr. Chisholm, *20 July 1923*

Balm to the heart your kind letter is. You know, *Scots are* nice; understanding and kind. (Did you know that my name was Cameron? Ha!) The article on New Australia[1] will interest me, but usually such articles hurt; for they are seldom even moderately fair. Usually they are like the picture in—I forget the name of book and man, but he was a teacher in New Australia, came out for his health, and had a Scottish name—anyhow he showed a picture of young barefoot ragamuffins on a fence, an Australian bush picture it might have been and underfooted it: 'This is how children are exposed to snake bite *under socialism*', or words to that effect. This man was in New Australia *not* in Cosme and in N.A. *after* it was Socialistic a long time.

You'll be thinking I am a dashed nuisance, but will you use those spring verses as soon as you can? I sent one in the same style, on birds, to the *Worker*, and being not so far, done here, and easily imitated, I wd. like the Daily Telegraph to get in ahead of the imitators. We have had imitations of most of the older poets, but this particular form has not been among them. Possibly because it was neither heroic, sporty nor erotic. Did not sufficiently lend itself to these expressions of, is it life or imagination?

I am wondering were you ten years old when you gave *Marri'd and Other Verses*[2] to your sister, or do grey hairs sprout on a young tree (never mind the mixed metaphor, expressiveness is more than fixities). When I am not fencing my grave and writing my last epitaph

[1] See note to letter, 5 August 1896.
[2] Mary's first book of poems, published 1910.

I am about nineteen. But the calendar says 59 next month. Sometimes I am ashamed that I do not feel like Methusaleh. A happy aspect of character I hope. 58! 58!! 58!!! (I was born in '65!!) . . .

Will you return the 'Times' article which I enclose. As to G. R.[1] he is one of whom there are very few like him in the world. Generosity is his name—generosity never advertises.

To A. H. Chisholm

The Hotel Imperial
Goulburn

Dear Mr. Chisholm,   27 August 1923

Thank you for returning the cuttings, also for what you are thinking of writing from them. I suppose I am about the least advertised (using the word in its 'push' sense) of any writer in Australia. I belong to no particular group and groups advertise one another. I am perhaps the one who has most constantly and most conscientiously (till lately) given others prominence over myself. So you see that I am really & truly grateful to you. I am sending with this an article on Writers and Painters. It rambles like a flock of sheep, but I have hopes that like the sheep it never quite gets off the grass. I shall be sending you some more verse later on. Thank you again for the 'spread' you put on the thinness of that last bit. It made it look quite important. I have a bad cold and am tired so excuse brevity.

As to that New Australia stuff:[2] If you notice it is always New Australia and never Cosme that is written up, and always the first few months of dissension and never the ten years of permanence. It is, also, always Lane as dictator and never Lane, the elected, who could have been deposed at any meeting the colonists chose to call!

Again thanking you.

To A. H. Chisholm

The Hotel Imperial
Goulburn

Dear Mr. Chisholm,   10 October 1923

You are more than kind! I have been moribund with flu and bronchitis and hadn't energy to write to say I have no photograph of Louisa

---

[1] George Robertson.
[2] See note to letter, 5 August 1896.

Lawson.[1] Not now; mine is gone. You got a better one than the one I had anyhow. Yours was of her in her younger years, and shows the fresh look of youth. 'Aussie' has blocks of the four—Louisa, her husband, and her father and mother (Albery). They are in Gertie Lawson's[2] articles, and if you haven't seen them you should. Gertie's articles are interesting as showing how like she writes to Henry. But she has the over emphasis of the dramatic of the mother, which Henry kept restrained and in its place as subsidiary to the story to be told.

Jessie Mackay has just sent me a 'gorgeous' notice of 'Hound of the Road', and someone else writes to add it as an 'epoch making book' to the great four: Geoffrey Hamlyn, For the Term of His Natural Life, Robbery Under Arms and Jonah. The writer has sense enough not to strain the comparison beyond saying that mine marks a period and an essay as they. I believe Jessie Mackay says something the same. Well, it's nice even if too good to be true, and I take to it like a duck to water!

Am very tired and will say no more except the Lord have you in His keeping and make you live a long time to be nice to people who want it!

To Nettie Palmer

The Hotel Imperial
Goulburn
Dear Mrs. Palmer,   *29 July 1924*

You will think me anything and everything.

I have waited to write partly for glasses and partly because I had much to say. I have your husband's book[3] and your letters and your request for names to answer. I haven't read the book: for two reasons: one I wanted to get new glasses so that I cd. *really* read it i.e. not only with eyes but with mind; and the other because every time I open it I get stuck on The Hermit.[4] I begin it anywhere and go to the end with the same sense of surprise, the same flash of vision, the same feeling of reality, the same thrust of unknown memory, and the same cry of something familiar, lost and nostalgic, that the first reading gave me, and that Lawson gives me. That last picture comes so startlingly that *I am it*: the poised-for flight: and I feel myself fall off the fence because there the story ends and there are no more words to carry

---

[1] Henry Lawson's mother.
[2] Henry Lawson's sister.
[3] Vance Palmer's *The World of Men*, published in London in 1915.
[4] 'The Hermit' is the first of twelve short stories which comprise the book.

me on in flight. I think it an astonishing thing. The art, and the suppression of any appearance of art, together make it remarkable. It wants for nothing; one can *hear* it; it tells itself with the sound of the things that echo and ache in it. I repeat that it wants for nothing. But if the others are like it, they or some of them will want for tears. Perhaps I should say 'want for falling tears' for tears lie behind this in an ache that cannot out, and yet is full of the bewilderment of life. It is the only thing I class with Lawson and I hope you will not mind me saying that. I put Lawson alone. There is in him the hot tears that no one else can give, that wash out weakness of construction and faults of execution.

I remember when I used to help Lawson in the young years, and long before he wrote sketches and stories. I urged him to write, I was only a girl but I used to say 'when you write, make the characters tell everything, not you.' And here it is. In 'The Hermit' is no author; the created is all. The stage nothing but the story. What a small, simple *little* story it is yet what concentrated years of history and of life lie in it!

There is something of the Russian in those stories—I have just turned two or three pages since I thought I had finished about the book. I think it is in dealing with the vast and forcing it to that which encompasses it, many a novel has in it less than this short story: most in fact.

Will you let me say I liked your husband and say it in my own way? I think I never met anyone more unconsciously sincere, and with so few subterfuges. Reticences, yes; but not the other thing. I would trust him with anything, knowing it would be treated with dignity and justice. And how sensitive!

Your Essay[1] has just been sent me by the 'Penny Post'. Not to notice it but to read, though I think they want my opinion. I have to thank you for putting me into it and in such a kind way. You are right about O'Dowd. Yet there is something in common between him and Vance Palmer, only where the one speaks in a small still voice the other shouts: comes trampling out of the forest, hair in his eyes shouting his discoveries. They both sweep a wide field, in your husband's case wider than appears on the surface.

I never told you with what feeling, what affection Henry Lawson spoke of do you mind if I say Vance? He saw in him the recognition of one who knew him as equals know each other: for what they were and are and not shallowly. The words were few and appreciative but the tone of the voice said so much. You know how the voice deepens

---

[1] Nettie Palmer's 'Essay on Literature', published in 1924 as *Modern Australian Literature, 1900-23*.

and the eyes get that interior look, well, that is how Lawson felt. 'The *only one*' he said *'the only one who ever really saw'*. And he told me if ever I saw Vance to tell him what he had said. The years have taken away the words, that one sentence excepted, but not the meaning. He also spoke of his character as a being and as a man, and if I put it into conveying words it would be 'gentle folk'. (It was another instance of how we saw things in the same way.) The word he used was 'gentleman', but it is so abused that in writing it loses the meaning given by the speaker—the meaning of character and capacity as well as of usage...

Now I must end and say good bye, and my love to your children. What recollections they will have in years to come! Also remember me to all remembering friends, and believe me Yours very truly,

To A. H. Chisholm

129 Phillip Street
Sydney
22 August 1924

Dear Alec,

To say Thank you. My heart is very warm when I think of you, for I always see the boy behind you who, still a boy, liked the things I wrote. As soon as I can I shall make some quotations from and references to your book[1] in The Worker. I am not supposed to 'review' or 'notice', but I can *quote*. So I shall quote and most appropriately for the children, knowing that all the grown-ups will read it, too. It has just struck me you have never looked out my window—or have you? Half my view, the Bradley's Head half, is already gone. The rest of the Bay will be gone soon. I weep, but I daren't gnash my teeth for I am a good socialist and have to regard the other person's apple cart as well as my own. But what a happiness that view has been to me. It has been like life.

If you haven't looked out my window will you bring your wife in—or come yourself—but it must be soon. The buildings in front are going up almost a storey a day now.

With my most respectable affection Yours

Mary Gilmore.

And I never said what a beautiful book it is! What a picture that is of the emu! I nearly weep over it for recollections that must die when I go.

[1] Alec Chisholm's book was probably *Bird Seeking in Queensland*, published in 1922.

To Nettie Palmer

The Hotel Imperial
Goulburn
7 November 1924

Dear Mrs. Palmer,

I have just laid down Vance's book 'The World of Men'.[1]

Three weeks ago I began a chapter of recollections. It deals with people and happenings of over fifty years ago—and later. It cannot be published with real names because some of the children are still alive. I cannot put my name to it because my name would give too many clues. Yet the matter is, in justice to those dead or gone, necessary to be published. I thought, as I wrote it, might I ask Vance to act for me in the matter—there are so pitifully few one can trust; leakage is so usual.

I have just read 'Father and Son',[2] and 'Under which King?'[3] and as soon as I can get the matter typed and in consecutive form, if you will, I shall send it to him. I know that it will be safe with both of you. Also I think of giving a m.s. copy with the real names (additional) for the children to keep till later years when it will have a greater value in our history.

I am reading 'The World of Men' in miserly fashion. I think it an outstanding book altogether. The pain in it! and not one weak splash of the sentimental in it. I suffer as I read, for I too have seen what he has seen. The young eyes saw, and the old heart aches. Life's curious division! A sort of seedtime and harvest of which we know nothing till half the seed is lost.

I sent you the Goulburn notice of your Essay on Literature.[4] I hope your hair did not stand on end that I quoted all you said about myself. But, for one thing, I wanted it in, and, for another, the people here know my name and because of that they will read what otherwise they wd. pass over, caught by it like a bit of wool on a burr.

If you *possibly can*, get 'The House of the Ravens' by Hugo Wast. A translation of the Argentine, or did I tell you before? It is one of the books which an Australian can read, in wonder that another land is so like his own, and from which he can realize how his own land can be romantically written about. It is a book the writer of 'The World of Men' should have—and his wife too.

All good wishes—and no need to write in a hurry. Yours sincerely,

---

[1] See note to letter, 29 July 1924.
[2] A story in *The World of Men*.
[3] A story in *The World of Men*.
[4] See note to letter, 29 July 1924.

To Nettie Palmer

The Hotel Imperial
Goulburn

Dear Mrs. Palmer,   23 December 1924

If the book is 'Cronulla'[1] I read it in serial, and cut out several chapters to send them away. This letter is not an answer to yours. That was written and got heaven only knows where. Some day it will turn up, probably when I am doing answers to corresp. or some such thing. No; this letter is for the purpose of asking Vance to do what I had planned for years to do and now never will do,—with the less regret that I think he can or will. Only keep quiet on the idea or some of the lesser fry will tangle it up with their *booted* (?) feet, or spoil it. The thing is to write an Australian stalking chapter—stalking a kangaroo with only one slug in the gun and not too good a sight or none at all on the weapon. A thing in which shadows are real, a tree trunk almost a second sense—where the feet are bare, and a grass blade between the toes a reality. Where the intensity of the hunter is contrasted with the placidity of the sylvan and the sunset-safety of that which does not know it is hunted. The long toil for a gain of a few yards; the sky, the trees, the birds, the herbage; the patience of the wood craft; then the tempest of alarm, speed, flight and pursuit over logs and between trees; hearing still following when sight was lost and then sight again, and recognition of a grey thing still as a statue; and so on and so on. Ever since I was fourteen I have seen that and wanted to write it. But couldn't and wouldn't touch it with the sacrilegious hands, I will not say of the incapable, but of want of technical knowledge of known things. It has never been done, not as a great thing. America has done it. Scotland has done it. But we haven't. I gave Henry Lawson *one* story of watching the snake ('The Drover's Wife').[2] People thought it *his* mother; it was us and my mother. I have never been *sorry* I gave it and I want Vance do this other, and without fear of making it too long. It is fear makes things short and meagre. All good wishes to you all.

[1] *Cronulla: A Story of Station Life*, a novel by Vance Palmer, was published in 1924.
[2] Mary's claim to have told Lawson of the incident which formed the basis of 'The Drover's Wife' would certainly not go uncontested by Lawson scholars. The Editors believe that claims such as this (which are difficult to prove or disprove) are an interesting feature of Mary's character and as such are valid inclusions in the selection. In a manuscript in the Harry F. Chaplin Henry Lawson Collection Lawson writes, 'The Drover's Wife was my Aunt Gertrude, wife of Job Falconer, then squatter at Lahey's Creek. They were drought ruined.' See *Henry Lawson*, Studies in Australian Bibliography, No. 21, collected and annotated by Harry F. Chaplin, p. 13. Brian Matthews, in a paper at the 1979 A.S.A.L. Conference in Canberra, argued that the story reflects an incident in the life of Louisa Lawson. For further comments on the Mary–Henry Lawson relationship see notes to letters 5 August 1896, 29 August 1928 (to the Henry Lawson Memorial and Literary Society) and 5 June 1926.

Some one wrote on stalking of a deer in the Highlands. The cocks crowed and the wind blew, the twigs broke and the wind carried scent. I think it ran into three days, wh. is not needed in this one. But it was a noble piece of writing. I read it in Paraguay. and never forgot it.

To A. G. Stephens

Upper Flat
40 Beach Road
Rushcutters Bay
7 July 1925

Dear Mr Stephens,

The lines are not Spanish though I probably wrote them in Paraguay. I had forgotten them but a third reading brought back a faint recollection of some of the phrasing. Very squashy but horribly true as an ordinary picture—say of the departure of the M. S. A. Fleet.

Last night was my first visit to the English Association. Heney's[1] carefulness as a once S.M.H. editor pursues him with all the intensiveness of habit. Slow death is very easy but a 'bust' emotionally is after all life's best sneeze. The Jewish legend that no man could live who sneezed—till Abraham or was it Jacob? got leave to do it and lived—shd. have been the other way about.

I am wondering if you are coming tonight to hear Dora Wilcox playread. Also I'd like you to give your version of Ada Cambridge as an early Victorian. The woman's power was partly smothered; but smothered & all it was there! A Gladstonian face with Gladstone (she told me) her hero. Thanking you for remembrance—fame has touched me: a man in England wants four of my verses for a calendar!

To Nettie Palmer

The Worker Newspaper
St Andrew's Place
Sydney
5 January 1926

Dear Mrs. Palmer,

Thank you for your remembrance and letter. I had your copy of 'The Tilted Cart' ready to send as soon as an errata slip needed was ready. I hope you will like it. I also came across a year-old letter I had written you in reply to one of yours. It reads like a thing without foundation now—an unrelated bubble that has no destination. I wonder do we go off at the end like that, or face eternity as the unrelated? Bodies relate, touch, tingle, and mourn. But do souls? Our belief in eternity—in

---
[1] Thomas Heney.

life after death—is rooted in our sense of justice. We may doubt revelation but surely justice is eternal and never to be doubted somehow, somewhere, somewhen! and what justice of reparation the world needs.

I hope you will like the notes at the end of the Tilted Cart. They are a new lot, no one has done early Church recollections, and these are fact. Some day I hope to do a whole lot of the same, but I must get among the old folk of Brucedale to revive and make them exact. 'Daily Tel' got the book one day and within the turning of the press had a third of a col. notice next the leading article. A most unusual thing! And wasn't I pleased. Although I thought the least important themes were chosen to praise the book. The old station melodrama I wd. have chosen, and the other tragic ones. But that's *me* and not *them*.

I was hoping my dear son would have had time to see you at Caloundra on his way back to Cloncurry, but I fear not. He went back on Sunday last and was pressed for time. Today is Tuesday and he will leave Brisbane as soon as he can.

While I think of it—if you have friends going to Detroit, Michigan, U.S.A. my brother[1] is British Consul there, and is always glad to see anyone from Australia. He is regarded as rather a big man by other big men. He is the one who wrote 'The Spell of the Bush'[2] (Bookstall series, and still a good seller—for *them* not for him.) . . .

I see your two remarkable girls,[3] standing, sitting, walking about. They'll do foundation work for Australia yet. Recollections and biog. probably. Two people to inherit from, which is more than most get. When I get to my next book, I want to make an extract from one of Vance's short stories, when I have the thing in shape I will see you somewhere and talk over the matter.

My kindest wishes for the New Year. You know that Lawson told me that Vance was the only one who saw the inside of his (H's) work? Equality—of work in difference. That sense of pity so few have is in both.

Yours as ever (hoping to see Kathy[4] who is said to be in Sydney)

---

[1] John Cameron.
[2] Published in 1909.
[3] Aileen and Helen Palmer.
[4] Katharine Susannah Prichard.

To Nettie Palmer

The Worker Newspaper
St Andrew's Place
Sydney
3 June 1926

Dear Nettie (my age writes it!)

I am a fool about papers, and if I say I do not know about where a field of paying papers exists in Sydney do not look on that as any guide! I sort of sit in my corner with my nose to my pen and only now and then glance outside; also I promise to go to see people and never go. So what *can* I know.

Mr. Cockerill, the new editor of the 'T' is a live man and is going to make something of the paper in time. He has a big leeway to pull up and not yet much room to do it in but he knows what's what and it might be worth your while to try him with something as a beginning. He asked me for verse, but it has bin 'squeezed out' for weeks and is not yet in. But that need not deter you. He has re-established the Nature Notes and uses some sketches and articles for Sat. Billy Moore[1] does work, but not quite what he had before. Don't know the difference in it, though. The 'SMH' is taking special articles largely for the Sat. issue. Also verse. The verse is an outrage, most of it. But it gave space to two of Neilson's, so I have forgiven it. Then there are the weekly and monthly Journals. The Triad is asking me for matter. But you know the Triad anyhow. And of course there's the blasted Bulletin—for it certainly is a blasted tree if ever there was one! But you know all this. So of what use am I as a guide to brains? My use is for charwomen and the like. I forgot 'The Wentworth Magazine', Miss FitzMaurice Gill is editor. It takes short stories, articles or verse, but it must be of the 'happy' order. No moods. I think it pays rather well. Miss Gill asked me for some verse which I sent according to specification—short and not too imposing.

I am returning you your Henry Lawson article as Vance may want it for a reference. It reminds me that in a recent 'Mercury' (London) there was an article on Australia from someone in Queensland and signed Dinning.[2] I think Vance might follow that (or you) with something like your brochure on Aust. Literature. St. John Adcocks Anthol has included Angus & R. Aust. writers, 'M' and Zora Cross among them. Today I get a letter from P. Serle asking permission to reprint as *he* is getting out an anthol.[3] to be published by Collins & Co. so England may be waking up, and may take matter denied its place here. There's no doubt about it Australia is at the ice age for writers. I never

---

[1] William Moore.
[2] 'A Letter from Australia' by Hector Dinning. *London Mercury*, April 1926, pp. 38-41.
[3] See letter, 16 September 1927.

knew it to be so hard and so much a patron of the worse than mediocre. It suggests to me either bankruptcy or the expectation of war—or a slump in all perceptive power and judgment: editorial I mean.

I like it that Aileen[1] has thought of Swans.[2] The romance of the world is in the swan. It is the lotus among birds. My own mind has always gone out to it, on it, and with it. 'Just as the sun like a fiery ball . . . such is the death of every day'. Two very definite pictures not niggard and yet in few words. I think her real work will be prose, though one can never tell what the loosening out of the mind in relation to language and its mastery will do. The instrument counts for quite a lot in poetry.

If you are writing to G. G. McCrae will you give him my best obedience and so make one letter do two pairs of eyes?

Curious how things happen! I have just had a letter from Gertie Lawson acknowledging that her mother intercepted Henry's letters to me. 'There was a letter for you', she said as a child, 'it was in Henry's writing'. 'There was *no* letter', said her mother, and ordered her out of the room. Now I have Gertie's letter of proof. Strange! Yours sincerely (all of you)

To Gertrude Lawson

The Worker Newspaper
St Andrew's Place
Sydney
5 June 1926

Dear Gertie,

I have had an envelope addressed long enough to write you, but every time I tried to begin to write a letter someone rang up or called.

I am glad of the kindness behind your letter. One never knows what life will do, and I may outlive you, but the chances are, that you will long, long outlive me.

I shall see Mr. Mutch as soon as I am able and see what can be done to secure that part 'Ownership' of the grave[3] to the people of the State, or for the *poets* of the State. Of course he may not be able to do any more than the other people interviewed seemed to think could be done. But that has to be seen.

I remember the day so well when I came in from teaching at Neutral Bay[4] and you told me there was a letter for me in Henry's hand

---

[1] Nettie & Vance Palmer's daughter.
[2] Mary named her 1930 volume of poetry *The Wild Swan*.
[3] Henry Lawson's grave. See note 2, p. 67.
[4] Mary taught at Neutral Bay for some months in 1890, and after that for five years at Stanmore, prior to leaving for Cosme.

A. G. Stephens, from the Bookfellow, 16 December 1919

Dowell O'Reilly

Vance Palmer

A. H. Chisholm

Mary as she looked in 1927

R. D. FitzGerald

The Palmers with Hugh Esson and E. T. Browne at Emerald in 1923

writing, and when I looked it was not there; and how when you came in and I asked you, your mother said to you 'there was *no* letter. Leave the room!' And you came next day to me privately and told me that there was a letter, and emphasized what you had said before; and how we both looked for that letter. And then, when Henry came back[1] and said that he had answered every letter I had written him that he *had received*, I realized that more than that first letter had come and I had never seen them. He told me then that it was his mother that had stopped them—and that he should have arranged for an address c/o my mother. And now without ever asking for, or expecting it, comes your letter confirming it all, forty years after or nearly. And in the end it was I who had to say where and by whom he was to be buried, for no one else knew of the grave in Waverley;[2] while today you give me your inherited share in that grave! How strangely things come about.

I hope you are very well and thank you very much.

---

[1] Henry Lawson and his brother Peter went to Western Australia in 1890, arriving there in May. Lawson returned at the end of September the same year. There are various accounts of the reasons for his sudden exit from Sydney. Mary has this to say in her 'Personal History. Henry Lawson and I' (see note to letter, 5 August 1896).

> Meanwhile she [Louisa] had arranged for Henry and Peter to go to West Australia 'to make money quickly ... if Henry was to marry'. Henry, loth to leave me, the night before he sailed, asked me to elope with him and go to a registry office that evening and get married and that somehow he would arrange my passage in the boat next morning. Some sense of unfitness, some realization that I was not ready for marriage, made me say no. He tried every way to persuade me. 'You don't care for me as I care for you', he said, 'or you would', and so we said goodbye and he sailed next day. But not before he had told me that his mother was turning against the idea of marriage through her coolness with my mother, so much so that she had set one of her employees (a girl) to watch how often Henry came to see me. When Henry sailed I went to stay with his mother. He had feared her so much that he asked me not to tell her anything of our arrangements. I promised I would not. She expected me to be open, treated me for the first few days as a prospective daughter-in-law. But when I said nothing, she (I know now), was wounded. Then she tried to draw me out. But I had sent Henry away, without what to me would have been a definite promise of marriage, and, I felt I had no right to talk; and also no right to break my promise of silence to him. The final result was that she became as bitter toward me as toward my mother ... In six weeks my mother was back [from Junee]. I left Mrs. Lawson and we went to live in a boarding house ... I had written to Henry regularly for all the while I was in his mother's house, and got only his first letter. It was not till he returned from the West, months after, that I found that his mother had intercepted all the others ...

[2] Mary's statement 'Personal History. Henry Lawson and I' contains a long account of the events immediately after Lawson's death, the efforts of herself and others to secure a state funeral for him, and the confusion surrounding the exact location of the grave. She concludes:

> The grave in which he lies was not Kendall's. [Henry Kendall's remains had been removed from the original site in Waverley Cemetery to a more imposing site some four years after his death. Mary refers here to the original Kendall grave]. It belongs to Peter and Gertie ... and Henry's heirs in common. Gertie tells me that Charley's share has been made over to her, so that she holds two shares.

To S. H. Prior

The Hotel St James
Hyde Park
Dear Mr Prior,[1] *9 October 1926*

This letter nearly began 'Dearest Angel' to express my feelings on reading your note, only I thought of your shock if it came too suddenly on your view. I would have seen you, or sent you something, by this, for the Christmas Number only I have been watching the Bulletin for its notice of requirement and I have been ill with congestion of the lungs for some weeks now, and haven't been able to go out. I love to be remembered, especially by the Bulletin, and will enclose something to choose from—one just written, on the Waratah, and which I think it deserves. But if you use it I want the notes at the end to go in as they are history, and history of a kind never before written. The person who says we have nothing romantic in Australia on which to base our novels doesn't know where he lives. This land is full of subject matter for great novels. If only I had the time what wouldn't I write. The land and its history, past and present, teems with romance, in meat for romance. What's the difference between The Rocks and The Bowery but distance? or between Bendigo or Araluen and California, or Woolloomooloo and Pyrmont and Limehouse, but in the eye that sees them and the pen that writes them. I said it to Lawson forty years ago, when he said 'But what is there romantic to write about in Australia?' and 'What romance is there in a bullock team!' and I have never ceased to say it. It is all a question of orientation. Our writers always orient with one eye on somewhere else and one vision blurs the other in when the other is the Australian vision.

To R. D. FitzGerald

16 Montana Flats
Cremorne Point
Sydney
Dear Mr. FitzGerald, *9 May 1927*

Whatever will you be thinking of me! I think I had flu and some pneumonia when your book[2] came and it was put away and I have just come to it again.

---

[1] S. H. Prior, the *Bulletin* editor, had written to Mary, 8 October 1926, requesting her to contribute to the 1926 Christmas number of the *Bulletin*.
[2] R. D. FitzGerald's first book of verse, *The Greater Apollo*, 1927.

That is a fine thought 'My years are built at tragic cost'. We are all so full of our *gains*—and our own petty worth—we say 'What a lot to learn' and never 'what loss!'

> It is enough that trees are trees
> That earth is earth, and stone is stone

They are the real letters, and the real name, which we try to put into the little twist we call an alphabet and words! That is why language defeats us; it would hold the universe and cannot.

But I like best the scored seacliff. There is tempest in the form, and a fine command of the form. But one sees behind it the things too big for little words.

May I, who write little things in little words and in simple form, pay homage to the bigger thing in you?

And now I haven't said Thank You!

To Percival Serle

The Women's Club
167 Elizabeth St
Sydney
Dear Mr. Serle,   *16 September 1927*

I have just bought a most beautiful thing, the first of its kind in Australia. It is your Anthology.[1] I am very proud of it as being the only anthology we have as our own which has concerned itself with the higher literary values, and not with catch cries and tag stuff. I had no idea we could have collected *so homogeneous* a body of poetry. It is poetry and not verse, and means a new standard for coming writers. For after all, example does count; few are so self-oriented that outside influence does not encourage, deter, shape or direct—and the latter so often to the hurt of the writer.

I think you have balanced the book well. Further you have not overloaded it with the long-established and the oft-quoted. The burden of the past does not exclude the present, for though we love the past, we do not want always to sit with the dead. We want the living (and the coming on) and you have given them. For myself I am very proud to be in your book. It sets *your* name in its good place anyhow.

Gratefully, yours sincerely,

I forgot to say how I like your preface. It is a fine thing. I like

---

[1] *An Australasian Anthology*, 1927, edited by Percival Serle, assisted by Frank Wilmot (the poet 'Furnley Maurice') and R. H. Croll.

your remembrance of Sir Henry Parkes; it is a dignified thing to have done, and a worthy. I love those two sincere Palmers,[1] and am glad of how you have valued them.

To Nettie Palmer

129 Phillip Street
Sydney
Dear Nettie,   7 April 1928

With this pen I wrote Hound of the Road[2] in the first draft, and I have only just found it again. (This to explain the difference, if any in the script.)

I am sending you by registered post my earliest *collected* writings, some written 41 years ago. Verse and thoughts—and all so young! and yet so much me of today. I did not read it all for somehow I couldn't. The book (MS.) has been packed and stored away for so many years unseen I have forgotten most of what is in it. It may give you the repayment of a paid article on beginnings and beginners.

I said 'Dear Nettie' when I saw your article in the 'SMH'[3] this morning. I shall put you and Vance into the preface of my next book. Verse; and I think the typing will be done this month. When the typing is done I shall send the children the m.s. copy, as it is only on newsprint it won't be worth binding or keeping, but it will be of a day's interest, and you can make comparison on the change age and a fountain pen make in the hand-writing of youth and a steel pen.

I like your article very much especially that Monbulk part. The translation of names did not lie with the black but with us; and with us in the hard narrow meaning in English by which we branded the aboriginal. I hope you manage to collect a lot of odds and ends, and, however small in 'area', feed them out with generous and adequate English, so that even if you and I and V. should be regarded as a lot of harebrained fools, we shall still have fed the bread of life to the young literary schools that follow us. Monbulk—where the tribes meet in safety—for it is a place of peace! Some people when they see a

---

[1] Vance and Nettie Palmer.
[2] Mary's small volume of essays and reminiscences, 1922. Of *Hound of the Road* she said in a letter to W. H. Ifould, 23 March 1924:

> It is only since I wrote *Hound of the Road* that I venture to call myself a writer, for, in it, I do what I always wanted to do, i.e., give the pioneer (his times and the land), a setting of poetry and natural romance, and so show his right relation to a literature which goes beyond mere chronicle and itemization. It is my aim and my hope now to continue doing this. It is where I began in the young years, it is where I hope to end.

[3] 'Our Once Green Tree', S.M.H., 7 April 1928. Nettie Palmer's article dealt with her own (and Mary's) anxiety to preserve Aboriginal lore.

telegraph pole only see a pole; some see the whole wonder of telegraphy and the land through which it goes. So most people only saw the telegraph pole in the aboriginal and his language. Who was that foolish person cavilled at what you wrote of Hardy?[1] It sounds blasphemous, but to me in his verse Hardy comes nearer to being God than any writer I know. His work however small is that of a Titan—is titanic. Struggle and strain and with it an implacable must and an equally implacable pity that suffers in all that it makes. His prose does not get me as his verse does. Perhaps his canvas is too large for me.

I have a dear delightful little flat that looks over Burdekin House to the North Head and even the ocean. But I am afraid the sea air coming straight at me out of the ocean is knocking me to pieces: I can't sleep. I am praying for cool weather and then I may be better. I should grieve to have to leave it. All good and best wishes to you all—

To Nettie Palmer

129 Phillip Street
Sydney
15 April 1928

Dear Nettie,

There is no need to return any of these things enclosed. You may have seen them or you may not. The summers increasingly tell on me, so I have begun to 'divide up' before it is too late; but all the same it is done with the very cheerful hope that I shall continue to dodge the scythe in spite of its occasional nearness. I don't know whether you will welcome being treated as my official assignee or biographer, or whatever it may be; but I am pouring my other self out to you, because for one thing you have the capacity of hitting straight what is essential, and of not exaggerating either praise or blame. Then, too, you may as I said out of the forty years (or nearly) collection I lately registered to you find something to give you a paid article knowing how well! that it would mean more to me and do more to *make* me when I am a wispy shade than it would mean, make, or do for you.

Dorothy Cottrell's book[2] is to appear serially in the Sydney Mail—in May or June.

By the way I had a thundering letter in the Brisbane Worker, 4th of April, I was angry when I wrote it or it wd. have much more bespoken a gentle manner, but the occasion justified me as I had been accused

---

[1] Thomas Hardy (1840-1928), English novelist and poet.
[2] *The Singing Gold*, 1928, a story of the south-western pastoral region of Queensland.

by a member of my Board, speaking in an A.W.U. Convention, as a conscriptionist. Me!!! The second part for my next book[1] (verse) is in the typist's hands, soon I hope to have it all there.

Best of wishes and boggins of thanks to you and yours

To Nettie Palmer

129 Phillip Street
Sydney
29 August 1928

For them Palmers—and their children.

I meant to wire Hurroo! but my husband[2] came down, and my time had to be his. When he left—half an inch of rain reported and he just flew, a possibility of grass and sheep being much more important than a wife! I had such an arrears, and so many things to see to for him that I am still meeting Apollyon[3] in the way or whatever is the equivalent of too much work. Dear Nettie, this has to be an answer to your letter for the time being. I am *not* Wynken de Worde. You must have forgotten or not received the letter in which I said that I thought it was P. O'Leary.

I have a hat that was Henry Lawson's, would them Palmers like to have it? I have had Vance in mind for it ever since it came into my possession because of what Henry thought of him.

My best love, trimmin's and all,

Mr. Davies
Publicity Secretary
The Henry Lawson Memorial and Literary Society

129 Phillip Street
Sydney
29 August 1928

Dear Mr. Davies,
Do not fail to invite Shaw Neilson to the Lawson celebration. His address is 160 Gordon Street, Footscray. I just now had a letter from him, will you tell him I said so, please, and that I will write (and with apologies) later on?

---

[1] Probably *The Wild Swan* which did not appear until 1930.
[2] One of Will Gilmore's rare visits to Sydney from his Queensland property.
[3] The 'foul fiend' met in John Bunyan's *The Pilgrim's Progress*, 1678.

Now as to Henry Lawson;[1] when I first knew him he hoped to become a writer. He had never seen a dictionary in his life and did not know what a dictionary was. He had never held a volume of poetry in his hands nor had he ever read a novel. He did not know what a novel was and I had to explain. He had never seen a copy of either 'Robinson Crusoe' or Bunyan's 'Pilgrim's Progress', and had never heard of either. I lent him both. 'Robinson Crusoe' he managed to partly read, 'The Pilgrim's Progress' he could not read. He had read so little that even 'Robinson Crusoe' was half empty to him. Parts of it interested him, but when he found it was fiction he lost all interest in it, his mind still being unawakened. He told me he had never seen a book of any kind in his home, except (he thought) a book of sermons. I lent him 'David Copperfield', which was his first novel. He did not care much for it, except as to Steerforth who, after argument, he admitted seemed a real being. My sister has that copy of 'David Copperfield' now. If I can, I shall get her to give it to me, and we will send it to your Society—as a possession. I lent Henry copies of Burns, Tennyson

[1] Mrs Ann-Mari Jordens who has assisted the Editors in the compilation of the notes and annotations to these letters (and who is working on Frederick J. Broomfield) notes that Broomfield in his address to the Fellowship of Australian Writers, 28 November 1930 on 'Henry Lawson and his Critics', attacked Lawson's 'literary friends' who claimed to have 'taught him to read, think, rhyme, etc.'. Lawson had 'a rough spin at the hands of his friends no less than from his foes', Broomfield remarked acidly. (*Henry Lawson and His Critics*, Sydney, 1930, pp. 13-14, 16).

Mary's written statement 'Personal History. Henry Lawson and I' (Volume 41, Gilmore Papers, Mitchell Library) gives many details of her relationship with Lawson. Although the present Editors, like others before them, have been unable to authenticate all her comments about Lawson, the document referred to above contains a wealth of details which certainly point to a close and continuing relationship between them over many years. Some of the details are included here:

> He used to take me out to see the wrong things, the things repressive of the rights of Australia; the things like a blot upon her and which prevented her being herself—the low wage workers, the Chinaman working at treadle-saws in the underground cellars lit only by a grating in the street, the huddled houses by the old Argyle Cut, and the Rocks where women hung their washing out on the roof and from windows, and where the pale seamstress sewed at a foot or hand machine from daylight to dark for a few pence, and last but not least the mixture of blood and the neglected children by the Quay and elsewhere. The wrongs of man were his theme, nationhood his dream, and we were both young, and reformers in ideals. At this time it was still customary for a man to give his arm to a lady, and Henry in the tradition of his elders offered the arm I expected. So hand in hand in a way, like two children out of a book we did the streets of Sydney and I look back and know we were children—so innocent and so eager, so young and so fresh in our dreams ... I urged him to write prose. I told him his prose was better than his verse ... I begged him to write Australia, and again Australia. To help him I even collected some aboriginal lore and words—very hard to get at that time, for no one was interested in Australia then. At that time we thought tags were needed to show that Australian matter belonged to Australia ... I introduced him to Le Gay Brereton. Brereton begged me to urge him to study form, rhythm, and a better English ... Concerned in the New Australia movement I was the more able to resist Henry. Affection I had and always would have for him; the affection of a friend who thought him wonderful, and for whom he had opened a newer and a wider world.

The meeting with Le Gay Brereton has been verified in his own memoirs.

(he thought T. 'sentimental' and returned it only partly read) Keats, Coleridge, Shelley, Browning, Poe, the Ingoldsby Legends and I forget what else (we had a good collection of good writers). Keats, Shelley, Coleridge and Browning he could not grasp. Poe affected him at once, and he liked the Ingoldsby Legends 'well enough', but Burns was a revelation to him and his master for all time. I gave him a copy of Poe which he carried about with him till his death; he showed it to me the year before, 'I still have it', he said, and 'There is not a word you ever said to me that I have forgotten'.

I made him get a dictionary. He brought it back to me in a rage saying what good was a book like that, that it did not have the words he wanted in it. I said it *must* have. He declared that it *hadn't*. I asked for a word; he gave it and I found it at once. He took the book from me in disbelief, and then when I put my finger on the word, he said in triumph, 'That's page 70, I read three times to page 24 without finding it'. 'But' I said (I think the word was something in the g's or farther on), 'that word begins with (whatever it was) and page 24 ends at so and so, and doesn't go so far'. He was bewildered, and I had to explain the alphabetic run of the letters, and that you could not find a word by just opening the book (*as he had thought*) and showed him and taught him how to find words.

He brought me 'Faces in the Street' in its first more or less completed form. The lines were of all lengths with broken rhymes, and of mixed metres. I explained metre and helped him correct it in places, told him about 'syllables', 'feet' being a word he could not grasp, and that *all lines must rhyme* if he began that way. He had not known this. The following Sunday (I think it was) he brought it back, metre regular, lines fairly even, but rhymes in the middle (on the strong stress) in some places. I said it did not rhyme. He insisted that it did and that every line 'had its rhyme'. 'Where?' I asked pointing to an unrhymed ending. 'There it is!' he said and pointed to the middle of the line. He was so sure that as long as it rhymed any where that it was right, that we had quite an altercation. I took down poet after poet, but as I could not hit on a verse *of his exact form* he would *not* be convinced. At last I thought of 'Meiklejohn's English' with its rules for prosody, and reluctantly he gave in. When I told him to take it to the Bulletin he nearly went mad with joy. He took it there with the result that everyone knows. One of my words in that poem is 'Mammon', he had 'masters', and I objected on the ground that there was no servility here and no slaves. I gave him a line with 'Mammon' and another with 'Moloch' in it. I had to explain both words from *every aspect*. When he brought me the script again he had used 'Mammon'. I preferred 'Moloch' as stronger, he preferred 'Mammon' as nearer to his idea.

He wanted to write revolution. I begged him to write Australia.

'What is there to write in Australia?' he said scornfully. I talked of the pioneers, of the teams and their names, of the wild horses, the wild cattle, the aboriginals, for I had lived among all these, and he in a settled (as compared with me) a settled district. Once when I had talked to drive things home he said almost with tears of appreciation and wonder in his eyes 'You see the same things as other people, but differently. I see them now as you see them. Why', he said, 'you make even a tin pannikin or a quart pot seem wonderful!' For three years I constantly fed his mind and helped him. The story of 'The Drover's Wife' was *our* story. The boy in it is now General Manager for the Northhampton Land Company in Queensland. He is my brother[1] next to me, and we were talking of it, for the first time since it happened to us as children, only last May or June, when he was in Sydney on holiday. Our father was a station building-contractor and the words Hughie used to my mother were, 'When I'm a man *I'll* not go away building, I'll stay at home and take care of you, Mamma!'—we used that word 'Mamma' in those days.

All this seems to be about me, but it is necessary as showing how Henry began, and through what an unawakened period he had to travel to loose the genius that was his, and only waiting to be given outlet and exit. But there can be no word from me of Henry Lawson without reference to that most faithful of all his friends, poor old Mrs. Byers.[2] She was beautiful, my mother said, when Lawson first took an apartment from her, She had flats, a good business, and £500 in the Bank. Whatever she had went on him in the years of his misery. From her he got his real knowledge and deep love of Dickens. She loved Dickens and had a complete pocket edition of his works. When Henry was moody she would read to him by the hour. When I first saw her at Yanko (Leeton) she still had most of the set. When I saw her a year ago there were but three volumes left. She would have given them to me, but I would have felt a robber. Now I am sorry I did not take them as they could have gone to your Society, for you would have valued them and kept them safe.

All my life it has been my lot to help others find themselves. My life from earliest years has been so full of observation and experience, and I realize now, too, that I had an exceptional father and mother for both were intellectual, and full of poetry and the historical sense, so that I see things in relationships unknown to most others, and can consequently show a path unseen to one seeking outlet. My last 'find' is Dorothy Cottrell[3] whose book 'Singing Gold' is to be published in both U.S.A. and England, and serially in U.S.A., Canada and Australia.

[1] Hugh Cameron.
[2] Isabel Byers.
[3] See note to letter, 15 April 1928.

She was offered £5,000 (and took it) for the serial rights alone for U.S.A. and Canada.

My heart is with your meeting and your efforts. Yours sincerely,

To Nettie Palmer

129 Phillip Street
Sydney
28 November 1928

Dear Nettie,

I'm nearly dead of MS novels since I wrote up Dorothy Cottrell, but I've got to send you a line somehow. In case you have not seen any of her story I am posting you two 'Sydney Mails', but *this* week's is the one—a bit about a lamb. I wept over the ms. and weep over the print each time I read it. It is so simple and so deep. Well, the Bulletin writes me that they are keeping my article (it is paid for) for Vance's 'Life'. I thought they meant Vance's own life, but at this moment wondered was it Henry Lawson's as I compared them a little.

I am devoured still by other people's affairs, and I am afraid I shall have to go out into the wilderness to escape them—and I starve in the wilderness for want of people. Only as I grow old do I realize how much I have been and am a hungerer for my kind. I swore I would not read another ms. this morning; and just now is gone a working man and his novel is written in an exercise book—script. Oaths seem to be no use to me. But I do so want to get at my own work; I do not grow younger. What a contrast this week between 'Singing Gold'[1] and 'Coonardoo'.[2] Get the Mail to see it. The gold so clear and warm, Coonardoo so cold and dirty—for it is dirty this week. And I am so disappointed, the first chapter was so good.

Well my dears, daughters and all, my love to you and a Happy Christmas.

Three parts dead and only one part alive—so tired—Did you see Sept. London Bookman? A good word for me in it—also Vance.

Am sending you Dorothy Cottrell's portrait for the children.

---

[1] Dorothy Cottrell's novel. See note to letter, 15 April 1928.
[2] *Coonardoo* was Katharine Susannah Prichard's novel about the north-west cattle country and with black–white relationships in the region. Mary's comments here are somewhat hard and do not reflect the general esteem in which *Coonardoo* was held.

To Hugh McCrae

129 Phillip Street
Sydney
26 December 1928

Dearest Hugh,

If you aren't the nicest thing in the world just at Christmas time! Of course you are the one poet, & of course you like best the two lines you quote because there is the possibility of a poet's vision in them. But me, though I write, am never less (& never more) than a housemother & a body with one eye to the children's welfare & *my* two lines are the optimist's vision and the 'Stand up to it laddie & take your knock' of 'Here's to the fox where'ere he lies. Here's to the hope that never dies, as we go etc'. As far as one reacts to the specific in one's own lines I react to those last lines and do you know what came with your note? A card from Guernsey from David & Clara Stevenson, David cousin to Robert Louis Stevenson & to whom I was engaged in the early New Australia days, and perhaps would have married but that another woman so broke her heart over it she married the first man asked her & suffered & suffered. When I went to Cosme & passed her house (she was then married) I used to hear her crying when she thought no one could hear. A year after I married Will. In 1914 Clara's husband swore himself of enlistment age & entered hospital to have an operation that would allow his passing for the war. He died, almost on the table. Through all those years she had been a faithful wife to him. David got to the war, a bullet near the heart sent him back to Paraguay—& he married Clara. Now they spend their days sometimes in Scotland, sometimes in Guernsey. It appears God has certainly rewarded the faithful ... It was due to me, & in a second degree to David that Lane did not abandon the New Australia project when we had the bailiffs in, sell the 'Royal Tar'[1] & repatriate everyone. I got David to go to Sidney Burdekin to see if he wd. lend enough. When he refused D. said 'I never was so near killing anyone in my life as at that moment'. In the end Miss Rose Scott to whom we were mortgaged extended our loan, & money coming in we got the Tar away.

When I look back what a life I have had! What things I have helped in! & how unknown to those not directly concerned. 'The deed! The deed!' is after all the one thing worth while. But you can understand with what joy I received, after all these years, that card from Guernsey.

---

[1] For details of the sailing of the *Royal Tar* see Gavin Souter, *A Peculiar People; the Australians in Paraguay*, 1968. Reverend G. Stuart Watts wrote to Mary, 13 August 1953, with the following details of the *Royal Tar*:

> My grandfather, John Campbell Stuart, was a pioneer shipbuilder on the North Coast of this state, and the *Royal Tar* was one of the ships built by him at Stuart Island, Nambucca River ... The *Royal Tar* was built originally for a Mr. Hastings, who, I am told, was so impatient to have her launched that she almost broke her back when she hit the waves.

What do you think of the Fellowship[1] being started after all? How long is it since I made the first move? 1916 was it? Connie Stephens[2] has kept my letter & could say. I have forgotten.

Most excellent & ever invisible thing my affection to you and yours—as ever

To Frank Dalby Davison

129 Phillip Street
Sydney

Dear Mr. Davison,   *13 July 1929*

I have just read the Cattle[3] stories and if you had not already found yourself I would be saying 'I have found another genius!' Man! You don't know what you have written in these! In these stories you speak our own—our very own language; our real language that is dying for want of use, and is going out of memory because *none* have really written it. You give the love of the bush in its own being, where others have only written *about* it. This is so different, it is history made real & facts made living. Don't give any of these four to Mr. Mackaness.[4] Give him the dog story if you like, but not these. Keep these together, work them out as one, break them into smaller chapters, & make *one book* of them—a book for men & boys, & a book for Australia. What a glorious knowledge you show! Not a sentence, not a line that does not count & is not packed, & yet there is no overloading, no trimming for the sake of trimming, & no ekeing out. I want you to come to see me so that I can talk to you about it. I so loved the writing, so felt it great that I could not help editing it in places as you will see. The reader's ear & eye made me do it. I hope you will not mind. My first impression was right; I have not read anything so good for years. It satisfies my knowledge of fact, my longing for the facts to be written, and my sense of English. And as you know I do not say these things idly.

I would like to see the book put out as one of The Cornstalk[5] series—a book with good print & margins, and pocket size. There needs to be an introductory chapter, long or short does not matter, telling of settlement, descriptive of horses, saddles & bridles, stock yards

---

[1] Fellowship of Australian Writers. Mary gives her version of its establishment in the letter to George Mackaness, 22 May 1935.
[2] Mrs Constance Robertson.
[3] Frank Dalby Davison's sister showed the *Man-Shy* stories to Mary. Davison later indicated that he was much encouraged by Mary's enthusiasm for them.
[4] George Mackaness had edited an anthology of Australian short stories the previous year.
[5] The Cornstalk Press was a subsidiary of Angus & Robertson. It published cheap editions and reprints in a series throughout the 1920s.

& the like, huts, fencing timber, and the making of a damper, with a little conversation breaking in as you have it elsewhere. Something that sets the key of man's hardness and nature's fullness and yet that does not belittle man, little though he be. And if you like you can give this letter to Mr Robertson[1] & tell him this is what I think of your work. This field is your own; no one else has touched it; keep it your own, for you know it to the full.

And now I find you have not left me your address! How am I to get in touch with you?

Don't let go I beg of you, but however hard it is for you to write, keep on. Yours sincerely,

To Hugh McCrae

Sydney
26 September 1929

Dear Hugh,

This is only like a bird's shadow in passing of what I would like to say of your work—of what I *feel* in regard to it. One cannot define that which is not confined to time and place. You are the one tall tree. The rest of us are only flowers in the garden & the best of us but wild shrubs in comparison.

Hugh McCrae

Meerschaum & sea birds,
    Albaster & dreams,
White doves in their wheeling,
    The pale moonbeams,
Pride & the strength of a man,
    Pity deep stirred,
Night with the stars
    And the voice of a bird:
These he has given us,
These he has made;
Beauty has spoken,
    Here unafraid.

Mary Gilmore

---

[1] George Robertson.

To Marjorie Quinn
The Hon. Secretary,
The Fellowship of Australian Writers.

Dear Miss Quinn,

The Lyceum Club
114A Pitt Street
Sydney
4 December 1929

As you know I have long suggested that one of the aims of our Society should be the collection of personal recollections of Australian writers, and not only of those who are gone, but of those who are still alive. So I am suggesting that Hugh McCrae, because of his outstanding quality as a writer, should be asked to give a series of public lectures or talks, either over the wireless, or directly to audiences in Sydney and the other capital cities and on the lines I have indicated. After Mr McCrae could come others. It would be an excellent thing for awakening interest in Australian publications as well as a means of keeping in mind the personal which as everyone knows is so easily lost if not made use of. One of the objects in founding this society of ours is this very thing. So I am proposing that you bring this letter before the next Committee meeting of the Fellowship of Australian writers, or, if too late for one before recess, before the President, Professor J. Le Gay Brereton, to ask his endorsement on behalf of the Society of Mr McCrae as the first speaker to be called upon to initiate the movement. I may say I am writing to the President of the Lyceum Club as I am writing to you, the Lyceum Club being so much concerned with literature as one of its sources of being. As it has thirty-seven branches in Europe and the Empire, we might well be glad of its co-operation in this should any of our writers travel overseas. Yours sincerely,

To Nettie Palmer

Dear Nettie,

129 Phillip St
Sydney
16 April 1930

I have just got the Bulletin with the story.[1] What a fine man's beginning, what a clearness of picture, and what values to Australia, inside and out, in the naming of things she possesses! *That* is what gives individuality to a country. Trout, which they all write about having read of it, belongs to all the world. So does salmon (when it isn't in Ireland—and thank God for Ireland in that individuality) and carp and pike. But

---

[1] The 'story' was Vance Palmer's novel, *The Passage*, then being serialized in the *Bulletin*. The first instalment appeared on the day Mary wrote this letter.

who has the parrot-fish and who the slugs that lie 'Like black cucumbers' and who the rainbow fish and the spotted sea bream but Australia—even if they feed and live in other waters! Our fish should say 'Australia' as plainly as tarpon say Florida or America. And here they are. And what a boy in those 'Bright miraculous mornings' when the Andes might possibly, as I remember, have poked up over the horizon in the slow turning over of the world!

There have been times, and not a few, when I have thought you gave up too much to your family, and Vance as of, and not of the group. Now I see your compensation, even if I do not see your own fruition.

'Even his loose-hung body seemed to be thinking about the job in hand'—you see I go back to it! It has the observation which has become part of the observer's own body and being, which is so notable here. And it is that absence of being soaked through with the accessories—the settings of the theme—that has hitherto made Australian writing so thin. It has not eaten enough in the subconscious to be able to trawl up a deep sea harvest from itself, in season or out of season. It has been all on the surface—or too much on the surface, and broken only by the emotions of the appetites. The perceptions of the poet, which are the reciprocal between nature and self, have been too much absent. We have lived *on* nature and not *in* her. In this story we have the 'in', with the 'on' as the subsidiary.

Veronica Mills[1] came yesterday shy as a bird and as full of little dartings. She is like what she writes, spurting up in unexpected perceptions and summarizings just when one has begun to think the field a little thin. What she wants is drilling as to the need and the way to grasp impression and response and make it thought, and how is she to get that away in the bush, wanting a hand to guide her? . . . [letter incomplete]

To H. M. Green

129 Phillip Street
Sydney
Dear Mr Green, 23 April 1930

I have just been able to get your book.[2] So far I have only 'walked' through it and I am struck by the absence of recurrence in its phrasing of criticisms. It is an astonishing thing to see how you have seen with

---

[1] Veronica Mills was one of Mary's young writers, who came to her for encouragement and advice.
[2] *An Outline of Australian Literature*, 1930.

a different eye everyone of the people you have touched upon. You perceive similarity and likeness, but nowhere do you lap two people in the same cloth and I do think that is a great tribute to your own many sided and varied mind. It's its measure—or one of its measures and you have been just. As to the 'University Group'[1] written of by Gilbert Mant, it is understandable that in the close association with the University and with the peculiarly defined common heritage in books of the University—that your mind would react to these as surely as a musician reacts to his type of music. The standard is there become a part of being. I do not know that I quarrel with that. It is a question of this or that as a standard.

There is another thing: the book has not tired anywhere. And yet the mind must often have felt a weariness of the subject; not because of the subject but because of the delving. And you have delved, because the book in its content is a big thing.

I may say that among the minor novelists—you left out my Aunt, Jeannie Lockett. Her novels were 'Judith Grant' (London 1893 Hutchinson & Co.) and 'The Mill' (I think published here but I have no copy of it). She also wrote serials, short stories and descriptive (scenic) articles. To the last (as a pioneer in this kind of thing) she had for years a gold pass over the state railways: the only woman to be given such a thing.

Also you forgot 'The Working Man's Paradise' by William Lane. Unimportant as a novel, its effects as a social influence was beyond that of most novels. You might be interested to know that the girl in this, and in my Aunt's book, 'Judith Grant' is more or less me.

I do not think with you as regards Robert Crawford.[2] I put him much higher than you do. But perhaps you had only his book—or was it his first book?—and I judge him by his later uncollected verse in addition.

But these are small things compared with the real and greater values in the work. May I say I am surprised at the space you give me? For I have always thought that, as regarding me from the University standard, you thought I had only very small values. So I thank you with surprise as well as in every other way. I shall be having the proofs of my new book almost at once, and I am wondering what you will think of it. With congratulations Yours sincerely

---

[1] Cecil Mann (not Gilbert Mant as Mary suggests) in reviewing H. M. Green's *An Outline of Australian Literature* in the *Bulletin*'s Red Page, 16 April 1930, said, 'Mr. Green too, appears to show a marked partiality for professors. In the work of Professor Le Gay Brereton and Professor L. H. Allen he can see nothing but good and very great good at that'.

[2] Robert Crawford (1868-1930) published *Lyric Moods*, 1904, and *The Leafy Bliss*, 1921.

To Yvonne and Joan Webb

129 Phillip Street
Sydney
6 May 1930

My two dear little girls,[1]

I thought I had replied to your joint letter a week ago! But I have flu' & my wits are flu'ed, too.

    I think the story quite out of the common and later on hope to have a talk to you about it. How old are you each & how long writing? The verse is not so unusual, but verse is usually of slower growth, so that it is not be be taken as a final criticism that I say it is not so unusual as the story. Besides two small stanzas are not enough to form opinions on. The story is an edifice, where the verses are only incidents, or incidental. I shall be glad to hear of you both when you have something more to show me. When my cold is better I hope to find time to have you come to see me. In the meantime write when you feel like it, but do not *force* the mind.

    With all good wishes Yours sincerely

To Nettie Palmer

129 Phillip Street
Sydney
8 May 1930

Dear Nettie,

I had nearly written you yesterday but hadn't a moment, and now your letter is here. What a last chapter in 'Men are Human'![2] *I felt stunned by it,* for the work was so quiet throughout that the end comes like the fall of a hillside, that *had* to fall, in a moment of quiet. The story has the relentlessness of Coonardoo[3] without its mannerisms, flat passages, and sordidness. What a piece of work! Not an overstress in it, and yet what room for overstresses!

    About yourself; not a martyr, of course, but the fictionist put out of sight. Possibly the fictionist might not have been greatly worthwhile—one never knows—but the door was closed; willingly, and with the eyes looking further afield.

    Yes, the verse is good: very much like father's verse, not like

---

[1] This letter is typical of the encouragement offered by Mary to the many young writers who devoured so much of her time. See also letters, 29 May 1930, 8 December 1931 and 28 December 1941.
[2] The novel *Men Are Human,* 1930, by Vance Palmer, won a prize in the *Bulletin* competition for that year.
[3] Mary's dislike of *Coonardoo* (by K. S. Prichard) is again evident. See also letter, 28 November 1928.

mother's. Mother's verse puts out a hand, catches a warm little bird and holds it close; father's verse builds a house, and in it you can go from room to room. You might not like the rooms, they may even seem austere and bare, but they are there, and father's books are father's verse extended.

About Hugh McCrae, he thought of a lecture here, but has given up the idea. I suggested one on his contemporaries and showed him that, as he was going away what an opportunity he had for saying all the nasty things he liked! But Hugh has no remembrance of grouches, and also he didn't realize that I was only pretending. I doubt if he would have had a paying audience here—and certainly not on his own publicity work! He is still an infant when it comes to facing the world. I told him when in France to write verse, however bad as French, for the French papers. He said how could he, as French verse was so fixed in its forms. I said his aberrations, being a foreigner's, would be an attraction, for of course however bad his French, his poetry would still be there.

For myself, pain is more constant than it used to be. Still I may again renew my youth. One never knows, and I have the first galleys of 'The Wild Swan'.[1]

My love to all them Palmers—

I am afraid you are right about V.M.[2] yet with practice the capacity to shape could and perhaps would grow. She thinks you like a warm bird—Now that is funny! I just remembered writing that of your verse! She was afraid you wd. be 'haughty' and 'Oh how different she was'!

To A. H. Chisholm

129 Phillip Street
Sydney
Dear Aleck, Alick, Alec, *Alexander*! *20 May 1930*

How glad I am to see you in your conquering role with your new book![3] I was so glad I nearly said 'Gosh!' or something even more improper at my age. Dear Man I am delighted. More power to the pen that is yours.

About your young writers: I have three regular visitors all fifteen— and one with a dash of genius in verse, one who, if she goes on, will be a Barnard-Eldershaw in one instead of two. The third will be an

---

[1] Mary's finest collection of verse to that time. It was published later that year.
[2] Veronica Mills.
[3] Probably *Birds and Green Places* published in 1929.

artist in line and colour. All of course, as it may be that adolescence does not change them as *it* changes. So with this little girl you write me about. She has faculty, thought, and feeling, and adolescence may leave her with the fire that is genius but which at present she lacks. Still one never can tell . . .

I had the loveliest letter last evening from Leslie Haylen,[1] just when I was having cold shivers in the spine as a result of shock: shock being (a) this cookery Book horror[2] as exposed by Smith's and of which I was ignorant till they came to me about the advertisement (b) tooth out and just kept alive on sips of brandy to get it out and (c) another worry that involves me because others did not take ordinary reasonable precautions. Had I known they did not I would have done it for myself. And into the midst of my misery comes Haylen's letter like an angel of kindness. He is another who sees beneath the surface of 'The Wild Swan'. . . Love to the family.

'The Rue Tree' is going into 12 point-Cloister type, but different shaped book as it is religious Verse and should go into an ecclesiastical coat pocket. I hope it will, and in a plenty. But it is not the money that matters to me. It is to see my book in shape as I want it.

To Roderic Quinn

129 Phillip Street
Sydney
Dear Rod,   *28 July 1931*

Today they unveiled the Lawson Memorial;[3] to-night I was taken to see it by moonlight. I came home and thought how there were those friends with him in his prime; and a few who also knew him in his years of triumph, but unlike those others, remained with him, still friends in his adversity. And, of those, the outstanding one was Rod Quinn. You, Rod, never changed with the times—as some who sat in the front places to-day did. To the last the old companionable ways remained between you. And thinking about you and the faithful heart in you, and the straight outlook which you have always given facts and life alike, and also of the limpidity of your verse, a few lines of

---

[1] Labor parliamentarian who shared Mary's views on many social problems.
[2] A question of plagiarism.
[3] A bronze statue of Henry Lawson, with a 'swaggie' and a sheep dog, was set on a rise in a secluded part of the Sydney Domain. The statue was the last work of the sculptor George Lambert. See *Sydney Morning Herald*, 29 July 1931, p. 10.

tribute came to me, and I have written these, just as they came, and here they are:—

To Rod Quinn

His are the songs that to the wind
The wheat makes day by day
And his the murmur where the waves
With whisperings make play.

Springs break no brighter than his words,
And, in the fountains fall
The drops no clearer are than is
The verse that hears his call.

He has a child's heart, and his Muse
Wrote him his name—Pellucid—
Within his eye her jewel shines
And all his song is lucid.

Affectionately,
Mary Gilmore.

To Nettie Palmer

129 Phillip Street
Sydney
Dear Nettie, 8 December 1931

I know who Brent of Bin Bin[1] is, but may not tell. It is 'he'; that much I think I can say to you. But do not publish it without B's permission which you may get if he writes to you. I had thought him my brother Jack because of certain family matter in the book and the spelling of Cooma as Coomer, and which I at the time did not think anyone but Jack (or I) could tell in the words (*our words*) used. Then remembered telling a certain person the stories *in* those words, and of Coomer for Cooma. During the winter I was writing this man and called him B. of B—'Dear B. of B.' I wrote. No denial has come. Equally no affirmation! But affirmation I did not expect. About Vance's books, and your H.B.H.[2] No, I do not want them just now. I am working on two books at once, prose and verse.[3] The verse now only needs final revision or selection; the other is going to the typist, as fast as my tired heart and eyes

---

[1] Mary loved a mystery and always jumped to her own conclusions about the true identity of writers who used pseudonyms. She was usually wrong. Brent of Bin Bin was Miles Franklin.
[2] *Henry Bournes Higgins*, a biography by Nettie Palmer of her uncle.
[3] The prose was *Old Days: Old Ways A Book of Recollections* (1934); the verse, *Under the Wilgas* (1932).

can get it into readable form. When these are off I am hoping to do no more at such speed. Then I shall see if I cannot do a few special articles on Vance and Nettie Palmer. And by that time, too, the papers may be in a better position to take articles from other than their staffs. But I want to put it on record here, if I did not do it before, that I think Vance's 'The way of all men'[1] (? *was* that the name? my brain is like a perforated sieve just now thanks to work and humidity) an outstanding study. It has all that 'Coonardoo'[2] has in it of the permanent, without its inhuman isolation of the main character (as a suffering unit) without its bald and arid areas (they *are* areas, not spots) and with a lovableness given to humanity that makes its men *all* men: they are not bounded by time, period, place or country, and they *are* men not effigies or shadows.

Some day I may ask you to requote this for me to give me my start. Till then I do not want to look at anything of yours or Vance's. I want it to come new and fresh, so that impressions will fountain and not merely flow or even just ooze.

I am to give a young girl, Joan Ryder, a letter to you. She has much in common poetically with Veronica Mills, but is steadier, and younger. She and her people have just gone to Melbourne to live. She and two or three others have been coming to me 'to talk' for the last couple of years. I trim their verse and it goes into the Herald. The whole group is promising—and each one different from the others. They are a very dear and interesting little hatching. So eager, so young, so ready to learn, and so fair, as youth, to look upon. I shall miss my Joan . . .

As to those books I sent—no thanks to me but all to Nettie Palmer. Affectionately and gratefully,

Am posting you a couple of 'Tilted Carts' to do what you like with.

To Percival Serle

129 *Phillip Street*
Sydney
Dear Mr Serle, 21 *January 1932*

Good Luck to your shop![3]

Coincidence is a strange thing. Three weeks ago, a Ms. book came to me, the only copy in the world of 'Evening Notes', our daily paper

---

[1] The correct title was *Men Are Human* (1930).
[2] See letters, 28 November 1928 and 8 May 1930.
[3] Percival Serle ran a second-hand book shop in the Eastern Market, Melbourne, from 1931 to 1936.

in Cosme,[1] Paraguay, all the rest having been burned by a fire in the Cosme Library. This copy was the accident of a friendship, it having been a copy of the original carried on for a year, for a man (H. S. Taylor) who had had to return to Australia owing to the death of his father. The copying was a work of love for Harry by Jim Sime, whose sister was married to Waterson of 'The Times' London. Harry is stricken with an incurable disease and as a parting gift he sent this prized Ms. book to me. The last pages are being typed in duplicate as I write this. The coincidence is that this Ms. contains eight months of the journal as edited by *me*! Last week came a letter from Helen Birks of Adelaide, and the last time I saw her or heard from her, was in Paraguay about 35 years ago; and this week comes *your* enquiry. There is no book on sale! But my intention is to publish 'Evening Notes' with annotations. Then there will be a book. I want you to get in touch with a wild, Irish–Argentine friend of mine, Daniel B. Cody. He is selling yerba mate (Paraguayan holly tea). The Tea Trade tried to stop him, so he raised an ancient law and beat them. You would find him a most interesting man—you and your group. He knows South America and our part in particular—and all sorts of interesting people here and elsewhere. Use my name in writing him.

Again Good Luck.

Just doing the final work on my next book of verse.[2] It has a new feature the others have not.

To George Robertson

Dear Mr Robertson,

129 Phillip Street
Sydney
15 March 1932

I have missed the sight of you about the shop however distant or however brief the word.

I have just sent 'Flynn'[3] up to my husband for his birthday. Set Flynn aside and yet there has never been a greater advertisement for Australia. No trade returns, no maps give the impression of space, and *habitable* space, that that book does. *Here* is space *lived*, not dreamed or speculated on. The writing is not as good as in Lasseter[4]—more spread; but if Lasseter had never been written first how we would have

---

[1] See note to letter, 5 August 1896.
[2] *Under the Wilgas* (1932). Its 'new feature' was a series of tributes to well-known Australians (e.g. Henry Lawson).
[3] Ion Idriess's *Flynn of the Inland*, 1932.
[4] Idriess's *Lasseter's Last Ride*, 1931.

praised Flynn! In any case, the less terse and more florid writing will take the crowd. Flynn should be translated at once into the emigrating languages of the North—and into Spanish for South America. Such a book does draw peoples together and shows itself internationalist.

John Flynn came to me with his dream twenty two or three years ago—before he got his Inland appointment. And he came to me later on with the first scheme, and later the first plans of his first Nursing Home. He went to many others, but I am glad I am among them.

I have just sent away the MS of another book of verse.[1] It is like 'The Wild Swan' yet different. I did not take it to you because later on I hope to write more fully on the aboriginals and perhaps use what is in the Wild Swan and what is in this, and I need the copyright of both to do this.

Also I have been too dead and alive to lift up a lightsome voice till this minute, so here's for the birthday whenever it is:

> Ken ye that man Robertson?
>   ou ay! ou ay!
> He's the bonny fit ahint
> Mony sailin hie!
>
> H'isted up among the stars
> Noo on thrones they sit
> But they hadna sat sae hie
> Wantin' yonder fit.

Wi my ain thanks to the fit. Yours sincerely,

                                      Mary Gilmore

To R. H. Croll

129 Phillip Street
Sydney
Dear R. H. C.   *1 September 1932*

You will be cussin' me twice over.

I put your book aside to go over it to you, got a nerve-panic & break & for three weeks was on the verge of a breakdown. High blood pressure is no friend to man!—not to me at any rate. Now I am packing for the chance of a hurried trip with friends who say 'Choose US or HOSPITAL!!' and I cannot lay my hand on your book.

But I remember one thought as I read it. And it was: 'At last Australia is emerging from the things of the flesh: at last, the door of things above those of herd level is opening.'

---

[1] *Under the Wilgas*, 1932.

No matter how great the writing of herd level (yes!) of blood and heat and hunger of the (yes!) belly—the living height is beyond it still. Hubert Church belonged above the Battle, and R. H. C. belongs there too. No time for more. Yours affectionately,

Am sending The Wilgas to Shaw Neilson c/o you. Will you kindly get it to him? perhaps even read him some of it? as you would I know if it is possible.

To Nettie Palmer

129 Phillip Street
Sydney
Dear Nettie,   20 September 1932

I am sending Nora Kelly a par from your letter about your Island[1] and Vance's books. The article I wrote on Vance over a year ago, and sent to the Bulletin is still there—somewhere. They promised to return, but it still is not returned.

It is curious to me how hard I worked for 'Man Shy'[2] and could not get attention to it, till people used my words, forgetting they were mine. (Not you, of course!) To both you and Mackaness I wrote of it (then in short stories) and begged you both to include one in your collections, as they were outstanding, non-localized, and yet Australian. But neither listened. At the F.A.W.[3], before he made a book of them, I declared them to be the beginnings of an era for Australian literature that would mean something to the world and not just the localized... Besides talking of it at the F.A.W. and to all sorts of people (for I never let up once I started, in, I think, about 1924) I wrote to Geo Robertson, and also talked to Mr. Ritchie and Mr. Cousins just as emphatically, and now A. & R. are bringing it out. And for that I thank the Lord that at last Davison and A. & R. have come together.

About my last book 'Under the Wilgas'. I knew you were away on some distant horizon up north but did not know where. Good luck for today, and Long Life for tomorrow to Vance's books. But about my own: That 'Black Bread of Night'[4] ran away from me, and became before the middle of it, the black bread of night of the street. Themes do that with one sometimes.'She dwelt Serene' was written at top speed to get another thing taken out of the galley proofs. Its date is 10.5.32. Most of the book was written '30 and '31 and '32. 'The Bull' was written

---
[1] Probably *The Enchanted Island* by Vance Palmer, 1923.
[2] Frank Dalby Davison's book of stories. See note to letter, 13 July 1929.
[3] Fellowship of Australian Writers.
[4] 'Black Bread of Night' and the other poems mentioned are all in *Under the Wilgas*, 1932.

practically at one sitting, and consequently I was never able to alter or reshape it. And the same with 'T.B.' except that in there is an addition (and one can feel it!) to the original stanza of reshaped extended lines, and that is in the first ten lines of the stanza about the 'thunderheads'— the ten were originally six. The first three and the last six had a paunch stuck in the middle of them, and I do not know that it adds to their dignity.

The misprint in the Sonnet 'The Fox Temptation Knoweth' does not worry me as the rhythm carries it, you notice it as an expert. And I have no Thesaurus and never had. My only one *is the crossword puzzle* as a distraction for a tired or spare moment. Once in about a million times it calls to memory a word known in younger years. Then I feel as if heaven opened and the Lord smiled on me. When I went to school at nine or ten the other girls used to say I used words they could not understand. I did! I used 'By my halidome' and 'Peradventure' and 'Verily, Verily' and 'Naithless' and 'scaith' and goodness knows what else.

You mention that re-reading some of the things leads to discovery. That was one of the things Frank Morton used to say. 'The more you read the more you find the work indefinably allusive'. I tell you I treasured that saying. For it is the unobviously allusive that is what I want. I do not *aim* at it. But it seems to come of itself.

That thing on Neilson: In all those on actual people there had to be the *interpretation of the person*, as well the verbal tribute. I think the verse on Parkes is *like* Parkes: neither delicate or feminine: and so on. The Lion Brereton one is I think *like* Lion in some way. Perhaps I am wrong, and merely imagine it. The subconscious is always the dictator in my writing, and I never know to what extent it is the impersonator or the subject to be treated, because (except for trimming afterwards) everything just comes!

A thousand good wish Hellos to you both and thank you for your letter, woman of wide sympathies.

The Labor Daily and also another paper said the Aboriginal verse was not poetry and then quoted 'Weenyah weenyah' in proof of the statement. My innermost soul said 'Gosh!' even if my lips withheld themselves from the utterance of such a word.

To George Robertson

129 *Phillip Street*
Sydney
Dear Mr Robertson, 24 *September 1932*

There has just come to hand the new Ion L. Idriess book 'Men of the

Jungle'. I have only just lifted the corners, but I am so glad to see that the illustrations representing the Australian aboriginals make them look what they really were, and not the debased caricatures of themselves, that so many have made them. It does not seem to be generally recognized (as it should be recognized) that every debased picture of an aboriginal is a reflection on Australia. For this reason: the white man is today a world-wide and universal: the coloured man is not; and to people outside he is his country. What the man is the country is in the eyes of the 'foreigner', and territorially every man is a foreigner who has not dwelt within a country. Pride in Australia should make people represent its native (inhabitant) decently. America, India, Africa, and New Zealand all do this, and with profit in the eyes of the world nationally. Especially is this so in regard to literature; Australia is the one step-child in regard to this.

There is a great debt owed to you, you and your Firm as publishers, in relation to 'Lasseter's Last Ride', 'Flynn of the Inland', and now this book 'Men of the Jungle', in that you have 'levelled up' Australia, and not in its aboriginals levelled it down as is so usual . . . Yours gratefully and sincerely,

To George Robertson

129 Phillip Street
Sydney
Dear Mr Robertson, *26 September 1932*

I had a hope that was as big as a tree—a whole mountain side of forest that you would look most closely on the lines to Isabel Byers[1] I could not live in my grave if I had not done something worth while in tribute to her. It is only worth while because it really does cover her, in her sacrifice: which never counted its loss or its pains: and I put it where juxtaposition would deepen its value as a tribute. I did some apparently ill-bred things in this book, but they were done to meet the tongue of a liar (and the word is the real one needed) when those who *could* meet it are gone.

These books by Idriess are seas where aforetime we had ponds and brooks. They have in them the power of ocean, they run like tides.

---

[1] Henry Lawson's close friend. The lines Mary refers to are on page 57 of *Under the Wilgas*, 1932. They are:

> She had an innocence no time effaced;
> And, as from heaven a star looks down,
> So shined she out for him whose life lay waste,
> Till sacrifice made her renown.

The lines follow on from the short poem entitled 'Henry Lawson'.

I wrote you at once about 'Men of the Jungle', and you should have the letter today. They are the voice of Australia come to standing upright on her own feet instead of lying like a child in the sand. And more than that: they are the voice of Australia indifferent to reproof. The tradition of the past, founded in other countries, is not laid on them.

As to you—I never think of you that I do not see Australia. You and she are inseparable. And each making the other. John Dunmore Lang, Parkes, G.R. and that little spider W. M. Hughes (who is as big as he is little), builders all.

Thank you for your letter of appreciation of the book. And thank you for so much more. Yours sincerely,

To Nettie Palmer

129 Phillip Street
Sydney
16 November 1932

Dear Nettie,

Your enclosed, Jessie Mackay's article on Hubert Church, and what you said, made me feel very sad—and also very glad, for I had written Hubert Church a tribute on some of his work to which he replied, 'Your very kind thoughts of the poem are such as I have never known. A few may like what I write—but they are silent. Fellow craftsmen are too busy to tell me their thoughts. Some are jealous—it is plain you are not.'

I am only allowed to use my eyes, again, a little so must be brief. About 'Man Shy'.[1] The actual first time I told you of the stories was in Melbourne when I went there from Goulburn and full of it because I had only that year read it. Then I wrote to you at Caloundra and I think in Melb. though both times may have been Caloundra. In one of the letters—the second?—I put forth a timid feeler about something of my own, and mentioned 'The Glove' in 'Hound of the Road' but whether in the first or second letter I forget. One letter you replied to, am not sure about the other.

My eyes, and my general health, troubling me I went first to the Eye man. First examination he said 'Bring me all your wasted glasses and all your specialists' prescripts. so that I can study them.' I took five pairs of glasses I had never been able to use, and about ten prescripts. After a second examination he said 'No worry, no writing, no stooping, no leaning forward. And live all day in the open air.' The third time after examining he sat down in front of me: 'You are

---

[1] See letters, 13 July 1929 and 20 September 1932.

a woman and so do not swear; but I am a man and I tell you your eyes are in a *hell* of a condition!' So that's that. As there is still, after various half recoveries, the blasted facial paralysis (you see I *can* swear) I don't know whether to pray for a speedy recovery or a speedy death. Once I would have suffered visible agonies; now I am old and age suffers them in repression. But don't say anything to me about it lest repression 'bust'. Now I must put the pen away . . . All good wishes to you and Vance and the children, word-clothes and other—

To Captain C. H. Peters

129 Phillip Street
Sydney

Dear Captain Peters, 17 December 1932

Your letter with Mr Ewers' review[1] of my work has just come to me. It is the sort of thing my heart has been hungry for—something with analysis and not just pretty-pretty platitudes or shallow condemnations. I do not agree with him that 'The Wild Swan'[2] is not my best book. I think it is; but that is a matter of opinion. I shall write to Mr Ewers with a twice-filled pen as well as a twice-filled heart. And this not only for the present and in my lifetime, but because I can feel that after I am gone there will be one—Nettie Palmer will be another—who will give my work a real assessment and who will place me, though I have written much that is small, where on the better things, I really do belong. There is *responsiveness* in this man's work, he is a swimmer in the water of a writer's work and not one who writes as a glider over it. I *am* so pleased! And to you so grateful. All good Christmas wishes to you and yours and as far away as John K Ewers.

I am sending him an annotated copy of 'The Tilted Cart' and possibly a dated one of 'The Wild Swan' or 'Under the Wilgas'

To J. K. Ewers

129 Phillip Street
Sydney

Dear Mr Ewers, 17 December 1932

I have just had a copy of a review you did in the W.A.Daily News

---

[1] The review by J. K. Ewers was in the Western Australian *Daily News*, 26 November 1932.
[2] Published 1930.

of 26. 11. 32 and if I say the same things to you that I at once wrote to Captain Peters—that kindest of men—it will be because I said my heart to him and can only repeat it.

Your review, or write-up, is the sort of thing I have *starved* for, my heart has ached for. It is analysis, and not just the platitude of custom, and the condemnation of the shallow glance. You respond to and contain the writer, you do not just go over him like a water glider on the surface of a pool. Most of the criticism one gets is of the water gliding order. The pool may be of any depth, it is only the surface that counts with such. You (and Nettie Palmer) are different. You see the pool and what is in it, and not just the reflections of things exterior to it. You get the reality that lies beneath the accretions. I do not wholly agree with you that 'The Wild Swan'[1] is not my best book. I do think it has (your lovely word!) more 'contagious freshness' than 'Under the Wilgas'.[2] Still 'Under the Wilgas' *has* thumped the stars a bit, perhaps in 'the cry of time-tormented man' (I forget what I called that) and in 'The Bull'. I saw that bull stand at his fence, it must be thirty years ago, and then suddenly, in 1924 it just flew into being, almost without additions, almost without corrections. Practically one sitting wrote it. But I do not know how many the few corrections took! They came years after and had to be few lest tonal quality altered. Many corrections would have meant re-writing and that would have meant a complete change.

And how grateful I have been to Mr Anderson[3] who printed the book! He looked after every possible error in my script as well as typographicals. I do not make many, and for that reason the scrutiny has to be unrelaxing. These books have made me two great friends to whom I never can be grateful enough. Captain Peters and Mr Anderson. There was nothing either could do they did not do. Nothing was too much. And patient! Now perhaps there is you. I wrote Captain Peters that I would write you with a twice-filled pen and a twice-filled heart. It looks as if I have done it, doesn't it?!

You are in Perth. I wonder if some day you could get me a copy of the Perth Herald article written when my mother Mrs. Cameron (Beattie) died? I think it would be about 1898-90 [*sic*]. I was in South America, and am a fool over dates. *The thing that happened* matters to me not the year. The happening is so much that the year melts in it. I wd. pay all necessary expenses in the copying if a paper could not be got. My brother, John Cameron, was Sub. under Vosper,[4] and afterwards editor of the Coolgardie Miner. He made history over the water

[1] Published 1930.
[2] Published 1932.
[3] Of Robertson & Mullens.
[4] F. C. B. Vosper.

supply scheme. Afterwards he started 'Clare's Weekly' for Clare the brewer in Perth, and had a small paper, I forget its name, in partnership with 'Milky White' (Emerson).[1] He married a Perth girl, coming back from South Af. war (where he had been a special corresp.) for the ceremony. Then went to London to work on the London Daily Chronicle and The St James Budget—or was it The Westminster Gazette—or was it both? After that he was on 'The Irish Packet' and later for years edited the 'Mentone and Monte Carlo News.' Later he had a small paper of his own in Eng. or German, on the Riviera at Monaco (you will presently realize why I am no good on dates!) and a couple of seasonal papers in Switzerland. The war broke his papers and he went as special corresp. for a time on the Italian Front. Afterwards he had a semi-literary and trade journal in Basle (and I cannot remember its name: the intense anguish of the war in which I suffered for everyone blotted out so much for me!) Next he was appointed Acting. Brit. Consul at Schauffhausen. Here he received British prisoners from Germany. Once there was an Australian among them. They talked all night of an Australia left years behind. From Schauffhausen he went to Berne for a time and from Berne to Bucovice, in the Balkans area, from Bucovice to build up the fallen British trade in Detroit. He was consul there for six years and made a friend of Henry Ford. Now he is at Danzig—a very difficult and responsible position. His daughter is very musical, and had a slim booklet of French verse (her native language was French) published when she was about fourteen. Donal, called after our father Donal Cameron, is a whale on languages. He studied at Cambridge, went to Peking and in 8 months was translating difficult Chinese documents. Was appointed Vice Consul at Tientsin and is now Consul with office and staff of his own, under the Consul General at Shanghai. Jack (my brother) wrote two novels or stories. One is well known and is the Bookstall publication 'The Spell of the Bush'.[2] You, with your critical and responsive faculty, wd. see likeness and difference between his work and mine written about the same ages. Mine being 'Marri'd' as I was too busy housekeeping to dare prose.

I have written all this family matter at length because my mother had the literary or a topical col. as well as the Woman's paper of the Perth Herald (she died there) and because of Jack's connection with Perth. Also it may yield you a paragraph or two when stuck for matter. If you see K. S. Prichard speak my name.

Now again let me thank you. Presently I shall send you a couple of books dated and annotated. Meanwhile I am praying like the very devil that you will live to be very old, *for it is by what is written after*

---

[1] Ernest Sando Emerson.
[2] Published 1909.

death that we live, and if you remember in thirty years time that once I wrote, I will be renewed as the eagles. The longing to endure is the longing to have been read, to have produced faithfully, however small the content or even the height.

You are right about the weakness of the bird and the aboriginal verse: it was in part intentional—which weakens it. But if I had not written who would? That was my reason. I was only a candle holder for others to follow. I had a knowledge others had not but through which they might reach and seek to fuller things.

Has my pen been twice-filled? It is not yet too empty to repeat that I thank you. Yours sincerely,

Lovely, that word 'contagious freshness'!

To Nettie Palmer

129 Phillip Street
Sydney
19 December 1932

Dear Nettie,

Awhile ago, an hour, ten minutes, I don't know, a boy came. But he brought a book.[1] A book that is all alive, not some darned Professor talking slow, but a woman's quick mind flying from point to point, with a thousand wings fluttering at a time, and picking up that, this because it shines, that because it can *be* shined, and putting it all into the fit and living words that such things deserve and so seldom get. It is your book of Essays, and I don't know how I have put it down long enough to write this!

And the quotations! No quotation is drowned in itself; there is just the glittering point; no more, whether from a tear or a diamond, the tip of a gum-leaf or the glint from a bird's wing. What it is to have scholarship, *and what it is to have knowledge*—'to observe' as you say, 'and be startled by what you see and hear'. My dear I can't tell you how delighted I am with your book. It is the expression of what I knew you had in you and which you had not, or rather had not had time to unloose.

Again and again I notice how important it is for a writer to be a poet—a singer poet, not a blankverser. In it lies that responsiveness which enables one to flick with a needlepoint what others take a pitchfork to. (and I leave that 'to' like a stake in a plain to emphasize—more!—to 'specification' what I mean. It dimensions it.)

My dear girl I am rejoicing for my country. We have a background,

---

[1] Nettie Palmer's collection of essays, *Talking It Over*, 1932.

now, a background is coming forward, we stand in line with the world's pride; we are one with the world—the world from which we have taken and which now can take from us. Funny thing ego, isn't it? Mine seems nailed to a mast.

To George Mackaness

No. 2 Claremont Flats
99 Darlinghurst Road
Kings Cross
Sydney

Dear Dr Mackaness,   *27 April 1933*

I shall be delighted for you to use any selections you think fit for your compilation for A & R., 'The Wide Brown Land'.[1] I hope, in the essays, that your choice will fall on the parts that contain names, and are directly historical (and therefore moving) rather than on the merely speculative. However the choice is to be yours and not mine, and with you it must rest.

I had not looked at those two things in prose, 'Roads of Remembrance' and 'The House of Memory',[2] for some years—not to *read* them that is. And I am thankful to you for drawing my attention to them, for I have found what is my quality above others: it is the quality of tears. Dr. Kelly of the Tablet in N.Z. always wrote of the *lachrymae rerum* (I hope my terminations are right! my Latin died long ago) and today for the first time I *fully felt* what he meant.

While I think of it. If you have any hesitation about Joan[3] being included, I'll father the choice if you like. You can give the verse an asterisk and have a note saying that the verses had been included after consultation with, or by, the advice of M.G. if you like.

Yours very gratefully and sincerely,

To R. H. Croll

Kings Cross
Dear Robert Croll,   *18 May 1933*

I know that it doesn't change. The heart's fellowship is not affected

---

[1] An anthology of Australian poetry published in 1934 by Dr George Mackaness in collaboration with his daughter Joan.
[2] These two essays were from *Hound of the Road*, 1922.
[3] Two of Joan Mackaness's poem's, 'In Early Green Summer' and 'Golden Green', were included in *The Wide Brown Land*.

by such little things in space and eternity as years and miles! If I came—
'went' isn't it to Melbourne?—I would fall on your neck with all the
abandon that my rich sixty seven years give me.

As to my address, 'Sydney Morning Herald' will always find me.
I left the Worker[1] about two years ago—or going on for that. Too tired
to go on longer, for one thing, and an objectionable manager as well
as a jealous editor: the two in league. Like a good ass I resigned, but
gave them both a kick (also like a good ass,) when I left and as I was
off the paper they could do nothing about it. But they have never definitely notified readers that I am off the paper and letters still come

---

[1] Mary's relationship with the *Worker* was from 1908 to 1931. See W. H. Wilde. *Three Radicals*, 1969, and note to letter, 1 June 1946. The final months of Mary's time on the paper were rather strained as the following excerpts from her letters indicate:

The Manager,   30.12.30
'The Worker Newspaper'.

Dear Mr. Donovan,
Some weeks ago, when I was last at 'The Worker' office to draw my salary, the pay clerk told me that you had given him orders that I was to sign as an outside contributor. As you had said nothing of this to me, I would be glad to know what it means, and how it affects the arrangements under which I joined 'The Worker'. As I have strained a tendon in my broken foot, I have not been at the office since then, nor have I signed the docket, as I hoped to see you. But stairs put too much pressure on the strained muscle, so I am writing.
                                                                                       Yours truly, Mary Gilmore

The *Worker* manager, T. Donovan, replied that he, as Manager, and Mr Boote, as Editor, had in a recent review of staff decided that Mary should be transferred from the salaried section to the literary contributors' section. Mary replied:

                                                                                                      [undated]

Dear Mr. Donovan,
I have to acknowledge your letter dated 6.1.31, which is a reply to my letter of earlier date and which is the first intimation to me personally of your intention to change my status on 'The Worker'. There are several things mentioned in it which require consideration—one of them being my arranged-for right to do literary articles and verse for magazine, book and other publications. There were for the whole of 1930 (apart from my book 'The Wild Swan', which makes the total five) four such contributions, two being verse—the one piece of verse consisted of eight lines and appeared in Stead's Review, the second piece was sixteen lines and appeared in B.P. Magazine, twenty-four lines in all—and the other two prose. One of the latter was on the aboriginal and historical, in Stead's Review, the other on a social but non-political subject in the magazine section of another publication. In each case I was specially asked to write as being an Australian authority on both subjects. Am I to understand that you are objecting to the publication of my books, verse, and other literary work? There is no other kind of work of mine appearing other than in 'The Worker'. Am I to understand that the suppression of my purely literary work is what is asked for, and if so, why? And why am I singled out? I shall be glad of an answer, as I shall then know where I stand. Also, if the matter is put in writing there can be no misunderstanding. My ankle is still weak—the tendon having been torn out of its supporting sheath which kept it in place—and I am afraid it can never be safe again as the sheath cannot again close round it once it is torn out of it. I had a copy of 'Desiderata' sent your daughter as I thought it might interest her. It does not pay for verse, but its literary value is high.
                                                                            Yours truly, Mary Gilmore.

In reply (9 January 1931) T. Donovan claimed that Mary's previous letter had no bearing on the matter at all. He flatly commented that as the *Worker* paid for only a portion of Mary's time, her former position on the staff of their fully employed members was anomalous. Shortly afterwards Mary resigned from the paper.

to me as if I were there. Also people wonder why 'my page'[1] is not as good as it used to be. Ha Ha! Joy to my heart,—even if I am blamed for the inferiority. (Sounds as if the good little ass was still kicking!)

My love to the Crolls—I suppose Robin is the tallest man in the family now.

To George Robertson

Dear Mr. Robertson,
Kings Cross
24 June 1933

It is so long since I sent you a 'birthday' line that you will be asking 'Is that woman dead? and if she isn't why isn't she?' So here is amends:

Being the good wish of a pious woman with a ricketty heart to Maister George Robertson.

> I wish ye noo, wish ye noo,
>   Wish ye, muckle man,
> Saut wi' meat, barley broo,
>   Siller tae your han.
> But anither wish hae I,
>   Wish it twice as mair (That bit is to show I am a Highlander)
> That ye had na stept sae hie
>   Up yon blastit *stair*!

What books you have been getting out! I have been looking upon 'Lasseter's Last Ride'[2] and 'Man-Shy'[3] as two books setting Australia over the fence on the high road, and out of 'the paddock' of the past. But now I am reading 'Jacka's Mob'[4] and here indeed is time written in a book and creation from the muck: And *what* muck! It is as enduring as the pyramids. What power there is in the unadorned. And what an untrimmed story! My thousand times over good wish to you.

To Alice Mackaness

Dear Mrs. Mackaness,
Kings Cross
4 September 1933

About forty million thanks to you and yours!

I shall be at the Lyceum Club tomorrow feeling like a child and Santa Claus. I have been such a one to do without things that I won't

---

[1] The Women's Page which she edited during those years.
[2] Ion Idriess, 1931.
[3] F. D. Davison, 1931.
[4] A novel by Edgar John Rule, 1933.

know where I am with more than three teaspoons—and to have *two* butter knives will be too bewildering! And yet no one ever loved nice things, and right-thing things and plenty of them than I. I have hungered for them all my life. But too many *other* things call me, and 'things' have been easiest to do without! So I have done without 'em.

About Sunday: I am trying to finish the final revision of my new book[1] and must not leave it. Not even for the Mackanesses. It has been held up so long through ill health and other interruptions that I dare not lose a day—a working day for me—while I have the cool weather. I am about over the functions[2] but I still have one lot of the flowers, for they kept coming. I am enclosing something I want you to keep till its appropriate moment in case I am not able to attend to it—you can see what it is. Now I must to my MS. while the daylight is good.

To W. G. Cousins

Kings Cross
27 October 1933

Dear Mr Cousins,

Herewith the MS of my new book, 'Old Days: Old Ways'.[3] (Tentative Title).

There is matter in it about the aboriginals that has never been published by anyone before, notably the fish-traps and the seed-planting. So I hope that for reading it will not go to anyone who might be tempted to make use of it either in print or in lectures. I have the *hope* that you may read it *yourself*. The matter deals with real people, so I am open to all and any advice in regard to the use of names where they occur. As far as I know none of the people dealt with are now alive—but there are their children as old as I am, their grandchildren and their great-grand children. Usually I have omitted names, but there are places where I have used initials and where occasionally a name, person and place, is given. I do not think I have done anything dangerous, but one never knows. If no names are used it makes a book valueless for historical purposes or for foundation reference—and I am hoping, as the preface shows, that this book *will be* a foundation to other books.

The typing has been a trouble. Each time I paid a typist I added so much and interlined so persistently that I had to learn to type in order not to go broke. But it is clear enough I think for a reader. For the printer it can be typed again if or where necessary.

None of the matter has been published before. But I would like

[1] *Old Days: Old Ways A Book of Recollections*, 1934.
[2] Mary's birthday party, held to celebrate her sixty-eighth birthday on 16 August 1933.
[3] *Old Days: Old Ways A Book of Recollections*, 1934.

to publish some of the matter beforehand unless you advise against it. I would like to use 'The Fish Trap' (Folio 176) and a few of the almost story chapters perhaps. Also the chapters on 'How the Aboriginals counted' (Folio 167) and perhaps the one on 'White sails and disease'—for there again is hitherto unpublished matter. Also I *am the first*, here, to point out *that the aboriginal gave no new diseases to the world*.

If there is more material than you want for the book (provided you *take* it,) I will be glad to have it for the next, which will be that much nearer completion. And I do very badly want this to come out as early as you can make it. If I can I will see you today. If not, then next week. If there are repetitions beyond reason in the book will you let me know? I am too close to it, as yet, to get a proper bird's eye view of it as a whole. Kindest wishes.

To Sarah Nixon-Smith

Dear Mrs. Smith,

Kings Cross
14 December 1933

I have not had breakfast yet, but I must answer your letter which just came by our early morning post. I shall be so delighted to see you and to have you drink out of my tea cups. But what a wonderful thing to have a letter from one born in the same house I was born in.[1] And you must give me a full description of it. There was a poplar planted there by my grandfather, planted for me when I was born, & from which (I was told) the poplars of the whole district came. The tree was new in Sydney in 1865 and Mrs. Reiby [sic][2] had two at Reiby[sic] House. My Grandfather was always a friend there & a guest, & she as a special favour gave him a young rooted tree which, with the earth bound on its roots, he carried on his saddle all the way up to Goulburn, & planted it there for me. This is history. There were only a few poplars in all Sydney then. The Reiby trees were still a landmark in Sydney in the 80's & early 90's . . .

Now I will post this, or rather address it & make my tea. Age likes its tea! I was 68 last August. But how I shall love to see you. I am in all day Mondays, so write if you cannot come on a Monday. And remember me to your brother Archie—

[1] Mary was born in her maternal grandmother's bedroom at the property 'Merry Vale', Cotta Walla, near Goulburn, 16 August 1865. The property later came into the Nixon family, of whom Sarah Nixon-Smith (she married a Smith) was a member. A poplar was 'rooted' by Mrs. Sarah Nixon-Smith from the original poplar planted by Mary's grandfather (Beattie) when she was born in 1865. This 'rooted' poplar was later transplanted to the Poets' Corner in the Sydney Domain. See also letters, 16 March 1934 and 27 December 1934.
[2] Mary Reibey (1777–1855).

To W. G. Cousins

Dear Mr Cousins,

Kings Cross
17 January 1934

I have revised the MS of 'Old Days: Old Ways', and then had it all retyped. Still in spite of that I had to do more markings, but not enough to make the printer curse me, I hope.

I have taken out two chapters. One on scalping the blacks and the bonuses paid to the scalpers, as I thought it too horrible for this book: whose aim is to suggest romance in Australian historical associations, to excite wonder at what was done and endured, and to awaken pity for both black and white. The other chapter was partly covered in other places in the book. These two I have replaced by 'Proud Men' (page 246) and 'Dust on the Trail' which are more fitting—and really needed.

And, I think that, without boasting, I can claim to have written a book that will not only stand, but which will mark an era in our historical and romantic writing. I think you will be glad to have had it. At least I hope so! So I hope you will say 'good luck' to it for its own sake. Yours sincerely,

To George Mackaness

Dear Dr Mackaness,

Kings Cross
6 March 1934

I have had the idea of the F.A.W.[1] doing something in remembrance of G.R.[2] and today I took it upon myself to ask Mr. Ritchie and Mr. Cousins could it be arranged that we as a society could put up a bronze or other tablet to say G.R. was our first Fellow, and that the tablet was for the purpose of recording that. Simple and not staring and in as few words as possible. I asked for a location either in his old office or in the centre of the wall among the portraits—'The Gallery'. I told them I wanted to know if it wd. be allowed before I moved for it to be done by the Executive. So I want to move at the next meeting that this Society, The Fellowship of Australian Writers, approach the representatives of A. & R. for permission to place a tablet on the wall of 'the portrait gallery' stating that Mr. Robertson was the Society's first Fellow, and first-elected Life Member.

As a matter of fact I would be glad to pay for the tablet myself (if need be to get a *good* one I will) but of course that is for the Society to decide—Yours sincerely,

[1] Fellowship of Australian Writers.
[2] George Robertson, one of the co-founders of Angus & Robertson, died in 1933.

To Sarah Nixon-Smith

Dear Sarah Nixon, otherwise Mrs. Smith,

Kings Cross
16 March 1934

How kind you are. I don't know which is nicer your needlework or your letter! The needlework came safely and I wish I could do half as well. Some day I will go out for a day with you . . .

I have been thinking of that poplar tree[1] that you said is still alive and on which Sister MacCallum wanted a recording plate. It seems incredible it could be the same one, and not one of its offspring. It would be 68 years old now, & a real record. Will you make sure if it is that old? Of *course* you would remember it as a girl & know quite well which it was! I forgot that.

My dear, I hope you & Jessie will come to see me again, if I cannot get out to see you. I am not strong yet after that illness, but can now go out of doors. My new book[2] is taking all my time and energy just now. Affectionately,

To W. G. Cousins

Dear Mr Cousins,

Kings Cross
8 June 1934

You shall have this 'first copy off the machines'[3] as my gift copy back to you again to thank you for all the trouble you have taken and the patience you have had. As to the jacket you could not have got anything to stand the name out better than this delicate colouring. The name comes out like old Florentine enamel. I am glad of the gum tree. It belongs to the people of the book and (let me confess it!) I had been a bit afraid it might have been (because of the beginning) crinoline, pelerine,[4] and poke bonnet. Though I did also feel sure it wouldn't. Still the underground fear, however small, was there. I was too much excited at the outside to look inside. I took the inside for granted—and now find I had a much bigger book than I expected. I thought the print would have to be wider spaced to fill it.

I shall annotate this book, and if names make it libellous you will just have to lock it up. I shall give you and Mr Ritchie the same marginal notes.

[1] See also letter of 14 December 1933.
[2] *Old Days: Old Ways A Book of Recollections*, 1934.
[3] *Old Days: Old Ways A Book of Recollections*, 1934.
[4] A name applied from time to time to various fashions of mantles or capes worn by women.

I must not keep the messenger so again with a thousand thanks. (and including your reader)

To Hugh McCrae

Dear Hugh,

Kings Cross
2 October 1934

I am posting you the Shaw Neilson book I showed you. For several reasons, one is that I want it to find home where its values will be understood. I am the woman who never can put her babies down on a hard bed. The pillow has to be shaken & the blankets smoothed out. For that reason I gave your special edition of *Satyrs & Sunlight*,[1] card & all to Alec Chisholm. I valued it too much to want it lost and my folk are dear folk but they stand in relation to editions as I do to sculpture—the instinctive worshipper who has no craft, & therefore no accepted & usual measure of quality, & no language by which to speak. For instance my husband, who in his day swore as profoundly as anyone else provided I was not by, wrote me of 'Landtakers' that B.P.[2] might have been more decent with his language: which (none of it for anyone but yourself) struck me as really funny. It is a new jest every time I think of it. The effect of a daughter-in-law & possible grand children, no doubt! All this is to make you feel at ease about having what you refused to take.

I told you that in Rayner Hoff's work there is a quality, or *the* quality, which gives me the feeling of a life hunger being fed. I tried to put some notes together, thinking I might by grinding it down to shape & conventional acceptability make an article. Also it released some of the tension of feeling I had about the work to write what it meant to me. I intended bringing in others. But I do not know enough to do anything with the matter so I have torn most of it up. But I am sending you the note I made on you because I walk in somewhat the same field as you, no matter how different our work is and am not so afraid to say to you. This is what I think, & so on.

I am in a joyful mood this morning. Last night I found someone who knew the swans & the swamps (& in a much smaller degree) the blacks as I knew them. I knew some of her brothers (or uncles I suppose) about fifty whole years ago . . . Also I have started a woman writing to a still keen 90 year old uncle for his recollections of the blacks (and incidentally on her own in Queensland, among them,) and I have a letter from a 72 year old woman born on Mount Rouse Vic. when it

[1] Hugh McCrae's book of verse published in 1928.
[2] Brian Penton.

was a Black Station (*as all the old big ones were*) & her recollections as to blacks & dogs. The Mount Rouse Manager had charge of 300 blacks as his working army & reserves. Her recollections confirm mine. So do in a lesser way one or two others. But they are younger & less important.

And Hughie Dear this is part of my way of saying Thank You for where you put me in the Aust. Quarterly article.[1] I wish I could believe it!

My kind regards to your wife & all your tree.

Dunno what this summer is going to do to me. My heart is already going wibble, wobble like a constant jelly. Soft. Have to cut walking to a minimum. Still one never knows.

Hugh McCrae: his line (& his design) stands up like a thin flame from stone. It is intensely individual, cold clear, with definition that rises above the hot impulse of the groundling. Even in his least thing he is still, however remotely an Olympian; the herbage never grew high about his feet. In his Bulletin work Alf Vincent was an unconscious futurist in angles, Hugh in the same work is futurist in the whorl. He lives in curves, yet his work is curiously stripped. It is moonlight on cloud without the cloud, or a rainbow with its cloudiness sharpened to a line. His line is whitely brilliant without denying the spectrum. Nothing he could ever do would be lost in the mass. In a million years he would still be Hugh McCrae, 'After-the-manner-of' has never been a part of him.

I really do feel it all this way.

M.G.

To H. M. Green

Kings Cross
Dear Harry Green, 11 November 1934

I am enclosing a bit of verse by one of my swans. It was written when he was fourteen . . . When this boy sent his verse to me, nearly a year and a half ago, I hardly believed he wrote it, and sent for him to come to see me and bring me something more. This he did in the winter of 1933. He is working very hard at the C. of E. Grammar School North Sydney. His mother is a widow, and money is not plentiful. Laurie plays the Organ in the Chapel, is studying to be a teacher of languages, is an *innocent* child, simple and sincere, without affectation, and under

---

[1] 'Mary Gilmore—our great national poet', *Australian Quarterly*, Sept.1933.

it all with the poise of ten mountains. He *knows* what he wants, and *moves unhurrying* toward it. I wrote him a year ago that I expected great things of him and that I expected him to stand between Masefield and Bridges—as I *do*. I am enclosing his last letter written last Wed. as I got it on the Thursday. You can judge the boy not only from his own exaggerated almost and non-mannerismed hand writing, but from the tone of the letter itself. 'Pandora' is the last long thing he brought me, a couple of months ago. I found it faulty and gave it back to be worked on again when his studies would give him leisure. But observe his last paragraph!! I marked it, as I thought 'what were all of us elders doing about Persephone at fifteen!' His signature at the end is his only break. I have never seen it so ornate before.

I have another youth—over twenty—in Victoria. He too does things not hitherto attempted here. But he is over-saturated by Keats and Catholic poetry. He will have to break from that to be really himself—if he can. But he is not Laurie Murchison.[1] He has not his powerful calm, as a controlling basis of storm. And I have a girl—with a nice fat baby—but I *fear*. Still I think she will emerge from the milky stage, and one day perhaps as a grandmother, do what Henry Handel R. has done, though in another way. Are my swans swans Harry? Or am I a goose among the geese?

I hope and hope your wife is feeling nearly herself, if it is too early for her to be quite well. I did not get to see her as I was months ailing myself and every 'ail' leaves my heart less able to stand fatigue.

Affectionately to you all

To Sarah Nixon-Smith

Dear Mrs. (Sarah Nixon) Smith,

Kings Cross
27 December 1934

You will be wondering why I have not written but I have had one untoward happening upon another, and letters have had to wait. Thank you so very much about the poplar[2] you have rooted from 'my' tree of '65—August 16th 1865—What a long time ago! Someone suggested that there should be a brass tablet put on 'my' tree commemorating its being planted as my birth tree & that it came from Mrs. Reibey's[3] garden who had been given its parent tree only a couple of years before by McLeay[4] when there were only three in the Botanic Gardens, &

---

[1] Now Canon Murchison who readily recalled his visits to Mary and remembers her with awe and affection—'a very gracious old lady'.
[2] See also letters, 14 December 1933 and 16 March 1934.
[3] Mary Reibey.
[4] Alexander McLeay.

which, with hers, had made the only ones in Australia. It certainly is an historical tree! And cuttings from it should sell at local Church bazaars for a shilling or two apiece, if people knew its age & the story.

I shall have a small present for your daughter later on. Just now, being the time of the year & my son & his wife in Sydney, I hardly know what I am doing even a day ahead. Billy and his wife have their own affairs, but I make my comings & goings wait on theirs, as I want to see as much of my son as possible while he is here.

I was writing to the Editor of the new woman's paper ('The Woman') & told him about your people & Merryvale, the poplar & Mrs. Reibey and gave your address in case they ever wanted a photograph of the tree, and the Nixons as owners. So you may hear from the paper. On the other hand they may not have the historical sense, in which case you will not hear.

I hope you had a happy Christmas, and I hope your daughter will be very happy in her marriage. Also if I forget to send her a remembrance as a present I shall think you very unkind if you do not remind me as I *want* to send *your daughter* something. The tie of sentiment & feeling, to say nothing of your thought & kindness, is too strong to be disregarded. I want to give her something of my own so that it will carry its special remembrance when I am gone . . . Now I must end. And thank you again & again for the tree. Billy will be here till end of Feb. so, till he goes, the tree is best with you. Affectionately,

Mary (Merryvale) Gilmore.

To W. G. Cousins

Kings Cross
Dear Mr Cousins, 7 February 1935

Herewith the galley proofs of 'Earth's Quality'[1]—which is *not* a good selling name for the book. 'The Weldons' or 'John Weldon' even, would have been better. There have been so many 'Earths' (Earth Battle, Red Land, Potters' Clay, Red Earth and so on) but the challenge with Dorothy Cottrell's 'Earth Battle' comes in at once.

I have made a few tentative markings and a suggestion in regard to the foreword all of which are for you and Winifred to accept or reject as you like. So much for that.

Here is indeed something new in Australian writing. That introductory chapter—the first—is astonishingly arresting. I went back and

---

[1] *Earth's Quality*, 1935, a novel by Winifred Birkett dealing with the influence of a pastoral property on the lives of several generations of an Australian family.

read parts of it three times, and the sound of the sheep never ceased! There is a note of the bizarre in the book, which without being in any way like, or of the same type as the twisted characters of 'Wuthering Heights' and one of Mary Webb's books—was it 'Run to Earth'?[1]—is the first real promise Australia has had of a writer of hers entering that field. The character could have more developed without affecting its naturalness under its circumstances; I refer to the mad boy Roy, driven out of himself by psychic shock.

John Weldon, Anthony, Roy, Alec even, and Jill are no fictions. They are real. And the outstanding thing is the knowledge of the land and the things of the land—a knowledge so a part of Winifred's life, that it is spun from her mind as silk is spun from a caterpillar's body. There is completely impersonal, unconscious, almost seemingly unconsidered knowledge set forth there. It flows by reason of the story. This to me is art, and art with beauty. For when the old man John Weldon's hands parted the fleece, one's own hands felt the parting with him; one's own touch caught the texture and the feel of the wool in the staple. Other things the same. But this (so simply done!) at the beginning of the book lived throughout the book and set its key. The ending of the book is as right as it is unexpected. Of this you can use what you like if you want it. For the rest, part of the latter half of the book where the girl comes in is just a little weak. But the book is so unsentimental this is inevitable in one at beginnings. Some of the scenes are too sketchy for the same reason, as where Charles and Stella come to understanding, and also where Roy fires the pisé house. In a later edition these should be packed out a bit. Also Roy, towards the end wants a bit more making, whether to mending or not does not matter.

But I am delighted with the work. The balance of tonal quality in the language shows that it is worth something to prose writing to have it rooted in a sense of verbal sound and rhythm, no matter how definitely it remains prose.

I forgot last time I saw you that I had been asked to do a week session for a month at 2KY,[2] I meant to mention it because it is publicity. I am working better on my next book[3] but the hindrances are innumerable: heart through heat among them. In haste

Please tell Winifred I doffs (dips!) my lid to her!

---

[1] The novel by Mary Webb was *Gone to Earth*, 1917.
[2] A Sydney commercial radio station.
[3] *More Recollections*, the sequel to *Old Days: Old Ways*.

To Hugh McCrae

Dear Hugh,

Kings Cross
18 February 1935

No, I wasn't cutting bread & butter when your letter arrived. I was making toast. I said 'Darlingest' nineteen times & the toast burned.

But what a gift! & what a letter! and thank you for what you said about the M. G. portrait.[1] So many astonishing people said it was a good portrait, that I wondered was I witless or somebody else. Yet there is something in Saunders' work, & I am not sorry I gave him his chance.

And thank you for Katharine P's[2] legs. They bothered me because I could not place them. Now I can think of them & be at peace. I liked the painting there, but not the portrait. She was given a bewildered look who never is bewildered, and the delicate feminine look so much hers was not brought out enough.

I am trying for the last month to get my new book[3] together, but under such difficulties, as the eyes are so often (through the cross lights from the clouds) a-never-tired-of-waiting trouble. However it really is begun, about a quarter of it ready (more or less) for typing. A. & R. want it in for March. I see it!

My son & his wife are somewhere. They left no address but 'bathing togs'. I am learning to be the mother of a daughter-in-law's husband & though I never at any time constrained my boy I do not like it. Be thankful yours are girls! I am of opinion now that the secret of happiness is in the possession of power even if never used—you at least can punch a son-in-law, but a daughter-in-law, however nice, is fireworks on her own. Me, I have to sing low in spite of your 'rules the waves' & 'peremptory'...

'My knees I break to you'.

To H. M. Green

Dear H. M. Green,

Kings Cross
9 March 1935

My apologies for delay in acknowledging your kindness in sending me your book.[4] Presently, if I can lay hands on one you have not got, I will send you one of mine.

---

[1] A pen and ink drawing of Mary done by Eric Saunders in 1931, now in the Pictorial section of the National Library, Canberra.
[2] Katharine Susannah Prichard.
[3] *More Recollections*, 1935.
[4] Probably *The Happy Valley and Other Poems*, 1935.

This is the day of the death of imaginative poetry, or poetry for the sake of its own qualities. It used to grieve me that I had no time (and no capacity) to write *real* poetry, that all my stuff was a web of human emotions, and without the silver web that *is* poetry. Now I grieve no longer. The new dispensation is at hand, and who or what will emerge the Lord only knows. I doubt if it will be us, at all events: you with your kind, me with my absence of your kind.

I am tired and my eyes are tired, so much so I am getting on very slowly with my new book.[1] However I can take time as the other[2] is still selling. So I will say no more except that I was mortal glad to see the improved look in your wife's face when I met her the other day. It is good to see her looking so renewed, even if strength is slow in returning. My thanks to you again.

To R. H. Croll

Dear Robert Croll and all the Crolls.

Kings Cross
25 March 1935

I am in doubt of your address my book not having it down, consequently I am sending this, and something you will value, to you c/o Percival Serle as I have his address. When you get this letter you will probably have the packet, I am registering it for security's sake. It is a proof copy of Neilson's first 'Heart of Spring'[3] given me by A. G. S.[4] and with his handwriting on it. On the back is pasted an envelope addressed to me by Shaw Neilson and containing the original copy of a poem he wrote to me years ago called 'The Smoky Parrot'.[5] I do not know if he kept a copy of it himself. I am sending my best beloved children, that Billy does not need, to homes before it is too late for me to send them, and to save making a nineteen page will. Also I will get the letters of thanks while I can read 'em, thank the Lord!

I am working hard, but how slowly now-a-days! on my new book.[6] A and R wanted it for a month ago, but it is yet only half done. Except for notes and rough writing. That and they are a yard high or at least a foot.

[1] Probably *More Recollections*, 1935.
[2] *Old Days: Old Ways A Book of Recollections*, 1934.
[3] John Shaw Neilson published 'O Heart of Spring' in the Sydney *Sun*, 5 November 1911 and in the *Bookfellow*, April 1915.
[4] A. G. Stephens.
[5] There are various titles attributed to the poem including 'The Smoker Parrot' and 'The Smoker Parrots' as well as Mary's title. The poem was apparently first published in the *Clarion*, May 1909.
[6] *More Recollections*, 1935.

My love to everyone who remembers me and especially them Crolls—

To T. Inglis Moore

Dear Tom,

Kings Cross
5 May 1935

I think I am old enough in years and mother enough as an Australian writer, to the young, to begin that way.

I have an aching wish that someone would have done for the natives of Australia what you have done for the Philippines in your book 'The Half Way Sun'.[1] The natives here had just as distinctive religious observances (apart from head hunting) and if a translator has capacity, just as distinctive ways of saying things! Turnbull[2] is doing it in this story now running through the 'S.M.H.' for New Guinea. He gives more than mere pigeon English, which you I am glad to say, have avoided—writing as it were from brain to brain, in the equalities of intellect and capacity, only different by subordination of the one side to environment and its form of culture. I think the death of the old man a remarkably fine piece of work. And that reference to the two smells, the one the father man smell! That stands on its own. I have never seen such a reference before, and yet it is a part *of every human life*, no matter where. There and always missed in literature. As to the reviews, they don't amount to much more than an expression of the reviewers' inability to grasp the essential values of the book or its place as a foundation or storehouse for future literature. Most of them, in any case, are only capable of seeing a book as a butterfly alighting, complete and without effort in the making, on a flower. Judgment is in the heels of asses, as far as most of them are concerned. If they saw a misprint (I think I saw one) they would notice it and think it an evidence of intellectual acumen (or is it acuity?) They have been good to me, but so often in regard to others there is only one thing to say and that is Let them fry! . . .

My blessing on the infant and the doorstep.

To Sarah Nixon-Smith

Dear Mrs. Smith—otherwise Sarah Nixon,

Kings Cross
10 May 1935

Billy said that, in the present dreadful drought in his part of Queens-

[1] *The Half-Way Sun. A Tale of the Philippine Islands,* 1935.
[2] Gilbert Munro Turnbull. The 'story now running' was *Mountains of the Moon.*

land, it would be no use expecting the poplar[1] to live if he took it with him. So I wrote the other day to the curator of the Botanic gardens, told him the history of the tree and asked would he accept it for the gardens. He says

'It has been very interesting to read the history of the Poplar to which you refer. I will be pleased to accept the tree and have it planted in a prominent position in the gardens.

Do you know the name of the Poplar? We have a collection of them here, & possibly we have the one to which you refer, but still we can find plenty of room for others.

Trusting the plant will thrive when planted in its new home & that you will be able to visit the gardens & note its progress.
Yours faithfully
                     (signed) G. F. Hawkey
                     Curator'
So I suggest that you ring up or write to the Curator, asking for a date to bring the young tree in, but *not* on a Monday, as I would like to be there when it is planted and perhaps bring a friend or two to see it done. I know, too, the papers would be glad to make a paragraph about it. And of course you should be present at the planting & your daughter as well. One thing should be done, & that is a brass plate should go on the tree giving its history. I think we must talk about that, but later on. I have not forgotten that I have something for your daughter as a wedding present.

All good wishes, and what thanks to you and yours for saving my poplar tree!

To George Mackaness

Kings Cross
Dear Dr. Mackaness,   *22 May 1935*

You should have had the documentary account of the foundation of the F.A.W. before this, but I have been in bed by Dr. MacPherson's strictest order (acute bronchitis, & tired heart) since last Friday. However I am up today. Will you keep the record very safely in case it is needed later on for reference . . . Yours in haste—very tired

FOUNDING THE FELLOWSHIP OF AUST. WRITERS

For years before I formally started it I had been proposing to found

---

[1] See letters, 14 December 1933 and 27 December 1934.

a society of men and women writers to be called a Fellowship.[1] I began so early on it that I had the endorsement in writing of Henry Lawson for it. I also had the endorsement of Mr. Roderick Quinn among others. In 1927, because of Mr. Quinn's urgency that I form my society, I promised him that I would get to work on it in the following year. I could not go further than I had gone just then, as besides my page in 'The Worker'[2] and my committees, I was working on the material of what shortly after was to become three new books. This took longer than I expected, and I delayed. Then Mrs. Cassidy[3] came to me with a message and a reminder from Mr. Quinn. The message was that if I did not get to work at once someone else would. I said I would prefer that, as I was so very busy. Mrs. Cassidy said that if others began it would probably be a society like the Casuals and that women might be excluded, whereas in my plan women and men alike were to be members. However my promise to Mr. Quinn was the thing that weighed most with me. I asked Mrs. Cassidy would she, if I founded it at once, do the immediate secretarial work for me (my table at the time was full of galley proofs to be back at Angus & Robertson's within twenty four hours). Mrs. Cassidy said she would, and that she could get the notices for the meeting typed for me without cost. I gave her all the silver I had (about one and ninepence I think) which she said would cover cost of first postage. I wrote the necessary notice for a meeting. I also said I would pay for notices in the papers and any other reasonable expenses. As I could not then fix a date for the meeting, as I wished to see the secretary of the Lyceum Club to arrange for it, I being a foundation member of the Club, I asked Mrs. Cassidy to call again when I would have everything settled.

As space is limited I omit many particulars. At the first meeting held I did not wish to take the chair, being a woman, and feeling it was more a man's position. I was definitely told that I must, as I had called the meeting, and that I must conduct the meeting because but for me 'none of us' would be there, so that I *'must'* take the chair.

---

[1] Mary wrote a number of letters to various people at this time, setting out her claim to be the founder of the Fellowship of Australian Writers. This letter is representative of them all. The *Bulletin* of 28 December 1938 gives the date of the first meeting of the F.A.W. as 23 November 1928, presided over by Mary Gilmore. It seems (from Mary's diary of 1928) that there was a preliminary meeting at the Lyceum Club on 8 November 1928. The first officials of the F.A.W. were John Le Gay Brereton (President), with vice-Presidents Mary Gilmore, Walter Jago, Steele Rudd, F. J. Broomfield, George Portus and S. A. Rosa. Marjorie Quinn was Secretary and Arthur Crocker, Treasurer. The Fellowship amalgamated with the Writers' Association, 16 February 1938. Arthur Crocker in *Fellowship*, June 1944, gives most of the credit to Roderic Quinn for the foundation of the Fellowship of Australian Writers. The controversy continued in succeeding issues of *Fellowship*.

[2] The Women's Page. See letter, 1 June 1946.

[3] Lucy Cassidy.

I took the chair, and I also recorded the proceedings of the meeting. This record I gave to Miss Marjorie Quinn when at the second meeting she was elected Hon. Secretary. A sub-committee consisting of Mr. S. A. Rosa, Mr. Aidan de Brune and (I think) Miss Dulcie Deamer, was formed to draw up a constitution and rules for the foundation of the society and a date for a second meeting set. Again I engaged and paid for the use of the Lyceum Club, and at the second meeting, again presiding, the rules as proposed were amended, accepted and passed.

The question of name coming up, and the name under which I had interested people being The Fellowship of Writers. Mr. Rosa, I think it was, proposed the inclusion of the word 'Australian' which made it 'The Fellowship of Australian Writers'. As I was more concerned with the founding of the society than in having my designation accepted, that became the name. Mr. Rosa proposed me as first President and gave his reasons. I refused to be nominated for the same reason that I had not wished to take the chair—I thought it better for a man to act as President over men and women than for a woman to rule over men. Consequently I agreed to Mrs. Cassidy's suggestion (to whom I had said I would not be President) that Professor J. le Gay Brereton be the first President. I was stepping down from the chair to conclude the meeting, all the foundation business being ended, when someone announced that the Professor (who had sent me word the day before that he would be late) had arrived. I went back to the chair and he was then proposed and elected President.

When the constitution was handed over for printing, Professor Brereton told me he had seen to it that my name as founder was sent with the document to the printer, and that my name would be on the printed copy. When the printed copies were delivered someone had removed my name or had neglected to print it. My name not being on the printed copies of the constitution, in order to legalize any action or ruling he might take or make on it, he asked me to sign his own copy, which I did. He also said it would be well to sign several other copies in case of loss, which I did, and added that whenever anyone asked for a copy it would be the Hon. Secretary's duty to see that I signed it, as otherwise it would not be in order. He also of his own will, said that when next the constitution was printed, he would see that the omission would be rectified, and that he would see that my name as founder would be printed on it. And again he assured me it was not his fault that my name had been deleted. My reply to that was that everybody knew that for years I had been interesting people and proposing the formation of the Society: that everyone knew the circumstances of its founding, and that even if my name had been omitted in the printing of the constitution, no one would dispute or question its right to be there, especially as no decision could constitutionally be made without it, or its recognition in some other way. And I said then (as I have always said) that I acquitted him of all blame or part in the omission. Actually, for years, I thought it a printer's error. To recapitulate: I had begun the work in the time of Henry Lawson, whose approval I had; I was not asked to begin or institute someone else's society, but to go on with my own; I wrote and was responsible for the notice sent out to call the meeting; I paid all preliminary expenses; I presided as the responsible person at all the meetings inaugurating the foundation; the constitution was formulated, submitted, shaped, and accepted under my ruling as chair, and which no one disputed as my right . . .

When the Education Department was approached for the use of its premises for our meetings, before we could get that use, I was asked as founder to give my positive assurance that there was nothing seditious or contrary to law in the constitution of the society I had formed, and in addition I had to give a further assurance that while in occupation of the premises (a) nothing political or religious would be discussed: (b) that there would be no introduction of subjects publicly contentious (c) no criticism of any government, our own or other, nor of any Government Department (d) and nothing done or discussed that in any way might embarrass, involve, or make difficulty for the Department whose premises we were using. Further, as the Professor could not always be present I had to promise that I would attend all meetings to see that the conditions of use were not broken, and as far as humanly possible I have done this.
Addenda.

Because Mrs. Cassidy came to me when she did, and because the arguments she used helped to convince me that my society should be gone on with *and at once*, I wrote in her book an inscription[1] which I never thought would be claimed as evidence that it was she who founded 'The Fellowship of Australian Writers'! As a matter of fact, an interruption during the time I was writing it, caused me to leave out certain defining words. I looked twice at the sentence when written, and decided that it would spoil the look of the inscription if I interlined it by the necessary addition, and left it as written. I realize now how foolish I was! When I handed the book to Mrs. Cassidy, she was the first to say that I was the originator, and that she had only come in later. I replied. 'Probably if you had not come to me just when you

---

[1] Mary presented Lucy Cassidy with a copy of *Pitt Head Poems* by Frederick C. Boden and inscribed on the fly-leaf:

'For Lucy Cassidy who started the Fellowship of Poets and got Lawson Day as a fixture in the Education Department, and who in more ways than one has been the friend of Australian poets'. (dated 6 November 1928).

did I would never have gone on, and so to that extent you have started the movement going'...

To Constance Robertson

Kings Cross
4 July 1935

Dear Connie,

Of course I have 'flu. That is why I did not get to the Wed. lunch. But I had a wire that my people[1] had seven inches (*inches!*) rain. They haven't had that in over ten years and it would not surprise me if they all got gloriously drunk as a result. Actually I suppose they all had to go out in bathers or raincoats and save drowning sheep. I hadn't dared to afford a doctor for this bout in case I had to use up my last penny keeping the roof over their heads. Now I feel like having two doctors just to show 'em. But what a relief for those poor things up there! And incidentally for me; but I do not count myself against the young. Not nowadays. But I am praying like Samson at the Gates of Gaza, 'Lord strengthen my arm this once I pray thee that I may finish this next book'. It may be no better than the last, but it will be as good.

Just had a nice letter from Capt. Peters to say that Mr. Lyons, the Prime Minister, specially asked their London Manager could he send him three of 'Mary Gilmore's books, Marri'd and Other Verses, The Rue Tree (de luxe edition), and The Wild Swan (ditto)' as he 'wanted to present them to someone in this country'. (England). Having got them Mr. Lyons replied 'Dear Mr. Maurice, It was exceedingly kind of you to let me have the three copies of Mary Gilmore's books. I was very anxious to obtain them, and appreciate, more than I can say, your courtesy in sending them to me. Yours sincerely, J. A. Lyons'. (Note he says *Mary* Gilmore). Without smashing nations could you make me a par from this.

Yours, living on O.P. Rum and Radiators.

To Percival Serle

Kings Cross
2 August 1935

Dear Mr. Serle, Along with the family. There came a surprise, an irruption, & a crowd to my door yesterday. The crowd depended not on its numbers but on its mass, and its mass on its qualities & what was in its hand. The crowd was R. Croll ... & Hugh McCrae, & what

---

[1] Her husband and son on their Queensland property.

was in its hand was Percival Serle's Christopher Smart's 'David',[1] I've looked at it & felt it, & I haven't cut it. It is a cut above being cut—or at all events at present. And my love back again to thank you for it. I had a million things to ask R. C. and not one of them got asked. But I gave them tea in the kitchen & beside the sink, & when they went I sent my love to every body I loved in Melbourne & that includes the Serles.

The book is lovely as a picture.

I am working like a maniac, & a lunatic & an over driven poor devil on my new book[2] having in a moment of aberration said it wd. be ready in a fortnight. I thought it was threequarters ready & it was nothing like it. But I believe tonight that the post is in sight. John Farrell's granddaughter is typing it—the only one of his descendants who reproduces John in his temperament & fancy. She writes verse, & for her age, good little Vignettes. I love to see the seed go on, thinking how glad the dead would be to see it.

I break my knees to you both—

To Hugh McRae

Dear extravagant Hugh,—

Kings Cross
9 November 1935

If I said Darling! seventeen times it might relieve my heart & put thumb prints on my debt. I got the book[3] today, and had a suspicion that the drawings were the 'roof & crown of things'. So I took it in (with my final proof of 'More Recollections') to Mr. Cousins, and ever since I have been scooping round in my mind asking 'What *can* I send him in return?' and 'What *have* I that is worth his while to have that I can send him?' and at the moment all that there is is my love: & you've had that such a very long time that there is nothing very startling about that!

A lovely lovely book. Delicate & lovely, & yet how pointed its arrows of honey! It is butterfly & dragonfly & yet the bee is in it. My dear, my country begins to have books. Hitherto its literature has been too much emotional, too little intellectual. Too much itemization, too little of the filled hand. Painting is the same. Sculpture was till Rayner Hoff came. I bracket you two together in my mind as the makers. Other people show their scaffolding too much. Some never get down off it.

---

[1] Percival Serle edited Christopher Smart's *A Song to David and Other Poems* in 1923 in a limited edition of 300 autographed copies.
[2] *More Recollections*, 1935.
[3] Probably Hugh McCrae's *My Father and My Father's Friends*, 1935.

It is good to have lived to see the things that are being done now. I have always had the ache in the heart for the things missed. We've had the gospels, but the diarist is the whole Bible in whom, & by whom, & with whom, & through whom & from whom all things are made manifest!

(I stole a pinch from Georgiana's Diary[1] about the aboriginals. You'll see it when the book comes out.)

But what can I say to you through whom all things are made manifest? The dead can never die as you have touched them. A gallery of sunlight.

My homage & my affections are with you.

To Hugh McCrae

Kings Cross
23 December 1935

Dear Hugh,

I am leaving a copy of 'More Recollections' with Mr. Cousins for you, as the postman's back is over-burdened. I wrote my heart into an inscription[2] & then found I had made a rhyme. Do not blame me too much for it. Also the grammar shakes, but that's no matter. One of the nicest things in the world is to shake one's fist at grammar, or to say 'I ain't' or something like that. I never let Billy say it when he was little, & now I feel as if I had robbed his young life of treasure & his years of remembrance. After which the good wish & the good years to you & yours.

To Hugh McCrae

Kings Cross
15 January 1936

Dear Hugh,

If anyone takes your place in my affections I'll be dead! And you can tell Nancy[3] that, & make her a recording witness!

Had two darling letters from dear Julian Ashton, the second in reply to mine answering the first which had made up to me for the spiteful 'write' of Dunbabin (I suppose) on 'More Recollections'. In it Mr. Ashton says: 'I have seen the notices of your last book. Not so cordial as is their wont. But my dear Mrs. Gilmore you surely have

---

[1] Hugh McCrae had published, in 1934, *Georgiana's Journal*, a transcript of his grandmother's diary of the day-to-day life in pioneer Victoria.
[2] Mary's own personal note in the copy of *More Recollections* which she sent to Hugh McCrae.
[3] Hugh McCrae's wife.

not forgotten those lines attributed to Sir Walter Raleigh, "Go soul the body's guest . . ." (I need not quote farther as you know them as well as he & I do: and follows on with) "For though to give the lie deserves no less than stabbing, yet stab at thee who will . . ." ' (and it never occurred to me till he quoted it that that 'For though . . . deserves no less than stabbing' refers to the duello! It used to puzzle me why the 'deserves'—nothing else was possible, 'the lie' being given.)

And the dermatitis—had you never heard a returned soldier curse iodine 'and the dam' fools' who poured it into their wounds & poisoned the susceptible? Alas poor man! He remains a child all his life, nursling of misguided women (his mothers) in infancy, and nursling of misguided doctors in his later life. Iodine! and there was 'Karraseen'— Kerosine being cheaper than iodine; & there was nicotine, & nicotine hardier than either, and both good old bush remedies. Where did the first hundred years of young Australia get *iodine* for tick bite?—white Australia that is! and what did the blacks use? That, no one bothered to find out, though there are hazy recollections still with me of men suffering terror of ticks, & what the blacks said to do. All I remember is that the blacks said the tick had to come out and that they were adepts at removing it without breaking it, or in any way adding to the trouble. And that reminds me, when you read the new book read all of it but the part about the blacks, only a few notices (or noticers) appear to have seen the other parts! and I have a soft spot in my own heart for them. I think I have put down things long due for such chronicling (is that spelling right?) and in collected form, for what has been done, so far, has been wholly personal, or scattered, a parag. here, a parag. there. The 'Trap Dams'[1] I wrote thirty years ago in the original 'New Idea',[2] could not find the cuttings, & had to rewrite it for the book and I am also hugging myself that I gave the boasting Anglo-Saxon one in the nose in showing what the Spaniard did—the derided Latin generally—under conditions Australia never had to face. I think that is partly why the N.S.W. notices are chill: that and the exhibition of our blood stained past. When all that stuff used to be written during & after the war about Australia's virgin page I used to stand in wonder. Not two hundred years old & our first hundred years saw the Convict System, the destruction of at least half a million blacks, and in the '80's the thousands of dead black-birded kanaka 'slaves'.—and after that the war. A virgin page! The 'cat' alone marked it.

After which you will ask have I the fire & fury of dermatitis! No; but I've had psittacosis or flu' or their twin for ten days, and am now

---

[1] An essay in *More Recollections*, 1935.
[2] A Sydney popular magazine.

feeling that the dragon is in the dust & I in the air above it which accounts for the length of this letter.

 After which I respectfully draw to a conclusion and remain
 Dear Mr. McCrae (with much sympathy)
 By these tokens your humble & obedient—
  What? servant? Admirer? fellow farer? or just
        Mary Gilmore

P.S. A wire last night my people up north have just had 3½ inches of rain. So there will be bread in the cupboard after all.

To Hugh McCrae

Kings Cross
18 March 1936

Hugh McCrae: So that *no one else* can claim it.
My dearest Lamb (That's a good beginning!)

I have been preparing for the TOO-M-B by going through old papers, etc. of which I have enough to build a continent and voyaging on the seas of print I found enclosed, which I send you in case you haven't a copy of it yourself. I am sure to come across some more, for I have only nibbled like a rat at the edge of a tip.

 Did you get 'More Recollections' from Mr. Cousins?

 I have just had a letter from Robert Garran. What grief & loss, his wife's death, and yet what an impression of eternal hope, behind the sense of loss, that what was continuing here must be continuing elsewhere. What a lovely thing faith is! I haven't got it but I have the next best thing. Fight. One fights life, & death, & everything else for continuity—so you write, & I write, and out of the dust the word arises & says I Am: & in that I Am are you & sometimes I.

 With my affections and the hope that Nancy has survived your illness from iodine poisoning.

I have just wired to ask my people what they are calling their *boat*: not such rains since the 70's.

To Hugh McCrae

Kings Cross
3 April 1936

Dear Childe,*

The years heap, & I have been making 'a tidy hoose' with an eye on the end on 'Some fine day'—though not immediate I hope. Flats are places; farms are homes. A home is a place where you can put your beloved garnerings to burn in a wood fire and under the sun. But a flat is a place where you take an enamel pie-dish & a factory-made match. I have such a pie dish & such a match, and a heap of ash by me as I write. When we were leaving Paraguay, I had Billy's first & only cot broken up, saved one piece, cut it into two: one for dad & one for me: and burned the rest. Better the clean ash than the dusty ending in a stranger's hands or a rubbish heap.

    I am going through all sorts of loved letters. Yours I feel like giving to Honey.[1] They range from years ago till a month or six weeks ago, except two, both of which because they contained private matter are burnt. Honey would treasure the letters, & because of friendship & affection, I want them treasured.

    Now I have to go to the occulist[sic], with the usual unspoken prayer of dread in my heart.

    My love to Nancy,[2] and my burned-up ashes of affections to you.

* Childe because heir of my heart—or one of them. They are not many & not all alive.

To Hugh McCrae

Kings Cross
26 July 1936

Darling! (and I hope Nancy[3] is looking over your shoulder)—what a dear thing it is to be able say out one's heart to one's friends! . . .

    Brennan[4] was the heroic. There was nothing little in him. He wandered with gigantic shades, with the giants, & was one with them. And if that is not the heroic, & of the heroes, I do not know what, above the flesh & the fist, is. Well now he is with Agamemnon and Menelaus & all the rest of them, & sometimes we can still hear the shields clash & the sound of far voices. As to genius unless it have an immortal physical body it is as intangible as life. Life goes and its perishable body falls to dust and one day my sole claim to fame will be that Rayner Hoff did my head. That will remain; all else gone. So with even Brennan, wanting rag. The mediocre lived when paper was rag; now even genius cannot survive unless survival is arranged for.

    (Jeremias[sic] she is today! She's been ill for over a month, poor thing; for six months she has had to nurse a damaged eyesight and

[1] Hugh McCrae's daughter, later Lady Cowper.
[2] His wife.
[3] Hugh McCrae's wife.
[4] C. J. Brennan.

you know what that means to one who lives in & by the eyes, so forgive her.) . . .

I am up & about again, glass with care, & hope that perhaps next week I may be given a left eye lens that will allow me to get at one of my four or five (rough MS. yet) books. What mountains of work to be done torment one's old age! Yet Keats was young & said it. 'Old before his prime.' I had six hours sleep last night & feel alive, as this letter shows.

My love to Nancy, & to you 'twice as more' as the Highlands say.

Seventy-one next month: can I believe it? I thought once it would be wonderful to live to be thirty. What an old age thirty was then.

To Hugh McCrae

Kings Cross
9 August 1936

Dear Hugh McCrae,

I wrote so full of myself over the verse you want to include in your next book that I overlookit or rather neglectit to say what a lovely sense of picture—drama it is—you have. The verse about the swans 'wide-winged, with caparisons streekt oot on high'[1] I never reached such an image, but it means the same wonder, & the inward cry 'O God! to think that someone sees them nightly, & can suffer heart break because the mightiness is lost!' that the very sound of the word wrings through me. The loss! the loss all over the world & through all time. Life everywhere perishing that other life might live. These for man, & man for powers & principalities. No wonder God takes a back seat & the devil ceases to exist. Life is great enough for the one, & man bad enough for the other. I think of the swans we killed, & the Moors in Spain: the broken beauty. No doubt the Moors are as good as we are. But not in Spain!

I heard a Greek fruit seller speak of the Turk. 'For three—or was it six?—centuries we were under his heel; the best of our young men were drafted into his army, & our young women were sent to his harems.' and the whole bitterness of a defrauded race, the grief of

---

[1] These lines and others in this letter are part of Hugh McCrae's poem *To Mary Gilmore*

> An' oh! again I mark *The Swans*
> (Brichter than angels come to Mons
> Wide-winged, with caparisons
> Streekt oot on high)
> As they, thine own commanded sons,
> Possess the sky

wrong perpetuated was in his voice. So might Spain say of the Moors.
To leave off raging & to turn from evil
'... far doon the street ('dune' you have it).
Hop-step-an'-jump, & rent the beat, my ain heart made withouten feet.'
Four hundred pages could not have wrought it. What is it in words
that makes the miracle? Something turns in a line & there is creation.
I have puzzled & puzzled over it. The ear within the ear hears & the
hand writes, & then the ear within the ear hears it & the eyes know
tears. 'Withouten feet'. No use trying to say what it holds in or of the
measureless. I know as you say, it refers narrowly to the bust without
body. But if our writing only held what we narrow the pen to at the
moment, it would not live. It sometimes seems as if a power within—
another captive self—forced utterance, or sang between the bars of the
external. The dimensionless self giving the dimensionless. Perhaps it
is out this the elder ones visioned the spirit & dreamed immortality.

The world is with us & immortality is far: so it may interest you
to know that I met & liked Zane Grey. I went to D.J.s[1] to say goodbye
to him on Sat. & to my astonishment when the girls heard I was there
I was rushed for my autograph. Out of that grows a half idea that A.
& R. should have a day when authors wd. autograph (especially you
& me) and sell millions of copies of books.

I came across a little painting Honey[2] did for me when a child.
I thought then it showed genius, I think it still. I have come to the
conclusion (or nearly have) that genius is the transference of self to
the work, otherwise it is ordinary & without character. After that the
measure of genius is the intellectual self. (How's that for a person who
knows nothing of ART?)

My dear, my thanks go to you.

To Lionel Lindsay

Dear Mr. Lindsay,
Kings Cross
9 September 1936

May I, as one to whom the thought of the Moors in Spain is a heart
break, thank you for your letter in today's 'S.M.H.'[3]

For the Catholic Church & the Catholic people I have the same
admiration as for any other historic & ameliorative body, whatever
the creed. But of any Church as a world power I have only dread no
matter what Church—even my own. When Queen Victoria had all her

---

[1] Popular diminutive for the Sydney emporium, David Jones Ltd.
[2] Hugh McCrae's daughter, later Lady Cowper.
[3] Lionel Lindsay's letter was entitled 'The War in Spain'.

family & relatives on the thrones of Europe, she had her hand on the greatest secret service body the world has ever seen. Edward had a small marriageable family, then came the world war, & in the revolutions the thrones went & the secrecy with them. Also went the power through crowned heads of the Vatican as a civil & secret arbiter. It is obvious that the moves & marriages of today's royal family is to re-establish the Victorian condition. A dictator is but a step from Kingship, and Kingship once more becomes the hereditary with all its powers of secrecy and a fixed aristocracy. You may recollect that it was England, even more than Italy, made the Vatican a civil & independent Kingdom. So much is this so that (though I have no time for their 'No Popery' cry) the Orangemen are dead as door nails ever since the Vatican became openly a throne among thrones. Nearly two years ago I said 'The next country the great powers will dismember is Spain.' It is in the Republics, & not in the Monarchic countries, that revolutions have been financed & engineered. So the Moors have been sent into Spain—what an impiety— & without a single church in the Empire (or out of it) raising a hand in protest. Why? Because the secrecy of thrones is behind the Moors, and the marriage of thrones in their victories; with the churches the herdsmen of Kings.

Once more let me say how I thank you.
Yours sincerely,

To Hugh McCrae

Dear Hugh,

Kings Cross
22 September 1936

I said 'Blast it!' twice this morning, so the effervescence being a'oot I begin soberly & with propriety. First to enclose a reprint; second to say that I have slowly begun Christina Stead's 'The Salzburg Tales'.[1] What genius! and to think that I remember her father bringing her to me in her later teens[2] to ask if I thought she would make a woman journalist! and when I said NO!! he huffed up & said 'But look at what she has written!' (Clipped from the 'S.M.H.') I replied 'It is precisely because of what she has written I say it. That girl is too big to write tea parties & frocks. She will be a publicist and writer of great special articles' (& so on.) But I never dreamed that that lank-haired pallid-faced anyhow-dressed girl would attain to the might—might not mere height—she has done . . .

[1] Published 1934.
[2] Christina Stead, in a letter to the Editors, was unable to recall this incident but did mention that her father and Mary were acquaintances.

Much or little genius stands alone. You know it; I on the fringes, know it; she knows it and with what a sentence she says it in 'Seven Poor Men of Sydney';[1] 'A thin heart must always be rubbing shoulders with crowds and sitting in the sun to get a little heat. If it does not exercise daily it is found defunct the next morning of inanition. But a strong passion moves in chaos and associates with death, its foot goes among hermits & ravens'.

When I am dead, Hughie, remember that I said Christina Stead would not make a social page woman journalist and make it my pedestal.

To Hugh McCrae

Dear Hughie,

Kings Cross
28 September 1936

I have just got 'The Home Annual', 1936. In the name of all things wise & foolish why do you not do a whole historical 'Camden Town'? Man alive! What a field you have; and what a chance for your own vital . . . scribbled illustrations to illustrate the work. And what folk-stuff there must still be about the area that is Camden, Picton, Cobbity and even farther out. Old chimneys, old houses, old broken orchards, old men, old women, old histories, old cups & saucers, old tables, stools & chairs! Don't tell me I ought to go up & do it: you can walk & I can't and it is walkin and talkin, and sittin down, and leanin over fences, and pokin pigs, and pattin horses, and strokin cows and No! that's wrong; you don't stroke cows: words belong where they belong, and that doesn't belong there. Anyhow that is enough of directioning.

I have gone through the annual and you & I (even if I say it as shouldn't) are the only young ones there. The others are old, old, old; with nostrils pinched to a tone & a cadence as a dummy, and the verse & the words fitted & trimmed over it. *Dressmakered*. Patch-bagged even if some of the patch bags contained silk.

I like the Adrian Feint decorations as a suite apart; but they don't key in with your vitality; they are pen & ink & ruler, & your verse is hawthorn & holly, stoups, farmers, & ale. As to my own 'and hear the flame sing all of a choir', the 'hear' is too soft, it should have been 'bid'. I notice the 's' is off tables; perhaps I did it. Also 'the cat will sing in his drowsy tone' should have been '*a* drowsy tone'. Mea Culpa. The cat that scrapes at my door to be let in, though not mine, is a lie.

But what a reprint of Gruner's 'Dissolving Mists'! I am always

---

[1] Published 1934.

tormented by an eye that sees forms where no one else does. Look over the feeding cow in the distance and see the Michelangelo face & head facing the squared end of the building; and in the man in the armchair on the other side note G.R.[1]

The laundry, the rent collector, & a visitor have intervened. But I wanted to say that I saw Chauvel's 'Uncivilised'.[2] What a country we have, & what beauty there is in planes & space. Seeing it I nearly cried for things I have seen & will never see again. The aboriginal children and the *authentic* aboriginal dancing were to me beautiful, too. But there was too much conventional decoration, & a wiggle-waggle solo dancer who might have been doing the snake dance but not the snake dance as I . . . saw it in the old & original corroborees. The girl in the water was a snowflake, or a thing of moonlight. No need of censorship there! The strangling was ugly in the last foot; the tongue protruded & was ugly. The girl & her nightgown was Pitt Street in the wilds. But with all its faults the picture was worth making, worth praising, and scenically one of the best of ads. for Australia.

No need to answer all this. It is just a moment's 'talk'. As ever,

Mary Gilmore.

I forgot. I saw the Rayner Hoff plaster head of you at the exhibition. However could he so have failed! Something must have gone shipwreck to have left so derelict a thing afloat. Derelict as to his power of interpretation of character, & derelict as to the subject to be transferred or interpreted. I think of it, unhappy, for I had hoped so much, for both of you. But the genius is in the Dale Collins head; there is all the beauty of the feature, and all the sensuality of the man. The belly (as I said) is in the face. I missed the private view being too tired to go that day.

I hope you are well & Nancy[3] too. I am thistle down, up & flying one moment—bruised & broken on the earth the next.

To Miles Franklin

Kings Cross
Dear Stella Franklin, 15 October 1936

I have not read anything so wise & fine as your 'All That Swagger'.[4] I would not like to tell you how often it has wrung—not brought but

---

[1] George Robertson.
[2] Charles Edward Chauvel. *Uncivilized* was published as a novel in 1936 but was also shown as a film.
[3] Hugh McCrae's wife.
[4] *All That Swagger* was Miles Franklin's S. H. Prior Memorial Prize novel for 1936.

wrung—the tears from my eyes. And tears again are all too scarcely produced in Australian writing. One of the things that has caught me in a whirl-wind is your astounding memory. I do not mean for facts, items, stories, and places, but the impressions of people singly, & in mass, of events. In this week's instalment. 'The Queen would be so pleased with the whelps.—She would invite them to Buckingham Palace'—things like that, for that is only one out of a thousand.

I must stop. There has just come in one of my last two Aunts (by marriage at that) and a girl she adopted, now here on furlough from a missionary station in Manchuria. But you don't know how I have felt about your work for Australia. All the flags in the world are but a circumstance compared with such a work as this. And the living style. 'Oh moi, Oh moi!' I haven't words to say what I would say.

Proud of you, proud for the country that brought you forth, yours very humbly by comparison

To Hugh McCrae

Dear Hugh,
Kings Cross
31 October 1936

(I had intended beginning my best beloved Hugh, but someone came in & interrupted & the whole thing went flat) anyhow here is the meat. I have been able to use my eyes a bit more of late, & have been going through about 40 Kilos of scrapped, 'under consideration', & fresh verse. Some of it's middlin', some of it's worse. But some of it seems worth while.

What is a broad sheet? A couple or more look broad-sheetish to me so I enclose copies for your consideration & advice. I have never been broad sheeted (not even as a ghost) and I would like to feel the feeling of a new adventure. Must they be illustrated? And if they must, could & would you? and if not you, WHOOOO? Are they done by hand? Are they machined? By hand would be distinguished, but I think, as the verse is patriotic and I want it to go as far abroad as possible, machining wd. be best. But, in any case it will go in the new book if the new book can raise a suit—a coat & jacket.

My dear, I hope you are doing what I wanted. The Canterbury Tales of Camden. For the love of God and Australia, do it. My love to you all.

To Frank Dalby Davison

Dear Frank,

Kings Cross
14 November 1936

You have done again in this Dark people story[1] what you did in *Manshy*:[2] brought reality to the imaginary. Those two children wander through the bush and in the distance I hear their voices just as if I were in the same bush, & they real & heard but not seen. You did that with the *Line* of horses in *The Wells of Beersheba*.[3] I did not see the horses individually, but I still see the *line*, I see it waver and move, I see it in mass at the gallop, I see the single gallop of scattered horses yet it is well over a year, perhaps two since I read the book. You are the only one of our writers who does that: makes a living entity of sound & movement so that they and not the structure built up on words remain alive in memory. The economy in outside description in which to clothe the figure & action is its own distinction. Most people spread the waters of description, & shallow the spring. You do the opposite.

Also I have wanted to thank you for arranging last month's meeting of the F.A.W.[4] for me. It gave me great joy to think Mrs. Cassidy was present & heard Adam McCay tell how I stood for Anti-conscription for she was said to be most active in maligning me in that very matter. I did not do more than a third of my life in its public work but it was something to get that much done. Also I deliberately left out the founding of the F.A.W. as I want to see you secure in the presidency for next year, & it might have stirred up antagonism.

There is another thing that I am pleased about, & that is that Frank Cotton remembers (& told Mrs. Lindsay) that I was on the first Executive of the A.W.U.,[5] & that I had to decide on the A.W.U. coming out in aid of the maritime strike.[6] So that is another witness of the very few who are left. If you remember I mentioned how at that decision I went white, my mouth dry, & my tongue stiff. I forgot to add that it was a matter of standing wonder among the men that anyone could go as white as I did and still be alive. They said I went white to the

---

[1] *Children of the Dark People: An Australian Folk Tale*, 1936. Illustrated by Pixie O'Harris.
[2] See letter, 13 July 1929.
[3] *The Wells of Beersheba: A Light Horse Legend*, 1933.
[4] Fellowship of Australian Writers. See letter to George Mackaness, 22 May 1935.
[5] Mary claims to have been co-opted (she said she was present under her brother's name of John Cameron) by the executive of the Australian Workers Union.
[6] A large-scale labour disturbance began in August 1890. It began with the Merchant Marine and later involved miners, transport workers and shearers. At stake was the recognition of Unionism on one hand, and freedom of contract for employers on the other. The strike ended in defeat for the Unions as the workers returned on terms imposed by or acceptable to the employers.

fingernails, and that my hand on the table looked like marble. It was talked of for years, & told again in Paraguay.

Glad to see you on the Bulletin Red Page. It should lead to permanency, there or elsewhere. It is 3 a.m. and as sleep will not return once I wake I write letters, so yours is first in the list & herewith.

To Hugh McCrae

Dear Hugh,

Kings Cross
18 January 1937

You & I are in much the same boat as regards looks & the grave. But after all looks count. Fancy having a face with a whine in it! Spos'n either of us looked like that? The Lord God has been good to us.

As to those touchy-tetchy people: I never can understand the ego that can never bear to be stood aside for a moment, & that must always be knelt to. But you love people as humanity, and I love people as humanity, and to such the world is wide, & toleration its main road. The person who hasn't called, or who hasn't acknowledged a letter, may have been too busy baking the bread, or ploughing a field and all their attention on their work to the exclusion of everything else—& necessarily. Man's a funny creature, and the Almighty was wise in not making him on the first day, or He wouldn't have been given range to make the other things. Ego is a great thing to make the world go round, but it is a wheel with spikes in most cases. Hence the origin of 'He's got the Spike'.

Just now I looked up techy-tetchy, to be sure there was a 't' & found a word new to me: 'teathe' ('talk') homely old English. Apart from its ruder cruder meanings there is one that my heart jumped at; the feeding of cattle on pasture to return what is taken from it. What an engine reciprocity is!

Also I was thinking over the newest scientific statement in regard to dietetics. And I was mentally railing at the tom fool—dam-fool—doctors who say to eat dry whether you want to or not and that all animals eat dry. *They* never saw an animal eat the dew! never saw a horse flap his lip & tongue over the top of wet grass to get more wet than the blade gave him! . . .

I seem to neglect Nancy in having so much to say about other things but she is in my mind all the time I write. I hope she keeps well.

An hour later.

Just had in a most interesting man from the North of Australia; a Mr. Bennett, Scottish Bennett, is 79 & has hawked with wheelbarrow, dray, waggons & camels, & now owns two stations. As a boy he attended

George Robertson

Hugh McCrae

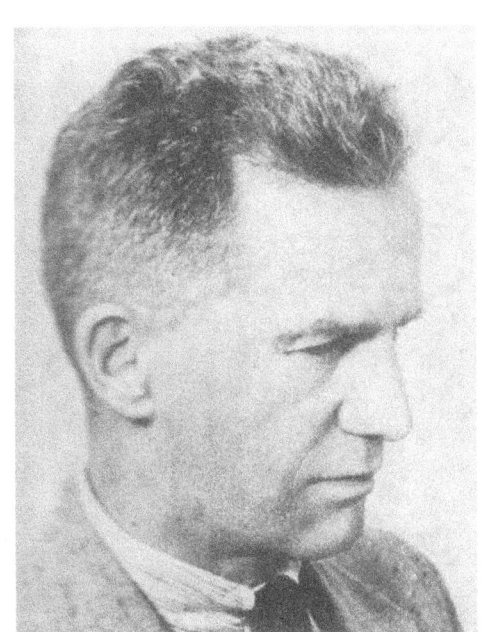
H. M. Green

Frank Dalby Davison and his family at 'Coorteai'

John K. Ewers

Dr George Mackaness

Lionel Lindsay

Tom Inglis Moore

Dr. John Dunmore Lang's Sunday school, & his first job was telegraphist when the G.P.O. was in Wynyard Square & the Telegraph office up opp. where Farmers is in George Street. Got away young (is the youngest of his family) & went bush; & bush (with intervals) he has been ever since. Thinks my books of recollections 'most accurate'—'more than most others'. I asked had he ever known aboriginals domesticate dingoes. '*Never*' he said 'they are untameable'.—As I also know, & have said. He has promised to write to me 'anything & everything'. A man of thought & culture & the quiet ways of the solitudes. These are the things that make me feel living & alive.

To Neville Cayley

Kings Cross
20 January 1937

Dear Neville,

When I think of the work you have done for this country I nearly break my heart with feeling. *Science* knew Australian birds through Gould,[1] but Australia *as a people* only learned them, learned that a bird's feather was beautiful, through your father.[2] He put the birds on the walls of houses, and after all it is in the houses that minds dwell and tongues meet and talk the things the minds think and the eyes see. No one has yet written what this country owes your father in this. And now come you, half Gould, half your father. The birds sing because of you even as we heard their dying cry through your father. Of course, I know that people say your father was conventional. His day was conventional, but in spite of that he made people see the living by and through the conventional. What your father's pictures did to arouse a feeling for the bird, the pity of its death, and the need of its preservation, will never be known now, and certainly never adequately told. But he set pity in the hearts of people who did not know a trite from a barrow . . .

And where we waked pity, you give beauty, and, by the very faithfulness of your colour and group, the birds sing. You people build Australia, and you, A. & R. and all the rest, give her what no masonry ever gave her: permanency of life. I love the very names of those who do this and here I had better end. Affectionately,

[1] John Gould.
[2] Neville H. P. Cayley.

To Joseph Lyons

The Rt. Hon. The Prime Minister,
Sir,

Kings Cross
2 February 1937

I beg to acknowledge and to thank you for your telegram of congratulations on the bestowal of an Honour by His Majesty The King on me.[1] And I also wish to thank you for the endorsement you gave my name (and work) when it came before you officially. Believe that I fully appreciate the honour done me, and in me to Australia. May my past work stand as the guarantee of my future.

I am, Sir, Yours sincerely
Mary Gilmore (D.B.E.)

To George Mackaness

Dear Dr Mackaness,

Kings Cross
18 February 1937

Thank you all for your good wishes.[2] I knew I had them whether expressed or not. As to the letters and wires! They came from every part of Australasia. I had to send word to Wm. St. P.O. not to send the wires singly, but to send them in batches. The letters came 40, and 50 a day the first week. Now thank heaven there are only 8 or 10 a day. Three people wrote me verses. One a beautiful thing was posted from Brisbane, no name, no clue, disguised hand writing on envelope. And the writer did not know I had left the Worker (four years ago) for in red ink block printing it said 'Not for Australian Worker'. The letters came from N.T. to Tas and from Perth to Brisbane. N.Z. letters have begun this week. Am tired!!! The callers, and then the functions! and I have to think of something worth while to say or people are disappointed. They think a writer talks in ordinary at the level of his or her emotional writing! However the worst rush is over. Now I have to go through the letters. So far I have only answered the official, the semi official, and societies, invitations and very pressing ones. But the interviewers came daily for *nine* days and took hours of time. They said they loved to hear me talk!!! I suppose a good lot of it went to 'the morgues' of the different offices. Two people want to paint me for the Archibald already. I shall be glad when things quieten down. Had a family party of 40 of my people in the gardens on Sat. afn. at my poplar tree. It is a cutting of one planted at my birth,

---

[1] Mary had been admitted, in the New Year Honours list, to the order of Dame of the British Empire, on the recommendation of the then Prime Minister, Joseph Lyons.

[2] Concerning her award of the D.B.E. See letter, 2 February 1937.

which came from Mrs Reibey who got hers from the ones McLeay[1] imported for the Gardens. My cutting was the first to go across the mountains I believe. That was one link with the gardens. The other: My last-living uncle is married to the grand daughter of Ferdinand Napoleon Meurant,[2] of an old landed French family. His first land here was taken from him when McLeay enlarged his space. An equivalent in nearly value was given him in exchange at Seven Hills. This Meurant was the first person married in the first Wesleyan Church here and he started the first Sunday School (in his kitchen) in Parramatta—History interests you, so I tell it. Now I must end. Again with thanks and *no forgettings*.

To Frank Dalby Davison
Mr. F. D. Davison
The President of the F.A.W.
Dear Sir,

Kings Cross
25 March 1937

I wish to express my deep gratitude for & my appreciation of the kindness shown me in the dinner held to celebrate the honour[3] conferred on me by the King, and in the fact that old & dear friends were asked to come to speak. The honour, being restricted to an order of forty only for the whole Empire is greater for that; that N.S.W. has six out of that forty is also matter for satisfaction.

To the Fellowship of Australian Writers & its Executive I again tender my thanks & repeat what I said last night that the best thanks are found in service. Yours sincerely,

To Frank Dalby Davison

Dear Frank,

Kings Cross
26 March 1937

Thank you. The one grief is always that my own people are not at hand on such occasions as the other night. But this time more than

---

[1] Alexander McLeay.
[2] In an article in the *Daily Advertiser* (Wagga Wagga), 4 July 1933, entitled 'The Beatties of Brooklyn', Mary wrote

> My uncle, Alfred, who died in May, was the youngest of six sons and six daughters. Eleven of these are gone and the only one left is William Hugh Beattie, now at Cheltenham, whose wife is the eldest daughter of the late Louis Meurant. And Louis Meurant's father, Ferdinand Napoleon, owned as his first Australian possession, what is now Hyde Park for which the then Government gave him the lands held so long at Pennant Hills [not Seven Hills]. and where I believe the remnants of the old family residence still stand.

[3] The award of Dame of the British Empire. See letters 2 and 18 February 1937.

at any other I had old & loved friends about me. (Had we known it Matt Charlton[1] wd. have come—the three ex-Labor Prime Ministers). I have just been writing W.M.H.[2] that while all the others being present, their words died on air, his, he being absent, live to be Mitchell Libraried or heirloomed as the case may be.

Again thank you. Thank you for what you did & for what you said. I told Harry Julius it wd. be a good time to die: I wd. have such a fine funeral! Yours sincerely,

I had forgotten the D.B.E.s were restricted to 40 for the whole Empire. The Order of the Bath is the coveted one, being also restricted to 300[3] I think. I was told by someone (not official) it was expected years ago only Clara Butt lived past her crisis. It seems horrible to think of it that way. It makes me feel a bit like 'blood on the bearskin'. But the closing does double & treble the value of the honour. Forty for the Empire & N.S.W. has six. That is big for N.S.W.

To Vance Palmer

Dear Vance,

Kings Cross
5 May 1937

A beautiful thing! Moving, powerful, sane. The action is absolute in completeness. It puts you where you ought to be.

Of course you know I am writing about 'Legend for Sanderson'.[4]

I hope Aileen[5] keeps well. What a time! What a world of schemers eating up the small! Death slavering at every door, as no one power lifting its voice or its hand to say Nay. Death itself is not so bad; it is the time-serving and the hypocrisy that is so degrading. No hope there!—but what a note of hope which is the child name of fulfilment, in your story ending. My love to you all,

To Miles Franklin

Dear Miles Franklin,

Kings Cross
17 June 1937

What stuff! It is the stars and the tears of man!

I have just run through the M.S.[6] which came this morning, and

---

[1] Matthew Charlton.
[2] William Morris Hughes.
[3] There are various categories of the Order of the Bath. Mary seems to have only a limited knowledge of these Orders.
[4] Vance Palmer's new book published that year by Angus & Robertson.
[5] His daughter.
[6] This letter, and some which follow, deal with the poetry of 'E' (Mary E. Fullerton).

it is either you, a priest, or a nun. And yet perhaps not any of these. There are the affinities—Emily Dickinson[1] a little too much—, but what pain, what vision; and what a self-determined hope! The work belongs to the group that includes Shaw Neilson[2] here, Housman[3] and Emily Dickinson overseas. The 'belonging' is innate and *not* intentional—except that Emily Dickinson is too much paralleled in mode in some of the smaller things.

I give you greeting for your find, whoever it is. I have put in some notes on slips. I could have put in a hundred in appreciation and wonder.

The work wants strong editing, both for inclusion in a final count, and for form. There are places where the whip crack ending needs modification, as too many such kill the effect of the better.

I am writing at once, and will post back the MS tomorrow or as soon as I can.

Again my Hail! and also to the writer. The gift is there.

To A. H. Chisholm

Kings Cross
14 July 1937

Dear Alec—otherwise A.H.C.—

If it had been me I couldna ha' been gladder. Indeed I'd sooner it was you because I am a modest person!

It is good to see the younger men in the thorny position of great editorship.[4] And especially now (and from now *on*) when Australia wants her own in blood and in opinion.

Good luck to you! there is no one gladder than I am of your high flight and lofty perch. And when y'are auld and grey, and hoary with the moss of tradition as the editor of a great Daily, peep back through the fallen years and remember one who was glad for you, and whose name was Mary Gilmore.

Am getting typed what will probably be my last book of verse[5]—perhaps the last altogether—unless I have rejuvenation or something!

---

[1] The American poet, 1830-1886.
[2] John Shaw Neilson.
[3] Alfred Edward Housman.
[4] Alec Chisholm had just been appointed Editor of the Melbourne *Argus*.
[5] Mary refers to *Battlefields*, published in 1939, but not her 'last book of verse'. *Fourteen Men* was published in 1954 when she was almost ninety.

To Miles Franklin

Kings Cross
22 October 1937

My dear Stella Miles Franklin (& if I know any more baptismal names I would put-them in: I know some names *not* baptismal I could call you!)—if you have my earlier letter 'with comments', & will send me a copy of it along with the MS.,[1] I'll bend my proud neck to the chariot.

And, my girl, you could have trusted your own judgement without any fear. The eyes that saw what old Danny[2] saw, & the heart & mind that created that old man, have not lost the gift. And the gift is perception: the one great foundation of painting, & writing, & sculpture, & poetry: you couldn't be blind in these things if you tried, though you might lack the skill of form. Not of form in general but of form that leapt to the vision & covered it.

With the letter & the MS. I'll stand to *you*; I think the poet could have stood on hir own feet (or, if you like it better, 'hes'.)

To Hugh McCrae

Kings Cross
18 November 1937

Dear Hewer,

We're gettin fewer
I look back
And cry Alack!
I look forward
And (what's a rhyme for forward?)
And when I come
On the good paper
I've saved for
Special occasions
I use it up
As now
(Which, if free verse,
Might have been worse)
In case it's left behind me
And I've never
Had (another line)
The pleasure of its use myself.
This is the kind of thing
I've wanted to write all my life
And been too cribbed and cabined to do it.

[1] See note on 'E' to letter, 17 June 1937.
[2] Danny Delacy of Miles Franklin's *All That Swagger*, 1936. Danny and his wife Johanna, immigrants from Ireland, are the first of four generations represented in Miles Franklin's novel.

My dear, how are you? What a curious thing belonging to a time is: it isn't blood, it isn't association, it isn't equality of years, of outlook, of work, and yet how it holds!

I haven't seen Bill[1] since he went to Gallagher's and yet now that he is gone I feel as if I had had my ribs torn apart. It isn't a case of tears, I have shed none; it is a feeling of cavity, of loss and a blank wall. The clan breaks and we weep the clan.

Perhaps after all the clan is life, & those who have most life most feel with & for & in the clan.

I had to write an ode for the Women's Book for the 150th Anniversary. The meaning & aim is good enough but the stuff itself is pretty awful. I just 'jouked' it out at the last minute, not being any good at writing to order and it looks like being written to order.

How are you? And Nancy[2] & the descending clan? I always envy you the descendants. I see them with the inner eye every time I see you; see them going walks, & dressed for Sunday & all the rest of it; the mind asking what? what? what? as to each one of the future; will they be Statesmen (or women), painters, poets, travellers, or just plain nice people.

That's me, my dear, the real me, and only some people know it.

To T. Inglis Moore

Dear Tom,

Kings Cross
19 November 1937

If ever there was one foolish in this world!! But first: Of course use anything you like from my letter. I am honoured both by your wish, the use for which you want to quote, and the company, M.S. and other, in which I go.

Dear man, if I had ever called myself a poet and not a verse-writer you might have worried. But I know the difference between poetry and verse just as well as you do. I have never, in writing, reached after the clothing—the jewelled or the silken words that are poetry. My house of words is a sawn timber house. It is neither a bower, a mansion, nor a battlement—all of which are poetry in its several forms. But I do rise above jingle in a sense of turning vowel sound, and, when I have time to do it, consonantal values. Usually I have not had time, and the dishes have been left to clatter on the literary shelf—or the literary dishes have been left, if that conveys it better.

In any case, Tom, you did say that I had written poetry as well

[1] William Gilmore, Mary's son.
[2] Hugh McCrae's wife.

as verse. What I did wonder at was that you did not mention Ada Cambridge, if only for her 'De Profundis'. Ada Cambridge was a great woman, a mighty among pigmies, I mean as a woman of power, intellect and feeling, and I realize that I would have died lonely if I had not once met her.

In regard to the place you gave Dulcie Deamer, knowing her reputation and the subject of the poem, could you resist it? As to poets and verse writers: when editing the Woman's page of 'The Worker', again and again, Rod Quinn and R. J. Cassidy berated me because I always spoke of myself as a verse-writer, saying it was 'an insult to them' that I did so. Also both used to berate me for publishing 'that rubbish'—that 'rubbish' being Shaw Neilson. They used to say 'no one could call *that* poetry who knew what poetry was . . . Why! The lines were not equal even!' Two great things I have done in my life. One is that I published Shaw Neilson in the face of Arthur Adams, Bert Stevens, The Worker Editor (Mr. Boote), Rod Quinn and R. J. Cassidy, and (2) that I said to her father, when he hoped for my recommendation, that Christina Stead[1] would never make a social writer. As to Shaw Neilson I have never read him unwrung. And, while I think of it, I remember why I chose 'wild' instead of 'warm' for the change in 'Love's Coming'.[2] It was the vowel—fall—warm—too near. I had reason; but vision would have been better. And now I have repented!

Just had the loveliest letter from a man: 'Now: I have taken liberties. I showed your letter to a friend who has taught me more about Wagga Wagga than I ever learned when there. May I bring him? . . . I only wish we could drive up with a buggy and pair'. A buggy and pair! I nearly smell the horses and the dust. I nearly weep for remembrance—in the quickness of remembrance.

Just remembered I have the MS. ready for my next book of verse.[3] Perhaps it would be well for you to see it before you finish your article. A lot of it has been in print in one paper and another.

---

[1] See letter, 22 September 1936.
[2] J. Shaw Neilson's lovely lyric 'Love's Coming'. Mary's claim to have changed the word 'warm' to 'wild' in the following verse is difficult to substantiate.

> Quietly as tears fall
> On a wild sin,
> Softly as griefs call
> In a violin.

[3] *Battlefields*, published in 1939.

To Miles Franklin

Dear Miles Franklin,

Kings Cross
17 January 1938

I had my matt proof of the article on your poet[1] this morning, corrected it, & registered it away by 10 a.m. (It is now 11.). I had been downhearted over it, thinking it was below level, unworthy of the poet & unworthy of my own best work. But I am delighted to find it is better than I feared. It really will do. I am struck more than ever—or as sharply as ever—by the arrow-point clearness of the work, The Selections I made are as good as those you had. That two uncollaborating people should choose, & choose examples throughout of equal outstanding distinction, is remarkable. But what a tribute to the writer!

But I must tell you that, as I read, it flashed through me, this time with the keenness of certainty, who the writer is. My blessing rest upon h—. I do not complete the sound lest even a thought on the air break the secret you want preserved till you tell it yourself.

The article will be out in Feb. It was held up to let the Brennan one go first. I believe it will stand, even with the Brennan article[2] & its Professor author. For your sake & the sake of the subject I pray it may!

To Miles Franklin

Dear Miles Franklin,

Kings Cross
31 January 1938

Just had an enthusiastic & appreciative letter from T. Inglis Moore on my article on your poet discovery.[3] He says: 'on your selections Great Stuff!!! Emily Dickinson herself couldn't have bettered those last 2 lines—& much of the thought, the reach outward & inward, & the *fresh* simple phrasing is very like Emily . . . I'd love to see the MS. if possible. Is there any chance?' I wrote that you were only too anxious for publicity & that perhaps he might do an article for London, in which case there would be no bar to quotation as there would be here (you & I being in the field) and that he would have the whole range of the work to choose from.

Is that not so? If so you might call & see Tom & the sooner the

---

[1] Mary E. Fullerton ('E'). See letter, 17 June 1937. The article was 'Poetry: And An Australian Poet', *Australian National Review*, February 1938, pp. 36-42.

[2] A. R. Chisholm's 'Prolegomena for a Study of C. J. Brennan', *Australian National Review*, January 1938, pp. 48-55.

[3] Mary E. Fullerton ('E'). See letter, 17 June 1937.

better. Fires of appreciation are best not let die right down if you want the good aromas to rise.

Heart terribly tired. But my husband's brother[1] who is 81, & who has always had some grumble, Will says, has just been riding & breaking a young horse. So I've *married into* a good family for life!

Good wishes—& bless the poet!

Hitherto I've been Australia's most considered woman poet; I won't be after this one comes out.

To W. G. Cousins

Dear Mr Cousins,

Kings Cross
19 March 1938

On the largest sheet of paper I possess I wish to say I accept (through you) the Broadcasting Commission's offer of £10.10.0 for Mr Tal Ordell to read my book 'Old Days: Old Ways'. My landlord has just raised my rent 3/- a week and I saw my homeless feet wandering the streets looking for a new location. This means they can stay at home here for another year; and in the state of the world today that looks like a long time!

I am grateful to you for entertaining the offer, for I know you could have refused, had you so chosen. It means publicity for me in a greater degree than you are in need of, and in that the kindness lies. Yours sincerely,

To Lionel Lindsay

Dear Lionel,

Kings Cross
8 April 1938

The years give kinder leave than ever youth could give for use of the name—I want to say what a pleasure, what a happiness it was to be your fellow as guest yesterday. While ever the day of causes exists there will be life. I who have lived for causes all my life know that. The Celt & the Latin are one in this. The strength of battle is in their bones. But mechanics have taken battle from the hand bound by the rule of chivalry, & has made it a mass monster, so that we now have to say not even *combat*, but *contest*, for a right word. (This is in continuance of yesterday's use of the word).

But what a grief for the De Baezas[2] that the young lad should

[1] Samuel Gilmore.
[2] A Spanish diplomatic family, in Sydney at the time of the Spanish Civil War.

have to go. Too young to face the demoralizing life of the trenches: though in the scattered fighting of the guerilla, adventure can make life clean. Mass has no room to be clean. In Patagonia[1] I knew a young Spaniard who shot himself rather than face it—mass life in war: the undeclared war then breaking out between the Argentine & Chile.

I am up to my eyes in the clan Cameron[2] revally—rally. We want to save the old Lochiel lands & the castle (Achnacarry) in perpetuity for the chief & the Clan. And we want all the other clans to follow suit, & in the end rehabilitate Scotland, but especially the Highlands.

My kindest word to your wife.

To R. D. FitzGerald

Kings Cross
9 April 1938

Dear Mr. FitzGerald,

You have written the one great poem[3] in and for Australia—the very first. I have just been through it and felt the luminosity through the cloud; for it is not easy reading. It is too big, too wide, too deep, and too sensitive in its thought to be easy. You have rent the veil and gone out into the light, where the rest of us have stayed indoors in little boxes—form mastered, instead of form being but the garment trailing behind us. You have it trailing from your shoulders, we have it wrapped round our heads and look out from it.

In everything else the world has given Australia; this is something Australia gives the world.

I cannot write more, as a visitor has come in and this is interrupted—But the visitor can wait while I say that your Uncle, J. Le Gay B., always thought you outstanding.

Thank God for something real at last. Yours sincerely,

To R. D. FitzGerald

Kings Cross
27 April 1938

Dear *Bob*—after your letter you've got to be Bob—Don't worry about writing little (except that one remains unexpressed perhaps and could express). To have written that one poem is to have done more than Daley and Quinn and Brady and Dorothea Mackellar and all the rest

---

[1] See note to letter, 5 August 1896.
[2] Mary was born Mary Jean Cameron.
[3] Mary refers to 'Essay on Memory', published in *Sydney Morning Herald*, 9 April 1938.

of us of a like ilk have done altogether. Do you know whom I put with you? A. G. Stephens. Only he had the same breadth. He was a mine and a mountain and so are you. The rest of us are just *shops*. All the toys in the windows and only the same kind in the *boxes*. One poem to date great writing from—great as the future may be or greater—is worth all the little no-daters, no matter how good or many

Your handwriting is small and tight where his is large and loose, but there is a curious likeness to Shaw Neilson's! I am interested in everything that appertains to race. There is a root key (or a key root?) somewhere if one could find it.

Probably it goes back to the hormone.

Where others have written the occasion you have written the timeless; and only the timeless marks a period—a start—an era—or an age. As to A.G.S.: the mountain only brought forward small blossoms but they showed the mountain.

To A. H. Chisholm

My dear Alec,
Kings Cross
6 May 1938

So long the intention, so slow the hand to do, and so short the years as they fill and overfill with life's accumulations of things to do, and things that cannot be left! So, though I have thought of you millions of times, letters have remained unwritten. Now you are in London. Will you go one day to Australia House and ask for John Cameron who was Diplomatic Representative two or three years ago at Danzig and who has a sister called Mary Gilmore?

Yesterday your Donald Charles Cameron and I talked here a lot about you and as we talked I said, 'He, too, is one of the lovable ones', and, hours after he had gone, I remembered that you had called him that to me. So I wrote and told him you had said it of him, and that when he wrote to you, as I hoped he would, would he give you my love.

Sir Donald is curiously like my father in ways, and my brother George, who was almost a double in appearance of the great Lochiel, and from whom father was descended. Last night he Sir Donald came, Clan Cameron 'Chief for Australia and her dependencies as appointed by Lochiel', and spoke to the newly formed N.S.W. branch of the Cameron Clan, and gave it a soul. And if any man ever looked a chief he did. The N.S.W. President, Col. Claude Cameron, was taller, but he only looked a withy-wand beside the other man. The magnetism of generations was behind the one, and only the pedigree behind the other. It is a curious thing how that blossom of inheritance only comes to some. Father and his father and all his uncles had it. But it is less in the descendants. Sometimes I feel as if my hand is almost on the key to the enigma, and then it escapes.

I hope you will be able to stand the cold of the North lands. And I do hope that if you go to the U.S.A. (and that seems more like your field,) you will get to Ole Virginny where there is a strong body of Camerons—there since God knows when, and still Cameron and still Highland. Also when you see Lady Game,[1] as you will, say she is not forgotten here, and that I know I owe her a letter a long time. But my eyes have been a trouble. There is a new Labor (Lang) Weekly to come out and talk of a Smith's Weekly Magazine. Don't let Deirdre[2] forget she once loved my verse, and that you wrote me a foreword—My dear that's all—

To Lionel Lindsay

Kings Cross
14 May 1938

Dear Lionel,

I wrote my people that you had said you wanted to give me something of yours, & I wrote that if it were only a bit of a broken frame I would treasure it. And that is fact. No, I have no choice. It is the fact that it is yours & came from you that matters.

It is good to have lived. To have known the people I have known is life. Nothing else seems to matter, yet it is hard to learn to be quiet . . .

I went to the Ashton exhibition and saw Howard's mother[3] painted as she was when I knew her half a century ago; curious how the heart can be wrung by a bit of paint!

To return: Send me anything, Because 'He nothing did or mean' whatever he did. My heart is hot with its thanks.

The sun be on you all.

I forgot to tell you that the Cwlth. Lit. Committee has granted me a year's Fellowship to collect my biographical material.

It was Mr. Curtin's[4] nomination. It will be a wandering collection, full of other people's sayings and doings. But others are my life, not me. Also I am hoping to have my family down this or next month, all being well.

[1] Wife of Sir Philip Game.
[2] Daughter of A. H. Chisholm.
[3] Mary Ann Pugh, Julian Ashton's mother.
[4] John Curtin

To Nettie Palmer

Dear Nettie,

Kings Cross
20 June 1938

I hope you are quite strong again. Miss Caton came here, and I met her again at Sra. de Baeza's[1] reception. I find that the people who come here do not talk with *power*, they are too routine; so they do not make much stir. However, Sydney has a very able pair in the Consul Gen. for *China* and his wife, and the myriads of China loom larger than Fascism and the Spaniards. Moreover Sydney is very Anglican and that means Papal and Franco. One State Church buttresses another when both have political power. The Church of England as a parallel is Franco. The Church of Scotland, a state church without political power, is Catalonia—is Madrid. The C. of E. has come out for Franco, the C. of Scotland has not. One can fight politics, but politics and Church, where one buttresses another, is another matter. Senor de Baeza tells me he has better news from Paris than from papers here. But I can see that he is weighed down by uncertainty and anxiety. Such nice, such sincere, such high principled people! They have a boy and a girl. The boy is 17 and must go. 'We cannot keep him' his mother said 'when others over there of the same age are fighting!'—He is just a boy, young, and slender and small for his years. 'He is mad to go' said his father. 'We cannot keep him'. But when I last spoke to him of it, and was he still determined to go, his chin quivered as he said yes.

My letter must be short as my eyes do not now stand much. 'Wonderful sight for your age', 'Perfectly healthy eyes' say the specialists, but the glasses are badly made and badly set, and so I have had 10 pairs in two years, only one of which I have worn more than a day. Now I am back on my six years old ones—Love

To Lionel Lindsay

Dearest & Dear Lionel,

Kings Cross
4 August 1938

What a surprise. Just come; & I can hardly hold the pen with excitement.
When I look at 'The Dancer'[2] I feel of all things I ever wanted in the world!' and when I look at the other[3] I think 'O God! What

[1] See note to letter, 8 April 1938.
[2] An etching by Norman Lindsay, published in *Art in Australia*, 1, 9 (1921), plate 33.
[3] A second, and unidentified, drawing or painting.

a possession!' All the hungers of my life for art fed at last. These things hold light & light holds all colour all line all movement.

I look back, as I once wrote Hugh McCrae, to the years of standing afar off looking from the distance at those I much wanted to know, and never hoped to know except from a distance, and they were Hugh McCrae & the Lindsays. I was so small compared with them; my work so scattered in kind & quality: the skirmishing, skirmished, scrapings & scraps of poverty so great I dared not go about for fear it would be known: and how I ached to be, not a stranger, but one amongst these. Now it has come to me before the end. First Hugh & now you. I need no more write 'I am as one looking out of a house,
Knowing the empty rooms'.

How many times I have looked at 'The Dancer' when shown, that miracle of drawing, of action, of space, of detail, of pride (*those proud feet!*)—I have not words. Actually as I write I have only tears.

I must post this at once or I will never dare to send it.—It says too much. But I kiss the hands of the giver and I kneel to the maker,—maker in the infinite & not the imprisoned sense.

Because we are one with Spain & because of the Spaniard somewhere in both of us . . .

To R. D. FitzGerald

Kings Cross
Dear Mr. FitzGerald, 7 August 1938

What a hand and what an eye! I have just been writing to Mr. Farmer Whyte to congratulate him on 'Miss Mary Ann Bell',[1] and how *rich* it is. No skeleton there, with a few pretty rags of rhythm and phrases hung on it! I have just told Mr. Whyte it is 'a good strong hedge, where others have only a (mostly merely) little flower in a pot—me among the number'—or words to that effect . . .

Again, and again, and again let me congratulate you—and us on having you.

To Nettie Palmer

Kings Cross
Dear Nettie, 14 August 1938

Just came across unposted enclosed. The exclamation on Vance will

---

[1] 'Miss Mary Ann Bell' was the title of poem XIII of R. D. FitzGerald's *Moonlight Acre*, 1938.

interest you. Yesterday, I think, or despairingly hope, that I have finished my next book of verse.[1] It is a mixed lot as it will probably be my last book of verse *seriously* published. Some of it was written many years ago, one bit yesterday. Not all of it good, but all of it still a part of my sheaf. The less good wd. seem better, if it were not for the actually better—or, shall I say, totally different? I hope you are quite strong again and that Aileen[2] is still safe and sound. What a fool-governed Empire (unless Chamberlain is moving secretly and underground) we belong to! And what a man W. M. Hughes is! What a vision beyond today!

Louis Esson came to see me some weeks ago. He said his wintering-in-Sydney flat was opposite mine, and, though I told him to come over any time he liked, nary a sign have I seen of him. Not even dangerous as it is at Kings Cross, to wave to him. He told me an astounding thing:— About 1909 I went to Melb., and one day in the gardens near me (shabby and deadly poor) two beautiful girls were standing talking books. Hungry for intellectual converse, but too shy, three times I tried to muster up courage to address these radiant beings. At last, as I feared they were going, I, nearly choked with dread of a snub, spoke. They responded when I gave them my name. They were Hilda Bull[3] and K.S.P.[4] The result was we all had morning tea together.

But, imagine my astonishment, when last month Louis spoke of it, and said how excited the girls were, as I was *the first real writer they had met!!!* It seems unbelievable. But I can still feel the choke of blood in my heart as I tried to bring up courage to speak to *them.* I was so shabby and poor; they were so fresh, fashionable, and up-to-date. I was wearing what was still my best dress—the one that had been my best when I went to South America seven or eight years before.

To return to the world: I don't swear, but all the same what a God-dam world we are living in. What a fertility of evil there will be after all these wars! Wheat, rice, and wine will flourish exceedingly. And we will eat and drink them.

Again I hope you are well and strong with the strength of ten. My love to Vance and the girls and you—

---

[1] *Battlefields,* published 1939.
[2] Nettie Palmer's daughter.
[3] Wife of Louis Esson.
[4] Katharine Susannah Prichard.

J. K. Moir & E. E. Pescott,
Melbourne Bread and Cheese Club

Kings Cross
15 August 1938

Dear Mr Moir and Mr Pescott, too:

This is in answer to both of you, to neither of whom for your last letters have I replied (Not sure of my grammar there!)

I did not reply to Mr Pescott's letter because I wanted to be able to say something definite, and could not because with limited use of my sight I was finishing what will be my next book of verse. Will you let me wait till next week before I say what I can send you? I ask this because I have to see Mr. Cousins this week (A. & R.) about this book, as, if they will not take it I shall have to send it to Robertson and Mullens. (This, of course, is private.) Both Firms are dear to me, but for sale purposes I am better known in Sydney than in Melbourne. On the other hand I really believe Capt. Peters to be the better sales manager. The one thing that is an advantage here is that there is no posting back and forward of proofs, and a sudden recollection in regard to a misplaced comma (and there are millions always) can be seen to here on the spot. You who publish and print will appreciate the position.

About your publications! It would be an honour to be one of them. That goes without saying. My trouble is that there is so much in my life that I have to choose between a mere indexing or 'sales-enumeration' of incidents, or a chapter—unless I can think of something else in a defined way. I have a certain amount of loose stuff set down at one time and another, and I thought of having it collected (it is only a fraction even so, of my life) and typed. I could send you that and let you make your own selection or collection adding what you wanted for completion. That might give you what you want.

You don't know how grateful I am or how warm my heart is to you both for your proposal! Recognition here is our only sure continuance, and what a thing it is to be remembered: not only remembered but to be still a working force when one is gone! This dust is nothing even when alive, it is what one gives the world that matters. That is your feeling, both of you. That is why you publish, not for money reward, but to be a stone in the building that is the nation—a step and a stair to others you will never know. Greater than all the kings is Chaucer, for all the Kings had was the pomp and the funerals! And so in a lesser way with us today—if we are any good at all. This shows how much I want to be one of yours.

I will leave it at that if you will please let me and next week go through all sorts of things for a collection. I have a greeting from your

'Bread and Cheese' Club, and have sent a copy of 'The Tilted Cart'[1] in return. I wrote it in the middle of finalizing 'Hound of the Road' just to show I could write that sort of thing. 'Hound of the R.' was written in three weeks but with years of interval between the two halves. During the second half I wrote The Tilted Cart. All my good wishes to you both

To R. D. FitzGerald

Dear R.D.F.

Kings Cross
17 August 1938

Two things before I forget them. We—the others—when we write take the outside within and reform it, not from itself as itself, but from itself plus us. You go to the object and the object (or objective) remains itself. You are never there, yet you are the recorder and creator.

Then this. 'Mary Ann Bell' in particular. The rest of us are hidebound by regularity—(It was forced on us in our young years by the times) and our regularity is obtrusive. In Mary Ann the regularity is there but always as a surprise. In other words it is fresh, ours is yardstick. Frank Morton, when I had written something irregular (and I do take my natural gaelic ancestral form sometimes) once said 'I wish to God I could break through, but I have written regular metres and forms so much, that now even if I try I cannot write any other way' his meaning being that he had become a cripple to regularity...

I love you because you're doing something for Australia in your work—something that will make the average German, French, English or American reading it say 'Gosh! there's a new note in this!' and by and by it will be said of it 'Yes that is Australia. An Australian wrote it' and *no comparison with Masefield or anyone else.*

To Hugh McCrae

Dearest Hughie,

Kings Cross
16 December 1938

This is just a line before I drop dead of the heat, to say how disappointed I am that my new book[2] is not to be my Christmas card to you, for it does not now come out till next year. *Early* I am *promised.* A. & R.

---

[1] Mary's book of poems, published 1925.
[2] *Battlefields*, published 1939.

are to bring it out, not because I don't love Capt. Peters,[1] because I do! but because here is handy & I love A. & R. too.

May the Lord God have an ice box under my throne in heaven! and don't be deluded by this strong language & this firm hand (more or less firm) into thinking that I am not a sufferer! Still, I retain my weight (some of which I could dispense with) & my immortal soul has to bear its weight as best it can. How are you & how is Nancy?[2] and the little buds of the children? Two tiny things came up to me in the street today to say 'Mummy saw you pass!' and I felt that it was Christmas & childhood the one thing that is immortal.

I wrote Tom I. Moore to thank him for 'Adagio in Blue'[3] & said I still think 'Hugh McCrae' his high water mark. I also told him that of all who have written, Hugh McCrae lives most in his work. Under the story, under the phantasy, you are there, bone & flesh. Your sinews draw the verses to form, & the light in your eye, the hidden heart, & the laughter that is philosophy cover them. Others are mostly moods—moods & emotions. And life has to have the ancient granite & the smell of the hillside in it if it is to be life. And these are in your verse. They are in your drawings too.

I agree with Hartley Grattan[4] that there are only four poets in Australia (you saw it?) Hugh McCrae, Shaw Neilson, O'Dowd & Baylebridge and that's with my love & good wish to you & to Nancy for Christmas.

To Hugh McCrae

Dear Hugh,

Kings Cross
22 December 1938

What a darling! No one has that quality of being astonishingly alive as you have it. Your verses kick up their heels & the click comes over the air. Before they go round the corner of a road they twist a look back & there are two shining whimsical eyes. Not in 'Mimshi'[5] alone,

---

[1] Of Robertson & Mullens Ltd, Melbourne.
[2] McCrae's wife.
[3] T. Inglis Moore's *Adagio in Blue*, published 1938, contained his poem 'Hugh McCrae', p. 56.
[4] This is a reference to Hartley Grattan's article, 'On Australian Literature, 1788-1938', *Australian Quarterly*, vol. X, no. 2, June 1938, pp. 19-33. Her account of it is not quite accurate. On p. 26 Grattan named five poets who, over the previous thirty years, had 'something to say and can say it effectively'. These were Bernard O'Dowd, Furnley Maurice, Christopher Brennan, 'William Baylebridge' and Shaw Neilson. Hugh McCrae was bracketed with Victor Daley as poets 'of the purely decorative variety'. Mary was nowhere mentioned in the article and did not meet Grattan during his term as Carnegie Fellow in Australia 1937-38.
[5] *The Mimshi Maiden*, 1938.

in everything. Capacity for a man's laughter, capacity for a man's pain, & the fun of a rascally boy! Faery & Cavalier & the melancholy Jaques[1] all mixed together. The past & the future fallen into the gap of today. Today is always the gap, for today means bread & bread means money, & money means a business head and you never had that, my dear.

What lunacy has got the Federal Ministry?[2] (And I *like* Archibald Galbraith Cameron, & not alone for his goodly name.) A man came here yesterday & said 'Fascism is so near it may fall on us any day!' I said 'I don't believe it.' He said *'You'll see'* and today I wonder which of us was right.

Did I tell you I have Billy & Dorothy down? Billy's hair is a shade thin on the crown, & every time I see it I feel like someone who has suddenly fallen on his nose. For how can that thin patch belong to *my little boy?* Are your girls still little girls or did they grow up? I mean to you & their mother? Life's funny! We have all the threads of the enigmas at our fingers & we never pick them up. This thin spot on a head, is yesterday, & today & tomorrow, I say it & don't see it.

To Hugh McCrae

Dear Hugh,

Kings Cross
29 December 1938

Of course it is not snobbish! You couldn't be if you tried; and if it were there is that in you so removed from it, that it would make it *not*. But when I think of people like Lady Stonehaven[3] (& others) I think what a centre you & I could have made, separately or on visiting terms, had we had their means to it! Kings & Queens wouldn't have been in it with us! Still we've both done our bit—in your case the Lindsays & the Ashtons will not be the only family of brains generation after generation! Australia owes a debt to the McCraes. They have polished up her front door, not a little, but a whackin' big lot.

I liked your 'Ballerina'. She's still dancing! But your praise of my work bewilders me. It seems incredible. But how life-giving! I know the uncritical like it, but that the critical & such a critic should, is like water to the thirsty, only the water is dew drops too beautiful to be true, and the thirst of unbelief rises up again.

---

[1] The character Jaques in Shakespeare's *As You Like It*. 'The melancholy Jaques grieves at that', II, i.
[2] The 'lunacy' is probably a reference to the debate at the time on compulsory military training. There was a division in Cabinet on the issue. See *Sydney Morning Herald*, 15 October 1938, p. 11.
[3] Ethel Keith Falconer.

Funny how we veer! I used to think Paterson[1] the wonder of the (Australian) age. Then I got past him as one gets past Wordsworth. And now I've gone back to him—though I haven't got back to Wordsworth quite. Strange how we never see-saw over Shakespeare! What a mind! and—

But I'm tired and must go to bed. But for days I have been saying in my mind:

'There is a path which no fowl knoweth, & which the vulture's eye hath not seen'.

Do you know your Bible, boy? That is Job 28, & verse 7.

I have just quoted it to R. D. FitzGerald. What a range that man has! Granite with a thousand eyes!

'There is a path which no fowl knoweth, & which the vulture's eye hath not seen:

'The lion's whelps have not trodden it, nor the fierce lion passed it by.'

Well, some poets have found it, & trodden it, & he is one. You are right about a poet being supreme in his orbit—though these are not your words.

Billy says of my verse; 'There's one thing about it, Mum, it has *no padding!*'

Finally, my brow is on the ground to Huntly's[2] children! God bless 'em. Also the wilful dog. Yours

To R. D. FitzGerald

Dear Robert—

Kings Cross
29 January 1939

If Adam McCay had had more *real* faith in himself what could he not have done! every quotation he makes is the measure of himself, himself left undone and undriven to being.

A week ago T. I. Moore asked me did I think you the greatest poet, so far in Australia. I said, *I do.* Repeating in that what I had said to him a year before. I said 'Brennan was spoken of as greatest, but that Brennan was dated because too mannered; that the mannered loses as the language changes; that Swinburne, on whom I as others became drunk, was a case in point; for he is largely gone except for those who *can* get drunk on him; but that FitzGerald's English would *still* be English when the language had so changed that no one would understand or

---

[1] A. B. 'Banjo' Paterson.
[2] Hugh McCrae's grandmother's maiden name was Georgiana Huntly Gordon. See note to letter, 3 June 1926.

feel or respond to the mannered'. You do not glitter till all is light and there are no dark places; you *shine*; You do not murmur and moan like winds and waves: you *blast*.

It is the root word of the language that shines; it is the root-word that blasts. Out of Job come all the elements, and the language is without clothes.

To return to Tom. I told him you would live because you had the Anglo-Saxon and its directness. That the fault of modern poetry is that it depends on emotion too much; that Brennan (and all the rest of us; me badly among the number) was perishable because of that. (Hothouse poetry is too sappy; the heather and the gorse may be uprooted or ploughed out; but let the plough stop and they cover the hills again.)

All of this is my good hard fist telling you never, never, for the sake of making a book or seeking variety, be less than you are.

My dear Hugh McCrae, though he does not range and indicate world beyond world as you, has done this. He has kept to the Austere in economy of word, and defined form (perfect in its way), and shot any tendency to emotionalize with laughter. This is genius down to its shirt, unhampered by deck houses and electric lights, sailing with sails full set where possible, but under bare poles (and always with the poles whatever the sail) where the inward force is fiercest.

I am a tired old woman, but I can still go crazy at the sight of gorse! and here's the result. Forgive it and do not reply—

The Committee for the Halstead Press *Kings Cross*
Farewell to Mr & Mrs Kirwan *30 January 1939*

Dear Sirs,
I write to thank you formally (as I did informally those I saw at the function on Saturday evening) for inviting me as one of the 'family'. I used to long and long to belong; the 'belonging' came, and has continued ever since it began; though the beginning was not like Saturday evening, when I was joined in the presentation to the gathering with the departmental heads. I cannot tell you how much I felt that, and how grateful I am for all your kindness.

The firm of Angus and Robertson[1] has played such an important part in our history, not only as to literature, but in shaping an Australian feeling for patriotism to this country! Every book sent out has been a brick in that edifice, if it only meant the stirring of one thought, or pride in the addition of one new name. This is patriotism in deeds, not words.

[1] See also notes to letters, 15 March 1932 and 31 January 1951.

It is an honour to belong to such a firm, it is an honour to be noticed by it, and to be published by it. I have felt this—I have felt the character of the Firm ever since I first entered the door nearly fifty years ago in Market Street I think it was, and only second hand books were sold. The shop showed the men that made it—and these were the men who shaped the Firm, and the Firm still follows them. There is an atmosphere in Angus & Robertson's that no other bookshop has; it has an individuality that marks it.

It seems strange perhaps that I should write at such length. But I cannot say two words and be done. I feel this place, and the work its people have done, as so much a part of the better development of Australia that when I begin to write I do not know when to stop. Yet here I do stop.

Again thanking you all—from roof-tree to doorstep—Yours sincerely,

To Julian Ashton

Kings Cross
Dear Mr Ashton, *? June 1939*

In accord with your wish I have written a condensed account of the New Australia venture as we founded it in Australia as an association and then as a Colony in Paraguay, together with some of the causes that led up to it. The record is brief and from memory my full file of leaflets and Journal having been given to the Commonwealth Library many years ago. That file, I may say, includes the New Australia Journal first printed in Wagga and later in Sydney; the Manuscript Cosme Monthly which William Lane, John Lane (his brother), David Russell Stevenson and I in turn produced on a gelatine multigraph pad; and finally the later 'Cosme Monthly' set up on our own printing press in Paraguay. This one became a quarterly in its last years. I mention this file, because I asked Mr. W. A. Woods and Mr Arthur Rae as two of the original Executive Committee, when they went to Canberra, to add their annotations to mine, and make any corrections necessary. This they did. Consequently this collection is of more than ordinary value to students of social experiments such as ours.

As a final word, to you, who have done so much for art and other intellectual cultural needs in Australia, I wish all the success in the world for your book, not only because it is yours, but because it is historical and Australia so much needs the historical mind and the historical collection. In this I am but one of a great company, for all who have known you belong to it. Yours sincerely,

THE NEW AUSTRALIA MOVEMENT

The New Australia Movement began when all Australia for a second time needed a stimulus, as when the affair of the Eureka Stockade catalysed public feeling and opinion, and law was compelled to recognize human standing rather than legal usage which had become legal tyranny. When William Lane landed in Australia from England we had not yet recognized Australia as an entity and with full moral right to self-duration and full self government. Currents of force and opinion everywhere were setting in a thousand directions, all good as showing vitality of thought but all unorganized. Federation, a White Australia, Eight Hours, Unionism as a force were all seventh waves (or leviathans as the seventh wave was still commonly called) in a sea that chopped and tossed to each new wind. To this William Lane came as a man poor in money, but rich in ideas; and in a little while, writing and talking personally, without ostentation, quietly, and even without seeming to do it, as far as the young Labor Movement was concerned he centred the uncentred. Others, even in those years claimed credit that was his, but he certainly gave the initial directional impulse. His was the mind that cleared and made plain the obscure.

His first intention was to make Australia as a whole his field. But the vastness of the continent, which was vaster than its area, because its settlement without connection, was fringing and not central, soon showed him that success would be a Jack-o'-Lantern as to achievement. (His own words.) His general idea given up, at least as far as Australia as a whole was concerned, he next turned his thoughts to the young and growing Trades Union Movement and preached the gospel of the New Unionism, i.e. the political and social as against the older trade and therefore class unionism. But here again he found insufficient verge for all that was needed. Here was 'class' still, and he wished to abolish the fixities of class. 'Class is still caste, no matter where it is found', he said to me later on in discussing the New Australia as a possible thing; and it was the rule of caste and class, and the consequent frictions and injustice arising from these that he wished to do away with.

William Lane believed in humanity, not in the possession of things; and in the fluidity of human life, individual and sectional, rather than in the fixed. 'No one is free who has no time for thought or enjoyment. Leisure is a human necessity', he would say and to him, indeed, leisure was as much a necessity to the individual as law to the community. So the end of his thinking and observation, based on knowledge of an older world, and fired by the freedom he had found in the U.S.A. *'Australia is half-way between England and the U.S.A.'* was the New Australia Movement, which apparently ended in Paraguay.

I say apparently, because the influence of that Movement never quite died out in Australia. It educated even its opponents.

The New Australia Constitution as drawn up by Mr Lane begins as follows:

'An association of *bona fide* workers has been formed to make an earnest effort to put into practical shape the co-operative ownership by the workers of land and machinery, the co-operative conduct by the workers of the industries by which they must live, and the co-operative protection by the workers against the risks which constantly threaten men, women and children with misery and want under existing conditions. It is felt that when such co-operation is shown to be not merely problematic but actually established, public opinion will endorse the social reform which all know to be necessary, but which is now prevented by ignorance, mistrust, and mistaken self interest.

...This association will be recruited in an intelligent population already accustomed to new country; its members will have been generally familiarized through Unionism with self-government; it will be of sufficient size to be almost wholly self-sustaining, to economize labour by systematizing it, and to open up scope for all abilities by specializing industry; in organization it combines the advantage of strong industrial order with the constant supremacy of the whole while socially it leaves each member absolutely unharassed by needless regulations. By the organization of industry it will be able to pen to all Art and Science, now the privilege of a few ... The agent whom the Association despatched to South America reports in the highest terms on the exceptional facilities for such settlements as this to be found in secluded parts of that continent, and that a most liberal concession of over four hundred thousand acres, free of charge, on settlement conditions and to be selected by him, is under offer. Messrs W. Saunders, President of the Australian Labor Federation, and C. Lėck, member of the Central Political Committee, have been sent to prospect this concession ... Those desirous of knowing more of a movement intended to prove, voluntarily and practically that the Co-operative Commonwealth is a commonsense reality, and those who see what is in the future if nothing is done to save Australian workers from old-world conditions are invited to communicate with the offices. More good will be done to the Australian Labor Movement in five years by such a grand object lesson worked out by Australian workers than could be accomplished in fifty years by theorizing and preaching.'

Then followed the basis of organization which was Ownership by the community of all the means of production-in-exchange and distribution. Conduct by the community of all production-in-exchange and distribution. Superintendence by the community of all labour-saving co-operations. Maintenance by the community of children under guardianship of parents. Saving by the community of all capital needed by the community. Division of remaining wealth production among all adult members of the community equally, without regard to sex, age, office or physical or mental capacity.

Further clauses summarized ran:

All authority was to be by ballot of all adult members: regulations affecting the community at large were to be confirmed by a two-thirds majority of all adult members; disputes were to be settled by arbitration; dismissal from the community for persistent or unpardonable offence against the well-being of the community could be decreed only by a five-sixths majority of all adult members; the individuality of every member in thought, religion, speech and leisure, and in all matters whatsoever whereby the individuality of others is not affected was to be held inviolable. The sexes were recognized as equally entitled to full membership.

The three fundamental principles which could not be broken or altered even by a unanimous vote were: (1) Monogamy, (2) Teetotalism, and (3) the Colour line. (It will be remembered that at that time 'a white Australia' was the outstanding Australian aim.)

The enrolment of members was rapid once we began seriously to work. Women paid nothing to join, men paid £60 as a paper minimum for when we thought a man worth while we took less. Needing a ship to trade when trading as a colony would begin, we bought 'The Royal Tar' for £1500, and began to fit her out for the voyage.[1] Also we began gathering in the people for the sailing. As they came to Sydney with their families and their possessions, we housed them in places we rented in Marrickville and Balmain. But the Government so hampered us in every way it could, hoping to deplete our cash resources as well as to disaffect our members, that while it did not succeed in the latter, it certainly did in regard to the former. The result was that we could not pay the baker, and the bailiffs were in for rent. But the landlord and bailiffs were so decent that it was pretended that the men in possession were members of the expedition, and the real members never knew how badly off we were. On top of this came a new exaction from the Government with the result that at a meeting of the Executive at which I was not present, it was decided to sell 'The Royal Tar', give up all idea of settlement, and repatriate everyone from what the ship would bring. When I was told of this, I said No, and that we must go on. 'But we cannot!' Mr Lane exclaimed. 'It is impossible to go on, for there is no money.' 'There will be money' I declared out of what subconscious depth I know not, adding, 'Wait, and see

[1] For additional details of the *Royal Tar*, see notes to letters 5 August 1896 and 26 December 1928. See also Gavin Souter's *A Peculiar People; the Australians in Paraguay*, 1968.

if I am not right.' I asked for a month's delay, then as that was refused for three weeks, then two, and in the end they agreed to a week. So I, who had no idea that I had any personal influence found myself a leader. Next day a large cheque came, and I was regarded almost as a prophetess. After that money rolled in, the ship was victualled, and the first batch of over 200 was ready for sailing. Meanwhile measles had smitten Sydney and our people did not escape. The order went forth from the Health Department that no New Australia child affected was to go on board. But Mrs Kidd, who had two children with measles, and the only two on board, who would neither stay behind nor be separated from her little ones, was a match for all opposition. She had already dressed both children in warm clothes, before she took them aboard, and when she saw the Port Health Officer coming up the gangway, she had ready two thick slices of bread, plastered with raspberry jam, handed one to each child, said 'Bite', and then smeared their spotted faces with the jam. The doctor saw no measles. Mrs Kidd was an able and a nice woman, a friend to many both in Paraguay and in Australia. In later years the family returned to its home town Albury, and I heard that Mr Kidd became Mayor for several terms. Critics who do not expect a Parliament of average and elected people to agree, expected us, with every kind of rebel and intellectual-thinking outlaw, to be meek as lambs. Yet among the people we had was, for instance, Jack Amor, on whose head, dead or alive was a price £1,000.

I think it was he, yet who, with the police hot on his track as he fled, stopped to feed a starving woman and children whom he found stranded in the bush; after that, in face of police and proclamations, rode to the nearest town, and bought enough provisions to last her till her husband who had been three days away after the strayed horses, returned to the camp. Another was poor Larry Petrie, son of a Scottish Writer to the *Signet* in Edinburgh—Larry, who had lost an arm in a Union railway scrimmage, who was tried for blowing a hole in the side of the 'scab labour' later state steamer, 'The Warrego',[1] as she went down in Sydney Harbour in the big '91 strike, and who died in Villarica, Paraguay, with three ribs driven through his lungs saving the station-master's little girl from an incoming train. He could have escaped himself, but he threw himself forward to save the child. In addition there was Louis Simon who, with T. Westwood and another man named White, arranged to capture a Spanish gun-boat that for safety had crept up the River Plate to Asuncion, during the Spanish-American war, and go privateering. Later, Louis Simon had the name of engineering or partly engineering a rising in one of the provinces of Brazil. However, all were not like these. Others less boldly spectacu-

[1] Mary is confusing the ship's name. It was the *Aramac*. The incident occurred on Moreton Bay, not Sydney Harbour.

lar were James Sime who was brother-in-law to the Editor-in-Chief (Walter) of the London Times; William Laurence, who could have made a world name with his beautiful voice, a silver tenor. He married our Nurse, Clara Jones, and when August 1914 came, understated his age, asked for an operation to fit him for the campaign, though the doctors told him of its danger, and died on the table. After him came David Russell Stevenson cousin to R.L.S., and also to Mr Russell French of the Bank of New South Wales, and who in the dark at dawn and evening, used to tie his clothes on the top of his head, and sharks and all, swim across the Harbour from the north side to the New Australia Office at 111 Elizabeth Street because he had not the tuppence needed for the back and forth of the penny ferry. When 1914 came he enlisted in Paraguay in a British unit, got a bullet in his heart on Gallipoli which no Doctor could remove, returned to Paraguay, married Clara Jones, the widow of William Laurence, and lives now between Scotland and the Channel Islands. Then there were H. S. Taylor, medallist of Roseworthy Agricultural College in South Australia, who in after years made his paper at Renmark, 'The Murray Pioneer', a standard of literature as well as the best all-round irrigation paper in the world; Thomas Tudor-Williams, whose half-sister became the Countess of Seafield, and whose hobby was music; William Saunders, ex-President of the Australian Labor Federation, son and grandson of slave-owning planters in California, and who in his last years was a member of the San Francisco Chamber of Commerce, his son being a Legal Adviser to the State of California; Alf Walker, I think from the Sydney 'Daily Telegraph', and who died just after he got a good position (through our James Sime) on the London 'Times'; J. Molesworth, who christened his son Voltaire. Long after Voltaire stood for Parliament in Australia, and was well-known on 'Smith's Weekly'. Yet others were Charles Holman, brother to W. A. Holman; A. K. MacDonald, a huge Scot who had led an exploration party in Central Africa, whose boast was that he had never lost a man there, who had been adviser to King Menelek in Abyssinia, and who after he left New Australia wrote an illustrated descriptive trade book for the Paraguayan Government; A. Brittlebank, reported afterwards as a Labor Member of Parliament in Cape Colony; Nurse Clara Jones, who, before she sailed for Paraguay in 1893, flew the Red Flag over Muttaburra Hospital (Qld) in celebration of a Labor victory in the election of that year. When the horrified Committee hauled it down she ran it up again; again they hauled it down, again it went up, after which she beat dismissal by getting her resignation in before the Committee could speak. Besides these there were John Sibbald, who was wheat-buyer to the West Australian Government during the war; the Birks families of Adelaide, the elder Mrs Birks being sister to Sir Kyffin Thomas, and for twenty years President of the W.C.T.U. in Adelaide. Mrs Birks wrote to me in her later years, as also Mrs Sibbald has done, begging me to write a true account of the New Australia movement, as the wonderful thing it was, since only opponents had written of it, and, she said without regard for truth when it suited them. To continue our list: there was Arthur Greenway, well-known in South Africa; Charles Pope, an Englishman who joined us in Paraguay, and of whom I heard never a syllable after he left New Australia, till, in 1937, I read a book on the Amazon by a Dutch or Belgian writer named Up de Graff. When I had last talked with Mr Pope he told me that he had been with this expedition as interpreter, as he knew French and as well several South American Indian dialects. He said that he had had a wonderful time and that he had been begged to stay on when he decided that he would go no farther. Delighted to find someone who knew French I aired my school-mistress French on him. He looked at me blankly. I tried again with a more defined accent. Mr Pope's face brightened. 'O.' he said with emphasis on the pronoun, 'I only speak Parisian French! That is why I do not understand yours!' Some of our own men going shortly after on a holiday up the Amazon territory, fell in with the Up de Graff expedition and when they returned to Cosme, our village, they said that when Pope would be asked to interpret for some Indian he would meet the case with the gabble of his own invention, and when the Indian would look the equivalent of the Indian Northern 'How?' Charles would turn to his chief and say 'This Indian does not know any of the dialects I speak. He has come from a far-off and little known territory and must be a stray.' So it went on till the party came on someone who knowing Guarini tried Mr Pope out. That was the end of him as interpreter, and also as cook. Mr Up de Graff, in his book, said Charles Pope was the worst cook he had ever seen. He also said some other much more nasty things about him.

No account of those we had with us would be complete without some record of the Lane family. Mrs William Lane was a granddaughter of Professor Errington of Edinburgh, and also a cousin of the great Professor Blackie; John Lane was long a teacher in the Queensland Education Department, and Ernest, the youngest brother, is now a retired Brisbane journalist. William Lane was born in Ireland, and educated at Colston Hall, Bristol. He passed the entrance examination (for Cambridge or Oxford) at so young an age, his sister Gertrude told me, that he was not allowed to enter. Family finances failing he learned typesetting, and at an early age went to Canada, and thence to Detroit. While there he met and married his wife, being only about nineteen I think. Later he decided to come to the new land of Australia, where, he thought the cruelties of the older world would not yet have found a footing. I will never forget with what anguish of spirit he told me that there was nothing new here but the land itself. Then here, as he would have done in any country in which he might have been he began his reform work. His entry into Australia and Australian journalism I have told to others and they have written it, so I need not give it again. But I may say that he refused a highly paid position (and a brilliant and powerful future had he chosen to accept it) for leadership in a poor and derided movement, and the shouldering of its burdens. Offered £20 salary a week on the then 'Daily Telegraph', together with the right of private work as well, he refused it and remained on at £3 a week on the little Queensland paper, which, he told me, was actually as near and as dear to him as his life. There he wrote 'The Working Man's Paradise', the story of what we were doing then, and in which, if I may be pardoned for saying so (others have written it) I was Nellie. In addition he founded the New Australia Movement, influenced all liberalized thought of the time in Australia, was the friend of the Judiciary, whose police, if they could have caught him out would have gaoled him; and gave Henry Lawson work and an ideal of mateship when he most needed it. 'The Cambaroora Star' was written about Lane and his paper and quite a number of the lines in it are Lane's. More than this, William Lane was No 1 during the great Shearers' strike of the '90's, and was the 'uncrowned king of Queensland', for whom 10,000 armed and mounted men would have risen as it were out of the grass all over Australia had he chosen to give the word. 'Why not give it' I asked, not realizing what a cruel thing a revolution could be. 'No', he said. 'Revolutions only put the same kind of men on top again that they pull down.' And in this connection I may say that 10,000 men faithful to their leaders, in those days of mobility and scattered populations, when there were neither high explosives, aeroplanes nor wireless, would have equalled an army of three times their size today. If a rising had been agreed to, and many wanted it, it would have been a shed burning guerrilla war. 'Guerrilla war' and 'Guerrillas' were words often in use just then. Yet with all this William Lane never ceased to be emphatically an Empire man, so that there was nothing strange in that, in the after years, he raised in New Zealand a troop of mounted men for the 1914 war and died Editor-in-Chief of the 'Auckland Herald'. All his life he held the belief that it was the mission of the Teutonic peoples (especially of the English branch) to rule the world. Even in deciding to settle the New Australia colony in Paraguay he never lost sight of this idea, his intention, known only to me and to W. G. Spence, being to raise the British flag there, when, as he hoped, our numbers would justify such action. Because England and Germany were so closely allied in blood and thought at that time, we could have counted on the German population of Matto Grosso, where even the negroes spoke German, and thence on by fighting or by negotiation to British Guiana on the coast. At least that was the plan. Bolivia, being nearer, was also thought of, but was dismissed because, if we took it, Mr Lane said, it would be of greater advantage to the USA than to England. He never used the name Great Britain, but always England, Scotland and Ireland, being Celtic and not Teutonic racially...

I have been asked, again and again, why we went to South America, and why we did not settle in Australia. The answer is easy. Neither Australia, New Zealand, nor Tasmania would give us even a foot of land. The nearest approach to an offer came subterraneously from certain big squatters, the Government secretly assenting was that we might have an area in what was then called 'the Wilcannia Desert' provided that we undertook to put a certain number of voters on the area in a certain number of years, and who would vote for a water-supply scheme that would make the surrounding station-owners millionaires. I was for accepting even that offer, as I hoped that by staying in Australia we would, in time win over the whole continent. Mr Lane, however, said 'No', adding that, inhospitable as the location was, it was a bribe, and he would have nothing to do with a bribe. After his refusal no other movement toward keeping us in Australia was made. So our 'prospectors', Messrs William Saunders, Charles Leck, and Alfred Walker, the Sydney journalist, were sent to South America.

The Spaniards, perhaps as a side inheritance from the Romans, understand colonization as no other race does. We were immediately offered, free, all the land we wanted, by the governments of the Argentine, Brazil (which of course was Portuguese) Chile, Bolivia, and Paraguay. This was not because of our excellence, but a matter of national foresight, for all these Republics in those sparse years gave free land for settlement to any immigrant nationality desiring it. So there were French, German, Welsh, Jewish, Russian, Italian and other colonies, each speaking its own language, publishing its own newspaper if it wished and had the money to do it, and each provided it kept the State laws, run self-governed. Consequently when we settled in Paraguay we spoke our own language, and had our own school. I followed John Lane as teacher when I went to the colony, which was after the break had come between the two parts. Like others we published our own Monthly journal. As far as I know, we were the only English-speaking community-settlement in South America, and though we were in a country which recognized only the Catholic religion, we had our own colony non-Catholic marriage service written by William Lane and published in the 'Cosme Monthly'. This was accepted as official by the Government, whoever was our Chairman at the time being gazetted as Registrar. No Protestant clergyman ever came to the country because there were almost no Protestants to minister to, but I believe that about eight years later one did come for a time.

There were two separate and separated settlements formed by

the New Australia people. This was the result of division over principles. As I have already mentioned, the sailing ship we had bought for our own use was 'The Royal Tar', one of the finest little barques ever built in Australia. She made two voyages. For the first she left Sydney on 12 July 1893, with, I think, 200 people, and arrived at Monte Video on the 12 September following, taking 57 days from port to port. For the second voyage with almost as many people she left Australia on 1 January 1894, arriving at Monte Video on 4 February a period of 53 days, or four less than the first trip. No special trouble broke out at sea, but the first shipment landing at Monte Video prior to transhipping up the River Plate for Paraguay, a number of men not only got drunk ashore, but they brought drink aboard, thus breaking one of the three unalterable laws without which no one could remain a member, and on the breaking of which expulsion automatically followed. The trouble this caused simmered all the thousand miles up the River Plate and during the early days of settling on the four hundred thousand acres of rivered land which had been granted us by the Paraguayan Government. More than that, some of the offenders began bartering things with the local Paraguayans, and they did this knowing that one of the clauses under which we held the land free, had all our furniture, etc, transported at the cost of the Government, and all our imports to come in free of Customs duty for ten years, was that we would not indulge in barter and so defraud the Customs—or help the inhabitants of the country to do it. The end was that certain persons were expelled and their sympathizers went with them. The three persons expelled were Louis Simon, T. A. Westwood and Fred White. Twenty-seven other men elected to go out with these three, and those who were married took their dependants with them. We paid them according to the number of children they had, the sum total being nearly twelve thousand dollars cash. More than this, the number of those who decided to remain on the settlement argued that we should make members of the Paraguayans and that the regulations under which they had joined in Australia were no longer necessary now that we were in Paraguay. To this Mr Lane would not agree, and the 'Split' occurred. Those who held by the original rules left the free land, and by giving up everything saleable, even to the women's wedding rings and the men's watches, we paid a deposit on what was roughly five leagues of land. Yet even here the Government stood to us. After three years, seeing the wonderful progress we made, the Government made us a full grant, subject to certain settlement clauses. The grant was for six leagues or roughly 16,000 acres . . . There were such complaints from the near-by Paraguayan people about the other colony which had at once given up Socialism as a colony basis—there being theft, brawls, drunkenness, and even worse—that the Government stepped

Mary E. Fullerton

Miles Franklin

R.G. Howarth

Colin Simpson

Mary wrote in 1940: 'This is the first Battle Cry written and set to music in Australia. It is based on an aboriginal corroboree theme which I heard on the Bland in 1872. The boomerang is Australian. It is a weapon of war and it returns. My thanks are greatly due to Mme Evelyn Grieg for arranging the setting for me and helping place it before those for whom it was written: The Fighting Forces of Australia.' (Education Gazette, 1 January 1941)

in, sent out a surveyor and assessor and subdivided the land. When the more reputable members of that settlement used to come to visit us, they said we lived in luxury compared with the way they lived. Yet indeed we were poor enough at that time. In the end we were known to South America as 'The Saints', and the non-Socialist colony as 'the Sinners'.

And now as to why we in Cosme failed. First, we were really too few to work the land as it should have been worked, and we had no capital to buy sufficient machinery. Everything that could be made by hand and made from timber in our own forest was so made. However we built the first fireplace and chimney in Paraguay, made the first corrugated iron tank in all South America, still called the Australian tank, taught along with our recalcitrant ones the Australian method of sheep-shearing first with blades and then as they were introduced with machines, and through my recollections of how when I was a child the Australian aborigines caused wattle-seed to germinate quickly, we, for the first time since the expulsion of the Jesuits over a hundred years before, successfully germinated mate seed. This has meant millions of dollars in trade to South America. I may say that, in fourteen years Cosme had no death from disease, not even when bubonic plague and small pox ran through the country; and in that time no policeman had to come except as someone's guest.

Again as to why Cosme failed.

The law of life is movement. The circumscribed dies. Exodus is as necessary anywhere there is life, as ingress. We were the only British colony of our kind in the world. There was no other similar place with which we could have reciprocity or exchange. So, when the human cry came for change of scene, the desire for new faces, from the need of food that we could not supply, or even for another kind of girl or man to marry (for not all is affinity that is adjacent) when, I say, these things happened, and natural frictions aggravated them, there was no similar colony to go to. There was only the alien world, which was still by earlier custom the familiar world. And so the drift away began. And yet the world today, even of Australia, approaches what we advocated, and in a degree that to me is sometimes almost incredible. Even in the matter of national or community barter, which is the one thing that will release Governments from being the servants of the accumulated dollar and the all-powerful pound, even in this the world begins to do what we of New Australia proposed as human. Abraham Lincoln, William Lane's hero, and for whom he called his eldest boy Charles Lincoln Lane, gave us the ideal by which we hoped to live as an abiding community, and that was 'Government of the people by the people for the people'. But we were ahead of our time. On that note I end.

To George Mackaness

Dear George,

Kings Cross
2 June 1939

Would you like me to tell you who it was for whom Dr. Lang[1] had the church-bell rung while he read (under that cover) his banns of marriage?

In the beginning of time in Australia, when there were only two classes of people, the free and the bond, here, a certain Scot who had money came out and took up land at—(I won't write it). Riding over his domain one day he came across a beautiful woman sitting under a tree drying her hair and reading a book. It was love at first sight on his part and he made an excuse to speak. The final outcome was that he bought her off her husband for a bullock dray and six bullocks. He sent her to Sydney and came back with a 'wife'. Either three, four, or five children were born (I forget now what father said, but it was a number) and the real husband either died or was killed. So a marriage at last could take place. Mr. Mac went to Dr. Lang—and you know how that great old man arranged for the secret of this well-known family to be kept, when years after Mr. Mac died, his will puzzled those who knew of it, for it named all the *elder* children for their respective inheritances, and did not do so with the *younger* ones. The *naming* precluded any claims against them by the younger and legitimate heirs. Dr. Lang never told, but there were Highlanders in the congregation who knew *the Gaelic*. The banns were in part in Gaelic, so that the ringing of the bell hid the clearness of those words from those who did not know it. Dr. Lang got the promise of those who did know it not to tell it. But Grandfather Cameron was one of them. I think there were only two or three recognized the gaelic forms of the names. I think I am the only person left who knows who this Mac was.

And now, I forgot to tell you I am on the first proofs of 'Battlefields' (verse), Angus and Robertson are doing it for me.

To Hugh McCrae

Kings Cross
30 June 1939

All that before I can burst out with 'What a darling thing!' and how essentially Hughie!

---

[1] John Dunmore Lang. The story in this letter is a winsome thing, typical of Mary's sentimental heart, but, of course, incapable of verification or identification. And, equally of course, needing neither!

I was writing to Mr. Menzies[1] on his remark about prestige & its need of honest pride—(a variation of what he said) & I cut your word Bombs out & enclosed it headed, 'Another good Scot!'

I am a Labor woman ever since there was a Labor section to belong to, but there are things that Menzies says that make me say in my heart 'Here is a man one could follow!' & I have never even begun to think it of any other leader outside my own side: *side* as a whole, not as to individuals always.

But O Hughie—some writing is hydromel,[2] and the Holy Grail is a thing to follow, keep on at it. My love to you all including the ink & paper.

My poor book promised for Sep. 1938, Oct. Dec. Feb. 1939, Easter is still God knows how far off yet. The tears of age are bitter, & I have wept them.

This paper is to be excused for its colour. It is 15 years old. Was stored at Goulburn since 1923 & only a while ago recovered along with *what* forgotten things.

In the grave one will forget like that, so that heart break will not matter. But I can't imagine forgetting an unpublished book, even there.

To Miles Franklin

Dear Miles Franklin,

Kings Cross
8 July 1939

(With the Stella still shining), I want to congratulate you (& Dymphna Cusack) on 'Pioneers on Parade'.[3] There is not a dull line in it, & there are some lovely terms of speech. I could only gallop through it because of my eyes. But 'life' in a book is felt and 'life' bubbles in it: the first written champagne we have had. Except that Winifred Birkett's 'Three Goats on a Bender'[4] is first, and that is Sauterne. Some ass in today's 'Sun' vents spleen instead of writing criticism. But what you will say is 'Let the galled jade wince', and some of 'em will.

---

[1] R. G. Menzies became Prime Minister of Australia on 4 May 1939 Mary is probably referring to a radio broadcast made by him.
[2] Spineless.
[3] *Pioneers on Parade*, 1939, a satire on Sydney society, was written in collaboration.
[4] An amusing story, published in 1934, of three women attempting to breed goats.

To W. G. Cousins

Dear Mr Cousins,

Kings Cross
2 August 1939

Your boy has been here, and now is gone. The book[1] is a gem, and a jewel. Everything about it—touch, weight, and what it is to the eyes. And how I do thank you! Now I will get at once to work to write to Hugh McCrae, Lawrence Campbell, and anyone else you may name, to have a meeting and discuss a friends of 'G.R.'[2] book. That is if you are agreeable. It only wants someone to start the idea, and to arrange for who shall edit it. When I wrote to Lawrence Campbell before, he said he had spoken to you and you were for the idea. Such a book, as I said then, could be written without recourse to any documents or other matter now denied for a life. Even if matter came in that was not politic to use, it could, with the writer's permission, be part of a collection from which a greater 'life' could be drawn. Those who could write are going—Hilary Lofting, Brennan, Lawson, Brereton, Dowell O'Reilly and how many more! All their debts to this man, and their recollections, dust. I think your boy could write—something he said and the way he said it—perhaps he could even edit as a collaborator with someone older. I feel this so much, lest it be lost, a good job I wrote 'Thank you' first! I might have forgotten.

To A. H. Chisholm

Dear Alec,

Kings Cross
10 September 1939

Three things happened—nay four. 'Battlefields' came out. I had a birthday, my first grandchild arrived last Sunday, and I put your letter, and therefore address, somewhere while I was what the doctor called 'Dangerously ill' (However I am on the mend.) So I am sending you a copy of 'Battlefields' and this letter C/- Capt. Peters. You may wonder at the inscription.[3] Wonder no longer! William (the IV) Wallace Gilmore being born, I thought as a good Celt I would celebrate fittingly and wrote him a telegram 'Cead Mille Failthe'[4] which the post master said was a *dead* language and a *foreign* language and refused owing to censorship to transmit. As soon as I could hold a pen I wrote him that it was 'the oldest national, official *living* language in the British

---

[1] *Battlefields*—at last!
[2] George Robertson.
[3] The inscription in the book *Battlefields* was to Hugh McCrae and Rayner Hoff. Probably there was a personal inscription in the copy Mary sent to A. H. Chisholm.
[4] Celtic for 'One hundred thousand welcomes'.

Islands' and that it was strange that though I could not send the language of men fighting for the Empire, I could send a line of long dead Homer and no one would object. Also as a final sting I said 'this language was pushed aside for a branch of German known as English, *and which was forced upon the islands by a German Conquest by the Angles and Saxons'*. Ha! Ha! *Nemo me etc.* So you see why I leave you to look up your family battle cry—Also you will see that if I am no longer dangerously ill, I begin to be dangerously well.

The boy William began well, then suddenly and alarmingly failed. Specialists came. The Mother's milk at fault, so science stepped in, artificial food came, and yesterday and today the child is better. May he continue so!

This is to thank you, Alec, for your birthday good wishes. I had pneumonic flu—and a strange doctor whom I now think the greater evil of the two. John MacPherson, my doctor and friend for years died— and what a careful doctor he was I now know! All good wishes

To A. H. Chisholm

Kings Cross
3 October 1939

Dear Aleck, Alic, Alec and the Gaelich if I only knew it—! (Elshender?)

I put 'Honing up the Hill'[1] in the book because it was Deirdre's[2] (more or less) and then forgot to tell you. I hesitated over the inscription wondering could I get it in, and then thought the G.P.O. might think I had written a whole letter, and I could not risk the surcharge.

I have just been to see William Wallace (and the rent man called in my absence, so that I will be broke when next he calls). The infant looks well, bawls well, I am told already shows temper. He may yet be a Dictator.

It is good to hear from you, Alec, and that the 'family' is well. I had a letter the other day from your Sir Donald Cameron. He has raised his Regt of Queensland Cameron Highlanders, and is in camp with them for a month. He refers to 'my old friend Alex Chisholm', returning me a cutting I had sent him where you mentioned that I had said 'in him was the magnetism of generations'. Mary Hughes[3] here the other day said of him, 'when he goes after being to see us we both feel as if a brother had gone'.

[1] A poem from *Battlefields*.
[2] Daughter of A. H. Chisholm.
[3] Wife of W. M. Hughes.

I hope you will like 'Battlefields'—'Prophetic name' wrote Billy,[1] when it came out. I did not want it to be prophetic, but I wanted it to help, in its small way, put the gulf wider between man and war.

Had Louis Esson in to see me last night. He has a flat across the street. He says Hilda (his wife) and Kathy Prichard are to be over presently, and that K.S.P. has been working very hard for Communism in the West. We all had wings once and soared on causes. That K.S.P. still does shows how young she is. However I can still see a possible swan in every new literary gosling that comes along, so that meat is good and water sweet, and a funeral wreath need not be ordered before I die finally!

I have just been given a copy of the 'Advocate' with a wonderful write-up of M.G. by P. O'Leary. I am twisted in knots of joy and humility over it: out of all crowns offered we only want *the* one. I look at this from a distance, not daring to put it on.

Now my dear bird of the mountain and salmon of Loch Lomond,—wherever the Chisholms came from, this is to say my affections go to you all.—

Mary Gilmore.

To R. G. Howarth

Dear Mr Howarth,

Kings Cross
28 August 1940

As you are loosening up in 'Southerly' I venture to send some of my looseness!

Now as to Australian themes, apart from goannas and kangaroos, koalas and emus, all un-Australian because their use solely depends on their names, will you let me say a word? As you know I have for so long pleaded for a place, not alone in biology, history and derisive and contemptuous writing, but in literature, for the continental fund of matter and inspiration that is aboriginal. And when I say literature I mean that creative, created and essential thing that derives from a national root and not from imitation or duplication of other literatures. Man is the voice of his land and in this we have, at present, to be one with the aboriginal if we are to have rugs to our (literary) beds, and a hearth for the fire. I belong to the past that counted its syllables. The past had to do that in order to be printed. But little by little we

---

[1] Mary's son. His son, William Wallace, is the infant Mary speaks of earlier in the letter.

have moved, and now we are right out where we ought to be—and in a time when there is almost no paper to print us. Still there is 'Southerly' and 'Southerly' is to loosen.

No country in its primitive state had any richer lore than Australia. Love-making in the 'Loo has no more pretty speeches (taking the 'Loo as a symbol) than a black's camp—and no less. So if we decorate our yokels with pretty love words why not our blacks? For we are taking a people in each case, and not this or that ungodly ruffian. So while I had to count my syllables to get a hearing, I wrote white man songs about black men as a means to an end, but knowing they were a foolish thing. And a foolish thing, not because life made them more applicable in one case and less in the other (for it did not) but because convention, become folly, had to be fought by equally foolish convention. I did what I wanted for it opened the door a little. In my last book 'Battlefields' I came nearer to what I wanted. Last night I had my reward. One came to me who will step forward—is stepping forward from where I shall one day leave off. I sometimes think we are a bold but not a brave people. Boldness is of the appetites and the body, bravery of the mind. Intellectually we have not dared. We have gone into the surf holding the same old lifelines as the rest of the world. I mean as to literature—and music. As to the musicians they never see the bee for the hive! They all say, when I ask them to try, that devil is 'nothing in aboriginal themes', and quote negro spirituals of all things. The negroes' own music is of the tom-tom and as monotonous as the Red Indian and the Australian aboriginal's. The spirituals come only from the U.S.A. and derive from Hebridean airs, Psalm tunes and plain chant. No one ever went to Africa for negro music!! And as with music, so with lore, song, legend, ritual and life. Am I raging? There is only one crime in life and that is waste. Analyse it and see if I am not right. And how we have wasted and thrown away what should have put us in the forefront of the world. Take 'Hiawatha'. Was the rhythm there an Indian rhythm? So if I send you something on a Scandinavian rhythm, say 'At least she carries a flag; and someone may follow. Who will do better?' I said earlier that there is someone. It is William Hart-Smith. He had a Spanish grandfather and that may account for it, the *Conquistador* belonged to the Spaniard. I have asked him to get in touch with you and to join the A.E.A. which he is eager to do. His wife is Mary Wynn and works in the Mitchell. And she also has gifts. When Hart-Smith goes to you, treasure him. He makes his own form. It joints at times like a waggon on a cobblestone road. But the individual and the stuff are both there; they are not blown glass from a factory and the jolt does not smash them.

What fine things Letters writes. He and Hart-Smith have a kinship but one uses a chisel and the other is blue metal. I wish I had been able to begin as blue metal; I might have done something worthwhile. My thanks to you for the patience I hope for. Yours sincerely,

To George Mackaness

Dear George,

Kings Cross
30 August 1940

Half a sec—no time to write the full word SECOND—and I shall reply to your just-come letter. What do you think happened, day before yesterday? Bartlett Adamson! And he came to ask would I give a message for the Cultural Conference to meet on Sunday. He said that as I had opened that first one they would like it. Of course I know what was wanted. My name there if not me, in person. Of course I said I would. So next day I sent this:—

'Dear Mr. Adamson, In response to your desire that as I opened the first of these Conferences I should send greetings to the present one, may I say that I have much pleasure in adding my tribute to the work that is being done by the Conference.

'Culture is the best of human thought made living and permanent. And any person or body, which helps to do this is doing patriotic work, and work which, though rooted in nationhood, extends *benevolently* beyond the bounds of either race or nationality—so helps to make and shape the world. Yours etc. M.G.' And may I say I like that 'benevolently' even if I am its parent! Next: Did you see the lovely thing Jim Donald wrote of me in his col. in last Sunday's 'Truth'? Only a paragraph, but every line and every word counts. Also did you see Ernestine Hill's tribute in the A.B.C. the week or so earlier? Bigger but no better, except for added items, than J. D's. I only saw Mr Donald once to speak to, and that was for a few moments ten years ago. And did you hear me over the wireless on my birthday? And what did you think of the verse at the end? I am coming to the conclusion that no one recognized it as verse, and that even you thought I was thundering out on my own personal (and not as a writer's) account. I have had letters from three States about that talk and how they 'loved' to hear my voice. One amazed writer said it was 'a *young* voice'. Another from Adelaide was full of regrets that she could have seen me only that measles struck the family, and all their boxes had to be taken off the 'Royal Tar',—so they never went to New Australia. Yet another to remind me I had known him when he was one of the Secretaries at 111 Elizabeth Street (the New A. Office) and that is all but 50 years ago. What a thing is memory! I had not seen or heard of him since. His recollections of the young M.J.C.[1] should be interesting!

[1] Mary Jean Cameron, Mary's maiden name.

Have been so long ill or ailing! But hope to mend a bit at least, so that I can go through my letters. I am and have been borne down, in my illness, by the burden of things to be done and which just had to lie,—and grow heavier the longer they lay.

Now as to your letter. At once I will set to work and type you 'Shakespeare'[1] (thank God you have chosen that! I think it is my high water mark as literature, and also no one else here has done it as I have) and later will send 'Lest We Forget'[2] and perhaps a later one or two: for things do get written in spite of eye and other miseries.

My love to Alice, and Joan, and John and George[3]

Have not seen Ernestine except for a second, for months and months. By the way you will have to include one of W. Hart Smith's, an aboriginal one. I must get him to send it to you.

To R. G. Howarth

Dear Mr Howarth,

Kings Cross
12 September 1940

... It is a fact that there is a difference between the writing, on literature and especially verse, of to-day and yesterday. Yesterday dealt more with its contemporaries. Certainly it had not the past that to-day has, as to-day's past was its present: and so it is perhaps that I am not quite fair—or is it reasonable? And more than that the past had A. G. Stephens, the man who was a golden mountain to the understanding, young, old, or middling, and who dealt with, or dealt it out, with something more than *acquired* knowledge. What an aura of knowledge there was behind and around everything he wrote! And when he blasted it was the lightning stroke. He did not know how to be a gnat. Did you know that for three (or more?) years I financed (and really owned though at the time I did not realize it) the Bookfellow? I went in rags and lived on bread and scraps to do it. But I did it because it was something for Australia, and because it put Australia, in criticism as a part of literature, among the world's great. And because the lesser critics hated him (probably with good *personal* cause). When Shaw Neilson's first book[4] came out they damned it with sneers and faint praise. When I spoke bitterly of it to Arthur Adams (and also to Bert Stevens) the

---

[1] Mackaness was preparing another anthology. 'Shakespeare' was published in *Under the Wilgas*, 1932. The poem is too long to quote here but R. D. FitzGerald included it in *Mary Gilmore: Selected Verse*, 1948, pp. 145-50.
[2] Published in *The Wild Swan*, 1930.
[3] George Mackaness's family.
[4] *Heart of Spring*, published by the *Bookfellow*, 1919.

reply was. 'It was done to get at A. G. Stephens!' So was Neilson wounded. I feel sick to this day when I think of it and that sickness this morning found parallel voice:—

> Where the black savage of the skies,
> Dropped down on angled wing
> Than the little new born lamb
> There seemed no frailer thing.
> One moment there was the harsh brute paused
> One moment there was peace;
> Then there was blood upon his beak
> Blood on the silken fleece.

So was the half-blind sensitive Neilson stabbed and wounded.
... While I think the past should be permanently recorded, I do not like to see it so often put as the green tree in the front of the garden ... If my work is good it will live according to its degree of worth; if it is not good, all the praise, all kindness of friends, all the emotions of the emotional, easily-stirred will not make it live ... Keep 'Southerly' going. It is a tree of hope.

M.G.

P.S. We who write the impulsive yet vital thought of today can so easily find another stimulus and an opposite point of view tomorrow. So put me down as one who knows that opinions are not an offence.

To Sir Lionel Lindsay

My dear Lionel,
Kings Cross
8 January 1941

What a treat to get your letter. I did not know your boy was away. He is still a 'little feller' to me, though he may be (or is he?) married and a father.

It wouldn't matter whether it was for your art as art or because you were a Lindsay that you have your honour,[1] because it is enough that you have always meant something to Australia. Enough? It is the only legitimate reason. *Earned*, & the honour in the *earning*.

Don't reply. Replies can be a burden, & one real letter once in a while is worth the lot. I am expecting a broken boy,[2] who, through drink, is out of the services. And I, who would gladly put dynamite under the hidden rulers who make war, am making another attempt:

---

[1] Lionel Lindsay was knighted in the New Year Honours of 1941.
[2] Mary's diaries of 1941 have much to say of this situation concerning a young serviceman whom she helped considerably.

this time to get him on to a ship. In the Navy he can only drink in port. At sea he would be as good as anyone else. Let me repeat your phrase: 'Up Bardia',[1] the tail that has no joint called Mons or Dunkirk.[2] I've got to say it again!

Hearts. Don't talk to me about hearts in this weather. If I did not write at top speed my writing would be like this! (That is an exclamation mark.)

To Miles Franklin

Dear Miles Franklin,

Kings Cross
17 February 1941

... When our soldiers went overseas to Great Britain there was a broadcast to Australia—The N. Zealanders spoke first. Asked for the N.Z. Battle Cry, they gave the magnificent 'Kumera! Kumera!' which in manner, even if it only means 'give us yams!' (or food), is so outstanding. Then Australia spoke. Asked for the Australian Battle Cry the astonished speaker said 'There is none!' 'But there surely must be one of some kind!' 'Not that I know of.' Pressed & prompted by someone near he gave that *yelp* 'Wacko!' As I have been telling everyone ever since, the seas between shuddered, so did the earth & heavens (& Farmer Whyte adds 'So did Mary Gilmore'). In the morning I got up & wrote the Battle Cry[3] enclosed herewith. As you see it has the endorsement of the Minister for Education, and the National Fitness Council asked for it for their camps & when I sent it to Mr. Hughes he said he wd. take it with him to Melbourne & ask for it to be sent to the Australian Squadron. All the soldiers who have had it think it just what was wanted ... It is given as you will see in the note on the MS. to the Defence Forces and no one else is ever to make money out of it. Perhaps because of it someone will one day do a better one. But it will still be the first. As I wrote the only Coronation Anthem (or Ode) written, composed, & officially performed in Australia I have two firsts to my credit! Well that's brag enough! But I am glad to have something to my credit.

All good wishes, & never let your ink pot empty. Yours

---

[1] A derisive expression. Bardia, in the Western Desert, was the first significant Allied victory in World War II. Australian troops played a leading role in the campaign for Bardia. See *Sydney Morning Herald*, 6-27 January 1941.
[2] Two Allied retreats, Mons in World War I, Dunkirk in World War II.
[3] Mary's Battle Cry was 'We're the Boomeranglanders'. Little came of her enthusiasm to have it set to music and taken up by the troops.

To W. G. Cousins

Dear Mr Cousins,

Kings Cross
5 December 1941

I have just read Ernestine Hill's novel on Flinders.[1] What a work! I feel as if my own writing is a child's besides it. The research is tremendous. I know nothing written here in which so often a single word is a match struck in explosion on things unsaid, but in the minds of those who know what lies behind. The shallow reader will not know this, the mind unstored will not be lit.

Two things stand out in regard to the book. One is the impression of impulsive force in the writing. I have known for the last seven or eight years that the book was a living hope and desire in the mind of the writer, and that she was collecting or incubating it though engaged on other work. But that that eager impulse should have kept its high water mark throughout all that time and then transferred itself to the book, still unbroken, is to me, astonishing. Actually she 'transfers' to the reader as a great actor 'transfers' to his audience. This is rare in any writing, here or elsewhere. Usually it is confined to poetry (i.e., to the recitational, if I may coin a word.)

The other quality that struck me is rarer still. I would be a lunatic to make a comparison between Ernestine Hill and Victor Hugo but in her lesser degree she has with him the quality of reverberation. The only other book written in Australia which has this is Marcus Clarke's 'For the Term of His Natural Life'. (I might say that among our critics A. G. Stephens had the same quality.)

And, finally, let me say you were right when you told me some time ago you had 'a book'! You had indeed! Yours sincerely,

To Yvonne Webb

Dear Yvonne,

Kings Cross
28 December 1941

Your booklet[2] came yesterday, & what a beautiful thing it is—inside and out. What are you selling it at? & how?

I saw Yvonne & her baby several times lately, had her here one day, & had a card from Joan. The babies are increasing. I have quite a lot now, one here, one there, all over the place—even in the country where my girls have married & gone. I often wonder if you ever remember when you three would come to Phillip Street (& here) how no matter

---

[1] *My Love Must Wait*, 1941.
[2] Probably *Selected Poems*, 1940.

how broken or weary I was I would drag myself up to give you help & intellectual food & training. A man, curiously enough, after fourteen years last week wrote me his still living gratitude. Almost I had forgotten him, I had only seen him once, & that so long ago.

My own last book, 'The Disinherited',[1] is coming out at once. An advance copy was pulled off the machine & bound so that I should get it on Boxing Day. Men worked almost to death, the Christmas rush of a big Printing & Publishing house, did that. And was I touched and grateful! I still tingle at the thought of it. It is only 30 pages, a psychological study (never done in Australia before,) & Capt. Peters wrote the Introduction. Two bindings, one paper, one (limited & autographed edition) hard covers. May good fortune spread the sales of your book as well as mine! And may you never look back. The verses are really lovely little things, delicate & almost translucent. Affectionately,

For the *first time* you forgot me on Mother's Day, & I wondered why.

To Mary Wynn

Kings Cross
Dear Mary Wynn, 7 February 1942

You are my rock and my salvation! Why did I not think of it before? It is this: will you copy for me the air, and only the air, of the Battle Cry?[2] If you could put the tonic sol fa under the notes so much the better. Angus & Robertson will bring me out a Battlefields leaflet for Army distribution at cost price. I want the air with the words, and will have the slogan, Matt Thynne's letter,[3] and the Toast all done on the same sheet. At least I hope so. If your notation will not reproduce you are almost sure to know someone who can do it.

I have looked through Bill's[4] work. What strong stuff it is and what unusual vision fills it. I regard him as first of his school here, as all others on similar lines are *softer*. Their concern is with words as the instrument—as the *kind* of instrument—and as an object in themselves. His use of words is as a medium of expression, the thing to be said being paramount and the words subsidiary. In another way the horses forge on, the vehicle behind them. Others caparison the horses and so run with them. The fringes rather than the horses are for the reader or catch his attention. Bill's strength lies in not doing that. Yours

[1] Published 1941.
[2] See note to letter, 17 February 1941.
[3] Matthew Thynne, then on active service, had written to Mary praising the Battle Cry.
[4] William Hart-Smith, Mary Wynn's husband.

To George Mackaness

Dear George,

Kings Cross
5 a.m. 2 March 1942

Only a line. I have copied out, 'No Foe shall gather our harvest',[1] as I have taken the printed one to send it to Mr. Curtin.[2] I pasted it on letterhead 'Worker' paper that belonged to 1914 when Mr Lamond[3] was issuing 80.000 copies of the paper a week and was proposing to go to either 100.000 or 120.000 copies. 'The Worker' was a power then: Lord Carmichael, when governor of Victoria told me in 1910 or 1911 that he based all his political reports to the British Government on The Worker, as it was the fairest of all the papers; he said his orders were he was to get it as soon as it came out, and he read every word I wrote. That is why he asked might he call on me, when he visited Casterton where I then was. We were so poor then I had not even

---

[1] The spirited, patriotic poem in which Mary echoed the prevailing mood of the Australian community to resist determinedly the Japanese threat. The poem, in large print, was displayed in the window of the Sydney department store, Murdoch's, where it drew much public interest.

> Sons of the mountains of Scotland,
> Welshmen of coomb and defile,
> Breed of the moors of England,
> Children of Erin's green isle,
> We stand four square to the tempest,
> Whatever the battering hail—
> No foe shall gather our harvest,
> Or sit on our stockyard rail.
>
> Our women shall walk in honour,
> Our children shall know no chain,
> This land, that is ours forever,
> The invader shall strike at in vain.
> Anzac! . . . Tobruk! . . . and Kokoda! . . .
> Could ever the old blood fail?
> No foe shall gather our harvest,
> Or sit on our stockyard rail.
>
> So hail-fellow-met we muster,
> And hail-fellow-met fall in,
> Wherever the guns may thunder,
> Or the rocketing air-mail spin!
> Born of the soil and the whirlwind,
> Though death itself be the gale—
> No foe shall gather our harvest,
> Or sit on our stockyard rail.
>
> We are the sons of Australia,
> Of the men who fashioned the land;
> We are the sons of the women
> Who walked with them hand in hand;
> And we swear by the dead who bore us,
> By the heroes who blazed the trail,
> No foe shall gather our harvest,
> Or sit on our stockyard rail.

[2] John Curtin.
[3] Hector Lamond.

a glass in which to offer him a drink. (We were keeping Will's father and mother at the time and building up the old home.) However he did not drink water and I had nothing else. I was the only person he called on in the town—and I was the shabbiest as to clothes. You should have seen the respect I got after that!

But I won two elections for Labor.[1] For the second campaign both Mr. George Reid and Mr Deakin were brought up to off-set me. Both failed. We won by over 2,000 Votes, thus doubling the first majority. 'We don't mind being beaten', said Mr Jacobs, campaign director against me. 'But we hate being beaten by a woman!'

I am sorry Alice is not well. She *shouldn't* be not well. As for me, h.b.p.[2] doesn't let me sleep, so I get up and work. My nerves won't stay still in bed, so I have to get up.

With my love to you both

Is that *Cwealth Lit.* scholarship fund still going?
I might put in a book of verse, if it is—Please let me know.

To Constance Robertson

Kings Cross
14 April 1942

Dear Connie,

... I have the stuff for a new book of a few pages, with some historical notes such as have never been published. I had been thinking of putting it in for C'wealth Literary Fund approval.

It seems strange that I have not seen 'No Foe'[3] in Murdoch's window, though it went there almost immediately after being published. But I have had letters about it.

Last week to go over 2CH in a session I was unable to hear, 'Singapore' has gone all over Australia loudly.

I had a letter from Lithgow read to me last night, and the writer said that the men in camp there had asked him (the writer) to convey to me their approval because I had said all that they wanted said. The men on one of the ships (Navy) from Singapore itself, wanted a copy of it, another woman told me. Dunno what cheers would have reached

---

[1] Mary was campaign manager for the Labor candidate for Wannon in the 1906 and 1910 elections, Labor winning by 962 votes in 1906 and 1180 in 1910.
[2] High blood pressure.
[3] See note to letter, 2 March 1942.

me if they had seen the *original*!¹ Only four copies. One went to Curtin, one to Gen. Gordon Bennett, one to Mrs. Jackson² (confidentially) and one for myself. I wrote on the margin of the one for the P.M.—'For Mr. Curtin, even if I have to go to gaol'.

Do you get the Canberra Times? Look up the file for 'Australia to America'.³ It begins 'John Curtin stood at the door', and ends 'Then

---

¹ From Dame Mary's diary of 16 February 1942 the following extract is taken: 'Singapore is fallen. I see those broken men carrying the white flag.'
To Leslie Haylen she wrote a note which said 'men and women from Malaya have said they were sold out, that the British heads ordered that nothing was to be destroyed as after the war they wanted everything in good order'. Then the original version of 'Singapore' follows in her diary on 1 March 1942. It reads:

> They grouped together about their chief,
> And each man looked on his fate,
> Should ever the sound of a restless foot
> Reach out to the foe in wait.
> And bitter the wrath in each man's heart,
> And savage the oaths they swore
> As they thought of how they had all been ditched
> By 'Impregnable' Singapore!
>
> Flat on her base she squatted the sea,
> But, bare as an old bald head,
> Her idiot face looked up to the skies
> To show she was profiteer bred;
> And there under heaven she naked lay,
> By the enemy planes confined
> While the craven --------- sat safe at home
> Till their pants wore out behind.
>
> She brought forth death as her eldest child,
> With defeat as her second son
> Then she hung a white flag out on a staff
> To show that her task was done.
> But black with rage the Australians stood,
> And God! how those Anzacs swore.
> Bennett and all his men alike
> At the old --------- Singapore.
>
> Was it her fault she betrayed our troops?
> Was it her fault she failed?
> Ask it of those who slaughtered the flag
> That once to the mast was nailed!
> Ask it of those who pandered for power,
> Traitors, whatever their rank.
> Who flung to the dogs the nation's pride,
> Till the very name, ---------, stank.

This was not the poem which was later published as 'Singapore' in the *Australian Women's Weekly*. Alice Jackson of that magazine wrote to Dame Mary on 4 March 1942:

> My dear Dame Mary,
> After a conference on your poem, we decided it was just a little too hot to handle. In its original form, it would not, we feel, survive the Censor's 'Blimping' eye. So we tinkered around with it a bit and achieved the watered-down result attached.
> Too well we know this is not packed with T.N.T. in the Gilmore manner but we trust you will do us the favour of giving it your blessing as its publication will then be achieved and that, we feel sure, will effect the good you aim to do with it.

² Alice Jackson of the *Australian Women's Weekly*.
³ The poem Mary refers to, published in the *Canberra Times*, 19 March 1942, was entitled 'Australia to Abraham Lincoln.'

foot to foot they turned to the foe, The Anzac and Lincoln men'. It was given a good place I believe. I did not see it. No copy of the paper was sent to me so I only know from others it was in. Not great verse but it just hit the moment.

Terrible tired, terrible busy, and growing terrible *old*. Love

Tom Gilmore just wrote this to me (and wasn't I proud!) 'You never forget, Aunt Mary; the important and the unimportant are all important to you, so vital is your attachment to life.'

To Hugh McCrae

Dear Hughie,

Kings Cross
18 April 1942

Clearing up against either the end or the bombs—which ever comes first—I found the following, & wonder if ever I sent it to you.

>   18.2.39
>   He has the joyous heart,
>   This Hugh McCrae,
>   Who, in a swallow dart,
>   Pierces the heavens,
>   On from the Arctic to the Torrid speeds,
>   or backward turns,
>   And, like the dragonfly above the reeds,
>   Poises an instant,
>   And then flits.

Affectionately—to all the generations.

To Miles Franklin

Dear Stella Miles Franklin,

Kings Cross
26 April 1942

Yesterday I finished 'The Pea Pickers'[1] and then I wrote a letter, to say that I was not asking questions, but that I felt Stella Miles Franklin's mind all through it. This morning I tore the letter up. But the feeling did not die, so this is written because of the beauty of the book as a response to life and to the living things that are Australia. I found all my own responses in it but for which I have never found words. I lived in it as I read. That is, up to the Celtic Bronze. The two later

---

[1] A novel by Eve Langley, 1942.

divisions gave me the impression of having been written (and the gold stretched to cover them) to fill a publisher's number of pages.

I have praised many books in my time, but none like this. This is a vine on its own. The teller emerges through it and takes all the other characters swirling after her like debris in a stream. She is so vital that the others are shadowy by comparison. Yet I can see the Indians, and the Italians are still talking—not as individuals but as mass. Jim is real. I hear him walk, as for months I heard the bullock driver walk in K.S.P's 'Working Bullocks'.[1] I did for months after I read it—heavy and slow. But Jim is not animal as they were.

Anyhow whoever Eve Langley is—you or another, you *and* another—I would like her to know that an old woman who loves her country was stabbed through and through, again and again, by the observation, the pity, the understanding and the response to creation that is in the book. Will you tell her this?

P.S. As a matter of fact I sometimes wondered was the writer Stella Miles Franklin plus the unknown poet S.M.F. found.[2]

To R. G. Howarth

Dear Mr. Howarth,

Kings Cross
9 October 1942

What a treat 'Southerly' is after the wish-wash and conventional stuff of other publications. It is the 'Bookfellow' born again, because it has 'identity'. Writing is an activity of life. Put the full-stop there and you have a sword, and a discovery. Everyone who has written has lived it, but with heads in the clouds. To bring it in with cooking and washing up is to make it life: and these things are. Once reading and writing were luxuries—things the then world thought miraculous but unnecessary. Even you, so much younger than I, must remember, in remnants, that. Now literature ceases to be miraculous and unnecessary. It has become 'an activity of life'. It is the bones of thought, not a skull here, a tibia there, a rib somewhere else. But a related structure, and recognized as such . . .

Later. To Mr. Leon Gellert.

To say thank you to whoever wrote the notice on 'The Disinherited' in today's 'Herald':

[1] *Working Bullocks* was published by Katharine Susannah Prichard in 1926.
[2] An amusing piece of detective work by Mary—Eve Langley becoming a mixture of Miles Franklin and Mary Fullerton ('E').

> I have no thunder in my words,
> Thunder is much too high;
> But I can see as high as birds,
> And feel the wind go by.
>
> And I can follow through the grass
> The darling breasted quail
> And so, although the thunder mass
> I choose the lesser grail.
>
> Age changes no one's heart, the field
> Is wider — that is all.
> Childhood is never lost; concealed
> It answers every call.
>
> So, when the wind goes blaring by,
> And in the driving hail,
> Or when some tempest shakes the sky,
> I run beside the quail.

I saw my first quail when I was about three. I see it yet.
M.G.

To Sir Lionel Lindsay

Kings Cross
Dear Lionel, 9 January 1943

How your letters matter! I, too, feel the want of a world sense (not merely an Australian want) of spiritual or ethical values. This war is proof, as the last was, of the same thing. When I read, 'his first Kill,' 'out on a Kill,' I feel sick, not only for today's use of the words, but in resurrection of the past when they were the familiar words of my childhood in relation to the blacks. But just as I, then, because of national usage, had no shock, but regarded them as a natural part of life, so people today, in relation to those they are fighting—& alike on both sides and in all countries.

I read just before your letter came, J. R. W. Taylor's article (that man can write!) on sharks, in today's 'S.M.H,' and as I read I thought 'Man is the world's shark, & great empires are the giant shark.' We live by destruction and by devouring. Even the drink & the drug traffic shows it. I have ever since the war started, been trying to help lads whom 'treating' as soldiers made drunken, till at last they were pitched out of the army, and in the cases where I have known the parents the training has usually been plenty of force, but no ethics. I blame the last generation, not this one for conditions. As to corruption, political & other, can you tell me any where it is not rife—perhaps even, the rule. My side does at least sometimes light a candle of hope, for people to follow! The failure of Menzies was a great blow to me, for he really did begin well as an Australian. Now there is only my own side for the flowering of hope and against what terrible odds outside him Curtin is working! For Curtin *is* straight . . .

To George Mackaness

Dear George,

Kings Cross
10 May 1943

Your letter an hour ago a great relief, for I was worrying over the autobiog. I hate to *owe*, and I felt the possibility of debt if I did not get it done, and *well* done. However when I remember what has gone (and what is to go yet) to the Mitchell I feel I am once more a self-respecting body. I have a lot of stuff in the rough already. Also I have copies of Henry Lawson's letters (some of them) from gaol to Mrs. Byers[1] with other related matter. And all that belongs to my biography . . . I have also put another person in the way of getting more Lawson matter from people who knew him. All the stuff that Mrs. Byers had treasured should still be available.

I have not heard anything of Hughey—McCrae—for some months. I am afraid his health for the last three years has been as bad, or perhaps more uncertain than mine. I forget mine in my new finds: geese most, but hope is strong. I have a new one coming tomorrow evening, and of course am hoping for a star!

Just got some new clothes, and don't I feel fine! Peacock proud in them. Fitted twelve months ago, and only now got them!! A bad cut, but mended by a good tailor since then. A good tailor is an artist just as a sculptor is. I never realized it till I saw what was done to what had been anything but Art.

My love to Alice. By the way, life has one crowning mercy! one's brain has no gall-bag. If it had life wd. indeed be intolerable. The good of life be yours.

To W. Hart-Smith

Dear Bill,

Kings Cross
14 May 1943

I have just now got your 'Columbus Goes West'[2] and what a book!

[1] Isabel Byers.
[2] Hart-Smith's volume of poetry, published 1943.

I have gone through it twice already. What lines! What thought! What newness! . . .

No more for the moment. I want to get you at once. I am so delighted and so filled with wonder, and pride for Australia. Yours

To George Mackaness

Kings Cross
Dear George, 3 June 1943

I owe you *two* letters. About Mrs. Byers[1] she had a small trunk full of stuff of one kind and another. But she died, I think it is ten years ago. Of Henry's small sheets of verse I know nothing. The *Worker* office should be able to help you unless Tom Mutch[2] has said all they can say.

A bibliography of my stuff! I never remember the occasional writings. But I wrote a lot of political matter for the 'Casterton Herald' (or whatever its name was. I forget even that!) and the widow of the Mayor of Silverton said a few years ago that I wrote most of the 'Silver Age'—the then only paper on the Barrier.[3] And Walter Jago told me his father had told him I wrote most of Louisa Lawson's paper 'Dawn'. I wrote some of its 'leaders' I remember as well as anything else she wanted. I did a lot for the 'New Australia Journal' (edited one issue) and for the 'Cosme Monthly'. In my teens sent all sorts of stuff to the 'Albury Banner', some to the 'Border Watch'. I did a weekly col. of Topical Notes (or something) for Stronach when he had 'The Echo'. I forget for how long. Did other stuff as well. Wrote for 'The Town & Country Journal', and my first cheque as a writer came from it. Did odd bits for the 'Sunday Times' and the 'Evening News', but few of any of these went over my own name. I used my initials M.J.C. and M.J., J.C. or Noms de plume—one I remember was 'Rudione' and again 'Rudione Calvert.' These in the 'New Australia Journal', and I believe, but am not sure, in the 'Albury Banner'.

Also I wrote in S.Am. for the Buenos Aires 'Herald' or 'Standard', (I forget which) prose and verse, but not a great deal. If she has not burnt them Nettie Palmer has the Buenos Aires and a little other stuff. I was very ill some years ago and sent her a tiny book of cuttings, a book of M.S. verse, (some published) and a book of my Mother's, containing verses she had written on me as a baby . . . My 'Beach Schools' went into the Vic. Education Gazette and into the 'Australian

---

[1] Isabel Byers.
[2] Thomas Davies Mutch.
[3] The Barrier Ranges were discovered by Charles Sturt in 1884 and the remote and forbidding landscape of the surrounding region took its name from them.

Worker'. So many of my schemes went into the 'Worker'! Perforated glass to build houses, made from Broken Hill Slag, Hollow Slag bricks to be keyed one into the other, glass legs for furniture—endless things! I proposed those airfilled spring mattresses years before they were made for sale. Any one going through the 23 years file of my page could get endless stuff. Also in my letters to the 'S.M.H.' I covered a lot of ground in those. Then of course there was the 'Bulletin', and even I think the 'Lone Hand'. Also 'Lilley's Magazine'. Perhaps even the 'Antipodean'. But of that I am not sure. I just remember John Farrell asking me to write for it. But there was the 'Queenslander' when Mary Hannay Foott was there. There was a Launceston paper too. W. A. Woods editor then. Others were the 'Temora Independent' and the Wagga and Goulburn papers. I wrote in the latter as 'Hill 17' when I got the hill for the Soldiers' Memorial.[1]

I never remember my own stuff. I only realized last week that Ruth Bedford did some children's verse of mine *years ago*, along with others and I wondered who had written the things. *I did not think much of them.* And that happened to me more than once! But if you keep this as a record. Yours

To Charles Barrett

Kings Cross
23 June 1943

Dear Mr. (Dr., Professor, Sir Charles) Barrett (whichever it is!— *why* can't I remember it!) You don't require any letters of introduction from anyone (though C.H.P.'s[2] an added grace) to come to see me! Anyway I am glad to hear from you.

What I would like you to include of my verse is 'Singapore'.[3] It is the beloved of the soldier. Ever since it appeared soldiers, soldiers' wives or families have written almost every week for or about it. The soldiers say 'It says just what we wanted said & couldn't say ourselves!' It is framed waiting for the return of P.O.W. husbands all over the place. I enclose a copy. If you don't want it send it back as I have had to have so many multiple copies made for those asking for it, that every copy counts now. As for my verse, you may have the run of the whole lot. Anything for the soldiers matters to me. 'Sweethearts' I don't remember. But then I have so little memory for my own stuff. People read it, & I ask 'Who wrote that?' And it is not senile old age.

---

[1] Mary drew attention to the hill overlooking Goulburn as a suitable site for that city's War Memorial. A monument was subsequently built there.
[2] Captain C. H. Peters.
[3] See note to letter, 14 April 1942.

It has always been the same. 'Why you wrote most of the "Dawn",' (Louisa Lawson's paper) 'Did I?' & then I remembered that Mr. Jago was right. 'You wrote half "The Silver Age".' 'Did I?', and then argument made me remember. But it is a long time since 'The Silver Age', it was the first & only paper on the Barrier.[1] But these are only two instances; so it goes on through all my writing.

But I do want to use 'Singapore'. It had to be watered down for publication I made only 4 copies of the original. One went to Curtin ('Even if I have to go to gaol for it!') & one to General Gordon Bennett. Yours sincerely

To Miles Franklin

Dear Miles,

Kings Cross
25 June 1943

I am in bed with bronchitis & pleurisy so excuse the writing.

Your book[2] came just now & I have opened it—& again, but even more than before, opened the gates of wonder. What a responser & what a responding heart & mind to life and all it gives!

I disagree with Tom Moore in some of what he says. He narrows where he shouldn't—I suppose we all do, because we all accept certain *cliches* as gospel & work from them. 'E' escapes all this, working only from her mind. There *is* a kinship with Shaw Neilson—of question, wistfulness, & the sense of loveliness, of beauty that is beyond expression. In other words of flight into the unbound, & then on the return, putting what can be held of it into containing words . . .

I think if I may I will try the 'S.M.H.' with a brief writing on 'E'—or writing based on 'E'. People have said to me that 'E' is Miles Franklin.[3]

If it all depended on 'Silhouette in Richmond Park'[4] I wd. say yes. For the bush bred have seen or said it. Miles Franklin is bush bred. There are other things too. But my mind is open, and I ask no questions.

How A.G.S.,[5] even to tearing his hair, would have revelled in this! Wherever 'E' went he would have been, whatever door opened he would have seen. What doors she opens! What windy, wordy, roadmetal stuff most of us write beside it. Stardust & manna, candle light & a fire on the hearth! If age has given me understanding of this kind of writing, then thank you for age!

How are you—well? To you my grateful thanks. Yours

[1] See note to letter, 3 June 1943.
[2] Actually 'E''s book (i.e. Mary Fullerton's). It was entitled *Moles Do So Little With Their Privacy* and contained a preface by T. Inglis Moore.
[3] Mary's own suggestion. See letter, 17 June 1937.
[4] The poem on page 45 of the collection.
[5] A. G. Stephens.

To Miles Franklin

Dear Miles Franklin,

Kings Cross
2 July 1943

Thank you for your letter. I did not tell all the story of poor Henry Lawson's starved hunt for food.[1] One of the things he said, & with what controlled inward bitterness, was how thankful he was when someone was clean enough to wrap a mutton bone in paper instead of just putting it in with every kind of filth. The locality (according to the papers) had quite a scare over this queer woman 'with big feet' & who 'would run like a deer when any man approached her'. 'She never accosted anyone'. I mentioned his runway (down a narrow lane between houses). But in the end he was caught. 'A raw young Irishman in the Force'—Carroll or some such name. He found the runway, chased Henry into it, & by a short cut met Henry who ran into his arms at the other end...

It was winter, towards midnight. He told Henry he was on his beat & had to finish, but there was a little shelter, & a tiny fire where he ate when he went off, & told Henry to go there & wait for him. When relieved he went there, shared his meal with Henry, & gave him 3/6 for food for next day. All this Henry told me himself. I have seen those great white feet ever since—seen them running to escape detection. And the other haunting thing is the little windy place where he sat to which he had run to escape being seen (when I took the food to the house), sweating with influenza, his legs bare to the wind. Henry Lawson, the man who shaped a literature in which the world could see Australia! I know (& I knew) it would have been fatal, but there are times when I almost wish I had been fond enough to marry him. How different his life would have been!...

About 'E': I will do what I can. I am still indoors with the bronchitis, but hope soon to get out of doors. Peter Hopegood's choice would have been mine too. How often I have seen those antlers[2], & those stars! As I know you too have done. It is a beautiful little knot of lines with a vast sky and perceptive experience behind it. I think again that 'E' has something warmer in her than Emily Dickinson. She is nearer the human heart & nearer the wonder that lies in a heart seeing intellectually but with a little friendly fire in it. In plain words, there is more wonder, less ego in her work than in Emily.

[1] For Mary's relationship with Lawson see notes to letters, 5 August 1896, 23 December 1924, 5 June 1926 and 29 August 1928 (to the Henry Lawson Memorial and Literary Society).

[2] Refers to the poem 'Silhouette in Richmond Park' with its lines:

> Are these oak or antlers,
> In the darkling
> Branched upon the sky;
> Star sparkling,
> Or bright eye?

As to yourself—get away from the weight of the sea for a while. You are of the inland & the altitude and your roots are crying for their native soil. Get back to Danny's[1] country, & remember what a doctor once told a friend of mine: 'The outside of a horse is good for the inside of a man'.

I preach but don't do, & TB results. But I am always hoping to do! Yours sincerely,

To Sarah Nixon-Smith

Dear Mrs (Nixon) Smith—

Kings Cross
20 August 1943

Your letter just came. What a loss, & what a grief for you!. But you have your *two* families and can see both. But it does not fill the empty place, or the empty house. You have written about the poplar[2] just in the way I wanted. Your letter will go into my Collection just as you have written it. It could not be better.

Some day I hope to see Goulburn, Roslyn & Merry Vale[3] again. Some day I wish you would get your family to drive along the old Castlereagh Road from Penrith & see Kerry Lodge where my mother was born two doors past the little (First) Wesleyan Church. In 1890 her poplar was still standing. When I again saw the place a few years ago there was only the huge butt of one left. The Pepperinas were still there, gnarled & old. If you told the people who own the place that you knew the family who built it & lived there they would give you a drink out of grandfather's (Beattie's) well and let you see the 100 year old grapevine. Part of the old fences still stand. It is as good as ever as a house, but the 'bird cage' someone put on the front spoils it . . .

To Hugh McCrae

Dear Hugh,

Kings Cross
28 August 1943

What it is to be a poet! Thank God, I never had the temerity to call

---

[1] Danny Delacy, the pioneer Irishman in Miles Franklin's *All That Swagger*, 1936.
[2] See note to letter, 14 December 1933.
[3] 'Roslyn' and 'Merry Vale' were the properties of Mary's grandparents (the Camerons and the Beatties) near Goulburn.

myself one. This is anent your 'The Butcher'.[1] If I had written—attempted to write—that it would have been dead meat. A poet wrote it, and it dances in, & dances out, tambourine and all!

Spoke for Mrs. Street,[2] and a Sunday later for Leslie Haylen, was 78 on the Monday, & spoke for Falstein on Toosday. Poets can't do that!

How are you? When I feel worse I feel the end is nigh. When I am not so worse (for I don't get better now) I do things. With the health of youth at the end of life what couldn't we do! For the years do give range.

My love to you all, small & middly—especially to grand children.

Talking of grand-children—my little grandson was taken to a rodeo, since when he has galloped everything moveable up & down the yard shouting 'Ride her, Cowboy!' When I heard it I thought of his father, when I brought him at about six his first 'horse', as he rode it up & down the backyard I heard 'Come up, you ----y virgin!' Very casually I asked where he had heard that! Our landlord. It was his pet adjuration to his mare, he being a Protestant Defence or an Orangeman.

To Colin Simpson

Dear Colin Simpson,

Kings Cross
19 September 1943

Yes! it's unbelievable but 'She's still alive!' as an astonished man said two years ago.

I thought you were still in England but your article on a soldier land scheme in the west (N.S.W.) says you are here. I have looked at the map you include and almost every proposed place is far from water in an area with an extremely limited rainfall. Who is to provide the water for house, irrigation of sorts, and stock? I enclose a copy (with its tail cut off) of my scheme for last war and again for this one. I wish you would look at it. But with a kindly eye please. If not, don't look.

Of course if the soldiers are to be provided with water at a reasonable cost to them, they will be safe. But what of the taxpayer? Yet the Darling, and the Queensland and the Northern Territory rivers

---

[1] McCrae's poem 'The Dying Butcher'. The lines Mary refers to are:
    All flesh is grass, but mine has turned to hay
    Mildewed, alas, just meet to throw away.
    If this pun pleases—please credit Hugh McCrae.

[2] Jessie Street was Labor candidate for Wentworth, Leslie Haylen for Parkes and Pilot Officer M. Falstein for Watson, an Eastern Suburbs electorate in Sydney.

pour into the sea and no man gathers them. Actually settlement, inviting erosion and consequent silting, destroys them.

The aboriginals told father, me a child standing by, that the white man was so careless he destroyed the soil and in time the land would become waterless. I have long written that to protect the forest that protected the land no aboriginal allowed a mistletoe to grow. Father followed their example when managing Cowabbie Station and nearly got sacked for 'wasting the men's time'. The taxpayer has paid since.

To W. M. Hughes

Dear Mr Hughes,

Kings Cross
19 September 1943

I meant to write, but I have been ill—Parliament would not have been Parliament without you! and though I am a good party woman, I still have my old loyalties to one who has meant so much and done so much for Australia.

Today I read again:—

'For whom does Mr Hughes speak?' asked President Wilson.

'I speak for 60,000 Australian dead', Hughes answered 'out of their six million people. Can the President of the United States speak for any more out of his hundred million?'

Abraham Lincoln might have said that, so simple, so unadorned, and yet with the directness and the steel of an arrow.

I sent you early (months ago) a copy of my last book, the numbered special edition, 'The Disinherited'. It was not acknowledged, and I have wondered if you received it. And that reminds me: I shall enclose a copy of my scheme for soldier settlement. The paper shortage cut the tail off it, but the body is there. I do hope you will read it—and in connection with the rainfall on the Western Lands resumptions! Only a fraction of the blocks are on the river—what is the water supply of the rest? These men who are to go there are soldiers—I need say no more to you than that. Again yours sincerely,

To A. H. Chisholm

My Darlingest Alec—

Kings Cross
24 September 1943

Note the distinctness of the word! It is the measure of expectation of favours to come. But I have done a good job and you will feel I did. I have got a Poet's Corner officially named in the Sydney Gardens, also I wrote Mr. Curtin about the same or similar for Canberra and

W.A., and am writing to you now and the other states today. I enclose a cutting from yesterday's 'The Standard Weekly' which will save my time writing and your eyes reading.

I wrote to thank you for remembering my birthday in the 'Herald', for it cd. only be you. The little lad who liked my verse is still the little lad God bless him! I grow so old now, that every remembrance (from friends; others are only a trimming) is a warm blanket against the winter cold.

Old friend J. J. C. Bradfield, who would have made rivers where there are none, is gone, and only this week I decided I would see him about my plan: 'River Farms for Soldiers' (in the March 'Queensland Digger': I wish you could see it. I am trying to get copies.)

What a draw to the Gardens in this or any State a hundred years— and even less—will be to the young. Tradition does not drop from heaven; it has to be recorded. And tradition is an essential part of defence as part of the fuel to or of patriotism. Think of it in years to come! Think what it will mean to school children on 'conducted tours' and on their own! Dreams? *Our* dreams, Alex, don't blast life out at the cannon's mouth. We build. And please God we will build when the cannon is rust—or I hope so. Every good to you and yours

Spoke for Mrs Street[1] in the Election, then on Sunday Mr. Leslie Haylen, was 78 on Monday and spoke for F/O Falstein on Tuesday. Not bad was it for a sick woman—Or did I make you this brag before? If I did, sigh and say 'She's growing old.'

To George Mackaness

Dear George,

Kings Cross
8 October 1943

I have got it! Last month! My long proposed Poets' Corner in the Botanic Gardens. 'You and I alone did it' the Minister said when I met him this week. 'There was *no one else* in it' he added, and repeated it again later.

I wired Kate Baker 'ask Government give Poets' Corner in Botanic Gardens. Furphy tree to be first in it' and I was not only told my message was *the* one . . . but my suggestion is to be followed.

For Tasmania I sent my circular letter to Dame Enid Lyons, saying I wanted one of her first acts to be for a woman, and also that I wanted her as our first woman M.H.R. to be in it. She was so pleased indeed she wrote twice to thank me.

[1] See note to letter, 28 August 1943.

The cutting enclosed tells the rest of the story except that Curtin came earliest—his reply to my letter. My grounds are unassailable, and the minute I put them they are acclaimed. Also it can only happen once in the history of a nation. I put it that small memorials go inside the gardens, big ones (if they come) outside with the Henry Lawson area. It is fitting that Kendall should be first inside, and Lawson in the wider area.

I said that memorials could be trees, statuary and tablets on the stone walls round the outside of the corner. *No lawns to be destroyed or lessened.* So I think taking it by and large I *done* something!

To Roland Robinson

Dear Mr. Robinson,

Kings Cross
14 December 1943

I am afraid I am not encouraging.

Your play is poetry. That is a fact. *But* it is not aboriginal anymore than it is Russian or English; it is not fact; and the day of fancy or fantasy is gone except as far as fairy tales are concerned. In a time of plenty you wd. have had no trouble in publishing, & repayment in cost. But not today, only what soldiers buy pays today.

There is in Sydney a man who knows the aboriginal & his lore in the same way my father did, & with the same feeling. He is in the (NT) Dept. of Native Affairs. His Book 'Taboo'[1] is out, his sagas are with me at the moment, (I am to write the Introduction). Prof. Elkin[2] is collaborating on his *big* book. But he is to speak at the F.A.W.[3] next Sunday. Go to hear him if you can. He was here when your MS. came & I took the liberty of letting him see it. 'It is poetry' he said 'but not a native story'. You can use this (or my name) in speaking to him. He *has* done a lot of speaking—16 lectures of two hours on native lore & customs to the soldiers up North, and each lecture a different one. If you have been about the Alice, or northward, you may know people he knows.

Don't be downhearted over my criticism. The bad times are part of it. Only for the times it would make a lovely booklet.

[1] *Taboo*, by W. E. 'Bill' Harney, 1943.
[2] Adolphus Peter Elkin.
[3] Fellowship of Australian Writers. See notes to letters, 26 December 1928 and 22 May 1935.

To Constance Robertson

Dear Connie,

Kings Cross
17 December 1943

This nearly demented person is besieged by National Anthemers wanting to set 'No Foe Shall Gather Our Harvest'.

If the 'S.M.H.' has any sense of being on the spot at the moment, a better (or at least more suitable) one will appear tomorrow on the Magazine page.[1] If it doesn't will you ask Mr. Taylor to let you see it and then bash him, for he will deserve it! (If you shrink from bashing him you can let him see this. It will be just as bad.)

My dear what can I give you for Christmas that you haven't got! You have my long affection every day of the year, added up it might be a good lump sum. Affectionately,

To George Mackaness

Dear George,

Kings Cross
12 February 1944

I owe you a letter, and you (and Alice) owe me a visit. Anyhow I would like you to see the amassed stuff I have relative to my future biography. I have already paid about £50 for the typing of some years of more or less diary. That includes cost of paper and duplicate. I could have it done cheaper in the house (if I could get a girl) but there is the likelihood that the unprofessional typist might talk, and *I* might be hanged for my opinions.

I have had no word of Ernestine.[2] Rene Foster wrote from Adelaide the same day as you, asking for news of any sort. I sent her your letter noted 'to be returned'. Ernestine may have more than outward circumstances beginning to attack her nervous condition. I am not particularizing, but you can guess. Her last letter to me said it would be a long time before she did any writing again... She needs every consideration for her dependence on Bob,[3] to help her continue writing. Bob might be good manure in a trench, but her books are Australia, and we can replace life (curious as it may seem) where we cannot replace the lost historical, without which we cannot build the spiritual and, actually, the directive to some extent. If I had my way I'd leave Bob to help Ernestine, and pack out half the fat-brained sitting in military offices!

[1] Apparently the *S.M.H.* was unimpressed for there is no mention of the new version of the National Anthem in the issue of 18 December 1943.
[2] Ernestine Hill.
[3] Ernestine Hill's son.

Have been (and am) ill. Had a splintered jaw, and a good tooth badly loosened at the dentist's and next day flu on top of it. No return of it thank goodness. I hope you are A1 in health, also Alice. As ever,

A writing and travelled soldier addressed me 'Dear Australia' and said that was what I am to most Australian soldiers. Did I nearly burst with pride? I'm telling you!

To R. G. Howarth

Dear Mr Howarth,

Kings Cross
21 May 1944

I wanted to write and not only express my agreement but thanks for your article on the New Pocket Library (S.M.H. 29.4.44) I do agree with you about Gordon.[1] But he is not only aphoristic, I would add he is Australian and add it emphatically. In the 70's you could not go to station, hut or shearing shed, but the name of Gordon wd. almost call a spell for someone to recite something of his. And why? Because he uttered *them*, who were unable to otherwise utter themselves, and the people, and the country they knew . . . I was about fourteen then and I know he was in the hearts of the people because they were his and he was theirs. In later years, after I came back from South America, I lived in his Western Victoria country.[2] Last month I gave my son a buckhorn handled knife came from his table. I knew people who were his friends and had tales and relics of him. And again I say he was in the hearts of the people because he was of them and not outside . . . The city bred criticize him from the desk and not from the hearts of the people. The re-publication of Gordon, in cheap form, would set the country reading and reciting again. The people want song not naked intellect.

As a child father took us (about 1871 I think) to Mt. Gambier to see where Gordon made his leap.[3] It was unfenced still. The fence was put up later because others were doing it (three or four; I think my mother's brother among them) because one man did go into the lake. His mates hauled him out. His horse was drowned. We *saw* this . . .

---

[1] Adam Lindsay Gordon.
[2] Near Casterton. See W. H. Wilde, 'Mary Gilmore—The Hidden Years', *Meanjin Quarterly* 4 (1973), 425-32.
[3] Known as the 'Blue Lake leap'. Gordon performed a daring but fool-hardy leap on horseback, risking a drop of some 200 feet into the Blue Lake near Mount Gambier. See, inter alia, W. H. Wilde, *Adam Lindsay Gordon*, 1972, pp. 7-8.

Mr Malloch,
Bread and Cheese Club,
Melbourne.

Kings Cross
25 May 1944

Dear Mr. Malloch,
My tombstone would have borne the words: 'she died of a broken heart', if I hadn't been in it! What a beautiful book it is and in what fellowship written. 'What book?' Yours, 'The Chronicles of the Bread and Cheese Club'. I would I could give you a bang, with a similar body of women! But men may be convivial and women may not, and that perhaps is the root of difference and the fence between them. There are no Armies of women. When there are they cease to be women. I said to a demobbed man yesterday, 'It must have been terrible, coming back to Civilian life after the fellowship of the Army'. 'For six months I nearly went mad' he said. He has been out nearly two years and yet under his words his inheld voice spoke agony. And I can understand it. And so I can understand your Bread and Cheese Club. I'd give the world to be in it, but I'd spoil heaven to keep out of it, leave it intact, which means I do understand things that matter. My name is all that I would ask to have there in your record and your memory. And (Happy Woman!) it is there . . .

    A visitor, and I must end. The book is a joy to hold in the hand as a printer and editor's production, and a lovely thing to read. But I must get some autographs in it for my collection at the Mitchell. I cannot have this left out! Yours (all of you) gratefully,

To Roland Robinson

Dear Roland,

Kings Cross
28 July 1944

Your book, 'Beyond the Grass-tree Spears'[1] came awhile ago & I have just laid it down. The verse is very sensitive & as sensitively finished. You are not like anyone else, though you write the same stars & seas. That is something to be thankful for on bended knees. While I think (as to the book) the 'accompaniments' are a bit obtrusive the printing of your verse is beautiful. Each page gives an impression of form or pattern in proportion. This too is rare.

[1] Published 1944.

I am glad of your inscription.[1] It is a grateful pleasure to me to have been associated with what is really the flowering of a mind. Of our writers I link you with Roderic Quinn & Shaw Neilson. You have the pellucid quality of Quinn, with the sensitive delicacy of Neilson. As to passion—Neilson has passion raised to pain; Quinn has none; it is wistful in you. In description, your reactions & expression are your own.

Now as to future publication. Keep *small in volume*. Delicacy cannot be served up on too large a dish. So again I say keep small. If you lose that elusive & delicate atmosphere you become as the mass of others. If you lose what others have not, you have to work with anvil & hammer, hardening steel. So many remain 'just-iron'.

I have not been at all well for some time. Working hard of course! I hope Barbara is happy in the book. She deserves it as much as you, yourself. Will you let Mr. Ingamells know what I think of the work? It will save a tired woman another letter. Finally I hope you are very well.

To A. H. Chisholm

Kings Cross
29 September 1944

Dear Alec—

I wrote you two days ago, and am now writing to tell you to get a book and never cease till you get it. It is 'The Yearling' by Marjorie Kinnan Rawlings. It went into 4 editions in three months. I don't know how a woman wrote it without being mannish or too woman-like. It is neither. The hunting is a man's hunting, bears, wolves, deer and small things, and yet the birds sing and the flowers bloom. It has the variety of Shakespeare. It is so close to life I felt lonely when I put it down. I wish you would write an Australian boy's book, not like it of course, but in its field. The boy in it could have been you.

Get it, and get it, and get it! or have you had it? My affections to you.

[1] The 'inscription' must have been a personal one to Mary in her copy. The first lines of the book are also a type of inscription. They read:

> I made my verses of places where I made my fires;
> Of the dark trees standing against the blue-green night
> With the first stars coming; of the bare plains where
>   a bird
> Broke into running song, and of the wind-cold shrub
> Where the bent trees sing to themselves, and of the night
> Dark about me, the fire dying out, and the ashes left.

To George Mackaness

Dear George,

Kings Cross
7 October 1944

... Presently, after the war, we will be surged with immigrants of every country. Our history of localities will be overlaid if we do not see that this is prevented. So I want you to read this, and present my other typed matter to the Historical Society,[1] and ask if they will back me in the proposition for a Day for local historical matter, in all schools in the State.

(You remember I have each time stressed this kind of thing to the Teachers' College when I talked there.) The smaller the school the nearer to the historical item of the beginners—fire, flood, adventure, or what! The examples I give in the enclosure indicate how wide can be the range. It will cost the State nothing, the Hist. Soc. or the Mitchell will reap without cost if they care to do so, as the local papers will collect by reporting the Day. I am telling you all this as I may not be able to write it all for the Historical Society in form. I have for this winter been facing the choice of having my health and losing my sight or of saving my sight and hastening down hill. Not a nice choice; but my sight now is most to me. And that's that! Yours

To A. H. Chisholm

Dearest Alec—

Kings Cross
7 November 1944

No doubt the Scots aye are it! (The Ministerial hieroglyph of dots and telegraph poles beat me. What is his name?) To return to Scots! I just had this from Walter Murdoch, and you never said anything nicer yourself:—

'I would it had been my lot
To have seen thee, and heard thee, and known,
'So says Tennyson of Scott, and so say I of Dame Mary Gilmore ...' I have done more than forward your letter to our Minister for Education,—I have gone to see him, and handed him the letter with my strongest possible recommendation.
... I'll try to get the public here to take up the project ... If your idea is taken up with enthusiasm future generations will bless your name, for all that you will have saved from oblivion. I bless it in any case.'

Do you wonder if I wrote to him as a heaven-sent angel? And another Scot, your (and my) Christina Mawdesley writes this morning 'Local Day for Schools is an inspiration, and wd. result in putting on record many things that wd. slip away ...'

[1] Mackaness was President of the Society, 1948-49.

I'm scared to death now that some of the other countries to wh. I have written, and will write, will start first, and Australia come in late. You'd think these people of ours had to build the walls of heaven, before they put up their country's flag to (or of) its people's history! ... Yours,

To Kenneth Slessor

Kings Cross
24 November 1944

Dear Kenneth Slessor (I am nearly old enough now to call you Ken!)

How kind to one who had not expected it, you were last night! I am as grateful as I am astounded that I should have been put with the high: those to whom I look up as from a far distance. I think you & Bob FitzGerald, now that Hugh McCrae is almost not writing, are the only two who really matter & will beat the grinding wheels of change & time. One reason is that you both must work terribly hard (& I use those words as praise) to get the form & phrase you want. The day of 'the little thing flung off', the little spout of emotion, is gone. Now it is the day of the mined & the quarried—the hard stone of intellectual thought & experience shaped & made beautiful. And more: made durable. And Douglas Stewart—There are ways in which he runs ahead of you both. But the fashion & glitter of words holds him more than you and Bob—doesn't hold either of you!—& when that fashion & glitter go, as it did with Tennyson, the ebb will begin, and a new evaluation be required. But he really is fire on the snow—fire on a berg—wonderful & beautiful.

I am worried about Hugh McCrae. I wrote him over a fortnight ago & have had no reply. That is not like him, & I am wondering if he is again too ill to care what happens. Also I sent him since then a piece of verse I wrote for the Hugh McCrae talk & reading last night at the Henry Lawson Society. Not poetry of course, but there are one or two lines that tell the true self that is Hugh. As I said to him he has always left the ferret to his hole, the weasel in his ditch. The jealous, the mean, the ignoble have never had part in Hugh. He has judged but never belittled another writer.

I wish when you or your wife are passing you would stop off & knock on my door. I am mostly in & it doesn't matter how early as long as you don't ask for chops for breakfast. Again & again since you came back I meant to write to you or ask to see you. But I had a bad winter, & things slipped. And again this quail in the wheat looks up at the heron & says Thank you for being a heron.

Later.
A letter from Hugh in answer to mine; & what a shaken hand,

& half wandering mind—& *yet* the gold is there. And the directness & generous judgment on two things I sent him before his last wh. he had evidently not received when he wrote. He is like the pine tree, that in decay retains its majesty—dignity—if you like it better.

His trouble is valvular heart. Doctor, he says, tells him to lie down with the lamb family; *he* says *Walk*, & he walks.

Still Later.
It has just struck me! I have some valuable matter for an article on my plea for a Local History Day in all schools. S. Aust. is sporadically collecting theirs, & is calling it 'door step history' & Harney, W.E. has sent me 'The Harney Herald Pioneer Number' full of stuff by child descendants of pioneer founders. I am wondering could you do an article from all this? My eyes have more than they can do.
I send you this because you praised Hugh.

To Hugh McCrae
Still tall the tower we thought could never be too tall,
The strong foundation stands unshaken at its base,
The engined might within drives on in rise and fall,
The proud exultant spirit holds its dear notorious grace.
And yet what weight—what weight the years have brought to bend
If not to break, the pride that would not own decay,
And which refused to fear we might one day attend.
A stage was ours, where now the stranger makes the play.
You had the gift for friendship, Hugh! The hidden knife
Within the jealous palm, that stabbed, then sought its lair,
That knife was never yours. For you—come peace, come strife—
Stood up to conflict face to face, & met it—knuckle-bare—

You were too generous to wound with cruel phrase;
You were too great in art to fray another's gold;
But, the rich-minded, in assessment. You gave praise
And helped the weak to strength until it stood up bold*
And in that hunting field where thought creative hounds,
Where envy spits in gall the venom of its itch,
You, in your fineness, put all meanness out of bounds,
And left the ferret to his hole, the weasel in his ditch.

And, Hughoc, though your stook above unkempt sheaf
Rose like the pine tree on our far ancestral hills
Through all its faults, you never made dispraise a thief,
To steal the little grain that broken sheaf, imperfect spills.

* A quotation, 'stood up bold', & to my shame I have forgotten if it came from the Bible or not.

M.G.

To Constance Robertson

Dear Connie,

Kings Cross
24 February 1945

Have you seen R. G. Howarth on your father[1] and Shaw Neilson as given in Devaney's Life.[2] I am sure it is a lie that your father spoiled any of Neilson's verse,[3] that he drove a hard bargain with Neilson over it, or made money (if any) out of Neilson. Neilson would be the first to combat that if he were alive.

You must have known the roughness of Neilson's verse at the beginning. Even I knew of it in one or two pieces. 'Green Days and Cherries' was accepted as a name by Neilson. It was I who said 'No, it is too intentionally pretty'. And your father took my advice. You can use this letter, Connie, if you take the matter up—as you should. Neilson always said that next to your father I was his encourager. Now a later comer wants to push your father out. Yet Neilson in his letters to me (now at the Mitchell Library) gave all (not just full) credit to your father. In a letter I gave to Dr. George Mackaness, he wrote that I was first after your father to encourage him. I believe he told Bob Croll (or someone who told me) the same thing. Affectionately.

These people yap at your father now that he is in his grave and would have thought it glory to have a word of praise from him living.

To W. G. Cousins

Dear Mr Cousins,

Kings Cross
20 April 1945

I have to thank A & R on my own behalf and for Australia for three valuable things, two books and a magazine.

Hugh McCrae's 'Forests of Pan',[4] handled by you, leaves every other writer behind. (R. D. FitzGerald excepted who is perhaps as perfect in his way, though so different in impulse and diction) because he (Hugh) adds no cotton to his silk, and his silk is real; *not* manufactured and artificial. Reading Hugh's work is like handling loveliness—texture, colour, form, vitality, art and the arrow in the bullseye every

---

[1] A. G. Stephens.
[2] James Devaney's biography of Shaw Neilson was published in 1944.
[3] On the subject of A. G. Stephens's editing of Shaw Neilson see Hugh Anderson, 'The Making of Shaw Neilson's "Honeymoon Song" ', *Biblionews*, 9 (1956), 23-8; the same writer's 'Green Days and Cherries', *Meanjin*, 10 (1951), 67-8; and H. J. Oliver's 'A More Versatile Neilson: The Manuscript Evidence', *Southerly*, 17 (1956), 29-33.
[4] A selection of Hugh McCrae's poetry by R. G. Howarth, published 1944.

time: these are Hugh McCrae. I regard myself as that much more worth while in that I perceive and feel Hughie's work as I do. It is my own pat on my own back. No matter how long ago written and first printed, the work is as new as this morning—Hugh, in the future, will be our Chaucer: a man to whom the word as well as the story mattered.

The second book is H. M. Green's 'Fourteen Minutes'.[1] That book gave me a bad half hour! (I had made a record on writers of my young years (for 2FC) and had said that Barcroft Boake had hanged himself with his stock whip. H. M. Green's book came just after that and *he* said Barcroft (who was a constant visitor of ours at Wagga) had *shot* himself. The National Library and a copy of Who's Who confirmed my over 50 year old recollection) However the book is excellent for the scope allowed it, and it is pocket size: another good thing. I was surprised at how often he mentioned me, and then I realized that it was not I, but my range, caught his attention.

The third publication is 'Southerly'—and how great a need we have of such a magazine, the English throughout is so good. English matters. Good English is a living, enduring, beautiful thing, poor English is a splay-footed reptile, and that no matter how good the material in its belly (I have to use the word as no other fits). The J. A. R. McKellar[2] appreciation and quotation gives a man (with Hugh McCrae's vision and a warmer English) the due that should have been accorded him long ago. He was the lightning where Hugh was the finished spear.

If any sentence of this is any use to you I shall find a place among the gods if you will use it.

My thanks and warm good wishes to you.

To Hugh McCrae

Dear Hugh,

Kings Cross
11 May 1945

I think the reference to Villon[3] (in the way it was made & meant) was shallow. I thought it at the time when I read it. Your work may express grief or loss, but there is no self-pain in it. That is one of the reasons why I find you like Chaucer. Not as a follower but as of the same sunlight & clay. That, and the loveliness of the words. Mad as it may

---

[1] An adaptation of a series of radio talks on Australian writers by H. M. Green.
[2] The *Southerly* article, 5, 4 (1944), 3-10 was 'John Alexander Ross McKellar, Memoir by J. W. Gibbes'.
[3] Mary refers to a review of McCrae's *Forests of Pan* in the *S.M.H.*, 5 May 1945. The review said that the 'influences of older poets from Villon to Catullus are perceptible'.

seem there is a greater fellowship between Lawson & Villon; the poles apart of form & idiom dividing most people from the fact. Self-pity is only one step beyond self-pain, in expression. But how beauty of form (in all its aspects) can wring the heart! So one weeps with Villon, but not with Henry. In you something triumphs over death though the heart suffer the throe of the wrung.

In other words, you do not know how to be morbid. So you are like Chaucer, and I see it again in your stripped form & diction. You wear neither poppies nor roses. You keep too close to life for either.

If you come Monday, well & good; & if you don't, I've got you all the same.

I wd. sooner see you doing a life of Menzies or George Finey than Watt;[1] I don't see him worthy of your best. I remember his Uncle, 'Old Billy Watt of Bumbaldery'. He had greater ideas than the nephew he endowed with his money. Silly little people thought him silly. He was not. They saw Australia as an island; he saw its future. Now I've got to tell a girl whose people object to her re-marrying to ask if they expect her never to smile again. She is only a girl & a whole life before her.

My hands are on yours,

To Kenneth Slessor

Kings Cross
9 June 1945

Dear Ken Slessor,

I have just been reading R. A. Morrison's review of your book[2] in 'Southerly' (just come) and I am like a compassless mariner on a wide sea, between you, Hugh McCrae, & R. D. FitzGerald. Which is greater? Which?

I know it is heresy to say it, but I put *you* before Brennan. Brennan is a lion roaring & you know the lion is there because of the roar. I begin to think you are the lion, stark, lean, watchful & stript of his roar. And not only that, but a stronger more swift & enduring lion than the Brennan lion, without the anguished thunder of his roar.

But what three points of a triangle you, Hugh & Bob are!

Did I ever tell you my grandmother told me, in childhood, the story of (Jane?) Mary Ann Bell, Bob's ancestress of whom he wrote 60 years later? Also she told me of Mrs. Lindsay who, with pots of boiling water (she got all the women to work) drove off the besiegers on the walls of Derry (Londonderry)? and I never heard it again till

[1] Ernest Alexander Stuart Watt.
[2] Slessor's collection, *One Hundred Poems*, 1944.

60 years later when Lionel told it to me. Both Irish, as my mother's people were for centuries.

And did you see Norma L. Davis's 'Remembering the Birds' in this week's 'Bulletin'? She brought back everything I knew & was as a child—the smell of every bird was known to us then (& the glades that smelled of Parrots.) The city has taken away our noses & given us stinks—dirt, rubbish-carts, fish & butchers' shops—instead. Norma is too opulent—but better that than the stretched thin tissues of ignorance. As to my triangle which ever way you lay it, the top one is in his right place.

It has always seemed strange, almost unbelievable that you should feel my work. It is so without finish, so (as some have said) over emotional; but it must be because life is behind it. In a book I am reading I find: 'The creative artist has an enormous advantage over other people. For he can comport himself into some other set of circumstances, or into some other world or era, every time he sits down at his desk'. The finished writer is in his creative world of finish, writers like me are in the world of others & have to express their reactions—incarnations—in haste or all will be lost. Finish, if it comes, is only the tail. With you it is forelock, mane & tail, and with the whole lovely coat.

To Kenneth Slessor

Dear Ken,

Kings Cross
16 June 1945

There was no need to write, no matter how glad I might be to have a letter.

The only person who does not live in the shadow of wreck & grief is the fakir whose range of affection is his prayer mat. What he loses he never misses. I hope & hope Noela[1] will be better.

In anxiety for you both.

Don't write till Noela is better.

To Hugh McCrae

Darlingest & Wonderfullest!

Kings Cross
19 July 1945

That 'dishonest hi'—I have got that far, & am on wings for that word.

---

[1] Kenneth Slessor's first wife, Noela, died in 1945 after a long illness. See Douglas Stewart, *A Man of Sydney*, 1977.

Who but you could have picked up & shined it! (Now I go back to the book.)[1]

A fountain, a brook, that spring up in jewels.

I don't like the last verse of Hob. The first two verses are mighty, & then he drops to being just a gone-to-sleep (but not to sleep) ordinary man. 'Beside his wife ... with book & candle (to the end) and 'The word of God ... and twenty balls ...' Power, fear, readiness, daring, all stripped to the bone, back-straight, and unbeaten even if ground to powder. The atoms speak. See what I mean?

'Some sweetheart field ...' Lovely.

'She walks the chambers of the air'—
One walks on the words as
Christ walked on the waters
of Galilee.

'Sleep, that is married to life ...'
(How different from the usual sleep the fellow or simulacrum of death. You make sleep a living fellow with life.)

'... and took with marble eyes a yet Unconquered gaze ... Man with his woman made a flood of kings & weavers ...'
That 'weavers'! what a lift that (social) dip gives to wings forward, backward and circling and darting every range of history & thought! (If I am in-coherent don't mind. It deepens the tribute.)

'Too old for merry-make'. who else would dare omit the 'ing' of common usage?

Later, & the end of the book which I leave untouched.

My dear, I have forgotten to remember your inscription,[2] in the work itself, for what is said or written to me is a small thing compared with what is written for time & the world. But how beautiful, & how characteristic of you it is. You were never niggard, Hugh. No miser's cradle was ever yours. And more than that: you have hidden pain behind a banner. The whimper is as far from your work as the miser from

---

[1] The quotations and references are from and to McCrae's *Voice of the Forest*. The lines from 'The Blind Man Said' are:

> While Menelaus pale
> First felt his spright
> Dishonest him, and quail.

[2] Apparently a personal tribute in Mary's copy. *Voice of the Forest* is dedicated to R. M. Crookston.

your heart ... There was a big man in the sky when you were born & when the little, the petty, the bric-a-brac, the gimcrack are forgotten, the big man will still be there high as the sky and the commentators will say 'That is Hugh McCrae' and I am saying it now hoping to be part of that time. To have seen a star & known it a star makes one feel immortal—that me at the moment is ME.—

Mary Gilmore!

To George Mackaness

Dear Dr. Mackaness,

Kings Cross
28 July 1945

I have just had a letter from Adam McCay, saying that he is without means, and is applying for a Literary Pension. If anyone deserves the Pension it is Adam! His work never fell in quality, whether as leading article, special article, political, topical, or other. He had knowledge as a reader and thinker, and a gift of English, which made everything he wrote a satisfaction and a food to the mind. He made his readers think. If his best work were collected and edited for book publication, there would be no question as to his standing as a writer ... Adam McCay has a Degree (M.A.) and was notable for his intellectual standing in a notable school before he went to the University. So it is not a case of one suddenly jumped-up, but of a life of continuous national service to form, educate, and lead public opinion. Surely this counts for more than a lot of tiddley-winking verse, a volume of feeble stories or an ordinary novel. Yours sincerely.

To George Mackaness

Dear George,

Kings Cross
29 July 1945

I posted you a letter this morning. The next moment I was struck. Billy[1] is gone. Pneumonia. Don't say anything. Don't tell anyone. And don't write. Not yet.

[1] Mary's only child, William Dysart Cameron Gilmore, born 1898. This is the only letter so far available to the Editors, in which Mary's personal grief is revealed over the death of her son, of pneumonia, in Queensland on 29 July 1945. Her diary however records her agony:

> I force myself to read, to work, to shut the door on thought, I only know now that everything I did was as much a part of my son as of myself. Now nothing matters ... The body eats, the mind thinks, the hands do their work, but as separate entities. There is no unity. The only unity is the subconscious everlasting consciousness of grief and loss.

Some two weeks later, 11 August 1945, she wrote:

I am telling you, because you George and Alice have been so much my friends.

My head feels in a vyce. My niece and her husband came with the news—long distance telephone news this morning. Billy went last night. I sent them home. I am best alone.

To William Bluett

Kings Cross
12 September 1945

Dear Billy Bluett—

We are old enough & long enough known to each other for that—I cried over your letter. Death is nothing. The agony, for people like you & me, is in leaving untold & unrecorded in permanency, the stories of those who made the real history of life as lived & endured & of this country. The individual is the doer & sufferer, but more & more I see that it is the mass in unity that is being built, & matters. Life & its stories are the cementing mortar, & the creator of the enduring. As to you—a man who can write as you can is a lunatic to sit by the fire & dream instead of doing. For God's sake—for Australia's sake—get to work! My heart is aching with all that your letter brought back to me. Ida[1] was no dramatic writer—no painter in words—but you *are*.

[1] Bluett's elder sister.

>   After the years of separation
>   Once again you are mine;
>   The loneliness is ended
>   And the burdens gone.
>   In my arms as a babe I held you
>   Now in the arms of earth you lie
>   There no evil thing can touch you
>   And no grief break.
>   I would have held you safe my son,
>   But you were a man, and
>   As a man you had to go . . .

1945 was a year of double tragedy for Mary. On 20 February her husband Will Gilmore had died of blood-poisoning in Queensland. He was buried in Cloncurry Cemetery. Her diary of 23 February 1945 records:

> My private life scarcely enters here. So there is something recorded here which affects me greatly. It happened that circumstances over which neither of us had any control compelled us to live in different places but dad had the life he wanted. He had everything he asked of life. This has always been a happiness for me to think of and remember. We were separated by distance but not otherwise. Dad's death was sudden and wholly unexpected. I cannot believe it yet . . . there has never been a day I have not thought of him, and now there will be no more letters to write to dad, no more paragraphs or articles to mark and cut out to interest him, no more books to send.

After many normal entries in the diary in the following days she ponders 'Queer how I can talk (and write) on or from the surface, and feel this dull endless ache underneath'.

Ida can be forgiven for not making a record, you cannot, for you have every gift she had not.

Now as to your request, *you* write the story of Etty's[1] life, bring in Mrs. Bogue Luffmann to widen interest, and I will take the matter to Connie Robertson. More than a paragraph is needed. Write two columns if you can so that it can be cut to what the woman's page will allow.

Etty's history will not lose by a little delay. The wait will give it a better chance, as the papers are expanding on the woman's section. Give plenty—part of the family history can come in. For I will suggest to Connie a series of articles on pioneer women. She has done me. She can do others & in the end make a book of them. Ida told me your mother was descended from William Wallace (I think I heard father say that, mention that too). The first sizeable telescope I looked through (we had a tiny one) was your mother's. Put that in, as it links one woman with another & today links become (& adorn) history. Nothing exciting or picturesque is too small, routine matters need only their recording. What I suggest is what I tell everyone, that is an exercise book & pencil by the bedside, & jot, & jot, as memories come. Collating & connecting can come later. In the exercise book put anything & everything, no matter how wide. Do not keep to one aspect or theme. That is how I wrote 'Old Days' & 'More Recollections' (*not* chapter by chapter.) You may do all this, but I write it in case you need pushing to it...

To William Bluett

Dear Bill—

Kings Cross
24 October 1945

The body of the chicken is over a low gas, & the legs & wings in a cool place for a later day. Thank you for the chicken, but ten times more for your thought. The chicken will warm my tummy, but the thought has warmed my heart.

Now about the writing. No matter how small, no matter how brief, no matter how unconsecutive, notes are history; they are the land, the road maker & the gardening can come later; in a hundred years time; and with that time your name is on the gate again. Your name & all your people, your times, & your past with it. You have no idea what ten minutes a day after you go to bed will gather! *I know* because my diary is a clothes basket into which everything goes and yet not everything, for most of what would hurt others I omit; & then there are

---

[1] Another sister of William Bluett.

the things one forgets or only realizes a year afterward are important. But a netful is better than none, so though I grieve, I don't grieve; for some loss is inevitable. But so few gather who should. That is the heartbreak. An instance, last month I met the grand daughter of the woman who stepped ashore in the first woman's hat to come to Australia. Think of it! They had not recorded it. But I had heard of it in childhood from father & how people said she was 'bold' (a bad word then) and now it is in my diary with what the family did not know & I remembered . . .

To W. G. Cousins

Kings Cross
4 December 1945

Dear Mr Cousins,

I am still alive, and am hoping to see you. But in case I feel too tired to go out tomorrow, I am writing.

I am sending you the MS[1] of what I hope *will* be, and what *should* be, our first Walt Disney order of film, and I am sending it by the hand of the author, Eleanor (Mrs Gordon) Smith, of Cottesloe, West Aust. She is taking it to you hoping for publication as a children's book. But I saw beyond the book. I saw the value to children all over the world as a film, and far beyond that, to Australia as an advertisement through the films if we can get it there.

I have suggested to Mrs Smith certain alterations by which to make it run more clearly, and which, I hope, your readers will endorse. She has the central figure at least a boy of ten, though not yet born. I have suggested that he has waited so long to be born that, tired of waiting and quite a boy, he has (as she shows) run away. There, as a ten year old straying lad he is accepted as a boy and has his adventures. Another thing is that instead of making a whistle some chapters on, he makes it early—even before he runs away perhaps—and that the air he plays follows far and near, actual and as haunting, throughout the whole story, till homesick for the Dream world he at last returns (as she too hastily makes him) and is 'dreamed' by his father-to-be to birth.

If you read the MS yourself you will see, as I have told Mrs Smith, that the kangaroo, 'the run-away dog that *hops because he swallowed a frog*' (glorious bit!), indeed all the animals and characters can be extended and extended and the stories go on like Ginge[2] to world without end!

[1] Apparently nothing came of this manuscript although Eleanor Smith did write several other books.
[2] Ginger Meggs, the famous boy of the comic strip series. See Bancks, James, in Appendix.

The language is not *written down*, which is a blessing to adults as well as children, and the whole thing is within the range of the child's mind.

I hope, and I hope, and I HOPE you will see this story (this MS) as I do. Yours sincerely,

P.S. The name will need to be altered to Bimbi or something as easy.

To George Mackaness

Kings Cross
Dear George, 23 January 1946

... Have you met William Harney yet? I told him some years ago Australia will one day raise statues to him! I am more sure of it than ever. He was unknown then. Now he has to refuse people who want him to address meetings.

He tells me there is a tremendous movement up North by writers and artists to recreate or capture the aborigine as a human being, as an artist and as a source of an Australian foundation in literature. The name I first gave him, 'our Australian Captain Cook', I still give him and more than ever, for what he is doing for us in regard to a source of art and literature independent of all the rest of the world.

You will see by all this that I am still alive. But not always sure of it myself these last few weeks!

My love to Alice. Yours as ever

To Peace Inglis Moore

Kings Cross
Dear Peace, 25 January 1946

What an astounding child. Pacita[1] of course. I have never seen anything so alert and vital. Every cell of her body has its own separate and personal life; every hair of her head capable of doing a pixie dance on its own account. At a hundred she should be the darling of everyone about her and the centre of Australian life. And how unpretentious and with what poise! No wonder Tom's heart is in her! She is both of you in one.

What honesty, what character, what a sense of standard is in the child!

[1] Pacita Moore, daughter of Tom and Peace Moore, now Mrs Alexander with three children of her own.

And I think if she came to take up experimental Science she would put the atom together again as a friend of man.

(Science or mathematics were my natural field. I *love* the sharp certainties of Euclid. And experiment made me a cook and a maker of jams no one else could make; also the whitest and lightest of bread in a district where bread was the age-long housewife's pride).

Well—all this has been boiling up in my mind—my stirred and wonder-filled mind—to say. And at last I have a moment in which to say it.

To see the growing up of these young things is the discovery of new continents and the development of new worlds...

Affectionately (and love to the child) to you and Tom.

To William Bluett

Kings Cross
3 February 1946

Dear Billy Bluett,

Just now a nice man came to the door from a nicer man! And he had a whopping big chicken for me from the nicer man. Thank you for the chicken, but how much more for the remembrance. I had been all strung up for a talk I had given over 2FC at 2 p.m. and was suffering the inevitable reaction. In the dumps. Now I feel like wings.

It has just struck me! Have you ever talked on the air? They are doing a series of Pioneer Stories, & if you felt like it I would send in your name as one who had a story to tell. They made me the first, I think because I am 80. They pay only £5.5 for 15 minutes, and claim the copyright, but I always write in my own proviso: 'copyright retained by author for book publication'. (I do that with the 'S.M.H.' & any other publication using my work).

This summer has not been kind to me any more than to anyone else. You are lucky to be above the humidity of the lower levels. Though perhaps you feel it proportionately.

The name Brindabella[1] brings back a vision of Farrer in his blue flannel jumper & moleskin trousers in the wheat, heavy-footed but with what a mind! I realize now he *loved* his wheat. Nothing else mattered to him and then came C. E. W. Bean, & what a different kind of man. One had his feet on the ground & the other on the mountain tops, & both servants of Australia.

How are the recollections going? Nothing is too small, & slowness does not matter. A stick here, a stick there, & the woodheap grows.

All this is to say Thank you & Thank you again. Yours, past & present.

[1] The picturesque mountain range near Canberra where Billy Bluett lived.

The Editor, Kings Cross
Sydney Daily Telegraph. 6 May 1946

SIR,—

'That word' has its origin in the Bible. It does not appear at all in the New Testament; it is entirely Old Testament, which, unlike the New, is imprecatory throughout.

The very Anglo-Saxon letters that form the word make it an explosion—a blasting and a force flung out. What it was in the original Hebrew I do not know, and a full and complete comparison might be interesting.

In the earlier books of the Bible there is no hint of the imprecatory, the word is merely descriptive. But when we come to the Psalms one gets the impression that David was a soldier, and, as could be, there is definitely a hint of the imprecatory. This is also found in Ezekiel, and it is in 'Woe to the bloody city!' even though still adjectival.

When Cromwell and his men rode England they made the word still more imprecatory. They talked of 'bloody-minded men', who were not monsters, but reputable followers of the King. Then it was that the word was lifted out of its narrowed use to become practically the imprecation it is today, so that when I was a child Irish people were still called 'bloody-minded Papists', though they had never shed a drop of blood and were our neighbours.

Actually, the word has great history behind it, and the Bible as its beginning; at all events, in English.

As to censorship, apart from this word, greatness in literature can travel any path. But if censorship did not exist, dirty-minded little boys, no matter what their ages, would have no check on what they would scribble on public and private walls. And can we call this literature?

To Miles Franklin

 Kings Cross
Dear Miles, 15 May 1946

You are a dramatic hussy, or a hussy for the dramatic! I have just read your article[1] (and revelation) on 'E' whom I had thought *a nun*, because of similarity in the examples of verse sent me, written in unconsciousness through pain & forgotten when consciousness returned. I felt bound—perhaps promised—not to tell this. Even now I have not named the convent, so that is safe. I think you will remember I once asked

---

[1] '"E". The Full Story', by Miles Franklin, *Bulletin*, 15 May 1946. See Mary Fullerton (Appendix) and note to letter, 17 June 1937.

if you were 'E', as I had an idea it might have been you all the time. Anyhow I am glad I saw her as individual & not an ex-stirp (if there is such a word!) of Emily Dickinson.

Keep going. I am fighting for my miserable chest again—Chill. Still astonished.

To The Chief Commissioner of Police

Dear Mr. MacKay,

Kings Cross
1 June 1946

It is a long time since Mr. Lamond[1] brought you to see me when I edited the Woman's Page[2] of the 'Australian Worker', but you may have some recollection of the Office, even if you have forgotten me.

I am writing you in regard to the suggestion I made (Daily Telegraph 24.5.46) that a sculptured recognition of the work our dogs[3] have done in establishing Australia on her pastoral and other foundations and with particular reference to your Police-dog, Zoe—that she be made the central figure if a group be decided on, and that she be the only one if a single figure be chosen . . .

We have no statuary of our own to the dogs that did so much for us, that brought the cattle and the sheep home, were the drovers' right hand, found lost children, and died of snake bite saving the children they went out with, and, in the case of the Police dogs, helped safeguard society individually and as a whole. Such a work as I suggest, in white marble, and not a crude thing like 'the Dog on the Tucker-box', would be an inspiration and an education to our children.

I am a tired old woman over 80, but I love my country and the things that made her, so I am asking you will you take this matter in hand, call the necessary Committee of public men and women, and allow your Services to raise the money either by a Concert in the Town Hall or a Ball if that is better, and see that the name of the Service

---

[1] Hector Lamond.
[2] From her isolated farming life at Casterton, Victoria, Mary wrote to Lamond suggesting a special page for women in the *Worker*. Lamond wrote back offering her the task. See 'Mary Gilmore—The Hidden Years', *Meanjin Quarterly* 4 (1973), 425-32.
[3] This was not the only attempt by Mary to highlight the contribution made by the dog to Australia's development. In December 1955 she wrote to the General Manager, Commonwealth Trading Bank of Australia, suggesting that the Bank give some permanent recognition of the sheep dog by incorporating a sculpture of a dog in one of its buildings. In 1959 the Bank decided to incorporate a feature mural of a sheep dog in action on its new bank, then building at Wagga Wagga. Bim Hilder, son of J. J. Hilder, on being commissioned for the mural, wrote to Mary for advice. She told him to go to the Homebush sale yards in Sydney to study the dogs in action. Mary was delighted with the Bank's response as she was with the response of Police Commissioner MacKay to this earlier letter.

(and your own) goes on the pediment as part of the record. It would be a great gift to Australia, and the first of its kind. Yours sincerely, and hoping,

To Donald Gordon Campbell

Dear Don,

Kings Cross
4 June 1946

... I have gone through your story (2 essays) and you have done a beautiful piece of work. That story of Patch, & the subsequent 'half naked drover', stand alone in Australian writing. No one has ever done that before except Charlotte Bronte in 'Jane Eyre'.

But I am sending all back to you to fallow. There are weak spots, parts that want filling out & fattening. (You know my word 'fattening' by now.) The work behind the weakness of execution is too good to be launched on the world in immaturity. Put it away, & do more. Every one that you do will add to your mastery of execution. When you write six as good as this, however different, then they can go to market. My suggestion wd. be a line of connection throughout; Patch if you like, or the locality if that appeals to you. Don't try a novel yet. You are not ready for it. You have the bigness of great inward force, & till you are 'set' you are liable to be too big for the 'joints'—in other words there wd. be weak junctions, weak patches & thinness in places. You have so much in you that you can take criticism. So I am not afraid to tell you to wait. Which was the great French writer who was held back, & held back for seven years, & then told to go out & conquer the world. Was it de Maupassant—the world's master of the short story for at least a century?

If you published your story now it wd. belong to the era of Henry Lawson's 'His Father's Mate'. But where that depended on sentiment (was 'sentimental', Henry, in later or more mature years always said) there is no playing to the gallery in yours. It is almost Greek in its defined onward movement. But while I think of it cut out all those 'Oh's'. They are said but not written, & they are very girlish.

My kindest regards to your mother.

To Hugh McCrae

Dear Hugh,

Kings Cross
13 June 1946

Have just been reading 'Southerly' Number 4, 1945 and what a treat it is to get it after the usual shallow (lettery) stuff of the big dailies!

But reading this, & loving every word, I have come to the conclusion that the critics don't think much of me[1] because I live in the world & not in an atmosphere above it. Of course I have written a lot of the silly I-don't-walk-on-common-footpath stuff myself. But I think when I have been best, & most myself, I have walked with feet on the earth. I can say this to you because you have given me a standing others have not; and perhaps this is why. Of course I know I am first a house-keeping mother-woman. I make jam with the same outward urge & sense of creation as I do everything else.

Which reminds me! Last night I could not sleep I was so delighted & excited over a letter from the Commissioner of Police. I wrote in the 'D.Tel.' last month, when 'Zoe' died, that because dogs had helped so much to found Australia in prosperity & production, they should have a statuary memorial; that 'Zoe' shd. be the central or chief figure in white marble set on a green lawn in the Botanic Gardens where children play; & I asked wd. Mr. MacKay,[2] as head of the police who had helped so many causes (but had never had more than a polite thank you & a par. in the papers,) take the matter in hand. Yesterday I had his reply (confidential of course!) and he agrees with me & is already seeing what can be planned and done. Hooroo! & Hooray! It can, if properly done, be made a great & a beautiful thing. (But I told him in my reply not to accept a pyramid of dogs or a haystack of them!) Well, capacity for this kind of vision is perhaps one of the reasons why I am not regulation coin among the critics.

Joshua Smith, in last evening from painting McKell,[3] I told him of what I had proposed. He thought bronze wd. be better for the purpose than marble, as being more fluid. What wd. be your idea, Hugh? And could you 'See' a group or a plan and in mind be the sculptor that you so much are? A sculptor with vision & not mere skill? One idea I have, probably impossible, wd. be a sunken garden, grass floored, where children could have stories read to them; 'Zoe' in marble in the middle, other dogs in bronze all round, backing on the wall or as a frieze. All private of course till MacKay makes a public move.

Just beating my old enemy, disseminated pneumonia. I get it like a baby. Affections to you.

---

[1] The *Southerly* number mentioned by Mary contained articles and reviews of Australian poetry but no mention of her—hence her comment 'the critics don't think much of me'.
[2] See letter, 1 June 1946.
[3] William John McKell.

To Hugh McCrae

Dear Hugh,

Kings Cross
14 June 1946

Again in relation to my place in the critics' eyes as a 'poet' (which I never call myself) most of them are concerned with execution in relation to language, and *not* with relation to life or humanity *through* language. My chief concern is relation to life. Language changes, but life does not. Language even grows, but life does not. It is still at its fundamentals. Language is leafage, the roots remain.
(and here, flick! this:—

> Loveliness lies with leaves!
> And what are words
> But leaves upon a tree
> Where we are birds.

Simple as ABC! But, like life, profound—if the profound is in the reader. At least I hope so.) To return, if I can.

A tremendous lot of what might have been permanent literature is lost, because the writers are too mannered & are over concerned with words (words meaning form of course.) There was a time when I might have said mellifluous instead of sweet, hyaline instead of clear (How I envied Francis Thompson! Now I don't. His lovely words belong to another age.) But 'straight' or strait words were all that would come. They had to be my prop & my stay. And perhaps because of that some future will find a critic who will say 'This woman wrote English!' meaning the permanent, & not just leaves that pass.

I am still on stilts over MacKay's[1] letter. If he fails me I'll fall like Satan 'from morn to noon, from noon to dewy eve' wasn't it, & then crash like stone.

If I had had my eyes I wd. have written a book on what our dogs have done for Australia. I indicated it a bit in 'More Recollections'[2] and another on horses, special ones, from The Camel owned by Christison[3] (Victoria) of Lammermoor (Q) & I think mentioned by A. L. G.[4] the most ungainly animal ever foaled, but he was a 'lepper',[5] a racer, & could outlast any horse ever put against him.

Interruption. Twelve country eggs packed in a thin cake tin, & eight of them squashed. I don't feel I can write after that!

Is all well with you? And how grown up are the grand children?

[1] See letters, 1 June and 13 June 1946.
[2] Published 1935
[3] Robert Christison.
[4] Adam Lindsay Gordon.
[5] Leaper.

To A. H. Chisholm

Kings Cross
28 June 1946

Dear Alec,

My first moment to attend to your letter. Three days this week I had my midday dinner at 3.p.m. (and breakfast at 6.a.m.) and that is a sample of life for me—(I could not endure, though, if people did not come like that. It keeps me from thinking).

Yesterday morning I had this from my Hughie McCrae, on 'Old Forthright'[1] in the last 'Southerly' Magazine.

'The greatest piece of writing produced in Australia. I've been in ecstasies ever since ... Extremely creative. I admire it too much to feel jealousy. (*And as if Hugh ever felt anything but admiration for anything another did if it was worth while! M.G.*)

... I'm grateful to you past expression for gratifying every sense I've got ... It's mine as well as yours. A God-gift to everybody ...'
The generous hearted Hugh! He never grudged praise to anyone! Of the two sisters[2] in the verse the one taught me music when I was about 16, the other was married to Old Forthright (not his name, of course) by the Wesleyan Parson ... Nuff sed on that subject. Affectionately,

To Hugh McCrae

Kings Cross
28 June 1946

My heavenliest and (must have room for the word!) Enthusiasticest of critics! and if anyone should believe in telepathy I should, for with this is a letter I wrote & held up, wondering where you might be; & then it got covered up.

And here is your blasted heavenly pound back again! I'd go on my knees for such a letter as you have written me. But if ever you find a holey thrippence, I'll put a string through it & wear it as an earring.

My *natural* verse writing is the pictured. The earliest published

---

[1] A poem of Mary's published in *Southerly* 4 (1945) and later included in *Fourteen Men*, 1954, pp. 8-11.
[2] 'Then the church people made him a match
With one of two sisters, gentle and sweet,
Whose delicate fingers stitched delicate lace,
Or on the piano played elegant airs.'

under Mary Hannay Foott was that. Then I wrote one in 'The Worker' on Larry Petrie,[1] an explosive who lost an arm trying to wreck a train, here in the 80's, & then died horribly in Paraguay saving a little child from a railway train there. It began

> 'The Crows kep' flyin' up, boys, the
>   crows kep' flyin' up,
> Rome he seen an' whimpered
>   Though he was but a pup...'

(I forget the rest: & of course it was immature). But when it appeared Henry Lawson came to me & said almost with tears of appreciation:
  'You have beaten me on my own ground.'
  Then fear hit him, & he said 'One of us will have to give up. There is not room for both of us. There is only "The Bulletin".' We argued, but fearing to break him at his beginning & realizing that a man could write stronger than a girl (as I was) on these root things, I said I would give up that field. And from then on till latterly, wrote the woman's world & the emotional. I think Archibald must have known of my sacrifice because 40 years later Perce Packham his friend told me Archibald said to him, 'I love the woman for the way she stood back & nursed Henry Lawson at his beginnings.'
  Well, Hugh, in your appreciation & 'Old Forthright'[2] I have come into my own at the end...
  You will be surprised at who the two old ladies were.[3] Their name was Coats, one taught me music when I was sixteen. And they were the sisters of Coats then at his beginnings. Coats Cotton. They told me he was beginning to prosper, & had sent the money for their return to Scotland. Miss Bray, who has been typing for me, & whose grandfather (Prince, Ogg, & Bray (or Co.) had the first wool office & store in Sydney, the old Stone place at the Quay that Goldsborough, Mort, later had, & which fools pulled down a few years ago, told me her mother in London (or Scotland?) visited the Cotton Coats. She must have seen my two old ladies as my Miss Bray is about 70.

---

[1] Mary's poem 'The crows kep' flyin' up' was published in the *Worker*, 9 September 1893. For details of Larry Petrie, see Appendix. In her statement 'Personal History. Henry Lawson and I' (see note to letter, 5 August 1896) Mary elaborates:

> The incident referred to a time when Larry was lost and dying of thirst in the bush; a boundary rider seeing the crows flying up came to look was it a sheep or was it a man... Larry was
>   'Lyin' like the dead,
> Crows a flyin' up boys, a goanna at his head'.

Although there was a gap of over twenty years between the 'Personal History. Henry Lawson and I' and this letter to Hugh McCrae, Mary's account of the incident with Lawson is substantially the same on both occasions.
[2] See letter, 28 June 1946.
[3] See letter, 28 June 1946.

And here is the first line of 'Leaves' amended

'What loveliness in leaves!'

A copy of 'Old Forthright' enclosed but will send script later. What a tower on a hill you are, Hugh, the sun turning it to gold. Affectionately,

To Hugh McCrae

Dear Hughie,

Kings Cross
3 July 1946

(I'm sparing the last clear corner of the other day's letter) I believe I've got it at last! I mean what I have taken many words to say and it is this: You do not deface or obscure your fundamentals with imagery. No, I had it in a few words and I believe it was: You do not overlay with imagery, others think they must, or even really must or be a dummy of hoops.

Time tarnishes trimmings, & they, in the growth of usage & language, go out of fashion.

That is why I say watch Nan McDonald.[1]

My dear, I hope you are well.

I am trying to complete the selection of my work of which my two dear friends Tom Inglis Moore and R. D. FitzGerald (how different in mode, their verse!) have been the father & mother. But my eyes make it very hard. Even with this they have tired. When I think of the years of suffering through that Macquarie St. specialist I wish for the days of witch craft, when you could put a malediction on an enemy without having to do the dirty work yourself.

The Bread and Cheese Club
Melbourne

Kings Cross
2 October 1946

Dear people who have been friends to me:—
You will notice I am still at Kings Cross. Awhile back a young fellow-Clansman, Cameron, was married. Looking for a flat or house I suggested considering Kings Cross—'I wouldn't dare!' he said. 'My people would disown me. It was the one place I was warned against when I was leaving Scotland.' I have been over 15 years in this flat at Kings

---

[1] Mary's high opinion of Nan McDonald was vindicated when she published *Pacific Sea*, a collection of poetry in 1947. The review of it in the *Bulletin* concluded, 'she has produced a book exceptionally beautiful in its short poems, and, read simply as pastoral poetry, attractive all the way through'.

Cross, and have seen no evil. Somehow that reminds me of Miss—. She is (or was) about 14 stone and looked more. 'I took a flat in Bourke Street for three months' she said 'and am still an honest woman'. Only the word she used was the more direct 'V--n' (as you see I am still a modest woman or I would have written the word in full—and in the first place). The antithesis between her huge rude size, with her reputation for (to put it nicely) 'tall' stories, and that she was the child of two of our 'very best families', and the implication of possible assault on all these, make a thing funny that would otherwise be merely vulgar, for she herself saw it that way—I mean the antithesis. As a piece of Australian broad wit by an Australian and a gentlewoman of the day, I think it worth preserving, so I give it to you to preserve.

Provided there was real wit, a collection—one that could be published—would not be amiss.

P.S.   For the rest:
God said, from out His heaven, 'I have made wonders seven' then man said, 'Add to these I made the Bread and Cheese!' As I am not a member that is not arrogant on the part of the Club!

To Jean Yeats

Dear Jean Yeats,
Kings Cross
7 October 1946

Cousin Marie[1] (Miss Marshall) has just sent me your letter about me, for which I thank you and Cousin Marie very much.

I see you have 'divisions' at your school and one called Gilmore for me—that makes another! There is one at the Domestic Science School at Randwick. Four are Gilmore, Bruce (Mary Grant B), Turner (Ethel) and I forget the other. Also there is one in, or near Melbourne, five others in N.S.W.

I like your 'But fiercely Australian'! I hope you are too. Australia may one day need everyone to be 'fierce' in her protection against outside enemies, though I do hope that all wars are over, and that the world will for the future be at peace, for all war that maims or kills is the enemy of man. Again thanking you.

[1] Cousin Marie was editor of the Young People's page in the Sydney *Sun* at the time.

To R. H. Croll

My dear and very dear Bob Croll,

Kings Cross
28 December 1946

You have beaten me to it. I had you in mind to write and your letter is first, having just come.

Your Mr. Malloch[1] was here yesterday morning, and I have news of you all. I suppose, from what he said, you are the best loved man in Melbourne. The years are eating us, Bob, but they can't eat that.

We have a very foolish man here (foolish because he knows nothing, but pretends he knows a lot). His name is Michael Sawtell.[2] I enclose two of his letters (which I want back as I have no other copies) one in the 'Daily Telegraph', one in the 'S.M.H.' With these is a copy of my reply to the 'S.M.H.' one, and that one you can keep as I have a script copy. He, Sawtell told me when I was on the 'Worker' and first met him, that he knew nothing of the blacks, that he had only done one six months droving in the Northern Territory, and had only seen the blacks with the drovers, and a few mission blacks... However, the blacks gave you your name 'the wise old man' and Harney[3] gave me mine: 'the Earth Mother', and said that I had begun what others had followed. I have been doing it for 60 years. When I was 23 I wanted Henry Lawson to write the blacks; gave him the material for the lore and stories. 'I am not going to be laughed at for writing about black fellows!' he retorted angrily. But after I came back from S. America, and was editing the Woman's page of the 'Worker',[4] in about 1913 he said to me:'You were right, and I was wrong'. And it was then he wrote his most beautiful poem about an old black in Sydney 'Trouble belong it to mine' [sic].

And that reminds me that yesterday there came a copy of 'The Mudgee Mail' with its front page heading 'Of Times that I have Known, By George Henry Cohen. Episode No. 162. More about the Lawson Family'.

Much of the article consists of a letter from an Albury priest, cousin of Henry, in which he says (you will love this!) 'After going to some trouble in trying to wipe away the fact that Henry was born in a tent (Mr. Cohen writes) my correspondent added a surprising post

---

[1] Of the Melbourne Bread and Cheese Club.
[2] Mary's description of Sawtell seems justified. In his letter of 11 December 1946 to the S.M.H. he argued against the payment of wages to Aboriginal stockmen because he believed they would be demoralized by money. His letter of 16 December 1946 to the Daily Telegraph argued that the Aboriginals were doomed and welfare would only hasten their extinction. Among a number of replies to his letters was one by Mary in S.M.H. 28 December 1946. See next letter.
[3] W. E. 'Bill' Harney.
[4] See letter, 1 June 1946.

script 'I don't suppose our Lord Jesus Christ's relatives liked it going down in history that he was born in a manger'. Truly a remarkable comparison . . .' and also he says and Mr. Cohen quotes, 'Last of all we resent the school history books for saying he was of Gipsy forebears. He was not . . .'.

And, I add, he was not. He was poor and wanted to be distinguished, and he adopted 'the gipsy blood' because I told him Albury was a gipsy name . . .

All this will interest you. My love to you,

To The Editor
Sydney Morning Herald   *Kings Cross*
Sir,   *28 December 1946*

Mr. Michael Sawtell says (23/12/46) that 'one of the great mysteries of the bush is how the aborigines make their smoke signals'.

When I was about eight years old, the responsible eldest of the then little family, father taught me and my brother to produce fire and make aboriginal smoke signals so that we could call the blacks (or him when away from home), if we were lost or in other danger.

Strangely enough, my brother, though the younger, made better rings than I did. Rings were a sign of urgency, puffs being the ordinary message code and S.O.S. of the day. Straight-up smoke meant safety or danger over.

We thought it a great game until the blacks complained to father that we were calling them without need.

Until the blacks were 'dispersed' men in the bush used the signals and taught them as a matter of course to their wives and children, so that they could get help in case of snake-bite, accident, sickness, fire on the wind, and men or children lost. The blacks would answer a call without hesitation. If those far away saw the signals they would send up messages so that others nearer could come at once.

There was nothing mystic either in the making of the smoke or in the meaning. You learned the code as a ship's flag-officer learns the shipping code.

All else required was a knowledge of the shrubs and grasses needed for the different densities and kinds of smoke, how to hit the smoke to make puffs or rings (the latter requiring some skill), and how to keep the blaze down.

To George Mackaness

Dear George (and all of you!),

Kings Cross
15 April 1947

Ernestine Hill's last address to me is 'Hotel Como. Perth. W.A.'.

I am shocked to think of the fall Alice had. The very word 'pelvis' in such case, goes through me like a knife! Such injury, when I was in my teens, never hoped for mending (except by aboriginal means, which no doctor would even look at; the aboriginals made the patient immobile in a sheet of bark, with Eucalpytus leaves and clay padding!).

Just had a letter from Captain Ridley, S.S. Lady Isobel. He had nearly completed a book (on which I had advised him) and in the cyclone off Townsville the other week, his cabin was flooded, and all his MS. pulped. Nothing left but pulp.

Do you know Ruth Park? What an all-rounder she is! Asking in a letter was I well and in want of help she said to let her know as she is quite good with mop and bucket. Radio plays, novel, verse, two babies,—and early twenties! What a record.

Just had a letter from my nephew Donal (my brother John's son). He has a big position at the British Legation in Bucharest. Some say breed in man will be studied as in horses, prize dogs and cattle. He sent me a photograph of his boy 10 years old, at school in England. People who saw my grandson a week ago thought it was he. Three generations from my father on each side, and three other families intermixed.

Arthur Fadden, M.H.R.
Leader, The Country Party,
Canberra.

Kings Cross
9 May 1947

Dear Mr Fadden,
With apologies for my inefficient typing, I feel that I must protest against an utterance of yours during the debate on C.L.F. appointments,[1] as you have certainly included me as one to whom a Literary Scholarship should not have been given (See S.M.H. Report 9.5.47).

I am an aged woman who has given life-long service to Australia and her people, allowing for age, more than you have given. I am still

---

[1] *S.M.H.* of 9 May 1947 reports a debate in the House of Representatives over the granting of a Commonwealth Literary Fund award to J. H. Rawling, an ex-member of the Communist Party. Some Government speakers, including Arthur Fadden, indicated their belief that the C.L.F. helped nurture communists. Mary's *Selected Verse*, 1948, was published with the aid of a C.L.F. grant.

giving it. Besides being one of the few left who worked for the founding of the New Unionism over fifty years ago, and which became the Political Labour Movement of which you are an opponent to-day, I helped to obtain the Old Age Pension (which your side said 'would destroy thrift if it became law'), I helped get the Maternity Grant (which your side described as a 'direct incentive to immorality' and called 'the Bangle Bonus'—wealthy anti-Labour women taking it and then brazenly boasting of bangles bought with it), I worked for Arbitration (in regard to which we had first to educate your side and then hammer it into your heads so that it might stay there). In addition I worked for Manhood Suffrage and Votes for Women (both opposed by your side until they became a popular cry): for the rights of the child born out of wedlock, and many other things your side opposed, but of which Australia on all sides now boasts, and of which a record, as regards me, can be found in my page of 'The Australian Worker'—a published record of twenty three full years. (I wonder if Sir John Latham remembers saying 'She hits hard but never below the belt'. And may I commend the last part of that saying to you) . . .

Apart from the above, my service to Australian Literature ranges from the young Henry Lawson ('All that I have done I owe to Mary Gilmore') to to-day's postal delivery—and that even if you think my own books do not count.

. . . Don't you think Mr Fadden that after all that, that I have earned and paid for anything the C.L.F. has given me? Especially as I have just sent another 700 pages (sealed till after my death) of my historical gatherings, to the Commonwealth Library.

Finally, toleration is not an enemy to loyalty, but bigotry is . . . Across No Man's Land. Yours truly,

To Donald Gordon Campbell

Dear Don,

Kings Cross
30 May 1947

No time for a line. Visitors, Visitors, Visitors! Some from overseas.

Thank you for your book,[1] will have to wait to read it. It came with Peter Hopegoods 'Circus at World's End'.[2] What a contrast! Two separate worlds, he impressed by fantasy, you by beauty.

I enclose the loveliest of verses, 'Ringbarked' by K. Dalziel.[3] I want it back please. But what beauty, what simplicity, what feeling,

[1] Probably *Song Unending and Other Poems*, 1947.
[2] Also published 1947.
[3] Kathleen Dalziel. The Bread and Cheese Club, Melbourne, published a volume of her poems, *Known and Not Held*, in 1941.

what perception, what a breadth of remembering knowledge is there! Study it.

My regards to all your kind nice family.

Have a look at P.H. when you come to Sydney, at the Mitchell, or A. & R. But study K.D.

To Colin Simpson

Dear Colin,

*Kings Cross
31 May 1947*

I listened last night, What a story![1] What pain, what suffering, what useless loss!

Radio necessarily crippled the full story, which should be made into a full-length play. As it was I thought I had only listened in for half an hour.

You kept the whole thing on its own base. No sentimentalizing, no empty heroics. 'Six men came out . . . six!' Six men in all the world . . . But what a drama of history and heroism it makes . . . I wonder would and could Douglas Stewart make it another 'Fire on the Snow' . . . They are parallel stories of human dignity, might and endurance, in which only the members are different. A handful of men or an army, they are one man in all the world in each case. The vast is with them and in them—and they all the time feeling no more than weariness, crawling along, and, in escape, as wandering ants in the grass . . . I would like to see the whole thing turned into the permanence of literature . . . If you, and the A.B.C. are not inundated with letters, I shall be very much surprised. I shall wonder if all the worth-while of Australia did not die on the Kokoda Trail[2] or in Borneo . . .

P.S. Call it 'Six Men from Borneo'.
P.P.S. Later in the day.
In view of the necessity for us (Australia) to have the Japanese Peace terms considered here—where the danger of the East is known . . . this 'Six' of yours should be publicized to the last world limit . . . It should especially be heard in the Commonwealth Parliament. Only a fool

[1] Colin Simpson's 'Six From Borneo', subtitled 'The Story of the Death Marches and the Fate of Prisoners of War in Northern Borneo', was broadcast by the A.B.C., 30 May 1947. Of 2000 prisoners only 6 Australians survived. The 'six' from the Australian 8th Division, captured in the fall of Singapore, told their own story in the documentary programme.
[2] The Kokoda Trail ran from the Owen Stanley Range outside Port Moresby to the coast near Buna in New Guinea. Along the Trail Australian soldiers repulsed the Japanese advance on Port Moresby.

would not know its meaning... Also I would have it done in all schools. I am an Internationalist, but I am Australia first, and before all others. If Australia had been secure when this war began, there would have been no Kokoda Trail, and no Death March in Borneo.

And such a story as you have here should have first call on every kind of publicity and publication.

To Colin Simpson

Dear Colin,

Kings Cross
19 June 1947

I have just heard your Wagga Wagga story.[1] And every word of it went home to my heart, the writing was so warm and understanding. I nearly wept at the droving, for droving was romance to us as children—romance & terror. I could *smell* the yards. I have always longed to write the history of Wagga. No town except the Palmer[2] in Queensland and Coolgardie in Western Australia had such a history as Wagga when it was a frontier town.

To R. G. Howarth

Dear Mr Howarth,

Kings Cross
23 June 1947

Heaven about us lies when 'Southerly' comes. The pots burn and the washing up stays till I go through it, for I look for it as I long ago looked for the Red Page under A.G.S.[3] and later the 'Bookfellow'.

Hart-Smith.[4] He is one of my bantlings. But I opened doors for him. 'Modern American Poetry' being one. And for its effect see 'Daniel Webster's Horses' (Elizabeth Coatsworth), 'The Distant Runners' (Mark Van Doren), 'The Spider' (David McCord). This does not mean that H-S is a copyist. But it does mean that their door was his. His force is his own. So is his observation and imagery. An Englishman, when in the Army he went to W.A. (where he had a break-down) he saw a new world of insect and other life, of vividly defined things

---

[1] Colin Simpson's 'Wagga Wagga' was broadcast 19 June 1947, as part of the A.B.C's 'Walkabout' series. It included interviews with colourful Wagga Wagga characters, including an old drover and a ringer at the Wagga Wagga horse sales.

[2] A gold-field settlement on the Palmer River in Queensland. Gold was discovered there in 1873 and it became the most prolific alluvial gold field in Queensland. It was often a violent and unruly settlement.

[3] A. G. Stephens.

[4] W. Hart-Smith had three poems in this *Southerly* issue (8.1.1947). The poems were 'Neptune's Horses', 'The Surrender of Granada' and 'Cosmic Argument'.

he has never dreamed of in damp England and dewy New Zealand (from whence he came to Australia). He found there the things I had watched in the dry Riverina as a child, and where I, a child, could only bring wonder, he brought thought. So he saw and wrote the spider, the goanna and so much else. He came to me with his mind teeming. W.A. made him.

I had a wonderful letter from Sidney (Sydney) Jephcott and in it a poem you should go on your knees for, for 'Southerly'. May Brahe was here. 'You know my uncle by marriage', she said, 'Who is he?' 'Sydney Jephcott'. I nearly fell at her feet. I met Jephcott once at John Farrell's in about 1893 or 4, before I went to South America. (The then young came to John as the young to-day come to me.) After I came back from S. America Jephcott once again came to see me. I had been told he had died, and till I saw May Brahe thought it true . . . I wrote to him on a hoped-for address and it found him. He replied beginning, 'Dear Madonna of the Underdog', and enclosed me part of a poem written on his 82nd birthday. . . I am nearly sure it was Sydney Jephcott planted the Albury saleyards with European acacia nearly 60 years ago and he is the father of the American red wood in Australia. He got two seeds on condition that he distributed their product. His land is an arboretum of varieties. Just had to stop to answer the phone. A descendant of Charlotte Yonge, who wants to talk Wagga history with me, though we have never met. So I must end . . . One word more of 'Southerly'. I loved 'Afternoon'.[1] It was me and all the things I know. But how beautifully written! The return (or repetition) was perfect. And how valuable the Brereton stuff![2] That is what literature in Australia needs, collection like that. The bucking horse began us, but the inkpot on margins is today.

To Donald Gordon Campbell

Dear Donald,

Kings Cross
7 August 1947

(That beginning was for Sir Donald Cameron; not used; so it does for you.) I sent you back your Old Towers[3] with some marginal notes. But had no time to write.

Now for it! You must leave out all mention of yourself, your own feelings (& the *Sentimental*) as a narrator. You have made yourself (the narrator) the head & front & king-piece of the story & the stories &

---

[1] A story by Arthur Ashworth.
[2] 'Some Brereton Marginalia' by S. Musgrove, academic and critic.
[3] Probably a short story by Campbell. See letter, 4 June 1946.

other characters are only your clothing. Old Tim (or whoever he was) came in, sat down by the fire poked it, the flames leaped, the shadows interlaced & danced, & he talked. You are only the recorder. You want to describe the old fire place, stones sticking out of the pug, cracks in the whitewash, the darkness behind the sitters, shelves on the walls etc. No need of 'mod. cons.' in an old time story. *Go back to the old man's time* & live in the pioneer surroundings, the more 'pioneer' the better. As you sit the wind blows in, the curlews & mopokes call, a lone trail of belated swans goes over head, their cry grown thin in the height. The fire is log, with the bark still on it, the small stuff the same. Even a bit of yellow fungus like a human ear burns & smells on the air (we always chopped these off). See what I mean? Live it & paint it. The conversation being sandwiched in. You have a gift for seeing things, & a gift in your own comparisons and similes. Don't be afraid to use them. Economy in these things does not give Australia. It only gives a townsman's writing. The town forgets or never saw the bush—so at it in the *big* way, Don—

To R. D. FitzGerald

Dear Bob,

Kings Cross
10 November 1947

There is a power, concentration, vitality and perception in your mind, that belongs to only a very few. Your letter is proof of it. You see the world, not the circumscribed life of a man. It is this in 'Fifth Day'[1] seemed to me so wonderful. The smallest thing was in it. But its smallness made it in your hands, part of the vast. That you do little is no matter. One great stone in the plain is worth all the ant heaps—even if the plain is dependent for its fertility on ant and worm. I do not belittle them. I look up with lifted eyes. The fewness of your pieces is the witness of what they are made of in sweep, delving down, and work to get it all in! Kittens can come in batches, elephants with their wisdom, and their longevity, in ones—and at long intervals. If I could write like you (I suppose it takes reading and knowledge to see it all), I would feel I was with God—A Creator, not just a recapitulator, a maker not just a modeller of clay already in being. I thought the 'Essay on Memory'[2] your greatest height. This 'Fifth Day' is higher. Memory was Philosophy. This is man. Here is Don Quixote in stature, without the foolish and the farce—and still the giant-figure in its fall. And if

---

[1] 'Fifth Day' by R. D. FitzGerald, later published in *This Night's Orbit*, 1953, dealt with the trial of Warren Hastings.
[2] Published in *S.M.H.* 9 April 1938, after it had won first prize in a national poetry competition held as part of the Australian Sesquicentenary Celebrations.

No Foe shall gather our Harvest

Sons of the mountains of Scotland,
Clansmen from corrie & Kyle,
Breed of the moors of England,
Children of Erin's green isle
We stand four-square to the tempest
Whatever the battering hail —
italics { No foe shall gather our harvest,
Or sit on our stockyard rail.

Our women shall walk in honour,
Our children shall know no chain,
This land that is ours forever
The invader shall strike at in vain.
Anzac! ... Bapaume! ... and the Marne! ...
Could ever the old blood fail?
{ No foe shall gather our harvest,
Or sit on our stockyard rail.

So hail-fellow-met we muster,
And hail-fellow-met fall in,
Wherever the guns may thunder,
Or the rocketing "air mail" spin!
Born of the soil & the whirlwind
Though death itself be the gale —
{ No foe shall gather our harvest,
Or sit on our stockyard rail.

We are the sons of Australia,
Of the men who fashioned the land,
We are the sons of the women
Who went with them hand in hand.
And we swear by the dead who bore us,
By the heroes who blazed the trail,
{ No foe shall gather our harvest
Or sit on our stockyard rail

Mary Gilmore

Copied for Dr. Campbell Mackaness
2.3.42

The manuscript version of No Foe shall gather our Harvest

The sheep dog memorial

you think of alterations, I wd. say leave them. Life is not a rhythm, it is a mass of rhythms. And that is what your work always is. Leave smoothness and flowers to us who are annuals. 'Consider the lilies' is all very well. But, the lilies are gone. It is the words remain. The centuries will come back to you. They won't know others even existed.

I left Wagga on Wed. morning 9th by the Riverina Express. If only I had known you were there! About my Verse and A & R., Frank Clune is much more important there than I am. It makes me sad; not for myself, but for old ideals.

In Wagga found a future good writer. Also I started the librarian at the Teachers' College collecting names of original stations and first owners—with all *that* means.

To Nan McDonald

Dear Nan McDonald,

Kings Cross
4 February 1948

I have just read with delight the Bulletin Red Page on your book.[1] For myself because the writer picked out 'Candles' and 'The Tollgate Islands'. They have no parallel anywhere in Australia or elsewhere. In them is the simple, the terrible and the note of eternal judgment: the Dies Irae. No one else but Brennan had the last, and in Brennan it was not the Dies Irae; it was something formless, and the D.I. is not.

What things I have lived to see grow and come to being in, and for Australia! The day of the tinkle is over. It is now the mass mind, the voice of mass; of past and present in one, even if by a single mind and hand.

I do not know if Douglas Stewart wrote the criticism or someone else. I hope *he* did, so that I can think twice as more of him, of whom I think so much. And if it is T.I.M.[2] (though I don't think so). then it is ditto. And if it is someone else, then it is more power to him!

I am nearly dead with the heat, but my heart had to speak.

I think of how you carry work and responsibility and how little time to sit and think. Yet out of that little what a voice and what power!

[1] *Pacific Sea*, 1947. For details of Red Page review see note to letter, 3 July 1946.
[2] Tom Inglis Moore.

To R. D. FitzGerald

Dear Bob,

Kings Cross
2 March 1948

It was *not* the 'Selected'[1] over wh. you rejoiced. The book just finished is 'Fourteen Men',[2] and is in the hands of Miss Bonn for typing. She says it will take to the middle of April, as she has to give it to her special typist—'who knows how'—The proofs of 'Selected' haven't come yet.

'Fourteen Men' has an appendix (Did you know me without one!) and it has two long notes that will in one case make some people's hair stand on end, and in the other tear that 'glory' or what is left of it. I wd. have liked you and Tom to have seen it as a special privilege and fellowship, but I had to get it out of the house, as every time I looked at, or even *saw* it, I found myself revising. So I just had to stop if it is to be out this or next year. But you will see the duplicate as soon as it is typed—and before anyone else even knows it is written. You two come first—

I have solved 'The Rose of Tralee'[3] letter ... Family likeness (as I think I once wrote you) comes in hand writing even if different. It must have been your father wrote me. Thinking it you, and being ill and too busy to think, I did not reply. Will you make my apologies? and tell him my grandmother told me his grandmother was the Rose of Tralee and I repeat—*that* is to go in to 'Selected', and by you and Tom, if I shd. not be here—It was a fact my grandmother told me—she taught the words to father who loved to sing it—in 1872—on. I cd. and want to write more, but the painter-paper hanger wants the room. So for the next few days I am an exile from etc as Brennan more or less said, and I shall be living on one chair—wherever it can be put.

If ever anyone comes on a letter with the signature on the very edge, like a shipwrecked mariner clinging to his boat the letter will be mine— Why can't I write one thing and have a nice margin at the end! I'd *like* to.

---

[1] Mary's *Selected Verse* was published by A. & R. later in 1948.
[2] *Fourteen Men*, Mary's final volume of verse, was not ultimately published until 1954.
[3] The song 'Rose of Tralee' was written by Charles William Glover (1806-63). It is difficult to substantiate this interesting little snippet that R. D. FitzGerald's great grandmother was the subject of the song.

To George Ferguson

Kings Cross
13 March 1948

Dear Mr. Ferguson,

You are 'G.R.'s[1] grandson. I have a capacity for worshipping people, and your grandfather was one of them. They weren't so many after all. They were my grandmother (Mary Beattie), my father, Lochiel, William Lane, A.G.S.[2] and your grandfather. It didn't matter whether I saw them or not. In the last three I saw their work. It made a halo over Australia. The first two were personal. They and the other three made me. So I am glad to have a note from you—for your *own* sake, as well as for what it says of 'Selected Verse;.

I am a terribly tired old woman, and I would like to see how the critics take that book!

As I have my next book of verse being finally typed, I would like 'Selected' out of the way when I can find a printer. I am trying to find out if any (or how many) other women have a book of verse at 82. Men have I think . . . but I can't recall a woman.

I could wish you had a better jacket artist! (if I may). It is a mistake to try to put the *book* into the jacket. Interpretation is a mistake. *Selling* is the object. *Cold Nose* should have had Zoe[3] stark against the sky to catch the eye of every child even. Ruth Park's slum[4] is enough in spite of its quality as work, to make one say 'Slum!' and turn away. But the Flying Doctor is good. Harney's[5] is over looked. You don't want an Encyclopaedia!

Do you mind my saying this? Yours sincerely,

To George Ferguson

Kings Cross
St Patrick's Day
17 March 1948

Dear Mr Ferguson,

I forgot the valiant day till reminded just now—so have apologized to the saint by writing in full.

About a jacket. At the moment I only like a plain cream one with a small coloured border 'Selected Verse' at the top, and 'Mary Gilmore' in a heavy black type halfway (or nearly?) down. My name is what

---

[1] George Ferguson (1910-), grandson of George Robertson.
[2] A. G. Stephens.
[3] Zoe was a police dog. See letter, 1 June 1946.
[4] The book was probably Ruth Park's *The Harp in the South*, 1948.
[5] W. E. Harney's book was probably *Brimming Billabongs: The Life Story of an Aboriginal*, 1947.

would catch the eye. You don't look for verse to find Mary Gilmore, but the name Mary G. leads to verse.

Joshua Smith is painting me again. So I asked his opinion. He said 'Make it like the cover on the Art Books'. So that is like my idea.

There *could* be a soldier, a ship, and an aboriginal in the faintest shadow painting (if that is what you call it) but the name of the book and author is the main thing. How does it strike you?

I think you know I wanted a life of G.R.[1] done before those who were his intimates were gone—a book warm from the hearts of those who loved him, a group of about four men to have done it. Unless you do it, that warmth will never come back. A section at a time, bits here and there, and then a sorting and collating would do it. My prose books 'Old Days' and 'More Recollections' were done that way. The patches joining made the chapters. Scraps jotted and kept are so easy! *Don't* let them go.

To George Ferguson

Dear Mr Ferguson,

Kings Cross
22 April 1948

I do not know if you wanted any sort of suggestion from me or not about the jacket for selected verse.

But here *is* a suggestion, if it is any good.

My name is known, and does count so I thought

              MARY GILMORE
            HER   )
            BOOK) smaller type
and in about the middle of the sheet or a little lower:
            SELECTED VERSE

and down in the bottom left corner a small reproduction of my bookplate, of the Joshua Smith painting in the gallery, or even a photograph. That or an aboriginal standing poised on a cliff, with or without a spear, background irregularly ruled for this. The rest in black on a white or cream paper, and a three or four line or mottled coloured edging all round.

As a craftsman you will see all the faults and difficulties in this. But it would be individual, I think. But of course, this is only a suggestion. I'd love one of those rich colour covers. But tired eyes think of and see the plain print best in a window or on a counter.

[1] George Robertson, Ferguson's grandfather.

Am going through the galley proofs and hope to finish them this week. I have some repetitional rhymes to alter. In separate books they did not matter, but when collected, the mind says I heard (or I saw) that before!

Galley proofs from A. & R. are a treat to tired eyes. I bless the printers and I bless your staff. They have all been kind to me. Yours sincerely

Mr Robertson told me that the head of an English Publisher out here complained that the window was full of Australian and not English books (Do you know that one? and what G.R. said?)

He also told me that a poor seamstress, with swollen legs came to sew for his wife. Mrs Robertson looked after her, the woman broke down at the kindness, and told her she had been sewing for the wife of a big barrister(?) at whose house she had been poorly paid and had had neither consideration nor care. G.R. waited for that man to come to the shop, where his least spending was £100 a year, brought up the case, and gave him, a rich man, a dressing down, and told him never again to enter the shop as he would give instruction he was not to be served. But the poor woman he sent for three months to his place in the mountains, gave her £3 a week and paid a doctor to see to her.

(Is it any wonder I worship the name of that man!)

To Alan Marshall

Dear Mr. Marshall,

Kings Cross
3 May 1948

Just now Miss Mary Mansfield[1] rang me (I have known her since she was a girl & am a sort of mother to her) to read me your letter to her about Mr. Robert Close and as words build no barns I enclose a chq. toward the fund she told me you were raising.

I have a horror of the dirty but that does not interfere with my sense of justice, and justice (if justice is even-handed) was the last thing meted out to Robert Close. As a matter of fact, last Tuesday week I wrote a letter to the Sydney 'Sun' to more or less say that. This I enclosed in a letter to Mr. Close C/- the Editor of the 'Australian Journal'. If he has had it you may have seen it, but it may still be at the office of the Journal. I made a point in the letter that no one else has made & which, even if rhetorical, might be useful.

Now about TB. I have been TB (given up at 13 when my chest

---

[1] The editor of Frederick Blakeley's *Dream Millions: New Light on Lasseter's Last Reef*, 1972.

fell in) off & on all my life—& I will be 83 in August. Broken Hill first saved me, & later Paraguay (I was woman leader next to William Lane in the New Australia movement & Colony in Paraguay).[1] If Mr. Close could get to the Darling, & live out of doors! Even Adelaide wd. be better than Melbourne. Paraguay was of course the Sanatorium of S.Am. People used to come there, for T.B. from Europe.

It wrung my heart to think of that man battling with broken lungs. And he *can* write. I read him in the 'Australian Journal'. If the family exchequer needs it, my chq. can go there. (I have just had a wind fall & can spare it.) But I don't want it published. Leave it as a friendly help & therefore private.

I had no reply to my letter to Mr. Close, but I can understand from your letter why (if he has it) . . . Mary Mansfield said you were Allan. Are you? or is it Alan?

The point I made in my 'Sun' letter was that brewers & hotel keepers create, *publish* & *sell* what demoralizes & causes every kind of crime. But, in trying a case of crime due to drink, I asked has any judge given a dressing down to either a brewer or a hotel keeper, and I ended by saying that compared with the crime (not those words though) caused by the publishing & selling of this product the name of Mr. Close's book was an invisible dot on a world wide horizon. (As of course it is!) Yours sincerely

To R. D. FitzGerald

Kings Cross
9 May 1948

Dear Bob—and this is for Tom too[2]—

If I am dead by the time you get this don't be surprised! I have just (*I hope*) this minute finished the Galley proofs of 'Selected Verse'. I am not at all surprised that a baby cries when it is born!

Snags! One is that in writing one book and then another you can use the same rhymes but *not* in a Selected or a Collected volume. The first even-Steven was quite interesting. The second was blue-metal in the eye. So prepare *now* for your selected or collected 40 years hence when you are 82, and with only one middling eye!

But it's done, and I thank you two from my heels to my head and from my head to my heels. I am so grateful I don't know how

---

[1] See note to letter 5 August 1896.
[2] R. D. FitzGerald (assisted by T. Inglis Moore) had edited the selection of Mary's poetry for the new volume, *Selected Verse*, 1948, and written the Foreword. *Selected Verse* was republished in an enlarged edition in 1969 with a further foreword by R. D. FitzGerald.

to say it. Except this: After going through this in these galleys I realize why you two said I could write and that I counted—I wonder why on earth I was big enough to have written lots of it. It may not have polish, but it has thought, force and feeling. And where the thought came from—but I do know: it came up out of the unconscious or subconscious at the call of need, or intent, or emotion. What this letter is for is to say that I put a note on your Foreword that it was to go to you for your correction, if correction in setting or punctuation is needed. I could not and would not touch it.

Also, in my bit, I put in 'The Rose of Tralee'.[1] In my grandmother's telling there was no doubt about it. 'The people loved her so much, she was so good to everyone, they made a song called "The Rose of Tralee" about her'. There was this: 'No cabin was too small or too poor for her to enter' and wherever she went she took food, there was hunger and starvation throughout the land.

I shall take the proofs in tomorrow. So will you ring A. & R. when you get this.

May repayment some day come to both of you.

To T. Inglis Moore

Dear Tom,

Kings Cross
27 July 1948

This is a skirmish note; later I hope to write a real letter.

I have just put up, for posting, the MS. of my new book, 'Fourteen Men',[2] to submit it to the Commonwealth Literary Board for publication. It is, I think, up to my usual level, though *not* up to some things in 'The Passionate Heart'[3] (philosophic and on the then war.) The main things are the notes, of which the two most important are on our early lynchings, and on the wattle as a mimosa-acacia cross. *These* are *history*. I want you, Tom, because you are *Tom*, to see them if you have the time and the wish. I would like Bob to see them, too, but Bob is not here and you are on the spot. But Bob *may* be a C.L. Fund reader (No. I am not asking,) in which case I would be happy.

'Selected Verse' is still . . . 'God Knows'—printers being what they are. As to 'Fourteen Men', 'Weeping Angels' may be regarded as too violent. But in the revulsion now against war, it might pass. I am open

---

[1] See letter, 2 March 1948.
[2] Not published until 1954.
[3] Mary's volume of poems published in 1918. For comment see T. Inglis Moore 'Mary Gilmore', *Southerly* 3 (1949), 122-30; R. D. FitzGerald, 'Mary Gilmore. Poet and Great Australian', *Meanjin* 4 (1960), 341-57; W. H. Wilde, *Three Radicals*, 1969.

to suggestion by the Board in such matters. But when I think of those who howled and hollered for the war that smashed the Empire and made it crawl on its belly to America for money, I think no thump on the nose too hard. Not that I believe in great Empires: I don't. I believe in small countries. But I don't want the Empire I belong to to 'bust', while another grows greater, and gobbles up everything!

Tom, my dear, I've written my letter after all!

To Hugh McCrae

My dear Hugh,

Kings Cross
24 September 1948

This is my third attempt at answering your letter.

My fourth attempt, Camden is not Kings Cross, nor is Kings Cross Camden and that's that, or Q.E.D. or whatever the phrase should be.

But if you know how anxious I am, & grieved because you are ill. You have no *right* to be ill! You have such energy of mind & heart. It wd. need a cast iron body to stand up to it. I wonder, if your trouble is the same as mine: the malnutrition of over work & over energy? I am on vitamins for the last nine months. The senses of smell & taste have been somewhat resurrected (they had died) along with increased ability to walk farther than across the street. But why all this? You have your doctor.

And I didn't forget you when Tom & Bob helped with 'Selected Verse'. But two years ago you had your own worries. So I thought I wd. ask your name in the new book, 'Fourteen Men'. It has to be recast, as it is too much an omnium gatherum and when it is recast may it find a place in your 'heart'!

Just read H. M. Green in 'English' (Mag. of English Ass.) No. 38 in which he says '. . . Mary Gilmore Australia's most distinguished woman poet, & Hugh McCrae who is one of Australia's two principal Lyrists . . .' Would I were a man for two minutes to bash that man! I never think him fair to you. He either can't see or he is jealous of you being the beloved of anyone & everyone worth while—including me; I burn joss sticks to you. (No need to answer this.)

To Hugh McCrae

Dear Hugh,

Kings Cross
28 September 1948

It is Wednesday 28th Sept! & I should be at work cleaning my house like a good woman. But I, fatally, opened a book at page 238. And as always I had to stop, too full, too stunned, too amazed, too lifted on high, too driven with wonder, to go on.

The book is 'Story Book Only',[1] & I stopped at page 243—Fancy, Phantasy, Imagination? It is vision & power.

Only the little mind could say this of it as its limit.

To Donald Gordon Campbell

Kings Cross
Dear Gordon, 2 October 1948

I read your verse[2] this morning without realizing it was you, & thought to myself 'This one can write!' You have a beautiful sonnet rhythm cadence & caesura on an octosyllable stanza, & I did not realize it till that 'tremendous' bumped me. I thought with a pang 'He has made a mistake!' Then I counted & found the Octo & not the Deca. For the sake of the verse get something with the same grace of movement as the other lines. The verse is vowelled & 'tremendous' rests on consonants.

Anyhow it is a beautiful & (what is more) wholly unpretentious thing. Good Luck to you!

To Constance Robertson

Kings Cross
Dear Connie, 8 February 1949

I saw your paragraph last week and thank you. I believe Canberra would like a portrait of me, but this one is too tired and 'documentary'. It began well, was finished, all but two sittings for the hands, in October, and then Joshua Smith painted out all the alert look. Also the hands are badly done. I had refused and refused to sit ever since the one at the Gallery. But in March last I was caught on the hop and by the promise that only 14 sittings would be wanted, that it would be quite finished in June, and no later. He took till the 23rd December, and nothing I could do or say would make him do the portrait before the

---

[1] *Story Book Only*, published by Hugh McCrae in 1948, contains some of his prose, including *My Father and My Father's Friends*, first published in 1935. Pages 238-43 contain snippets of anecdotes and comment, beginning with 'The Comedy of Manners' and ending with a comment on Captain Cook.

[2] Campbell's poem 'Symphony' appeared in the *S.M.H.*, 2 October 1948. The lines which seemed to concern Mary read:
> And soon it folds me in the flight
> Of some tremendous dream.

background and dress. These took most of the time. Friends who saw it, are as much bewildered as I as to why he altered it after saying it was finished, and only two sittings wanted for the hands. (The hands are odd sizes people tell me). I had to go on sitting or ruin his chances of the prize if William Dobell did not exhibit . . .

I loved *your* portrait. But I'll swear you painted it, even if Mary Edwards held the brush. She has done nothing like it and never will again. Her portraits are saints in haloes. This is Connie Robertson in a hat. It is a lovely thing. Even the hand is you—slender, defiant and impish. You need not reply to this, because just as I am here you are there. Affection touches even if hands don't. And I am happy in your standing and success. Also that you are properly painted. For a loosening out from the stolid and the conventional, I put your portrait next to the Margaret Olley[1] one. It may even be a better portrait, but for the Public (and posterity) there needs to be the picture as well as the portrait, and Dobell is the leader there. Love,

To Harold White

Dear Mr. White,

Kings Cross
22 February 1949

Yesterday I register posted a further packet of my diary of personal and historical gleanings. It runs from 1.1.48 to 30.6.48; and if there is less of me than of others, it is because others are worth while. Did I tell you that I have by will left the copyright equally between the Mitchell Library, the Commonwealth Library and my grandson? (This of course is confidential).

I also sent Mr. Temby[2] what I call 'the first (Phantom)' Coat of Arms[3] of Australia, with a full history of its inception, making, & 'investment'. The design is chalk-filled for a copy on cardboard which Joshua Smith made for me. (It went to the A.J.A. collection). This will brush off. The copper is black with age. But I saw it burnished. I leave it to you to decide, in which condition, it is best as a historical record.

---

[1] Margaret Olley was the subject of Dobell's successful entry in the 1948 Archibald Prize competition.

[2] H. S. Temby.

[3] The 'coat-of-arms' was a very tarnished copper breast-plate made by Edward David Stewart Ogilvie (1814-96) and presented to the chief of the Aboriginal Yugilbar tribe which lived on the Clarence River near Tabulam where Ogilvie established a 'run' called 'Yugilbar' in 1840. Ogilvie was on very friendly terms with the Aboriginals giving them hunting rights on the 'run'. By 1850 'Yugilbar' extended to about 300 square miles. By 1866 Ogilvie had built a great Moorish castle on the property (Mary claimed in the letter of 9 March 1949 to have been shown its secret passage). Mary had a chalk copy of the 'coat-of-arms' made on cardboard and presented it to the Australian Journalists Association.

I love that thing ... suddenly, out of the past it came back to me—to memory and my hands. It is with a full heart I have given it to the country foretold by it in its design and in its intent.

I am not sure if you are Librarian-in-Chief ... I met you when at Canberra years ago, you were young and eager faced. A National Librarian needs vision, and while we have vision we are young—Yours sincerely,

To Mrs E. O. Schlunke

Kings Cross
Dear Mrs. Schlunke, 3 March 1949

There have been people & people otherwise I would have replied on the instant. You certainly have the sense of & feeling for poetry. But the 'Bulletin' is a man's paper, and you write a woman's feelings & a woman's verse. That verse on the Plover & the sick child could have been mine. My hair nearly stood on end, the feeling, the subject & the manner were so one between us. Then I got hold of it and realized that with you, as with me, the children have to come first, the writing second. But keep on writing, only writing can give you mastery of form & words. Keep everything, & then in quieter years you can shape & reshape the young thought and impulse that unless kept that way, never comes back again.

I have made a few 'Marks' as a guide, one learns that way. Don't bother about rhyme till it comes easy. Rhyme puts hobbles on Pegasus, & Pegasus is winged. Remember there is free verse (*vers libre*) in which lines follow the thought & are not sawn off regularly like flooring boards.

My eyes are tired & I must stop.

I am returning the verse with this. And anytime you or Mr. Schlunke are in town remember where my door is.

Try collecting bits of prose ... the colour of a clod, the dew on the cabbages, why life at all—anything & every thing from gossip to the stars. Patches make a quilt, scraps of thought & observation make a book. But write, if only as an outlet. Yours sincerely,

Try the 'Aust. Womens Weekly' with something, prose or verse, but short. The plover one I am thinking of—write to the Editor, Kenneth Wilkinson & use my name—address MS. to the Editor, The Aust. Women's Weekly, Box 4088W G.P.O. Sydney—(Enclose stamps for return).

To Harold White

Dear Mr. White,

Kings Cross
9 March 1949

I cannot say what a happy woman I am to have your letter this morning and find that you think about the (phantom) coat-of-arms as I do. You even feel about polishing (or not) the breastplate as I do. Polished it would catch every eye; left as it is it has the years of time and history written on it. Could one erase these? The polishing can come in a thousand years. The history written on it by the years can never come back once it is gone—and yet?

I have just had a monetary wind-fall, not great, but money means little to me personally, and I am considering sending you something to stand against the need of retyping the diaries—which will come in a few years time. The war prevented me getting the good and durable paper they should have had and Miss Dorothea Bray who has done the last four years under my roof, tried and tried to get better paper and good ribbons, but failed.

There is in the diary a fuller account (in bits) of the breast plate, Mrs. Ogilvie, and Yugilbar, than you have with the breast plate. And (or did I tell you before?) till I wrote it, and gave a copy of the account to Jessie Street, as Ogilvie's grand daughter, I was the only person left who knew the small secret cell in Yugilbar Castle. I wrote it for publication, but did her the courtesy of asking her leave. She said 'No. People might tear the place to pieces looking for it'. But it is in the diary. Also I could go straight to the spot where it is if I went. And it is 78 or 79 years since I saw it. Only father and I and Ogilvie's eldest son were told and shown. The secret was to go to eldest son to eldest son through the generations for which he built. It was (and is) partly this failure made me see the necessity of the nation and the state or its institutions as the custodian of things that matter to the future. Mr. Ogilvie even made a 'spell' for his hopes; that Yugilbar would stand while Ogilvie, or Ogilvies dwelling there, should continue. And the stranger inherits there.

But in the diaries I send you Ogilvie still stands, and Yugilbar with him.

The world is losing what it once had—Europe at all events—the look of race and family! I saw a girl yesterday in a delicatessen shop, who said her name was Cameron and she was related to me. I believed it—or her look—she had the look of 'the Great Lochiel'[1] whom

---

[1] Cameron of Lochiel (c.1695-1748), known as 'Gentle Lochiel', a Highland chieftain, whose reluctant support of the young Pretender in 1745 encouraged that of other chieftains.

Macaulay[1] called 'the Pericles of the North'[2]— our common ancestor. This girl's great great grandfather and my grandfather were first cousins. It takes a lot of intra-breeding to make a look last like that ... Yours sincerely,

To R. D. FitzGerald

Dear Bob,

Kings Cross
24 March 1949

I have read your letter just come and am answering before I read your criticism,[3] because I want to say that I have two Grüner[4] sketches (and a Grüner artist's proof etching) because I have see-sawed between you and Tom for them and the National Library at Canberra—see-sawed ever since you considered 'Selected Verse' for me. Now I am settled and I am telling you at once, as I don't want you to feel that it is a new up-spring of wish because of the kindness I know I will find in this criticism. I shall leave the things with A. & R. (upstairs), and you and Tom can decide which to which because in this matter (and more than this) you are both one to me. The one oil is a Cow,[5] the *first Cow* that mothered so many of Grüner's later and other Cows. This was given me as from his Mother; the other came later and is pepperinas—wh. I called 'willows' !!! (The poor artist)

I saw Hughie[6] on Monday (my first day out for months) and if ever a man was his work and his work him, it is Hughie. His very joints transliterate or sing his words. And his hearing is back! I had not known it. Anyhow I felt as if I had seen archangels and the Almighty in the joy of seeing him look so alive and well.

Now I end so that my straying eye can have its fill of the manuscript of which it is so conscious.

[1] T. B. Macaulay.
[2] Macaulay actually called the 'Great Lochiel' the 'Ulysses of the North'.
[3] R. D. FitzGerald's review of Mary's *Selected Verse*, 1948, which appeared in *Meanjin* 3 (1949), 182-4.
[4] Elioth Grüner.
[5] R. D. FitzGerald chose the cow painting.
[6] Hugh McCrae.

Mr. Malloch
Bread and Cheese Club
Melbourne.

Kings Cross
28 March 1949

Dear Mr. Malloch—

The address to be given (3.4.49) on early steam navigation of the rivers of Riverina (N.S.W.) is of interest to me. It may interest the Club to know that in the Eighties Wentworth was the third largest port for tonnage in N.S.W. 'Sailings' were a daily entry in the newspapers then.

My late brother, Hugh, married Emily, daughter of Captain Brown who owned a little fleet of five steamers on the Darling, the 'Florence Annie' (written of by Dr. C. E. W. Bean, the war historian, as 'The Dreadnought of the Darling'),[1] 'The India' and I forget the others. Mr. Brown was a religious man, and wd. not take Cargo on Sundays. So the rival fleet got the Sunday lading (must use the right word for ship travel!) As he was making an income of £1.000 to £2.000 a year, he could afford to be religious. But he was really sincere, and always held service on board on Sundays for his 'crew', wh. included his wife and one of his daughters, and any shore people who liked to come. I forgot to add that one of the Brown Passengers was Gilbert Parker, writer of 'when Valmond came to Pontiac'[2] and who was afterwards knighted.

When Bean wrote 'The Dreadnought of the Darling' he was a staffman on the 'S.M.H.' and did it for the paper. I never knew how vast our inland wheat fields (and possibilities) were till I read that, though I was familiar with Riverina from end to end. In the years that followed, and the war of 1914-18, Bean forgot he had written this till I reminded him one day at a Journalists Institute luncheon. I think it was reprinted a year or two ago. On the old Murrumbidgee in the 70's one boat was called the *Marian* for my mother. Yours sincerely,

To R. D. FitzGerald

Dear Bob,

Kings Cross
26 April 1949

Don't you *dare* thank me again for the Grüner![3] I have to thank the Lord I had them to give them to you and to Tom; and to thank the Lord they are in a place where they will be individually valued. Had they gone to the Mitchell or the National Gallery they would have been mere studies amongst his greater work—so everytime you or Tom

---

[1] Published 1911.
[2] *When Valmond Came to Pontiac: the Story of a Lost Napoleon*, 1899.
[3] See letter, 24 March 1949.

say 'That is Grüner's work' I shall be exalted and he too—or rather what would have been two of his less understood and finished paintings. I had a great regard for Grüner's mother. She fought like a Trojan, through poverty and hard work, to make him a painter, i.e. to give him the freedom of his genius and no life of Grüner can ever be properly written without full recognition of her and this. This long paragraph means that I am always glad one of the pictures was given me in her name. I had intended beginning: 'You have a warm heart, Bob!' So it goes in here . . .

No need to answer this, Bob, *Not* with your overworked and tired eyes. I am dreading September—England declared war in 1914 in September, and in 1939 in September. The harvest was in. This Conference in London is possibly for that purpose, though I hope to God not—Death has been abroad enough.

To George Ferguson

Dear Mr Ferguson,

Kings Cross
2 May 1949

I have to thank you for a copy of McKeown's last book 'Nature in Australia'.[1] It is a book should be in every school library, to be read as a part of the curriculum. This because it is so informative, the information being in good and *very* readable form. One of the things I like about it is its generous reference to contemporaries in all the fields it includes in its scope. The chapter on erosion, in view of the meat contracts with Great Britain which mean cattle with their destroying hoofs on vast areas of surface land, should be specially marked and sent to Mr Chifley:[2] this because, while closer settlement would do good and conserve the land, wide areas will mean not conservation, but destruction in a part of Australia which should be its garden, but which because of winds and rainfall is easily destroyed.

I said the book is informative. It is a treasure house of reference and knowledge. Another thing I like is that there are a few references to places in Australia, as defined by some personal observation there, as when felling trees and scrub near streams to save the anglers' lines which starved the trout for which the lines were made.

I write this appreciation to thank you for sending me the book. My copy goes presently to my collection at the Mitchell Library.

By the way the Giant Toad (page 112) used to wake me up in Paraguay, slap-slapping its tongue against the flooring boards under

[1] Published 1949.
[2] J. B. Chifley.

my bed as it caught night insects. And there was a story that, as a new comer, one of our men in the dusk thought they were little pigs, and proclaimed 'a find'. Yours sincerely,

To Donald Gordon Campbell

Dear Don,

Kings Cross
18 May 1949

Your news came yesterday, & I am more than pleased that you thought of *me* in regard to your news! That I am glad for you goes without saying. I believe in early marriage as it helps people grow together—that is, of course, where there is a home to live *in* & enough to live *on*. For marriage is the most difficult of all things life has to face. When fellowship grows, it can replace romance, & without hurt or loss.

I have friends at Parramatta who may know your Elizabeth. If you had given me her surname I could have written her & sent their address. And of course, I shall be glad to see her—any time. I look on you all as, in a way, part of my family, father, mother, David & all.

Yours sincerely and affectionately,

To T. Inglis Moore

Dear Tom,

Kings Cross
4 June 1949

Just come,[1] & I am replying instanter even if what I write has been in mind since before Selected Verse even began. And that is what a debt for recognition, appraisement, and kindness I owe you two. Others have praised verbally, but you two have *written*, and *again written*. You are tied up to your written word; others remained free of recording.

Another astounding thing to me is that Bob whose writings are star high where mine are grass & tree-top has given so much of his heart to my work. The two writings are fields or worlds apart. It is for all the world like the Almighty coming down to look at the trees in the Garden of Eden, & having a talk to Adam.

Every writer here has a warmth and sometimes some hint of iron—the newer strong ones especially. He has the coldness of forged steel: *and* there is nothing more alive & living than steel! Or for another simile:

---

[1] T. Inglis Moore's article 'Mary Gilmore' which later appeared in *Southerly* 10, 3 (1949), 122-30.

He has the knit of granite, & with it its glint. I have seen the granite walls of St Peter's (R.C.) in Goulburn in the late afternoon dark green instead of blue grey, & the flashes of sun from its crystals as the sun moved on so that it lit all over, but in sparks. I expect big things of Judith Wright[1] & Nan McDonald. (Unless they stand still) but they are rock & iron; they are not steel. And so I am astounded at his regard for my work, which is mostly a cry.

(And now I have to attend to my *house-keeping*, in case someone comes & finds it & me in dressing-gowns).

Later

What a piece of work! *What* a writing! I have read it as work or creation, & not about me, I have read *it*, not something written about me. You have knit closer in this than in anything you have written (to my knowledge, that is) except 'A Drum for Hugh McCrae'. Of course I know it is about me, & I am filled with feeling again & again & some point of assessment, so sure & (I hang for it!) so accurate. These things ... may or may not be true, may not be permanent in time. But it is the work that is the monument, the monumental, the enduring, and the tribute to Tom Moore! It will be read, in years to come, not as about the verse of M.G. but as Tom Inglis Moore, and his work for Australia, hammered in on the less critical. And what a standard, what a widening of horizon in the application of the quotations! I read them with wings; they gave me wings. And they gave ideals.

I don't know how you are going to write about others after this! Where will you get more material than you have here!

I am dizzy with the thought of it. You have entered into the work as I did when writing it. I was consumed in it; and I was it and it was life I wanted to write, and I wanted it for Australia to be part of the land on which I stood. How right you are there.

It seems like putting polish on the stars and the sky to make suggestions, but I pencilled in one, if you don't mind. And have you the name, Mary G. popping out like a star in the sky a little often? That kind of thing is one of my faults. Mr. Howarth asked me for some verses to go into the issue of 'Southerly' with your elogium. (That is the word isn't it?) Since reading this I feel I shd. send him something more worthy of your writing. I sent him the last things I had written. I never had time to write long sustained work, and did the best I could under the circumstances. My scrub flourished because there were no big trees to eat up the ground. But today I notice, as others must have done, how age runs to slick little bits, compasses only the small, and the

---

[1] One of the earliest forecasts of Judith Wright's potential. Mary lived to see Judith Wright recognized as one of Australia's greatest poets.

little last spark in the ash. So 'Fourteen Men'[1] will be very much combed out, combed out, and the little sparks put into booklets on their own.

My sight? Least said soonest mended and no one is to know. One eye can still read and write. I forget names horribly now, but my hearing is still a friend. Had flu and the two ancient T.B. spots begin to say hello, but I think have stopped; for the deadly sense of weakness has lessened. My dear Tom, Peace and Pacita, may someone be as generous to you as you have been to me, and Bob will not grudge you this if I say you have done a richer piece of writing than he did, and not only because he was confined for space. It is something in you.

Later

You will never believe it, but I have read your appreciation through twice at full gallop, and haven't a word of it left in my mind! (I used to read the original 'Bookfellow'[2] like that down in the scrubs of Western Victoria). I have tried to find the root of that (wh. is the highest praise) whether because of its force, its homogeneity of vibration, its put over to the reader as creation or what. Beyond the words there is the 'it', and it is the 'it' one is racing with; that one is apprehending. (Comprehension belongs to the words as the moving or speaking factor). But I am returning the M.S. without another reading. I shall wait for 'Southerly' and its appearance. And, *of course*, put in about you and Bob! There wd. be loss to me, without that. Linked with you (and him) makes me somebody...

Nothing I could ever say or do would repay you and Bob for what you have done for me to put me in a high place, not just for now, but for future assessment. I *know* I have value for ordinary people. They come to me, and they write to me, from everywhere. I am in scrapbooks in all sorts of places. I hear it so often. 'I have been keeping you in my book since I was a girl' etc. etc. That makes me one with the people, but it is not literature. It is you and Bob who have insisted there is literature too—insisted as no one else (except Hugh McCrae) has done. What you and Bob have done stands with Hugh McCrae's 'Twa Heads'[3] (or whatever he called it. My memory is not as good as my capacity for impression and thought, now). For in that Hugh lifted me from the ruck to the level of fellowship without criticism and you two have done it *by* and *with* criticism. Is it any wonder I am grateful?

[1] Her volume of poems then in progress and published in 1954.
[2] See the letters written by Mary to A. G. Stephens in the period 1903–9, especially letter, 29 January 1907.
[3] Mary appears to mean McCrae's poem 'To Mary Gilmore', part of which, in his handwriting, was used by Mary as a foreword to *Fourteen Men*, 1954. See note to letter, 8 February 1953.

To R. D. FitzGerald

Dear Bob—

Kings Cross
8 June 1949

Your letter just came and I reply at once (there is no need for an answer! there never is.) Tom sent me his 'M.G.'[1] I read it through at a gallop (i.e. breathlessly) and not a word remained in memory. I read it a few hours later. Some fury, *furore* (or whatever the word is) and no word left in memory. And this is the highest tribute receptive man can give any writing. The whole (and not the parts, piecemeal) goes down at once and becomes part of being. That is how our elders read their Bibles. One text at a time, for more would blot out by inclusion, the item or individual bit. I did not—could not read it as M.G. It could only be read for itself. It had no hangers-on or poor bits. Your word 'It is magnificent'... is the right word. But what a trio to pay tribute to this 'all among the barley' writer, you two and Hugh McCrae. I try to believe it is more than goodness of heart and the result is so startling and dazzling that I just retreat and say 'Cant be!' and yet I do know I come near to human life, for the *little* people come to me. or write to me. Of course it is the difference between literature and life, the grass and the sun-bird. Somebody, A.G.S.[2] or Frank Morton was it once said, 'She never tries to rise above her natural height' or words to that effect. And that is mostly true. I love the height. I go into it on the wings of others. But I know my wings are a quail's wings. Once in a while a skylark's perhaps. I lived with the earth as a child, and I loved it. It was part of me then. I only have it in memory now. (What was that A.G.S. said, or quoted, about writing in tranquillity what was felt as storm, or something like that?)

Well here's something else. 'Storm' reminded me of it. Did you see last Sat. week's 'Daily Tel' with a letter of mine,[3] put in under the heading 'Poetess (abhorrent word!) on War and Cant'. That was storm, remembered and in being. I did not expect it to be printed. But I have had tribute from Qld. to W.A. over it. I hope I did not tell you this before. Memory begins to be a sieve of wide mesh. As eyesight goes I find memory goes. Eyesight is probably the root of memory being the greatest sense or root of observation. Perhaps the root of man's rising intellect. The eyeless do not build by invention only by accretion as the oyster. Think of the sudden eye of a spider and his marvellous web! And now I hope I haven't talked your head off!

---

[1] The *Southerly* article. See letter, 4 June 1949.
[2] A. G. Stephens.
[3] In a letter to the *Daily Telegraph*, 28 May 1949, Mary attacked those who criticized the violence and degradation depicted in Norman Mailer's *The Naked and the Dead* yet failed to attack war itself which initiates such behaviour in men.

To T. Inglis Moore

Dear Tom,

Kings Cross
24 June 1949

I wrote Leon Gellert that three men had been most generous to me! Tom Inglis Moore, R. D. FitzGerald and Hugh McCrae, and that now, in spite of the fact that he had 'poked borak' at me, there was a fourth! 'Poking borak' was aboriginal for 'poking fun', in case you don't know it.

I am posting today your two copies of 'Selected Verse', for, though the one has a request for your 'letter' in it, it was already yours!

After I had in-written the other I wondered if it was what you wanted. If not I shall send you another one (additional).

About the South American thesis on its poetry, plus or in contrast to Australian, your versions need not be letter perfect parallels of the original *words*. The feeling and the singing or poetic quality is the main thing. It would be a new departure for Australia, and, new to the judges, would catch their imagination, if not their historical knowledge . . .

Ruth Bedford has a copy of the famous 'The Gaucho'[1]—I think it is called. I had it once but it is gone long ago. I forget to whom now. Perhaps Bernard O'Dowd. The Argentine sets great store on it. It is Gaucho life and customs written, I think, nearly 100 years ago. It is simple verse, of the Heney[2] simpler type, but is a continuous poem of the easy verse type. I am sure Ruth Bedford would lend it to you if no other copy can be found. But 'Tabare',[3] because of its possible Australian parallel of racial pain and suffering, is in my heart. Moreover it has power and majesty. 'The Gaucho' has neither; it is simple narrative, and by an uneducated or unliterary gaucho.

Someone just came, so must end. The books will be posted with this—as to my biography you are to be the first to see my diaries after I am gone. So keep this as your authority—Affectionately,

To George Ferguson

Dear Mr Ferguson, (otherwise G.F.),

Kings Cross
28 September 1949

I was about to write to ask for 6 more copies of 'Selected Verse' to my account, and also a copy of Hugh McCrae's 'Story Book Only'.

---

[1] 'The Gaucho' by Jose Hernandez, 1938.
[2] Thomas Heney.
[3] *Tabare, An Indian Legend of Uruguay*, by Juan Zorrilla de San Martin, 1888. An epic poem set in the 16th century, dealing with the tragic love of Tabare, son of a Spanish woman captured by an Indian tribe, for the sister of a Conquistador.

I want to give it to my grandson, a boarder at Scots Prep. School, but it is to stay in the library at Scots when he leaves to show that he had been there. (How the Scottish blood loves to proclaim itself!) The book is to stay with you till I can come into town.

Thank you for the Colin Roderick book[1]—and the double-dyed varmint left me out![2] Or was he to use only books now in print? I have been for months trying to get time to add some notes (proving things I was first to write) to 'Old Days' and 'More Recollections' and submit them for resurrection: they have been buried a long time. If you won't touch them I shall send them to Collins (in Scotland) or some London firm. People constantly ask me where can they get them. Sometimes through the 'Bulletin'. Yours sincerely,

I want Hugh McCrae's autograph for the 'Story Book Only', but I want to write in it before he sees it.

To George Ferguson

Dear Mr Ferguson,

Kings Cross
10 October 1949

On Thursday I took in 'Old Days: Old Ways' and 'More Recollections'[3] for your consideration. You were out and I saw young Cousins,[4] who seems his father over again, though looking different. If he is manager, tradition will be kept. But he is surely the youngest manager since when A. & R. began!

Besides my two books, I took in the copy A. & R. sent me of 'The Holy City',[5] which I am giving my grandson at Scots' Prep School but which is to stay there when he leaves ... (Is there *no* good ink nowadays!?!) I wrote an inscription (of sorts) in the front, and referred to Captain Hurley and his work. *I hope* you saw it, as I thought the Firm might like a copy of that part—to send to Captain Hurley, as I called it an Iliad in pictures, and no one else might have thought of that.

Of 'High Valley'[6] I wrote a 'High Praise' to Mrs. George Johnston

---

[1] Probably *Wanderers in Australia*, 1949, an anthology of travel writings.
[2] Roderick took no account of Mary's *Old Days: Old Ways* (1934) and *More Recollections* (1935). They are not, of course, travel writings.
[3] Her two books of reminiscences and anecdotes of pioneer life, published in 1934 and 1935.
[4] Aubrey Cousins, the son of W. G. Cousins (editor of Halstead Press) and also a director of Angus & Robertson.
[5] James Francis Hurley, *The Holy City. A Camera Study of the Holy City and Its Borderlands*, 1948.
[6] A novel by Charmian Clift and George Johnston, 1949. It won first prize in the 1948 *S.M.H.* competition.

c/o the Sun, and am wondering did she get it, as I have had no reply. Also I wrote Colin Roderick about his book.[1] I hope you find something in that too. It is all little enough for the books you have sent me. Yours sincerely,

To Constance Robertson

Dear Connie,

Kings Cross
28 October 1949

I am worried over you. You are working at a too continuous high tension and no make-up can hide how small your face has become and how thinned to the bone you are.

Life drives, I know, and work is salvation. Nothing I can say will alter that—either for you, me, or anyone else who finds creation in work.

You have a tremendous inheritance of healthy tissue from both your father[2] and your mother, but don't drive it too far or you will snap—yet you should be alive and alert at 90—the root of energy is there.

With love—and I do not often write that.

Birds of Paradise? What was it the old aboriginal said to Jean Devanny? 'The bird of paradise sits in the tree-top and the wind blows through its tail'.

To R. D. FitzGerald

Dear Bob,

Kings Cross
24 November 1949

Your hand at writing, like Hugh's, has something to it. It isn't just something you have written. It is something in itself. And if I say it is like something driven out of, and on stone, that is also part of it—and it walks on its own feet, as your verse does.

Yesterday I came on 'This Understanding'.[3] It bit, as it did on its first reading. Presently I hope to come on the other one and that too I shall send you. All that for the envelope in 'Meanjin'.

[1] *Wanderers in Australia*.
[2] A. G. Stephens.
[3] A poem by R. D. FitzGerald in the *Bulletin* earlier that year, 29 June 1949.

For the inside: what a lucky woman I am! I believe I said before (to you? to Tom?) I shall die at peace knowing hands have built me into the fabric of Australia—of this land under my feet.

And what a lot of the definite, of arrowed points, you have put into so little. Both as to me as a person, and my verse. I *want* to be more than my verse, I want to be this person who once lived here.

That my verse is a woman's verse, and not the lord, their shadow (excuse the *lord* simile) of a man's, makes the inward ego turn catherine wheels of joy. It is a thing I would not know myself, but when it is said, I realize, and for the moment, perceive it as a reality.

I am anxious about Hugh. He was here a couple of days ago. Outside, he looked fine and alert and alive. But I had a feeling that this is more due to the will than to the body as its foundation. Beatrix Esmond[1] is not all fiction. A brave face to the world is necessary to some of us. There was always Nancy,[2] no matter what came or went. Nancy was home to the bird. Now there is no Nancy . . . I heard an older man say long ago—Professor Anderson after his first wife died. 'It was so lonely to come home. The place was so empty'. He made a sufficient second marriage. Hughie didn't and I think that left a relic of shock—and that shock still hurts.

You'll never guess what I did last Friday! I spoke (very briefly) at an open air meeting (my first) at Taylor Square,[3] for Eddie Ward![4] The scattered audience made it like talking to a body of people with no face. They had ears, and that was all.

It was quite different from talking over the air. The air is like writing. Your nose is on the paper in front of you; and the people are all about you. Distance is not distance. Here it was scatteration. But they were nice to me, one woman even said 'We could listen to you all night!' I thought that a good note to end on!!!

Your grateful pensioner,

To Hugh McCrae

Kings Cross
Dear Hugh,   25 November 1949

I wrote to you C/- A. & R. the other day. This is a forgotten P.S. to that & the earlier letter.

I think part of your trouble is *deferred psychic* shock. You had all

---

[1] A character in Thackeray's novel, *The History of Henry Esmond*, 1852.
[2] Hugh McCrae's first wife, Annie Geraldine (Nancy).
[3] In Sydney.
[4] Edward J. Ward.

the ordinary shock when, so suddenly, Nancy went. And that is all that most people have, or are ever aware of.

But people who do creative work draw it from within, no matter how well the outside self is able to mould & dress it. Genius is artesian & from the unconscious mind or the psychic. Most people are sub-artesian or just reflector pools & lakes. These suffer no deferred shock.

When I was about fifteen, I saw a man thrown from a bucking horse. I heard his neck crack. I was sent into the house for brandy to prevent me knowing what had happened, & later was told the man had taken his own horse & gone away. Over 40 years later, at an Inst. of Journalists luncheon, on a gruellingly hot day, in the annex I saw the collapse of an old Herald man, Mr. Cunningham. As they lifted that flaccid body I had the sudden attack of deferred shock. I saw 40 years back, in him, the flaccid body of the young man as he lay on the ground: I had to fight, & refuse to meet, that deferred shock for years. When I remembered, the place & the happening then became a tragedy, & only then, Deferred shock has to be fought, Hugh, and rejected.

To T. Inglis Moore

Dear Tom,

Kings Cross
12 December 1949

'Southerly'[1] came this morning. I said before, on the MS, that I read, and re-read, as though not already read. It is still like that, only more so. There are things I had not seen (or is it *perceived?*) before. Richness deepened. You say that my verse is me. *This* is *you*. You see the tree in the slip just up through the ground. I don't think anyone has had such a generous analysis and appreciation and it is intensified by illustration in quotation from and on other writers. And how curiously illustrative of your work that portrait is! It came unexpectedly and it fits unexpectedly. It has what no painted portrait has ever said or expressed. It shows power, and power is what you say I have. Well, if I have done a quarter of what you say is in my work. I am somebody; I am worth while.

I am very tired and must end. But I could not rest till I had said thank you.

I thought Bob had done wonders in his article in 'Meanjin'.[2] This goes farther and wider and it has you in it, as though emotion drove.

I must end. A visitor has just come.

My dear friend. Only with tears could I really thank you.

[1] *Southerly*, 10, 3 (1949).
[2] *Meanjin*, 3 (1949), 182-4, review of *Selected Verse*, 1948.

To George Mackaness

Kings Cross
3 January 1950

Dear George: and what a co-incidence! The verse on my calendar-block for today is,

> 'He slept beneath the moon,
> He basked beneath the sun;
> He lived a life of going-to-do,
> and died with nothing done,
>   James Albery!

When I first knew Louisa Lawson[1] I asked her how she spelt her maiden name. She spelt it, 'Albery'. *That* I think is as nice a New-Year's Gift as I cd. give to a history hunter like you. This means that your letter has just come. Thank you and Alice and Joan—Ha!—

> With you and Alice and Joan
> Friendship is never a loan!

I am nearly dead with the heat, but am still crazy over T.I.M.'s appreciation in 'Southerly'. It is its *literary* value matters so much. *That value* will keep something of me alive, when this me is long dead and forgotten.

And then the last sentence in the '12 Australian'[2] living men, in its last two lines (Sunday Sun, 1.1.1950,) what a New Year Card to wake up to! Good job I know what's what in work, and not what's what in bubbles, no matter how lovely they look, or I wd. be a bust bubble that floated too high. I had a line from Ernestine[3] saying she hoped to be in Sydney soon. (I wonder!) Also a letter from Jacqueline Deschamps (and Noel) from Germany—I met her long ago as an anxious friend of Ernestine, and before that a friend of E's. mother. She wants Ernestine to stay with them in Germany and build up her health (and incidentally her knowledge of foreign countries and literature.) How I hope she will go!

Young Bill, my grandson, flew up to his mother, near Cloncurry for Xmas. His seventh flight there alone. She had a pony and a pup waiting. So his mind will be on them for some time yet. The heat wave there is terrific. But Western N.S.W. goes (and is) as high.

[1] Henry Lawson's mother.
[2] Leaders in the various fields of Australian life were asked whom they considered to be the twelve Australians who had made the greatest impact on the lives of people in the past half century. The sentence Mary refers to is: 'Nearest claimants for inclusion among living women are Sister Kenny and Dame Mary Gilmore'.
[3] Ernestine Hill.

Don't forget a copy of my history of founding the F.A.W.[1] is (not yet for the public) at the R.A.H.S. for you to see any time you like. Might be a good idea to see it, in case any point is not clear and can be asked about. The originals are at the Mitchell.

By the way see Roland Robinson's 'Language of the Sand':[2] It is Australia from itself, from within; and not *about* Australia. He is authentic. He was taken into the life of the tribes, and has a lot of tribal lore. Every good wish and all my heart to you and Alice and Joan, whose friendship is never a loan—

To Clive Turnbull

Dear Mr. Turnbull (on a crippled sheet of paper!)

Kings Cross
15 January 1950

Thank you for your notice a while ago of Roland Robinson's 'Language of the Sand'.[3] He is the best on native Australia, so far. Everyone else writes explanatorily and patronizingly and from the outside. He writes as *it*—from the inside. In other words, he is one with this land, its life and its people whether birds, camps, or natives.

He is a great hulking fellow, with the nicest little wife—red hair and golden freckles ... He is equally himself as an artist's model, a railway navvy, or in a black's camp. He brought his first verse to me, and when he told me he was going North I gave him W. Harney and told him to learn all he could from and about the blacks. Now his heart is with them.

I gave him your notice and suggested that he write to you and thank you. He is sure of himself, but modest and grateful for help. He is doing an article for the 'S.M.H.' on his railway fettling at Alice Springs. (By the way isn't 'fettle' Scottish Anglo-Saxon? I love words with the original earth in them.) By the way (not twice!) I thought of a big back-handed comparison the other day which years may make legitimate. 'That Mozart is the Shaw Neilson of Music'. He is, isn't he? Yours sincerely,

To R. G. Howarth

Dear Mr. Howarth,

Kings Cross
27 January 1950

... Brennan looked on me as one with the mind of a woman or a child.

[1] On this controversy see letter, 22 May 1935.
[2] Published 1949.
[3] Published 1949.

I never had any *real* conversation with him. (I had or have ideas but no scholarship. I have known and felt that all my life.) Once I had the temerity to ask him what he thought of my verse. I asked with the timidity his greatness demanded. He came down slowly from the heights, looked at me for a moment to see if he could find anything to arrest him, and replied 'I had rather not say . . . There is nothing I *can* say.' I wasn't then, and never have been, hurt by that moment. It was only what I expected, knowing the difference between his height and mine.

Now that he is gone, that reply of his is one of my treasures. I know I am only a daisy in the grass in comparison with the great, but I try to be really a daisy, and not just a pretentious weed—

To R. G. Howarth

Dear Mr. Howarth,

Kings Cross
6 February 1950

Your letter just came. When (this is a continuation of Brennan)[1] Brennan said of my verse 'I had rather not say . . . There is nothing I *can* say', there was nothing unkind, and nothing hard. He was just speaking to a child, a child whose world was eons of space and time away from his own. He had no egotism. He *knew values,* and on values he stood. He stood on the rock of reality, and not on the heaving sea of self—of which he was the ocean.

The other night a knock as I was at my tea, the door open a chink on the chain. I smelt the whisky before I reached the door. 'Can you tell me where Dame Mary lives?' 'Here' I said. He was about 26, a sailor, with an accent. He said he was Scottish. 'Your accent is not, or not wholly', I said. He spoke German, and came off a Dutch ship. He wanted me to write his life, 'a wonderful life'. I said I would give him the names of some newspaper men. 'I don't want newspaper men. I can get them for myself. I want a writer like you, so that the book will be sure to be published'. After some talk he brought out, as the high water-mark of persuasion, 'Do you remember the man who murdered his wife with *fifteen cuts of the axe?* . . . I was *there!* I *saw* it!' Believe it or not, I refused *that!*

I wrote and sent you two hitherto unpublished (in any form) aboriginal myths or legends and suggested an aboriginal number of 'Southerly'. I expect Mrs. Kingsley-Strack[2] on Wednesday to let me see her versions again, with a view to adding them to mine. Roland

---

[1] See previous letter, 27 January 1950.
[2] Mrs Joan Kingsley-Strack, a keen collector of Aboriginal stories, legends, and myths.

Robinson has some too. He is to address the English Association in May, so you will have him. I told him of 'Southerly' and my suggestion—no more just now.

16 February 1950
Held this till I saw Mrs. Kingsley-Strack. She is prepared to let me have her version of the creation. It has a lot that mine hasn't, and where my leader is the emu, hers is the dingo. Mine is Riverina, hers South Coast.

To R. D. FitzGerald

Dear Bob—

Kings Cross
28 March 1950

If I hadn't mislaid the paper, this wd. have gone to the 'Daily Tel' instead of to you. (The papers being gone I cannot quote it). In Mr. Bartlett's article on Aust.Lit.[1] he says you owe something to T. S. Eliot. This idiotic ascription always *did* enrage me, even when young.

I saw a thing you wrote when you were about 17, I think, shown me by your uncle.[2] I told you of it before, so I need not repeat that. But what I want to say is that, in that verse, there was, in embryo, everything that comes out in your work today. T. S. Eliot's allusiveness is feathery, yours is direct. He skips and skims, you slash, and no matter how controlled the slash is.

In the name of (you can put it in) what has the Essay on Memory or H. Shoals[3] to do with or in common with T. S. Eliot and his pirouetting slippers and cups of tea? There are no pangs in Eliot, there are only flicks and stings, and little ones at that.*

I might have written you all this before. But this is a nice new rage.

So my indignations to you *at once and hot*

*Don't think I do not see his values, though.

Mr. Malloch,
The Bread & Cheese Club,
Melbourne.

Kings Cross
1 May 1950

Dear Mr. Malloch,
... Having read Mrs. J. S. Litchfield's[4] fiery spark, you may be interes-

[1] Norman Bartlett's article 'What Our Poets are writing About', *Daily Telegraph*, 28 March 1950, surveyed the work of living Australian poets.
[2] J. Le Gay Brereton.
[3] *Essay on Memory* and *Heemskerck Shoals*, two of FitzGerald's works.
[4] Jessie Sinclair Litchfield.

ted to know that at Neutral Bay State School,[1] I taught her there when she was-none-so-old. I went to South America, and it was years before we met again, but many many times I thanked a writer up North who defended, by her pen, the North against all comers, never dreaming that she had been Jessie Robertson! As you know she was one of the evacuated during the war. Not given time to pack, she locked her house, and in Sydney faced up to life off her own bat (for the most part: being one of those independent Scots.) When at last she went back, her home had been looted; the MS., diaries, scrap-and-cutting books of a life time all gone—a loss neither she nor the North will ever be able to make up and mend. We are 'sib' in race, she is a great Australian, and I am very proud of her—if only for the family she has given Australia & proof of the health of the North.

As for me I feel as if I am carrying the Fiery Cross throughout the land! Why because I was asked to be the first to sign the Australian plea for self-government for Scotland. Judging by Mrs. Litchfield's letter, she may be the first in the North! Yours sincerely

To A. H. Chisholm

Kings Cross
3 May 1950

Mine Nalec—you see I can still be frivolous!—It was like you to think I might like to see 'Gallipoli'.[2] I wrote it with a breaking heart for Gallipoli seemed to me (and all of us) to be the place of, and to cover, a world's grief. Adam McCay said it was one of the finest things ever written. And perhaps, size for size, he had a degree of reason. Seeing it again unexpectedly and after so many years it brought back the old ache and cry . . .

I had Hugh McCrae and Donovan Clarke in some days ago. Donovan Clarke I had not met before, and Hugh has renewed his youth

[1] Mary taught there briefly in 1890 after returning to Sydney from her teaching position at Silverton, near Broken Hill.
[2] 'Gallipoli' was one of Mary's short poems in *The Passionate Heart*, 1918. She refers here to its appearance in the Melbourne *Argus*, 25 April 1950.

> Only above the grave of murdered faith
> The grass grows never green.
>
> But thou, Gallipoli, though thou art battle-scarred,
> And heardst the endless cry of death and pain
> Strike through the thunder of thy guns,
> Yet, when the spring shall come again
> Thou shalt call back the robin and the wren,
> And clothe with fresh green grass thy piteous plain
> And every broken grave and shard.
>
> O Memory, so like the little lark that runs
> To nest among the graves of far Gallipoli,
> Oh, cover thou thy griefs as tenderly!

in that hearing aid. I had never realized before, what an enraging thing and what a strain on the nerves, going deaf, must be.

I wish I had known when I last saw you that I was about to be recorded for my last Wednesday's talk[1] a subject never given anywhere before: the inheritance of aura, vibration, wave length or what you like to call it. Everyone feels it some time or other; it is as inheritable as a nose; but I am the first to give proof of it. Here it is in brief: I knew a man as child, boy and man. He lived for years in Qld. One day at Crookwell I felt him enter the room where I was. The man coming in was his opposite in size, colour and weight. Later I found this man was the father of the son he had never seen. (That was in about 1922.)

About nine years ago in this flat, I felt the presence of a man dead about 14 years. A girl, whom I had never seen before came in. No doubt whose daughter she was! She had her father's aura, as the till then unknown man at Goulburn had given his to the son I had known.

When the talk comes out in the A.B.C. Weekly I shall send a copy to the Sorbonne (Paris) and other scientific bodies. I ended the talk with: 'We measure the wave lengths of stars; why not man?' The very day after I was recorded, there was an item in the 'Daily Mirror', from Vienna, where a scientist has written books on 'human radar'. But mine is on its *inheritance* of aura or whatever it is. And it is 'inheritance' that is my proposition. (Inheritance is not telepathy, as people might at first think.) One woman writing me after listening in reminded me that aura is really what the blacks call their 'shadow self'. Their shadow self goes with them always.

By the way, what about a quotation from the ABC for the Encyclop.?[2] Just thought of it!

Always remembering the little boy who liked my verse

M.G.

To William Bluett

Dear Billy,

Kings Cross
8 June 1950

In the midst of writing to Mr. Chifley, Mr. Menzies, Mr. Speaker Cameron, Dr. Evatt, Mr. Calwell & Mr. Ward, your chicken arrived. It is still crowing (or is it?). And by Post! It seems unbelievable. And what a surprise!! (But just like you.) My thanks are in pieces, like this letter, but between beginning & ending they are 'a flock'.

[1] Mary was a guest on the A.B.C. programme, 26 April 1950, entitled 'Where Old Friends Meet'.
[2] Chisholm was editor of the *Australian Encyclopaedia*.

The letters I am writing are on Byram Mansell's[1] re-creations of aboriginal art. He has something to give the whole world as Australian, and I am putting all my life's effort behind him, seeing in his work the fruition (in another way) of my own life—longing and fighting. I have always said that we had here, in the blacks, their lore & work, as much to give the world as Egypt, the Red Indian, & all the others, But no one seemed to see it (no one worth while) till now Mr. Mansell is illustrating beliefs in aboriginal ways, using native modes & colorings ... The value is of the ages. The U.S.A. has long seen this, & if we do not move quickly the U.S.A., & not Australia, will show this work to the world. You can guess my feeling of urgency in this matter. Like your chicken, may the Australian cock crow first.

Dear kind Billy, here, too, are my thanks.

To T. Inglis Moore

Dear Tom,

Kings Cross
21 June 1950

Did you know that Judith Wright had (and still has) a baby?!? (Have just written her.) It makes clear why she wrote so understandingly in 'Woman to Man'.[2] She is now Judith Wright McKinney.

I am a very tired old woman, but that baby lifted me up, and also Byram Mansell's adaptations and interpretations of Aboriginal paintings. He hopes to hold an Exhib. in Canberra when it can be arranged. He has the *real thing*. Others have reproduced or copied; he *interprets*—and it means the same with our so misrepresented blacks, as Gilbert Murray did with his 'Trojan Women' and their originals. He is giving their work and Australia their place in the world's record of peoples. He is doing, not a personal, but a national work in this and if we are not alert, the U.S.A. will claim to have discovered our blacks. Namatjira[3] is a black man painting in the white man's way. Byram Mansell is a white man painting in the blacks' way: and what a difference in interpretation!

Well that's that and now I am tired. By the way did you see Inigo Jones' article in 'Bulletin' for 7th June. 'Sun Spots and Cycles'—what a work that man is doing. And to think that I knew Clem Wragge!—at his beginnings. The miracle is still here.

[1] William Arthur Byram Mansell.
[2] Judith Wright's daughter Meredith was born in 1950. *Woman to Man*, with its sensitive appraisal of love and motherhood, was published in 1949.
[3] Albert Namatjira.

To Colin Roderick

Dear Colin Roderick,

Kings Cross
27 June 1950

Your book[1] has just come, and I have gone at a gallop through it. You are sounder, stronger, and more authoritative in this than in the earlier two.[2] Your English is straight out of the palm of your hand now. And *that* I like above everything. (There is too much *pen* in most people's work.) The whole collection you are making is above and beyond anything we have had before, as a scythe is in regard to a sickle—no matter how good and inclusive the sickle. I can't see anywhere, in looking back on what I have read, where you have gone 'thin'. The smallest assertion stands as soundly as the widest. I am glad of what you said of Ruth Park. Her people may hang like figures from a dome of circus-trapezes, but what human, to-be-loved even if reprobated figures they are! She has in this what Kylie Tennant misses. They both use a wide-meshed, loose-knit canvas. But where Ruth stitches in roses, leaves, thorns and all, Kylie only gets as far as grass. Another thing: the intent to write is almost absent in Ruth's work. Anyway Australia stands up with the rest of the world in these (or at least this one) of yours. And for this it needs the writing as well as the subject.

To W. Farmer Whyte

Dear Bill,

Kings Cross
16 July 1950

I am wondering when you (or someone equally trustworthy!) are likely to be in Sydney. I have two things I want to give the National Gallery (when it comes to being in Canberra). They are not large but difficult for me to pack and send—now I am dodderingly old.

One is a small tray, painted on plastic, by Byram Mansell; an aboriginal design in aboriginal earth-paints. It is beautiful, it is interpretive and yet is true. Most others just copy, and their copy is a *dead* copy. This is alive and the convention of the aboriginal is maintained. It has a second value in that it is one of the first pieces of aboriginal art so used and adapted. I want it hung on the wall as any other painting. It is not to be used as some smoker's tray. It is to be perhaps the beginning of a collection of native art, adapted or collected.

The second thing is a silver-point etching by that woman-genius

---

[1] Probably *An Introduction to Australian Fiction*, 1950.
[2] *The Australian Novel*, 1945 and *20 Australian Novelists*, 1947.

Kenneth Slessor

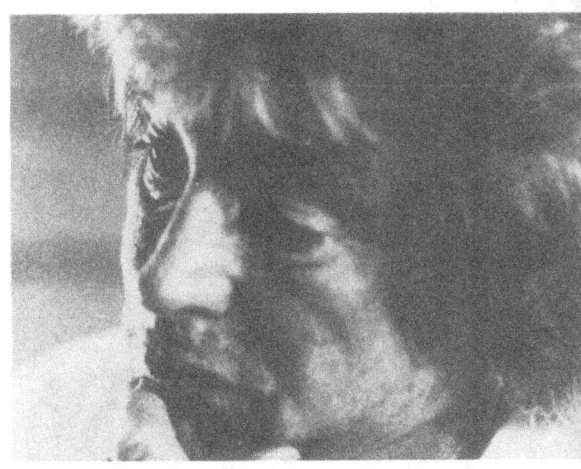

Roland Robinson

Nan McDonald

Douglas Stewart

On the way to her 90th birthday party with Albert Namatjira

Maria Kuhn, our own Australian-born woman. It is thistledown, it is so transparent. Three negro spiritualists, and all singing . . .

To Judith Wright

Kings Cross
22 July 1950

Dear Judith Wright, (as a writer you still are) that verse[1] of yours brought only one word to me and that was (I never verbally use it) '*Gosh!*' You are mighty! Such a simple verse; but what inclusions! All the suns in a drop of water; eternity in a little smile; nothing and everything. Might in an atom. Well, we have the atom bomb, but yours is not explosive and cruel, yours is life out of death, and the long evolution of time. I could wish I were as big as you! My parallel piece is 'The Word'[2] or whatever I called it—the invisible might of breath—a word—which holds the world together, as it is now built on language, man and nation alike. I have it as naked statement, you have yours as poetry.

But you will have to write at least one long poem or the future will not hold you for bigness. Link and link what you have (of a kind) into one Iliad of theme or of the mind. I never had time for this, nor will you if you have to bake the family bread, and make the family clothes, as I did: with the husband and child always first till age gave more time. But I hope there is more money in your house, money giving rest and time. Don't hurry; hurry makes shoddy. But keep the notes however poor and thin. The young impulse never comes back, but it can live in a line, and later on be built up and clothed. Rex Ingamells is coming tonight, with his thousands of words poem,—born to failure as there are not enough years to harvest under it. These things are best in prose.

Must get dressed, (this is 5 a.m. after re-reading your verse) as I want the house tidy when visitors come: and they come so early!

With your letter came one from Mr. Chifley[3]—on the world situation and Australia (confidential of course, and now ashes;) But what a day! One letter as important as the other in a way.

---

[1] As the poem referred to was included in a letter to Mary from Judith Wright it is, at present, impossible to identify.
[2] Probably 'Word-Held'. See *Fourteen Men*, 1954, p. 58.
[3] J. B. Chifley.

To J. K. Moir

Kings Cross
16 August 1950

Dear Mr. Moir (convention says 'Mr. Moir' but my heart says 'J.K.')

As last year you, Mr. Waite, and the Bread and Cheese Club arrived before I was dressed in full decorum. Did I mind? I felt the honour of the occasion.[1] Mr. Waite says the flowers came from Mildura, Brisbane, Sydney and Melbourne—and all full of scents: stocks, daffodils, carnations and hyacinths, the last word reminding me of Greece and the heroism and culture of that and other small one-people nations. I am a tolerant internationalist, but how I regret the loss to the world of racial interbreeding of a single stock and what it means in blood, bone, and culture to a people! There is the difference of the hand-made between them and the factory-made—if that is good English! . . .

All this is my thanks—my grateful thanks—for remembrance by a club that has never seen me, but which has been so good a friend to me—

To J. K. Moir

Kings Cross
15 October 1950

Dear 'J.K.'—There are nice people in the world! *You* will be missed when you are gone aloft. For over three years I had a hard time making ends meet on a quarter of the income the Qld. Trustees[2] shd. have sent me. I found a good Solicitor, and he made them pay the arrears, so, if I look shabby now, it is because I am too old to spend time on clothes and that I badly need for writing.

I am trying to get my next book (small) of verse[3] ready for printing. It is slow work, as so many people come and I cannot use my eyes at night. But I would love to see Melbourne again, and you and all the other people there whom I know or don't know.

Later on I may feel free to move. Then you will hear from or see me. But I warn you that I am a very tired old woman. The seas are beating hard on the base of the lighthouse.

My heart is warm every time I think of your letter. Judging by your interest, if you have £20 'to spare', you must have 'met' a miracle.

---

[1] The recognition by the Bread & Cheese Club of Mary's 85th birthday.
[2] Trustees of the estate of her late husband, William Gilmore, who had died in 1945.
[3] *Fourteen Men*, published in 1954.

I felt it like a blow when you gave up being head of the Club, you and it have so long been one. I suppose you had your need otherwhere and had to. Also the child has sooner or later to stand on its own feet—so Salud and Hasta Luego.

Hasta Luego is the equivalent of the U.S.A. 'So Long', means 'until soon'.

Mr. Malloch,
The Bread & Cheese Club,
Melbourne.

Kings Cross
27 November 1950

Dear Mr Malloch,
Thank you for giving place to my suggesting letter in, just come, 'Bohemia'.[1] Women Writers' Society here is appointing a Filing Sub-Committee to carry out the collection of autographed letters as proposed here by me. Think of all the old ones now gone and the history lost! In the aged, the far back ungathered events, personages, and other, history lies.

How many, for instance, remember Rush, the Sculler, when Sculling was new and almost startling in Australia, and who recalls the story of him after winning his championship (Don't know now how big or small) when in a pub he declared to the world, 'I'll row any man! I'll row him on the sea, I'll row him on the rivers, and I'll row him in the dew on the grass!' I think I was about fourteen then and now I am eighty-five. And there are thousands of such stories and incidents banked-up and covered-over in the minds of the old, only waiting for a touch to bring them up again. *These* stories are not war; they are humanizing.

I have just sent the Sydney 'Daily Tel' the history of the naming of Australia Street (Avenida Australia) in Buenos Aires, in honour of William Lane as a Liberator...

To Mrs E. O. Schlunke

My dear Olga,

Kings Cross
13 December 1950

You have your 'Bulletin' Xmas card, & I am delighted! Congratulations. What a song that thing would make—either as a thing of wild passion or as something delicate & flute like.

---

[1] The journal of the Bread and Cheese Club.

I am so sick of butter like margarine that I nearly wrote to you last week to send me a small tin, even if it came as oil; *as* of *course* it would in the weather that we are having. But don't send it now, wait till the boys are back at school & the ravaged butter dish at peace again. In any case your cows may be dry.

I am feeling 85 +, the plus repeated. So no more. But when I heard that plover call it went through me, & I was hearing it across the night—as so often as a child. We had to leave our place, Jindra,[1] because there were so many plovers they gave my mother 'the blues'. That was about 1871. 'Jindra' meant—'the place of plovers'. It was an aboriginal plover sanctuary. The birds were never hunted there, or the eggs taken. And with that I have written a whole letter!

All *good* to you & yours for Christmas & the New Year.

To Douglas Stewart

Kings Cross

Dear D. S. (*No* mistake in spelling *there*!)   15 January 1915 [Sic] 1951

... There is the pine-tree which reaches, slender & lovely from every aspect, to heaven, and there is the vine, sometimes a pumpkin vine, sometimes grape—the grape leaves glinting in the sun and smelling of the earth. Wouldn't I love to be the grape vine!

The immediate thought arises, which is most the friend of man? Or should I say life instead of man, as being wider. The co-incidences of life must be part of the root of belief in witchcraft & the supernatural! Before me lies a loose leaf from an old 1947 calendar;

> Better build schoolrooms for 'the boy'
> Than cells and prisons for 'the man'.
>   Eliza Cook—

I look at that & think either might have been the other.

To George Ferguson

Kings Cross
31 January 1951

Dear G.R.F.[2] (That is better than just G.F. or Mr Ferguson.) and might

---

[1] Mary wrote a poem entitled 'Jindra', in which the plovers feature. See note to letter, 9 July 1952. Jindra was probably Jindera, south of Wagga Wagga.
[2] George Ferguson is the grandson of George Robertson.

I suggest that you 'devise', or whatever the word should be, that every descendant Head of A. & R. be G.R. with whatever other surname initial may follow? Tombstones are a long way off. The familiar appellation remains. More! It is a guide, a light, and a reminder. Also an affirmation.

Anyway, if the parenthesis may be forgiven, I have to thank you for your letter (30.1.51) reaffirming Mr Cousins' renunciation (to me) by the Firm of any of my copyrights held by it.

I have loved the shop—the Firm[1]—ever since I first found it in the '80s in Market(?) Street—a little one-roomed shop that might have been the widened front room of a dwelling. G.R. once told me that was the happiest period of his (book) life. There were no worries then, and he and Mr. Angus were the whole thing. However it was not the most exciting! And, in power, something was added that made greatness more than just *being*!

May there never be a time in a thousand years when a descendant of G.R. is not a G.R. head in his own right.[2] What a blossoming of Australian writing that man brought about. The salt of something real to say was in everything he published. He *made* men write.

To George Ferguson

Dear G.F.

Kings Cross
2 February 1951

When I opened your parcel and saw the inscription you had written in the book I just cried out of my surprise and my heart 'The darling! ... What a darling!'

I am so used to books from the Firm that the fact of this coming from you flew me right up into the sky; and that you put such an inscription in it means that forever it will remain that I was a friend of 'The dark people'.

For a long time I have wanted to be of those who call you George. I think I shall just say it without asking . . .

To return to the Battarbee[3] book on Modern Aboriginal Art, what a debt this poor, derided and destroyed people owes Rex Battarbee! In years to come it will stand out like a red light on a mountain, and this book will be like a Shakespeare first folio in our history, or to

---

[1] In 1887 Robertson and Angus joined forces at 110 Market Street, Sydney. They had previously conducted separate book shops, Robertson in George Street and Angus in Market Street. In 1890 they were at the corner of Market and Castlereagh Streets, and in 1891 at 89 Castlereagh Street. The present shop is in Pitt Street.
[2] Angus & Robertson is no longer controlled by the original founders.
[3] *Modern Australian Aboriginal Art*, 1951.

collectors. Angus and Robertson have done more for Australia, in its publishing, than anyone else, or people realize—G.R.[1] is alive in his grandson. What a book, and what production!

My thanks to you personally for the book, but more for not letting tradition die.

This copy goes to my collection at the Mitchell Library.

Again with my thanks 'twice as more' (I hope you are Scottish enough to know the phrase!).

To W. Hart-Smith

Dear Bill,

Kings Cross
12 February 1951

'On the Level'[2] just came and I could not stop till I was through it.

All that reaching out in other men's thoughts has ended for you. You have found yourself; have found that to be worthwhile a man has to be himself. What a triumph! And what a book! It is as direct and individual as a flint axe. The ballooning of the world is forced down into an arrow head. No wonder Douglas Stewart thinks so much of you . . .

My heart is lifted up over what is in the book and how it is shaped.

To George Ferguson

Dear Mr Ferguson,

Kings Cross
16 March 1951

I hope you won't say 'What wild cat idea has this woman now!' But three days ago I had a shock at how easily a great man *can* be forgotten after those *who touched his life* are gone.

I took a couple of friends to the 'Bulletin' Office, *one* a Bulletin publicator, the other not—and who had never seen the Bulletin or its people. Talk of G.R.[3] came up, and a Bulletin *head* (second generation) said G.R. was one of the tightest and hardest of men to deal with. 'He may have been in the business side,' I said, 'but he was the opposite privately.' The other looked at me astonished and said 'I had never heard anything like *that* of him!' I said 'In his private generosity his right hand never knew what his left hand did.'

'That is news to me!' was the comment.

[1] George Robertson.
[2] W. Hart-Smith's *On the Level*, 1950.
[3] George Robertson.

I could hardly believe that in that place of writers and their stories, G.R.'s friendly hand to so many of them could be forgotten.

So I am wondering could Idriess[1] do a light G.R. like 'Flynn of the Inland'[2] and 'Kidman'.[3] The great biography could be written ten even twenty years hence. But the time to do the fishing, even for *that* is now.

G.R., Archibald,[4] and A.G.S.[5] (in a more limited way) brought writers together and made a family of them. That on the one side. On the other, they published them. Publishing still goes on. But that a-family-at-one-hearth is gone.

That period, with G.R. and Archibald as giants, and Lawson and the general train as the following and the setting would make a marvellous saga—if the writer had the vision and the warm heart needed for its reproduction! Yours sincerely,

It would make a good screen picture which people are sure to remember.

To Mrs E. O. Schlunke

Dear Olga,

Kings Cross
16 March 1951

The 'Little Coo'[6] timed herself perfectly—the Show[7] opened yesterday! Thank you so very much!

Mrs. Myrtle White ('No Roads Go By') has been for some weeks in Sydney staying with my cousin, Mrs. Roy McNiven. On Monday I took her to the 'Bulletin' Office for an introduction there, as she had not known even where it was. I saw Ken Prior[8] whom I had not seen for years and we all had a long talk, Miles Franklin with us. He spoke of the old dusty stairs of the older building. He told me he had bought them. I asked what he intended doing with them. He said 'I have an idea of putting them up at the back on this floor'. I told him they should belong to the nation & should go to Canberra. So, as he knows Mr. Menzies well, he said he would write to him at once.

[1] Ion Idriess.
[2] Published 1932.
[3] *The Cattle King*, 1936, the story of Sir Sidney Kidman.
[4] J. F. Archibald.
[5] A. G. Stephens.
[6] Perhaps a reference to a gift of fresh butter.
[7] Royal Easter Show at Sydney. The Schlunkes may have had some connection with the cattle at the show—hence the butter.
[8] Henry Kenneth Prior.

I loved those old stairs. The feet of all the foundation writers of Australia went up & down them. He showed us a card given him when he went to the 1914 War, with twenty 'Bulletin' names on it. Only one is left—MacMahon,[1] now 90 or over. And I knew every one of those twenty as a friend. I am here in Sydney, Bernard O'Dowd younger than I in Melbourne, W. H. Ogilvie in Scotland—somebody said Bayldon[2] was alive a year ago. I wish some painter or story writer would do a 'Blessed Damozel'[3] of those old shadowy stairs & their 'Angles'. What about Eric?[4]

But you will be sick of this! How are you all? That blind boy still haunts me—as you wrote it—not as I amended it.

Thank you again for the 'Coo'. When I address this I shall have a cup of tea & some thin fresh bread & *butter*—from your place & hand. Affectionately,

To T. Inglis Moore

Dear Tom,

Kings Cross
22 March 1951

Only two days ago I managed to get the A.B.C. with your talk.[5]

When I think of the years in which I looked upon Bernard O'Dowd as a sun in the sky where I was a glow-worm on the earth, and then to find myself bracketed with him in a talk, I am like a dog turning round and round how best to make a comfortable lie down!

Of course the years have taught me something. I realize that O'Dowd has a sky of his own, that Hugh McCrae has a wider summer sky, that R.D.F's[6] heights are ocean deeps, and that perhaps I am a grapevine, the sun on its leaves. I hope I am. A pumpkin vine is too sappy and unenduring, and I do think I have written some things that have the concentration of vision that gives living force, and in that, life or continuity. The ones you quote being these.

I have had a bad time. I think what I thought was a slight stroke was polio or both. Observant friends say how I have lost weight, and unobservant ones 'how well' I look—for wh. I wd. like to knock their heads off, because I know how little they see while pretending to really see. (What a yap about myself!)

I met Sir John Northcott the other day, after meeting him in

---

[1] Tom MacMahon, the well-known cashier of the *Bulletin*.
[2] Arthur Albert Bayldon.
[3] Dante Gabriel Rossetti's poem, 'The Blessed Damozel', 1850.
[4] Olga Schlunke's husband.
[5] A talk on Mary and Bernard O'Dowd as social poets.
[6] R. D. FitzGerald.

personal letters. I liked his unpretentious letters. I liked the man. It was at a Veterans' affair, and the way those old fellows' faces brightened, and their shoulders lifted up, at sight of him, showed what he meant, as a man and an ideal, to them. Lord Wakehurst[1] had more enquiry in his brains perhaps, but this man has something—a broader human soundness—that Lord Wakehurst hadn't.

Now I must stop. Even my brain is tired; memory and concentration are a tax.

You will never know, Tom, how grateful I am for your so long and so fully continued evaluation and lifting up of my work. With you it is not just a word and on — the word dropped and chance the arbiter. You *build*. And whether the building is to be a hut or a four-roomed cottage, it will be of permanent material. Of wh. as I said I hope and believe there is some.

Now I must stop, I feel a little blackout hovering in the brain. Affectionately

To R. D. FitzGerald

Dear Bob,

Kings Cross
4 April 1951

Your generous mind in your letter just now. What is the good of the invisible if there is no visible to express it? The mist in the sun—almost in any condition—is beautiful. But what does it beget or bring forth if the particles do not become flesh i.e. solidify?

There was a strange parallel in opposites in a beautiful poem by Arnold Wall the issue before 'The Flesh'[2] (or whatever I called it) came out. His was the spirit as the bride. I was glad mine had gone in weeks ahead or he might have thought I had in obverse lifted from him. Different as poetry. The scholar was in his. Last week I had a girl in, Reba Ginsburg, of Russian descent on the one side. She works at the C.S.I.R.O. and for her B.A. took up every different course she could. She has that mind that looks through both ends of the telescope at once. She brought me a long poem 'Phoenix' which she had entered for the S.M.H. prize. It was mentioned. Judging by the lines quoted from the winners I would have given *her* the prize on her mind, and let the faults of construction and obscureness go. Her idea (I don't say theme, which was her word, because the work was in parts so

---

[1] John de Vere Loder. See Appendix (Wakehurst).
[2] 'The Flesh' was published in the *Bulletin*, 28 March 1951. The poem by Wall that Mary refers to in this letter was 'The Far Journey', published 21 March 1951. Douglas Stewart wrote appreciatively of Wall in *The Flesh and the Spirit*, 1943.

obscure) was the one-ness of time and of all things. That something, in so much of Russia, is in her, and was in the verse.

As to the Churches (and 'Russia' reminded me) their idolatory in teaching hymns is appalling. I am thankful to be a Presbyterian because we keep the Psalms. There is no idolatry in the Psalms thank heaven—or should I say thank God? I don't go to Church (not since years ago James McLeod left) but I can see God even in the back of a shark. And more and more I regard that (in Isaiah) 'I form the light and create darkness. I make peace and create evil.' (Never heard in the pulpit of course!).

To return to me and Judith Wright, I suppose in 'Dominions of the Boundary'[1] O'Dowd was first.

I also had in last week a beautiful (as to mind, poise, and character) black girl. 'Where do you belong?' I asked. 'My mother is Indian, my father was brought to Australia as a slave,' she replied (in the blackbirding days). She is interested in the Youth Peace Movement, works for it, and does sewing as a living. And last night there came a friend of hers, a school-teacher, to say she would do typing I want done. I said I must pay her. She said 'No. To do something for Australian culture is payment enough.' These things are God in a grain of sand; these things are life: not just living. And your letter is the same. It is good to hear from you. How are your tired eyes?

To Donald Gordon Campbell

Dear Gordon,

Kings Cross
17 April 1951

Your booklet 'For Friend & Fireside'[2] came yesterday. Today I read it. There is no doubt you are a poet, even though not yet quite found. The lovely 'unbookish' similes, that are the utterance of observation, & which no one else has ever said, or thought of, run all through the lines. I hope you will never lose that, and its *freshness*. But if you never wrote anything else, my faith in you is justified in 'Henry Lawson Westward'.

I like 'Philemon'. There is in it the continued uncontinued. Also it seems, without losing freshness, more purposeful & material.

But I have a bad chest—& must stop . . .

Remember me to your people, to your wife & to yourself.

---

[1] Bernard O'Dowd's collection of poems, 1907. For comment see, inter alia, W. H. Wilde, *Three Radicals*, 1969, pp. 24-5.
[2] *Friend and Fireside*, 1951, contained the two poems Mary mentions—'Philemon' and 'Henry Lawson Westward'.

To W. Hart-Smith

Kings Cross
13 June 1951

Dear Bill,

Thank you for my being delighted that there is an infant! And eight months old now! You are evidently a bad (or a poor?) father as you did not tell me her name. She is evidently still 'it' to you. I hope her mother is better. And treats her as a responsible and important personage. Anyway I have pasted the snaps into 'Columbus'[1] against the day she shows she is a Genius and expresses all that was inhibited and seeking outlet in you when you first came here. How you have surprised me and how very far you have travelled in the mastery and power of self-expression. The lame man walks and is free.

I do not often now, cut out and keep verse, being near the end of my way and not wanting burdens. But I kept (and will keep) 'Eight Affirmations of Judgment'.[2] I said 'Here is Australia's outstanding piece of verse'. Others are finished, polished, shapely and running on even wheels. But here is passion independent of a yet walking form; and power that itself is wheels. In that comparatively short poem is the sweep of eternity and the covering of all men. In the ending only one piece in my recollection parallels it and that is one of Hugh McCrae's. Hugh is the Alps in his work, but you, and especially in this, are the fighting, struggling ants that are humanity.

This is so, even in 'Columbus'—which stands alone. Someone wrote here who has never written so before or since. My remorse is that I did not see all this when you were here—fighting your way on.

To T. Inglis Moore

Kings Cross
22 June 1951

Dear Tom,

Will you look up today's 'Sun', for a letter of mine proposing 'the first International University' to be at Canberra? I know difficulties would be mountains high: But it could start with *one* foreign college, and no one after that steal our 'first'. I shall write to Walter Murdoch and to Prof. Julius Stone about it and then perhaps overseas.

Did you hear Mr Casey[3] last night? *What* an address! What perfection of enunciation and diction, and what balance! Very well-hidden

---

[1] *Columbus Goes West*, Hart-Smith's book of verse, published 1943.
[2] Hart-Smith's poem, published in the *Bulletin*, 30 May 1951.
[3] Richard Gardiner Casey.

pro-American of course. And for that I am against him. But as art I have only admiration for it.

People are talking about Mr Hughes,[1] and that he should not have been asked to speak. But that little man is too big for it to matter what he says or how poorly. His past is too great as a servant and maker of Australia, for anything else to matter. But it broke my heart to hear him—that mind never should have aged; decay should never have touched it.

My love to you all (including the blackberry jam)

To George Mackaness

Dear George,

Kings Cross
27 June 1951

... I called Henry, Mister Lawson[2] as a matter of course whenever I first met him. Christian names were not the first-day acquaintance familiar things then that they are today! Henry was tickled to death over it. 'No one ever called me Mr. before!' he said. I said it was the usual thing with people till fully acquainted and leave given and taken. He replied 'Not among the people I am used to ... *You* belong to a different *class*! In my class no one is Mr. Everyone is called Henry, Harry, or whatever his name is'. He laughed again each time he came, over the words 'Mary called him "Mister" '. Then about the third time he said, 'I will write a poem on that! (He never used the word verse at any time, for his work. Not in conversation.) Next time he came he had the verse. It was in a way a tentative love-letter. He gave me the copy he had with him. Later on he published it in a collection under the heading 'The Free Selector's Daughter'[3] *so that I should not be embarrassed*. I was so much annoyed at him publishing it at all, that I tore my copy up. I had had no idea he would 'sell' it! ...

---

[1] W. M. Hughes.

[2] Mary's story of the origin of Lawson's poem 'Mary Called Him "Mister" ' is interesting, even whimsical. The poem, however, tells of a stock situation where two people in love fail to break through the stuffy barriers of convention and part without confessing their love. Such a situation appears to bear little resemblance to the Mary-Henry Lawson affair. Her comment that the poem was 'in a way a tentative love-letter' is scarcely substantiated. The poem was published in the *Bulletin*, 1 October 1892.

[3] 'The Free Selector's Daughter' tells of the poet's romantic interlude with a girl called 'Mary' but it is not the same poem as 'Mary Called Him "Mister" '. 'The Free Selector's Daughter' was published in *In the Days When the World Was Wide*, 1896.

To the Writer of 'The Austro-Vert'[1]   Kings Cross
Dear Sir,   9 October 1951

I wish I knew who you are!

Your Journal is the only publication of its kind that has a good hard stone at its heart! (Most have pumpkin). Do I owe a subscription, how much is it, and where do I pay it?

I think A. G. Stephens used more polish in his English than you do, but I think that in values *and evaluation* you are his successor. Perhaps indeed if the stone in the sling is sufficiently hard, packed, and fine—is as direct and unwasteful as an arrow—it does not need more polish than nature gave it. Polish is a thing of dates; or, if you like better, of a period (See how my mind wags!)

May you grow, whoever you are. Yours sincerely,

For a comparison, see the Battarbee[2] book. A. G. Stephens was Namatjira.[3] You are the other fellows—and, being old, I begin to think the other fellows best. Their idiom is their own. I am wondering if you aren't P. R. Stephensen—if not one of the young ones.

To George Ferguson

                                                                                Kings Cross
Dear Mr Ferguson (otherwise 'G.F.'),   11 December 1951

The Bligh book[4] came an hour or more ago, and I have just laid it down in wonder. The research astounds me. Even the page annotation and references are a mountain-range of time, observation (and which had to be exact: which is more than merely accurate) patience and continual attention. Only the writer of such a book as this could measure even these brief entries and notes. What pages, and their numbers noted, must have been turned! Even what books lifted and returned to place!

This book is the log of the George Mackaness's voyage—a voyage which, in its way, parallels that of Bligh. It is not what the ghost of Bligh owes Dr Mackaness in this book, it is what Australia owes him! Part of what my grandmother said, and almost her words. James Cook did routine work; he followed maps and directions of centuries before

---

[1] *Austro-Vert*, see Appendix.
[2] *Modern Australian Aboriginal Art*, 1951.
[3] Albert Namatjira.
[4] The second edition of *The Life of Vice-Admiral William Bligh* by George Mackaness, first published in 1938.

him. This man Bligh had neither map nor even occulting stars to guide him.

When I was a child, in the early 70's the name of Bligh was that of a monster, that is to most people. But once, when I was about eight or nine, my grandmother (Mary Beattie) told me this was unjust to Bligh. She said (and I use her words) 'He was a Godly man' (a word which then whitewashed all iniquity) that he 'had to be severe in order to be just' (on the voyage,) that 'through all that time he had kept his men alive, so that he had not fed himself at their expense'. There was much more, but these things are all that remain clear in memory. But in a world of blame and hatred she saw clearly, and this is what Dr Mackaness has done. In doing this Bligh is his monument. No history of great voyages can again be written without reference to this book.

Ghosts only walk in theatres but if they could only come back and walk in publishing houses what history would be revived and what confirmations learned! In this I am thinking both of my father and of my mother's mother, for in my childhood they would talk every kind of philosophy and history by the hour.

Thank you for sending me the book, and G.M. for writing it. Yours sincerely,

To George Ferguson

Dear 'G.F.',

Kings Cross
23 January 1952

On Monday I gave a letter of introduction to you to Mrs. E. M. Burrows[1] (her first name, she told me is aboriginal for 'woman'.) She has deep roots in early Australia, and a remarkable 20 years in the Pacific Islands. The MS (of which she read me some) is vital and different from the usual conventional stuff.

She is a woman of great force, and if in the parts not read to me there is 'smoke-room' *please exonerate me.* I don't know those parts. (I don't like that kind of thing.) But I really do think her work worth while, even if it should need a censor.

Just had a letter from Ernestine Hill hoping for a word from me about her book.[2] She should have had *five* letters from me about it by now. Every place I have dipped into struck a bell in my heart. I told her it was 'the Iliad' of Australia. Sales today depend on city readers. But no city critic gets beyond the range of his inkpot. There are no horse-bells in an inkpot. Yours sincerely,

[1] Probably Ena Maud Burrows (Mrs E. M. Dalhunty). She appears not to have published this book of which Mary read the manuscript.
[2] *The Territory*, 1951.

To Judith Wright

Dear Mrs. McKinney,

Kings Cross
17 February 1952

This is to introduce Miss Reba Ginsburg, who is appointed as a Junior Lecturer in English (i.e. she is not a Professor). She writes verse, as different from yours as syringa from blackboy,[1] and yet with a small kinship of an underneath question. She is Jewish of Russian descent.

If she is ever near you in Brisbane, will you ask her to call? She is a stranger in the North.

I hope you and that great baby of yours are well, Are you still on the Wyndham Diaries?[2]

What I would like—what I *want* you to do—after the baby and the Diaries are more off your hands, is to write a long, deep poem. Too few of these today in Australia. Half your shorter ones, joined up by blank verse and general theme could go into it. I wanted to do my aboriginal verse, incorporating all I have done on them, in that way. I had not time, when I had time. Now time is ending. So it will not be done. Too much else to do now and eyes and body worn out. But will you think of this bit as years go on.

Every good wish.

To Judith Wright

Dear Judith Wright,

Kings Cross
23 February 1952

I hope you didn't feel hurt by my saying you and Reba Ginsburg were as different as syringa and blackboy![3]

The blackboy is the invincible thing of the bush, its leaves are spears, only fire can consume it, but when it flowers, the honeylovers cover it, and the wind is scented from its flowers.

I woke up this morning thinking of Henley:[4] 'My head is bloody but unbowed' and I thought of you and your ear bones.

I *saw* Henley in London. Huge in his wheeled chair, the table hiding his crippled (polio) legs; his eyes were dark pools of light. There was only one chair for visitors. I sat, my husband stood on my side, on

---

[1] Syringa is an ornamental shrub with creamy-white, sweet-scented flowers. Blackboy is a native plant which, from a distance, resembles a native in grass skirt with an upraised spear.
[2] Judith Wright's research into the family diaries resulted in the publication *The Generations of Men*, 1959. For additional information on the Wyndham diaries see that book.
[3] See note to letter, 17 February 1952.
[4] William Ernest Henley.

the other Henry Lawson who had brought us on Henley's invitation, as we had come from Paraguay and Patagonia (and how shabby as to clothes!) Henley asked me to write him some thing for Blackwood's. But I was too conscious of my own inferiority and too shy to send him even a line. I think at times what a fool I was. But mostly know I was right.

All good to you.

To Peace Inglis Moore

Dear Peace (May I, or did I before?)

Kings Cross
15 March 1952

I received last night and looked at this morning the loveliest boxed picture! What colour and what bloom! I begrudged taking anything out but I had a plum for breakfast and beans for midday dinner with your jam at the end of the feast. Talk about poetry, after your jam! Did I say Thank you? I couldn't say it often enough.

I think I never saw Tom looking better. The gardening must be good for him. As for myself 87 is not an improving age, and with last year's polio added it is wuss! However the brain is not bad yet for which the Lord be thankit.

I wrote Pacita[1] before I began this (in case I shd. forget), and congratulated her on being at the Women's College,[2] and said I hope when she settles in she will come to see me. I hope she will.

My grandson is in Scots Upper school now, growing tall, and an avid reader. But 'Greenwood'[3] (near Cloncurry) has had no rain, and the monsoonal season is over till next summer.

Again thanking a woman I greatly admire—Affectionately

To R. D. FitzGerald

Dear Bob,

Kings Cross
16 June 1952

I have been going down hill so fast that the old exuberance of letters is itself failing. A thing in a slender way I had in common with that genius at it, Hugh McCrae, and in wh. we expressed, not our relationship to others, but to ourselves. (That I can *see* this shows how far from life's high peak I have slipped. It is now in the distance.) Hence you have had no letters. Neither has Tom. But I have wondered how you

---

[1] Daughter of Peace and Tom Inglis Moore.
[2] The University of Sydney.
[3] The Gilmore property.

were and what doing, for I miss your hour once in a while, *or your verse*. A few odds and ends of things I valued are left—I couldn't part with them—and there is one for you and one for Tom. They will go to you both later.

This is not my last Will and Testament, as I am writing odds and ends for the 'Tribune',[1] they having given me space (or leave) for things the other papers will not even look at. I enclose some, wh. you can send on to Tom when you are writing. As you know, to me the killing of children in war is the last thing in human degeneration.

And that recalls another thing: when William Lane was initially forming the Political Labor Movement, and stirred Australia from end to end with his sincerity and ideas he was twenty-six years of age (I was 25 when I met him, then well known) Holman[2] was roughly the same, and W. M. Hughes (both later than Lane in the Movement) also twenty-six. Where are such young leaders today? War ate them. Their power and their gospels died with them. But in the history of Australia what a phenomenon these three and W. G. Spence (on whom they all relied as sober and wise) all were! Douglas Stewart saw it as regards Lane—for wh. he has my everlasting gratitude. Here endeth (The last kick of the dying fowl?)

To A. H. Chisholm

Dear Alec,

Kings Cross
9 July 1952

For years I have wanted to inscribe or write something to you, but it wouldn't write: i.e., not good enough. At last I think I have what I want, and hope you like it.[3] I have sent it to open a Magazine page to begin in the 'Tribune' (which gives me space the daily papers won't) and hope your hair will not stand on end. Herewith is a copy from

---

[1] Mary's column 'Arrows' was published in the *Tribune* from 1952 until her death.
[2] William Arthur Holman.
[3] Mary's poem 'Jindra', inscribed to A. H. Chisholm, was first published in the *Tribune*, 9 July 1952, and included also in *Fourteen Men*, 1954, p. 54. The poem contains lines which tell much about Mary and ends with the words:

> All things I loved . . .
> My father heard a plover cry
> The night that I was born, and thistle-seed had wings
> The day they christened me.
> How then shall I sit, in quiet by a hearth,
> And never hear the wind blow through the yarran till it sings.

The notes to the poem in *Fourteen Men* (p. 86) are copious. She says that in Aboriginal folk-lore the plover itself and its cry symbolized one who would walk-about, mentally and physically, i.e., one who had 'wings to the mind'. The name 'yarran' tree means 'the tree that sings when the wind blows through it'.

the paper, and the notes, to which, as remembrance comes when I look back, I could add more or lengthen.

I was very young at Jindra Plain[1] (as it was then) but there were plovers crying day and night, till my mother said she could not stand the lonely sound, and we had to move. Father was building the first Falkiner[2] sawn and shingle house. (The old one was of split slabs and a bark roof).

As to the plovers at my birth, I was born in the afternoon. But father was a born poet, and a just appreciator of the blacks, and I remember (when I was about five) he said of me that he had heard the plover's cry when I was born. My mother replied how could he when I was born in the afternoon! He told her he had, and that it was one in the distance. 'The sound was faint, but it was a plover'.

The fence he put round the larks' nesting ground stood for several years. But not being eaten down, the grass became better there—the lovely fine Riverina grass—and travellers broke panels and put their horses in. Twice he came from distance to mend it. Then little by little it had more gaps, and in the end was fire wood . . . Two sapling rails with the bark on; top and bottom rails. I wonder how many guarded larks with a fence? Dorothy Cottrell's uncle, who called them 'The Singing Gold'[3] was the only other man I would think might do it. Father had the same feeling as the blacks' belief: of the right of the wild to be preserved. They hunted nothing for sport. We do.

Well, Alec, though 'Jindra' is about me, it is you in essence.

My affection with it.

I felt that for you. I should have put lyre bird. But I kept to the lark, as it *was* the lark, as an end. Also I wanted to put what father did in the notes—the lark and the aboriginal song 'our shadows meet together in the moon'.

To George Ferguson

Dear 'G.F.',

Kings Cross
1 August 1952

I thank you for the Judah Waten book.[4] It is something to possess. The Mackenzie Editorship of Poetry does not impress me; though, of course, he may have been hampered by circumstance.

[1] Probably Jindera, south of Wagga Wagga.
[2] Franc Sadlier Falkiner.
[3] The title of Dorothy Cottrell's book, 1928.
[4] A volume of short stories, *Alien Son*, 1952.

I have written Mr. Waten, and, if you like you can read my letter before sending it on. I say this because I think he is something we never had before—a kinship with the great literature of the *world*, past present and future, and which in prose we have never had before. The Celt gives a glitter of fancy to literature, but the Jew gives richness ... a wealth that is gathered *in homely ordinary fields*. That is where he stands up above us all.

My long affection is with the Firm.

Have been very ill. Have had trained nurse for two or three weeks, but am now up, and again *able to write letters*. As you see!

To R. D. FitzGerald

My dear Bob,

Kings Cross
17 August 1952

I can't say the happiness it gave me to have you three ... here and all together yesterday.[1] Men get together like that more than women. I found that early, in the early Labor Movement, because somehow I was often admitted. When I am gone my hope is that you will all remember yesterday.

'G.F.' gave me Douglas Stewart's last book.[2] When I look at it (*not* the little things) I feel like a worm, or a thing beaten to my knees in comparison. I don't feel like that with you because between your work and mine there is no common ground or field of comparison. But we are silver and you all gold. I hate to say it, but there are times when I feel you stand above Hugh McCrae. I have loved his work so long—so long that I hate to see him outfaced. But you both have one quality in difference yet in common: that austerity of language that lives beyond all the arabesque scintillation and beauty of language and metaphor that, drink to the thirsty in its own day, is flat in the next generation.

I don't know how much of this is addle-headed, because I am too tired for anything but thought; and not too much of that. But I see more and more that in writing the anvil gives the living, the canvas gives a picture. Thank you again for yesterday—You and the others

[1] Mary's 86th birthday.
[2] Probably *Sun Orchids*.

To R. D. FitzGerald

Dear Bob,

Kings Cross
16 October 1952

I wrote you a letter yesterday morning, that now, having read the unimaginably wonderful thing you call 'Landfall'¹ seems too shallow for words.

No time, no change in language, no deepening of rational thought and feeling can ever pull that work down from the height.

I consider Brennan in young years, could, with the will to force behind him, have done what you have done? But he needed the *out* of the drugged mind. You make your *out* come back to you, bees laden with pollen! Most others' bees come back with honey. The pollen creates and recreates in other minds, the honey doesn't.

What forests and sands of history and thought you have kneaded and hammered into that small handful of words! I can be stunned by beauty, I love honey, but here is creation.

I think of all the mushroom growths to wh. I have given praise.

Well here is something that takes words from me. But at least I said one thing yesterday. I said you shaped the Grampians. I am looking at the Grampians; the rock, the form, the foliage. Now I am running to words, and what shallow things they are without power behind them!

To J. K. Moir

Dear Jock,

Kings Cross
27 October 1952

Your letter just come. Thank you for Father Dunlea.² No man more needed the outlet of interesting and intellectual people than he does at this moment. He had so long a heart breaking struggle to keep Boys' Town³ going and 'himself' a man who had no more idea of money than a child! I wd. like if he cd. give a talk to the B & C Club on his youth in Ireland, the men he met here during the depression, Protestant and Catholic (His Boys' Town is non-Sectarian) when (he mightn't tell this himself) he wd. go out with whatever money and food he could find in his Presbytery, with socks and singlet on, and come home without any of them. His shirt hiding the want of his singlet—his boots his missing socks. His successor is a Maltese and a man of the world. I spoke of Father Dunlea to him, when I met him. 'He has only one

---

¹ 'Landfall' is the first part of R. D. FitzGerald's *Between Two Tides*, 1952.
¹ Father T. V. Dunlea.
² A settlement for delinquent and orphaned boys near Engadine, New South Wales.

fault', he said, 'he is too good ... In this wicked world you have to meet it with its own weapons' (or words to that effect). He is keeping Father Dunlea's flat for him, and said he 'could not allow anyone else to use it'. As a collection increases in value in age, I have started him, Father Cianta on a collection of envelopes, in their own handwriting sent me by distinguished people. I put a note on each. On yours I wrote: 'John Kinmont Moir, O.B.E. descendant of the family of the old Border ballad of Kinmont Willie, who was "hangit at bonnie Carlisle". Mr. Moir is the well-known collector of Australiana, and founder of the Bread and Cheese Club'. I started John Farrell's g. daughter two years, supplying the scrapbook and envelopes already pasted (or fastened) in. The envelope has not only the handwriting, but the postage stamp, with the date and place stamp. And, if that doesn't appeal to you then I'm Dutch!
About C. J. Dennis:—

Anyone who knew Dennis found him in his writings, and in them heard even his voice speaking.

My first knowledge of him was in the 90s, when, in Adelaide, he and someone else had a paper called (I think) 'The Gadfly'[1] to wh. I sent some verse and other matter before I went to South America. My next meeting was when 'The Sentimental Bloke'[2] was in typescript and he was selling copies for 5/- each in Sydney. This, I might add, was a strictly limited edition as money was scarce and typing cost money! the world was the richer for his being, and the poorer for his going. Yours sincerely,

To R. D. FitzGerald

Dear Bob,

Kings Cross
27 October 1952

Thank you. Your letter has helped me find the solid instead of shifting sands: In writing one only feels the urge of expression or creation; in reading one finds *outlet. The wings!*

I am glad you are (or have I misread?) dreaming, hoping or planning for a lengthening of 'Between Two Tides'.[3] The Iliad is a picture on the screen. It is action in the foreground. The hinter land is in yours. Yet one would love to say, even as a lie, that you will have written Australia's first Iliad! We do so need one; and it means the permanent even as a word.

[1] Founded by C. J. Dennis in 1906. Mary may be confusing it with *The Critic*, a South Australian weekly magazine on whose literary staff Dennis worked in the 1890s
[2] C. J. Dennis's major work.
[3] Published 1952.

There is something Spanish in 'Between Two Tides'; not wholly Anglo-Saxon in bluntness.

Am expecting Judah Waten who is in Sydney and whom I would like to meet. It was Brian Fitzpatrick wrote, 'Christ on an Ash Tray', as you know. I saw those trays myself, in Pellegrini's.[1]

Bob what a marvel the Iliad is. History, drama, epic, short stories, and a novel—the first?—and all else that it is.

To R. D. FitzGerald

Dear Bob,

Kings Cross
28 October 1952

The old friend[2] is gone; the man whom history will make great & not less. I had written him two or three years ago, knowing he would not mind, that I hoped he would take his last step, say his last word and draw his last breath in the House he had done so much to make.

A few months ago someone wrote in the papers that that was his wish—well, it is true, for his deeds for Australia have been the walls of that house.

Saturday before last I gave a brief reading of my verse for the 'Tribune' at a meeting in some hall in Regent Street. I chose 'The Ringer'.[3] When I got to John Dunmore Lang, I paused to mention his statue in Wynyard Square. Then I looked down and found the last line, 'and one was William Morris Hughes'. At a gathering hostile to W.M.H. Discretion said 'no one will know if you leave it out'. But I could not be a coward, & I could not turn my back on an old friend. I read it. To a dead silence. But, I added, 'W. M. Hughes did more for Australia than any other one man. He fought for Australia wherever he went. It is thanks to him that we are not more under the heel of the U.S.A. than we are'—and on that I ended. His life for Australia defends him wherever you look, no matter what the accusations.

To George Ferguson

Dear 'G.F.',

Kings Cross
14 November 1952

I thought when Ingleton's book[4] came it was the top of the tree—as

[1] Roman Catholic shop supplying devotional goods and religious literature.
[2] W. M. Hughes, who died early in the morning of 28 October 1952.
[3] Mary read her poems 'The Ringer' and 'Doin' the Boots for Sunday' at the *Tribune* Festival, 18 October 1952. She was given a standing ovation.
[4] *True Patriots All: or, News from Early Australia as Told in a Collection of Broadsides*, 1952, edited by G. C. Ingleton.

in its way it is. But today Tyrrell's book[1] came. I am dumb before it. What completeness out of an enormous field, what perfection of sequence, what a living yet not too mannered English! To anyone knowing his times he must have acres of notes not needed for the purposes of this book. And how discreet where a self advertiser would have wanted to boast his knowledge. Every fact is a fact, yet no one is hurt and how living, warm-hearted, direct or wrong-headed, everyone is. I couldn't put the book down once I looked at its first page. A gallop through, of course, but what a peopled city to live in again!

As to the make up of both books, A. & R. are out of the wilderness and have come home again. How G. R. would have held and handled those books. His hands were as sensitive (and as executive) as his mind. Even my hands feel 'Here is something!'

This book holds the makers of this land—the makers whose bricks were words, whose mortar was ink. The forgotten walk in it. They can never be forgotten again.

I wrote Mr Tyrrell that I hoped, before he went there would be 5,000 pages, and more from the other world. And this book is why I can't turn round with a quiet mind and tell you what I think of Ingleton's book, which is perhaps equally good, in its way, and equally necessary. One thing Ingleton's book does do (as far as I have gone, which is not very far yet) and that is testify to the innumerable blacks in the country. A white man only had to appear and they came out of the bush on the instant as though the bush were alive with them. As to you, my grateful thanks for these two books . . .

To Hugh McCrae

Dear Hugh,

Kings Cross
26 December 1952

What a delight to get your Christmas card. The clouds are a lovely place to be in! But when I get down to earth & see your handwriting firm again—so different from a while ago—I thank God for the solid earth.

I hope you admire this nice print and paper. It is a gift from a Melb. man for whom I wrote a foreword. As a matter of fact I will be more known for Forewords presently than anything else. I am doing so many—not that I want them—that I am getting housemaid's knee over them. Didn't you get housemaid's knee once in one of your letters?—Just thought of it so I am not original. Alas! Not even smart.

---

[1] *Old Books, Old Friends, Old Sydney*, 1952. Although supposedly by James R. Tyrrell there is some suggestion the book was 'ghosted' by Cecil Mann. See Douglas Stewart, *Writers of the Bulletin*, 1977 Boyer Lectures, pp. 31-2.

What work R.D.F. is doing! I know all about & accept the magnificence of Brennan, but I think R.D.F. more enduring. He has a kinship with you in that the roses (rosiness? what you will) of flesh is set on bone. The opulent thunder of Brennan is too vast for its bone.

Then again, you are racial, Brennan is personal. I do not know what R.D.F. is. He is neither, But you both having something that time-altered values cannot blot out. I wonder why I inflict these infernal pen thinkings on you! & not only you!

I had polio last Feb. & virus pneu. flu in Sept. But at last, I have been able to work on my long-hung-up next book of verse[1] & finish it—that is provided I do not look at it again. A friend is typing it. When it comes home I shall let you see it, humbly wondering if you would write four lines, if no more for it? When you see it you will know. And if you feel like No, say No. I am not a bigot as to my own side in verse.

Of all the immortals you are one. Where other people's letters (your card is a mile of letters all equally wonderful) are vapor or news compendiums yours walk on their own feet & have shining eyes.

Be thankful for the grand children, I think Australia will see all that Greece ever saw in this next flowering. The five year olds (under & over) astonish me

May the years be good to you.

To Hugh McCrae

My dear Hughie,

Kings Cross
4 January 1953

(I am so enraged I put an 'ie' in your name without intending it). If they could give me a D.B.E. & Lionel Lindsay a Knighthood, how much more they should have done the same for you! Of course the OBE[2] is a limited Order & the Knighthood isn't, wh. does give it value! But your work, equal, & more, in intellectual & aesthetic value to Lionel's, reaches 100,000 unabatingly through the years, his reaches 1000. If his work was 100,000 points above 1000, to you, it wd. be all right. But it is the other way round! Who writes prose like you? Even if verse—my verse—in centuries can become dated your prose never will.

As wrath increases with utterance I had better stop. So on the OBE. I congratulate you, but not *us*. We, nationally, should have done better.

[1] *Fourteen Men,* published in 1954.
[2] Hugh McCrae was awarded the O.B.E. in the New Year Honours list for 1953.

Yesterday Lady Isaacs[1] took me a drive and we went to see Dame Mary Hughes.[2] On our way there & back I did my day's good deed. I got a promise from Lady Isaacs to consider writing her recollections. She has the stuff in her, has humor & five languages (Sir I. spoke seven). We have never had a woman's book from the High Politics of Gubernatorial standing, & the people met here & overseas. I put in a little wedge on Mary Hughes—her need presently when she is fit for 'an object' in life. Told both to say 'Not to be opened till after my death,' & leave the MS with a light heart, to the Mitchell Library—May the Lord Smite you if you neglect to do the same!

To Hugh McCrae

Kings Cross
8 February 1953

Dear Hugh,

Thank you for the *permission*.

There is one thing which I love to think is true, & that is no matter what the difference in ages, no matter that we are at opposite poles as literature, there are some things in which, thank the Lord, we are idiotically alike, & it is for that 'idiotically' I am delighted we can both laugh, & both hear laughter, and it doesn't matter if it is inside us, at us, or afield.

Most people are afraid of laughter. But every time I have thought of that inscription[3] I have laughed, not a repetition laugh, but a new one—as if I had never seen it before.

As to it as a Foreword, I had wondered if Foreword wd. be best in your script. But think not, as the conventional above the unconventional leaves the unconventional the more outstanding.

Have been going through piles of old letters. Of them all Ruth

---

[1] The widow of Sir Isaac Isaacs, the first Australian to be appointed Governor-General of Australia.

[2] The widow of W. M. Hughes.

[3] Hugh McCrae's verse inscription was published in a facsimile of his own handwriting after the title page in *Fourteen Men*, 1954. There was no Foreword. The inscription reads:

>To Mary Gilmore
>Nae sun need shine the time we meet
>   Or whaur ye gae.
>Gin ye come here through stress of weather
>To snuff wi'me the Muses' heather;
>Despite the world an' a' its blether
>   We'se hae a crack:
>Syne pit oor lyart heids thegither—
>   An' na gae back.
>Hugh McCrae.

Park's are most like yours. She has the generous heart: the same kind of generous heart. She knows nothing of acid, constriction or rationing.

Just been reminded by a cousin that the Surgeon Beatty[1] of Nelson's bullet was an ancestor . . . I saw the bullet. Surgeon Major Beatty (retired), M.O. Liverpool Old Men's Home inherited it. He showed it to me. It went to his Surgeon M. son, of the 'Venus', who, some years ago, gave it to the R.N. or the Nation—or I think so. There is still at Shane Park, a plough my Beattie grandfather made. Not a particle of iron in it. Just the foot of a tree—bullet & plough!

To Katharine Susannah Prichard

My dear Katharine Prichard

Kings Cross
17 February 1953

I cannot say how glad I was to see you yesterday, but disturbed that you looked so frail.

I don't want to unsay your doctor, but seeing that your heart could stand Sydney, after Perth, and then the altitude of Canberra, I should say the trouble was not structural (disease) but a nervous or an exhausted heart—on your appearance the latter. You look bloodless, i.e. without red corpuscles, and want feeding up. Good ripe tomatoes and oranges and milk by the gallon, and cream from the dairy, if you can take it. Meat, of course, and not much bread. I have weetbix and cheese and lettuce or tomatoes, coffee half milk in the morning, no starch at mid-day, bread, butter, salad or cooked fruit and cream, an egg at night. The compartmenting gives *rest* to sections of the systems, I think. But any time I feel like a change I make it. Also, I nearly boil the spine or back of the neck with hot showers. It brings the blood to the marrow and nerve centres. Now-a-days it is bi-carb, bismuth. Vitamins off and on, and tonics *ditto*. Nothing fixed or constant to form habit. My trouble is want of sleep. But I just put up with it. I am writing this at 3 a.m. after over an hour of trying to sleep. No good trying. I am writing all this in case there is a hint of something useful to you. I have had 'a heart' all my life (as well as TB in spells since I was seven. Given up by doctors more than once). I can't go to heights for 30 years and even the up-slope of our flat entrance is often too much of a strain and I have to *stop* or come up *backwards* pretending I am admiring the view—at your age I was nearly dead of TB with, of course the high pulse and worn out heart that went with it. My lesson came in an A. G. Stephens' Bookfellow article—'Fight on damn it-all' being a sentence in it. I fought on and left the damning to others.

[2] Sir William Beatty.

Well, as I said, this is all me. But it might give a hint somewhere that in time would make you look less like a bit of thistledown. You are too white and too thin.

And that is all the lecture for *this* time. Also don't sit writing continuously too long—the body (and the heart) needs movement—for circulation and the brain is too full of tired blood. May your shadow *increase*.

To J. K. Moir

Dear Jock,

Kings Cross
9 April 1953

Your letter just come bewilders me! You describe Hal Gye[1] as puckish and 'James Hackston'. The James Hackston and wife who came to see me two or more years ago looked like a retired Gippsland farmer, and his wife ditto. They were over from Victoria (as far as I remember) on a visit. So what?!?!

When I am too old and feeble to be my own centre I shall go to Melbourne and be taken in a wheelchair (or a litter?) to your evenings—Me an' my nurse! But I'll probably spare you.

Yesterday James Tyrrell came with a limited edition book, 'Stone Walls',[2] by Mary Quick. She did the drawings, made her own blocks, and I think bound the book. But you probably have it. It deals with Berrima.

In about 1869 or 70 father took my mother to see Berrima. He showed her one of the dark cells. It was just a tomb, a little wider than a coffin. He put me inside, to my dread and terror, and though holding it, closed the door. I thought I would smother. I screamed and screamed even after I was taken out and held in his arms. Perhaps the aura of suffocating men remained there. But it shows the kind of child I was (for it was that I felt; not myself) and what men are when no law binds them.

About Morris Miller:[3] I wrote him the story of my mother's sister, Mrs. Jeannie Lockett and Havelock Ellis, whom she knew at Scone, N.S.W. and later helped. He later on sent her 'An Idyll'[4] which I saw, and which later on he added to and extended. I believe, at the instance of Olive Schreiner. (How many 'later ons'?) For fear of any more I end.

Good wishes and a long life of *hard work*,

[1] Hal Gye ['James Hackston'].
[2] *Stone Walls: Engravings of Old Buildings at Berrima, N.S.W.*, 1952, by Florence Mary Quick.
[3] Edmund Morris Miller.
[4] *Kanga Creek: An Australian Idyll*, 1922.

To T. Inglis Moore

Dear Tom,

Kings Cross
12 April 1953

I have been intending to write, but this shock of the fire at the University[1] has shaken me into a line. What it must mean to all concerned is beyond words. Universities *don't* burn, not enough to create loss of the irreplaceable!

I can't understand why such papers were not in a fire-proof strong room.

My writing days are lessening. Old age and over-tired eyes—I tell no one about the latter. With no time to look at it for four weeks now I have what I hope is the last typing of 'Fourteen Men'. I see by 'Southerly' you are working on your poets,[2] me among them—I must send you a script of 'Fourteen Men' if it is any use to you. It has stuff in it you have not seen—though you did see some of it, when some years ago I submitted it to the Commonwealth Literary Board, and it was rejected.

Had a letter from J. K. Moir who said he had had you and Peace as guests. There are times when he almost tempts me to go to Melbourne. Unfortunately I put all my wool money (which suddenly came to me thanks to a good lawyer) into C'wealth Bonds. Now they have dropped so much I can only sell at a loss, and am 'living small' in order not to do that, hoping for something nearer par again.

Again the University! What a shock.

Every good wish and remembering thanks for all the kindnesses you have done me.

To David Martin

Dear Mr Martin,

Kings Cross
7 May 1953

Thank you for your letter. You are not the only one needs encouragement! Here is another. We hope and so often do not achieve, aim and so often miss and to fail seems a calamity.

Our range is so small, time and the universe so vast in change, interchange and being, that after all failure, in the end, does not matter. I got something of this in the last thing written.

---

[1] The fire, 12 April 1953, at the Canberra University College, which destroyed many books, notes and manuscripts of A. D. Hope, C. H. Manning Clark and T. Inglis Moore.

[2] A reference to T. Inglis Moore's *Australia Writes*, an anthology edited for the Canberra Fellowship of Australian Writers. Mary's poem, 'The Flesh', was published in it.

> Here came I and sat me down
> Asking if life were cross or crown.
> When comes the end, said life to me,
> They're tweedledum and tweedledee.

It ran more or less in those words. In other words: In the final vastness there is neither good nor bad—there is one-ness. Christian Science dimly sees it; but is too narrow in its application. Especially when trying to be a religion. (What a lecture for a poor man to get!)

About your verse. In a way it bewildered me. We here are so much one people, with a one-people's mind that even (and this includes our young would-be moderns) when we try to be different we are still the same. We are just variations of one tree.

You have lived and thought and learned in many countries, and just when you are beginning to be like us, one or other of the other nation influences comes in. Minds are like babies,—one all over the world. Languages are different. So you show the effect of these languages; because you have not school boy learned them; but you have lived them.

When I read the few extracts I have seen of Lorca[1] I get what I mean. You are related to him, we are not; not even when we try to make corkscrews of mountains and bubbles of deserts (as some are trying to do, being too narrow to do more.)

I am used to a garden where all the plants are staked and tabbed. Your verse is full of plants without stakes, and which do not belong to our tabs. But it is an entity in itself, it walks on its own feet. In it is something of that terrifying thing I find in the Lorca bits I have seen; Not power that coalesces, but power that thrusts. Scrolled iron may be beautiful but it has no force—Force is in the spear. But only there as the projection of the thrower.

I wonder if you will understand all this? Written words can become very flat. I saw your verse in 'Meanjin'.[2] It certainly wasn't suet pudding. It hit like a bag of broken crockery! The made unmade, and yet an entity. Yours sincerely,

To David Martin

Kings Cross
18 May 1953

Dear Mr. Martin,

It is only once in a lifetime one gets a letter like yours of last week. It feeds and it builds. It is eaten and yet not lessened. It remains itself. Every question one asks of life is there, and in every question is the answer. I can't say how much I thank you for writing it. The miracle

---

[1] Frederico Garcia Lorca.
[2] 'To Me Peace is Three Simple Things', *Meanjin* 1 (1953).

is the mind—that can, without hands or feet, suddenly expand and perceive the infinite.

This is not a reply. It is just to say Thank you—

To H. M. Green

Dear H. M. Green,

Kings Cross
22 June 1953

Accuracy being a virtue (or is it?) the following will interest you. Some time ago my writer–Consular–brother John's widow wrote from London for a copy of his birth certificate as born 21.3.1869. I wrote for it here and found it dated him 21.4.69—and suddenly memory jumped over 84 years and I remembered it being said in 1869 that a mistake had been made in the month given—the proper month being March. Wishing to find out if I were Jean or Jane as a second name, I wrote for a copy of my own birth certificate.

It came. I am neither Jean, nor Jane on it. I am just plain Mary. The Jean or Jane must have been added at my baptism. This was by the Rev. Augustus James[1] (who had a black wife: from his missionary days) Wesleyan (then) minister in Goulburn in 1865. So I still don't know if I am Jean or Jane.

I am a very tired old woman, but for a year I have been writing regularly for 'Tribune' and less regularly for 'The N.S.W. Presbyterian'. (I hope you like the conjunction!)

I enclose an item[2] from the latter which I would be glad to have returned. So far, no one has bludgeoned me over it so my head is unbowed and not bloody.

The last word reminds me that Cynthia Stephens[3] is here from London, she uses that word in conversation as English as possible, but with her, because of her powerful intellectual quality it is actually only a floral decoration, and no more! She wants to write a life of her father.[4] A *real one*, not the usual conventional kind. I not only think you should see her; I think you could help. Cynthia is *outstanding*. She can be found through Connie. Yours sincerely,

To Douglas Stewart

Kings Cross
4 August 1953

My dear Mr. Blarney Man otherwise Douglas Stewart—Did you say

---

[1] Apparently a lay-preacher then in the Crookwell–Goulburn area.
[2] Mary's article from *The N.S.W. Presbyterian* of 5 June 1953 concerning British Royalty, pointing out that the sovereignty derived from Scotland, not England (i.e. through James VI of Scotland).
[3] Sister of Constance Robertson.
[4] A. G. Stephens.

praise was pleasant? Your letter took nearly 60 years and all their woebegones off me—& me 88 two Sundays away.

I am glad you liked 'Old Shep' or whatever I called it—with all the thanks in the world for using and talking of it. You have given me a new vision of the heroic. Old Shep probably wore kangaroo skin chaps (for trousers) instead of a coat-of-mail, & a small sapling with a hook left on the end for a lance. And, thanks to you, I see him as the greater Knight. On Sunday, when I was little, father wd. drive us out to see some old hutter—they had not yet become hatters, though they wore dingle-dangles on their hats to keep away the flies; also hutters had not the delusions of hatters when the transition began. Year in year out we wd. be the only people they wd. see, except the squatter whose sheep (or cattle in handful beginnings) they tended. Sometimes one wd. be a disgraced, or disgraceful Honorable; sometimes a man who 'had been to college', sometimes one—several indeed—with a wad of M.S. inches thick in his watch box by the sheep cote. What wouldn't I give to have one of those now! As simple and unexpectant as a little family in a Bethlehem stable, the Holy Grail was in their keeping—and its last name was 'the future of Australia' and us.

I just love you for showing me this; i.e. not just 'the pioneers' receding in a shadowy and misty group, but each man as I knew him.

I think I have finished 'Fourteen Men' for the everlastingly last time. The letter to Mr. Temby for whether or not the C.L.B.[1] will look at it is sealed and stamped—air mail stamps as nailing it to the Post. And, if I didn't send you this before here is another 'old shep' which appeared in 'Bohemia'. It grew into 'Fourteen Men' of course. It touches feeling but is not sentimental.

ON ONE-TREE HILL

Old Bill & I,
On One-tree Hill,
Looked on the plain
When all was still.
Nothing was there,
Where, once, the larks
Rose in a cloud
Of singing sparks.
Nothing was there,
Twixt earth & sky,
Save One-tree Hill,
Old Bill & I.

I'm glad I lived when I did, & had the father I had. Thank you again, Douglas—Dhu Glas.

[1] Commonwealth Literary Board.

To George Ferguson

Kings Cross
22 August 1953

My dear 'G.F.',

At last I have a moment in which to say how much I felt that the old Firm[1] should remember me. I am so seldom in the shop, and there are so many of a new generation, that it would be easy to forget. At the end of life these things are like a warm hearth stone to sit by. I know it is you, and perhaps Aubrey,[2] whom I have to thank. But the flowers came in the name of the Firm, and my thanks are to it as well as to you. In my (appalling) 89th year.

To Hugh McCrae

Kings Cross
22 August 1953

Dear Hugh,

You don't know what it meant to me yesterday! For though R.D.F. & Douglas Stewart were later & you had gone, somehow it seemed as if the four (you the first) who thought I had something in my verse & I were all together.

As to you—you are the world's miracle of laughter. A stone wd. laugh with you, *Not* have to. Fellowship has no compulsion.

Also I want to re-iterate that you & Neilson stand alone. Impossible, even moderately or passably, to copy. You both have that something that your friend Walter de la Mare has. There can never be a Neilson or a Hugh McCrae school. The unencompassable individuality stands alone. It is neither twin nor quintet.

Just now had a letter from Rex Battarbee about his school of aboriginal painters now seventeen & one the mother of five children, which (he says) gives the lie to the white man's statement that these people are lazy. I sent him a couple of verses from 'Fourteen Men' & the aboriginal notes to them. I asked him to let the natives see them for confirmation, for one thing, & to awaken memory or research among them for their own lore & customs which we destroyed & did not let them keep. They may, by research, find more than we can or have. Print makes us immortal. They had no print.

I am older than you, I look for the end. What a day yesterday was as a send off for me!

[1] Angus & Robertson.
[2] Aubrey Cousins, the son of W. G. Cousins (editor of Halstead Press) and also a director of Angus & Robertson.

To David Martin

Kings Cross
29 August 1953

Dear Mr. Martin,

'From Life'[1] came this morning, and I have been through it twice. It still astonishes me. It bewildered me, I told you, at first and seeing that it did, I did better than I thought in the Foreword. (I could do better now,—at least as to punctuation!)

The verse is astonishing. One thing is the controlled force, another the nearness to ordinary life in the unordinary—which is war; and that its rhythms are whatever you wanted them in the irregular and yet they are inheld. Where we ride with others in a sulky on wheels, with you we climb up and up from the ordinary on hands (or rather) *with* hands and feet. You are something new to Australian writing. The nearest we have to you is Judith Wright, but your reach is wider.

I am glad you include 'A Letter to President Eisenhower'.[2] I thought it power speaking out beyond its words when it appeared. I realize in some ways that in it you walk the field with Whitman, but it is on your own feet.

The type and make up are excellent. It is nice to hand and eye, and one forgets that it is not stitched. (tho' why wire is not stitching, too, I do not know!) Being only a shilling I am sending for a number of copies to send as replies for birthday wishes that must be answered. I suppose I can get them through the 'Tribune', the address of the 'Current etc' not being given. I hope it makes some of our young writers widen their field, in subject and manner. We need it—

Every good to the book

To Rene Foster

Kings Cross
1 September 1953

My dear and much neglected Rene Foster,

First, Ernestine[3] is at Mackay (Queensland) and having the time of her life finding out (for writing) the origin and history of the place and revelling in the sunlight and warmth. (I haven't answered her letter yet). She came here (from Western Australia) looking the picture of health; she went North looking the picture of misery. Cold just withers and kills her.

---

[1] David Martin's small booklet of poetry, 1953. Mary wrote the Foreword. In it she wrote: 'The writer is intensely masculine, yet in it there is pity deeper than any woman's. Women flower in pity, this man digs.'
[2] *From Life*, p. 23.
[3] Ernestine Hill.

Myrtle Rose White at her son's (bought) station 'Lalla Rook', Western Australia, hopes to be home before the end of the year, when her son will be married and his wife take over the house. She is one of the Crossings, of N.S.W.

I have sent the MS. of the book 'Thank God it's done!' of 'Fourteen Men' to the Commonwealth Literary Board, and am living on the postman's whistle ever since the Board met on the 28th ult, just over. Also, as I have always so much high blood pressure when I work, it ended in a minute 'stroke', and my hearing, sight and balance have slipped a bit. Not for the first time of course! I can't help working too hard; the h.b.p. drives me to it.

This 'S.M.H.—Daily Tel.—and Sun'[1] business worries me. It means another suppression of a public voice, and a move to monopoly of public expression...

No more for the moment, as I have an ever mounting heap of the unanswered—love,

A week ago had a visit from a man who was born on and grew up to 16 on Cosme (Paraguay) and is still in touch with those left there—now grandparents or ggps.

To Constance Robertson

Dear Girl Connie,

Kings Cross
2 September 1953

Doing things on the set day of the year too often is just remembrance of a date, not of a person.

Your flowers came yesterday, and if they were to come on 31st July, 1954, it would be all the same.

Memory is its own flower and its own remembrance. We—you, Cynthia, Donald and I all belong. The 'Bookfellow' kept me sane when, in the black scrubs of Western Victoria, we came back from the wide and international life of South America and Cosme (for though we might have had shortness of food there was no shortage of brains, new experiences, and new lands there) to the solitude of the bush and the unused brain of its people. Once a month the doors of the mind and the world were opened. I would prop up 'The Bookfellow' unopened just to look at it, and read only a little at a time to make the mind-feeding spin out. That is a debt that never lessens in my mind.

That astounding sister of yours![2] Is she still here? I advised her,

---

[1] John Fairfax & Co. purchased the whole of the unissued ordinary shares in Associated Newspapers (publishers of the *Sun, Sunday Sun, Woman, People* and *Pix*).
[2] Cynthia Stephens. See letter, 22 June 1953.

against the need of Australia, to go back to Europe and London—or to go to South or North America where even if population grinds there is scope. Give her my love—also Margot and her offspring if and when any come—as to you, you are always where you always were.

To David Martin

Kings Cross
Dear Mr. Martin, *3 September 1953*

I have my batch of copies of your verse, from the 'Tribune'. They were brought yesterday.

If it goes into a second edition (or more) I would like you to add a word to the sentence in the Foreword[1] where I wrote, 'Women flower in pity, this man digs'. I want to add, 'this man digs. His pity comes in clods from the earth that is life itself'. (Got it at last, and as I *meant* it from the first). 'This man digs. His pity comes up in clods, and from the earth that is life itself'.

I read the 'Letter to Eisenhower'[2] to a woman a few days ago (from the copy you sent me). When I finished she turned to another woman she had with her and said what an impression of pity the verse left in her mind—(She meant 'implied' but 'not directly expressed', of course.)

I see Bernard O'Dowd is gone. No one knows now, except a few of us who are left, how his 'Dominions of the Boundary' and 'Dawnward?' burst open the doors of narrowness when he wrote them. Today, because liberty is abroad and theirs, the writers refer chiefly to his later verse. They did not know the need of his early times for the reformer, and (hackneyed though the word be) the standard bearer. Yours sincerely,

To Hugh McCrae

Kings Cross
Dear Hughie lad, *11 September 1953*

When I think of the mind behind your letters, the depth, the breadth, the swallow-dip to a thousand things not said but within, the mind that wrote, I don't just think, I see miracles. Or one would be enough. These are the things that make us stand up & say, 'There must be eternity. These things live, & no death can touch that from which they sprang!'

[1] See note to letter, 29 August 1953.
[2] *From Life*, p. 23.

I could have wet towels with tears yesterday! I spilt boiling soup on my wrist, but immediately said 'Thank Heaven it is my left one!' I took out the heat under the cold tap, put on borofax & cotton wool, & hey presto! Still sore, I can use it this morning . . .

Later. Somebody came in & brought the Hurstville paper with a paragraph to say the Hurstville Council has renamed 'Park Road, West Oatley, Dame Mary Gilmore Road'. There's fame for you, my lad! I feel the horses' hoofs trotting on my back as I think of it! With this small smile I end. May it make you smile too.

To David Martin

Dear Mr Martin,

Kings Cross
15 September 1953

Yesterday I posted you a letter and a copy of 'From Life'[1] and hope I stamped it sufficiently.

In the evening I listened in to your 'Spiegel the Cat'[2] (and if my spelling is wrong please pardon me). If I say your version, in its execution, astonished me it is no less than the truth. The form of verse was so astoundingly simple, yet it was never monotonous—and more, it was never threadbare—But what a satire on man and his social condition; and his standard of life and morality generally. And what force in your version behind a light hand.

And that reminds me; when I wrote in the Foreword that line of the clod I suddenly realized that my thought had been used before, and that I had quoted it—Alex Comfort's,[3] 'They are like fists'. Both meant force; the blow, the sudden impact.

You will have heard the production over the radio of Spiegel the Cat. I thought the man who did the cat did it well. He was the part not just a man doing it. He was impressive; the others were not, though they did sufficiently well to carry the story. Am desperately tired now-a-days, but I wanted to write—

To David Martin

My dear David Martin—

Kings Cross
6 October 1953

I sent a copy of 'From Life' to R. D. FitzGerald among others in return

---

[1] David Martin's book of verse, published in 1953.
[2] *Spiegel The Cat: A Story Poem*, by David Martin, was broadcast by the A.B.C., 14 September 1953 and was later published, in 1961.
[3] Alexander Comfort.

for their birthday wishes. His reply dated 5.10.53 has just come. He says: 'Thank you very much for sending me David Martin's 'From Life'. I was most impressed . . . his verse is musical expression besides being just expression of ideas. It is very noticeable that while no doubt David Martin holds strong political views the approach in his poems to world and human problems is not really political but social. I think this is right and to the advantage of his work as poetry. Here is material wh. lends itself to propaganda of a party or partisan nature; but Martin ignores that aspect, rightly, and concentrates on the human aspects . . . Thank you again'.

Because you may not know R.D.F. I thought you might like to have this.

I have read 'The Stones of Bombay'.[1] How terribly real. But that last chapter is ruinous—anti-climax alike in force and as writing. It is just a journalistic addenda. Was it to indicate a possible second book?

The English of the book is so powerful, so concentrated in the use of words that I am dumb before it. It is creation in being; there is no creation in the loose.

You must have lived among the people, or you must be terribly responsive to atmosphere and observant of surroundings. The book is a thing lived, and the reader lives with it and its people.

I dislike—I shun—the unclean. You write that life (such life) is dirty, but you do not write that dirt is life, and what a difference that makes to a reader like me!

I haven't time for more and must end—

To Marjorie and Muir Holburn

Dear Marjorie & Muir Holburn,

Kings Cross
8 October 1953

'Freedom on the Wallaby'[2] came at mid-day & I have been through it, and with what a rising up of memory & feeling, things of the young years that I had not seen for a life time are there, with names this generation never knew. For this the collection is most valuable indeed. Collectors of Australiana and students shd. hunt for it.

Just as a personal matter & one of delight, I lived again in Hugh McCrae's 'Pegasi'[3] a thing as true and as living as if it were written

[1] A novel by David Martin, published 1949.
[2] *Freedom on the Wallaby: Poems for the Australian People*, 1953, edited by the husband and wife Holburns.
[3] 'The House for Pegasi' by Hugh McCrae was written in 1903 but not included in his volumes of poetry until R. G. Howarth's *The Best Poems of Hugh McCrae*, 1958. It was in the Holburn anthology.

yesterday and next to it Francis Adams & after Adams Ada Cambridge. No one today knows the way Francis Adams swept the feeling, young, and just-awaking minds of Australia when he wrote. I wd. say that ninety percent of the revolutionary verse & feeling (social &, from it, otherwise) sprang from Adams. And when I read him today—tired, the edge of reading worn down by too much reading (& too much doing) the old magic was still there.

As to Ada Cambridge, old & bed ridden from partial paralysis when I went to see her, she was I think the greatest woman in personality, & breadth & power of mind, I ever met. Like a fallen tree she was still a giant & noble trunk. I don't know if in the Mitchell Library there is a copy of her first little book called (I think) 'Chains'.[1] Because she was the wife of a clergyman, & it was too daring for the church (& respectable people) she had to withdraw it. There were only six copies that I know of left undestroyed. I *think* the Mitchell had one, I know Rose Scott had one, for it was at her house I saw it and she Ada Cambridge herself had one so had A.G.S.[2] I was too young to understand its inner meaning of revolt (against the then compulsory sex life of marriage) but I realized the beauty of the verse & its English. It was almost all in words of one syllable. But if you have seen it you will know that.

And then Barcroft Boake. He used to come to our home week ends when with Surrey or Lipscomb at Wagga Wagga. He never parted with his whip, even when at table; the whip with which in the end he hanged himself. His father did the first scenic colour photography in Sydney. His sister (Mrs Smith) lived next door to me at Cremorne Point, in the first house built there & long ago pulled down. One day when I came home from 'The Worker' office I found a pot of basil & a note at my door. That was her introduction to me.

These things rose up in memory as I read your book. Much else of course, & many others— dear old Sydney Jephcott among them who, in about 1890, planted the Albury sale yards with European acacia trees for shade for the cattle blinded by the sun & made hollow log water troughs for their thirst, and of course Shaw Neilson who said that next to A.G.S., I had most & earliest encouraged him, John Farrell of course. But I must stop, I am tired & my page at an end. Yours gratefully,

Of course your book goes to the Mary Gilmore collection at the Mitchell Library.

---

[1] In Ada Cambridge's *Unspoken Thoughts*, 1887, there is evidence of these sentiments in occasional poems, e.g. 'A Wife's Protest'.
[2] A. G. Stephens.

To David Martin

Kings Cross
13 October 1953

My dear David Martin,

Thank you for listening in and for your criticism of the 'feature'.[1] I took the liberty of quoting part of it in my letter of thanks to the station—gave it as from one who knew what he was talking about. As for me, it is the first time that, I think, perhaps my best and most worthwhile work came over the air. Usually the small and sentimental is chosen. John Thompson who did the work—he came here—is himself a poet, though I do not know his verse. But judging by what he chose and made of mine he must be worth while. About 'The Stones of Bombay',[2] don't misunderstand me. The only bit I thought hurried up was the end chapter. The atmosphere of the book had left it. I wd. have ended on 'He rolled over onto his side and remained so'.

I believe in an ending remaining a bit up in the air. Continuity lies in a question. To tie up too well ends everything.

I like your 'Dim Sims Man'.[3] But don't smash your cup in a sudden flare if I point out that you have 'faded' twice in two lines—lace and chart. I am fighting that in two little bits I have just done. I have the right and only word for both pieces, but it will have to go out of one or I cannot use it in my book. Yet the piece is as good as the other, and will go flat for want of that particular word...

I never think of you without seeing the picture of Elizabeth Fry in a little old black covered book of her life wh. I had to read as part of my education when I was about eight years old. It seems wonderful to touch the skirt of that great woman in your wife being her descendant. As to the book it wd. be a collector's find today. A very early Collins I think.

Thank you again

To Patricia Excell

Kings Cross
14 October 1953

Dear Miss Excell,

You shd. have my 'Bernard O'Dowd'[4] before this. I had the chance

---

[1] John Thompson devoted his 'Quality Street' programme on A.B.C. Radio, 11 October 1953 to Mary's poetry.

[2] David Martin's novel, 1949.

[3] See *Poems of David Martin*, 1958, p. 76.

[4] *Meanjin* 4 (1953), 407-19, contained tributes by Walter Murdoch, Mary Gilmore, F. T. Macartney, Nettie Palmer and others to Bernard O'Dowd who had died earlier that year.

of getting it weighed for air mail, a friend being here, & just wrote full-bat not to keep her waiting too long. I had no time to run over it to put in missing punctuation, lost letters or omitted words—which I hope you may be able & kind enough to place & for which I apologize. But my years are a burden & I am dependent on friends for posting & shopping, as neither sight nor legs are friendly to me, now, out of doors. As I said in the brief note with the MS. I had no idea I have been the only person asked for something about O'Dowd, & had regarded myself as one of many, & not to be missed if I did not write. I made no mention of why I ceased to write to O'Dowd wh. was because of the way he treated his too faithful & self-sacrificing wife ... I do not know if you listen to the Radio, but in Quality Street[1] last Sunday I had the finest 'feature' on me that anyone has ever had. For the first time my best & most unusual verse was chosen (usually it is the small & sentimental) and beautifully given. The readings included 'The Bull'[2] wh. I thought no one wd. ever give, & 'Old Forthright',[3] of whom we were terrified as children.

To return to the MS. I enclose stamps for its return if not suitable. Yours sincerely

To R. D. FitzGerald

Dear Bob—

Kings Cross
20 October 1953

Some day write something on the Fist, for the blows of the fist has come. I repeat—*has*, not have. *'and a thought without eyes* that runs lost in my head', was ever a line greater? Were ever words put together more beautifully, running like a ball of grass before the wind—yet every syllable an arrow?

But you have beaten me (in print) with 'Wonder'[4]—Also there is one thing writers *do*: 'Bring your thought home in your hand'. The fox is thought, the hunter reason, the hound skill—(How your work makes me think, and coalesce thought!)

> This hunger the gods give,
> This once to live.

Isn't it all we have and Isn't it all that God has? How else can God *be*, except in things, or in things like us?

---

[1] See note to letter, 13 October 1953.
[2] Published in *Under the Wilgas*, 1932.
[3] Published in *Fourteen Men*, 1954.
[4] 'Wonder', 'Heemskerck Shoals', 'Fifth Day' and 'The Face of the Waters' were all published in *This Night's Orbit*, 1953.

>   Let them all drown:
>   Living needs more than this twist of the head
>   looking up stream then down.

What iron there is in your work. Time withers the flowers, takes the edge from steel, but iron remains; iron remains iron even in disintegration—which means that students and scholars will be trying to fit meanings to R.D.F. when all the rest of us are nothing. I write this and post it, in the stir of feeling your book has given me.

Later
   No one coming this morning my letter is still unposted so I add this.
   You only asked me how I liked 'Heemskerck Shoals', (Someone said it was your best) I think it wd. make an outstanding monologue or a dramatic recital. But 'Fifth Day', to me is greater, and 'The Face of the Waters' is all that I wd. think, feel or propound if I only could.
And what a beginning! 'Once again the scurry of feet—'The beginning of all time, life, lives, thought and space, I somehow find in those few words and then the question formulates, and the answers come so slowly long after.
   'The egg-shell collapses in the fist of the eternal instant—' The eternal instants. I leave it at that.

To Rene Foster

Dear Rene,
Kings Cross
31 October 1953

... I am a very tired old woman now-a-days, though the brain still wags a pen. But polio left its mark, and a small 'bust' on the brain two months or more ago has not mended matters as it left me a little deaf. However I disguise it fairly well!, and only a few notice it. But there are times when I wish I were 60 again! There is so much to do, and so much mass pours in—and that reminds me: *Have* you seen R. D. FitzGerald's last two books[1] 'Between Two Tides' and 'This Night's Orbit'? Australia has touched great literature at last—and the lingually untrimmed quality of the work! Any word is not a poet's word, but poetry is in any word when there is vision behind it—and R. D. F. has vision as no one else so far has it.
   Every good wish and all power to your pen.

[1] *Between Two Tides* was published in 1952, *This Night's Orbit* in 1953.

To R. D. FitzGerald

Dear Bob—

Kings Cross
1 November 1953

I was dizzy over 'This Night's Orbit', but I have just laid down 'Between Two Tides'[1] after not seeing it for months, with its intensity and long continuity (so different from my flits of thistledown!) and I felt like Moses must have felt when he came down from Sinai after talking with God. Apart from the Bible and Whitman[2] at his highest, I know no writing in the world like yours. The immensity of vision is always like the sky—the filled and changing sky, for no sky is ever vacant,— behind and above a grain of sand, and both are one—and it is all so unpretentious, so bare of trimming. Creation needs no decoration. It is itself all of it. I don't know anything so independent of other aid as your work. The Bible has prophecy and the roar of the prophet. You have power in almost pages of words of one syllable and neither roar nor banners to help. Literature has touched Australia at last. How you must have lived this thing to have written it! How lived in research and preparation for it.

To R. D. FitzGerald

My dear Bob—

Kings Cross
9 November 1953

Of all the myopic visions! Do you think this small, parochial Australia of today is going to live for ever? That she will *always* be outside the great universal, thinking world? If I thought that I could wish she wd. shrivel up tomorrow and become dust. I saw the great world—once I wd. have said 'In South America' But I know now it was 'From' and not 'In', as it is 'From' not 'In' in Australia and the parochial no longer held me. I write for the man leaning on a lamp-post, the ordinary average all-round-the world common man, who may sometimes feel the sun and see the moon—you write for the same man, but you take him on top of a mountain where he sees the stars.

And how far and how many the stars are beyond the moon!

I think again of the simplicity of 'Between Two Tides',[3] men and women in ordinary clothes over ordinary minds, and yet with what a revelation of things beyond the little. The florist gives us the cut-flower. You give us the stem and flower, the roots and the earth about them. And if that isn't part of the making of a *permanent* Australia—

---

[1] See note to letter, 31 October 1953.
[2] Walt Whitman.
[3] Published 1952.

permanent as part of the world—then I don't know what is. And that reminds me (I don't know how or why) that when I laid down 'Between Two Tides' with its simple language, and its tremendous rhythm, the broken links of a chain, a thought fell into place and I got something I had wanted for a long time. In other words 'a thought (or thoughts) without eyes' walked home, and an undefined hunger ate and was satisfied. That thought, thinking of words was: 'any word is not a poet's word. But poetry is in any word when vision is behind it' (So any word is and can be a poet's word, and what a thing that makes language!)

And if by now you don't feel you have had a 'hit with a kick of (or is it 'on'? no 'of') the leg,* then my days of buffeting are over. But to come back. Man is not parochial; but times and conditions are—and that reminds me of Prof. Huxley and when he said man reached his highest in evolution. Hasn't evolution said that at every stage of evolution for all its millions of years? I don't agree with him. We are only at the fringe of things. As vision widens with height so does capacity. And that brings me back to words. Bunyan using words showed us the Delectable Mountains and Christian fighting Apollyon. With the same kind of words R. D. F. shows perhaps a greater field . . .

*Old North of Ireland from my childhood. 'Hit him a kick o' the leg'.

To Hugh McCrae

Me darlin Hugh,

Kings Cross
Saturday—& this very minute
14 November 1953

Our book is through. See 'S.M.H.' 14.11.53, Page 5, Col. 5, last paragraph, & nearly last line.[1]

—& just about saved from giving up the ghost. And the last phrase reminds me, what lovely old sayings this language (& this country) once had!

The other day, writing to R. D. FitzGerald, after not being heard for 80 years, one such sprung up without a moment's delay or hesitation, in the voice of my Irish grandfather. It was (could you get a better?) 'Hit him a kick o' the leg!' Immediately I saw every Irish Fair that had ever existed & heard the shouts. Also I used it on R.D.F. & delighted to do so.

[1] *S.M.H.* of that date carried this statement in a report of the Commonwealth Literary Fund meeting: 'It was also proposed to assist the publication of a new book of poems by Dame Mary Gilmore'.

To Rene Foster

Dear Rene,

Kings Cross
23 November 1953

What an interesting letter, and what an interesting time you have had or are having at Canberra! Time you realized you are an important woman, and should be given a good time. Did you see 'our first phantom coat-of-arms'[1] in the Library at Canberra? Mr. White[2] said he had it framed with my letter of explanation, and hung on the wall as a most valuable historical gift. (I shall send this to Canberra in case you are still there.) Mr. Temby[3] wrote me last week that he had sent my MS. on to Miss Beatrice Davis at Angus & Robertson's, which saved me doing it, and with the added eclât of his connection with it and the Commonwealth Literary Fund. As I said in a letter I sent to Adelaide last week, and which may await you there, it is time you collected your own book of criticisms (and notes on authors you have reviewed and met) and sent it to the Commonwealth Literary Board for consideration.

I have just been making some notes on my recollections of the daughter of Loveless,[4] the leader of the Tolpuddle martyrs. And also recollections of the Botanic Gardens, here, when I was a child. Simple things then. Now valuable history. So what about you and all the people and places you have met and written about in Adelaide?

Am half-dead with the humid heat; so no more. But so glad you are being a bit fussed over! Affectionately,

Tell your brother that this S.M.H.-Sun amalgamation has ruined two good Sunday papers and given us a rag-bag in return.

To George Ferguson

Dear G.R.II[5]

Kings Cross
26 November 1953

(If Queen Elizabeth can be Eliz II of Scotland there is no reason why you should not be G.R.II of A & R)

I have a letter from Mr Temby[6] (Canberra) saying A & R has accepted 'Fourteen Men' for publication, and of course am delighted.

---

[1] See note to letter, 22 February 1949.
[2] Harold White.
[3] H. S. Temby.
[4] George Loveless.
[5] Mary liked to link George Ferguson with his grandfather, George Robertson, one of the founders of Angus & Robertson.
[6] H. S. Temby.

Though I had 'Fourteen Men' first that Antarctic expedition called their book 'The Fourteen Men' and with good reason, being fourteen. So I will have to get another name in case of clash in sales. Or will I? Anyhow it is a thing easily settled later on.

Already I am on my next book. Prose. Most of it in the rough I think—all sorts of old and new stuff, facts, theories and the like. All necessary for the Mitchell and Canberra Libraries if nothing more.

What work R. D. FitzGerald is doing! World stuff of the highest and how he encompasses his field, and in what English! I wrote David Martin in Melbourne that I was almost in a delirium over 'This Night's Orbit'[1] and I really was. The sense of wonder expressed in fact, the unlimited made sane, outstands (and will outlast) anything anyone else of this period (except Hugh McCrae) has written. He has gone beyond the parochial of time and place into the world. He has given wings to thought yet kept his feet on the ground. I think what this means to Australia in future years. As you see, he makes me write in spite of myself — and you are too busy for that — so again my grateful thanks.

To John Hetherington

Dear Mr. Hetherington,

Kings Cross
18 December 1953

I write to congratulate you on your Life of Field-Marshall Blamey.[2] I am one of the very few left (if *any* others) who knew his father, mother, and his maternal grandparents. When I was little his father used to pull my curls and say to my father: 'This child will be heard of some day'. I didn't know then (nor anyone else!) what *his* son would be! Jim Blamey, now at Manly, I taught in the Infants' School in Wagga Wagga; Tom came as a small brother now and then—the nicest little boy you ever saw. But as a child he loved 'soldiers'—tin soldiers we called them then. When he was about five, I think, or a little older, father wanted to buy him something for his birthday. 'Not soldiers!' said his father. 'He has them in hundreds!' and he went on to say that the child would arrange his soldiers as opposing armies, put one side (or a section) in a difficult position, and when his father would offer to extricate them, Tom would refuse to let him, as he wanted to do it himself.

I think you would like to have this story, and I would like that you should have it. A man who can write as you can deserves it.

[1] Published 1953.
[2] *Blamey*, 1954.

Blamey's sister married a distant cousin of mine, but I saw nothing of the family after I grew up, till the last twenty years, and then only sometimes . . .

I had turned against Blamey because of his bad reputation in Melbourne. But just as I learned in my young 'New Australia' (Paraguay) days that a man could drink and *swear* (!) and yet be a good mate, so you have shown that a man of Blamey's morals can also do great things. For this I want to thank you. Also for your manner of writing. (What an Editor Blamey would have made, where power was the goal, here or in the U.S.A.!) Yours sincerely,

To Hugh McCrae

My Hewie Lamb,

Kings Cross
29 December 1953

If I had not had a Christmas line from you I wd. have thought the end of the world had come.

We both have our suitcases packed for them other places. You for Tartarus as your card says, me, longer than you, for its feminine (perhaps a Sunday School) counterpart. And I don't know which wd. be worst or, rather, I do. *You* wd. have the best of it.

By the way has it ever struck you what an affection humanity has for the devil & all his tributary imps & little devils? Just search English, if no other language, for proof of this. There are no Churches preaching for the devil. Apparently affection needs no Churches.

I had the nicest surprise last week. A. H. Chisholm & George Ferguson (G.R.II. I had written him that if Q Elizabeth cd. be E. II, he *certainly* cd. be G.R.II) Lovely to see them. And did it make me feel Somebody!! Which makes me wish you cd. have gone to England to see Walter de la Mare, as such a visit wd. have meant John Masefield too.

After which the Benediction.

To T. Inglis Moore

Dear Tom,

Kings Cross
29 December 1953

Your 'Australia Writes'[1] came this morning & the afternoon being cool I was able to go through it. The thing that strikes me is that 'it is different' i.e., not according to routine pattern.

---

[1] *Australia Writes. An Anthology,* edited by Tom Inglis Moore, 1953.

It is of the prose I think, not of the verse. We have had so much verse that practically any selection can only differ from others in items chosen. But stories are different—or yours are. There is, if I may use the word, a nobility of standard, an absence of the sensational for the sake of effect, that has not been found in any other collection that I have seen. The outside world will find something here as a book, to hold it—and what an ending! The choice of that simple, unaffected piece was a stroke of genius. Even its brevity counted. Actually I did not know Alan Marshall could write like that. It has set him high in my opinion. And what a lovely thing Henrietta D.B.[1] wrote of Miles Franklin! I like your biographical notes. They too are 'different'. And to my astonishment I find R.D.F. is David & not Desmond! Was it his father was Desmond? And as to your inscription to me in giving the book, you are as bad as R.D.F. in his. What do you two mean? However R. D. F. is world great. Some day we may have a painter to put with him. He goes beyond anything any other Australian writer has done. He gives us Moby Dick[2] in words of one syllable; the sky's boundary is in them. When I think of what he makes simple words do I need telescopes! However this is not your book; there you have made something the world can take in its hand & say, 'This is not what we generally get'.

Had a girl of twelve here today who wants to be a writer. From her maturity of mind I am wondering will she be another Christina Stead...

Thank you, Tom, for all your kindness to me. You have never changed in that—you, Hugh McCrae & R.D.F.

Am desperately tired, & will end. Affectionately,

To J. K. Moir

Kings Cross
My dear J.K.M. *14 February 1954*

I haven't got over it yet! The astonishment and pleasure of seeing you yesterday. All morning I had been feeling about to die, the day before grieving that I shd. die without having seen you, (fact)! but there was nothing I cd. do about it. And then Walter Stone brought you. Of all the astounding ten minutes! And I don't know which was the more excited, Walter Stone or I.

I wrote W. S. last night to thank him and said, 'What poundage, what energy, what force!' and I say it again. You could correct the

[1] Henrietta Drake-Brockman.
[2] Herman Melville's classic American novel of the great white whale and Captain Ahab, 1851.

slant of the Poles with your force and energy, and then look round to see what next you could do.

In my long life I have met and known many men of deeds and force: Henry George (I almost knelt at his feet) Henry Parkes, Archibald, Hargraves, Farrer (I didn't like him, but I liked his wife and she liked me. I remember it being said at the time. *'She* is a lady, but he isn't!' They were so opposite and so different), William Lane, A. G. Stephens, Sir Thomas Carmichael and now you. And all these men thought I had understanding. They talked to me as to an equal. What a remembrance!

Well, that's some of the excitement worked off! And thank you for coming...

To C. B. Christesen

Dear Mr. Christesen,

Kings Cross
16 February 1954

What an interesting script,[1] & what an astonishment to me to see it. I had no idea I or my work mattered so much. It is something new to me! I have made one note wh. I hope you will use. It really is essential. Also it covers the whole field indicated by the omission of the verse mentioned.

I had J. K. Moir here for ten minutes last week, brought by Walter Stone & over to see his mother. What a human dynamo (if I may use the now hackneyed expression) & the very opposite of what I had expected, wh. was not poundage & power at all. I thought he was worn thin—nerves & body—with overwork. Yet here is a man on whom overwork falls, & falls off, like rain on a duck's back.

I'd like to see his mother. She must have given him a tremendous inheritance.

He is an example of a man thought to be an egotist because he pours out what he is doing. He isn't; he tells, not because of himself, but because of the deeds or events. *They* are his interest. I do that too, in notes to my books. He & I are only the vehicle.

I wrote to thank you over the Bernard O'Dowd issue.[2] It (the O'Dowd) was beautifully done; no one person's style clashed with another's while each had its own meat.

Every good wish

[1] An article, 'Mary Gilmore: A New Poem and Textual Autographs', by A. G. McLeod, *Meanjin* 4 (1954).
[2] See note to letter, 14 October 1953.

To Dorothy Catts

Dear Dorothy Catts,

Kings Cross
5 March 1954

Your book on your husband's life[1] came to-day. I ran through it and write at once. What a strong piece of writing! Naturally strong I mean. If you did not refer to yourself as the writer no one would know a woman had done it. The sense of history is marked, and the absence of the indirect and sentimental. Another thing: you do know (so many do not) the value of humour and the weakness of the merely funny. The humorous incident and story you include makes no clash with the style and manner of the book. They are solidly a part of it. I thank you for including me in the life, but more for the inscription. It is generous.

To J. K. Moir

Dear J.K.M.,

Kings Cross
28 March 1954

I am the most excitedest person in this City! My book is on the way to coming out before Xmas. It is Verse, and called 'Fourteen Men' and passed on to A & R by the Commonwealth Literary Board. I had begun to think I would only see it in Kingdom Come, the heat (and the burden of age) has so knocked me out. I wonder how many women of 88 have a book of verse—not recollections or diaries—coming out.

Frank Clune sent me his and P. R. Stephensen's new book, 'The Viking of Van Diemen's Land'.[2] In it they have lifted Australian literature out of its old rut. They have gone into the world and out of the parochial—the credit of course is due to P.R.S. as a writer of English which he does know and can use, though it may be Frank chose the subject. Anyhow it is a move away from the squatter, the drover, the convict and Ned Kelly as parts of our history...

Every good wish.

To Hugh McCrae

My dear Hugh,

Kings Cross
12 June 1954

After all dignity does count! Where my choice was just a whimsy

---

[1] *James Howard Catts, M.H.R.*, published in Sydney in 1953.
[2] *The Viking of Van Diemen's Land: The Stormy Life of Jorgen Jorgenson*, 1954.

& a tiny whirlwind up sprung in the mind, this is a glorious light. My heart is higher than it has been for ages! And what a piece of your own hand-writing![1]

I shall ask for it to go in a page without anything but itself i.e. no 'Foreword' above it or anything. A note can go in the Appendix saying it is from 'Twa Heads' (was that the heading?) or in any form you wd. like.

Yesterday I had the agreement to sign, so the book is to the fore.

With what a grateful heart!

To T. Inglis Moore

Dear Tom,

Kings Cross
14 August 1954

First your letter and then the boronia; and how kind to remember! But what a garden you describe. I wonder could I add something to it. If a white Canadian poplar could be cut back to grow in a tub, I could.

When I was born at Merry Vale a white poplar[2] was planted for my birth. It still stands. It was a cutting from Mary Reibey's tree at her gate. Hers was a cutting from the first ones came to Australia for McLeay and planted in the Botanic Gardens. People named Nixon bought Merry Vale and the descendants still own it. Sarah Nixon (Mrs. Smith) some years ago struck me a cutting of my tree at her old home and I planted it in the top lawn of the Botanic Gardens, not fifty yards from where (behind the Kendall seat) the very first ancestor grew. The ancestor I last saw in my twenties, when father, who was a friend of McLeay's and through whom the hanging stair and cupola were added to Elizabeth Bay House. I could get you a cutting from my descendant tree in the gardens or from the Nixons at 'Merry Vale' Roslyn, near Goulburn. (Roslyn was my grandfather Cameron's place and there was only a fence between it and Merry Vale, my Beattie grandparents place). However a white poplar might not grow in a tub. So I must think of something else. What about bits from other writers' gardens till you have a Pantheon of shrubs?

My book[3] is to be out this year. I have had the galley proofs and as I notice the critics are now talking the value of the simple, I have hopes it may live. The Australasian Book Publishing Society is giving

---

[1] For the inscription see note to letter, 8 February 1953.

[2] For other details of the 'poplar' story, Mary Reibey and Alexander McLeay, see letters, 14 December 1933, 27 December 1934, 10 May 1935 and 18 February 1937.

[3] *Fourteen Men.*

me a birthday Party on the 23rd—Frank Hardy ('Power Without Glory') will call for me and bring me home according to my age.

I forgot to say that I hear the 'Daily Tel' took a good photograph for tomorrow (?). Two were taken, one with one of the first four Webster's Dictionaries to come to Australia. One came to the 'D.T.' for review. John Farrell reviewed it, it was given to him, he gave it to me. It went round the world with me and yesterday completed the 'D.T.' circle—sixty years later.

Every good wish to you all (and think about 'a writers' garden').

To Rene Foster

Dear Rene,

Kings Cross
12 September 1954

Of course you could ask about 'if my biography'! But I wrote you two or three years ago that I had given up all thoughts of a biography in my life time. Too old, too tired, and no time. That is why I left in my Will provision for it—you had my letters I know, as you replied, in regard to the provision, that 'the laborer is worthy of his toil'. I told Tom Inglis Moore who also wanted to do it, the same as I told you.

I am nearly 90, have no daughter to do things for me, and the work and help for others just piles up. I am never free from appeals from young people, and *they* must be answered.

I had the delight of my book[1] being out (and *brought to me*) for my birthday[2]—I said 'I can die happy now. I have seen and held it'. Also last Friday a visitor who had been at A. & Rs. for a copy said there was none. The first printing had sold out (in under three weeks). The second printing is out this week—one, two reviews[3] so far: Ken Slessor, and R. McCuaig in the 'Bulletin'—this one after its edition had sold out! I have been very ill but better this week. Every good to you and yours.

To Nan McDonald

Dear Nan McDonald—

Kings Cross
1 October 1954

Forgive my delay in thanking you for your book 'The Lonely Fire'.[4]

---

[1] *Fourteen Men.*
[2] 16 August 1954.
[3] *Fourteen Men* was reviewed in the *Bulletin* 8 September 1954 and by R. D. FitzGerald in *Meanjin* 4 (1954).
[4] *The Lonely Fire* was published in 1954. The title poem of the volume had been first printed in the *Bulletin*, 7 December 1949.

What a sense of *powerful drama* you have! You hit with an opening line, and do not tail off. You and Judith Wright have what no one else has in anything like the same degree—if they have it at all!—the blow of the fist in poetry. But you are more a poet than she is; the dream captures your words.

I have been very ill. Went too hard and fast for 89, and now am paying for it. So will end. May you go from strength to strength.

Yours sincerely—and again saying Thank You—

To Katharine Susannah Prichard

Dear K.S.P.,

Kings Cross
24 November 1954

As your friends in Perth are giving you a birthday party may I add my good wishes to theirs.

It is a long time since I first saw you—you and Hilda Bull[1] together, but the picture is as plain today as it was then. What two beautiful and eager souls you were. Hilda is gone, but you have never altered. Affectionately,

To Gavin Greenlees

Dear Mr. Greenlees,

Kings Cross
14 July 1955

You are doing great work with your editing the 'Forbes Advocate'! And how glad I am to see you are collecting the Old Hands recollections. You can tell Mr. Goodburn that I often saw Bundaburra Jack when I was staying with my Uncle and Aunt, the James Beatties, at their store, hotel and Post Office at Bundaburra Gap, in about 77-8.

About the article on Lake Cowal. Father said the native name could be translated almost as the garden of Eden it was such a place of singing birds and flowers. I remember the flowers like a carpet, the wading and swimming birds in thousands, the bittern booming in the night. Also I remember the Dorkins. There were people named Currie had a coaching place on the road to or from Lake Cowal. They had two girls who were identical twins. So that they would be known apart one had a blue bow on her hair, and the other a pink one. Not knowing they were *two* and not *one* girl, I wondered in bewilderment why each time 'she' left the room, waiting on table as we ate 'she' changed the

---

[1] This incident is described in letter, 14 August 1938.

colour of her hair ribbon. Saying so I was told 'she' was two and not one. Perhaps Mr. Goodburn may remember this and the Curries.

During the time I was at Bundaburra Gap I saw a migration of kangaroos from the dry hills toward the Lachlan. They loped along about three abreast and there must have been at least two thousand, great and small. On the ground they made a sound like a distant thunder, which was what caught my ear before I ran out of the house and saw them.

All good wishes to yourself, your wife and the 'Old timer'.

I am recovering from a major operation. Have been in Hospital since November last. Was a dying woman—three months to live and thought I would die on the table and save trouble. I didn't, am physically weak, but mentally as you see.

To Stephen Murray-Smith

Dear Mr. Murray-Smith,

Kings Cross
8 August 1955

What an astounding tribute![1] I don't know how to thank you and those who made it. One way is to send out 'Overland' to everyone I can, instead of writing letters. The batch ordered is already gone. So will you send me another lot please? I enclose a cheque, for £5 to cover cost and year or two's sub., the rest to be a donation to your funds. (You need not put my name in the magazine!) It wd. be a pity if it came to an end. It is just as good and easier reading than 'Meanjin'—that is for ordinary people. It begins to look, here and abroad, as if Australia is at last coming into her own in the Literary (or film) field. Part of the courtship of Australia by Britain as against the cowboy of the U.S.A: and the U.S.A. its heel on England. I hope this pro-USA, Liberal Govt. goes out next election, for though I do not idolize Gt. Britain, I do think the British Cwealth members shd. stick together, and *not* disintegrate in favour of others. Tell your young writers from me that to write their own generation or times is not enough, but to write so that the next generation can say we are there too. i.e. to include depth: or the trunk of the tree as well as the leaves. We do too much temporary work.

[1] *Overland*, Winter 1955 number, was a tribute to Mary who was then approaching her 90th birthday. Tributes were written by A. G. Mitchell, Judith Wright, K. S. Prichard, Eleanor Dark, Ernestine Hill and Dorothy Cottrell.

To Rene Foster

Dear Rene,

Kings Cross
7 September 1955

... I have given Mr. Dobell[1] two sittings, and so the beginning is made. Even if he gives me a pink eye and a blue nose it will still be a Dobell! I was astonished to be told, the other day, that the portrait was to be mine. So I wrote the Australasian Book Society (Melbourne) at once to say that if so it is to be given to the National Gallery at Canberra in the Society's name and mine, Dobell to have the right of the Archibald. I am very tired yet ... But thank heaven my voice holds out, and doesn't squeak or crack. A bold front has its values! Every good to you and yours.

To Peter McGregor

Dear Mr. McGregor,

Kings Cross
12 September 1955

I hope my telephone message of yesterday reached you, after the rebroadcast.[2]

I can't say how much I thank you, not only for *how* it was done by you but that I heard it. I was so strung up for the party that I had no recollection whatever of what I or anyone else said that evening. Now I am astonished and bewildered, especially at what Dr. Evatt[3] said. It is unbelievable—thanks to you I now know, even if unbelievable.

I had two sittings for Mr. Dobell, over a week ago, and yesterday I read in the 'Sun-Herald' that he said I had 'Koala eyes'. And am I proud of that!! A new and wholly Australian word, and on *me*.

More than this: I was lately told that when finished the portrait was to belong to me. I wrote, I instantly wrote, the Australasian Book Society (Melbourne) that I would not dream of keeping it—but would give it to the National Gallery at Canberra in their name and mine. (Is there a Gallery or is it yet to be?). Years ago they wanted one of me. Now it will be a Dobell. I doubt if they have one of his portraits there; and if he gives me a pink eye or a blue nose, it will still be a Dobell. However, it will not go so far from normal.[4] Yours sincerely,

---

[1] This is the first of several letters in which the controversial Dobell portrait of Mary is introduced. The portrait was an entry in the 1957 Archibald Prize competition. See letters 23 September, 24 September, 12 October, 20 October 1957.

[2] Peter McGregor, Supervisor of Talks in N.S.W. for the A.B.C., made recordings at Mary's 90th birthday party. The programme was broadcast as 'I Remember Dame Mary'.

[3] H. V. Evatt.

[4] There were many who were to quarrel with Dobell's interpretation of Mary in the portrait. See especially letters 24 September, 12 October, 20 October 1957.

To David Martin

My dear David Martin—

Kings Cross
24 September 1955

I am a long time in replying to your letter, and if I plead old age, weary body after hospital and want of time, just let it go.

About a poetry market for 'range', blame politics—Labor or advanced papers can't pay—and those wh. can are biassed against more than their own particular views, national, popular or international. Even if we started a good poetry magazine, having range, we could not carry on, as ads would not come in, and ads. wd. be needed—But all the same such a magazine might be thought of with a view to a possible co-operative future. As to my 'germ killing kerosene stove' as you call it, am not stout enough on my feet to risk it. Not much matter if I went up in smoke, but I have some more arrows[1] I want to plant and my new book I want to finish before I finish. Mrs. Dorothy Catts drove me to it. It is my childhood[2] (in part anyhow) I suddenly realized that I was the only person left alive who knew me as a child! You, so far from where you belong, shd. get to work on the unrecorded child (and surroundings so changed) wh. was you.

No need to 'big book' (verse) while small ones go out. They can make a big one later on. And if I am sufficiently alive when the time comes to improve the Foreword to 'From Life',[3] it will be an honour to be asked to do it.

Your 'Mission'[4] verse went to my heart. I wish you had time to visit round and *write* a book like it. The crassness of believing that aboriginal brains were any more 'primitive' than ours! Only our own 'primitive' brains could believe it. You have no idea how often I think of Elizabeth Fry—I think her the greatest woman England ever produced. Like our Caroline Chisholm 'she was a female Moses in a bonnet and a shawl' or words to that effect. But her fight was greater, and against more fearful and entrenched odds than in Caroline Chisholm's case. For Caroline the gates of a free world were already opening. Keep Elizabeth Fry in mind for a book. *Do*. Some years ago, where or in what paper I have forgotten, but perhaps the Magazine Section of 'S.M.H.', there was an article wd. give you almost a full foundation. Florence Nightingale is used to dim Elizabeth Fry and what she did. She acted for the army, and armies were the weapons of power and

---

[1] Mary's column in the *Tribune*. See letter, 16 June 1952.
[2] Mary dictated an outline of her early childhood to Mrs Catts but it was not published. There is a copy of it in the Mary Gilmore Collection at the Mitchell Library. See also letter, 6 November 1955.
[3] See letter, 29 August 1953.
[4] 'Mission Station, North Queensland'. See *Poems of David Martin*, 1958, p. 86.

of the entrenched privileged. In the prisons were the victims. They had no panoply and glory. They were only human beings.

Now I must say thank you to you and all those who made me a birthday party in Melb. But not only that, but made it an entity that stood up on its own feet, and like a stone in a desert. I did write to Mr. Stephen Murray-Smith, but in case I was not adequate enough I want you to say it, not once, but again and again for me. What else? You are a strong man in literature, and a strong man in person and in literature, for Australia. And that, no matter what the themes in your writing.

All good wishes to 'Elizabeth Fry', you, and your boy,

To David Martin

Dear David Martin—

Kings Cross
5 October 1955

Your letter came yesterday. They tell me you out-did yourself at the birthday Party.[1] I wonder what on. In any case you could never be small, no matter what the subject.

About your letter: It is not the individuals as the people but the *aim* that matters. I had to learn that. It is being young makes us apostles to *people*; age teaches us that people, as such, are a heartbreak. We confuse people and aim, thinking one includes or is the other. They aren't. Man can only compass the finite. The aim is finite, the people infinite—and they must be. Only death—only the dead are uniform.
(And now I am wondering was that your worry! or was it just that ordinary human up and down as to values; self and other.)

I saw your wife's verse in the 'Tribune' and thought it probably yours—or someone writing like you—not you. The kinship of minds, inwardly, even if different outwardly! Anyhow it was a strong and a good piece of writing; and as a first piece there is power—the same kind of power that you have in your work.

Am dead tired, but I have outletted something asking outlet, in all this. Every good to you and yours.

To David Martin

Dear David Martin—

Kings Cross
26 October 1955

'New World—New Song'[2] just came. Strange that last week I sent

[1] Mary's 90th birthday was celebrated by a party in Melbourne as well as Sydney.
[2] *New World, New Song*, edited by David Martin, 1955. It was 'a good range of some of the working-class poets in recent years'. Martin wrote the verses 'Our Poets' to sum up his thoughts on the volume. See *Tribune*, 5 October 1955.

S.M.H. a piece of verse wh. I shall send you when published wh. in a way is playing your note.

And about ideals being more lasting etc. Ideals are the tree of life—some are ever-green losing leaves one at a time only, some all at once. Ideals rooted in life are the former, ideals rooted only in aspiration, fancy or imagination lose all their adherents at once. Mixed metaphor no doubt. You can enlarge on the meaning.

Of course people are wonderful! even if they are the leaves that fall.

My childhood (book)¹ has now taken shape; it only wants pummelling now. When that is done *I* can sit back and rest for awhile. The child is only part of the book, but on it hang the variations. Kind (Mrs.) Dorothy Catts insisted on my writing it and equally insisted on typing it—sitting by my bedside for the first part and taking it from dictation. As I grew stronger I got up, made notes, and dictated from them. She says we have a script of 40.000 words. I may lessen or increase them, as I finish it off. Parts of it are worth while; not so sure of the rest. All the leaves on the tree as good wishes to you and yours.

To R. D. FitzGerald

Dear Bob,

Kings Cross
29 October 1955

See my verse in today's 'S.M.H.'² and find your subject for the 'Herald' poetry competition—and the glory of Australia as an old-new field for myth and literature. Only you and John Manifold have it in you (but in what different ways!) to do this. The stories are in the Mitchell, the inkpot on your table.

Byram Mansell is doing it in paint and tiles (and what a battle against narrow prejudice it has been for him and for me as his backer!) You do not need a flag waver before your engine. So, Bob, will you think it over?

I see the shape to be of my little book³ now and hope to finish it for next year's A & R. If they take it. Ninety years is as un-self-confident as the beginning years. So I have no brag to offer.

Mrs. (Dorothy) Catts has been my right hand in the typing. She came, in the early weeks, to my bedside and took it down from

---

[1] See letters, 24 September 1955 and 6 November 1955.
[2] The poem was 'Our Fleece Unbound', dealing with the Parramatta River. In exhorting R. D. FitzGerald and others, Mary is probably referring to the lines

> What shall we write if not this land of ours?
> But we, who have the place, the ancestry,
> the need.
> Our tale is still untold, our fleece unbound.

[3] On her childhood. See letters, 24 September 1955 and 6 November 1955.

dictation. What that saved me in work. Later I made and dictated from notes. Sometimes I gave her script. She never tired, and how grateful I am to her. The book is wholly mine, the generosity of typing is hers.

Every good wish and may your pen light your page!

To T. Inglis Moore

Dear Tom,

Kings Cross
6 November 1955

This time last year I had only three months to live, this time this year I have a new book done—and in three months. So I have done something for the Literary Pension you, as Acting Chair, allowed & allow me. Mrs. Dorothy Catts wanted to do my biog. As usual I said no. She said I need only dictate it. Again I said No & that I didn't know how to dictate. Then (as I have told everyone) I suddenly remembered that I was the only person left alive who knew me as a child. So my childhood began, & the period covered is '65 to '75 with (& what!) divagation—the divagations to make it interesting. Mrs. Catts says I have dictated 50.000 words. I can't believe it! Now there is the editing & the trimming of facts, phrases & words. I have an idea it is the first 'My Childhood' written here. If not who is there that you know of? Have two possible names for it, but may find a better as I go through the stuff.

I hope you saw my verse, 'Our Fleece Unbound',[1] in the Sat. 'S.M.H.' a couple of Sats. ago. Am hoping it will spur someone to do something on our lost tribes. Do you know G. G. McCrae's saga?[2] I can't think of the name now. He sent it to father when written in, I think the '70s. It was too conventional I thought though I was only a child or little more.

Every good & best wish.

To R. D. FitzGerald

Dear Bob,

Kings Cross
6 November 1955

There's no question about your being a writer! I read your 'Roads'[3] when the 'Bulletin' came, and wondered why on earth you had gathered up odds and ends to make something to publish. A couple of days later I read it again to try to find out why. I *did*, and each time I have read it it grows, and is still growing: in wonder, and deeper and wider.

---

[1] See note to letter, 29 October 1955.
[2] The Story of Balladeädro or Mämba, the 'Bright-Eyed', 1867.
[3] The poems were entitled 'Roadside: Eleven Compositions' and were published in the *Bulletin*, 2 November 1955.

If you hadn't two words of poetry in the lines what is behind would put it there...

Yesterday Dobell came again, and for the first time is satisfied with the sketch he made. His third visit only. His memory is his drawing board. What a saving of my time—and his.

All the best,

To R. D. FitzGerald

Dear Bob,

Kings Cross
8 November 1955

What a generous letter! It is like you. About the critics. Critics have the set idea that a writer has only one way of writing, and that if he departs from that he is going down hill. He may be, but not for their reason. One is that youth goes and thought has to take up what the young vitality leapt at or flung out. In other words we become the flourmill (of recollection and intellect) where once there was the growing corn. Another is that in the end words (and form) take possession of us. The habit of the furrow grows. It becomes the easy chair of composition. Frank Morton, who could sit at his typewriter or run off verse after verse without needing to alter a word, once said he wished he had never done it: it had tied him to the lighter verse. Then there is the third thing: we empty the scoop of first things as maturity comes, and though the mind widens the world narrows. And I suppose I am telling you—or rather giving you—stale hay. So I am done.

Mrs. Catts just rang to say she is coming with a copy of her new book,[1] just air-mailed from London yesterday. And about 'our tale untold', if you do anything it will come to you as your own. My part (or hope) wd. be only a tree in distance. What troubles me is that fools will rush in where angels fear to tread—you being one of the angels. In other words the idiotic or the shallow and imaginary will come instead of the deep and wise, and people will take these as a basis for the future. Better nothing than the tin-whistling of fools.

Well, my first remembered glimpse of 'Old Father Parramatta' was at Joubert's home[2] in Hunters Hill in about 1869 or 1870. I still see the water shining through the trees on the lower side of the grounds: too young to know what it was.

[1] The new book was *Those Golden Years*, 1955.
[2] The Joubert home was St Malo in Hunters Hill, acquired by the National Trust in 1955. Didier Joubert also bought Reibey Cottage from Mary Reibey in 1847.

To Stephen Murray-Smith

Dear Mr. Murray-Smith,

Kings Cross
13 November 1955

Your second letter came just now. It seems incredible that I should be one of the joint choice for nomination with Katharine Susannah Prichard (so long a friend!) for the World Peace Prize.[1] To be nominated seems to me to be more important than to win. The prize comes from the world, the nomination from my own people and my own country. While ever I have breath I shall try to justify that choice. Will you please convey to the Australian Peace Council my appreciation and grateful thanks for the honour they have done me . . . Yours sincerely,

To L. J. Blake

Dear Mr. Blake,

Kings Cross
19 December 1955

I had practically to drive Winifred Hamilton to writing of Steele Rudd in these later years. She now realizes how foolish she was, in destroying all or practically all his letters to her. However it is done, & she, poor girl, has enough to think of in her suffering health.

As to Steele Rudd, I only met him a few times in his attractive & fine young years, & avoided him in his dreadful (to me) last years. Of these you will get enough from others & the contemporary Sydney paper that wrote about him & his fall.

In his young years he was everything one could wish, — healthy, attractive, good looking, eager, friendly & earnest. I sat beside him in the theatre at the first night of his first play, 'On Our Selection', & felt proud to be beside him. I did not see him again till he was in his middle years; still likeable but the white ants had already begun.

Thank you for remembering me in your Lectures to students, & for what you say as to their response. My work is simple & direct in expression, & they can grasp that. Inner meanings, or application, come with experience, & that also holds them. But how glad I am to be told the verse matters—Thank you.

The Season's Greetings, Yours sincerely

Still on ticket-of-leave, from Hospital, & not yet strong enough to go out of doors.

---

[1] The Australian Peace Council, of which S. Murray-Smith was National Organizing Secretary, supported the joint nominations of Mary and K. S. Prichard for a World Peace Prize (value £7000). Among the sponsors of the nomination (unsuccessful) were Vance Palmer, C. B. Christesen, Alan Marshall and the Melbourne Bread and Cheese Club.

To W. Hart-Smith

Dear Bill,

Kings Cross
28 December 1955

Your letter is a revelatiôn, and clears much that I felt but could not define.

I always felt that you were allowed a limited free range, beyond which, if you went, you were pulled back.

I just thought, without going farther, that you were born that way. But you were born with a hindrance. Now that the aneurisms are gone how far will you range? In any case don't let the range flatten and shallow your work because the range is wider. It could mean continuity—i.e. novels or philosophy. Also you have your choice of studying yourself as you were or as you now begin to be. What are the children like or likely to be? And what a patient understanding wife you must have! She will have relief from strain as well as you ...

I was given a tremendous 90th Birthday party by The Australasian Book Society and The Fellowship of Australian Writers. There were 1000 people passed in and out and cards and letters from Russia to Kingdom Come.

Robert Close sent a beautiful letter from Paris. He began by quoting one of mine 'Though I wouldn't have your book inside my door I believe in justice'. He was then being prosecuted for 'Love Me Sailor'. Now he has a home in Paris and a yacht on the Mediterranean.

The A. Book Soc commissioned Wm. Dobell to paint my portrait. They said 'It is to go to you'. I said 'To Canberra'. So to Canberra it goes.

The F.A.W. commissioned a woman sculptor to do a bust, so that too will go to Canberra as the Rayner Hoff bust[1] and the Joshua Smith portrait[2] are in the National Gallery here.

But the greatest thing of all is that justice begins to turn towards the aboriginals at last. There is to come out (for world art) a book of their earlier nature paintings which are said to be more remarkable than that of any other primitive people and that they show a standard of genius in the expression by simplicity. Also that by thousands of years they antedated Picasso and those later schools.

To Roland Robinson

Dear Roland Robinson,

Kings Cross
23 February 1956

I want not only to congratulate but to thank you for what you have

[1] See note to letter, 2 October 1934.
[2] See note to letter, 13 June 1946.

done in regard to Aboriginal lore in last week's 'Bulletin'.[1] I wanted to write at once, but time has only come now.

Every literature has its dialect of its native or primitive people. This is a distinction we have never had. *You have begun it.* That is a distinction no one can take from you. Work it up a little more from the aboriginals as they tell you their stories. But don't *overdo it*. Overdone would destroy it as literature. The odd, the characteristically quaint, but not the bizarre, will create a language that will live. The Hoosier[2] dialect (Brer Fox and Brer Rabbit) is a case in point. Yours sincerely,

To David Martin

Dear David Martin—

Kings Cross
19 March 1956

Radar, telepathy—what you will! Also yesterday a woman visitor who knows another g.g.daughter of Elizabeth Fry.[3] She lives in Sydney and I am to get her address and perhaps see her.

Now about your book. I wd. say don't let the word propaganda appear on the jacket of all places. That means leave out A. D. Hope there.[4] I think the publishers wd. know best what to say. Have you 'The Gay Gordons'[5] in it? (I read it only yesterday!) In that you have one of the best pieces of balladry written anywhere, for it has the authentic form, sound (and matter) of ancientry, and yet in it is the story and the grief of today—the Flowers of the Forest[6] with today's tears (and if you like to quote that, *do*. I shall be honoured.) There is another suggestion. You know what my appendices mean to my books. They just about make them; to the critics if not to the general public. Don't use the word 'appendix' for fear someone seizes on it, but say 'Notes'. And *there* put what you will as to A. D. Hope, propaganda and other analytical or informative matter. In that you can put 1. 2. 3 etc. and

---

[1] *Bulletin* 15 February, 1956 contained an article 'As Told to Roland Robinson'. It comprised several Aboriginal legends including 'The Myth of Irringa the Devil-Dog' as related by Torrnunga (Albert Namatjira) of the Aranda tribe.

[2] The stories of Brer Fox and Brer Rabbit were written by Joel Chandler Harris (1848-1908) in authentic southern (U.S.A.) negro dialect. Based on native legends they were the first, and remain the greatest, in the school of negro folk literature. Whether the 'Hoosier' dialect is correctly applied to the Uncle Remus stories by Mary is doubtful as the Hoosier dialect refers to the Indiana dialect and the stories of Harris are based in Georgia.

[3] David Martin's wife, Richenda, was a descendant of Elizabeth Fry.

[4] A. D. Hope wrote a critical review of David Martin's *From Life*, 1953, stating 'It is nearly all red-hot propaganda of the crudest sort . . .'.

[5] The poem was actually 'Lament for the Gordons'.

[6] 'Flowers of the Forest', a song by Jane Elliot (1737-1805) was the most popular version of the old lament for Flodden.

quote A. D. Hope and your reply with full force (no explanatory matter of course.) and in the same way what you wrote on, was it Stephen Spender? There will be other things of course! And it has just struck me, my note here on 'The Gay Gordons' cd. go there too. *The critics will look at and note these things and the critics, not the jacket, counts* with the book-sellers who direct the counter public sales. I come back to 'The Gay Gordons'. Could you have a coloured pictorial jacket? I know that if you are publishing cost will count, expenses are so high today.

About R. D. FitzGerald, I am doubtful as far as my letter is concerned. I honestly think a first-hand letter wd. be best, for I am sure he said he wd. like to meet you, and a letter wd. be next best to the personal.

As to anything *I have written about your verse* you can use it, for I meant it and have not altered in my thought. I am sure of that, and of course with source you can quote anything by anyone that has been printed—as that Foreword.[1] Go through the verse for notes, if only a line of a note. It does build up a book. As to a name what about 'The Gay Gordons'? 'Songs of David' is a spark! But most people wd. think they were Biblical versions and, *today*, how many of *them* wd. sell!! (Not sure of my grammar there). There is another matter, the world is full of secret apprehension. It wants something bright as an enticement as a jacket, no matter what the inside maybe. Of course if I knew the body of the book I might unsay all this, for another name suggested from or by something else. So don't feel in anyway driven or bound by what I have written.

By the way in notes, if you make them, give your wife's descent, and send copies autographed by both to the heads of the Quaker, Cadbury and Fry people.

Don't skimp the Notes, if used, but keep them from over-flowing into the unnecessary or what cannot be included in the concentrated.

What a long tell-you-how to one who does, or should on his work, know how!

As for me, my feet are no longer young and how hampered I feel! I'd buy seven-leagued boots if they wd. help me walk a mile in the open world and air. But I don't repine, so many old people are bedridden in *mind* and body—(Hugh McCrae, I am told, is a sick man, and Ethel Turner knows no one, I heard). All good wishes to you all—may this letter give you some help.

[1] The Foreword to *From Life*, 1953, was written by Mary. See letter, 29 August 1953. A. D. Hope, in his review, said: 'The book has a kindly introduction by Dame Mary Gilmore which is remarkable as well for quoting a comment on Martin's verse by that arch-apostle of the muddled mind, Alex Comfort'.

P.S. and I don't usually descend to those letters: You will perhaps not have seen or had lent you a copy of 'Woman' wh. I am posting with this. It deals with the aboriginal loss to our literature and I am astonished at myself for it was just 'talked' without a note. I didn't know I cd. dictate till last year. Also in a 'Bulletin' of last month there are three word-of-mouth aboriginal legends told to Roland Robinson[1] by Namatjira and two others. I have begged and begged that the mind and manner of the aboriginal be given in writing their lore, instead of doing it as English and not native. Roland Robinson has in part done this, and what a different value it gives the work. It is the beginning, I hope, of an Australian Hoosier[2] or other dialect. I said all this lately to Alan Marshall and he immediately lit up on it and said so, So, when he goes North, I hope he will do something that way too. But R.R. to the extent he did it, is first.

Once again the top of the Tree to the new book.

I think 10,000 girls in bikinis on a beach infinitely less harmful to youth than this cover of 'Woman' (1.2.56) wh. I am sending. Girls move—this is still and can be pored over—I wd. tear it off only that wd look—self righteous?

To George Ferguson

Dear G.R.II,

Kings Cross
16 April 1956

I had your letter last week, and thank you. I would feel like being sliced up to have 'Old Ways'[3] cut up—even more than 'More Recollections'.[4] Every word in both is almost forgotten Australian history. Major Towner's sister lately told me the Major has 'Old Ways: Old Days' and that a neighbouring squatter having borrowed it offered £25 for it, which was refused on the spot. People all over Australia have written saying they have had the secondhand book shops looking for copies for them for years and years and they are so valued there is never a copy to be got. I am glad to know that all my books, even my Cookery book, are hoarded—the Cookery book over 30 years in some cases. (Good to be celebrated for something!) That celebrated reminds me that when the French had their part in the Easter Show I was told a French attendant there said there was a picture or portrait of me at

---

[1] See note to letter, 23 February 1956.
[2] See note to letter, 23 February 1956.
[3] Her book of reminiscences and anecdotes *Old Days: Old Ways A Book of Recollections*, 1934.
[4] The sequel, *More Recollections*, 1935.

Mary's flat in Kings Cross

At work in the flat

Judith Wright with her daughter Meredith   Katharine Susannah Prichard

Dame Mary at home

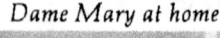

the Louvre! Of course I said impossible as when told some years ago by a touring Australian. Last week Mrs Catts said the Louvre is now up-to-date in its arrangement of paintings—each section or era in its own group—and that there are also collections of 'Notables' from different countries, Canada and Australia among them. So it may be I am in one of those. If *I am* G.R.[1] should be there and also you and A.H.C.[2] in any case Angus and Robertson should see into the matter and not leave too much to perhaps unliterary people—like political and other leaders (and followers).

To return to my MS. I know it wants fixing as to sequence. It also wants dates that Colin Roderick could, I am sure *would* give. But I also very sadly know I can not now face continued, concentrated work—that I must now leave to others—to the Old Firm in its charity and kindness. But will you give me this week to think things over. But what people I have seen and talked to—Farrer, Hargraves, James Tyson, Kidman, G.R., G.R.II and all the rest of them . . . And these are only some. But topping them all was Dr John Dunmore Lang, who, patting me on the head, said to my father, 'Ah, Donal! She's a bonny Scotch lassie!' and that patting means much more to me than being Dame Mary—Dame Mary is only an outside thing, that is in my heart.

In some things sent me after my mother's death and again just lately looked at, there is one of her letters to my father dated 1867 from Cowabbee. I was 2 years and 4 months old. Yet a large part of the MS you have belongs to that place and period. Recollections clear as daylight all my life. No need for you to answer this. I know how work-driven you are. As ever to you all.

To R. D. FitzGerald

Dear Bob,

Kings Cross
26 April 1956

What a story![3] and the first of yours I have seen. It filled me with that warm nostalgia that is the height of fellowship and loneliness—not loneliness for people today, but for the past. I hope that you wake up every night, driven to write books and books . . . These things are real and eternal. No change in language by time can make them out of date. Chaucer and his time—his England—lives in his people—his men who never had any children but to whom the cockney looks back (or we do) whenever he intones (I forget the exact words) through his

[1] George Robertson.
[2] A. H. Chisholm.
[3] 'A Garibaldi Veteran', *Bulletin*, 25 April 1956. Republished in FitzGerald's *Of Places and Poetry*, 1976.

nose (so sweetly)? When ever I read things like this 'Garibaldi Veteran' I feel like going on my knees in worship for it.

Last week in the 'Bulletin' there was 'The Ruzilla' by Mena Abdullah and Ray Mathew—the first writing in Australia akin to that of Hans Christian Andersen. The same was in the verse 'The Red Koran'.[1] It made me feel that in the admixture of races Australia is about to produce an independent literature of her own, one not based on English or U.S.A. as shapers—shears and scissors to pattern.

Anyhow, may Hunters Hill kick you out if you don't keep an exercise book and pencil by your bed for midnight—or early morning—use and may your hand never shake in age as you write—

To George Ferguson

My dear GRII,

Kings Cross
2 May 1956

I said give me a week. I am still thinking and want more. The MS is safe, being with A & R and I need not hurry, for if I went out before deciding things, you would still publish it, if only as a memorial.

But what I have thought is this: what about printing the autobiog. section with 'Hound of the Road'?[2] The other two books 'Old Days'[3] and 'More Recollections'[4] could be each on their own, for the longing letters from every part of Australia I get through the years they are out of print[5] show how interest lives and the books are living in content, though unpurchasable no matter how many secondhand shops have been hunted. Australia everywhere is waking up to the need of the preservation, and the knowledge of *settlement*, people's history.

I have lately urged Mr Heffron[6] to have schools called for historical local or adjacent people. Neutral Bay School in Ben Boyd Road (did I write this before?) is a case in point. Also I wrote Mr Palethorpe, acting Ed of 'Woman' and suggested a regular 'early days' from Australian towns, and in time what a collection of otherwise forgotten history! He said he would be glad to consider it. It is because in 'Old Days' and 'More Recollections' matter going by so rapidly that it will never be gathered again, that I do not want them cut up and half emptied out.

[1] A poem by Mena Abdullah, *Bulletin*, 15 June 1955.
[2] Mary's book of essays, 1922.
[3] *Old Days: Old Ways A Book of Recollections*, 1934.
[4] *More Recollections*, 1935.
[5] *Old Days: Old Ways A Book of Recollections* was eventually republished by Sirius Books in 1967.
[6] R. J. Heffron.

Another floating idea is that if I could get above or beyond immediate pressures on my eyesight and time, I have enough special articles to collect (on the blacks, for instance and which no-one else knows because they date back to the 60's and 70's) which perhaps could fill up to needed size. If I could get the annotations on letters for my collection at the Mitchell Library of my books I could get at these—that and the constant letters and visitors from everywhere. (Of course I would die *without* these!)

Well, here it all is, and you need not answer unless you think that 'Hound of the Road' is the solution. As to that Mrs Burke (husband, editor of Kodak Magazine) told me last week that . he thought it one of the most beautiful books she had read. 'Have you a copy?' I asked. 'No', she replied, '' could only borrow it from someone who had a copy.'

Just had yesterday, a medical student in his last year in Bombay, asking for a letter for his collection of world notables. Imagine me a world notable! Have you ever handled a lock of wool? A lad came yesterday from North Qld. I enclose a bit for you. Every good to all of you.

Unwashed wool. Note length of staple, quality and elasticity.

To Stephen Murray-Smith

Kings Cross
Dear Mr. Murray-Smith   25 June 1956

Having met you, you are no longer the nebulous being who can be addressed as easily as the Almighty. Hence the formal beginning. I am sending in a small item,[1] which gives its reason for finding a place in 'Overland'—wh. I hope it will. If not please send it back and I can use it in the 'Tribune'.

'Truth'[2] 40 years ago made itself popular with thousands by its 'Old Times' column dealing with the land, and the past. 'Swag'[3] partly goes that way, but is not yet identified with it, it being scattered. Could you regularly put a last item 'Old Time' (like mine is in part, though applied to today and the future)? It wd. identify the spot and build up a name. We are travelling so fast the past is going over the precipice of time like the herd of Gadarene swine. I hope you know your Bible! I heard one of the elder Broughtons tell father he had called his station

---

[1] Probably 'Time The Eternal Now', published in the Spring 1956 number of *Overland*.
[2] A Sydney Sunday newspaper.
[3] The column of short comments, usually on literary topics, in *Overland*.

Gadara because of the Gadarene Swine. But that also is past history, yet worth saving. The first Broughton was Anglican Bishop of Calcutta wh. included Australia. Was that Bishopric a prophecy as regards us?

I write from bed and hope the penmanship is legible. Old age being non-resistant I have a long bad attack of fibrositis.

Lately, asked to have a 91st birthday party I said, NO! ABS[1] was all I wanted and I didn't want it rivalled. But when I was told its *real* purpose (money for the Chair of Aust. Lit)[2] I had to agree. However I think the Dobell portrait will be the attraction—and that again is due to the ABS., and how grateful I am for it! Give my warm regards to Mr. Turner.[3] Yours sincerely

To T. Inglis Moore

Dear Tom,

Kings Cross
20 July 1956

Your letter just came and thank you for all you have been doing for me in your lectures.[4] I hope my work stands up to it in years to come!

I had two surprising things the last two months. One a letter from the Chief Moscow Lit. Soc. (or what ever it is) saying that they had followed my 'career', had one of my books, and wanted my biography. The other is that the editor of I WEN, the Literary Magazine of the Chief Lit. Soc. of Peking, gave Alan Marshall a 1955 copy of the Magazine to give me as it had a picture of me and something in Chinese for my last birthday. The only words I know in the page is Mary Gilmore, in our script. The magazine is in Chinese script.

As to this birthday, it is in August. When I was told it was to be kept up I said NO!! But when Colin Roderick said it was to gather money for the Aust. Ch. of Lit.[5] I had to be the peg!

What else? My *biggest* work is a fragmentary collection of ideas on world health, and all the rest of it based on my early knowledge of 'The bad lands' and what we now call trace elements wh. cure the bad lands. The scraps have been appearing in 'Tribune' as arrows,[6] the last one next Wed. I hope. To my surprise I had my copy of 'Soviet News' this week by mail, and in it (24th May) I find a Russian Scientist talking of the need of Geohygiene. *Geo*! Also since I began someone

---

[1] Australasian Book Society.
[2] Mary's fervent wish to see a Chair of Australian Literature established at the University of Sydney was not realized in her lifetime.
[3] Ian Turner.
[4] T. Inglis Moore had given lectures on Mary at several universities as part of a series of Commonwealth Literary Fund sponsored lectures on Australian Literature.
[5] See note to letter, 25 June 1956.
[6] Mary's column in the *Tribune* was called 'Arrows'.

in England says we are creating a carbon-dioxide blanket in the upper air. So it wd. seem I am not alone in my alarms, fears and conclusions! My work is only my usual candle. Science will follow.

All good to you and yours, Tom and again thank you. Am terribly tired bodily. Thank heaven the pen still works.

The Secretary, *Kings Cross*
The Seamen's Union of Australia. *2 September 1956*

Dear Mr. Elliott,
I want to say my own word of thanks and gratitude to the ships whose crews sent me letters, flowers or telegrams for my 91st birthday.

The sea matters. Man came from the sea and goes back to it. The little old sailing ships sailed round the world almost in the dark. They were the world's educators before astronomy charted the heavens. They did and dared as no aeroplane has ever done. Now the leviathans have everything that science can give, but the sail, like a leaf in the wind, gave them their charts and their courses. The brutality of the time goes, but the greatness and the heroism remain.

My first ship was an aboriginal bark canoe, my next an aboriginal dug-out, made from a big log with a hand scraper and fire to char. It would hold four men, and its rudder was a small bough held in the hand of the steersman. It was used on the Murrumbidgee, even when running hard.

Looking back over all this, 1870 or thereabouts, perhaps after all I come within coo-ee of the Union! In any case . . . men with ear-rings, men with long plaits tied round the head and strange tattoo marks on the fore and upper arms—men who had run away to the bush, nursed me, cut me damper made in the ashes, sang me 'The Golden Vanitee'[1] (which I sang for Henry Lawson at his beginnings), and told me tales of the sea.

Much has been written of the sea, but the great book of the sea still needs its Homer.

The sea has always been a man's world. Land and air belong to women as much as to men, but not the sea.

I have written all this because I feel so much being remembered by the Union.

And here is a little story of a man of father's kin (Scottish counting, of course) which reaches far. He was a Captain McKay, and sailing south a pirate with more guns than he came up beside him, threw out grappling irons and boarded his ship.

[1] A folk song, the first line of which was 'A ship I have got'.

He was six feet four or six in height, and as he walked the deck talking to the pirate Captain, he suddenly stooped, took the pirate under the knees and threw him across to his own deck, breaking his legs (I think it was legs). The pirates cleared out. Seventy years later I heard that from Donald Gordon Campbell (I think I may give his name), a writer, a dreamer, a collector of history, and a practical farmer and a descendant of Captain McKay.

He has his ancestor's sextant or quadrant and something else on his walls. 'And', he told me 'they are so accurate they could be used today'.

After that, isn't it time the Seamen's Union began to collect for a Museum and Library of its own?

I have a letter today from a birthday good-wisher. 'I read that you were a member of the New Australian expedition that went to Paraguay. My great-grandfather, John Campbell Stuart, built the 'Royal Tar'[1]—'our little ship of sail; she made a record voyage to and from Monte Video'.

Once again my grateful thanks to you and to those others who also belong.

To T. Inglis Moore

Dear Tom,

Kings Cross
24 December 1956

... I don't know how to thank you for thinking of inscribing your new book[2] to me. It is something living—as though one came alive everytime the book was lifted up. Not many books are inscribed to women—apart from mothers and wives. All my books are inscribed to men, though I remember Grace Bardsley in 'Fourteen Men'. But even that is not inscription. But I do thank you, Tom, and am most grateful. But all the time I am asking why? and again why? with Hugh McCrae, R. D. FitzGerald and others near and far.

I am up to my eyes in Christmas cards, letters and callers. But I have found time to suggest to the Mayor and Aldermen of North Shore that they send a letter to their long long resident, Mrs. Rodgers, the last grandchild of George Lavender and his wife (a daughter of Billy Blue) and that they take care of the old Lavender home—a beautiful building still in good order. Also that they remember Henry Lawson's

---

[1] For details of the letter from Rev. G. Stuart Watts see note to letter, 26 December 1928. See also Gavin Souter's *A Peculiar People: the Australians in Paraguay*, 1968, for further details of the *Royal Tar*.

[2] *Bayonets and Grass*, 1957.

friend Mrs Byers[1] (née Ward). She told me she was Thunderbolt's[2] niece, but that her father did not like it mentioned. My love to Peace and Pacita and that includes yourself.

To George Ferguson

Kings Cross
Dear GRII, 3 January 1957

I sent my seasons greetings to the firm a while ago, but here are yours personally even if late.
    I had an astonishing post on Monday last.
1. A letter from The Australian Literature Society saying I had been awarded their Col. Crouch gold medal for the best book in 1954— 'Fourteen Men'. So A1 to A & R. I wrote back and asked the Society to keep the medal, and award it verbally, in perpetuity, for the *second* best book in any gold medal year.
2. Letters from China, Vietnam and USA.
3. The following letter from the Ed-in-Chief of Foreign Literature in Moscow (who had earlier written saying he would like me to send something for publication and my biography or notes on it). Now I have his reply:

'Dear friend, thank you very much for your letters, for clippings, and for the promised book of your verses. We are looking forward to getting it. We shall find the interpreters here and will pay their royalties.
    'We believe that someone of our best women poets will find your verses close to her heart, moods and creative style and will make good translation.
    'The interesting article from the 'Melbourne Herald' will be certainly used when we will be publishing your verses.
    'With profound respect, Yours

A. Chakovsky'

Not dreaming of *book* publishing I sent (by ship mail) 'Fourteen Men'. This letter says 'book', and now I am wondering about the copyright. It belongs to A & R.
    I can replace 'Fourteen Men' by my own copyright books, but I think it best for me as a writer, and best as representing Australia. Will you tell me what about it and where I stand? Also whether you or I make the necessary agreement. I want to be safe in this matter, and not a trespasser against the old Firm.

[1] Isabel Byers.
[2] Frederick Ward. See glossary.

I had a visit, when they were here, from the Director and some members of the Chinese Classical Theatre as I could not use their invitations. One danced Chinese fashion (body, arms, hands) and one sang for me. The very next week two Russian writers came. One, Mr Sofonov, is Editor of the biggest weekly paper in Moscow (1,000,000 a week). He wrote 20 books, I was told, and is a poet. The second, not such a big paper, writes scientific books. They flew from Melb in the morning to see two people, I being one, and flew back that evening. Mr Sofonov said I was known to Moscow, but he wanted to write a personal article for the people. Am wondering what he will write as neither spoke English but through an interpreter we talked chiefly of the early Labor movements and of New Australia and Cosme.[1]

Nearly dead of the heat. So no more. All good to the Auld House and to you and yours *and* A.H.C.[2]

To R. D. FitzGerald

My dear Bob,

Kings Cross
10 January 1957

What a generous letter. But you are like that. The curious thing is that I myself did not think much of that verse![3] Mr. Pringle[4] did, someone else on the staff did, and now you. I thought that Roland Robinson was sky high above me and still do. It is the first time the aboriginal as to his ages of culture and what that gives of and to a people, has been presented. My letter[5] in Tuesday's 'Herald' is an unintentional P.S. to 'The Swan-Men', even if on a different subject. I have not yet seen 'The Feathered Serpent',[6] but the criticism in the Daily Tel. did mean understanding. Especially the quotation re the naming of everything in the Australian scene. That wide, inclusive and universal naming is a testimony to the past population that was here when the white men came, and also to its antiquity and continuity. As a parallel, small town and scattered populations do not number the houses in their roads and streets. Only increased and *settled* populations do that.

Nearly blind today, and half dead. Television. I was rung in the

[1] See note to letter, 5 August 1896.
[2] A. H. Chisholm.
[3] Mary's poem 'Yea and Nay', *S.M.H.*, 5 January 1957. It was printed just above Roland Robinson's 'The Swan-Men', a poem based on an Aboriginal myth.
[4] J. M. D. Pringle.
[5] Mary's letter 'Aborigines: Keepers of History' told of Aboriginal accounts of volcanic upheavals and the formation of Mount Gambier.
[6] *The Feathered Serpent*, a collection of Aboriginal myths and rituals, by Roland Robinson, was reviewed in *Daily Telegraph*, 5 January 1957.

morning yesterday to ask wd. I sit. Did you ever see a donkey after
a carrot? That's me (grammar or not) for anything unknown to me.
It was for a three minute T.V. appearance, I thought about half an
hour wd. do it. It took three hours—I got a grand-nephew and niece
into it, and had to go on for their sakes. Young and attractive looking
they shd come out well; and what an experience for them! They had
come in quite by accident.

You say we, you and I, are romantic. That looks like it. I agree
with your criticism of most of to-day's poetry, whether real or so-called.
It reads like the children of old parents—You can disentangle the
metaphor by visible racial experience. There is one good new voice
in story and verse; Mena Abdullah. As to R.R. I told him (after he
had in a small way begun it) to use the aboriginal locutions always
in his stories, to give them individuality and set a line for later comers.
Practice and his ear will establish a basic perhaps for a legitimate form
or dialect. This we should have had long ago. What about you? You
are literature in yourself more than he is and if begun, it shd. be good,
however small, and not cheap. The *Hoosier*[1] dialect was never cheap.
My grateful thanks to you Bob, and the Best of New Years to all of
you.

To T. Inglis Moore

Kings Cross
Dear Tom,   12 January 1957

I have just read your critical article[2] on the Macartney–Morris Miller
anthology. What a piece of writing! The subject did not hold or interest
me but the *writing did*. The anvil has done its work there. To be adequate
as English is not enough; not for you. Now you have put aside the
ease of the early years for the ease of handled steel. Polish is not enough,
nor is lovely language. The delight of these passes with the changes
in times and language. Only scholars and students read Francis
Thompson and Swinburne[3] now. Yet they are still giants—or the latter
is. And he is a giant not for the beauty of his lines but for what is
in them. So I am delighted with this work of yours in 'Southerly'.

My one eye has to be nursed (don't mention that, please! I don't
want to have it forced on my attention any more than I can help) so
my reading is mostly hop-skip-and-a-jump, but this I could not lay
down till it was finished. I hope your arthritis is reduced, at least—I

---

[1] See note to letter, 23 February 1956.
[2] T. Inglis Moore's 'Catalogue and Commentary', *Southerly* 3 (1956) discussed the
E. Morris Miller and F. T. Macartney bibliographical work, *Australian Literature*, 1956.
[3] Algernon Charles Swinburne.

mean the pain; and I hope you will not forget the 'ancient-needle treatment' of China...

For a change of subject, I had yesterday a letter from a woman asking had I read her book on the origin of world races, written on evidence she had received from *Mars*! So after that what are you and I!

All good to you and yours—

To C. B. Christesen

Dear Mr. Christesen,

Kings Cross
27 January 1957

What an issue of 'Meanjin'![1] That story of David Martin's[2] is outstanding. It reads as if really Russian; quality, manner, presentment—everything. And then Professor Oliphant.[3] What English! The vowels turn in such a way one asks, Is he a poet? His grandmother, the Scottish novelist as you probably know, wrote like that. It was in the 70s I read her. I forget the novels but I remember the English. Then there is the Baxter[4] poem.

But you always give us something beyond the reach-out of our other magazines; sometimes our own, sometimes the strong meat of overseas. Papers & writers do not mind being loud, but they do seem to be afraid of being strong. There is loudness everywhere, now, & so little for it.

Well, you can write or feel all this for yourself, so no more.

Good luck to the magazine, & still more to your holiday (?) to Europe...

Again all good wishes to you & yours.

To David Martin

My dear David Martin,

Kings Cross
28 January 1957

What a story![5] 'The Russian' in this issue of 'Meanjin', and what a number of the Magazine! Professor Oliphant's 'Men and Knowledge', your story and James Baxter's (2) and the verse (his)...

[1] Vol. 15, no. 4 (1956).
[2] 'The Russian'.
[3] Marcus (later Sir Mark) Oliphant.
[4] 'The Race-Book Seller and the Self-Killed Girl'. James Baxter also had two stories in this issue of *Meanjin*: 'The Town Under the Sea' and 'Walking up Castle Street'.
[5] See notes to letter, 27 January 1957 for the 'story' and for the other items from *Meanjin* 15, no. 4 (1956).

'Meanjin' always gives something none of the other magazines give—sometimes our own, sometimes of other lands. It stands out in this.

I have to thank Richenda[1] (I have the name right this time!) for remembering me at Christmas time. And in this letter are my thanks and reply to her. Tomorrow I have to talk for 3 minutes over T.V. Hope I don't founder! Always before I have had a note or two to keep me safe. Here, I suppose, there is nothing.

Had a letter from Eric Lambert, in London again. In his 'Five Bright Stars',[2] he took the idea of Angus Tallon from father's cousin Angus (?) Cameron of Clun-es (his station) pronounced in the then Scottish way)—I recognized him and asked if I were not right. I was.

He says he has a new novel, 'Watermen',[3] just out, the draft of another on his travel in Malaya and the first chapters of a third 'which is an attempt to put the Hungarian situation' as it really was, with 'so many innocent people' caught up in it, one side or the other. He says the work is very difficult as he is still too full of grief over it, and not objective enough—

Every good to you all—

To Peter McGregor

Kings Cross
1 February 195⁻

Dear Mr. McGregor—

Clan Alpini! Those were the Kings of Scotland. (I couldn't remember the name when you were here).

This is to thank you for your letter wh. came a while ago. And first—I have to apologize for not recognizing anyone at the studio.[4] My eyes, of course. But interesting!! Peter Dawson whom I had not seen for 20 years or more, Dr. Currey,[5] ditto, Janet[6] (her name has just gone) with whose grandmother I had been a fellow pupil teacher and whose g.g.m. always claimed to have taught me music (she still played in her 80's). Janet is on your TV staff and is writing children's stories between times.

But the oldest friend, Dr. Currey brought, not knowing I wd. be in the session. It was the ex-convict's hat—wh. weighed about 12 pounds

---

[1] David Martin's wife.
[2] *Five Bright Stars*, 1954.
[3] *Watermen*, 1956.
[4] Mary refers to a television programme, 'Picture Page', in which she participated. It was part of the first Australia Day television programme after the introduction of television.
[5] C. H. Currey.
[6] Janet Ashworth.

when I first saw it in 1872 on the maker and wearer's head; the hat or helmet was made from the big knob of a eucalyptus tree. Talking to the wearer then, father asked didn't he feel it heavy—he said *he had* but the muscles of his neck had strengthened, and did not feel it now. But if he wore an ordinary hat, he caught cold. The next time I saw that hat was in 1923 or thereabouts, stuck on a stump in the sun, the wind and the rain! 'We don't want it' said the then owners and gave it to me. And the third time I saw it was last Tuesday night—and what an old friend it seemed.

I was so nervous over the TV broadcast for fear I should fail and let you down, that your letter comes like balm to the soul. And to think your mother saw it! We are old acquaintances now as a consequence. But what an experience it was to me and what a bewilderment. I shall be able to face lions after it—

I want to thank everybody for kindness and helping my stumbling mind and feet—and you for arranging it all.

Yours sincerely and thankfully,

To R. D. FitzGerald

Dear Bob—

Kings Cross
22 March 1957

You are always so generous. You (and Hugh McCrae) saw value in my work when no one else did. And what an analysis—or shd. I say evaluation. (Dorothy Catts to talk over her King O'Malley book[1]— which is a *big* thing. Big really; not as to size.) What a phrase; 'For the sake of spoiling silence': who else wd. have thought of it?

I am so easily tired; the old lady ain't what she was! So will end with a word about the Dobell portrait[2]—not yet finished. He brought me the 'plot'—or am I wrong? The first thing that hit me was the sense of Power. I felt it before I saw the features *as* features. The second thing was that it had no connection with the conventional (painting). It stands alone. He is coming in two or three weeks to do the hands. I gave it (when it comes to me) to Canberra, but the right of exhibition is reserved to him, and I hope it may go to Paris, even if it has to be borrowed from Canberra.

This morning 'The Poetry of Australia'[3] came to me, from Imogen Whyse and her poetry circle. Beautifully got up, and worth getting

---

[1] *King O'Malley: Man and Statesman*, 1957. Mary wrote the Introduction to the biography and wrote also to the *Daily Telegraph* about the book, 10 October 1957.
[2] See note to letter, 7 September 1955.
[3] *The Poetry of Australia*, the first anthology of the Poetry Society of Australia was jointly edited by Imogen Whyse and Wesley Milgate.

if only for two small Hart-Smith 'prisms'. Dear kind Bob—again thank you—not only for now, but for long and long before now.

To Constance Robertson

Dear Connie,

Kings Cross
28 July 1957

I hope you have come back from your travels with the world at your feet. I noted at once the sure hand on the 'Herald' women's section and told Mr. Pringle[1] so. I asked him, 'What is it that jumps up from the page and says I and the writer are one!' (again and again that has puzzled me).

At the moment I want you to give a paragraph to the *Aboriginal Australian Fellowship* of which the Hon. Sec. is Mrs. McIlrath, 11th Floor, 247 George Street to provide money for winter clothes for the needy aborigines. The A.A. Fellowship is holding a Fair or Jumble Sale (Not sure of the name) and should be helped. I am the Patron and asked for an aboriginal name for the word as I hate 'patron'.

To Douglas Stewart

Dear Douglass,

Kings Cross
Après mid-night
8 August 1957

(I am always in trouble over the one s or two in your way of spelling your name: having been stuck in childhood on the Gaelic Dhu glas of my father's tongue). Will you use enclosed *tu wanst* if you can? The enclosed cutting from the 'Tribune' may start others before you can be first.

I say 'first' because you can extend what I have written—from the 'Bulletin' last old man and the files.

You have a grand niece of mine at the office. She is my brother Hugh's grand daughter, & ditto of 'The Browns of the Rivers' published by her cousin, Ken Barrett, some months ago in the 'Bulletin'. Her mother's uncle, Frank Brown, wrote a book of Bush Ballads[2] (she may know the name) wh. is well thought of. Another uncle was an entomologist, while I added further back ancestry, in the 'Bulletin', to Ken Barrett's article: which was a good one. She (my g.niece) rejoices in the very *Scottish* name of Maureen Gallagher! As old as Cameron no doubt, but what a yoke-fellow.

[1] J. M. D. Pringle.
[2] Probably *Songs of the Plains*, 1934.

As 'Bulletin' office history: you had my uncle James Beattie's daughter, Nellie, on the 'Mirror' for years, & later *her* niece was in the 'Bulletin' Office—Nellie's sister is Mrs. Reg MacDonald, Managing Director of the Brisbane 'Telegraph' (*He* wrote a book.)

A Family Tree is well-known, but a Press Family Tree is just as important (or more) to the history of a country *and* a journal. So here it is. Also it is time that a few of today's writers began to boast that their ancestors were on the 'Bulletin'! (How Bill Fitz Henry[1] wd. have loved that.)

All good wishes,

To William Bluett

Kings Cross
5 September 1957

My dear Billy Bluett,

I have to thank you for two things. One the mass of daffodils just come, and for your letter in defence of the aboriginal over bush fires & erosion in the Snowy Mountains water shed. The aboriginals it was who taught the early white *not* to start bush fires! Coming from lands where they never saw a bush fire they never thought of them as dangerous unless they were near the early settlements. Then, if one started, they called on the blacks to put it out by the blacks' way—of fighting it with small curtailing fires, lit ahead of it. I have helped them do this when a child. So I *know*.

I have done some writing now & then for the Daily papers, but there are so many callers who want to know this, that, & the other thing about the past, or lives of other writers! Just had a priest in about Henry Lawson. He is a Father Maher, of Mudgee, who bought land, & is having a replica of the house where Henry Lawson was born, built there, to be a passing refuge for poor women with children till they can get help; & this no matter what their creed. A pity all the Churches wd. not do the same.

Had to stop as John Farrell's daughter, Olive, came in.

My dear Billy, no use asking about your eyes unless it is cataract. An eye surgeon lately told me he had operated successfully on a woman of 90 for cataract. A bit better than when, a few years ago, 60 was the limit!

It is good that you still have 'the eyes of the mind'—& memory. But how few are left now of those who went to school with you & my brothers!

All good to you old & dear friend.

[1] W. E. Fitz Henry.

Mr. I. Turner
The Australasian Book Society

Kings Cross
23 September 1957

Dear Mr Turner,
The presentation of the Wm Dobell portrait[1] to me, on Friday, was, the President said, the 'biggest crowd they had had in the National Gallery at a function'. (The 'Daily Tel'. said there were 1,000 people). In speaking I mentioned the A.B.S. though a new and young publishing house, as the first (and therefore the pioneer) to do such a thing as they had done, and said I hoped it would give a lead to others to do the same. I went on to say that there was no National portrait of 'G.R.' (Mr Robertson of A and R) or of J. F. Archibald, yet that, in their time, no two men had done more for Australian art and literature than these two men.

In my thanks at the beginning of the function, I said I thanked (1) the Australasian Book Society for having done me the honour of commissioning Mr Dobell to paint my portrait, (2) Mr Dobell, whose work wd. be recognized anywhere in Europe, for painting it, and (3) Sir John Northcott for presenting it . . .

What I want to say, now, is what you will say and do:—that it is the A.B.S. wh. made the painting possible, Mr Dobell who did it, and that in presenting the portrait as a gift to the nation, I do it in the name of the A.B.S. which made it possible! (Words to that effect, only better put.) I want the A.B.S. to be regarded as the primary giver even if the public did subscribe, as, if it did not, the Society had taken the responsibility of it. I think it was a great thing for a young house to do—the strong and long established Houses (and the 'Bulletin') not having done such a thing, either for Art, Literature or the Nation . . . No more for the moment except my grateful and doubly grateful thanks—

Mrs. E. M. Colman,
Queanbeyan

Kings Cross
24 September 1957

Dear Mrs. Colman,[2]
Your very honest and fiery letter this morning. Thank you for your championship of me. But there are two sides to portraiture. One shows

[1] See note to letter, 7 September 1955.
[2] This correspondent appears to have been Elsie Marion Colman of 'Kawaree', Tharwa Road, Queanbeyan. She wrote several letters to Mary, criticizing the Dobell portrait because she felt that Mary had been belittled by it. Mary attempts, in this and other letters, to reassure her. Mrs Colman's son, G. A. Colman, a prominent citizen of Canberra, supplied the above details.

the features and not the character, the other shows the character as the main thing, and the features as less important. And (though the face is only a little like mine) it is me. All my relatives and friends say so. When Mr. Dobell was given the commission to paint my portrait, everyone knew his way of painting. No one was blind to it. The painting (as such) is outstanding. I was told yesterday that if I had not (from the first) given it to the nation (Canberra Gallery) I could have put a reserve on it of several thousands at auction, and got it. But of course I could not keep or sell it. And the more valuable the better for Australia and her people.

At the same time your letter warmed my heart; it was so open and there was no personal malice in it. Yours sincerely,

Did you know that the Aboriginal pronunciation of Queanbeyan was Que/*an Be* an (short 'an')

To Colin Simpson

Dear Colin Simpson,

Kings Cross
10 October 1957

Your 'Adam with Arrows'[1] came yesterday with its heavenly inscription—for which bless you back again.

Of course I darted at it like a woodpecker, a kingfisher, or what you like, just to get the taste of it, and it struck me that you had got right away from the iron-clad limits (mostly galvanized iron) of the radio demand.

The language is limber, more fluid, leaps more in the sun—what you will. In other words that it was written for the joy of writing, rather than as something to be done.

You wrote New Guinea and its people before they were skeletons, dried flesh and fragments. If only Australia had been written at the same full period.

Your bodies on a platform—I have seen our blacks on a platform, not sitting (they sat in trees or between logs though) but lying down, their weapons with them and four carved totem poles or uprights at each corner to guard them, and a tiny handful of slow burning sticks under them to make the fat run and the body dry—sometimes there was a canopy above the body to keep the birds away—sometimes it was just a covering of bushes over the face & the lower part of the body.

... 'This is the last brave land'. Man alive what a back-look is

[1] *Adam With Arrows*, 1953, carried no printed inscription to Mary. Colin Simpson's personal inscription is here referred to.

carried in those words! And behind them what a cry of grief and things lost . . .

The Editor, Kings Cross
Daily Telegraph. *12 October 1957*

Sir,
You have just published two letters[1] dealing with the portrait of me which was commissioned by the Australasian Book Society and painted by William Dobell.
    The second letter moved me very much.
    But to this writer and to all others for or against this work, may I say:
    It is the painter, not the sitter, who makes the great work.
    In my opinion, this painting is one which time will increasingly acclaim and the future history of Australian art be thankful for.
    I repeat that it is the painter and not the sitter who really counts.
    The great galleries of the world prove this.

As an example take 'The Last Supper' by da Vinci. Who cares tuppence for the sitters. You do not even ask their names or what they were.
I will mention only one other thing here.
    Of course I know that measured by the calipers, this portrait calls for adverse criticism.
    But there is another aspect by which to judge portraiture. No one is born without ancestors.
    At my first sight of this portrait, for one second I saw my father looking at me.
    Then the looker disappeared, and the painting was there.
    After the unveiling a lady who I had not earlier known, came to see me.
    She said 'When I put my hand over the lower part of the face the upper part was my grandmother Mackinnon'.
    To emphasize her point she said this twice.
    Her grandmother Mackinnon was my father's niece and my first-cousin.
    If a portrait carried in it the likeness to one's own people, however little, and whom the painter has never seen that is real portraiture.
    If it does not do this it is merely camera.
    Our ancestors in us are not there.
    I think I am the first to put forth this theory.

[1] The letters were published in the newspaper on 9 and 12 October 1957. This letter of Mary's was published as a feature article, 16 October 1957.

Mr. I. Turner,   *Kings Cross*
The Australasian Book Society   *18 October 1957*

Dear Mr Turner,
Thank you for this morning's letter, and you must have heard in Melbourne the sighs of relief in that 'Thank you'! The last thing I want to do is to handle the portrait. It has been your (the A.B.S.) work, and if any publicity comes from it you should have it. I *want* you to *have it* and if any authority for this from me is needed, here it is. I have said this earlier to Grace Bardsley, and even drafted her a letter to this effect (and more) to be signed and sent on to you. The 'more' is that I wd. like (and want) the A.B.S. to be a more or less Trustee to see that the portrait does not go to a cellar at any time after it is handed over to the Commonwealth. Can the A.B.S. and will (or would) it do this?

    I asked Grace to insure the portrait. She suggested Lloyds, and when done I said I wd. send the necessary cheque for the insurance.

    One other thing: my old town, WAGGA WAGGA, shd. see the portrait. The Head of the Teachers' College, Mr. Blakemore, has asked for it for the college wh., in a way, could include the town. But the City Council shd. be the responsible body.

    As to the portrait itself: I have had every sort of letter for and against, and before it was unveiled I was for a whole week battered by critics, Radio people and others trying to make me say or inadvertently slip an adverse *quarter of a word*. But I beat them! As one radio man said, 'In all the years I have been doing this, you are the first and only one who has beaten me.'

    In conclusion I enclose my first letter[1] on the subject. The 'Daily Telegraph' did me a singular honour. For the first time in its history a correspondent's letter was made a feature article.

    All good wishes and my grateful thanks to you and the A.B.S.

To William Bluett

                                                               Kings Cross
Dear Billy Bluett,   *20 October 1957*

. . . My portrait by William Dobell[2] has for weeks been the talk of Sydney, and called everything from 'a monstrosity' to 'wonderful'. It is to go to Melbourne next month. I was told artists & others were offering to pay £1 a head to see it privately so that they could study

---
[1] The letter of 12 October 1957.
[2] See note to letter, 7 September 1955.

it. Am wondering if it is true. I look like something out of the Middle Ages, but the painting is alive, and that is the important thing. I am giving it, after it goes round to Newcastle, Melbourne & Wagga Wagga, to the Nation—at Canberra. But with this letter I am enclosing the 'Bulletin' criticism,[1] which you need not return, as. I have other copies. I wrote a letter[2] to the 'Daily Telegraph' giving my point of view. David McNicoll[3] sent a photographer to take me for it, & made it really a feature article.[4] It is the first letter ever sent to the Telegraph, to be so treated in all its history. I tell you that I felt somebody! I gave a new point of view to portrait painters. It is that, to be a true portrait, ancestry must show much or little; or it is only camera work. I believe all Sydney (artistically) is talking of it. This portrait is not the usual 'likeness' but it has ancestors in it—father & his great uncle painted by Raeburn[5] & a first cousin . . .

Old age is telling on me, in lots of ways, sight being one. No use talking about it, but I have a vision of myself taking up trout fishing & living in your *barracks*!

No more, my dear old friend. I think of you so often & what a dreadful thing your loss of sight is to you. But how lucky to have your family!

Every good to you.

To Stephen Murray-Smith

Dear Mr. Murray-Smith

Kings Cross
1 November 1957

Your letter this morning about the Russian Magazine (wh. I leave you to spell,): In case you want a copy for someone else, I can send it back, as one came to me last week from Moscow—to my great bewilderment for I don't know even one word of Russian. My thanks to you for presenting me there! I discovered enough to see the portrait and to realize that some of my verse had been translated. A naturalized Russian is coming one day next week to tell me more about it. Now I find you are the angel Gabriel who has raised me to the height of what is so important and notable a magazine. But how glad I am that you write for it! This is the first step in internationalism. Thousands and millions read, but only a few meet—so the pen is mightier than the (traveller's) foot.

[1] *Bulletin*, 2 October 1957.
[2] See letter, 12 October 1957.
[3] Editor of *Daily Telegraph*.
[4] *Daily Telegraph*, 16 October 1957.
[5] Sir Henry Raeburn.

I expect you will presently have the Dobell portrait[1] in Melbourne. I am told Melbourne is already waiting to consider intellectual civil war over it.

I am a desperately tired old woman, but have let a sculptor, Mr. Lyall Randolph, come 'to look' at me for a bust he had begun on his own initiative. The bust has the features but that is all, Dobell's portrait is me without the features—mouth and chin. But what deep and intense painting has gone into it! . . .

All good wishes and thank you a thousand times—

Mrs E. M. Colman,   Kings Cross
Queanbeyan,   7 November 1957

Dear Mrs. Colman,[2]

An instant line to thank you for your most beautiful roses, which have just come. I at once stood them on their heads in water to give them a good drink after their journey. I have kept violets fresh over a week by that method and revived half dead other flowers. But I have found standing them in boiling water and leaving it to get cold is best in winter. But perhaps you know all this. Or is it only people who have no gardens need to know it?

My time is eaten up by other people so I am writing at a gallop. People come from all parts of Australia. However if I can help them, while I can, it is well and good. I used to get quite a lot of bee-in-their-bonnet people. Not so many now. But one said she was a granddaughter of Queen Victoria; that Q.V. had left her, by will, £10,000,000, and that she had written to King George to say she knew times were bad in England and she would only take £1,000,000—which is my odd rose for yours! In haste,

To A. H. Chisholm

Kings Cross
My dear, dear Alec,   15 December 1957

The first dear is for your card (and an earlier presscutting), but the double dear is for the way you spoke up for the black swans.[3] The

---

[1] See note to letter, 7 September 1955.
[2] See note to letter, 24 September 1957.
[3] Swans were much loved by Mary. They were celebrated in many of her poems and her 1930 volume of poems was entitled *The Wild Swan*. As a child she had listened and watched as the swans, compelled by Nature's rhythm, left the swamps and billabongs of the Murrumbidgee on their seasonal migration. As this letter shows, the memory of the swans brings to her heart both joy and pain but the dominant feeling is one of protest at the careless ravaging of natural beauty and the needless extermination of bird and animal life that have accompanied Man's march over the land.

swan-hopping of the 70s and 80s was bad enough, when the swans had open country and half Australia. But today, when tens take the place of thousands and they have no places of their own, to talk of having them proclaimed for destruction is like wanting to put out the stars of the Southern Cross. Fishermen, as a class, are not dependent on the waters where swans feed for a living. We don't proclaim quails because they eat wheat! The news of the demand went through my heart like a spear. I will give my mite for a petition against it if one should be thought of and if this letter or anything in it is of use, *Use it*. The swans of Australia need our defence—and we should give it.

All good to you in this, and in everything.

To George Mackaness

Kings Cross
28 December 1957

Dear George (Alice and Joan),[1]

Your card just came, and I hasten to say thank you. The post brought me a card from William Dobell, with writing on it so fine, a hair would be like a cable to it.

Had a letter from a friend to say that someone lecturing on Australian Literature in Moscow (by invitation and all expenses paid by Moscow), had written her that apart from Henry Lawson, the other Australian writers translated in Moscow were Katharine Susannah Prichard, Mary Gilmore and John Morrison—Stephen Murray-Smith had 4 pages about me in the leading Literature Russian Magazine—which was sent me from Moscow. In Russian of course, of which I do not know even a letter, let alone a word. After about two months I found a Miss Wheatley, in a foreign literature book shop, who translated it for me. China also has given me a place, but a small one by comparison. And do I feel proud!!!

Olaf Ruhen did a big thing in his 'Naked Under Capricorn',[2] I felt every line of it. I don't know of which he has most: the sense of drama or of character. He has both, and notably also he is historically true, and *that* counts.

Am going down hill of course, a bit hard of hearing ever since I had polio five years ago next February—which also left trouble in walking. But I can still chase or appreciate an idea. For which I am duly thankful. With all my warmest wishes for the New Year to you all,

[1] Wife and daughter of George Mackaness.
[2] *Naked Under Capricorn*, 1958.

To William Bluett

Dear Billy Bluett,

Kings Cross
8 February 1958

What a letter! &, except for a few words that have to be looked at twice, what readable writing. About your memoirs—recollections—what about a tape recorder for you to talk into? I think it is Elyne Mitchell (or someone up her way) writes all her later books that way. But I cannot help thinking what patience you must have taken to write so long a letter in letters you could not see but which I, or anyone, could read. I shall put this letter with my collection because of its historic value, in case you do not get a recorder for your own use. You might perhaps rent one.

I wish I had tried one out years ago. Now I am too near the end, & too tired, to bother.

Three old friends gone almost together—Hugh McCrae, Mary Hughes[1] & now Ethel Turner.

I had the sudden & unexpected arrival yesterday of Len Fox & his wife (Mona Brand) after two years in Vietnam. They only arrived from Hong Kong on Saturday. Like most other people I had (when not thinking,) the vague idea that the Vietnamese were a half wild forest people. Now I know they write poetry, paint, do sculpture, live in up-to-date cities, and their wives wear Paris fashions. What eyes travel gives people! Mona Fox (née Brand) writes plays. Len paints, writes, & is a journalist. His Aunt was Mrs. Phillips-Fox, she & her husband both painters.

I saw your picture in the papers where you more or less kissed the Queen Mother's hand! Life and Australian history has come a long way since you sat on a form (good old *cedar*,) in the Gurwood Street Public School at Wagga Wagga.

The same for me, & that old school, when under Miss Galloway as Head Mistress. A Peter Durie grand-daughter years ago topped the score in the Uni. for Mathematics. Now I think she is an elderly woman doctor at the Royal North Shore Hosp. Miss Galloway remained unmarried. But she had nieces, one of whom wrote to me years ago.

Well this is hoping your health is not a trouble, & all goes well with you.

Affectionately, old friend.

---

[1] Dame Mary Hughes, widow of W. M. Hughes, died in 1958 aged 83.

To Angus & Robertson

Dear Angus & Robertson's,

Kings Cross
18 February 1958

Per George Ferguson (GRII and for GRI[1] who would want it)
Not just this member of the Firm, or that, for he belonged to every book and shelf of being—I enclose my cheque for £5 to start a memorial scholarship to Hugh McCrae—I have just read the news.

You will know how and what to do to start it.

Only a fortnight, or less, ago, I wrote in your care, my last letter to him, not knowing the end was so near. In that letter, after reading the Hugh McCrae and the Brennan numbers of 'Southerly'[2] I told him he was greater than and would outlive Brennan. Brennan is dated; he wrote from and of himself even if (as I told Norman Lindsay,) he wrote in thunder. Hugh McCrae threw a wider net and is not dated, for he wrote life, not himself. Consider his poetry. He touched life at every point. Things that people (and critics) took as incidental, had the deep of life behind them. (Thank God I told him that years ago!)

I am sending this to you, George, because the tradition of the past and its fellowships are in you, and know you will respond.

I write my cheque now.

To George Ferguson

Dear G.R.II,[3]

Kings Cross
9 March 1958

Time I answered your letter and acknowledged return of cheque[4]—I thought, afterwards, that I had been too impulsive. For one thing you have the Chair of Australian Literature on your mind, next, when that comes into being, bursaries, etc. can then be established for it and named. Hugh might be first though I am half-a-mind thinking old Professor Badham (who established the Bursaries and knew literature) should be first.

Had this from Moscow a few weeks ago:

'Foreign Literature' Magazine is approaching the most prominent writers, artists and other cultural workers of various countries of the world with the following questionnaire:
1. What are you working on at present?
2. What are your plans for the nearest future?'. . .!

---

[1] George Robertson is GRI and his grandson George Ferguson GRII.
[2] *Southerly* featuring Hugh McCrae was 3 (1956) and that on Brennan was 4 (1949).
[3] Mary's abbreviation for the grandson of George Robertson.
[4] See letter, 18 February 1958.

An answer was requested at the earliest convenience.

The Magazine must be going to make some feature or record of work in other countries.

Tomorrow I am taking Ernestine Hill to St. Vincent's Private Hospital to meet Mr. Dobell. I told him I hoped he would want to paint her. They have never met but her boy, Bob, was in his art class when at College. (She comes to me after her appointment with A. & R.)

As to A. H. Chisholm, he must feel like a mile diameter sputnik[1] with two balloons attached. (One or two?)

May the Auld Hoose be the first one established beyond the moon.

To Vance Palmer

Dear Vance Palmer,

Kings Cross
7 April 1958

Just now I read your 'Mary Gilmore' in 'Hemisphere',[2] and I am astounded. It is as close and inclusive a piece of work as William Dobell's portrait.[3] I had looked at it before. But this time I really read it and with new eyes, as I was about to send it to the Editor of Foreign Literature, Moscow and to Rewi Alley in China . . .

This writing of yours seems as far from being the dimensional me as Dobell's painting. I am the stone dropped in the pond. The waves are there but I am not the waves. You and the painter look at the waves. The waves belong as much, or more, to the water as to the stone.

But in between moments of sanity, am I pleased! am I delighted. I stand off and look at the waves—with perhaps the sunset on them—on me and them, and a good thing for me, I remember I am the stone.

Well this is to thank you and Nettie for all you have been (and done for me) to Australia. What a national centre your house has been. Its waves wash the whole round of Australia.

If you get the 'Tribune'[4] you will have seen what I wrote of Hugh McCrae. I sent the cutting to Honey.[5] She wrote back saying she used to read my letters, when he was ill, to her father, and that he loved them. How I wish I had written more!

About the best thing in the Catholic Church is Purgatory. Purgatory gives you a chance to make up to people for what you didn't do or did unkindly in their life time. We poor wretches haven't a chance of that.

---

[1] The name given to a series of Russian space satellites much in the news in the late 1950s.
[2] *Hemisphere* 2, 3 (March 1958).
[3] See note to letter, 7 September 1955.
[4] *Tribune*, 26 February 1958, p. 7.
[5] McCrae's daughter, Lady Cowper, wife of Sir Norman Cowper.

Dobell is a mended man. He has come up out of the pit and his work is ahead of him again. He hopes shortly to be out of hospital. I took Ernestine Hill . . . as I hope he would like to paint her. He may but I am afraid not: yet she has the face and the look that should attract him or any below-the-surface painter. She has been nervously ill a long time but is at last able to finish one of three half written books—or she hopes so—

My grateful thanks to you—

To H. M. Green

Dear H. M. Green,

Kings Cross
12 April 1958

No mistake about who *that* means! I am so pleased as a reader, and so much impressed as a thinker, by your verse, 'God and the Child of Man'.[1] If the churches would cease their shallow idolatry which they call worship, and think as you have thought, they would lead the world. Bernard O'Dowd *saw* depths but wrote from the surface. You have *lived* your depths, or from the deep have written. Australia moves forward in the world in such writing. As to 'Southerly'[2] I think this is the best issue we have ever had.

I have forgotten if you are in Toowoomba or in Brisbane—perhaps even elsewhere. But if ever you go to Brisbane *do go* to see my friend Mrs. Edward Kuhn, Maria Kuhn, the sculptor. And you might see Reg MacDonald[3] of the 'Telegraph'. His wife is my first cousin or his ancestors and mine belonged in the past. Reg wrote one book during or after last war. You will be sorry to hear that Wm. Dobell (who is our only poet and creator in painting) has been very ill. Operation; but is really mending. 50 years of work are before him. Australia needs such men as he in painting—people who see (or go) beyond the leg-chains of convention. He shocked convention in my portrait,[4] but in your verse you don't, because you stand above it.

Every good wish

[1] Published in *Southerly* 4, 18 (1957).
[2] This particular number of *Southerly* 4, 18 (1957) contained verse and stories by Nancy Cato, Dal Stivens, Colin Thiele, Francis Webb, Geoffrey Dutton, Nan McDonald, Frank Moorhouse, Bruce Beaver, Ray Mathew, R. G. Howarth. There were critical articles by S. E. Lee, P. K. Elkin, H. J. Oliver, John Thompson and Charles Higham.
[3] Walter Reginald MacDonald.
[4] See note to letter, 7 September 1955.

To T. Inglis Moore

Dear Tom,

Kings Cross
17 November 1958

I am writing in a state of gratitude and astonishment. I first read your Judith Wright in 'Meanjin'.[1] So much absorbed in Judith Wright. as you *presented* her, that I only now, re-reading the article, have found you made more than one comparison and reference to me. It is a tribute to your writing—because it *was* your writing—that swallowed me up like that! And the re-reading did not lessen the first effect of the writing. It is powerful but the power does not dominate the beauty of the English. It is there all the time but runs under and through. I can't think that anyone else has written anything as good. Either power, thought (as such) or intent has been dominant. But here is movement without spur or whip. It moves from within and makes its own being as a whole—or a fact in being. (That sounds silly, but I can't find my right word, and I want to finish this and post it.

And having interpolated all that I am done. The heat has gone out of the iron.)

But you have done a beautiful piece of creative work, and, as I said before, I don't know anyone else who has equalled it. Yet with the kind of form and narrowed verse that is Judith Wright you could have done a pillar of salt in a desert—a pillar enduring and remarkable, but against wh. no one ever wanted to lean. Instead you have given warmth to cold light. Or, thinking of the range of allusion, you have burned wood from a forest instead of just turning on the gas. I thank you for this but how grateful I am for what you have done for me.

To George Ferguson

My dear G.R.II,[2]

Kings Cross
12 December 1958

On my special 60 year old paper which very few get, hoping to spin it out—this is for you, for the past, for the present of Angus & Robertson, and for A. H. Chisholm, to wish two dear and very dear friends, all that life can give them. So often I feel like O. W. Holmes 'lost leaf', or the one lone tree after a place has been cleared. But when I think of A. & R. I feel as if I am still part of a forest—*the* forest, a *real* forest. May that family and that forest which you keep going never die out, for you are an integral part of Australia. 'The coin outlasts Tiberius.'

The same with literature. Literature gives identity to a country and pedigree to a people—may the season give you all you wish.

[1] 'The Quest of Judith Wright', *Meanjin* 3 (1958).
[2] Her abbreviation for the grandson of George Robertson.

To C. B. Christesen

Dear Clem Christesen (which includes 'Meanjin')

Kings Cross
19 December 1958

Thank you for your card & the gift of 'Meanjin' for next year. If any verse *worthwhile* comes along you shall have it but I am afraid that at 93½ (don't forget the half) the harp strings are rusted—perhaps even broken.

You certainly get out a worthwhile magazine, & what an absence of the sentimental!—it mars so much of our other writings.

The Seasons Greetings back again—with 'twice as more' for the New Year.

To Rene Foster

Dear Rene,

Kings Cross
29 December 1958

Thank you for calling me friend—And indeed we have long, long remembrance of friendship between us. But you have done infinitely more for me, in your reviews & notices, than I could ever do for you.

I feel for you in your waiting grief over your mother. Nothing one can say makes any difference there, and nothing is sadder than that long wait at the end. *My* prayer is that I go out suddenly. It would be kind to me and to every one else.

The polio I had five years ago is still my enemy. It makes walking a slow & heavy thing instead of the joy it once was. However the mind (though not so much the memory for names) still steps out, & what a pleasure that is!

My grandson is Jackarooing on a 1,000,000 acre station near Charleville (Queensland). Their drought has broken—after over 30,000 sheep had died. (So much for monopoly instead of closer settlement!)

No more, my dear, except to give you the formal New Year's wish, & to double it as the way *you* would wish—Affectionately,

To Rene Foster

Dear Rene,

Kings Cross
25 April 1959

... Not feeling top of the tree, but, if no worse, I am hoping I can accept the invitation of the May Day Committee to lead their May Day March next Sunday (in a flower decorated car no less!) I was asked several years ago, twice, but had to refuse being too uncertain of myself. It will be my last public appearance I expect, or my last outing, physically of course; the mind is always outing!

With every good wish,
Yours gratefully and affectionately,

To Colin Roderick

Kings Cross
3 July 1959

Dear Colin,

I thought it was wonderful of you to want to write a 'Profile'[1] of me for my coming birthday; which I take it includes G.R.II[2]—and perhaps A.H.C.[3] along in spirit at least. But now that I have seen the script of the profile I am lost for words to say what I feel. The work is *literature* and the quotations from my verse—the *comprehension* and *apprehension*—show that they could have been written by *you*, had it come your way to do them. I can't tell you how grateful I am. I can't find words to thank you. You have put my life into my own verse; you have made it tell *me*—rebuild me—and not as a matter of events, but as my inner self. I could not have done it because I do not know myself either as an entity or as an influence.

You will do great work for Australia before you are done. And one of the things I hope you will do is write A & R, they and the firm being one identity in G.R.[4] and in G.R.II.

With my grateful thanks,

To Colin Roderick

Kings Cross
3 July 1959

Dear Colin,

Though I wrote my grateful thanks to you earlier there is so much more to include, and that I hope in some part to add to the other letter. One thing is, in your M.G. profile,[5] your saying I was Australia's most religious poet. Apart from 'The Rue Tree'[6] which was intentionally so, it wd never have struck me to say I was definitely religious. Yet when you mentioned it and quoted the witnessing verse, as I looked

---

[1] The Profile by Colin Roderick was published in the Melbourne *Age* Literary Supplement, 15 August 1959, on the eve of Mary's 94th birthday. It was entitled 'Dame Mary Gilmore: Australia's Grand Old Lady of Letters'.
[2] George Ferguson.
[3] A. H. Chisholm.
[4] George Robertson.
[5] See previous letter, 3 July 1959.
[6] *The Rue Tree*, 1931. For comment see W. H. Wilde, *Three Radicals*, 1969.

back I realized that such verse could only come out from a religious innerness. And, it is not a question of measuring by formula, I realize how right you were. The religious is an integral part of my being. Not only integral but essential. I can't define it, I can't put it into words, but I wd be lost without it.

Then there is your power to put an evaluation into a few telling and fully inclusive words. That kind of thing always gives me a sense of being fed. The whole being responds to it. Another thing is your *wide and accurate* knowledge. I have always admired knowledge and accuracy, even as a child. I wd sit all ears and wonder on my father's knee and listen to my elders' talk. They went into a world wider than I knew, but I went with them.

In this profile you went with me as I talked, and what you took for your purpose was *it and accurate*.

Next is the literary value. There is an enduring quality in the English as well as in the manner of writing. You have used today, but not the fashion of today—the non-enduring trimmings that are no more permanent than any other fashion.

But I must end though my gratitude for what you have done goes on and on. There will be a new era of good writing in Australia in the next twenty years. You will see it—and you will be part of it, part of its advance guard.

To Leonard Phillip Fox

Dear Len,

Kings Cross
16 July 1959

You might send this back if you can't use it—

> Henry Lawson
> (A Memory)
>
> 'Poor fellow me!' the old
> Man said, and all his race
> Spoke to the ear the grief
> That marked his face.
>
> 'Poor fellow me!' he said,
> And Lawson, as he heard,
> Caught the tribe's history
> In that sad word.
>
> So for the lost he wrote,
> To set his feelings free,
> Just what the old man said:
> 'Poor fellow me!'
>
> Mary Gilmore.

Note: I remember one day Henry Lawson coming into 'The Worker' office, and telling us how he had just been talking to an old aboriginal who had told him how the white man had robbed and massacred his people. Though born in what were still the aboriginal times (in the 60s) Henry knew nothing about the blacks, and this was his first contact with their story and treatment. He asked me was it true. I said it was, and told him a lot more. Next day (he) came back with the verse 'Trouble Belongit to Mine',[1] another of the old man's sayings. The verse was at once published in 'The Worker'. From then on Henry's sympathy was with the aboriginals—but as a people apart. M.G.

To Stephen Murray-Smith

Dear Mr. Murray-Smith—

Kings Cross
6 August 1959

In regard to my education, I went to school in Wagga Wagga for about 2 years from 1875 to 1877 and then for a short time to a small country school, Downside, out of Wagga Wagga. My real education was home study of lessons set by my father and mother in earlier years—father teaching me my letters when about five, and when, about 8 or 9 he gave me arithmetic generally. I owe my Latin, Algebra and Euclid and History to him and also he helped me, as a pupil teacher, with my French and its *accent*! My mother set and heard me my book-lessons: spelling, syntax, geography, reading and writing. As I was a voracious reader and loved any form of learning I was regarded by everyone as a wonder-child. At Wagga Public School I paid 1/- a week, my brother Hugh 9d, my brother John (afterwards War Corresp. in the Boer and 1914 wars, British Consul in Switzerland and Detroit, and finally Minister Plenipotentiary in Riga) paid 6d and my sister 3d each a week. There was no free, compulsory, secular education then. At 13 I went as unpaid Usher to the Public School at Cootamundra (to my Aunt's husband there, he being the one and only teacher for the school), then to my Uncle, John Beattie at Yerong Creek School, out of Wagga, teaching by day and studying by night. At sixteen I sat for my pupil-teachership and passed highest in all N.S.Wales. Apptd. Pupil teacher in Wagga Wagga. In all, my school days were about 2 years and six months. The rest was personal study. In the Wagga School I had such a name for composition that my slate was always kept to

---

[1] Colin Roderick makes the following comment on this letter.

Lawson wrote it ['Trouble Belongit Mine'] in 1914. Mrs. Byers tried to place it with the *Bulletin*, but it was rejected. It was published in the *Worker*, 31 December 1924—two years after Lawson's death, when his admirers were scratching about for any literary remains to link themselves with Lawson.

show visitors, and once the Mayor and councillors visited the school to hear me read, answer questions and do a composition on a set text.

As a Certificated teacher in later years, I sat for examination in Sydney. I expected IIIC and got IIIA. Three years later sat for IIB and was given IIA. I thought there must be a mistake, wrote the Dept, and IIA was confirmed. I was then interested in the Labor Movement under John Farrell (the poet) and William Lane, and in 1895 resigned from the Education Dept and left for Colonia Cosme[1] (New Australia) in Paraguay, met William A. Gilmore and was married in May 1897. My baby was born in 1898 (August) and in 1890 we went to the Argentine, then to Patagonia (then an Argentine Territory), where I was asked by the British Estancieros to start a movement for Great Britain to annex the Territory. I declined and wrote Lady Jersey to sow the Territory with British Migrants. She said she wd. consider it later as she was then doing it for S.Afr. (but it was too late then). I hope this will suit your purpose.

My literary Educators were my own people, The Bible, John Bunyan, Walter Scott, John Farrell, William Lane, J. F. Archibald (The 'Bulletin') and A. G. Stephens (The 'Bookfellow').

To George Frazer

Dear Dr. Frazer,

Kings Cross
8 October 1959

Since acknowledging your book,[2] I have read it fully, and I am filled with wonder at it as an expression of so many people's questing minds, even if the book is only yours. But we have, so far, had nothing quite as inclusive and yet far ranging as the section 'Poems of Speculation'. I think these especially the first one, 'Multi Dimensional' and 'Egocentre', in that order, stood out for me, as when your book came I had for several years been wandering through the same fields.

As my space in the 'Tribune' is limited I have not yet written a paragraph and made a quotation. But as soon as I can get at it I shall. But I wanted you to know how much I think of your work.

By the way, as a Frazer you shd. be anciently (if no more) related to the Cameron Clan. My father was descended from 'the great Lochiel'.

[1] See letter, 5 August 1896.
[2] *Poems of Life and Time*, 1957.

To C. B. Christesen

My dear Clem Christesen,

Kings Cross
17 January 1960

Your letter came yesterday, & I am still gasping. What an astonishing letter to get. For one thing it clears one thing that R. D. FitzGerald said to me last month, & that was that more than anyone else I was a religious writer—that it went through all my books. I had never thought of such a thing. But when told I could more or less see it could be so.

    A couple of weeks ago I came across forgotten MS. (a number of copies of which I had had made some years ago.) It is a list of things I had done, & is chiefly taken from my page in 'The Worker'.[1] I am sending a more or less dated copy which you can keep. There are two or three copies elsewhere . . . One is at the Mitchell in the M.G. Collection. But yours is better because of the additions, small as they are. Its chief value is that it shows a ranging mind. I have always refused to bother about a biography. Too busy to think of it; and I think the work one does, & can do, is more important . . . In any case there are my diaries, still going on, which will certainly contain me among the other people recorded, you among the number! I don't know if I told you, but Judge Ferguson (Trustee for the Mitchell) told me about 6 years ago that 'though it is small, it is one of the most valuable we have' i.e. The Mary Gilmore Collection. I am contemporary of so many & my contemporaries matter. And that I have always felt.

To C. B. Christesen

Dear Clem Christesen,

Kings Cross
18 January 1960

The small headstone in Cloncurry Presbyterian Cemetery which I had put on my husband's grave there, the Inscription reads (more or less as the actual copy is at the Mitchell Library in the M.G. Collection there):—'In family record of William A. Gilmore, born Horsham, Vic., 1866, Mary, his wife of Cotta Walla, Goulburn, N.S.W., 1865, and their son William Dysart Cameron Gilmore, born Villa Rica, Paraguay 1898.' Not sure of the exact wording now. But a letter to the Trustees of the Cemetery should bring an exact copy & a photograph if asked for.

    There was a paragraph in some paper (Qld.) sent me which said it was strange to find the name of a living person (mine) on a headstone.

---

[1] The Women's Page. See note to letter, 15 January 1910.

Drinking Yerba Maté South American style

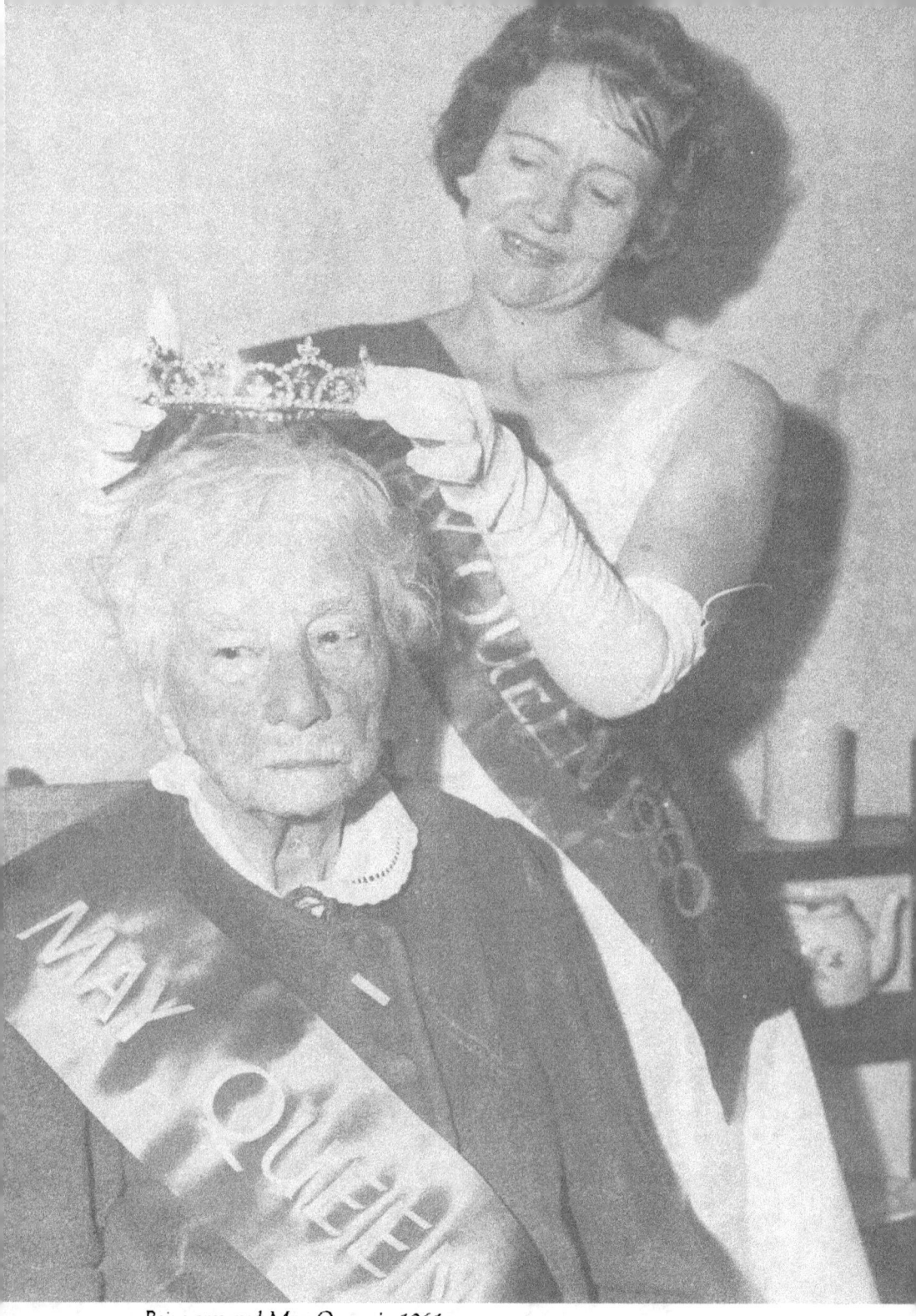
Being crowned May Queen in 1961

I did it so that in that way we would all be together, & my daughter-in-law had my son buried at Julia Creek.

I was born 16.8.1865, in my grandmother Mary Beattie's room at 'Merryvale', Cotta Walla near Goulburn. 'Merryvale' was bought by the Nixon family (neighbours) & is still owned by a Nixon descendant. Cotta Walla was the coldest spot near Goulburn. There is a Railway Station near there now, called 'Roslyn' after my Grandfather, Hugh Cameron's place, Merryvale and Roslyn (the name of the ancestral home in Lochaber) were adjoining properties. The trees grandfather Cameron planted still surround the old home—added to as new owners came. The poplar[1] planted for my birth as was then customary was still standing twenty years ago at Merryvale, the present Nixons told me. It was a cutting from Mary Reibey's poplar at Reibey House, Newtown, Sydney, & her tree was a cutting from the first poplars grown in the Botanic Gardens, Sydney. I have since had cuttings planted from my tree, & given me by the Nixons, on the top lawn near the Henry Kendall Seat, in the Sydney Botanic Gardens, and (planted for me by Mrs. Garth Fisher (d. of Sarah (Nixon) Smith, born in the same room I was born in) 23 Elimatta Street, Reid, Canberra.

I wrote the history of the cutting in the Sydney Botanic Gardens for filing there, & Mrs. Garth Fisher gave the same to Canberra.

My father[2] was Donal (usually Donald) son of Hugh Cameron, (heir to the Erskine earldom in Scotland) at Fort William, Argyle Shire. He came to Australia when about five. His mother died at sea. She was a sister of Hugh McColl, early M.P. in Victoria known as Canawl McColl because he talked canals for irrigation. He was also called 'the father of Irrigation in Australia'. Senator James H. McColl, M.H.R., was his son.

My mother was the daughter of Hugh Beatty (changed to Beattie in Australia) direct descendant of Sir William Beatty, a Knight in the train of James VI & I (of Great Britain). He was granted the Barony of Armagh, & his tomb is in Dublin C. of E. Cathedral. Earl Beatty is a relative. My mother's mother was Mary (Ralston) descendant of Ralph the Rover who took the bell from the Inchcape Rock ('The Abbot of Aberbrothock etc.') & was himself wrecked there as a result.

---

[1] See letters, 14 December 1933 and 20 August 1943.
[2] The details of Mary's ancestry, as given here, are not yet fully authenticated. The linking of her Grandmother, Mary Beattie (Ralston) with Ralph the Rover of Inchcape Rock fame is a delightful touch but no supporting evidence by Mary has come to the Editors' notice.

To Leonard Phillip Fox

Dear Len Fox,

Kings Cross
26 February 1960

Can you use the following? Had a visit from Julian Stuart a while ago, son of Julian Stuart who was one of the 'political prisoners' in 'St. Helena', Brisbane for his part in the Shearers' Strike of the 1890s, and afterwards Editor of 'The Brisbane Worker'. Another son of the elder Julian Stuart is Donald Stuart, writer of 'Yandy'.[1] A sister (I have forgotten her name) came to see me in 1959, she writes short stories.

The blacks taught me, as a child, to 'yandy' for seeds. A shallow bark coolamon was used to separate grass seed, for food, from the husks. Just shaking was no use. There was a special, easy twist of the arm, and, when done properly the seeds would be at one end of the yandy and the husks at the other. My father used to yandy gold specks from crushed quartz when looking for colour (gold traces). Today white people yandy but not with the skilled movement of the early blacks.

All good wishes to you and Mona and a blessing on your house.

Glad 'Common Cause'[2] is writing past history—men and events—as there is *too much* that is forgotten as time goes on. The past is part of the present, in action and result.

To R. D. FitzGerald

My Dear R.D.F.,

Kings Cross
28 May 1960

You ask will I think it good news about your Essay and Lecture on the person who *was* me and now is the falling embers left behind, but if you knew how many times I read your letter you would know! I am hung between the longing to hear (and read) as soon as possible the lecture and the essay, and the equally deep desire to prolong as long as possible the joy of anticipation. Your own work is such that it measures the mind behind the thinking, creative, analytic, *stored* mind, the lecture and the essay; when I am gone, you and William Dobell will be the Gods who created me part of Australia, and I haven't words, now, to say how happy and how grateful I am for it . . .

I have long given up to put you ahead of Hugh McCrae. You are *there*—and without any help from the critics. As to Hugh, he would have looked up to you, for Hugh never measured others meanly or with a niggard mind . . .

[1] *Yandy*, 1959.
[2] *Common Cause*, the official journal of the Miners' Federation.

Secretary, Kings Cross
Mary Gilmore Award Committee *28 June 1960*

Dear Mrs. Cross,
In reply to your request for a 'few words' for the Mary Gilmore Award for a novel (this year) I send the following which I hope will suit:—

> The printed word is the first step toward co-hering and coherent civilization, and literature is its ladder. This committee and its work is part of the world's forward Movement and not just an isolated entity for and of Australia, and nowhere else. Because of this I feel it is of the highest honour that my name should be associated with it and its work—an honour I am privileged to accept.
>
> Mary Gilmore.

and I do think it an honour in itself, and because the work is not only important in itself but will grow with Australia through the years. Yours sincerely,

To R. D. FitzGerald

Kings Cross
Dear Bob, *4 July 1960*

Your letter and cuttings came this morning. What a kind and generous thing you have done! Also Tom Moore. I hope Mr. Kahan's[1] drawing of you will be as good as the one in this last 'Meanjin'.[2] He has something in his work, of the living *flesh*—of life—that Dobell has. I thought when I read your letter how I am kept alive by friends. As to you reading 'Old Days Old Ways',[3] I had a copy of 'More Recollections'[4] sent me for an inscription, by Stephen Murray-Smith over a week ago, and not having seen it for years I began to read it as something not seen before and written by someone else and I was astonished to find that I am (or was) really a writer! It seemed unbelievable. But how glad I am that I did it, for so much in it I had completely forgotten—though it came back through the reading, but not so exactly. So, Bob, don't put off your own recollections. Tie up the dog, no matter on how short the chain. Memory is a new plant in man, and when it goes it does

[1] Louis Kahan.
[2] Kahan's sketch of Mary accompanied R. D. FitzGerald's article 'Mary Gilmore: Poet and Great Australian', *Meanjin* 4 (1960) and it was repeated with W. H. Wilde's 'Mary Gilmore—The Hidden Years', *Meanjin* 4 (1973). Kahan did sketch R. D. FitzGerald but it did not appear in *Meanjin Quarterly* until 1965.
[3] Published 1934.
[4] Published 1935.

not come back again. This the forest of the mind and in this changing period, what a forest.

Especially in Australia where the primitive became today in little more than a lifetime. And of course, I am looking forward, even with a little of the old gnawing hunger of the eager young muses for your essay when it comes out.

All good to you and yours, Bob—Gratefully—

To C. B. Christesen

Dear Clem Christesen,

Kings Cross
12 August 1960

I was in such haste to get the corrected verselets[1] back to you that I forgot to thank you for wishing to give me 'a do' at the University if I could go to Melbourne. Too old & too tired for going anywhere now—though I would love to see you all and be amongst you, all friends talking together.

I want to say again what a wicked & cruel thing (seeing what you have sacrificed for it, & given as a gift to Australia,) if 'Meanjin' is allowed to end for want of *Official*, University & Literary support. It is such an outstanding, proud representative of Australia, & not just here, but to all the world. Dr. Evatt[2] is out of the House or I would write to him about it. The State Parliaments are not big enough. But Canberra is all Australia, at home & in the eyes of the world. What or who is there to be approached? If this letter is any use, at all, you have my authority to use it . . .

I feel very badly about the want of realization as to the value of 'Meanjin' to Australia internationally. Insularity is not only vulgar, it is ignorant—and disloyal if it comes to that. Yours sincerely,

To Nettie Palmer

Dear Nettie Palmer—

Kings Cross
3 September 1960

What a kind remembrance you sent me in your second letter. It brought back all the happy astonishment of when the quatrain was sent me.

My first card came from China, and two wonderful cables from Moscow. The first (timed to reach me *on the morning* of my birthday)[3]

---

[1] Entitled 'Arrows', they were published in *Meanjin* 4 (1960).
[2] H. V. Evatt.
[3] Mary's 95th birthday, 16 August 1960.

from the writers, and the other from a society I do not know, but in wh. after saying I had the 'warmest heart and youngest spirit' and my 'human words widely read in our country' they said they were 'celebrating the anniversary' in Moscow Friendship House. What an astonishing thing! If it were K.S.P.[1] it wd. seem natural. But me? I have done so little.

    I gave your name and address to Mrs. Hazel de Berg, who is doing tape recordings (now for storage at Canberra) of Australian writers. (She may have done you when she was last in Melbourne.) By great good luck and long search she found a Bernard O'Dowd record and was able to get it. I have had letters from one of Bernard's granddaughters—trying to be a writer, on a farm and with a large family. Trying to write orthodox verse she cripples herself, but now and again, in what she sends me, Bernard breaks through. I had told her to write Bernard not ordinary verse and so find herself. My love to you, Nettie

Don't forget to see the next 'Meanjin' with R.D.F's analysis of my verse.[2] I feel broken hearted over the possibility of 'Meanjin' coming to an end—Our only magazine of international standing!

    Can't Australia stand up on its own feet and save it? And all the years, life—money Christesen put into it, and then to have to give up. It is too cruel—and it is wicked to Australia.

To Mrs Smith

Dear Mrs. Smith,
                              Kings Cross
                            5 September 1960

Your little book of verse with inscription came just now, and I hasten to thank you for it.

    It is rather curious to note that in this Springtime of 'Meanjin' there is an analysis of my verse by Robert D. FitzGerald, the Poet, in which he told me he has written that a characteristic of my work is that 'it is religious'—not all of it of course.

    I had not realized it till he mentioned it. As a matter of fact my book 'The Rue Tree'[3] written in tribute to the Sisters of the Convent of Mercy, Goulburn, was said by the critics of the time to be the best book of Catholic poetry written in Australia,—and me a good Presbyterian; but that book was a tribute and after all true religion is not sectarian.

[1] Katharine Susannah Prichard.
[2] 'Mary Gilmore: Poet and Great Australian', *Meanjin* 4 (1960).
[3] *The Rue Tree*, 1931. For comment see W. H. Wilde, *Three Radicals*, 1969.

It has no bounds and that no matter where it is found. It is like the sunlight.

It belongs to and goes to all. Again thanking you—

To R. D. FitzGerald

Dear Bob,

Kings Cross
12 September 1960

I return Clem Christesen's letter herewith. He had written me earlier that he was holding back some small verses *I* had sent him, but had not mentioned your article[1]—your article which *he had asked you* to write. And what work and time you had given it. I feel it is unfair to you to hold it back, but—as you say his own life has been sacrificed (and his heart broken) for 'Meanjin'. If I were younger I wd. stump the country to keep it alive. It is a disgrace to Australia that it shd. go. It is our only Magazine of international standing. However you know all this, and I am only letting off steam over my own sense of unfair play to a man who deserved better of his country, and my own sense of loss. And also of the unfairness of circumstances to you.

My grandson was 21 on the 4th of this month, a fine tall upstanding, healthy boy. He will go for a year to 'Landsdowne' (Qld) to study genetics, and then perhaps take over the property—it is his of course—near Cloncurry. He is a Scots College boy.

All good wishes and all my grateful thanks—

To R. D. FitzGerald

Dear Bob,

Kings Cross
6 October 1960

'Meanjin' came a while ago. What a noble poem you have written![2] How different from all the other verses in the magazine.

Fibre and thought, bone and gristle, life and strength, the inevitable and resistance—all there, all condensed: nothing spread out or watered. I said once I hated to put you above Hugh McCrae. But Hugh never reached where you are and in this especially. I am glad to have lived to see it.

On Tuesday last I signed a contract handing over my portrait[3] by Dobell to the Sydney Art Gallery to hold in trust for the nation.

---

[1] 'Mary Gilmore: Poet and Great Australian', *Meanjin* 4 (1960).

[2] 'Bog and Candle', *Meanjin* 3 (1960).

[3] See note to letter, 7 September 1955.

Hal Missingham brought the portrait so that I could see it—I had only half-seen it before and had no idea it was so big! Mr. Buckley (my solicitor) brought the deed (or contract) for me to sign, and Mr. Max Dupain came with Mr. Missingham to take photographs for the gallery record. I had left the portrait, by will, to Canberra, but heard that Dobell wanted it here. So cancelled the codicil to my will, and made the portrait over to the gallery as a gift. The work as a painting will grow in value with the years; there is so little of the conventional in it that it stands out no matter how good the conventional may be.

President, *Kings Cross*
Board of Trustees, *14 November 1960*
Art Gallery of N.S.W.

Dear Professor Waterhouse,
This is to say how glad I am to have your letter (and that of Mr. Tuckson) saying how glad you are to have the Dobell portrait[1] I gave to the Gallery. Money wd. not buy it, so I gave it, and what a painting it is! It will still be a treasure when people will wonder whom he painted. The man who can put your ancestry—your kin—whom he has never seen into your portrait as well as his wonderful painting, leads in Art. We have had too much photography—just features and colour—in our portraits. I think of Longstaff's Henry Lawson[2] (As soon as my little boy of five saw it, he exclaimed 'That is Mr. Lawson'), Sir Henry Parkes[3] by Julian Ashton and then of the decorative, the flat and the conventional—what a level!

However you do not want me to lecture you on art! I am only trying to say Thank you to you, to William Dobell, and to the future. My father's people stood by Raeburn[4] at his condemned beginnings. (That is why he painted so many of the Camerons.) When the portrait of Mrs. George Cameron was lent the Gallery some years ago I eagerly went to see it to look for a likeness to me in it. There was *no likeness* and I was so taken back I never told anyone of the family relationship—months later I suddenly remembered she was not related. She was only 'married in'! And what a relief to my mind. What Raeburn did for portraiture, in his day, Dobell will do, I hope, for Australia. His lamp will light the way—I am honoured that he painted me.

All good wishes and again my thanks.

[1] See note to letter, 7 September 1955.
[2] The portrait of Henry Lawson was painted by Sir John Longstaff in 1900.
[3] The portrait of Parkes was painted in 1889 when Parkes was Premier of New South Wales.
[4] Sir Henry Raeburn.

To R. D. FitzGerald

Dear Bob,

Kings Cross
15 December 1960

The Postman has just left 'our' 'Meanjin'[1]. I have only read the first page, but, Man! you have made me Immortal!!!! I can't get over it. But before I read any further my astonished, grateful, wondering heart had to write to you, and say—what *can* I say? I must feel like Moses on Mount Sinai receiving the tablets of Stone—the sky widening like a flash of lightning, *all* horizons in one—every thing everywhere visible and felt in the forever.

But I'll have no words and no ink left (see below) if I go on, and I want to begin that page over and over again, & (later) to write you on *you* in that article. I already realize that no one, not even A. G. Stephens, has analysed as dearly, as deeply, and evaluatingly as you have done in this piece of work. What a book on Australian literature you could write for the Sydney University—Staff and Students alike. Timeless it would be.

If I don't stop I never will, and I want this posted at once and my housekeeper is waiting... May everything that is good and everything you want come to you—the man who wrote not only 'Bog and Candle'[2] but this on

Mary Gilmore.

To R. D. FitzGerald

Dear Bob,

Kings Cross
18 December 1960

R.D.F. on Mary Gilmore.

I lose the power of judgment in reading the above.[3] I began the article as relating to me, and then find myself reading for the *work*—the writing—as literature and not at all as relating to me. I cease to exist and only the writing remains—and what writing, what concentrated thought, what phrasing, and what arrows of penetration, perception. The searching eye never lifts from the page; there is no speculative wandering—wondering indeed—reaching out and drawing other writing or other horizons. The limit of my horizons in the different fields of writing, is kept by the wider and deeper mind of R.D.F. everywhere, and throughout the whole work. Spread out as a literary article

---

[1] *Meanjin* 4 (1960) contained R. D. FitzGerald's 'Mary Gilmore: Poet and Great Australian'.
[2] *Meanjin* 3 (1960). See letter, 6 October 1960.
[3] The *Meanjin* 4 (1960) article. See letter, 15 December 1960.

what wider a ranging of related matter could have been included. Here there is only the writer's own brain in action. There is an entire absence of the usual critic who buttresses the thinmindedness of his own thought by constant quotation from and comparison with other writers. R.D.F. grows his own wheat, he does not buy it (as print) in shops.

22 December 1960.

I am sending you this, untrimmed as I wrote it (and the only copy) as it came to me when reading a paper and getting no farther. I wrote this at waking.

Funny thing I wrote in the above is my second agricultural simile—the other one went in a letter to you. Tom's essay was more literary and deliberate. This is sudden, concentrated, and in feeling I think is deeper. It never struck me I had a style and am a style—I just try to get what I think in the fewest but absolutely necessary words—I may never write more than this on your analysis till distance quietens response.

M.G.

Mr. Thomas, *Kings Cross*
Art Gallery N.S.W. *31 December 1960*

Dear Mr. Thomas.
Hogmanay tonight! Have been too much knocked about by the heat to get at this fully till now. The generous appreciation of my gift to the nation of my portrait by Wm. Dobell[1] is better than any money payment could be. As years go on its value to the nation will increase. In which case the Gallery is the only safe place for it.

About sittings for the portrait. There were only two, one (about an hour) I think in October (Not sure now but it is recorded in my diaries wh. are not to be opened till after my death.)

The second sitting was some months later, and was only about 20 minutes (to confirm the first). It was (and is) a case of the portrait being 'in the eye of the beholder'—and what a tribute in the result to Mr. Dobell! But the ancestry is in it—as I have written more than once, and it is ME, and not just a specification of dimensions in paint. And what a lucky woman I have been to have it done. You can tell Dobell this when you see him again. He has given me futurity in time and Australia as nothing else could have done. The least comprehending mind can look at this and remember it. But *my* work has to be found and read—wh. limits remembrance.

[1] See letter, 7 September 1955.

The two sittings were here in my lounge room, in wh. I am now writing. Later on Dobell brought a draft painting with a long bare ugly neck. I told him I did not want a Joshua Smith neck and asked him to put a velvet band or some lace around it to lessen the Joshua Smith resemblance. That was all I saw of the portrait till the final painting was presented to me at the Gallery.

I forgot to say that I first saw the finished portrait at Dobell's Agent's Shop . . . It was there I saw my father's eyes looking at me. And it was there I smashed the leading Sydney Critic's opposition to it. I told him . . . that a portrait that did not show the ancestors in it was not a portrait. It was only a photograph in paint. I said much more. He took his already written criticism out of his pocket and tore it to little bits and wrote a full-value one in his paper. At the moment this is not for publication. After my death you can use it, if you like. It is all in my diaries for use then. Again I want to say how glad I am of what you say of the gift and that 'the painting is a master piece'. It is more. It is a light in the convention-ridden darkness of Australian Art that will never go out. Yours gratefully

Private
Sorry that my writing is now so hard to read. Only one eye and that is not much good.

To C. B. Christesen

Dear Clem Christesen,

Kings Cross
5 January 1961

I am still in a state of wonder over R.D.F.'s essay[1] on my work. I start to read it as being about myself, & suddenly I am aware I have forgotten its connection with me & I am reading it as literature—which it is. Will you send me ten (10) copies of the issue as there are so many I want to send it to . . . There are some to go to China & Russia.

From Russia I have just received this morning a card & this: (in English)—'Happy New Year! Let this New Year bring you health & energy so that the arrow of Mary Gilmore should strike at everything obnoxious in this world. Yours, Boris Polevoi'.

I expect your wife knows him as a friend as well as a writer.

At last had a letter from Ernestine Hill. Thursday Island. She has been ill so long (& latterly 4 months in hospital) but says she is well again & working hard.

All good wishes especially for the New Year.

[1] See letters, 15 and 18 December 1960.

The Bread & Cheese Club,   *Kings Cross*
Melbourne   *20 February 1961*

Dear Mr. John Lynch,
You dear and generous people, one and all of you! What a lovely thing to do. Your letter has just come saying you are making me Ng Cobbera (a cobber, a fellow, and a mate.) and allowing me the club badge to wear. How glad and proud I will be to do it and thank you for the honour.

    Years ago J. K. Moir said (and wrote) that if ever the Club allowed a woman member it would be me, and me the only one. So as an associate (Ng cobbera) I thank you through J. K. Moir, for though less than he said, the honour is, to me, just as great.

    When the Lyceum Club here, of which I am a local founder, fell on depression times I had *associate* Members brought in. This included University Students. Might I suggest the same to you, so that Asiatic and other students could be ng.cobberas?[1] These not being *Members* could not rule the Club but they would noise its name abroad, and would be a Club asset. You need the young as well as the established. Besides these there could, of course, be heads of businesses, Law, Medicine and so on. All men of course. You might think of the idea, and if it turned out possible and well, you could say, 'Good on you, Ngcobbera! even if I am a woman. For the Asiatic students you might have a page in Bohemia and not only help pay for it but extend its range, literary and in sales.

    So again my deepest thanks, and may you last forever!

The Mary Gilmore Award Committee.   *Kings Cross*
                                                                     3 May 1961

Dear Sirs,
First I wish to express my gratitude to the May Day Committee and to the Trade Unions which gave my name to the Mary Gilmore Award and its monetary prize. There is first my own personal uplift and then there is the value to this call to Australian writers. None are left out as the subject for each year is a different one and ranges from fiction, poetry, drama, short stories and later, I hope, to include, localities, people and even our language.

    This brings me to the immediate question of the latest award,

---

[1] There is no record of the Bread and Cheese Club's response to this rather surprising suggestion.

'The Tracks we Travel'[1] a collection of short stories by the wide range of our best known writers in these.

The stories are Australian. The diction (and this is important) is typically Australian. It owes nothing to any other country for its *style*. Words are common property, but style belongs to the country of its origin.

We are old enough now to be users of our own individualized speech.

This award book, 'The Tracks We Travel', being a collection, gives variation to the language used. The idiom of a one-man book wd. still be Australian; even though every story bore the writer's own style—recognizable manner of speech and construction. But with a collection the basic is Australian, but the style in each case is personal.

The Australasian Book Society is the publisher of the book for this year's award. But it had an earlier one, a novel, 'The Last Blue Sea'[2] by David Forrest. There is a measure of the work this Publishing House is doing. From first to last its aim has been to help Australian writers, and establish Australia as a country whose literature stands on its own feet among the other older and more populous countries of the world. We may be new, but we grow tall trees.

To George Ferguson

Kings Cross
17 June 1961

Dear GRII,[3]

Thank you for your letter and what it says. And, except as regards 'Old Days: Old Ways',[4] don't worry about not coming to see me. Friendship as long as ours is not dependent on the visible. It stays.

About 'Old Days': It has the advantage of going farther back than the ones just published, Myrtle White's and some man's. Also the critics don't suggest 'editing' for the English. So, if you don't take it, if you do not object I shall submit it to the Commonwealth Literary Board—it is so long since it appeared. More than that, though so long out of print people still ask where they can get it—one about two weeks ago. After all these years!

---

[1] *The Tracks We Travel*, 1961, edited by Jack Beazley, included the Mary Gilmore Award Stories. The Foreword was written by Mary. The Introduction to the book outlines the history of the Mary Gilmore Awards and the May Day Committee Short Story Competitions.
[2] *The Last Blue Sea*, 1959.
[3] Mary's abbreviation for George Robertson's grandson.
[4] *Old Days: Old Ways A Book of Recollections* was first published in 1934. It was republished by Sirius Books, 1967.

Some people have their names down at the second hand bookshop for years, hoping for a collection or a library to be sold and a copy in it.

I do hope Alec is better than he was. I have such a long affection for him. He is (as you) a part of my life. (I missed even Adela Pankhurst, Mrs. Walsh, when she lately went and how glad I was that after so many years I had written to her since Xmas! Yet she was only a long acquaintance, *not* a part of my life.)

Just had a ring from St. Vincent's. My eye doctor will be here in 10 minutes.

My dear (GRII) the old lady sends her love.

P.S. 12.30 p.m. Dr. (Clement) Walsh just gone. Nothing can be done, except as a last resource. Cataract—as he found two or more years ago. If you want a good man I can recommend him. He told me he did an operation for cataract on a woman of 95 (four years ago) and she is still going strong. Another of 101—this operation was successful, but she tore a bandage off, and that was fatal (to her sight).

The Bread & Cheese Club,   *Kings Cross*
Melbourne.   *6 September 1961*

My dear John Lynch,
When I first saw Jessie Litchfield she was about twelve and a pupil in my class at Neutral Bay Public School[1] there. Even then she stood out in character, personality and intelligence. All that life had to do for her was develop her. Her interest went beyond the local to international and world affairs. In Northern Australia, in and beyond Darwin, she was an influence, a builder and a historian. Her interest never dulled and her spirit never failed. She was a loss to Australia when she died.

To Constance Robertson

                                                            Kings Cross
Dear Connie,—ME TOO!   *19 December 1961*

'Still at it'. Which means that your card and flowers have just come. (This morning it was a card from Donald). May all the good in the world and happiness be yours for the coming year and every other year to follow. I have been wondering since the flowers came (and

---
[1] Mary taught there for a brief period in 1890.

Donald's card) about the rest of the family—who are left, who are gone and what of grandchildren.

My grandson (just over 22) went up to the property at Cloncurry three weeks ago to take over the working and management of what had been his father's place. He has never been alone in his life—'I have been here two nights' he wrote me 'and it is very lonely'.

I wanted him to engage a married couple, as it is not well for him to be alone. But his reply was 'married couples cost money, but a tin-opener is cheap'. But some other arrangement will have to be made. (His mother can go up for the Winter, she has L.b.p. and has to Summer south). He is only 13 miles from the homestead where the (married) manager lives and should sleep there, driving back and forward to work each day.

As for me: I am full of halleluyahs over the A and R victory for the old management[1] (we don't want to see the A and R home another 'Bulletin'!) and after it had propped up the finances of Associated Press perhaps sold to the highest bidder in America! I have long pointed out that invasion by investments is as bad (for independence) as by an army.

For the rest: I am going down hill fast now. But as long as I can follow and curse and worship a leader, I am still alive.

As to you, good be yours, my dear child and may you be happy in the grandchildren. Love.

Did I tell you that the writers in Moscow kept up my birthday last year? I thought I was first but I am sure Katharine Prichard was before me. Dymphna Cusack's last book—130,000 copies sold out in a week. And Gavin Greenlees and wife back from China told me that he went to an outlying province in China. The mayor took him to a hall and showed him two of Namatjira's paintings on the wall. What about us?!?!

---

[1] S.M.H., 15 December 1961, reported that Consolidated Press withdrew its nominees from the contest to elect two of its representatives to the Board of A. & R. at the annual general meeting, 15 December 1961. Consolidated Press had acquired a majority (25% of ordinary capital) of first preference shares. A. & R. Directors had opposed the appointment of two representatives on the Board. Mary had earlier voiced her hopes for A. & R. to continue its historic publishing work. See letter, 31 January 1951.

To R. D. FitzGerald

Dear Bob,

Kings Cross
16 April 1962

I am growing past letter writing—age and want of sight. But I have to write you of this:—Sybil Thorndike has been nearly every day of their short visit to Sydney; all four came yesterday, and I proposed this (which I had already written G.R.II—George Ferguson).

It is that Sybil and Lewis include in their recitals Australian verse. I gave G.F. a list beginning with 'Out Where the Dead Men Lie', 'Clancy of the Overflow' and including you in my list. Some of your important verse lends itself to stage recital very much . . .

What started the idea is that I gave Sybil my 'Fourteen Men'[1] while they were here, and, looking into it she said eagerly 'I must get Lewis to read some of these!' I at once thought of Australia—what it would mean to have the best read. She just loves Australia, 'its vast spaces', and they may come here to live. Do you think you could send them one of your books to meet them in London.

But what a vital and alert-minded couple they are and how young for their years!

All good to you and yours—I am writing this in bed and hope you can read it.

To R. D. FitzGerald

My Dear R.D.F.

Kings Cross
8 June 1962

I did not write yesterday when your letter came though that was what I wanted to do. But what a piece of work! And how much in gratitude I owe you for it. It is a whole book[2]—and I expected it to be about 5 or 6 pieces in all, to be sandwiched in with others. And to think you are writing the introduction! Knowing how you have written of my verse before, and the value and standing you have given me for it, I feel lifted up beyond my human everyday standing. I become a part of Australia, one of its makers, for literature makes nations, it shapes their futures and their characters in the shaping of their people's characters. I am afraid I am always harping on this but so few people think either it or of it.

[1] Published 1954.
[2] *Mary Gilmore*. Selection and Introduction by R. D. FitzGerald, 1963. Australian Poets Series.

I just had a Russian book sent me. I thought, by the look of it, it was an anthology of poets. But I, of course, haven't a word of Russian, so I lent it to an office where some of its people read Russian, and they told me it was a book of writers of the world. They have two pieces of mine which I had forgotten about but I wondered if you were there. You should be! I also had a Miss Glendenning here from Perth, but born in Iona (Scotland), which is certainly a distinction. She is collecting material for a book on William Lane. You can't help her there, but you might find her interesting if she would call.

All good to you and yours Bob from this most grateful woman.

To R. D. FitzGerald

My Dear Bob,

Kings Cross
17 June 1962

I am writing from up among the stars down to the earth. I have just read your Foreword for the Verse.[1] *What* praise! and what analysis. I am wondering if A & R won't think it too much to publish. And such a long piece of sustained writing. Literature of course. How can I thank you?!!

Of course (unless you want it back) it goes into my collection at the Mitchell Library—as a tribute to this humble person.

A Million thanks!

---

[1] This final letter tells of Mary's joyous reaction, less than six months before her death at the age of 97, to R. D. FitzGerald's acclaim of her poetry. He said that her best poetry was the 'complete fusion of distinctive material and satisfying form'. He insisted on the permanence of Mary's best verses—'they will live because they are concerned with the common interests of mankind'.

His comments come from the Introduction to his selection of her verse in the Australian Poets Series, published in 1963.

Mary Gilmore

Appendix

PEOPLE, PUBLICATIONS, PLACES AND EVENTS
MENTIONED IN THE LETTERS

Abdullah, Mena (1930-). Born in Bundarra, N.S.W., she has published short stories, often in collaboration with Ray Mathew, e.g. *The Time of the Peacock*, 1965. See Beatrice Davis, *Short Stories of Australia: the Moderns*, 1967.

Adams, Arthur Henry (1872-1936). A New Zealander by birth, he edited both the *Bulletin* Red Page, 1906-9, and the *Lone Hand*. He published several books of verse (*London Streets*, 1906, and *Collected Verses*, 1913) as well as novels and plays. See B. G. Andrews and W. H. Wilde, *Australian Literature to 1900*, 1980, in the Gale Information Guide Library series.

Adams, Francis (1862-93). Adams was born in Malta and came to Australia from Great Britain in 1884, writing for the *Bulletin* and William Lane's radical weekly, the *Boomerang*. His best writing is in his essays, *Australian Essays*, 1886, and *The Australians*, 1893. He also wrote verse, e.g. *Songs of the Army of the Night*, 1888. See B. G. Andrews and W. H. Wilde, *Australian Literature to 1900*, 1980, in the Gale Information Guide Library series.

Adamson, George Ernest Bartlett (1884-1951). Born in Tasmania, he was a journalist with *Smith's Weekly*. His publications include poetry—*Twelve Sonnets*, 1918, *Bringer of Light*, 1944, *Comrades All and other Poems for the People*, 1945; fiction—*Mystery Gold*, 1925; and short stories—*Nice Day for a Murder and other Stories*, 1944.

Alley, Rewi (1897-). A New Zealander who as a young war veteran, went to China and lived and worked there. There is an account of him in Helen Palmer's article 'Rewi Alley: Interpreter of New China', *Meanjin*, 3 (1953).

Amor, Jack. A Queenslander who burnt down a woolshed during the shearers' strike and had a reward of £1000 placed on his head. He went to Cosme in May 1895 under the assumed name of Dawson.

Archibald, Jules Francois (John Feltham) (1856-1919). Founder of the *Bulletin* and *Lone Hand* magazines, Archibald imparted to the *Bulletin* many of the nationalist and radical characteristics which made it important in the literary history of this country, especially in the period of the 1890s and early twentieth century.

Ashton, Julian Rossi (1851-1942). The distinguished artist and teacher who founded the Sydney Art School. He was President of the Art Society of N.S.W. 1886-92.

Aussie. A soldiers' magazine (usually with an essay on an Australian writer) published 1918 to 1931. It was originally issued in France (January 1918-April 1919) and later (1920) reprinted with the title *Aussie: the Australian Soldiers Magazine*.

Austro-Vert. A literary periodical published in Melbourne from December 1950 to June 1953.

Badham, Professor Charles (1813-84). He was appointed Professor of Classics, University of Sydney, in 1866.

Baker, Kate (1861-1953). Born in Ireland, she came to Australia as a child. As a schoolteacher, boarding with the Furphy family, she encouraged Joseph Furphy to write and promoted his work. She was co-author (with Miles Franklin) of a biography, *Joseph Furphy*, 1944. She was awarded the O.B.E. for her services to literature.

Bancks, James Charles (1889-1952). Bancks created the now legendary comic-strip 'Ginger Meggs' which began as 'Us Fellers' in the *Sunday Sun* in 1921 and continued in that newspaper until 1951, when after a court case, Bancks won the right to publish it in the *Sunday Telegraph*.

Bardsley, Grace. A close acquaintance of Mary from the 1950s. She was in 1962 on the editorial board of *Outlook*, an independent socialist review edited by Helen G. Palmer. There is a tribute to her by Mary in the Acknowledgements in *Fourteen Men*, 1954.

Barrett, Charles Leslie (1879-1959). A noted naturalist, interested in all aspects of Australiana, and a prolific writer on this country's flora and fauna.

Battarbee, Rex (1893-1973). An artist himself, Battarbee was the teacher and mentor of the Aboriginal artist, Albert Namatjira.

Battlefields. Dame Mary's book of verse published in 1939. See, *inter alia*, W. H. Wilde, *Three Radicals*, 1969.

Bayldon, Arthur Albert (1865-1958). Writer of fiction and poetry. His works included *The Western Track and Other Verses*, 1905, and *Apollo in Australia and Bush Verses*, 1944.

Bean, Charles Edwin Woodrow (1879-1968). Editor and chief historian of the *Official History of Australia in the War of 1914-1918* (12 vols), 1921-36. Bean also wrote some reflections on New South Wales outback life, e.g. *On the Wool Track*, 1910, and *The Dreadnought of the Darling*, 1911.

Beatty, Sir William (died 1842). Surgeon to Admiral Nelson at his death at Trafalgar. He published *Narrative of the Death of Lord Nelson*, 1807.

Bedford, Ruth (1882-1963). Author of *Think of Stephen*, 1954, and prior to that *Rhymes by Ruth*, 1893 and *Sydney at Sunset and Other Verses*, 1911.

Benham, Dr Rosamond Agnes (1874-1923). A poet as well as a practising physician, she graduated from the University of Adelaide in 1902 and worked in the Sunbury and Kew Asylums. A. G. Stephens collected her poetry, which is in the Mitchell Library. See R. B. Chivers, *The Benham Family in Australia*, 1970.

Bennett, Lieutenant-General Henry Gordon (1887-1962). Commanding Officer of the 8th Australian Division in Malaya. Controversy surrounded his escape to Australia after the Allied surrender of Singapore in 1942.

Bernhardi, Friedrich (1849-1930). German soldier and military writer who argued that war was inevitable and Germany was entitled to secure victory at any cost. His gospel of force convinced the world at large that Germany was in an aggressive mood. In 1915 he was serving on the Eastern front.

Birkett, Winifred (1897-). Author of *Earth's Quality*, 1935, a novel dealing with the influence of a pastoral property on succeeding generations of an Australian family. She also wrote *Three Goats on a Bender*, 1934, the amusing story of three women attempting to breed goats.

Blake, Leslie (Bamford) James (1913-). Victorian schoolmaster interested in Australian literature. He wrote *Australian Writers*, 1968, a pot-pourri of comment and biography about a host of Australian literary figures.

Bligh, Vice-Admiral William (1754-1817). One of the early Governors of New South Wales 1806-8 but best known for his role in the legendary mutiny on the *Bounty*. His voyage of 3618 miles in an open boat from Tahiti to Timor in April 1789, was an epic of seamanship.

Bluett, Etty. A sister of Ida and William Bluett. Headmistress of the Woollahra Primary School, she became well-known to generations of pupils of that school.

Bluett, Ida. An elder sister of William Bluett.

Bluett, William P. (1871-1968). Forced to leave his career of journalism in the city because of ill-health, Bluett took his family to a farming property in the remote Brindabella mountains in the early years of this century. The establishment of the property 'Koorabri' is a saga in itself and it captured the imagination of Mary Gilmore. The property passed out of the family in 1972. A great granddaughter of Billy Bluett, Miss Pam Capsticks (Mrs John Finn), helped type this manuscript.

Boake, Barcroft Henry (1866-92). A bush balladist who hung himself with his stockwhip. His *Where the Dead Men Lie and Other Poems* was edited by A. G. Stephens in 1897. See B. G. Andrews and W. H. Wilde, *Australian Literature to 1900*, 1980, in the Gale Information Guide Library series.

The *Bookfellow*. Launched by A. G. Stephens in 1899 as a diminutive literary magazine it was incorporated by him with the *Bulletin* Red Page for a time, then it lapsed. It was revived in a larger form by Stephens in 1907 and survived precariously until 1925. At its best its literary standard was sound. At one stage Mary claims to have been associated with it through a form of ownership.

Boote, Henry Ernest (1868-1949). Editor of the *Worker* and himself a writer, Boote wrote *A Fool's Talk*, 1915, and *Tea With The Devil*, 1928.

Botha, Louis (1862-1919). South African general and statesman who at the outbreak of World War I declared that South Africa, as part of the British Empire, was also at war. By February 1916 he had crushed rebellion in Transvaal and the Orange Free State against his invasion of German South-West Africa.

Bradfield, John Job Crew (1867-1943). The brilliant engineer whose chief memorial is the Sydney Harbour Bridge.

Brady, Edwin James (1869-1952). Writer of bush ballads, short stories and sea shanties, his works include *The Ways of Many Waters*, 1899, and *Wardens of the Seas. Poems by E.J.B.*, 1933. See B. G. Andrews and W. H. Wilde, *Australian Literature to 1900*, 1980, in the Gale Information Guide Library series.

Brahe, May Hannah (1884-1956). Melbourne song composer who published over 300 songs some of which, e.g. 'Bless This House', 'To A Miniature' and 'It's Quiet Down There', have become known all over the English-speaking world.

Brand, Mona. See Fox, Leonard Phillip.

Bread and Cheese Club. An all male society formed in Melbourne 5 June 1938 with 12 original members to foster a knowledge of Australian literature, art and music and to cultivate an Australian sentiment. Its first president was J. K. Moir and its monthly journal was *Bohemia*, which commenced March 1939.

Brennan, Christopher John (1870-1932). One of Australia's most renowned (and controversial) poets. The one truly international poetic figure among Australian writers of late nineteenth and early twentieth centuries, he is best represented by his *Poems*, 1913. See the special Christopher Brennan issues of *Southerly*, 10, 4 (1949), 37, 4 (1977), G. A. Wilkes, *New Perspectives on Brennan's Poetry*, 1953, and B. G. Andrews and W. H. Wilde, *Australian Literature to 1900*, 1980, in the Gale Information Guide Library series.

'Brent of Bin Bin'. The pseudonym used by Miles Franklin to write numerous books including *Up the Country*, 1928, *Ten Creeks Run*, 1930, and *Back to Bool Bool*, 1931. Mary was unable to penetrate this pseudonym.

Brereton, John le Gay (1871-1933). Professor of English at the University of Sydney, poet, dramatist and prose writer, Brereton was a close friend of Henry Lawson and helped him in his early struggling days as a writer. See B. G. Andrews and W. H. Wilde, *Australian Literature to 1900*, 1980, in the Gale Information Guide Library series.

Bruce, Mary Grant (1878-1958). A journalist and writer of children's books, the most famous of which were the Billabong series and *A Little Bush Maid*, 1910. See Brenda Niall, *Seven Little Billabongs*, 1979.

Bull, Hilda (1891-1953). The wife of Louis Esson. She was a doctor, interested especially in the diseases of children, and wrote articles on the immunization of children against diseases such as diphtheria and scarlet fever.

Butt, Dame Clara (1873-1936). English singer, rewarded for her services to music by the award of D.B.E.

Byers, Isabel. Proprietor of the North Sydney Coffee Palace, 145 Miller Street, North Sydney, where Henry Lawson lived at various periods. His relationship with her was close. Lawson spent a total of 159 days in gaol from 1905 to 1909 for failure to pay maintenance to his wife. He wrote to Isabel Byers a number of times while in gaol.

Cambridge, Ada (1844-1926). Poet and novelist. Her *Thirty Years in Australia*, 1903, described her experiences in Victorian country centres. Her poetry included, *Unspoken Thoughts*, 1887, and *The Hand in the Dark and Other Poems*, 1913. See B. G. Andrews and W. H. Wilde, *Australian Literature to 1900*, 1980, in the Gale Information Guide Library series.

Cameron, Sir Donald Charles (1879-1960). Queensland Member of the House of Representatives (1919-37) and a distinguished soldier of World War I. He wrote the foreword to *Battlefields* (1939).

Cameron, John Alexander. Younger brother of Dame Mary. He had a varied career as writer (*The Spell of the Bush*, 1909), newspaper editor, war correspondent and diplomat.

Campbell, Donald Gordon (or Gordon Campbell). His published poetry included *Song of the Snowy River and Other Poems*, 1945, and *Gone Wandering*, 1947. Despite Mary's encouragement he seems not to have published stories or a novel.

Campbell, Lawrence, M.B.E. President of the Speech Association of New South Wales and an elocution teacher for many years.

Carmichael, Sir Thomas David (1859-1926). Governor of Victoria, 1908-11, where he encouraged literature and art.

Casey, Right Honourable Richard Gardiner (Baron Casey of Berwick) (1890-1976). Prominent Australian statesman who was Governor-General 1965-69. He was also a distinguished soldier, writer and speaker.

Cassidy, Lucy. Publicity Officer and Treasurer of the Fellowship of Australian Writers in the 1930s she was the wife of R. J. Cassidy who wrote bush ballads under the pseudonym of 'Gilrooney'.

Cassidy, Robert John. See Cassidy, Lucy.

Catts, Dorothy Marguerite (1898-1961). A friend of Mary, and herself a writer, she wrote biographies of the politician King O'Malley and of her husband, James Howard Catts, M.H.R., 1953-54, as well as fiction, e.g. *Dawn to Destiny*, 1946, and *Cornerstone*, 1947.

Cayley, Neville H. P. (1850-1903). Known as the 'Kookaburra Painter' he did considerable illustration work for books and journals and greatly stimulated interest in Australian birds.

Cayley, Neville William (1887-1950). Son of Neville H. P. Cayley and author of one of Australia's best-known ornithological studies, *What Bird is That*, 1931.

Charlton, Matthew (1866-1948). Began life as a coal and gold miner, later (1910-1932) Member for Hunter in the House of Representatives. Leader of the Federal Labor Party, 1922-28.

Chauvel, Charles Edward (1897-1959). One of the first independent Australian film-makers. Between 1925 and 1955 he produced many successful films on Australian subjects.

Chifley, Joseph Benedict (1885-1951). Labor Prime Minister of Australia 1945 to 1951. The achievements of his Government included the beginning of a mass immigration scheme, the establishment of the Snowy Mountains

Hydro Electric Authority and Trans Australia Airlines together with other similar attempts to implement and expand the Welfare State.

Chisholm, Alexander Hugh (Alec) (1890-1977). Newspaperman and enthusiast on all things Australian. He shared with Mary an interest in conservation and joined her in a campaign against the slaughter of egrets for women's hat feathers. He edited the Melbourne *Argus* and was General Editor of the *Australian Encyclopaedia*. He also wrote biographical studies of the explorer, Leichhardt and the poet, C. J. Dennis.

Chisholm, Caroline (1808-77). One of Australia's greatest women pioneers. In 1841 she established an Immigrants' Home in Sydney to assist girls and women waiting for employment, and later persuaded the British Government to grant free passages to wives and families of transported convicts.

Christesen, Clement Byrne (1912-). Writer, editor and critic, he is best-known as the editor of the literary magazine *Meanjin* from 1940 until 1975. He has numerous publications of his own including verse, *Dirge and Lyrics*, 1945, and edited works, e.g. *Australian Heritage*, 1949, and *On Native Grounds*, 1967, the latter a selection from *Meanjin*.

Christison, Robert (1837-1915). Pioneer pastoralist who in 1863 explored the country west of the tracks of the explorers Burke and Wills, and acquired a licence to land which he called 'Lammermoor'.

Church, Hubert Newman (1857-1932). A Tasmanian who lived mostly in New Zealand. He published a number of books of verse, e.g. *The West Wind*, 1902, and *Poems*, 1912.

Clarke, Donovan (1907-). Writer, academic and critic who held a teaching position at the University of Sydney. He was interested especially in the colonial poets, Harpur and Kendall, editing a Selection of Harpur's verse in 1964. His own poetry included *Ritual Dance and Other Verses*, 1940, and *Blue Prints and Other Verses*, 1942.

Close, Robert (1903-). Author of the once-banned novel *Love Me Sailor*, 1945, he wrote autobiographical works, e.g. *Morn of Youth*, 1948, and *Of Salt and Earth*, 1977. The controversy over *Love Me Sailor* and the general question of censorship raged throughout the late 1940s. See Mary's letter to *Daily Telegraph*, 6 May 1946.

Clune, Frank (Francis Patrick) (1893-1971). A prolific writer of travel and popular Australian books, e.g. *Dig*, 1937; *Roaming Round Australia*, 1938, and *The Wild Colonial Boy*, 1948.

Collins, Dale Cuthbert (1897-1956). Fiction writer who wrote numerous novels connected with shipboard life and oceanic places, e.g. *Ordeal*, 1924, and *Vanity Under the Sun*, 1928.

Colman, Elsie Marion. A resident of Queanbeyan who felt Mary had been belittled by the Dobell portrait and wrote several letters to her criticizing it.

Comfort, Alexander (1920-). British medical biologist and writer of numerous novels, books of verse and essays.

Corelli, Marie (1854-1924). An English novelist who wrote a number of melodramatic romances from 1886 to 1921, including *Barabbas, The Mighty Atom* and *A Romance of Two Worlds*.

Cosme. William Lane's utopian settlement in Paraguay which Mary joined in 1896. See Gavin Souter, *A Peculiar People; the Australians in Paraguay*, 1968.

Cosme Evening Notes. The colony's news sheet which Mary claims to have edited for eight months.

Cosme Monthly. The colony's magazine which first appeared in January 1895 in William Lane's handwriting. See Gavin Souter, *op. cit.*, pp. 154 and 182.

Cotton, Frank (1857-1947). One of the earliest members of the Australian Labor Party, being the M.L.A. for various inner Sydney suburbs in the 1890s.

Cottrell, Dorothy (1902-57). Author of *The Singing Gold*, 1928, a story of life in pastoral Queensland, and several other books. See *Sydney Morning Herald*, 27 October 1928, for Mary's article on her.

Cousins, W. G. Chief of the publishing department of Angus & Robertson during the 1930s.

Croll, R. H. (1869-1947). A Victorian writer who contributed frequently in prose and verse to Australian magazines and newspapers. He edited Shaw Neilson's *Collected Poems* in 1934. Croll's own verse, entitled *By-Products*, was published in 1932.

Cross, Zora (1890-1964). A teacher, actress, free-lance writer and journalist for the *Boomerang*. She wrote of bush life and the impact of city life on a country girl.

Currey, Charles Herbert (1890-1970). President of the Royal Australian Historical Society 1954-59, academic, and author of numerous Australian historical works, e.g. *The Irish at Eureka*, 1954.

Curtin, John Joseph (1885-1945). Labor Prime Minister of Australia 1941-45. He succeeded Scullin in 1935 as the leader of the Labor Party. A quiet, persuasive man, almost reluctantly accepting the post of Prime Minister, he did much to establish a successful Australian-American alliance in the difficult war years after Pearl Harbour.

Cusack, Ellen Dymphna (1904-). Best-known for the novel *Come In Spinner*, 1951 (written in collaboration with Florence James) which won the *Daily Telegraph* award of £1000 for the best wartime novel. She has also written plays, *Three Australian Three-Act Plays*, 1950, and collaborated with Miles Franklin in *Pioneers on Parade*, 1939.

Daley, Victor James (1858-1905). Lyric poet, who, with Roderic Quinn, stood out from the emphasis on balladry in the 1890s. His collections include *At Dawn and Dusk*, 1898, *Wine and Roses*, 1911, *Creeve Roe*, 1947. See B. G. Andrews and W. H. Wilde, *Australian Literature to 1900*, 1980, in the Gale Information Guide Library series.

Dalziel, Kathleen (1881-1969). The Bread and Cheese Club, Melbourne, published a volume of her poems, *Known and Not Held*, in 1941.

Davey, Mary and Alfred John. A couple who arrived in the Cosme colony 23 January 1897 from New South Wales. Later that year their infant daughter died. Davey was a miner and gardener who had emigrated from England to Australia ten years previously.

Davis, Arthur Hoey (1868-1935). Better known by his pseudonym 'Steele Rudd', he is famous for his *On Our Selection* writings and his magnificent

Australian rural characters, Dad and Dave. See B. G. Andrews and W. H. Wilde, *Australian Literature to 1900*, 1980, in the Gale Information Guide Library series.

Davis, Beatrice. Editor, for a number of years, of the publishing department of Angus & Robertson. She has edited *Short Stories of Australia: the Moderns*, 1967.

Davison, Frank Dalby (1893-1970). He first made his reputation with the book *Man-Shy*, 1931. His other works include a children's book *Children of the Dark People*, 1936, and his major novel, *The White Thorntree*, 1968. For a full list of his works see Grahame Johnston, *Annals of Australian Literature*, 1970.

Dawson, Peter (1882-1961). Popular Australian baritone and song writer. At the time of his death he had recorded 2500 songs and sold a total of 13 million records. See Melbourne *Age*, 27 September 1961.

Deakin, Alfred (1856-1919). One of the architects of Federation. He was Prime Minister of Australia 1903-4 and 1905-8 and was a leading intellectual of the day. He wrote numerous important political works including *The Federal Story: The Inner History of the Federal Cause 1880-1900*. See J. A. La Nauze, *Alfred Deakin: A Biography*, 1965.

Deamer, Dulcie (1890-1972). New Zealand-born actress, free-lance writer and novelist. Most of her fiction was set in antiquity. Her poetry collections included *Messalina*, 1932, and *The Silver Branch*, 1948.

De Brune, Aidan (1879-). Canadian-born editor of *Fifty Years of Progress in Australia 1878-1928*, 1929.

De la Mare, Walter (1873-1956). Author of many poems in which dream and reality, fairies and humble natural creatures are delightfully blended. He published *The Listeners*, 1912, and *Memoirs of a Midget*, 1921.

Dennis, Clarence James (1876-1938). The Australian folk poet, well-known for *The Songs of a Sentimental Bloke*, 1915, and similar verse such as *The Moods of Ginger Mick*, 1916, and *Doreen*, 1917.

Devaney, James (1890-1976). Literary critic, freelance journalist and teacher. He published the biography of the poet Shaw Neilson in 1944, and also edited Neilson's last volume, *Unpublished Poems*, in 1947. He wrote fiction (*The Currency Lass*, 1927) and poetry (*Where the Wind Goes*, 1939).

Devanny, Jean (1894-1962). Author of numerous novels of the sugar-growing country in Queensland. She also wrote more reflective works, including *By Tropic Sea and Jungle*, 1944, and *Bird of Paradise*, 1945.

Dick, Andrew. Dick and his wife arrived in Cosme, November, 1897. In February 1899 Alexander Dick arrived, and in May 1899 James Dick also arrived from Scotland.

The Disinherited, 1941. Mary's small volume of poems published by Robertson & Mullens, Melbourne. The thirty brief & fragmentary verses are loosely linked by the theme of deprivation. See W. H. Wilde, *Three Radicals*, 1969.

Dobell, Sir William (1899-1970). Outstanding Australian portrait painter and landscapist whose controversial portrait of Mary aroused much discussion in 1957. Dobell won numerous Archibald prizes for portraiture, including the 1944 prize with his portrait of fellow-artist Joshua Smith.

Donald, Jim. Sydney journalist, for many years a columnist in the Sydney Sunday newspaper, *Truth*.

Drake-Brockman, Henrietta (1901-68). Writer of short stories (*Sydney or The Bush*, 1948), novels (*The Wicked and the Fair*, 1947) and a prize-winning play (*Men Without Wives*, 1938).

Dunlea, Father Thomas V. (1894-1970). In 1939 he founded a settlement for delinquent and orphaned boys called Boys' Town at Engadine, about 30 kilometres from Sydney, and remained its Principal until 1952.

'E'. See Fullerton, Mary Elizabeth.

Edwards, Mary. Chiefly a portrait artist, she was a regular contributor to the Archibald Prize competition. Mary Edwards was one of the plaintiffs in the court case over the award of the Archibald Prize to William Dobell for his controversial portrait of Joshua Smith. Her own work was largely picturesque canvases of South Sea Island exotica.

Elkin, Adolphus Peter (1891-). Professor of Anthropology for more than 20 years at the University of Sydney. A leading authority on Aboriginals, his publications included *The Australian Aborigines*, 1938.

Elliot, Jane (1727-1805). Writer of the most popular version of the old lament for Flodden, 'Flowers of the Forest'.

Ellis, Henry Havelock (1859-1939). English sociologist and essayist who came to Australia in 1875 and remained four years. While here he was in charge of a school at Sparkes Creek, near Scone, New South Wales. He wrote *Kanga Creek: An Australian Idyll*, 1922. He later gained high repute for numerous books on sociology and sex.

Emerson, Ernest Sando (1870-1919). Journalist and writer of prose and verse. He wrote mainly for the *Bulletin*, *Lone Hand* and *Sydney Mail* under the pseudonyms of 'Milky White' and 'George Mather'. *A Shanty Entertainment*, a collection of bush stories and poems, was published in 1904.

Esson, Thomas Louis (1879-1943). Playwright and poet who struggled hard in the early years of this century for worthwhile indigenous Australian drama and with Vance Palmer and others founded the Pioneer Players in 1922. His own plays were published as *The Southern Cross and Other Plays* in 1946. See Leslie Rees, *The Making of Australian Drama*, 1973.

Evatt, Herbert Vere (1894-1965). Long-standing Labor parliamentarian who was Leader of the Labor Party in opposition 1951-55. He wrote *Rum Rebellion*, 1938.

Ewers, John Keith (1904-78). A writer and critic whose novels *Men Against the Earth*, 1946, and *For Heroes To Live In*, 1948, give a faithful picture of life in the Western Australian wheat country. He also wrote *Tell The People*, 1943, a discussion of the writings of Joseph Furphy, and *Creative Writing in Australia: A Critical Survey*, 1945.

Excell, Patricia. A staff member of the literary magazine *Meanjin* in which some of her poems were occasionally published.

Fadden, Sir Arthur (1895-1973). Leader of the Australian Country Party, 1941-58, and Prime Minister of Australia for three months in 1941.

Falconer, Ethel Keith. See Stonehaven, Lady.

Falkiner, Franc Sadlier (1833-1909). An Irish pastoralist, who acquired the station Boonoke on the Western plains of New South Wales in 1878.

Farrell, John (1851-1904). Brewer, journalist, poet, and one of the earliest balladists of the *Bulletin*. He is best known for his volume of verse *How He Died and Other Poems*, 1887. Mary regarded him (together with A. G. Stephens and William Lane) as among the most important influences on her life. See B. G. Andrews and W. H. Wilde, *Australian Literature to 1900*, 1980, in the Gale Information Guide Library series.

Farrer, William (1845-1906). An Australian agriculturalist who developed improved strains of wheat which could flourish in Australia. His experiments paved the way for a thriving wheat industry in this country.

Feint, Adrian (1894-1971). A painter, mainly of decorative and surrealistic flower pieces, who studied under Julian Ashton. Widely known for his etched and engraved book plates.

Fellowship of Australian Writers. The literary society founded in Sydney in 1928, and now Australia-wide. Mary played a leading role in its establishment, although in later years bitter controversy arose over rival claims to its origins. See letter, 22 May 1935.

Ferguson, George Adie (1910-), C.B.E. Director and Publishing Director of the firm of Angus & Robertson from 1930 until the change of ownership in 1969. Mary appointed this grandson of George Robertson, the co-founder of Angus & Robertson, as her nominee in the matter of her personal diaries in the Mitchell Library Mary Gilmore Collection. Ferguson is the author of *Some Early Australian Bookmen*, 1978.

Finey, George Edmond (1895-). Newspaper cartoonist on *Smith's Weekly* and *Daily Telegraph* in the 1930s. A special number of *Art in Australia* was devoted to him, June 1931. A collection of his cartoons was published entitled *George Finey's Caricatures* in 1931. In 1978 his 'Finey's Approach to Music' comprising paintings in collage was exhibited in the Sydney Opera House.

Fisher, Mary Lucy (Lala) (1872-1929). Journalist, poet, and friend of Henry Lawson. She edited the *Sydney Theatre Magazine* and an anthology of Australian prose and verse, *By Creek and Gully*, 1899.

FitzGerald, Robert David (1902-). One of Australia's leading modern poets and a staunch admirer of Mary's verse. FitzGerald's numerous books of verse include *Moonlight Acre*, 1938, *Heemskerck Shoals*, 1949, *Between Two Tides*, 1952, *This Night's Orbit*, 1953, *Forty Years' Poems*, 1965.

FitzHenry, W. E. A great friend of Mary Gilmore, he died in 1957. He had been secretary to three *Bulletin* editors and died in the *Bulletin* office where he had worked for over forty years. He was the author of *Australian Authors and Artists Handbook*.

Fitzpatrick, Brian Charles (1906-65). He helped found, in 1935, the Australian Council for Civil Liberties. One of the pioneer economic historians of Australia, he published *British Imperialism and Australia, 1783-1833*, 1933. Editor of *Australian Democrat*.

Flynn, John (Flynn of the Inland) (1880-1951). The Presbyterian clergyman who pioneered medical services to people of the outback. He was Moderator General of the Presbyterian Church 1939-42.

Foott, Mary Hannay (1846-1918). The literary and social editor of the *Queenslander* from 1884 to 1894, she published *Where the Pelican Builds and Other Poems*, 1885, a popular book of bush ballads.

Forrest, David (David Denholm) (1924-). Author of *The Last Blue Sea*, 1959, which won the Mary Gilmore Prize.

Forrest, Mabel (1872-1935). A prolific writer of sentimental and descriptive verse, e.g., *The Rose of Forgiveness*, 1904, and *Alpha Centauri*, 1909.

Foster, Rene. A close friend and frequent correspondent of Mary's. As this book is published she is living in Adelaide and is still vitally interested in things Australian.

Fourteen Men. Mary's last collection of poems, published in 1954. See inter alia W. H. Wilde, *Three Radicals*, 1969.

Fox, Leonard Phillip. He and his wife Mona Brand are both established writers and political figures. Len Fox wrote two novels as a result of time spent in Vietnam, *Chung of Vietnam*, 1957, and *Friendly Vietnam*, 1958.

Franklin, Stella Maria Miles (1878-1954). Best-known for her fiction and autobiographical writings, including *My Brilliant Career*, 1901, and its sequel *My Career Goes Bung*, not published until 1946. She also wrote several books under the pseudonym 'Brent of Bin Bin', e.g. *Up the Country*, 1928, *Ten Creeks Run*, 1930, and *Back to Bool Bool* (1931). For a full list of her works see Grahame Johnston, *Annals of Australian Literature*, 1970.

Frazer, Dr George. Author of *Poems of Life and Time*, 1957.

Fry, Elizabeth (1780-1845). The English Quaker and philanthropist who spent much of her life campaigning on social problems such as the improvement of prison conditions in England, especially for women.

Fullerton, Mary Elizabeth ('E') (1868-1946). Author of two books of short pointed lyrics suggestive of Emily Dickinson—*Moles Do So Little With Their Privacy*, 1942, *The Wonder and The Apple*, 1946. Mary was much intrigued by the identity of 'E'.

Game, Lady Gwendoline Margaret. Wife of Sir Philip Game, Governor of New South Wales, 1930-35, she published *A Few Words*, 1934.

Garran, Sir Robert Randolph (1867-1957). A distinguished constitutional lawyer, he was the author of several legal works, e.g. *The Coming Commonwealth: An Australian Handbook of Federal Government*, 1897. He also compiled *The Book of Songs: by Heinrich Heine* (a translation), 1924.

Gellert, Leon Maxwell (1892-1977). Poet, essayist, journalist and literary columnist of the *Sydney Morning Herald*. He published in 1917 *Songs of a Campaign* (an anthology of World War I poems), *The Isle of San*, 1919 and *Desperate Measures*, 1928.

George, Henry (1839-97). American economist and reformer, regarded as the founder of the single tax movement. His principal work, *Progress and Poverty*, was published in 1880.

Gilmore, William Alexander (Will) (1866-1945). Mary's husband, whom she met at the Cosme settlement of William Lane's New Australia experiment. He was a shearer from Victoria and some years after they returned to Australia he went on the land in Queensland.

Gilmore, William Dysart Cameron (Billy) (1898-1945). Mary's only child, born in 1898 while she was in South America. He accompanied his mother to Sydney to complete his secondary education. On leaving school he rejoined his father in Queensland. His son (Mary's grandson), William Wallace Gilmore, has been instrumental in having this correspondence published.

Ginsburg, Reba. Author of *At the Initiation: Four Poems*, 1951 and *The Numberless Sands*, 1952 (both limited editions of 140 copies). In 1951 she edited a national university students' magazine, *Brolga*, for which Mary wrote a foreword.

Gordon, Adam Lindsay (1833-70). The forerunner of the Australian bush balladists, best-known for his poem 'The Sick Stockrider'. See inter alia, W. H. Wilde, *Adam Lindsay Gordon*, 1972, and B. G. Andrews and W. H. Wilde, *Australian Literature to 1900*, 1980, in the Gale Information Guide Library series.

Gordon, Georgiana Huntly. See *McCrae*, Georgiana.

Gould, John (1804-81). Ornithologist and world authority on the birds of many lands including Australia, New Guinea, Asia and the Himalayan region. His book, *The Birds of Australia*, was published in 1848.

Gould, Nathaniel (1857-1919). A journalist in Australia from 1884 to 1895. On his return to England he published numerous novels about the sporting life, especially the turf. He is now recognized as one the the leading writers of popular fiction of that genre. See B. G. Andrews and W. H. Wilde, *Australian Literature to 1900*, 1980, in the Gale Information Guide Library series.

Grattan, C(linton) Hartley (1902-). An American free-lance journalist who first came to Australia in 1927 where he met Percival Serle and Frank Wilmot and began collecting Australiana. His articles on Australia on his return to America attracted the attention of Nettie Palmer, Miles Franklin and others. In 1936 the Carnegie Corporation sent him to tour and write about Australia and his questioning attitude prodded many Australians into articulating their aims and beliefs more rigorously than before. His publications include *The South West Pacific to 1900* and *The South West Pacific since 1900*, 2 vols, 1963.

Green, Henry Mackenzie (1881-1962). Librarian of the Fisher Library at Sydney University for twenty-five years and pioneer literary critic. He compiled *A History of Australian Literature*, 1961, and the earlier *An Outline of Australian Literature*, 1930. He was also a writer of poetry and essays. His wife, Dorothy Green, poet, academic, and noted critic, is at present writing an up-to-date history of Australian literature.

Greenlees, Gavin. One-time editor of the *Forbes Advocate* and amateur local historian. His poems were published in *The Art of Rosaleen Norton*, 1952, and later he spent a year in China working on a Peking newspaper.

Grey, Sir George (1812-98). He explored the Arnhem Land country between 1837 and 1839. He was later Governor of South Australia 1841-45 and of New Zealand 1845-53 and 1861-68.

Grey, Zane (1872-1939). The popular American fiction writer (especially of the 'Western' novel) who sometimes visited Australia for the big-game fishing season.

Gruner, Elioth Lauritz (1882-1939). Australian artist who studied under Julian Ashton and became Ashton's assistant at the Sydney Art School. He won the Wynne Prize for landscapes in 1916, 1919 and 1921.

Gye, Hal ['James Hackston'] (1888-1967). He published *Father Clears Out*, 1966, and *The Hole in the Bedroom Floor*, 1969.

Hadow, Lyndall (1904-76). A Western Australian short story writer (*Full Circle*, 1969). Her father was Julian Stuart who was one of the shearers' strike prisoners of 1891 imprisoned on the Island of St Helena, five miles from the mouth of the Brisbane River. He was released in November 1893. He was also concerned in fostering William Lane's New Australia experiment. See Gavin Souter, *A Peculiar People; the Australians in Paraguay*, 1968.

Halstead Press. Angus & Robertson's book manufacturing department which grew from the Eagle Press established in 1923. W. Kirwan became Manager of Halstead Printing Company as it was first known. Halstead was the name of the town in Essex where George Robertson (of Angus & Robertson) was born in 1860. W. G. Cousins succeeded Kirwan.

Hamilton, Winifred. Author of *Three Poems*, 1920, and friend and contemporary of 'Steele Rudd' (Arthur Hoey Davis).

Hardy, Frank (1917-). Hardy first made his reputation with his social propagandist novel set in Melbourne, *Power Without Glory*, 1950. He has also written the extravagant *The Yarns of Billy Borker*, 1965, and other short stories, as well as numerous prose works.

Hargraves, Edward Hammond (1816-91). One of the discoverers of gold in Australia.

Harney, William Edward (Bill) (1895-1962). Author of *Taboo*, 1943, a book which dealt with the author's experiences while a Patrol Officer in the Native Affairs Branch of the Northern Territory. Harney lived and worked in remote areas of Australia waging a constant fight for the cause of the Aboriginals and for the preservation of their culture.

Harris, Joel Chandler (1848-1908). Author of the Brer Fox and Brer Rabbit stories in the Hoosier dialect of the negroes of southern U.S.A. Based on authentic legends they were the first, and remain the greatest, in the school of negro folk literature.

Hart-Smith, William (1911-). His numerous collections of poetry include *Columbus Goes West*, 1943, *On the Level*, 1950, and *The Talking Clothes*, 1966.

Haylen, Leslie Clement (1899-1977). Labor Member of the House of Representatives for Parkes 1943-63, he shared Mary's views on many social problems. He was also a writer and published plays, short stories, novels and historical works.

Heffron, Hon. Robert James (1890-1957). Labor Minister for Education and Child Welfare in New South Wales 1944-66 and Premier 1959-64.

Heney, Thomas William (1862-1928). Critic, poet, fiction writer and journalist, he was associated with Sydney newspapers from 1878 until his retirement as Editor of the *Daily Telegraph* in 1925 and was the author of several novels and two volumes of poetry.

Henley, William Ernest (1849-1903). A close friend of R. L. Stevenson and editor of several literary magazines, he wrote considerable poetry and drama. Mary must have seen him in London as she was returning from Paraguay to Australia in 1901.

Hetherington, John (1907-74). War correspondent, author and columnist. His best-known work is *Blamey*, 1954, the biography of Field-Marshal Sir Thomas Blamey, but he had numerous other publications including *Airborne Invasion*, 1943, the story of the battle for Crete in World War II; *The Winds Are Still*, Sydney Morning Herald £1000 prize War Story, 1947; and *Norman Lindsay: The Embattled Olympian*, 1961.

Higgins, Henry Bournes (1851-1929). Uncle of his biographer, Nettie Palmer. Founder of the Court of Conciliation and Arbitration, he was also its President 1907-21.

Hill, Ernestine (1900-72). Her best-known works include *The Great Australian Loneliness*, 1937; *Water Into Gold*, 1937; and *My Love Must Wait*, 1941, the story of Matthew Flinders.

Hoff, George Rayner (1894-1937). Australian sculptor whose works include the figures on the exterior of the Anzac Memorial in Hyde Park, Sydney, and the central group of figures in the Memorial's interior. He did a bust of Mary.

Holburn, Muir (1920-60). He and his wife, Marjorie Pizer, edited *Freedom on the Wallaby: Poems for the Australian People*, 1953.

Holman, William Arthur (1871-1934). Prominent early Trade Unionist and Labor politician. He was Premier of New South Wales in 1913.

Holmes, Oliver Wendell (1809-94). American poet, essayist and novelist whose publications include *The Professor at the Breakfast Table*, 1860, and *The Poet at the Breakfast Table*, 1872.

Hope, Alec Derwent (1907-). Distinguished Australian poet whose chief publications of verse include *The Wandering Islands*, 1955, *Collected Poems*, 1966, *New Poems*, 1969. See Leonie Kramer, *A. D. Hope*, 1976 and J. Hooton, *Bibliography of A. D. Hope*, 1979.

Hopegood, Peter (1891-1967). Journalist, free-lance artist, poet and outback wanderer, he wrote *Circus at World's End*, 1947.

Hound of the Road. Mary's book of essays and reminiscences, published in 1922.

Housman, Alfred Edward (1859-1936). English poet who wrote *Shropshire Lad*, 1896, and *Last Poems*, 1922.

Howarth, Robert Guy (1906-73). Academic, literary critic and author, who was Professor of English at Cape Town University, South Africa. He founded the literary magazine, *Southerly*, in 1939.

Hughes, William Morris (Billy) (1864-1952). One of Australia's most colourful politicians, he was Prime Minister during World War I and was often affectionately labelled 'The Little Digger'.

Huxley, Julian Sorell (1887-1975). His popular writings on evolution have greatly influenced modern intellectual thinking on anthropology and sociology.

Idriess, Ion Llewellyn (1890-1979). A prolific writer of documentary and semi-fictional works on the Australian outback. His chief works include *Lasseter's Last Ride*, 1931, *Flynn of the Inland*, 1932, and *The Cattle King*, 1936.

Ingamells, Reginald Charles (Rex) (1913-55). Founder of the Jindyworobak school of writers whose purpose was to emphasize, in literature, native Australian subjects. His own poetry is represented in *Selected Poems*, 1944.

Ingleton, Geoffrey Chapman (1908-). Editor of *True Patriots All: or, News from Early Australia as Told in a Collection of Broadsides*, 1952, and author of *Charting a Continent*, 1944.

Jago, Walter. Probably the son of Walter Francis Jago, formerly Lord Mayor of Parramatta.

Jephcott, Sydney Wheeler (1864-1951). The poet of the beautiful Corryong district on the New South Wales–Victorian border. His publications included *The Secrets of the South*, 1892, and *Penetralia*, 1912.

Jones, Inigo (1872-1954). The Queensland meteorologist who pioneered the technique of long-range weather forecasting.

Joubert, Jules Francois (1824-1907) and Didier, Numa (1816-81). Entrepreneurs who had large land holdings at Hunters Hill near Sydney where they built 'St Malo', which was acquired by the National Trust in 1955. In 1847 Didier Joubert bought the adjoining Reibey Cottage from Mary Reibey.

Julius, Harry (1885-1938). Artist and designer, he studied under Julian Ashton and illustrated for the *Bulletin* and other newspapers.

Kahan, Louis (1905-). Vienna-born portrait artist, illustrator and stage designer. In 1960 he began the series of portrait sketches of important literary figures in *Meanjin* and won the Archibald Prize in 1962 with his portrait of the novelist, Patrick White.

Kaleski, Robert. Authority on dogs and sheep, and a contributor of dog stories to the *Bulletin*. He was the author of *Australian Barkers and Biters*, 1914.

Kelly, Nora. Social Editor of the *Bulletin* for many years. She published a book of poems entitled *Poetry 1940-42*, 1944.

Kendall, Henry (1839-82). One of Australia's best-known lyric poets of colonial times, he is recognized for poems such as 'Bell Birds', 'September in Australia' and 'Bill the Bullock Driver'. See W. H. Wilde, *Henry Kendall*, 1976, and B. G. Andrews and W. H. Wilde, *Australian Literature to 1900*, 1980, in the Gale Information Guide Library series.

Kidman, Sir Sidney (1857-1935). Millionaire pastoralist who began by purchasing the Owen Spring Station on the Hugh River, south of Alice Springs, in 1880 and expanded into enormous land holdings in New South Wales and Queensland.

Kuhn, Maria. Brisbane sculptor and teacher, some of whose pieces are reproduced in *Art in Australia* by N. MacGeorge, 1948. During World War II she made studies in clay in New Guinea of soldiers in action and in later years she prepared an *Atlas of Anatomy*, published in London. Her statue of Queensland Premier Hanlon is in the grounds of Brisbane General Hospital.

Lambert, Eric (1921-66). Author of several works including *Five Bright Stars*, 1954, and *Watermen*, 1956.

Lamond, Hector (1865-1947). Editor of the Sydney *Worker* who persuaded Mary to leave Casterton to join the staff of the *Worker* in Sydney to write the Women's page.

Lane, John. Brother of William Lane, he left *Cosme* in 1904.

Lane, William (1861-1917). Social reformer who edited the *Boomerang* from 1887 to 1892 then founded the New Australia settlement in South America in 1893. When the venture was abandoned in 1899 he returned to Australia and became editor of the Sydney *Worker* in 1900, then of the New Zealand *Herald*. See Gavin Souter, *A Peculiar People; the Australians in Paraguay*, 1968.

Lang, John Dunmore (1799-1878). Presbyterian clergyman and author who was instrumental in the building of the Scots Church in Sydney and was its minister for more than fifty years. Much interested in immigration and colonial matters, he was Moderator of the General Assembly of the Presbyterian Church in N.S.W. in 1872.

Langley, Eve (1908-75). Author of *The Pea Pickers*, 1942, she also wrote *The White Topee*, 1954. Married a New Zealand artist Hilary Clark and had one daughter and two sons. She died a recluse in the Blue Mountains in 1975.

Lavender, George. An identity of early Sydney after whom Lavender Bay is named. He married the daughter of Billy Blue, a Jamaican sailor who settled in Sydney in 1805 and was given a grant of 80 acres on the north side of Sydney Harbour. Blue operated a ferry from Blue's Point to Dawes Point.

Lawson, Gertrude. Henry Lawson's sister.

Lawson, Henry (1867-1922). Probably Australia's most popular literary figure. He was a poet and short story writer who has become closely identified with the upsurge of Australian nationalism and radicalism in the 1890s. See, inter alia, A. A. Phillips, *Henry Lawson*, 1970; C. Manning Clark, *In Search of Henry Lawson*, 1978, and Colin Roderick (ed.) *Henry Lawson Criticism 1894-1971*, 1972.

Lawson, Louisa (1848-1920). Mother of Henry Lawson. She exercised a strong influence on her son's early literary efforts. An individualist and feminist she founded and edited the journal, *Dawn*, 1888-1905 and began the Dawn Club for women. There is a good account of her in Manning Clark's *In Search of Henry Lawson*, 1978.

Letters, Francis Joseph Henry (1897-1964). Poet, essayist, academic, and author of *Darkness and Light and Other Poems*, 1934. He was made a Papal Knight in 1960 for his classical scholarship.

Lewis, F. Known in Australia as Alec Forrester, he joined William Lane's Cosme settlement. See Gavin Souter, *A Peculiar People; the Australians in Paraguay*, 1968.

Lindsay, Sir Lionel Arthur (1874-1961). Writer, artist and art critic, and a foundation member of the Australian Academy of Art. A member of the Lindsay family, most influential in the Australian cultural and literary society of the 1920s.

Lindsay, Norman (1879-1969). One of the most influential figures in the development of Australian culture in this century. A legendary figure who was bohemian, artist, novelist, poet, critic and writer of books for children. See John Hetherington, *Norman Lindsay*, in the Australian Writers and their Work series, revised edition 1969. Lindsay's letters were published by Angus & Robertson in 1979, the year of Lindsay's centenary.

Litchfield, Jessie Sinclair (-1954). A cousin of J. K. Moir, she wrote, inter alia, *Far-North Memories*, 1930, an account of ten years spent on the diamond drills.

Lochiel. The title given to the head of the Clan Cameron. The 'Great Lochiel' was Sir Ewen Cameron of Lochiel (1629-1719), the Highland Chieftain knighted by Charles II for campaigns on his behalf. He was noted for his enormous strength and size and was dubbed by Macaulay, the 'Ulysses of the Highlands'.

Lockett, Jeannie (née Jeannie Beattie). Mary's mother's sister. Apart from the novels Mary mentions in letter, 23 April 1930, Jeannie Lockett also wrote several social tracts including 'Female Labour in Australia. An Appeal for Help', *Nineteenth Century*, 1885, and 'The Labour Question in Australia from an Australian Point of View', *Westminster Review*, 1889.

Loder, John de Vere. See Wakehurst, Lord.

Lofting, Hilary Joseph Francis (1881-1939). Brother of Hugh Lofting (author of the 'Dr. Dolittle' books). Hilary wrote stories and critical articles for the *Bulletin*, sometimes using the pseudonym 'Francis Osborn'. He edited the 1929 unabridged edition of Marcus Clarke's *For The Term of His Natural Life*.

The *Lone Hand*. Created by J. F. Archibald and launched by the *Bulletin* in 1907, *Lone Hand* was a general journal with strong literary interests. Of a high standard in its early years when it published the work of many of the important literary figures of the period, it declined just before its demise in 1921.

Longstaff, Sir John (1862-1941). An Australian who studied art in Paris and was commissioned to paint official portraits of people important in Australian life. He painted Henry Lawson's portrait in 1900.

Lorca, Frederico Garcia (1899-1936). Spanish poet, dramatist and essayist who enjoyed wide acclaim outside his own country. He was executed in the Spanish Civil War.

Loveless, George (1797-1874). Leader of a farmers' trade union in the village of Tolpuddle near Dorchester. He and five others were transported to Australia for seven years in 1834 for 'unlawful oaths'. They became known as 'The Tolpuddle Martyrs'.

Luffmann, Laura Bogue (1845-1929). She wrote novels under the pseudonym Laura M. Lane before coming to Australia where she played a leading role in the feminist movement. She edited the *Women's Voice* and wrote for the Sydney *Daily Telegraph*. Mary addressed a poem to her in *Under the Wilgas*, 1932. See obituary articles, *Sydney Morning Herald*, 29 June 1929.

Lynch, John. Secretary of the Melbourne Bread and Cheese Club in 1961.

Lyons, Dame Enid Muriel (1897-). The first woman elected to the House of Representatives being the Liberal member for Darwin, Tasmania, in 1943. She was the wife of Joseph Aloysius Lyons (1879-1939), Prime Minister of Australia 1931-39. Her publications include *So We Take Comfort*, *The Old Haggis* and *Among the Carrion Crows*.

Macaulay, Thomas Babington (1800-59). One of the founders of the so-called Whig interpretation of history, he became famous for his 5-volume *History of England*, 1849-61.

McCay, Adam Cairns ('Dum') (1874-1947). The first literary editor of *Smith's Weekly*, he was also, at one time, associate editor of the Sydney *Daily Telegraph*. He published *The Boy at the Dardanelles*, 1916.

McCrae, Dorothy Frances (Mrs C. E. Perry). Sister of the poet Hugh McCrae, she published five volumes of verse from 1909 to 1926 and was a contributor to the *Bookfellow*.

McCrae, George Gordon (1833-1927). Father of Hugh McCrae, the lyric poet. He was a significant literary figure in nineteenth century Melbourne, publishing *Mamba* and *The Story of Balladeadro* in 1867. See B. G. Andrews and W. H. Wilde, *Australian Literature to 1900*, 1980, in the Gale Information Guide Library series.

McCrae, Georgiana Huntly (1804-90). Mother of George Gordon McCrae. A diary she kept from 1838 to 1848 was edited and published by her grandson, Hugh, as *Georgiana's Journal*, 1934.

McCrae, Hugh (1876-1958). Son of George Gordon McCrae, he was an important Australian lyrical poet of the early twentieth century. His numerous volumes of verse (some of them illustrated by Norman Lindsay) included *Satyrs and Sunlight*, 1909, and *Poems*, 1939. He was an admirer of Mary and her verse, and they wrote often to each other until McCrae's death in 1958.

McDonald, Nancy May (Nan) (1921-). Author of a collection of poems *Pacific Sea*, 1947. She also published *The Lonely Fire*, 1954, *The Lighthouse*, 1959 and *Selected Poems*, 1969.

MacDonald, Walter Reginald. During World War II he was invited by the British Information Ministry to see Britain at war. He wrote *By Bomber to Britain*, 1944. Later General Manager of the Brisbane *Telegraph*.

McGregor, Peter. Supervisor of Talks in New South Wales for the ABC in the late 1950s.

Mackaness, Dr George (1882-1968). Scholar, author, editor and President of the Royal Australian Historical Society in 1948-49. He compiled various anthologies of Australian verse and prose, including *Australian Short Stories*, 1928, *The Wide Brown Land*, 1934 (in collaboration with his daughter Joan), and *Poets of Australia*, 1946. Alice was his wife.

Mackay, Jessie (1846-1938). A leading New Zealand poet and a friend of Mary.

McKell, Sir William John (1891-). Prominent Labor politician who, after being Premier of New South Wales, was Governor-General of Australia 1947-53.

Mackellar, Dorothea (1885-1968). Widely known for her poem 'My Country'. A volume of her verse *The Witch Maid* was published in 1914.

McKellar, John Alexander Ross (1904-32). An extraordinarily brilliant and energetic young Australian whose early death in 1932 coincided with the publication of his poetry, *Twenty-six*. His *Collected Poems* was published in 1946. See *Southerly*, 5, 4 (1944), 3-10 for biographical article by J. W. Gibbes.

McKeown, Keith Collingwood (1892-1952). Assistant entomologist at the Australian Museum, he wrote many books on Australian insects including *Nature in Australia*, 1949.

McLeay, Alexander (1767-1848). As a reward for his Government service as Colonial Secretary 1825-37, he was granted 54 acres in Elizabeth Bay. His garden there, famous for its valuable and rare plant specimens, proved a stimulus to ornamental gardening in Sydney.

McLeod, James. Minister of St Stephen's, Macquarie Street, Sydney, from 1933 until he went to New Zealand.

McNicoll, David Ramsay C.B.E. (1914-). After being a war correspondent in World War II, covering the Normandy invasion, he returned to journalism in Australia. He was Editor-in-Chief of Australian Consolidated Press, 1953-72. His publications include verse, e.g., *Air Mail Palestine*, 1943, and *The Round Dozen*, 1947.

Malloch, Henry William. Journalist, accountant and foundation member and secretary of the Bread and Cheese Club, Melbourne. He published *A Brief History of the Bread and Cheese Club*, 1940, *Fellows All. The Chronicles of the Bread and Cheese Club*, 1943, and was the first editor of *Bohemia*, the Club's journal.

Manifold, John (1915-). A poet whose writings were usually critical of the existing order. His *Selected Verse* appeared in 1946. Other works include *The Death of Ned Kelly*, 1941, and *Who Wrote the Ballads?*, 1964. He edited *The Penguin Australian Song Book*, 1964.

Mansell, William Arthur Byram (1899-). Creator of a new style of painting in the Aboriginal way using Australian earths. His works include *Legends from Australia*, 1950, and *How the Sky was Lifted*, 1951, an Aboriginal legend decorated with native clay pigments.

Marri'd. Mary's first collection of verse published in 1910. See note to letter, 30 November 1909.

Marshall, Alan (1902-). Crippled by poliomyelitis as a boy, he spent much time travelling in and writing about Australia. His best-known works include the autobiographical *I Can Jump Puddles*, 1955, and numerous short story collections.

Martin, David (né Ludwig Detsinyi) (1915-). Born in Hungary, he wrote in German until he was 23. He came to Australia in 1949 and has written novels, short stories, verse and plays. Among his best-known works are *Tiger Bay*, 1946, *The Stones of Bombay*, 1949, *Poems*, 1958, and the Australian classic, *The Hero of Too*, 1965.

Martinez, Zuviria Gustavo. Popular and prolific Argentine novelist noted for his description of country people struggling against adversity. His *La Casa De Los Cuervos* was published in 1916.

Masefield, John (1878-1967). English Poet Laureate 1930, he was a vigorous, talented but uneven poet whose forcible style, strong, concrete vision and vivid realism made an original contribution to the complex mass of modern poetry.

Mathew, Ray (1929-). His collections of poetry include *With Cypress Pine*, 1951, and *South of the Equator*, 1961. He collaborated with Mena Abdullah in short story writing e.g. *The Time of the Peacock*, 1965.

Mawdesley, Christina. Author of *The Corroboree Tree: and Twelve Shorter Poems of Melbourne's Early Days of Settlement*, published by the Melbourne Bread and Cheese Club in 1944.

Menzies, Sir Robert Gordon (1894-1978). Australia's longest serving Prime Minister (having held the position 1939-41 and 1949-66) and one of this country's most notable statesmen. Much esteemed by Queen Elizabeth II who made him a Knight of the Thistle and Warden of the Cinque Ports. He published his memoirs, *Afternoon Light*, in 1967.

Meredith, George (1828-1909). English poet and novelist. He wrote numerous novels between 1856 and 1895 of which *The Egoist*, 1879, is outstanding.

Meurant, Ferdinand. He came as a convict under life sentence to Sydney in 1800, was pardoned, and lived at Seven Hills on a 160-acre grant. He had five native-born ('currency') children.

Miller, Edmund Morris (1881-1964). An interesting mixture of professional psychologist and literary historian. He was Professor of Psychology and Philosophy at the University of Tasmania, 1922-52. He published, in 1940, *Australian Literature. A Bibliography to 1938*, a descriptive and bibliographical survey and this was extended to 1950 with the assistance of F. T. Macartney. In spite of some errors and omissions, it has proved a most valuable bibliographical work for students of Australian literature.

Miller, Robert. Miller sailed in the *Royal Tar* from Adelaide in March 1893. He took a year's leave of absence from Cosme in 1897 to visit Scotland and Australia but never returned. He died in 1900 of Bright's Disease.

Missingham, Hal (1906-). Director of the Art Gallery of New South Wales from 1945 until his retirement in 1971, he is also a painter and graphic artist of considerable skill.

Mitchell, Elyne (1913-). Born in Victoria, the daughter of Sir Harry Chauvel. She travelled widely, writing novels, general books and children's stories. Her novels include *Flow River, Blow Wind*, 1953, and *Black Cockatoo Mean Snow*, 1956. Her most recent publication is *Light Horse*, 1978. Her father's biography *Chauvel of the Light Horse* by A. J. Hill was also published in 1978.

Moir, John Kinmont, O.B.E. (1893-1958). Co-founder of the Melbourne Bread and Cheese Club and its first President, he was a strong supporter of Australian literary and historical studies and a collector of Australiana. He edited *Shaw Neilson: A Memorial*, 1942.

Moore, Tom Inglis (1901-78). One of Australia's eminent literary scholars and writer of poetry, fiction, drama and criticism. His considerable body of critical work includes *Six Australian Poets*, 1942, and *Social Patterns in Australian Literature*, 1971. His wife Peace and daughter Pacita were also known to Mary.

Moore, William (1868-1937). One-time art critic of the Melbourne *Herald* and the Sydney *Daily Telegraph*. He wrote the two-volume *The Story of Australian Art*, 1934, and edited with T. Inglis Moore, *Best Australian One-Act Plays*, 1937. His wife was the poet Dora Wilcox.

More Recollections. Mary's book of reminiscences, published 1935.

Morrison, John (1904-). A sometime contributor to *Tribune*, and the author of several novels and collections of short stories, e.g. *Black Cargo and Other Stories*, 1955, and *Twenty-three*, 1962.

Morton, Frank (1869-1923). Journalist, poet, novelist and editor of *Triad*, a New Zealand magazine of high reputation. He spent his last years in Sydney and contributed to the *Bulletin*.

Murchison, Lawrence Maxwell (1919-). Scholar and Tutor at St Mark's Institute of Theology, Canberra, and Canon of St Saviour's Cathedral, Goulburn.

Murdoch, Sir Walter (1874-1970). Academic and writer, popularly known for his essays, e.g. *Collected Essays*, 1938, the earlier *Speaking Personally*, 1930, and *Saturday Mornings*, 1931. He also wrote the biography, *Alfred Deakin*, 1923.

Murray, Gilbert (1866-1957). Classical scholar noted for his series of verse translations of Euripides. He helped to make Greek drama real to ordinary audiences, his drama being performed in London, notably at the Court Theatre, 1902-27.

Murray-Smith, Stephen (1922-). Editor of the magazine, *Overland*, from its beginnings in 1954. He also edited *An Overland Muster*, 1965, being selections from *Overland* from the decade 1954-64. His other writings include the critical analysis, *Henry Lawson*, 1962. *Overland* incorporated *The Realist Writer* (1952-54) and took as its motto 'Temper, democratic; Bias, Australian'.

Mutch, Thomas Davies (1885-1958). New South Wales parliamentarian who first met Lawson in the *Worker* office in 1902. They remained firm friends. He published 'The Early Life of Henry Lawson' in the *Royal Australian Historical Society Journal*, 1933, and *The First Discovery of Australia*, 1942.

Namatjira, Albert (1902-59). The first Aboriginal painter to have his work widely acclaimed in Australia. His landscapes of Central Australia gained great popularity during the 1950s.

Neilson, John Shaw (1872-1942). One of Australia's finest lyric poets. Despite the handicaps of inadequate schooling, defective eyesight, and a hard life as a labourer, he published (with the assistance and encouragement of A. G. Stephens) many poems of imagination, delicacy and beauty. See the enlarged collection of his work by A. R. Chisholm, 1973, and his biography by James Devaney, 1944.

New Australia. The name of William Lane's original settlement in Paraguay. See Gavin Souter, *A Peculiar People; the Australians in Paraguay*, 1968.

New Australia Journal. A monthly journal edited in New Australia by Walter Head (W. A. Woods). It first appeared in 1892. See Souter, *op. cit.*, pp. 26 and 56.

Nixon-Smith, Sarah. A correspondent of Mary's whose family had acquired the property 'Merryvale' at Cotta Walla, near Goulburn, where Mary was born.

Northcott, General Sir John (1890-1966). Governor of New South Wales, 1946-57. A distinguished Australian soldier of two world wars, he was Commanding Officer of the British Commonwealth Occupation Forces in Japan 1945-46.

O'Dowd, Bernard (1866-1953). In the eyes of Mary Gilmore O'Dowd was the 'standard-bearer' of the nationalist radicals of the 1890s and early 1900s. A leading intellectual and writer, O'Dowd advocated a poetry of social purpose ('Poetry Militant'). See inter alia W. H. Wilde, *Three Radicals*, 1969.

Ogilvie, William Henry (1869-1963). He came to Australia from Scotland when he was 20 and his Australian experiences of horse-breaking and droving led him to become one of the most prolific of the Bush Balladists. His verse included *Fair Girls and Gray Horses*, 1898, and *The Australian and Other Verses*, 1916.

Old Days: Old Ways A Book of Recollections, published by Angus & Robertson in 1934, is a book of anecdotes and discussions in which Mary presents the Australia of the pioneering days. The book is partly factual, partly fanciful, often based on personal experience but also on hearsay and legend. See inter alia W. H. Wilde, *Three Radicals*, 1969.

O'Leary, Patrick Ignatius (-1944). One-time editor of the *Advocate*, Melbourne. He published the anthology, *The Bread and Cheese Book*, 1939, containing poems by Quinn, Brady, Neilson and others. He also wrote on various Australian poets, e.g. *Bard in Bondage: essays of Patrick Ignatius O'Leary*, selected and edited by Joseph O'Dwyer, 1954.

Oliphant, Sir Mark (Marcus Laurence) (1901-). Atomic research scientist who was Director of the Research School of Physical Sciences, Australian National University until 1966 and Governor of South Australia 1971-76.

Olley, Margaret (1923-). A portrait artist of some distinction, she was the subject of Dobell's successful entry in the 1948 Archibald Prize Competition. She won numerous prizes for her own paintings including the Finney Centenary Prize, Queensland, 1963.

Ordell, Tal. A popular narrator of stories and poems and producer of radio plays for the Australian Broadcasting Commission.

O'Reilly, Dowell Phillip (1865-1923). Teacher, member of New South Wales Parliament, and public servant, he was a psychological novelist, sensitive short story writer and poet, and the father of the novelist Eleanor Dark. His works include *Tears and Triumph*, 1913, *Five Corners*, 1920, *Prose and Verse*, 1924.

Palmer, Janet Gertrude (Nettie) (1885-1964). Her publications include the collections of poetry, *The South Wind*, 1914, and *Shadowy Paths*, 1915, a collection of essays, *Talking It Over*, 1934, and criticism, *Modern Australian Literature, 1900-23*, 1924. She was the wife of Vance Palmer and mother of two daughters, Aileen and Helen. A volume of the letters of Nettie and Vance Palmer has been edited by Vivian Smith, 1978. See below, *Palmer, Edward Vivian (Vance)*.

Palmer, Edward Vivian (Vance) (1885-1959). Novelist, short story writer and critic. For a full list of his works see Grahame Johnston, *Annals of Australian Literature*, 1970. See also H. P. Heseltine, *Intimate Portraits*, 1969, and *Letters of Vance and Nettie Palmer 1915-1963*, edited by Vivian Smith, 1978.

Park, Ruth. A novelist whose best works deal with life in the Sydney slums, e.g. *The Harp in the South*, 1948, and *Poor Man's Orange*, 1949. Her husband D'Arcy Niland was also a novelist.

Parker, Sir Gilbert (1862-1932). Author of *Round the Compass in Australia*, 1892, *When Valmond Came to Pontiac: the Story of a Lost Napoleon*, 1899, and other works. For further biographical information on Parker, see the *South Australian Institute Journal*, February 1933.

Parkes, Sir Henry (1815-96). Statesman, historian and writer, he is known as the 'father of Australian federation'. He was Premier of New South Wales five times between 1872 and 1891 and wrote *Fifty Years in the Making of Australian History*, 1892.

The Passionate Heart. Mary's volume of poems, published in 1918. Unfortunately there appear to be no letters of Mary's available from the years when she was preparing *The Passionate Heart* and after its publication. For comment on the volume see inter alia T. Inglis Moore, 'Mary Gilmore', *Southerly* 3 (1949), 122-30; R. D. FitzGerald, 'Mary Gilmore: Poet and Great Australian', *Meanjin* 19, 4 (1960), 341-57.

Paterson, Andrew Barton ('Banjo') (1864-1941). Australia's supreme bush balladist, his most famous poem, 'The Man From Snowy River', gave its title to his first volume of poetry in 1895. As well as verse he also wrote stories and a novel. See Clement Semmler, *The Banjo of the Bush*, 1966, and B. G. Andrews & W. H. Wilde, *Australian Literature to 1900*, 1980, in the Gale Information Guide Library series.

Penton, Brian (1904-51). Novelist, journalist, and one-time editor of the Sydney *Daily Telegraph*. His fiction included *Landtakers*, 1934, and *Inheritors*, 1936. He also wrote *Think—Or Be Damned*, 1941 and *Advance Australia—Where?*, 1943.

Pescott, Edward Edgar (1872-1954). Botanist, historian and government pomologist (1917-37), he wrote *The Life Story of Joseph Furphy*, 1938. His wife was Violet Furphy of Shepparton, Victoria.

Peters, Captain C. H., M.C. (1889-?1950). He served in World War I winning the Military Cross and Bar and was between the wars Managing Director of Robertson and Mullens Ltd, the publishing house of Melbourne.

Petrie, Larry. A violent revolutionary who was supposed to have blown up the ship *Aramac* off the Queensland coast in the maritime strike of the early 1890s. He joined the Cosme settlement in Paraguay in August 1896 and died there in 1901 while attempting to save the life of a child in a railway accident.

Pindar, John. He, his wife and three children, arrived at the Cosme settlement in Paraguay in January 1897, but he was expelled in May 1898 for breaching communal rules by eating a weaner pig acquired by Joseph Sims who divided it among a few friends. He and his family remained, however, in Paraguay.

Pitt, Marie E. J. (1869-1948). Balladist, descriptive poet, feminist, socialist and close companion of Bernard O'Dowd in his later years. She published *Poems*, 1925.

Prichard, Katharine Susannah (1883-1969). Poet, short story writer and playwright, she also wrote several novels with an Australian setting, e.g. *Working Bullocks*, 1926, *Coonardoo*, 1929, and a trilogy about life on the goldfields of Western Australia.

Pringle, John Martin Douglas (1912-). Former editor of the *Sydney Morning Herald* and writer of several books including *Australian Accent*, 1958, and *On Second Thoughts: Australian Essays*, 1971.

Prior, Henry Kenneth (1893-1967). Chairman and Managing Director of the *Bulletin* from 1933 to 1961.

Prior, Samuel Henry (1869-1933). Editor of the *Bulletin* (which was owned by his family) from 1915 to 1933. His name is commemorated by a number of annual prizes for literature.

Quick, Florence Mary. Artist and author, she produced and published *Stone Walls: Engravings of Old Buildings at Berrima, N.S.W.*, 1952, *Green Crowns: an Account of Native Trees on the Hills Around Robertson, N.S.W.*, 1955, and *Letters to Scotland, 1860*, 1961, compiled from the letters and diaries of J. McD. Stuart.

Quinn, Roderic (1867-1949). Sydney freelance journalist who published short stories and a novel but was best known as a lyrical poet of charm and grace. He formed, with Victor J. Daley, the school of poetry that has come to be described as the Celtic Twilight. His verse included *The Hidden Tide*, 1899, *The Circling Hearths*, 1901, and *Poems*, 1920. See B. G. Andrews and W. H. Wilde *Australian Literature to 1900*, 1980, in the Gale Information Guide Library series.

Rae, Haidee. Daughter of Dick and Eleanor Rae, she was born at Cosme in 1898, the same year as Billy Gilmore, Mary's child.

Raeburn, Sir Henry (1756-1823). Known as the Scottish Reynolds, he was the most successful and fashionable portrait artist in the Edinburgh of his time.

Randolph, Lyall (1901-75). He was well-known as the sculptor of the famous Bondi Beach mermaids. He did a bust of Mary in 1950.

Reibey, Mary (1777-1855). Sentenced in 1790 to seven years transportation to Australia for horse stealing, she married Thomas Reibey in 1794 and later became an important business woman in Sydney. She acquired property in the Rocks area and in Macquarie Street, and Reibey Cottage, built in 1847 in Hunters Hill, still stands.

Reid, Sir George (1845-1918). Australian Prime Minister in 1904 and Australian High Commissioner to London in 1910.

Ritchie, A. A. Born in Australia, he had overseas experience in the book trade with William Stevens Ltd of London and Edinburgh. From 1909 he worked with Angus & Robertson Ltd and was Manager of the Sydney shop for more than 20 years, becoming, in 1954, Chairman of Directors.

Robertson, Constance (Connie). Journalist and feminist, daughter of A. G. Stephens. She joined the staff of the *Sun* in 1917 and after being social editor of the Sunday *Sun* she built up the women's section of the evening

Sun. In 1928 she married, and also attended the first Pan Pacific Women's Conference in Honolulu. In 1930 she became editor of the *Women's Budget* and later of *Woman*. In 1932 she edited *Ink*, the magazine of the Sydney Society of Women Writers, and in April 1963 she addressed the English Association on her memories of Mary. This talk was published posthumously in *Southerly*, 4, 1965. See also *Opinion*, June-July 1935, p. 18.

Robertson, George (1860-1933). He founded, in 1886, with D. M. Angus, the famous Australian publishing house Angus & Robertson. Mary later came to address him as GR and later still his grandson, George Ferguson, as GRII.

Robinson, Roland (1912-). Irish-Australian poet and presenter of Aboriginal legends. His writings include *Beyond the Grass-tree Spears*, 1944, *Legend and Dreaming*, 1952, *Black-feller, White-feller*, 1958, and *Aboriginal Myths and Legends*, 1966.

Roderick, Colin (1911-). A prolific writer on Australian literature and an authority on Henry Lawson, having collected his verse and letters and written voluminously on him. See Grahame Johnston, *Annals of Australian Literature*, 1970.

Rosa, Samuel Albert (1866-1940). Associated with the newspaper, *Truth*, from 1901 to 1923 and later with the *Labor Daily*, he was an advocate of revolutionary socialism. He was expelled from the New South Wales Labor Party in 1919 and formed a short-lived socialist party.

Royal Tar. Ship on which the first emigrants to Paraguay sailed with William Lane. See Gavin Souter, *A Peculiar People; the Australians in Paraguay*, 1968.

'Rudd, Steele'. See Davis, Arthur Hoey.

The Rue Tree. Mary's volume of verse published in 1931. A collection of almost 100 poems it traces the course of a particularly powerful religious experience she underwent during the years 1920-26. Writing of *The Rue Tree* many years later (see letter dated 5 September 1960) she said the book was a tribute to the Sisters of the Convent of Mercy, Goulburn.

Ruhen, Olaf (1911-). Best-known for his novel, *Naked Under Capricorn*, he has written numerous other books including *Land of Dahori: Tales of New Guinea*, 1957, *The Broken Wing*, 1965, and *Harpoon in my Hand*, 1966.

Rule, Edgar John. Author of *Jacka's Mob*, 1933.

Sawtell, Michael (1883-1971). Author of two books of poetry, *The Wisdom of a Vagabond*, 1925, and *Pilate Answered*, 1925, he was a member of the Aborigines' Welfare Board of New South Wales in 1940. His views on the Aboriginal question did not find favour with Mary Gilmore. See letter, 28 December 1946.

Schlunke, Eric Otto (1906-60). Author of several books about life in the Riverina such as *The Man in the Silo*, 1955, *The Village Hampden*, 1958, and *Stories of the Riverina*, 1965. He also contributed short stories to the *Bulletin*. His wife Olga was a poet and friend of Mary's.

Schreiner, Olive (1844-1920). South African feminist, novelist and public figure, she met Havelock Ellis after the publication of her novel *The African Farm* and the two became close friends.

Scott, Rose (1847-1925). Sydney suffragette and social reformer, she was a friend of William Lane, the founder of New Australia in Paraguay.

Selected Verse. A collection of Mary's poetry published by Angus & Robertson in 1948. R. D. FitzGerald, assisted by T. Inglis Moore, selected the poems in consultation with Mary.

Serle, Percival (1871-1951). Chief clerk and accountant at the University of Melbourne. Bibliographer, biographer and anthologist, he was the author of the standard reference works, *Bibliography of Australasian Poetry and Verse*, 1925, and *Dictionary of Australian Biography*, 1949. He edited (with R. H. Croll and Furnley Maurice) *An Australasian Anthology: Australian and New Zealand Poems*, 1927.

Simpson, Colin (1908-). Author of numerous travel books, mostly about Asia and New Guinea, e.g. *Adam in Ochre*, 1951.

Sladen, Douglas (1856-1947). Anthologist, literary critic, biographer and minor versifier, he came to Australia in 1879, took a law degree at Melbourne University and was lecturer in Modern History at Sydney University. He returned to England in 1884. His critical work was not highly thought of by A. G. Stephens. Particularly interested in Adam Lindsay Gordon, Sladen was largely responsible for Gordon's bust being placed in the Poets' Corner of Westminster Abbey.

Slessor, Kenneth (1901-71). One of Australia's finest modern poets, notable particularly for poems such as 'Five Bells' and 'Five Visions of Captain Cook'. See Douglas Stewart's fine biographical and critical work, *A Man of Sydney*, 1977.

Smart, Christopher (1722-71). Author of *Song to David*, 1763, a collection of extraordinary stanzas, at times scarcely intelligible but rich in language of considerable beauty. This work was edited by Percival Serle in 1923 as *A Song to David and Other Poems* in a limited edition of 300 autographed copies.

Smith, Eleanor. She wrote *Isle of Girls*, 1953, and *The Beckoning West; the story of H. S. Trotman and the Canning Stock Route*, 1966.

Smith, Joshua (1905-71). Sydney portrait artist whose realistic portrait of Dame Mary was hung in the Art Gallery of New South Wales. Smith himself was the subject of William Dobell's controversial Archibald Prize portrait of 1943.

Spence, William Guthrie (1846-1936). Labor leader and politician who was, in 1894, General Secretary of the Australian Workers' Union. A member of both the State and Commonwealth Parliaments he was finally expelled from the Labor party in 1916 over the issue of conscription.

Spender, Stephen (1909-). British poet who voiced the economic, social and political dissatisfaction of the 1930s. Professor of English, University College, London University from 1970. His *Collected Poems* was published in 1954 and *Selected Poems*, 1965.

Stead, Christina (1902-). An Australian writer with an international reputation who made a considerable impact with *The Salzburg Tales* and *Seven Poor Men of Sydney*, both published in 1934. See inter alia R. G. Geering's *Christina Stead*, 1969.

Stephens, Alfred George (1865-1933). Editor, journalist and critic, he joined the *Bulletin* in 1894 and in 1896 instituted the famous Red Page, wherein Australian literary talent of the day was prominently featured. Stephens worked assiduously to promote Australian writers, publishing verse by Boake, Quinn, O'Dowd, Neilson and many others. His own numerous publications include *Oblation*, 1902, and *The Red Pagan*, 1904, while he edited the *Bulletin Story Book* and the *Bulletin Reciter*, both 1901. See P. R. Stephensen, *The Life and Works of A. G. Stephens*, 1940.

Stephensen, Percy Reginald (1901-65). Manager of Endeavour Press in Sydney and at one time (1936-42) editor of the magazine *Publicist*. He wrote prose and verse, sometimes of a satiric nature. His critical work included *The Foundations of Culture in Australia*, 1936, and *The Life and Works of A. G. Stephens*, 1940.

Stevens, Bertram (1872-1922). Art and literary critic who succeeded A. G. Stephens as editor of the Red Page of the *Bulletin*. He also edited the *Lone Hand*, 1911-17, and several anthologies of Australian verse as well as the works of individual poets, e.g. Kendall, Farrell, Daley.

Stevenson, David Russell. Probably born in 1862, he was a handsome bushman who was described by a fellow colonist at Cosme as a 'sardonic Hemingwayesque type of man'. He went to Paraguay in the *Royal Tar* and was one of Lane's chief lieutenants at Cosme. Earlier in Sydney he had attracted Mary and also a nurse, Clara Jones. In Cosme, however, Mary married William Gilmore and Clara Jones married William Laurence. Stevenson served in France in World War I, returned to Cosme and later married Clara Laurence, who was by then a widow. When Stevenson inherited some money they left Cosme in 1927 and went to Guernsey.

Stewart, Douglas (1913-). Poet, dramatist, critic and anthologist, he joined the staff of the *Bulletin* from New Zealand in 1938, editing the Red Page. Later he was on the staff of Angus & Robertson. His own writings include plays (*Ned Kelly*), radio plays (*The Fire on the Snow*), poetry and fiction.

Stone, Professor Julius (1907-). Challis Professor of International Law and Jurisprudence at the University of Sydney 1942-72, he was the author of many legal publications, e.g. *The Atlantic Charter, New Worlds for Old*, 1943, and *Law and Society*, 1949.

Stone, Louis (1871-1935). School teacher and novelist, he wrote *Jonah*, 1911, a story of larrikin life in Sydney, and *Betty Wayside*, 1915. See H. J. Oliver, *Louis Stone*, 1968.

Stone, Walter (1910-). Critic and bibliographer, he is well-known for his association with *Biblionews* from 1947 and for his bibliographical works on Lawson, Furphy (with Hugh Anderson), Brennan, and his publication (with George Mackaness), *The Books of the Bulletin*, 1955.

Stonehaven, Lady (Ethel Keith Falconer). Wife of Viscount Stonehaven, Governor-General of Australia from 1925, who revisited Australia in 1938.

Street, Jessie Mary, Lady (1889-1970). Feminist and Labor leader, the wife of Sir Kenneth Street, at one time Chief Justice of the Supreme Court of New South Wales.

Stuart, Donald (1913-). Author of *Yandy*, 1959, *The Driven*, 1961, and *Yaralie*, 1962.

Swinburne, Algernon Charles (1837-1909). English lyric poet of the Pre-Raphaelite movement.

Tale of Tiddley Winks, The. A booklet of verse for children by Mary Gilmore, published by the *Bookfellow*.

Taylor, James Richard William. Member of *S.M.H.* and *Mail* literary staff. His documentary-style works include *Gold from the Sea*, 1942, the story of the recovery of bullion from the *Niagara*, and *Prisoner of the 'Kormoran'*, 1941, the experiences of W. A. Jones on the German raider.

Temby, Henry Stanley. Assistant Secretary, Prime Minister's Department, 1949-55, and Secretary of the Commonwealth Literary Fund from 1938.

Tennant, Kylie (1912-). A novelist whose sympathies lay with the adventurous and more vagabond elements of society and with those who toiled hard physically for a living. Her novel of the Depression days, *Tiburon*, won the *Bulletin's* S. H. Prior Memorial Prize for 1935, while *The Battlers* shared the 1940 prize with Eve Langley's *The Pea Pickers*.

Thomas, Daniel (1931-). Curator of Australian art at the Art Gallery of New South Wales, and afterwards curator of Australian Art at the National Gallery in Canberra.

Thompson, Francis (1859-1907). Late nineteenth century English religious poet whose work recalls the Metaphysical poets of the seventeenth century.

Thompson, John (1907-68). Author of several volumes of verse: *Three Dawns Ago*, 1935, *Sesame*, 1944, *Thirty Poems*, 1954, and *I Hate and I Love*, 1964. He also edited, with Kenneth Slessor and R. G. Howarth, *The Penguin Book of Australian Verse*, 1958.

Thorndike, Dame Sybil (1882-). English actress who toured Australia with her husband, Lewis Casson, in 1962.

'Thunderbolt'. See Ward, Frederick.

The Tilted Cart. A small booklet of some forty or more ballad-like poems, published by Mary in 1925. The poems are both factual and fanciful reminiscences of bush characters and events. The copious appendix of Notes attached to the poems represents the beginning of Mary's long struggle to record, and to have recorded, the folk history of the outback of bygone years. One delightful character piece from *The Tilted Cart* is 'The Brucedale Scandal'.

Tregear, Edward (1846-1931). A New Zealander who wrote poetry as well as books about the Maoris and Polynesians.

Turnbull, Gilbert Munro (1890-1938). A prolific writer on New Guinea, his works include *Paradise Plumes*, 1933, *Mountains of the Moon*, 1935, and *Portrait of a Savage*, 1943.

Turnbull, Stanley Clive (1906-75). Poet, biographer and historian whose works include *Poems*, 1944, *Essington Lewis*, 1963, *Australian Lives*, 1965, and *A Concise History of Australia*, 1965.

Turner, Ethel (1872-1958). Children's writer whose many novels include *Seven Little Australians*, 1894, and *The Family at Misrule*, 1895.

Turner, Ian (1922-79). Radical, academic, historian, author of *The Australian*

Dream, 1968. He was Secretary of the Australasian Book Society when it commissioned Dobell's portrait of Mary.

Tyrrell, James Robert (1875-1961). Sydney bookseller and author. He wrote *Old Books, Old Friends, Old Sydney*, 1952.

Tyson, James (1819-98). Millionaire pastoralist who bought huge runs in south-western areas of New South Wales and in Victoria from the profits of his butcher's shop at the Bendigo gold diggings.

Under the Wilgas. Mary's book of verse published in 1932. It differed from her earlier publications in that it contained tributes to Australian personages such as Henry Lawson.

Villon, Francois (1431-63). The mainspring of modern French poetry who possessed a remarkable lyric gift and was capable of humorous and compassionate as well as mercilessly satirical writing.

Vincent, Alf (1874-1915). Staff artist for the *Bulletin* from 1898 to 1915. His work is represented by a collection of prints in the State galleries in Sydney and Melbourne.

Vosper, Frederick Charles Burleigh (1867-1901). Born in England, he came to Queensland in 1883 where he was active in the early Queensland Labour movement. He was arrested and tried for sedition during the 1891 shearers' strike. Vosper was editor of the *Coolgardie Miner* from 1894 to 1897. See 'F. C. B. Vosper: An Australian Radical', *University Studies in English*, vol. 5, no. 1, pp. 38-53.

Wakehurst, His Excellency Lord (John) de Vere Loder (1895-1970), Governor of New South Wales, 1937-46.

Wall, Arnold (1869-19). Poet, prose writer, mountaineer and botanist, he contributed to the *Bulletin* for over fifty years. He was at one time Professor of English at Canterbury University College, Christchurch, New Zealand.

Walsh, Adela Pankhurst. Daughter of the English suffragist Emmeline Pankhurst, she came to Australia in 1911. She took a leading part in the women's movement in Australia and wrote a play, *Betrayed*, 1917.

Ward, Edward John (Eddie) (1899-1963). Flamboyant Labor politician who was the member for East Sydney for thirty-two years and a minister in the Curtin and Chifley governments.

Ward, Frederick ('Thunderbolt') (1835-70). Bushranger in the New England area 1865-70. He was a 'gentleman' robber specializing in courteous robberies. He was killed at Uralla, 25 May 1870.

Wast, Hugo. See Martinez, Zuviria Gustavo.

Waten, Judah (1911-). Born in Russia, he came to Australia at the age of three. He has written short stories and novels, including *Alien Son*, 1952, *Time of Conflict*, 1961, *Distant Hand*, 1964, *Season of Youth*, 1966.

Watt, Ernest Alexander Stuart (1874-?). Ship owner and director of Gilchrist, Watt and Sanderson, he was at one time owner and joint-editor, with Hugh McCrae of *Triad*.

Webb, Mary (1881-1920). Popular English novelist whose stories were set in the Shropshire countryside. Well-known were *Gone to Earth*, 1917, and *Precious Bane*, 1924.

Webb, Yvonne. A poet whose publications include *Into the Wind: Collected Poems*, 1939, and *Selected Poems*, 1940.

White, Charles. Author of *Early Australian History*, 1889 and 1891-1902, and *Old Convict Days in Australia*, 1906.

White, Sir Harold Leslie (1905-). Librarian of the National Library from 1947 until his retirement in 1970.

White, Myrtle Rose (1888-1961). Author of *No Roads Go By*, 1932, a narrative of the northern borderland between New South Wales and South Australia. She also wrote *From That Day to This*, 1961.

Whitman, Walt (1819-92). American journalist and poet whose *Leaves of Grass*, 1855, was probably the most significant American collection of verse of the nineteenth century.

Whyte, William Farmer (1879-1958). Editor of the Sydney *Daily Telegraph* from 1921 to 1928. He wrote on Australia and the Pacific Islands, as well as the biographical *W. M. Hughes*, 1957.

Wilcox, Dora (1873-19?). New Zealand poet who published a play *Commander Capstan: A Comedy in One Act*, 1931, and three volumes of verse. In 1923 she married drama and art critic William Moore.

The Wild Swan. Perhaps Mary's finest collection of verse, published in 1930. See W. H. Wilde, *Three Radicals*, 1969.

Willis, Henry (1860-1950). Both a State and Federal politician, being speaker of the New South Wales Legislative Assembly and a member of the first Federal Parliament.

Woods, Walter Alan (1861-1939). Formerly Walter William Head, secretary of the 'New Australia' movement. He was also editor of *New Australia*, the journal of the New Australia Co-operative Settlement Association. There was some trouble with the New Australia accounts and Woods, then Head, left Sydney for Tasmania. There he founded the Labor periodical, the *Clipper*, and was a Labor member of the Tasmanian House of Assembly in 1906, being Speaker, 1914-16 and 1926-28.

Worde, Wynkyn de (d. 1534). Printer and stationer, at first apprentice to William Caxton then his successor.

The *Worker*. Sydney newspaper for which Mary wrote from 1908 to 1931. See notes to letters, 18 May 1933 and 1 June 1946.

Wragge, Clement (1852-1922). Inaugurator of Australian Weather Bureau in 1887. His weather forecasts were for many years a feature of Australian meteorology.

Wright, Judith (1915-). One of Australia's principal modern poets. Her first volume of poetry, *The Moving Image*, was published in 1946. See inter alia A. D. Hope, *Judith Wright*, 1975.

Wynn, Mary. Wife of the poet William Hart-Smith.

Yonge, Charlotte Mary (1823-1901). English novelist who expounded the religious views of John Keeble in her fiction. Works included *The Heir of Redclyffe*, 1853. She edited the *Monthly Packet* from 1851 to 1898.

Index

A & R, see Angus & Robertson Ltd.
A.B.C., see Australian Broadcasting Commission
A.B.C. Weekly, 256n
Abdullah, Mena, 324, 331, 373, 392
Aboriginal Myths and Legends (Roland Robinson), 397
Aboriginals, 70, 89, 92, 97, 101-3, 105-6, 120, 127, 168-9, 189, 191, 208, 219-20, 236n, 246, 248, 253n-4, 257, 262-3, 275n-6, 281, 290, 313, 316, 319-20, 322, 327, 330n-1, 335-6, 338, 352, 356, 381, 385, 391, 397
'Aborigines: Keepers of History' (Mary Gilmore letter), 330n
Achnacarry Castle, see Cameron, Clan, 141
A. D. Hope (*Australian Bibliographies*) (Joy Hooton), 386
A. D. Hope (Leonie Kramer), 386
Adagio in Blue (T. Inglis Moore), 149
Adam in Ochre (Colin Simpson), 398
Adam Lindsay Gordon (W. H. Wilde), 193n, 384
Adam With Arrows (Colin Simpson), 338
Adams, Arthur, 138, 171, 373
Adams, Francis, 296, 373
Adamson, G. E. Bartlett, 170, 373
Adelaide, 232, 302, 383, 392
Aden, 23
Advance Australia—Where? (Brian Penton), 395
Advocate (Melbourne), 168, 394
African Farm, The (Olive Schreiner), 397
'Afternoon' (A. Ashworth), 225
Afternoon Light (Sir Robert Menzies), 392
Age (Melbourne), 42, 350n, 380

Ahab, Captain, 305n
Air Mail Palestine (David McNicoll), 391
Airborne Invasion (John Hetherington), 386
Albery, also Albury, 58, 220, 251
Albury, N.S.W., 14, 157, 225, 296
Albury Banner and Wodonga Express, 183
Albury Border Post, 183
Alexander, Mrs Pacita, 208-9
Alfred Deakin (Sir Walter Murdoch), 393
Alfred Deakin: A Biography (J. A. La Nauze), 380
Alice Springs, 252
Alien Son (Judah Waten), 276, 401
All That Swagger (Miles Franklin), 127, 136n, 187n
Allen, Leslie Holdsworth, 82n
Alley, Rewi, 346, 373
Alpha Centauri (Mabel Forrest), 383
Among the Carrion Crows (Dame Enid Lyons), 390
Amor, Jack (Paraguay), 157, 373
Andersen, Hans Christian, 324
Anderson, Hugh, 199n, 399
Anderson, W. G., 95
Andes Mountains, 21
Andrews, B. G., 373, 375-7, 379-80, 382, 384, 387, 390, 395-6
Angel Place, Sydney, 48n
Angus, D. M., 263, 397
Angus & Robertson Ltd., 78, 90, 92, 98, 103, 110-11, 114, 124, 131, 134n, 147-9, 152-3, 164, 175, 199, 223, 227-8n, 231, 233, 239, 247n, 249, 263n-4, 281, 290, 302, 307, 309, 315, 323-4, 329, 337, 345-6, 348, 350, 368n, 370, 379-80, 382, 385, 389, 394, 396-9

403

Annals of Australian Literature (G. K. Johnston), 380, 383, 395, 397
Anthem, *see* Australian National Anthem
Antipodean, 184
Antwerp, 53
Apollo in Australia and Bush Verses (A. A. Bayldon), 374
Apollyon (*The Pilgrim's Progress*), 72, 301
Aramac, S.S., 157n, 395
Aranda tribe, 320n
Ararat, Victoria, 33
Archibald, J. F., 216, 265, 306, 337, 353, 373, 389
Archibald Prize, 132, 236n, 312, 380-1, 387, 394, 398
Argentina, 4n, 8, 20-1, 61, 246, 353
Argus (Melbourne), 135n, 255n, 378
Arnhem Land, N.T., 384
'Arrows' (Mary Gilmore verses), 358n
'Arrows' (*Tribune* column), 275, 313n, 326
Art Gallery of N.S.W., 361, 363-4, 392, 398, 400
Art in Australia, 144n, 382, 387
Art of Rosaleen Norton, The, 384
Art Society of N.S.W., 374
Ashton, Julian, 3n, 119, 143n, 150, 153, 361, 374, 382, 385, 387
Ashworth, Arthur, 225n
Ashworth, Janet, 333n
'As Told to Roland Robinson', 320n
Asunción (Paraguay), 157
As You Like It, 150n
At Dawn and Dusk (V. J. Daley), 379
At the Initiation: Four Poems (Reba Ginsburg), 384
Atlantic Charter, The (Julius Stone), 399
Atlas of Anatomy (Maria Kuhn), 388
Aussie, 58, 374
Aussie: the Australian Soldiers' Magazine, 374
Australasian Anthology, An (Percival Serle), 69n, 398
Australasian Book Society, 308, 312, 319, 326, 337, 340, 366, 401
'Australia to Abraham Lincoln' (Mary Gilmore), 178n
Australia Writes (T. Inglis Moore), 286n, 304
Australian Aborigines, The (A. P. Elkin), 381
Australian Academy of Art, 388
Australian Accent (J. M. D. Pringle), 396
Australian and Other Verses, The (W. H. Ogilvie), 394
Australian Authors and Artists Handbook (W. E. FitzHenry), 382
Australian Barkers and Biters (R. Kaleski), 387

'Australian Battle Cry' (Mary Gilmore), 173
Australian Broadcasting Commission, 170, 223-4n, 256, 267, 294n, 297n, 312n, 390
Australian Consolidated Press, 292, 368, 391
Australian Council for Civil Liberties, 382
Australian Democrat, 382
Australian Dream, The (Ian Turner), 400-1
Australian Encyclopaedia (A. H. Chisholm), 256n, 378
Australian Essays (A. H. Adams), 373
Australian Heritage (C. B. Christesen), 378
Australian Journal, 231-2
Australian Journalists' Association, 236n
Australian Labour Movement, 155, 177n, 222, 275, 277, 330, 353, 377
Australian Literature (E. Morris Miller & F. J. Macartney), 331n
Australian Literature: A Bibliography to 1938 (E. Morris Miller), 392
Australian Literature Society, 329
Australian Literature to 1900 (B. G. Andrews & W. H. Wilde), 373, 375-7, 379-80, 382, 384, 387, 390, 395-6
Australian Lives (Clive Turnbull), 400
Australian National Anthem, 192
Australian National Gallery, 312, 338, 400
Australian National Library, *see* National Library of Australia
Australian National Review, 139n
Australian National University, 394
Australian Novel, The (Colin Roderick), 258n
Australian Peace Council, 318
Australian Quarterly, 106n, 149n
Australian Sesquicentenary Celebrations, 226n
Australian Short Stories (George Mackaness, ed.), 390
Australian Women's Weekly, 178n, 237
Australian Worker, *see also Worker*, Sydney, 183-4, 211, 222
Australian Workers' Union, 72, 129, 398
Australian Writers (L. J. Blake), 375
Australians, The (A. H. Adams), 373
Austro-Vert, 271, 374
Avenida Australia (Australia Street, Buenos Aires), 261
A.W.U., *see* Australian Workers' Union

Bab Ballads, The (W. S. Gilbert), 27n
'Bacchus' (Bernard O'Dowd), 46n
Back to Bool Bool ('Brent of Bin Bin'), 376, 383

Badham, Charles, 345, 374
Baeza, Senor de, 140, 144
Baker, Harry (Paraguay), 11
Baker, Kate, 190, 374
'Ballerina' (Hugh McCrae), 150
Balmain, Sydney, 156
Bancks, James C., 207n, 374
Banco Agricola (Paraguay), 9n
'Bangle Bonus, The', 222
Banjo of the Bush, The (Clement Semmler), 395
Bank of Argentina, 20
Bardia, 173
Bard in Bondage: essays of Patrick Ignatius O'Leary (Joseph O'Dwyer, ed.), 394
Bardsley, Grace, 328, 340, 374
Barrett, Charles Leslie, 184, 374
Barrett, Kenneth, 335
Barrier, The (Broken Hill), 183, 185, 232
Bartlett, Norman, 254
Bath, Order of the, 134
Bathurst Free Press, 23
Battarbee, Rex, 263, 271, 290, 374
Battle Cry (Australian), 173, 175
Battle Cry (New Zealand), 173
Battlefields (Mary Gilmore), 135n, 138n, 146n, 148n, 164, 166n-7n, 168-9, 175, 374, 377
Battlers, The (Kylie Tennant), 400
Baxter, James, 332
Bayldon, A. A., 266, 374
'Baylebridge, William' (C. W. Blocksidge), 149
Bayonets and Grass (T. Inglis Moore), 328n
'Beach Schools' (Mary Gilmore), 183
Bean, C. E. W., 209, 240, 374
Beattie, Alfred, 133n
Beattie, Hugh (Mary Gilmore's maternal grandfather), 102n, 187, 284, 308, 355
Beattie, James (and Mrs), 310, 336
Beattie, John (Mary Gilmore's uncle), 352
Beattie, Mary (Mary Gilmore's maternal grandmother), 102n, 228-9, 233, 271-2, 355
Beattie, Nellie, 336
'Beatties of Brooklyn, The' (Mary Gilmore), 133n
Beattie, William Hugh, 133n
Beatty, Sir William, 284, 355, 374
Beaver, Bruce, 347n
Beazley, Jack, 366n
Beckoning West, The (Eleanor Smith), 398
Bedford, Ruth, 184, 246, 374
Bell, Mary Ann, 201
'Bell Birds' (Henry Kendall), 387
Benham, Rosamond, 47-8, 374
Benham Family in Australia, The, 374
Bennett, General Gordon, 178, 185, 375
Bennett, S., 130-1

Berg, Hazel de, 359
'Bernard O'Dowd' (Mary Gilmore), 297n
Bernhardi, Friedrich, 53, 375
Berrima, N.S.W., 285
Best Australian One-Act Plays (T. Inglis Moore & W. Moore, eds), 393
Best Poems of Hugh McCrae, The, 295n
Betrayed (Adela Pankhurst Walsh), 401
Betty Wayside (Louis Stone), 399
Between Two Tides (R. D. FitzGerald), 278n-80, 299-301, 382
Beyond the Grass-tree Spears (Roland Robinson), 194, 397
Bibliography of Australasian Poetry and Verse (Percival Serle), 398
Biblionews, 199n, 399
'Bill the Bullock Driver' (Henry Kendall), 387
Billy Watt of Bumbaldery, 201
Binalong, N.S.W., 54
Bird of Paradise (Jean Devanny), 380
Bird Seeking in Queensland (A. H. Chisholm), 60n
Birds and Green Places (A. H. Chisholm), 84n
Birds of Australia, The (John Gould), 384
Birkett, Winifred, 108n-9, 165, 375
Birks, Helen (Paraguay), 88
'Black Bread of Night' (Mary Gilmore), 90
Black Cargo and Other Stories (John Morrison), 393
Black Cockatoo Mean Snow (Elyne Mitchell), 392
blackboy, 273n
Black-feller, White-feller (Roland Robinson), 397
Blackwood's Magazine, 274
Blake, Leslie James, 318, 375
Blakeley, Frederick, 231n
Blakemore, G. L., 340
Blamey (John Hetherington), 303n, 386
Blamey, Field Marshal Sir Thomas, 303-4, 386
Blamey, James, 303
'Bless This House' (May Brahe), 376
'Blessed Damozel, The' (D. G. Rossetti), 266
Bligh, Vice-Admiral William, 271n-2, 375
'Blind Man Said, The' (Hugh McCrae), 203
Blue, Billy, 328, 388
'Blue Lake leap' (A. L. Gordon), 193n
Blue Mountains, N.S.W., 388
Blue Prints and Other Verses (Donovan Clarke), 378
Blue's Point, Sydney, 388
Bluett, Etty, 206, 375

Bluett, Ida, 205-6, 375
Bluett, William, 205-6, 209, 256-7, 336, 340, 344, 375
Boake, Barcroft, 200, 296, 375, 399
Boden, F. C., 116n
Boer War, 96
'Bog and Candle' (R. D. FitzGerald), 360n, 362
Bohemia (Bread and Cheese Club), 261, 289, 376, 391
Bombay, 23
Bondi, Sydney, 47, 49
Book of Songs: by Heinrich Heine, The (trans. Sir Robert Garran), 383
Bockfellow, 33, 34n-5, 37n-9n, 52, 111n, 171, 180, 224, 244, 284, 292, 353, 375, 390, 400
Books of the Bulletin, The (G. Mackaness & W. Stone), 399
Boomerang, 373, 379, 388
Boonoke (Falkiner Station), N.S.W., 382
Boote, H. E., 99n, 138, 375
Border Watch, see *Albury Border Post*
Borneo, 223-4
Botanical Gardens, Sydney, 107, 113, 189-90, 213, 302, 308, 355
Botha, Louis, 53, 375
Bounty, H.M.S., 375
Boy at the Dardanelles, The (Adam McCay), 390
Boys' Town, Sydney, 278, 381
Bradfield, J. J. C., 190, 376
Brady, E. J., 141, 376, 394
Brahe, May, 225, 376
Brand, Mona, see Fox, Mona
Bray, Dorothea, 237
Bread and Cheese Book, The (P. I. O'Leary), 394
Bread and Cheese Club, Melbourne, 147-8, 194, 217-19n, 222n, 240, 254, 260-1, 278-9, 318n, 365, 367, 376, 379, 390-2
Brennan, C. J., 122, 139, 149, 151, 166, 201, 227-8, 252-3, 278, 282, 345, 376, 399
'Brent of Bin Bin', see Franklin, Stella Maria Miles
Brereton, John le Gay, 35, 73n, 80, 82n, 91, 114n-15, 166, 225, 254n, 376
Brer Fox, 320, 385
Brer Rabbit, 320, 385
Brief History of the Bread and Cheese Club, A (H. W. Malloch), 391
Brimming Billabongs (W. E. Harney), 229n
Brindabella Mountains, N.S.W., 209, 375
Bringer of Light (Bartlett Adamson), 373
Brisbane, 260, 347
British Imperialism and Australia, 1783-1833 (B. C. Fitzpatrick), 382

Brittlebank, A. (Paraguay), 158
Broken Hill, N.S.W., 232, 255
Broken Wing, The (Olaf Ruhen), 397
Brolga (Reba Ginsburg, ed.), 384
Bronte, Charlotte, 212
Broomfield, F. J., 73n, 114n
Brown, Captain, 240
Brown, Emily, 240
Brown, F. H., 335
Browning, Robert, 74
Bruce, Mary Grant, 218, 376
Brucedale, 14, 64
'Brucedale Scandal, The' (Mary Gilmore), 400
Buenos Aires, 8, 12, 20, 22, 183, 261
Bull, Hilda (Mrs Louis Esson), 146, 168, 310, 376
'Bull, The' (Mary Gilmore), 90, 95, 298
Bulletin, 24, 27, 29, 33, 40, 51, 53, 65, 68, 74, 76, 80, 82n-3n, 90, 106, 114n, 184, 202, 210, 216-17n, 237, 248n, 257, 261, 264-7n, 269n-70n, 309, 316, 320, 322-3n, 324, 335-7, 341, 352n-3n, 368, 373, 381-2, 387, 389, 393, 396-7, 399-401
Bulletin Reciter (A. G. Stephens), 399
Bulletin Story Book (A. G. Stephens, ed.), 399
Buna, New Guinea, 223
Bundaburra Gap, N.S.W., 310-11
Bundaburra Jack, 310
Bundarra, N.S.W., 373
Bungowannah, N.S.W., 14
Bunyan, John, 72n-3, 301, 353
Burdekin, Sydney, 77
Burke and Wills, 378
Burns, Robert, 74
'Burnside', Strathdownie, Victoria, 12, 24-5
Burrows, E. M., 272
'Butcher, The', see 'Dying Butcher, The'
Butt, Dame Clara, 134, 376
By Bomber to Britain (Reg MacDonald), 390
By Creek and Gully (Lala Fisher), 382
By Tropic Sea and Jungle (Jean Devanny), 380
Byers, Isabel, 75, 92, 182-3, 329, 352n, 376
By-Products (R. H. Croll), 379

Caloundra, Queensland, 64, 93
Calvin, John, 38n
Calwell, A. A., 256
'Cambaroora Star, The' (Henry Lawson), 160
Cambridge, Ada, 63, 138, 296, 377
Camden, N.S.W., 126, 128, 234
Cameron, Angus, 333
Cameron, Archibald G., 150, 256

Index 407

Cameron, Charles (Mary Gilmore's brother), 5
Cameron Clan, 141-3, 229, 238-9, 353, 389
Cameron, Colonel Claude, 142
Cameron, Donal (son of Mary Gilmore's brother John Cameron), 96, 221
Cameron, Donald (Mary Gilmore's father), 13, 38, 75, 142-3, 193, 228-9, 272, 276, 289, 308, 310, 316, 323, 334-5, 339, 341, 352, 355, 364
Cameron, George (Mary Gilmore's brother), 142
Cameron, Hugh (Mary Gilmore's brother), 75, 240, 335, 352
Cameron, Hugh (Mary Gilmore's grandfather), 164, 239, 308, 355
Cameron, John Alexander (Mary Gilmore's brother), 22, 31, 64n, 86, 95-6, 129n, 142, 221, 288, 352, 377
Cameron, Mary Ann (née Beattie — Mary Gilmore's mother), 13, 67, 75, 95-6, 183, 187, 202, 240, 272, 323, 352, 355, 389
Cameron, Mary Jean (maiden name of Mary Gilmore), 4, 15, 141n, 170n
Cameron, Mrs George, 361
Cameron, Sir Donald Charles, 142, 167, 225, 377
Campbell, Donald Gordon, 212, 222, 225, 235, 242, 268, 328, 377
Campbell, Elizabeth, 242
Campbell, Lawrence, 166, 377
Canberra, 110n, 209, 235, 237, 239, 265, 269, 284, 302, 312, 319, 334, 341, 355, 358-9, 361, 393
Canberra Times, 178n
'Candles' (Nan McDonald), 227
Canterbury University College, Christchurch, New Zealand, 401
Carlyle, Thomas, 15
Carmichael, Sir Thomas, 176, 306, 377
Casey, Richard Gardiner (Baron Casey of Berwick), 269, 377
Cassidy, Lucy, 114-16, 129, 138, 377
Cassidy, R. J. ('Gilrooney'), 377
Casson, Lewis, 369, 400
Casterton, Victoria, 12n, 24-5, 27, 29, 32-3, 36, 38, 40, 42-3n, 176, 193n, 211n
Casterton Free Press, 36
Casterton News, 34, 36n, 183
Castlereagh Street, Sydney, 263n
'Catalogue and Commentary' (T. Inglis Moore), 331n
Cato, Nancy, 347n
Cattle King, The (I. Idriess), 265n, 387
Catts, Dorothy M., 307, 313, 315-17, 323, 334, 377
Caxton, William, 402
Cayley, Neville H. P., 131n

Cayley, Neville W., 131
Celtic Twilight, the, 396
Chair of Australian Literature, 326, 345
Chakovsky, A., 329
Chaplin, Harry F., 62n
Charlton, Matthew, 134, 377
Charting a Continent (G. C. Ingleton), 387
Chatterton, Thomas, 50
Chaucer, Geoffrey, 200-1, 323
Chauvel, Charles, 127, 377
Chauvel of the Light Horse (A. J. Hill), 392
Chauvel, Sir Harry, 392
Chifley, J. B., 241, 256, 259
Children of the Dark People (F. D. Davison), 129n, 380
Chile, 21
China, 144, 326, 329, 332, 343, 346, 358, 364, 368, 373, 384
Chisholm, A. H., 55-7, 60, 84, 105, 135, 143n, 166-7, 189, 195-6, 215, 255-6n, 275, 304, 323, 330, 342, 346, 348, 350, 367, 378
Chisholm, A. R., 139n, 393
Chisholm, Caroline, 313, 378
Chisholm, Deirdre, 143, 167
Chivers, R. B., 374
Christesen, C.B., 306, 318n, 332, 349, 354-5, 358-60, 364, 378
Christian (*The Pilgrim's Progress*), 301
Christina Stead (R. G. Geering), 398
Christison, Robert, 214, 378
Chung of Vietnam (Len Fox), 383
Church, Hubert N., 90, 93, 378
Cianta, Father (Boys' Town), 279
Circling Hearths, The (Roderic Quinn), 396
Circus at World's End (Peter Hopegood), 222, 386
Clan Alpini, 333
Clan Cameron, *see* Cameron Clan
'Clancy of the Overflow' (A. B. 'Banjo' Paterson), 369
Clarence River, N.S.W., 236n
Clare's Weekly (Perth), 96
Clarion, 111n
Clark, C. H. Manning, 286, 388
Clark, Hilary, 388
Clarke, Donovan, 255, 378
Clarke, Marcus, 174, 389
Clift, Charmian (Mrs George Johnston), 247n
Clipper (Hobart), 402
Cloncurry, Queensland, 47, 64, 205n, 251, 274, 354, 360, 368
Close, Robert, 231-2, 319, 378
Clune, Frank, 267, 307, 378
coat-of-arms (Ogilvie), 236-8, 302
Coatsworth, Elizabeth, 224
Cody, Daniel B., 88

Cohen, George H., 219-20
Cold Nose, 229
Coleridge, S. T., 74
Collected Essays (Sir Walter Murdoch), 393
Collected Poems (A. D. Hope), 386
Collected Poems (J. A. R. McKellar), 391
Collected Poems (Shaw Neilson), 379
Collected Poems (Stephen Spender), 398
Collected Verses (A. H. Adams), 373
Collins, Dale, 127, 378
Colman, Mrs E. M., 337n, 342, 378
Colman, G. A., 337n
Colombo, 23
'Columbus Goes West' (W. Hart-Smith), 182, 269n, 385
Come in Spinner (Dymphna Cusack & Florence James), 379
'Comedy of Manners, The' (Hugh McCrae), 235n
Comfort, Alexander, 294, 321n, 378
Coming Commonwealth, The (Sir Robert Garran), 383
Commander Capstan (Dora Wilcox), 402
Common Cause, 356n
Commonwealth Library, 49, 55, 153, 222, 236
Commonwealth Literary Board, *see* Commonwealth Literary Fund
Commonwealth Literary Fund, 143, 177, 221-2, 233, 286, 289, 292, 301n-2, 307, 326, 366, 400
Commonwealth Trading Bank of Australia, 211n
Communism, 4, 6, 10, 12, 168
Communist Party (Australia), 221n
compulsory military training, 150n
Comrades All and other Poems for the People (Bartlett Adamson), 373
Concise History of Australia, A (Clive Turnbull), 400
Condobolin, N.S.W., 37n
convict system, 120
Cook, Captain James, 235n, 271
Coolgardie, Western Australia, 224
Coolgardie Miner, 95, 401
Cooma, N.S.W., 86
Coonardoo (K. S. Prichard), 76, 83, 87, 396
Cootamundra, N.S.W., 14, 352
Corelli, Marie, 378
Cornerstone (Dorothy Catts), 377
Cornstalk Press, the, 78
'Coronation Anthem' (Mary Gilmore), 173
Corroboree Tree, The (Christina Mawdesley), 392
Cosme, Paraguay, 3n-4n, 5-9n, 10-11, 17-19, 49, 55-7, 66n, 77, 88, 159, 163, 292, 330, 353, 373, 379, 383, 388, 392, 395-6, 399
Cosme Evening Notes, 3n, 87-8, 379
Cosme Monthly, 49, 153, 161, 183, 379
'Cosmic Argument' (W. Hart-Smith), 224n
Cotta Walla, N.S.W., 102n, 354-5, 394
Cottesloe, Western Australia, 207
Cotton, Frank, 129, 379
Cottrell, Dorothy, 71, 75-6, 108, 276, 311n, 379
Court Theatre, London, 393
'Cousin Marie' (Sydney *Sun*), 218
Cousins, Aubrey, 247n, 290
Cousins, W. G., 90, 100, 103-4, 108, 118-19, 121, 140, 147, 166, 174, 199, 207, 247n, 263, 290n, 379, 385
Cowabbie Station, N.S.W., 189, 323
Cowper, Lady Norman (née Dorothea H. McCrae), 122n, 124, 346n
Cowper, Sir Norman, 346n
Crawford, Robert, 82
Creative Writing in Australia (J. K. Ewers), 381
Creeve Roe (V. J. Daley), 379
Cremorne Point, Sydney, 68, 296
Crete, 386
Critic, The, 279n
Crocker, Arthur, 114n
Croll, R. H., 69n, 89-90, 98, 100, 111, 117-18, 199, 219, 379, 398
Cromwell, Oliver, 210
Cronulla: A Story of Station Life (Vance Palmer), 62
Crookston, R. M., 203n
Crookwell, N.S.W., 256, 288n
Cross, Zora, 65, 379
Crouch, Colonel R. A., 329
'Crows kep' flyin' up, boys, The' (Mary Gilmore), 17, 25n, 216n
C.S.I.R.O., 267
Currency Lass, The (James Devaney), 380
Currey, C. H., 333, 379
Curtin, John, 143, 176, 178, 182, 185, 189, 191, 379
Cusack, Dymphna, 165, 368, 379

Daily Advertiser (Wagga Wagga), 130n
Daily Mirror (Sydney), 256, 336
Daily News (Perth), 94
Daily Telegraph (Sydney), 55-6, 64, 158, 160, 210-11, 213, 219, 245, 254, 261, 292, 309, 330, 334, 336, 339-41, 378-9, 382, 386, 389-90, 393, 395, 402
Daley, V. J., 141, 149n, 379, 396, 399
Dalziel, Laura Kathleen Natalie, 222-3, 379

Dame Commander of the British Empire, 132n-4, 282
'Dame Mary Gilmore: Australia's Grand Old Lady of Letters' (Colin Roderick, *Age*), 350n
Dame Mary Gilmore Road, Hurstville, Sydney, 294
'Dancer, The' (Norman Lindsay), 144-5
'Daniel Webster's Horses' (Elizabeth Coatsworth), 224
Dark, Eleanor, 311n, 394
Darkness and Light and Other Poems (F. J. Letters), 388
Darling River, N.S.W., 232, 240
Davey, A. J. (Paraguay), 11, 379
Davey, Mrs A. J. (Paraguay), 11, 379
David Copperfield (Charles Dickens), 73
Davis, Arthur Hoey, *see* 'Rudd, Steele'
Davis, Beatrice, 302, 373, 380
Davis, Norma L., 202
Davison, Frank Dalby, 78, 90n, 100n, 129, 133, 380
Dawes Point, Sydney, 388
Dawn (Louisa Lawson, ed.), 183, 185, 388
Dawn Club, 388
Dawn to Destiny (Dorothy Catts), 377
Dawnward? (Bernard O'Dowd), 293
Dawson, Peter, 333, 380
D.B.E., *see* Dame Commander of the British Empire
Deakin, Alfred, 177, 380
Deamer, Dulcie, 115, 138, 380
Death of Ned Kelly, The (John Manifold), 391
de Brune, Aidan, 115, 380
'Delacy, Danny', 136, 187
'Delacy, Johanna', 136n
de la Mare, Walter, 290, 304, 380
Delugar, Leon (Paraguay), 6
Dennis, C. J., 279, 378, 380
Derry, Ireland, 201
Deschamps, Jacqueline, 251
Deschamps, Noel, 251
Desperate Measures (Leon Gellert), 383
Devaney, James, 199, 380, 393
Devanny, Jean, 248, 380
Dick, Alexander (Paraguay), 380
Dick, Andrew (Paraguay), 9-11, 380
Dick, James & Mrs (Paraguay), 9, 380
Dickens, Charles, 75
Dickinson, Emily, 135, 139, 186, 211, 383
Dictionary of Australian Biography (Percival Serle), 398
Dig (Frank Clune), 378
'Dim Sims Man' (David Martin), 297
Dinning, Hector, 65
Dirge and Lyrics (C. B. Christesen), 378

Disinherited, The (Mary Gilmore), 175, 180, 189, 380
Disney, Walt, 207
Distant Land (Judah Waten), 401
'Distant Runners, The' (Mark Van Doren), 224
Dobell, William, 236, 312, 317, 319, 337-43, 346-7, 356-7, 361, 363-4, 380-1, 394, 398
Dobell Portrait (of Mary Gilmore), 312, 317, 326, 334, 337-42, 346-7, 360-1, 363-4, 378, 380, 401
dogs (tribute to), 211, 213-14
'Doin' the Boots for Sunday' (Mary Gilmore), 280n
Domain, Sydney, 102n
Dominions of the Boundary (Bernard O'Dowd), 46n, 268, 293
'Don Quixote', 226
Donald, Jim, 170, 381
Donovan, T. (*Worker*), 99n
Doreen (C. J. Dennis), 380
Downside, N.S.W., 14, 352
Drake-Brockman, Henrietta, 305, 381
Dreadnought of the Darling, The (C. E. W. Bean), 240, 374
Dream Millions: New Light on Lasseter's Last Reef (F. Blakeley), 231n
Driven, The (Donald Stuart), 399
'Drover's Wife, The' (Henry Lawson), 62, 75
'Drum for Hugh McCrae, A' (T. Inglis Moore), 243
Dunkirk, 173
Dunlea, Father T. V. (Boys' Town), 278-9, 381
Dupain, M., 361
'Dust on the Trail' (Mary Gilmore), 103
Dutton, Geoffrey, 347n
'Dying Butcher, The' (Hugh McCrae), 188n

'E', *see* Fullerton, Mary
' "E". The Full Story' (Miles Franklin), 210n
Eagle Press, 385
Early Australian History (Charles White), 402
'Early Life of Henry Lawson, The' (T. D. Mutch), 393
Earth Battle (Dorothy Cottrell), 108
Earth's Quality (Winifred Birkett), 108-9, 375
Ecclesiastes, 25n
Echo (Sydney), 183
Edwards, Mary, 236, 381
Egoist, The (George Meredith), 392
Egypt, 53

'Eight Affirmations of Judgment' (W. Hart-Smith), 269
Eighth Australian Division (2nd A.I.F.), 375
'Eldershaw, M. Barnard', 84
Eliot, T. S., 254
Elizabeth Bay, Sydney, 391
Elizabeth Bay House, Sydney, 308
Elizabeth II, Queen, 302, 304, 392
Elkin, A. P., 191, 381
Elkin, P. K., 347n
Elliott, E. V., 327
Elliott, Jane, 320n, 381
Ellis, H. Havelock, 285, 381, 397
Emerson, Ernest Sando, 96, 381
Enchanted Island, The (Vance Palmer), 90n
English, 234
English Association, 234, 254, 397
'Englishman, The' (A. G. Stephens), 37n
'Essay on Literature' (Nettie Palmer), 59n, 61, 65
'Essay on Memory' (R. D. FitzGerald), 141n, 226, 254
Essington Lewis (Clive Turnbull), 400
Esson, Louis, 146n, 168, 376, 381
Estancia Condor, 21-2
Eureka Stockade, 154
Evatt, H. V., 256, 312, 358, 381
Evening News (Sydney), 183
Everitt, Miss, 15
Ewers, J. K., 94-5, 381
Excell, Patricia, 297, 381

'Face of the Waters, The' (R. D. FitzGerald), 298n-9
'Faces in the Street' (Henry Lawson), 74
Fadden, Sir Arthur, 221, 381
Fair Girls and Gray Horses (W. H. Ogilvie), 394
Fairfax, John & Co., 292n
Falconer, Ethel Keith (Lady Stonehaven), 150n, 381, 399
Falkiner, F. S., 276, 382
Falkland Islands, 20-1
Falstein, M., 188, 190
Family at Misrule, The (Ethel Turner), 400
'Far Journey, The' (Arnold Wall), 267n
Far-North Memories (Jessie Litchfield), 389
Farrell, John, 17, 23, 25-7, 30, 55, 118, 184, 225, 279, 296, 309, 336, 353, 382, 399
Farrell, Olive, 336
Farrer, William, 209, 306, 322, 382
'Father and Son' (Vance Palmer), 61
Father Clears Out (Hal Gye), 385
'F.C.B. Vosper: An Australian Radical', 401
Feathered Serpent, The (Roland Robinson), 330n

Federal Story, The (Alfred Deakin), 380
Feint, Adrian, 126, 382
Fellows All. The Chronicles of the Bread and Cheese Club (H. W. Malloch, ed.), 194, 391
Fellowship, 114n
Fellowship of Australian Writers (Canberra), 286n, 319
Fellowship of Australian Writers (Sydney), 73n, 78, 80, 90, 103, 113-17, 129, 133, 191, 252, 377, 382
'Female Labour in Australia' (Jeannie Lockett), 389
Ferguson, George A., 229-30, 241, 246-7, 262-4, 271-2, 276, 280, 290, 302, 304, 322-4, 329, 345, 348, 350, 366-7, 369, 397
Few Words, A (Lady Game), 383
'Fifth Day' (R. D. FitzGerald), 226, 298n
Fifty Years in the Making of Australian History (Sir Henry Parkes), 395
Fifty Years of Progress in Australia (Aidan de Brune), 380
Finey, George E., 201, 382
'Finey's Approach to Music' (George Finey), 382
Finney Centenary Prize, 394
Fire on the Snow (Douglas Stewart), 223, 399
First Discovery of Australia, The (T. D. Mutch), 393
'Fish Trap, The' (correct title 'Fish Balks and Traps', Mary Gilmore), 102
Fisher Library, University of Sydney, 55n, 384
Fisher, Mary Lucy ('Lala'), 382
Fisher, Mrs Garth, 355
FitzGerald, R. D., 68, 141, 145n, 148, 151, 171n, 197, 199, 201, 217, 226-7, 232-3, 239-42, 244-5, 248, 254, 266-7, 274, 277-80, 282, 290, 294-5, 298-301, 303, 305, 309n, 315-17, 321, 323, 328, 330-1, 334-5, 354, 356-64, 369-70, 382, 395, 398
  Works:
  Between Two Tides, 278, 299-301, 382; 'Bog and Candle', 360n, 362; 'Essay on Memory', 141n, 226, 254; 'Face of the Waters, The', 298n-9; 'Fifth Day', 226n, 298-9; *Forty Years' Poems*, 382; 'Garibaldi Veteran, A', 324; *Greater Apollo, The*, 68n; *Heemskerck Shoals*, 254, 298-9, 382; 'Landfall', 278; 'Mary Gilmore: Poet and Great Australian', 357n, 359n-60n, 362; 'Miss Mary Ann Bell', 145, 148; *Moonlight Acre*, 145n, 382; *Of Places and Poetry*, 323n; 'Roadside: Eleven Compo-

sitions', 316n; *This Night's Orbit*, 226n, 298n, 300, 303, 382; 'This Understanding', 248; 'Wonder', 298
FitzHenry, W. E., 336, 382
Fitzpatrick, Brian C., 280, 382
'Five Bells' (Kenneth Slessor), 398
Five Bright Stars (Eric Lambert), 333, 387
Five Corners (Dowell O'Reilly), 394
'Five Visions of Captain Cook' (Kenneth Slessor), 398
'Flesh, The' (Mary Gilmore), 267, 286n
Flesh and the Spirit, The (Douglas Stewart), 267n
Flinders, Matthew, 174, 386
Flodden (Battle of), 320n, 381
'Flowers of the Forest' (Jane Elliott), 320, 381
Flow River, Blow Wind (Elyne Mitchell), 392
Flynn, John, 382
Flynn of the Inland (I. Idriess), 88-9, 92, 265, 387
Fool's Talk, A (H. E. Boote), 375
Foott, Mary Hannay, 184, 216, 383
For Heroes to Live In (J. K. Ewers), 381
For the Term of His Natural Life (Marcus Clarke), 58, 174, 389
Forbes, N.S.W., 37n
Forbes Advocate, 310, 384
Forests of Pan (Hugh McCrae), 200n
Forrest, David D., 366, 383
Forrest, Mabel, 35, 383
Fort William, Scotland, 355
Forty Years' Poems (R. D. FitzGerald), 382
Foster, Rene, 192, 291, 299, 302, 309, 312, 349, 383
Fourteen Men (Mary Gilmore), 135n, 215n, 228, 233-4, 244n, 259n-60n, 275n, 282-3n, 286, 289-90n, 292, 298n, 302-3, 307-8n, 309, 328-9, 369, 374, 383
Fourteen Minutes (H. M. Green), 200
Fox, Leonard P., 344, 356, 383
Fox, Mona (Mona Brand), 344, 356, 383
'Fox Temptation Knoweth, The' (Mary Gilmore), 91
France, 373
Franklin, Stella Maria Miles, 86n, 127, 134, 136, 139, 165, 173, 179-80, 185-7, 210, 265, 305, 374, 376, 379, 383-4
Frazer, George, 353, 383
Free Church of Scotland, 40n
'Free Selector's Daughter, The' (Henry Lawson), 270n
Freedom on the Wallaby (M. & M. Holburn), 295, 386
French, Russell, 158
Friend and Fireside (D. G. Campbell), 268n
Friendly Vietnam (Len Fox), 383

From Life (David Martin), 291, 293n-5, 313, 320n-1n
From That Day to This (Myrtle White), 402
Fry, Elizabeth, 297, 313-14, 320, 383
Full Circle (Lyndall Hadow), 385
Fullerton, Mary ('E'), 134n, 136n, 139n, 180n, 185n-6, 210n-11, 381, 383
Furphy, Joseph, 190, 374, 381, 395, 399
Furphy, Violet, 395

Gadarene Swine, 325-6
Gadfly, 279
Gale Information Guide Library, 373, 375-7, 379, 382, 384, 387, 390, 395-6
Gallagher, Maureen, 334
Gallipoli, 53, 255
'Gallipoli' (Mary Gilmore), 255n
Galloway, E., 344
Game, Lady Gwendolen Margaret, 143, 383
Game, Sir Philip, 143n, 383
'Garibaldi Veteran, A' (R. D. FitzGerald), 323n-4
Garran, Sir Robert, 121, 383
'Gaucho, The' (José Hernandez), 246
Geering, R. G., 398
Gellert, Leon M., 180, 246, 383
Generations of Men, The (Judith Wright), 273n
Genoa, 23
Geoffry Hamlyn (Henry Kingsley), 58
George Finey's Caricatures, 382
George, Henry, 306, 383
George VI, King, 342
George Street, Sydney, 263n
Georgiana's Journal (Hugh McCrae), 119n, 390
Germany, 251
G.F., *see* Ferguson, George
giant toad, 241
Gibbes, J. W., 200, 391
Gilbert, W. S., 27n-8n
Gilchrist, Watt & Sanderson, 401
Gilmore, Dorothy (Mary Gilmore's daughter-in-law), 150, 251
Gilmore, Mary:
Biographical information (*see also* separate entries)
Australian Battle Cry (her ideas on), 173; Australian Labour Movement, 165, 177, 222, 275; Australian Workers' Union (her role in), 129; biographical article by Colin Roderick in Melbourne *Age*, 350-1; birth, 275n-6; *Bookfellow* (impact of), 35-6; bust by Rayner Hoff, 122, 319; childhood and schooldays, 91, 313-16, 352-3, 356; Christian names, 288; contributions to news-

papers and journals, 183; Cosme (life and activities in South America), 3n-4n, 8, 11-12, 49, 153-63; Dame Commander of the British Empire award, 132n-4; Dame Mary Gilmore Road, Hurstville, Sydney, 294; Dobell portrait, 334, 337-42, 361, 363-4; drawing by Eric Saunders, 110; 'Drover's Wife, The' (her version), 62n; electioneering activities, 188-90, 249; Elioth Grüner paintings (gifts to R. D. FitzGerald and T. Inglis Moore), 239; Fellowship of Australian Writers (her role in), 78, 114-17; funeral service, 38n; Goulburn War Memorial (her role in), 184; health, 49, 144, 231-2, 284; Henry Lawson (her version of their relationship), 3n, 35, 62n, 66n-7n, 73-5, 186, 216, 270; husband (marriage, 3n, 11; to Queensland, 43n; death, 204n-5n); Local History Day for schools (her role in), 196; marriage, 3n, 11; Mary Gilmore literary awards, 357, 365; May Day Queen, 349-50; ng cobbera (nomination by Bread and Cheese Club), 365; noms de plume, 183; patriotism, 233; pioneer history (her enthusiasm for), 205-7; poplar tree at 'Merry Vale', 102n, 107-8; portrait by Joshua Smith, 235-6; Red Page (*Bulletin*) article on her life and work, 24n, 30n; socialism (her early thoughts), 4, 6, 56, 60; social reformer (her achievements), 222; soldier settlement scheme, 188-90; son (death of), 204n-5n; Strathdownie, Victoria (life at), 24-5; Trade Union Movement (her role in), 222; war (her thoughts on), 168, 181; wife and mother (her view of her responsibilities as), 27-8, 40, 48; Women's Page (*Worker*), 42n, 184; *Worker* (activities with and resignation from), 42n, 99n, 184; World Peace Prize (nomination), 318

Comments on Art, Literature and Prominent People (*see also* separate entries) *Adam with Arrows* (Colin Simpson), 338; Adams, Francis, 296; analysis of her own work, 137, 213-16, 244-5, 249, 266, 268, 300, 350-1, 355, 359; Angus & Robertson Ltd., 152-3; *Australia Writes* (T. Inglis Moore), 305; Blamey, Sir Thomas, 303; *Bookfellow*, 35-6; Brennan, C. J., 252-3, 282, 345; 'Brent of Bin Bin', 86; *Bulletin* (Red Page article on Mary Gilmore), 24n, 30n; Burrows, E. M., 272; Byers, Isabel, 75; Campbell, Donald Gordon, 268; Chisholm, Caroline, 313; contemporary Australian poetry, 331; *Coonardoo* (K. S. Prichard), 76, 83; Davison, F. D., 78, 93; Dobell Portrait, 334, 337-42, 361-4; 'Drover's Wife, The' (Henry Lawson), 62n; Dunlea, Father T. V., 278; Fellowship of Australian Writers, 78, 114-17; FitzGerald, R. D., 151-2, 242-3, 277-8, 282, 298-301, 303, 305, 356, 360, 362-3; *Flynn of the Inland* (I. Idriess), 89; *Freedom on the Wallaby*, (M. & M. Holburn), 295; Fry, Elizabeth, 313; Fullerton, Mary ('E'), 134-5, 139, 185-6; Gordon, A. L., 193; Gruner, Elioth, 239; Harney, W. E., 'Bill', 208; Hart-Smith, W., 269; Hill, Ernestine, 192; Hughes, W. M., 280; *James Howard Catts, M.H.R.* (Dorothy Catts), 307; Lane, William, 154, 159-61; Langley, Eve, 179n-80; Lawson, Henry, 3n, 35, 62n, 66-7n, 73-5, 186, 216, 270; literary critics, 317; McCay, Adam, 205; McCrae, Hugh, 79, 152, 199, 217, 234, 277, 282, 293, 345; McDonald, Nan, 309-10; Mansell, Byram, 257; Martin, David, 286-8, 291-5, 297, 321; *Meanjin*, 358-60; Moir, J. K., 306; Neilson, J. Shaw, 54n-5; Nightingale, Florence, 313; O'Dowd, Bernard, 266, 293, 298; *Old Books, Old Friends, Old Sydney*, 281; Park, Ruth, 258; poetic composition—Mary Gilmore's methods, 44-6; 'Quest of Judith Wright, The' (T. Inglis Moore), 348; Quinn, Roderic, 86; Robertson, George, 231; Robinson, Roland, 252, 319-22; Roderick, Colin, 258, 350-1; 'Rudd, Steele', 318; Saunders, Eric, 110; Slessor, Kenneth, 197; Smith, Joshua, 235-6; Stephens, A. G., 52-3; Tennant, Kylie, 258; *Tracks We Travel, The* (J. Beazley), 365-6; *Viking of Van Diemen's Land, The* (F. Clune & P. R. Stephensen), 307; Women's Page (*Worker*), 42n, 184; Wright, Judith, 259, 310

Works:
'Australia to Abraham Lincoln', 178n; *Battlefields*, 135n, 138n, 146n, 148n, 164, 166n-9, 175, 374, 377; 'Bernard O'Dowd' (*Meanjin* article), 297n; 'Black Bread of Night', 90; 'Bull, The', 90, 95, 298; 'Coronation Anthem', 173; 'Crows kep' flyin' up, boys, The', 17, 25n, 216n; *Disinherited, The*, 175, 180, 189, 380; 'Doin' the Boots for Sunday', 280n; 'Dust on the Trail', 103; 'Fish Trap, The' (correct title 'Fish Balks and Traps'), 102; 'Flesh, The', 267, 286n; *Fourteen Men*, 135n, 215n, 228, 233-4, 244, 259n-60n, 275n, 282-3n, 286,

289-90, 292, 298n, 302-3, 307-9, 328-9, 369, 374, 383; 'Fox Temptation Knoweth, The', 9; 'Gallipoli', 255n; 'Glove, The', 93; 'Henry Lawson', 92n; 'Henry Lawson (A Memory)', 351; 'Honing up the Hill', 167; *Hound of the Road*, 58, 70, 93, 98n, 148, 324-5, 386; 'House of Memory, The', 98; 'Jindra', 262n, 275n; 'Lest We Forget', 171; *Marri'd and Other Verses*, 42n-3n, 56, 96, 117, 391; *Mary Gilmore* (Australian Poets series), 369-70n; *Mary Gilmore, Selected Verse*, 171n, 221n, 228n-30, 232n-4, 239n, 242, 246, 398; *More Recollections*, 109n-11n, 118n-21, 206, 214, 230, 247n, 322, 324, 357, 393; 'No Foe Shall Gather Our Harvest', 176-7, 192; *Old Days: Old Ways A Book of Recollections*, 86n, 101n-4n, 109n, 111n, 140, 206, 230, 247n, 322, 324, 357, 366, 394; 'Old Forthright', 215-17, 298; 'On One-Tree Hill', 289; 'Orientation', 40; 'Our Fleece Unbound', 315-16; *Passionate Heart, The*, 233, 255n, 395; 'Poetry: And an Australian Poet', 139n; 'Proud Men', 103; quail poem (untitled), 181; 'Ringer, The', 280; 'Road to Appin, The', 40; 'Roads of Remembrance', 98; *Rue Tree, The*, 85, 117, 350, 359, 397; 'Shakespeare', 171; 'She Dwelt Supreme', 90; 'Singapore', 177-9n, 184-5; 'Sweethearts', 184; 'T.B.', 91; *Tilted Cart, The*, 63-4, 87, 94, 148, 400; 'Time The Eternal Now', 325; 'To Hugh McCrae', 198; 'Trap Dams, The', 120; *Under the Wilgas*, 86n, 88n-90, 92, 94-5, 171n, 298n, 389, 401; 'We're the Boomeranglanders', 173n; *Wild Swan, The*, 66n, 72n, 84-5, 89, 94-5, 99n, 117, 171n, 342n, 402; 'Word-Held', 259n; *Worker Cook Book*, 85, 322; 'Yea and Nay', 330n

Critical Works on Mary Gilmore:
Bulletin (Red Page) by A. G. Stephens, 24n, 30n; 'Dame Mary Gilmore: Australia's Grand Old Lady of Letters', (*Age*) Colin Roderick, 350-2; *Mary Gilmore* (Australian Poets Series), Introduction by R. D. FitzGerald, 369-70n; 'Mary Gilmore' (*Hemisphere*), Vance Palmer, 346n; 'Mary Gilmore' (*Southerly*), T. Inglis Moore, 233n, 242n-5, 250-1, 395; 'Mary Gilmore— our great national poet' (*Australian Quarterly*), Hugh McCrae, 106n; 'Mary Gilmore: Poet and Great Australian' (*Meanjin*), R. D. FitzGerald, 233n, 357n, 359n, 362, 395; 'Mary Gilmore: The Hidden Years' (*Meanjin*), W. H. Wilde, 12n, 193n, 211n, 357n; *Three Radicals* (Australian Writers and Their Work), W. H. Wilde, 42n-3n, 99n, 233n, 268n, 350n, 359n, 374, 380, 383, 394, 402

Gilmore, Samuel (Mary Gilmore's brother-in-law), 43, 140n
Gilmore Thomas (Mary Gilmore's nephew), 179
Gilmore, William Alexander (Mary Gilmore's husband), 3n-4n, 5-8n, 9-12n, 13, 18-23, 33, 42n-3n, 47, 72, 77, 89, 105, 117, 122, 140, 177, 205n (death), 260n, 353-4, 383
Gilmore, William Dysart Cameron ('Billy') (Mary Gilmore's son), 3n-4n, 5-12, 18-23, 26, 33, 38, 42n-3n, 48, 53, 64, 108, 110-12, 117, 119, 122, 137, 150-1, 168, 193, 204n (death), 353-4, 368, 384, 396
Gilmore, William Wallace (Mary Gilmore's grandson), 166-8n, 236, 247, 251, 349, 360, 368, 384
'Ginger Meggs' (J. C. Bancks), 207, 374
Ginsburg, Reba, 267, 273, 384
Gladstone, William Ewart, 63
Glebe Point, Sydney, 50-1
'Glove, The' (Mary Gilmore), 93
Glover, Charles William, 228n
'God and the Child of Man' (H. M. Green), 347
Gold from the Sea (J. R. W. Taylor), 400
'Golden Green' (Joan Mackaness), 98n
'Golden Vanitee, The', 327
Gone to Earth (Mary Webb), 109n, 401
Gone Wandering (D. G. Campbell), 377
Gordon, Adam Lindsay, 51, 193, 214, 384, 398
Goulburn, N.S.W., 13, 38, 54-8, 61-2, 93, 102n, 165, 184, 187, 243, 256, 288, 308, 354-5, 393, 397
Gould, John, 131n, 384
Gould, Nathaniel (Nat), 34, 384
G.R.I., *see* Robertson, George
G.R.II, *see* Ferguson, George
Grattan, C. Hartley, 149, 384
Great Australian Loneliness, The (Ernestine Hill), 386
'Great Lochiel, The', *see* Cameron Clan
Greater Apollo, The (R. D. FitzGerald), 68n
Greece, 260, 282
Green, Dorothy, 384
Green, H. M., 81-2n, 106, 110, 200, 234, 288, 347, 384
Green Crowns (Mary Quick), 396
'Green Days and Cherries' (Hugh Anderson), 199n
'Green Days and Cherries' (Shaw Neilson), 199

Greenlees, Gavin, 310, 368, 384
Greenway, A. (Paraguay), 159
'Greenwood' (station), Queensland, 274
Grey, Sir George, 384
Grey, Zane, 124, 384
Griffiths, Annette Agnes, 48n
ground lark, 276
Grüner, Elioth, 126, 239-41, *385*
Guernsey, Channel Is, 399
Gurwood Street Public School, Wagga Wagga, N.S.W., 344
Gye, Hal ('James Hackston'), 285, 385

'Hackston, James', *see* Gye, Hal
Hadow, Lyndall, 385
Half-Way Sun, The (T. Inglis Moore), 112
Halstead Press, 152, 247n, 290n, 385
Hamilton, Winifred, 318, 385
Hand in the Dark, and Other Poems, The (Ada Cambridge), 377
Happy Valley and Other Poems, The (H. M. Green), 110n
Hardy, Frank, 309, 385
Hardy, Thomas, 71
Hargraves, Edward, 306, 323, 385
Harney, W. E. 'Bill', 191n, 208, 219, 229, 252, 385
Harp in the South, The (Ruth Park), 229n, 395
Harpoon in my Hand (Olaf Ruhen), 397
Harpur, Charles, 378
Harris, Joel Chandler, 320n, 385
Hart-Smith, William, 169, 171, 175n, 182, 224, 264, 268, 319, 335, 385, 402
  Works:
    Columbus Goes West, 182, 269; 'Cosmic Argument', 224n; 'Eight Affirmations of Judgment', 269; 'Neptune's Horses', 224n; *On the Level,* 264; 'Surrender of Granada, The', 224n
Hastings, Warren, 226n
Hawkey, G. F., 113
Haylen, Leslie, 85, 178n, 188, 190, 385
Head, Walter, *see* Woods, W. A.
Heart of Spring (Shaw Neilson), 171
Heemskerck Shoals (R. D. FitzGerald), 254, 298n-9, 382
Heffron, R. J., 324, 385
Heir of Redclyffe, The (Charlotte Yonge), 402
Hemisphere, 346
Heney, Thomas W., 63, 246, 385
Henley, W. E., 28n, 273-4, 386
Henry Bournes Higgins (Nettie Palmer), 86
Henry Kendall (W. H. Wilde), 387
Henry Kendall Seat, Botanical Gardens, Sydney, 355

Henry Lawson (A. A. Phillips), 388
'Henry Lawson' (Mary Gilmore), 92n
Henry Lawson (Stephen Murray-Smith), 393
'Henry Lawson (A Memory)' (Mary Gilmore), 351
Henry Lawson and his Critics (F. J. Broomfield), 73n
'Henry Lawson and I' (Mary Gilmore), 3n, 67n, 73n, 216n
Henry Lawson Criticism 1894-1971 (C. Roderick), 388
Henry Lawson: His Books, Manuscripts, Autograph Letters and Association Copies, etc. (H. F. Chaplin), 62n
Henry Lawson Memorial and Literary Society, 3n, 62n, 72, 186n, 197
'Henry Lawson Westward' (D. G. Campbell), 268
Herald (Auckland), 160, 388
Herald (Melbourne), 329, 393
Herald (Perth), 95, 96
'Hermit, The' (Vance Palmer), 58-9
Hernandez, José, 246n
Hero of Too, The (David Martin), 391
Heseltine, H. P., 395
Hetherington, John, 303, 386, 388
Hidden Tide, The (Roderic Quinn), 396
Higgins, Henry Bournes, 386
High Valley (Charmian Clift & George Johnston), 247
Higham, Charles, 347n
Hilder, Bim, 211n
Hilder, J. J., 211n
Hill, A. J., 392
Hill, Ernestine, 170-1, 174, 192, 221, 251, 272, 291, 311n, 346-7, 364, 386
Hill, Robert, 192, 346
'Hill 17' (Mary Gilmore nom de plume), 184
'Hilltop', Strathdownie, Victoria, 27, 29, 32
'His Father's Mate' (Henry Lawson), 212
History of Australian Literature, A (H. M. Green), 384
History of England (T. B. Macaulay), 390
History of Henry Esmond, The (W. M. Thackeray), 249n
Hoff, G. Rayner, 105, 118, 122, 127, 166n, 319, 386
Holburn, Marjorie and Muir, 295, 386
Hole in the Bedroom Floor, The (Hal Gye), 385
Holman, Charles (Paraguay), 158
Holman, W. A., 158, 275, 386
Holmes, Oliver W., 348, 386
Holy City, The (James Francis Hurley), 247
Home Annual, The, 126

Homebush Sale Yards, Sydney, 211n
'Honing up the Hill' (Mary Gilmore), 167
Hoosier dialect, 320, 322, 331, 385
Hooton, Joy, 386
Hope, A. D., 286, 320-1, 386, 402
Hopegood, Peter, 186, 222-3, 386
Hornsby, N.S.W., 50
Horsham, Victoria, 354
Hotel Imperial, The, Goulburn, N.S.W., 54-8, 61-2
Houlder Bros, 8
Hound of the Road (Mary Gilmore), 58, 70, 93, 98n, 148, 324-5, 386
'House for Pegasi, The' (Hugh McCrae), 295n
'House of Memory, The' (Mary Gilmore), 98
'House of the Ravens, The' (Hugo Wast), 61
Housman, A. E., 135, 386
How He Died and Other Poems (John Farrell), 382
How the Sky was Lifted (Byram Mansell), 391
Howarth, R. G., 168, 171, 180, 193, 199n, 224, 243, 252-3, 295n, 347n, 386
'Hugh McCrae' (T. Inglis Moore), 149
Hugh River, Central Australia, 387
Hughes, Dame Mary, 167, 283, 344
Hughes, E. F., 36n
Hughes, W. M., 93, 134, 146, 167n, 173, 189, 270, 275, 280, 283n, 344n, 386
Hugo, Victor, 15, 174
Humbug Creek, N.S.W., 37n
Hunters Hill, Sydney, 317, 324, 387, 396
Hurley, James Francis, 247
Hurlstone Training College, N.S.W., 15
Huxley, Julian, 301, 387
Hyde Park, Sydney, 133n, 386

I Can Jump Puddles (Alan Marshall), 391
I Hate and I Love (John Thompson), 400
'I Remember Dame Mary' (A.B.C. radio programme), 312n
I Wen, 326
Idriess, Ion, 88n, 91, 100, 265, 387
Ifould, W. H., 70n
Iliad, 279-80
Imitation of Christ, The (Thomas à Kempis), 37n
'In Early Green Summer' (Joan Mackaness), 98n
In Search of Henry Lawson (Manning Clark), 388
In the Days When the World Was Wide and Other Verses (Henry Lawson), 3n, 270n
Inchcape Rock, 355
Ingamells, Rex, 195, 259, 387

Ingleton, G. C., 280-1, 387
Ingoldsby Legends (R. H. Barham), 74
Inheritors (Brian Penton), 395
Ink (Society of Women Writers, Sydney) 397
Intimate Portraits (H. P. Heseltine), 393
Into the Wind: Collected Poems (Yvonne Webb), 402
Introduction to Australian Fiction, An (Colin Roderick), 258n
'Invictus' (W. E. Henley), 28n
Ireland, 374
Irish at Eureka, The (C. H. Currey), 379
Isaacs, Lady, 283
Isaacs, Sir I., 283
Isle of Girls (Eleanor Smith), 398
Isle of San, The (Leon Gellert), 383
'It's Quiet Down There' (May Brahe), 376

Jacka's Mob (E. J. Rule), 100, 397
Jackson, Alice, 178n
Jago, Walter, 114n, 183, 185, 387
James I, King, 355
James, Florence, 379
James, Reverend Augustus, 288
James Howard Catts, M.H.R. (Dorothy Catts), 307n
Jane Eyre (Charlotte Bronte), 212
Jephcott, Sydney, 225, 296, 387
Jindera, *also* Jindra, N.S.W., 262n, 276
'Jindra' (Mary Gilmore), 262n, 275n
Jindyworobaks, 387
'John Alexander Ross McKellar, Memoir by J. W. Gibbes', 200n
Johnston, George, 247n
Johnston, Grahame, 380, 383, 395, 397
Jonah (Louis Stone), 58, 399
Jones, Inigo, 257, 387
Jones, W. A., 400
Jordens, Ann-Mari, 73n
Jorgenson, Jorgen, 307n
Joseph Furphy (Kate Baker & Miles Franklin), 374
Joubert, Didier, 317n, 387
Joubert, Jules Francois, 387
Judith Grant (Jeannie Lockett), 82
Judith Wright (A. D. Hope), 402
Julia Creek, Queensland, 355
Julius, Harry, 134, 387

Kahan, Louis, 357, 387
Kaleski, Robert, 34, 37n, 387
Kanga Creek: An Australian Idyll (Havelock Ellis), 285, 381
Karlsruhe, S.S., 8n
Keats, John, 50, 74, 107, 123
Keeble, John, 402
Kelly, Ned, 307

Kelly, Nora, 90, 387
'Kelpie', 37n
Kelpie dogs, 37n
Kempis, Thomas à, 37
Kendall, Henry, 67n, 191, 308, 355, 378, 387, 399
Kenny, Sister Elizabeth, 251n
'Kerry Lodge', 187
Kidd, F. (Paraguay), 157
Kidd, Mrs F. (Paraguay), 157
Kidman, Sir Sidney, 265, 323, 387
King, E. W., 37n
King O'Malley: Man and Statesman (Dorothy Catts), 334n
Kings Cross, Sydney, 217-18, 234
Kirwan, W., 385
Known and Not Held (Kathleen Dalziel), 222n, 379
Kodak Magazine, 325
Kokoda Trail, the, 223n-4
Kong Sing, Justine, 52
'Koorabri' (W. P. Bluett property), N.S.W., 375
Kramer, Leonie, 386
Kuhn, Maria, 259, 347, 387

La Casa De Los Cuervos (Zuviria Gustavo Martinez), 391
La Nauze, J. A., 380
Labor Daily (Sydney), 397
Labour Movement (Australia), 155, 165, 177
'Labour Question in Australia from an Australian Point of View, The' (Jeannie Lockett), 389
Lachlan River, N.S.W., 311
Lady Isobel, S.S., 221
Lake Cowal, N.S.W., 310
Lambert, Eric, 333, 388
Lambert, George, 85n
'Lament for the Gordons' (David Martin), 320n-1
'Lammermoor' (Robert Christison property), Queensland, 214, 378
Lamond, Hector, 43n, 176, 211, 388
Land of Dahori: Tales of New Guinea (Olaf Ruhen), 397
'Landfall' (R. D. FitzGerald), 278
Landtakers (Brian Penton), 105, 395
Lane, Charles Lincoln (Paraguay), 163
Lane, John (Paraguay), 11n, 16, 48, 153, 159, 161, 388
'Lane, Laura M.', see Luffmann, Laura Bogue
Lane, William, 3n-4n, 11n, 16, 23, 57, 77, 82, 153-5, 159-63, 229, 232, 261, 275, 306, 353, 370, 373, 379, 382-3, 385, 388, 393, 397-9

Lang, John Dunmore, 93, 131, 164, 280, 323, 388
Langley, Eve, 179n-80, 388, 400
Language of the Sand (Roland Robinson), 252
Lasseter's Last Ride (I. Idriess), 88, 92, 100, 231, 387
Last Blue Sea, The (David Forrest), 366, 383
Last Poems (A. E. Housman), 386
Last Supper, The, 339
Latham, Sir John, 222
Laurence, Clara (née Jones, later Clara Stevenson), 158, 399
Laurence, William (Paraguay), 158, 399
Lavender, George, 328, 388
Lavender Bay, Sydney, 388
Law and Society (Julius Stone), 399
Lawson, Charles, 67n
Lawson, Gertrude, 58, 66-7n, 388
Lawson, Henry, 3n, 17, 22-3, 25, 31, 35, 54-5, 58-60, 62, 64-5, 66n-8, 72-6, 85, 88n, 92, 114, 116, 160, 166, 182-3, 186, 191, 201, 212, 216, 219, 222, 251, 265, 270n, 274, 327-8, 336, 343, 351-2, 361, 376, 382, 388-9, 393, 397, 399, 401
Works:
'Cambaroora Star, The', 160; 'Drover's Wife, The', 62, 75; 'Faces in the Street', 74; 'Free Selector's Daughter, The', 270n; 'His Father's Mate', 212; *In the Days When the World Was Wide and Other Verses*, 3n, 270n; 'Mary Called Him "Mister"', 270n; 'Trouble Belongit Mine', 219, 352
Lawson, Louisa, 58, 62n, 66-7n, 183, 185, 251, 388
Lawson, Peter, 67n
Leaves of Grass (Walt Whitman), 402
Leck, Charles (Paraguay), 155, 161
Lee, S. E., 347n
Legend and Dreaming (Roland Robinson), 397
Legend for Sanderson (Vance Palmer), 134
Legends from Australia (Byram Mansell), 391
Leichhardt, Ludwig, 378
'Lest We Forget' (Mary Gilmore), 171
'Letter from Australia, A' (Hector Dinning), 65n
'Letter to President Eisenhower, A' (David Martin), 291
Letters, F. J., 169, 388
Letters of Vance and Nettie Palmer (Vivian Smith, ed.), 394-5
Letters to Scotland (Mary Quick), 396
Lewis, F. (Paraguay), 388

Life and Works of A. G. Stephens, The (P. R. Stephensen), 399
Life of Vice-Admiral William Bligh, The (George Mackaness), 271n
Life Story of Joseph Furphy, The (E. E. Pescott), 395
Light Horse (Elyne Mitchell), 392
Lighthouse, The (Nan McDonald), 390
Lilley's Magazine, 184
Lincoln, Abraham, 163, 189
Lindsay, Norman, 144n, 345, 386, 388, 390
Lindsay, Sir Lionel, 124, 140, 143-5, 150, 172, 181, 202, 282, 388
Listeners, The (Walter de la Mare), 391
Litchfield, Jessie, 254-5, 367, 389
Little Bush Maid, A (Mary Grant Bruce), 376
Liverpool, England, 22
Local History Day, 196, 198
Loch Lomond, 168
Lochaber, Scotland, 355
Lochiel, *see* Cameron Clan
Lockett, Jeannie, 82, 285, 389
Loder, John de Vere, *see* Wakehurst, Lord
Lofting, Hilary, J. F., 166, 389
Lofting, Hugh, 389
London, 22-3, 31, 386, 393
London Mercury, 65n
London Streets (A. H. Adams), 373
Lone Hand, 33n, 48n, 184, 373, 381, 389, 399
Lonely Fire, The (Nan McDonald), 309, 390
'Lonely Fire, The', (Nan McDonald), 309n
'Lone Star Spring, The' (station), Queensland, 47
Longstaff, Sir John, 361, 389
Lorca, Frederico Garcia, 287, 389
Louis Stone (H. J. Oliver), 399
Louvre, The, Paris, 323
Love Me Sailor (Robert Close), 378
Loveless, George, 302, 389
'Love's Coming' (Shaw Neilson), 138
'Love's Treasure-House' (D. M. Ross), 34n
Luffman, Laura Bogue ('Laura M. Lane'), 206, 389
Lyceum Club, Sydney, 80, 100, 114-15, 365
Lynch, John (Bread and Cheese Club), 365, 367, 390
Lyons, Dame Enid, 190, 390
Lyons, Joseph A., 117, 132, 390

Macartney, F. T., 297n, 331, 392
Macaulay, T. B., 239, 389-90
McCay, Adam C. ('Dum'), 129, 151, 204, 255, 390

McColl, Hugh, 355
McColl, James H., 355
McColl, Mary (Mary Gilmore's paternal grandmother), 355
McCord, David, 224
McCrae, Dorothea H., *see* Cowper, Lady Norman
McCrae, Dorothy F. (Mrs C. E. Perry), 35, 390
McCrae, G. G., 66, 316, 390
McCrae, Georgiana Huntly, 118n, 151n, 384, 390
McCrae, Hugh, 35, 77, 79-80, 84, 105-6, 110, 117-19, 121-3, 125-6, 128, 130, 136-7, 145, 148-52, 164, 166, 179, 182, 187-8n, 197-204, 212-17, 234-5, 239, 244, 246-50, 254, 266, 268, 274, 277, 281-3, 290, 293, 295, 301, 303-5, 307-8, 321, 328, 334, 344-6, 356, 360, 390, 401
Works:
Best Poems of Hugh McCrae, The, 295n; 'Blind Man Said, The', 203n; 'Comedy of Manners, The', 235n; 'Dying Butcher, The', 188n; *Forests of Pan*, 199-200; 'House for Pegasi, The', 295n; *Mimshi Maiden, The*, 149n; *My Father and My Father's Friends*, 118n, 235n; *Satyrs and Sunlight*, 105; *Story Book Only*, 235, 246-7; 'Twa Heads', 244, 308; *Voice of the Forest*, 203n
McCrae, Nancy, 119, 121, 127, 130, 137, 149, 249-50
McCuaig, R., 309
Macdonald, A. K. (Paraguay), 158
McDonald, Nan, 217, 227, 243, 309-10, 347n, 390
MacDonald, R. (and Mrs), 336, 347, 390
McGregor, Peter, 312, 333, 390
Mackaness, Alice, 100, 177, 182, 192, 205, 221, 251-2, 343, 390
Mackaness, George, 78, 90, 98, 103, 113, 129, 132, 164, 170-1n, 176, 182-3, 190, 192, 196, 199, 204, 208, 221, 251-2, 270-2, 343, 390, 399
Mackaness, Joan, 98, 251-2, 343, 390
McKay, Captain, 326-7
Mackay, Jessie, 24, 34-5, 58, 93, 390
Mackay, Queensland, 291
MacKay, W. J., 211, 213-14
Mackellar, Dorothea, 141, 391
McKellar, J. A. R., 200, 391
McKell, Sir William J. 213, 390
McKeown, Keith C., 241, 391
McKinney, Judith Wright, *see* Wright, Judith
McKinney, Meredith, 257n, 273
McLeay, Alexander, 107, 133, 308, 391
McLeod, A. (Paraguay), 6

McLeod, A. G., 306n
McLeod, James, 268, 391
MacMahon, T., 266
McNicoll, David, 341, 391
McNiven, Mrs R., 265
MacPherson, John, 167
Macquarie Street, Sydney, 396
Maher, Father, 336
Mailer, Norman, 245n
Making of Australian Drama, The (Leslie Rees), 381
'Making of Shaw Neilson's "Honeymoon Song", The' (Hugh Anderson), 199n
Malaya, 375
Malloch, H. W. (Bread and Cheese Club), 194, 219, 240, 254, 261, 391
Malta, 373
Mamba, The Bright-Eyed (G. G. McCrae), 316n, 390
'Man From Snowy River, The' (A. B. 'Banjo' Paterson), 395
Man in the Silo, The (Eric Otto Schlunke), 397
Man of Sydney, A (Douglas Stewart), 202n, 398
manhood suffrage, 222
Manifold, John, 315, 391
Mann, Cecil, 82n, 281n
Mansell, Byram, 257-8, 315, 391
Mansfield, Mary, 231-2
Man-Shy (F. D. Davison), 78n, 90, 93, 100, 129, 380
Mant, Gilbert, 82
maritime strike 1891, *see also* shearers' strike, 129n, 395
Market Street, Sydney, 263
Marrickville, Sydney, 156
Marri'd and Other Verses (Mary Gilmore), 42n-3n, 56, 96, 117, 391
Marshall, Alan, 231-2, 305, 318n, 322, 326, 391
Martin, David (née Ludwig Detsinyi), 286-8, 291, 293-7, 303, 313-15, 320-1, 332, 391
   Works:
   'Dim Sims Man', 297; *From Life*, 291, 293-5, 313, 320n; 'Letter to President Eisenhower, A', 291, 293; 'Mission Station, North Queensland', 313; *New World, New Song*, 314; 'Our Poets', 314n; *Poems of David Martin*, 297n, 313n; 'Russian, The', 332n; *Spiegel the Cat*, 294n; *Stones of Bombay, The*, 295, 297; 'To Me Peace is Three Simple Things', 287n
Martin, Richenda, 314, 320n-1, 333
Martin Place, Sydney, 48n
Martinez, Zuviria Gustavo, 61, 391

'Mary Called Him "Mister" ' (Henry Lawson), 270
Mary Gilmore (Australian Poets series), 369-70n
'Mary Gilmore' (T. Inglis Moore), 233n, 242n, 245, 251, 395
'Mary Gilmore' (Vance Palmer), 346n
'Mary Gilmore—The Hidden Years' (W. H. Wilde), 12n, 193n, 211n, 357n
'Mary Gilmore: A New Poem and Textual Autographs' (A. G. McLeod), 306n
Mary Gilmore Award Committee, 357, 365-6n
'Mary Gilmore—our great national poet' (Hugh McCrae), 106n
'Mary Gilmore. Poet and Great Australian' (R. D. FitzGerald), 233n, 357n, 359n, 362, 395
Mary Gilmore: Selected Verse, 171n
Masefield, John, 148, 304, 392
maternity allowance, 222
'Mather, George', *see* Emerson, Ernest Sando
Mathew, Ray, 324, 347n, 373, 392
Matthews, Brian, 62n
Maupassant, Guy de, 212
'Maurice, Furnley', *see* Wilmot, Frank
Mawdesley, Christina, 196, 392
May Day Queen, 349-50
Meanjin, 199n, 239n, 250, 287, 297n, 306n, 309n, 311, 332-3, 348-9, 357-60, 362, 373, 378, 381, 387, 395
Meanjin Quarterly, 12, 193n, 211n, 233n, 287
'Meggs, Ginger' (J. C. Bancks), 207, 374
Melba, Dame Nellie, 50
Melbourne, 54-5, 87n, 93, 99, 118, 146, 218-19, 232, 260, 266, 285-6, 303-4, 314, 340-2, 358-9, 374, 376, 395
Melville, Herman, 305n
Memoirs of a Midget (Walter de la Mare), 380
Men Against the Earth (J. K. Ewers), 381
'Men and Knowledge' (Sir Mark Oliphant), 332n
Men Are Human (Vance Palmer), 87n
Men of the Jungle (Vance Palmer), 91-3
Men Without Wives (Henrietta Drake-Brockman), 381
Menzies, Sir Robert G., 165, 182, 201, 256, 265, 392
Meredith, George, 26n, 392
'Merry Vale' (Beattie property), N.S.W., 102n, 108, 187, 308, 355, 394
Messalina (Dulcie Deamer), 380
Meurant, Ferdinand Napoleon, 133, 392
Meurant, Louis, 133n
Mildura, Vic., 260

Milgate, Wesley, 334n
'Milky White', see Emerson, Ernest Sando
Mill, The (Jeannie Lockett), 82
Miller, E. Morris, 285, 331, 392
Miller, R. (Paraguay), 8, 392
Mills, Veronica, 81, 84, 87
Mimshi Maiden, The (Hugh McCrae), 149n
'Miss Mary Ann Bell' (R. D. FitzGerald), 145, 148
Missingham, Hal, 361, 392
'Mission Station, North Queensland' *(David Martin)*, 313
Mitchell, A. G., 311n
Mitchell, Elyne, 344, 392
Mitchell Library, Sydney, 3n, 49, 55, 73n, 134, 169, 182, 194, 196, 199, 223, 236, 240-1, 252, 264, 283, 296, 303, 313n, 315, 325, 354, 370, 374, 382
Moby Dick (Herman Melville), 305
Mockbell's Cafe, Sydney, 48n-9
Modern Australian Aboriginal Art (Rex Battarbee), 263n, 271n
Modern Australian Literature, 1900-23 (Nettie Palmer), 59n, 65, 394
Moir, J. K., 147, 260, 278-9, 285-6, 305-7, 365, 376, 389, 392
Moles Do So Little With Their Privacy (Mary Fullerton, 'E'), 185n, 383
Molesworth, J. (Paraguay), 158
Molesworth, Voltaire (Paraguay), 158
Monbulk, Victoria, 70
Mons, Belgium, 173
Montevideo, Uruguay, 3, 162, 328
Monthly Packet (Charlotte Yonge, ed.), 402
Moods of Ginger Mick, The (C. J. Dennis), 380
Moonlight Acre (R. D. FitzGerald), 145n, 382
Moore, Pacita Inglis (Mrs Alexander), 208-9, 244, 274, 329, 392
Moore, Peace Inglis, 208-9, 244, 274, 286, 329, 392
Moore, T. Inglis, 112, 137, 139, 149, 151, 185, 208-9, 217, 227-8, 231-4, 239-40, 242-3, 245-6, 249-51, 257, 266-7, 269, 274-5, 286, 304, 308-9, 316, 326-7, 331, 348, 357, 363, 392-3, 395, 398
Moore, William, 65, 393, 402
Moorhouse, Frank, 347n
More Recollections (Mary Gilmore), 109n-11n, 118n-21, 206, 214, 230, 247n, 322, 324, 357, 393
'More Versatile Neilson: The Manuscript Evidence, A' (H. J. Oliver), 199n
Morn of Youth (Robert Close), 378
Morrison, John, 393
Morrison, R. A., 201

Morton, Frank, 91, 148, 245, 317, 393
Moscow, 341, 343, 345-6, 358-9, 364, 368
'Moss', 37n
Mountains of the Moon (G. M. Turnbull), 112n, 400
Mount Gambier, South Australia, 193, 330n
Moving Image, The (Judith Wright), 402
Mudgee, N.S.W., 336
Mudgee Mail, 219
Murchison, Canon L., 106-7, 393
Murdoch, Sir Walter, 196, 269, 297n, 393
Murdoch's, Sydney, 176
Murray, Gilbert, 257, 393
Murray-Smith, Stephen, 311, 314, 318, 325, 341, 352, 357
Murrumbidgee River, N.S.W., 240, 327, 342n
Musgrove, S., 225n
Mutch, T. D., 66, 183, 393
My Brilliant Career (Miles Franklin), 383
My Career Goes Bung (Miles Franklin), 383
'My Country' (Dorothea Mackellar), 391
My Father and My Father's Friends (Hugh McCrae), 118n, 235n
My Love Must Wait (Ernestine Hill), 174n, 386
Mystery Gold (Bartlett Adamson), 373
'Myth of Irringa the Devil-Dog, The' (Roland Robinson), 320n

Naked and the Dead, The (Norman Mailer), 245n
Naked Under Capricorn (Olaf Ruhen), 343, 397
Namatjira, Albert, 257, 271, 320n, 322, 368, 374, 393
Narrative of the Death of Lord Nelson (Sir William Beatty), 374
National Library of Australia, Canberra, 49, 110n, 200, 239, 302-3, 402
Nature in Australia (K. C. McKeown), 241, 391
Ned Kelly (Douglas Stewart), 399
Neilson, John Shaw, 54n-5, 65, 72, 90-1, 105, 111, 135, 138, 142, 149, 171-2, 185, 195, 199, 252, 290, 296, 380, 393-4, 399
Nelson, Lord, 284, 374
'Neptune's Horses' (W. Hart-Smith), 224n
Neutral Bay, Sydney, 16, 66, 255, 324, 367
New Australia, Paraguay, 3n-4n, 17, 49, 55-7, 73, 77, 153-63, 170, 232, 304, 330, 353, 383, 385, 388, 393, 398, 402
New Australia (journal), 49, 153, 183, 393, 402
New Australia constitution, 155
New Guinea, 112, 223, 338

New Idea, 120
New Perspectives on Brennan's Poetry (G. A. Wilkes), 376
New Pocket Library, 193
New Poems (A. D. Hope), 386
New World, New Song (David Martin, ed.), 314n
New Zealand Battle Cry, 173
Newcastle, N.S.W., 49, 341
Newman, Dr Frank, 54-5
Newtown, Sydney, 355
Ng Cobbera, 365
Niagara, S.S., 400
Niall, Brenda, 376
Nice Day for a Murder and Other Stories (Bartlett Adamson), 373
Nightingale, Florence, 313
Niland, D'Arcy, 395
Nineteenth Century, 389
Nixon-Smith, Sarah, 102, 104, 107-8, 112, 187, 308, 355, 393
'No Foe Shall Gather Our Harvest' (Mary Gilmore), 176-7, 192
No Roads Go By (Myrtle White), 402
Norman Lindsay: The Embattled Olympian (John Hetherington), 386, 389
North Sydney Coffee Palace, 376
Northcott, Sir John, 266-7, 337, 394
N.S.W. Art Gallery, see Art Gallery of N.S.W.
N.S.W. Presbyterian, 288
Numberless Sands, The (Reba Ginsburg), 384

O.B.E. (Officer of the Order of the British Empire), 282, 374
Oblation (A. G. Stephens), 399
O'Dowd, Bernard, 42n-3, 46n, 54, 59, 149, 246, 266, 268, 293, 297n-8, 306, 347, 359, 394, 396, 399
Official History of Australia in the War of 1914-1918 (C. E. W. Bean), 374
Of Places and Poetry (R. D. FitzGerald), 323n
Of Salt and Earth (Robert Close), 378
Ogilvie, Edward D. S., 236n-8
Ogilvie, W. H., 266, 394
'O Heart of Spring' (Shaw Neilson), 111
O'Harris, Pixie, 129n
old age pensions, 222
Old Books, Old Friends, Old Sydney (J. R. Tyrrell), 281, 401
Old Convict Days in Australia (Charles White), 402
Old Days: Old Ways A Book of Recollections (Mary Gilmore), 86n, 101n-4n, 109n, 111, 140, 206, 230, 247n, 322, 324, 357, 366, 394

'Old Forthright' (Mary Gilmore), 215-17, 298
Old Haggis, The (Dame Enid Lyons), 390
O'Leary, P. I., 72, 168, 394
Oliphant, Sir Mark, 332, 394
Oliver, H. J., 199n, 347n, 399
Olley, Margaret, 236, 394
O'Malley, King, 334n, 377
'On Australian Literature, 1788-1938' (C. Hartley Grattan), 149n
On Native Grounds (C. B. Christesen), 378
'On One-Tree Hill' (Mary Gilmore), 289
On Our Selection ('Steele Rudd'), 379
On Second Thoughts: Australian Essays (J. M. D. Pringle), 396
On the Level (W. Hart-Smith), 264, 385
On the Wool Track (C. E. W. Bean), 374
One Hundred Poems (K. Slessor), 201n
Opinion, 397
Ordeal (Dale Collins), 378
Ordeal of Richard Feverel, The (George Meredith), 26n
Ordell, Tal, 140, 394
O'Reilly, Dowell, 47-8, 50-1, 166, 394
'Orientation' (Mary Gilmore), 40
'Osborn, Francis', see Lofting, Hilary
'Our Fleece Unbound' (Mary Gilmore), 315n-16
'Our Once Green Tree' (Nettie Palmer), 70n
'Our Poets' (David Martin), 314n
'Out Where the Dead Men Lie' (Barcroft Boake), 369
Outline of Australian Literature, An (H. M. Green), 81n-2n, 384
Outlook, 374
Overland, 311, 325, 393
Overland Muster, An (Stephen Murray-Smith, ed.), 393
'Owen Spring Station', Central Australia, 387
Owen Stanley Mountains, New Guinea, 223n

Pacific Sea (Nan McDonald), 217n, 227n, 390
Packham, P., 216
Paddington, Sydney, 52
Palmer, Aileen, 64n, 66, 72, 134, 146, 394
Palmer, Edward Vivian ('Vance'), 58-62, 64-6, 70, 72, 76, 80-1, 83, 86-7, 90, 134, 145-6, 318n, 346, 381, 394-5
   Works:
      Cronulla: A Story of Station Life, 62; *Enchanted Island, The*, 90; 'Father and Son', 61; 'Hermit, The', 58-9; *Legend for Sanderson*, 134; *Men are Human*, 83, 87; *Passage, The*, 80; 'Under Which

King?', 61; *World of Men, The*, 58, 61
Palmer, Helen, 64n, 72, 146, 373-4, 394
Palmer, Nettie, 42n, 58, 59-66, 70-2, 76, 80-1, 83, 86-7, 90-1, 93-5, 97, 144-6n, 183, 297n, 346, 358, 384, 386, 394-5
Works:
'Essay on Literature', 59, 61, 65; *Modern Australian Literature, 1900-23*, 59, 65; 'Our Once Green Tree', 70; *Talking It Over*, 97
Palmer River, Queensland, 224
Pankhurst, Adela, 367
Paradise Plumes (G. M. Turnbull), 400
Paraguay, 3n, 19, 49, 55, 63, 77, 88, 122, 130, 153-4, 157-8, 160-3, 216, 232, 241, 274, 292, 304, 328, 353-4, 379, 386, 393, 395, 397-9
Parker, Sir Gilbert, 240, 395
Parkes, Sir Henry, 70, 91, 93, 306, 361, 395
Park, Ruth, 221, 229, 258, 284, 395
Parramatta, N.S.W., 133, 242, 387
Parramatta River, N.S.W., 315n, 317
Passage, The (Vance Palmer), 80n
Passionate Heart, The (Mary Gilmore), 233, 255n, 395
Patagonia, 4n, 8n, 19-20, 22, 141, 274, 353
Paterson, A. B. ('Banjo'), 151, 395
Pea Pickers, The (Eve Langley), 179, 388, 400
Pearl Harbour, 379
Peculiar People; the Australians in Paraguay, A (Gavin Souter), 3n-4n, 9n, 77n, 156n, 328n, 379, 385, 388, 393, 397
Peg Woffington (Charles Reade), 31
Pellegrini's, Sydney, 280
Penetralia (Sydney Jephcott), 387
Penguin Australian Song Book, The (John Manifold, ed.), 391
Penguin Book of Australian Verse, The (R. G. Howarth, K. Slessor & J. Thompson, eds), 400
Pennant Hills, Sydney, 133n
Penny Post, 59
Penrith, N.S.W., 187
Penton, Brian, 105, 395
People (Sydney), 292n
Perth, Western Australia, 95-6, 221, 284, 310
Pescott, E. E., 147, 395
Peters, Captain C. H., 94-5, 117, 147, 149, 166, 175, 184, 395
Petrie, Larry (Paraguay), 17, 19, 157, 216, 395
'Philemon' (D. G. Campbell), 268
Philippine Islands, 112
Phillips, A. A., 388
'Phoenix' (Reba Ginsburg), 267

'Picture Page' (A.B.C. T.V. programme), 333n
Pilate Answered (Michael Sawtell), 397
Pilgrim's Progress, The (John Bunyan), 72n-3
Pindar, J. (Paraguay), 11n, 18, 395
Pioneer Players, 381
Pioneers on Parade (Dymphna Cusack & Miles Franklin), 165, 379
Pitt, Marie E. J., 395
Pitt Head Poems (F. C. Boden), 116n
Pitt Street, Sydney, 48n, 263n
Pix (Sydney), 292n
Plate River, South America, 157, 162
plover, 275n-6
Poe, E. A., 74
Poems (Hubert Church), 378
Poems (Hugh McCrae), 390
Poems (Marie Pitt), 396
Poems (Roderic Quinn), 396
Poems (Clive Turnbull), 400
Poems of David Martin, 297n, 313n, 391
Poems of Life and Time (George Frazer, 353n, 383
Poet at the Breakfast Table, The (O. W. Holmes), 386
'Poetry: And An Australian Poet' (Mary Gilmore), 139n
Poetry 1940-42 (Nora Kelly), 387
Poetry of Australia, The (Imogen Whyse & Wesley Milgate, eds), 334n
Poetry Society of Australia, 334n
Poets' Corner, Botanical Gardens, Sydney, 189-90
Poets' Corner, Westminster Abbey, 398
Poets of Australia (George Mackaness, ed.), 390
Poor Man's Orange (Ruth Park), 395
Pope, Charles (Paraguay), 159
poplar tree, 102n, 104, 107-8, 113, 132-3, 187, 308, 355
Port Moresby, New Guinea, 223n
Portrait of a Savage (G. M. Turnbull), 400
Portus, George, 114n
'Postman, The' (*Bookfellow*), 33n
Power Without Glory (Frank Hardy), 309, 385
Precious Bane (Mary Webb), 401
Prichard, Katharine Susannah, 64n, 76, 83, 96, 110, 146, 168, 180, 284, 310-11n, 318, 343, 359, 368, 396
Pringle, J. M. D., 330, 335, 396
Prior, H. Kenneth, 265, 396
Prior, S. H., 68, 127n, 396, 400
Prisoner of the 'Kormoran' (J. R. W. Taylor), 400
Professor at the Breakfast Table, The (O. W. Holmes), 386

'Profile' (Colin Roderick), *see* 'Dame Mary Gilmore—Australia's Grand Old Lady of Letters'
Progress and Poverty (Henry George), 383
'Prolegomena for a Study of C. J. Brennan' (A. R. Chisholm), 139n
Prose and Verse (Dowell O'Reilly), 394
'Proud Men' (Mary Gilmore), 103
Pugh, Mary Ann, 143n
Punta Arenas, 21

quail poem (untitled—Mary Gilmore), 181
'Quality Street' (A.B.C. radio programme), 297n-8
Queanbeyan, N.S.W., 337-8, 378
Queensland Digger, 190
Queenslander (Brisbane), 184, 383
'Quest of Judith Wright, The' (T. Inglis Moore), 348n
Quick, Florence Mary, 285, 396
Quinn, Marjorie, 80, 114n
Quinn, Roderic, 35, 85-6, 114, 138, 141, 195, 379, 394, 396, 399

'Race Book Seller and the Self-Killed Girl, The' (James Baxter), 332n
Rae, Arthur (Paraguay), 153
Rae, Dick & Eleanor (Paraguay), 396
Rae, Haidee (Paraguay), 7, 396
Raeburn, Sir Henry, 34, 361, 396
Raleigh, Sir Walter, 120
Ralph the Rover, 355
Ralston, Mary, 355
Randolph, Lyall, 342, 396
Rawling, J. H., 221n
Rawlings, Marjorie K., 195
Ray, Charles (Paraguay), 7
Reade, Charles, 31n
Realist Writer, 393
'Red Koran, The' (Mena Abdulllah), 324
Red Pagan, The (A. G. Stephens), 399
Red Page, the (*Bulletin*), 24n, 30n, 33, 40, 82n, 130, 224, 227, 373, 375, 399
Rees, Leslie, 381
Reibey, Mary, 102, 107-8, 133, 308, 317n, 355, 387, 396
Reibey, Thomas, 396
Reibey Cottage, Sydney, 317n, 387, 396
Reibey House, Sydney, 355
Reid, Sir George, 177, 396
'Remembering the Birds' (Norma L. Davis), 202
'Rewi Alley: Interpreter of New China' (Helen Palmer), 373
Rhymes by Ruth (Ruth Bedford), 374
Richardson, Henry Handel, 107
Richmond, Queensland, 47

Ridley, Captain, 221
'Ringbarked' (Kathleen Dalziel), 222
'Ringer, The' (Mary Gilmore), 280
Rio Gallegos, Patagonia, 8n, 20-1
Ritchie, A. A., 90, 103-4, 396
Ritual Dance and Other Verses (Donovan Clarke), 378
Riverina, 225, 240, 254
'Road to Appin, The' (Mary Gilmore), 40
'Roads of Remembrance' (Mary Gilmore), 98
'Roadside: Eleven Compositions' (R. D. FitzGerald), 316n
Roaming Round Australia (Frank Clune), 378
Robbery Under Arms ('Rolf Boldrewood'), 58
Robertson, Constance (née Stephens), 50n-2, 78, 117, 177, 192, 199, 206, 235-6, 248, 288, 292, 335, 367-8, 396
Robertson, George, 42n, 53n, 57n, 79, 88-93, 100, 103, 127, 166, 229-31, 262-5, 281, 323, 337, 382, 385, 397
Robertson, Mrs George, 231
Robertson & Mullens Ltd., 95n, 147, 149n, 175, 380, 395
Robinson, Barbara, 195
Robinson, Roland, 191, 194, 252-4, 319-20n, 322, 330-1, 397
Robinson Crusoe (D. Defoe), 73
Roderick, Colin, 3n, 247-8, 258n, 323, 326, 350-2, 388, 397
Rosa, S.A., 114n-15, 397
Rose of Forgiveness, The (Mabel Forrest), 383
'Rose of Tralee, The', 228, 233
Roseworthy Agricultural College, South Australia, 158
Ross, D. M., 34n
Rossetti, Dante Gabriel, 266n
'Roslyn' (Cameron property), N.S.W., 187, 308, 355
Round the Compass in Australia (Sir Gilbert Parker), 395
Round Dozen, The (David McNicoll), 391
Royal Australian Historical Society, 196, 252, 379, 390, 393
Royal Tar, 3n, 77n, 156-7, 162, 170, 328, 392, 397, 399
'Rudd, Steele' (Arthur Hoey Davis), 31, 114n, 318, 379, 385
Rue Tree, The (Mary Gilmore), 85, 117, 350, 359, 397
Ruhen, Olaf, 343, 397
Rule, Edgar John, 100n, 397
Rum Rebellion (H. V. Evatt), 381
'Rus', 37n

'Ruzilla, The' (Mena Abdullah & Ray Mathew), 324
Ryder, Joan, 87

St Helena, Queensland, 356, 385
St James Hotel, Sydney, 68
St Malo, Sydney, 317n, 387
St Patrick's Day, 229
St Stephen's, Macquarie Street, Sydney, 38n, 391
St Vincent's Hospital, Sydney, 346, 367
Salonika, Greece, 53
Salzburg Tales, The (Christina Stead), 125, 398
San Martin, Juan Zorrilla de, 246n
Santa Cruz, South America, 8
Sapucay, Paraguay, 19
Saturday Mornings (Sir Walter Murdoch), 393
Satyrs and Sunlight (Hugh McCrae), 105, 390
Saunders, Eric, 110
Saunders, William (Paraguay), 155, 158, 161
Sawtell, Michael, 219-20, 397
Schlunke, Eric Otto, 237, 266n, 397
Schlunke, Olga, 237, 261, 265-6n, 397
Schreiner, Olive, 285, 397
Scone, N.S.W., 285
Scots College, Sydney, 247, 274, 360
Scott, Rose, 77, 296, 397
Scott, Sir Walter, 353
Seamen's Union of Australia, 327-8
Season of Youth (Judah Waten), 401
Secrets of the South, The (Sydney Jephcott), 387
Selected Poems (Nan McDonald), 390
Selected Poems (Rex Ingamells), 387
Selected Poems (Stephen Spender), 398
Selected Poems (Yvonne Webb), 174n, 402
Selected Verse (John Manifold), 391
Selected Verse (Mary Gilmore), 171n, 221n, 228n-30, 232n-4, 239n, 242, 246, 398
Semmler, Clement, 395
'September in Australia' (Henry Kendall), 387
Serle, Percival, 54, 65, 69, 87, 111, 117-18, 384, 398
Sesame (John Thompson), 400
Seven Little Australians (Ethel Turner), 400
Seven Little Billabongs (Brenda Niall), 376
Seven Poor Men of Sydney (Christina Stead), 126, 398
S. H. Prior Memorial Prize, 400
Shadowy Paths (Nettie Palmer), 394
Shakespeare, William, 20, 150-1, 195, 263
'Shakespeare' (Mary Gilmore), 171
Shane Park, N.S.W., 284

Shanty Entertainment, A (E. S. Emerson), 381
Shaw Neilson: A Memorial (J. K. Moir), 392
'She dwelt Serene' (Mary Gilmore), 90
shearers' strike, 1891, 160, 356, 373, 385, 401
sheep dog (tribute to), 211n
Shelley, P. B., 74
Shepparton, Victoria, 395
Short Stories of Australia: the Moderns (Beatrice Davis, ed.), 373
Shropshire Lad (A. E. Housman), 386
Sibbald, John (Paraguay), 158
'Sick Stockrider, The' (A. L. Gordon), 384
'Silhouette in Richmond Park' (Mary Fullerton, 'E'), 185-6n
Silver Age (Broken Hill), 183, 185
Silver Branch, The (Dulcie Deamer), 380
Silverton, N.S.W., 16, 183, 255n
Sime, J. (Paraguay), 88, 158
Simon, Louis (Paraguay), 157, 162
Simpson, Colin, 188, 223-4, 338, 398
Sims, Joseph (Paraguay), 395
Singapore (fall of), 178n, 223n, 375
'Singapore' (Mary Gilmore), 177-8n, 184-5
Singing Gold, The (Dorothy Cottrell), 71n, 75, 276, 379
Sirius Books, 324, 366n
Sisters of Mercy, Goulburn, N.S.W., 359, 397
Six Australian Poets (T. Inglis Moore), 392
'Six From Borneo' (Colin Simpson), 223n-4
Sladen, Douglas, 33, 398
Slessor, Kenneth, 197, 201-2, 309, 398
Slessor, Noela, 197, 202
Smart, Christopher, 118, 398
Smith, Eleanor, 207, 359, 398
Smith, Joshua, 213, 230, 235-6, 319, 364, 380-1, 398
Smith, Vivian, 394-5
Smith's Weekly, 85, 143, 158, 373, 382, 390
smoke signals (Aboriginal), 220
'Smoker Parrot, The' (Shaw Neilson), 111
Snowy Mountains, 336, 377-8
So We Take Comfort (Dame Enid Lyons), 390
Social Patterns in Australian Literature (T. Inglis Moore), 392
socialism, 49, 56, 60
Sofonov, M., 330
soldier settlement scheme, 188-90
'Some Brereton Marginalia' (S. Musgrove), 225n
Some Early Australian Bookmen (George Ferguson), 382

Song of the Snowy River and Other Poems (D. G. Campbell), 377
Song to David and Other Poems, A (Percival Serle, ed.), 118n, 398
Song Unending and Other Poems (D. G. Campbell), 222n
Songs of a Campaign (Leon Gellert), 383
Songs of a Sentimental Bloke, The (C. J. Dennis), 279, 380
Songs of the Army of the Night (A. H. Adams), 373
Souter, Gavin, 3n-4n, 9n, 77n, 156n, 328n, 379, 385, 388, 393, 397
South Africa, 53, 375, 386
South Australian Institute Journal, 395
South of the Equator (Ray Mathew), 392
South West Pacific since 1900, The (C. Hartley Grattan), 384
South West Pacific to 1900, The (C. Hartley Grattan), 384
South Wind, The (Nettie Palmer), 394
Southerly, 168-9, 172, 180, 199n, 200-1, 212, 215, 224-5, 233n, 242n-5n, 250, 253-4, 286, 331, 345, 347, 376, 386, 391, 397
Southern Cross, the, 343
Southern Cross and Other Plays, The (Louis Esson), 381
Spanish Civil War, 123, 125, 144-5
Speaking Personally (Sir Walter Murdoch), 393
Spell of the Bush, The (John Cameron), 64, 96, 377
Spence, W. G., 160, 275, 398
Spender, Stephen, 321, 398
'Spider, The' (David McCord), 224
Spiegel the Cat (David Martin), 294n
Springbank Station, Queensland, 47, 117, 121
sputnik, 346
Standard Weekly (Sydney), 190
Stanmore, Sydney, 16, 66n
Stead, Christina, 125, 138, 305, 398
Stead's Review, 99n
Steele Rudd's Magazine, 34n
Stephens, A. G., 17, 24n-7, 29-30, 32-3, 36-8, 40-1n, 43, 45n-6, 50n-2n, 63, 111, 142, 171-2, 174, 185, 199, 224, 229, 244n-5, 248, 265, 271, 284, 288, 296, 306, 353, 362, 374-5, 382, 393, 396, 398-9
Stephens, Cynthia, 288, 292
Stephens, J. G., 52n
Stephensen, P. R., 271, 307, 399
Stevens, Bertram, 50, 138, 171, 399
Stevenson, David & Clara (Paraguay), 8, 77, 153, 158, 399
Stevenson, R. L., 26, 52, 77, 386

Stewart, Douglas, 197, 202n, 223, 227, 262, 264, 267n, 275, 277, 281n, 288-90, 335, 398-9
Stivens, Dal, 347n
Stone, Julius, 269, 399
Stone, Louis, 53, 399
Stone, Walter, 305-6, 399
Stone Walls (Mary Quick), 285, 396
Stonehaven, Lady, *see* Falconer, Ethel Keith
Stones of Bombay, The (David Martin), 295, 297, 391
Stories of the Riverina (Eric Otto Schlunke), 397
Story Book Only (Hugh McCrae), 235, 246-7
Story of Australian Art, The (William Moore), 393
Story of Balladeadro, The (G. G. McCrae), 316, 390
Strack, Mrs J. Kingsley-, 253-4
Strand Magazine, 36n
Strathdownie, Victoria, 12n-13n, 24-5, 27, 29, 32
Street, Lady Jessie Mary, 188, 190, 238, 399
Stuart, Donald, 356, 399
Stuart, John Campbell, 77n, 328
Stuart, Julian, 356, 385
Sturt, Charles, 183
Suez Canal, 23, 53
Sun (Sydney), 49, 111n, 165, 218n, 231-2, 248, 269, 292, 396
Sun Orchids (Douglas Stewart), 277
'Sun Spots and Cycles' (Inigo Jones), 257
Sunday Sun (Sydney), 195, 292n, 302, 374, 396
Sunday Telegraph (Sydney), 374
Sunday Times (Sydney), 53, 57, 183
Sun-Herald (Sydney), 312
'Surrender of Granada' (W. Hart-Smith), 224n
'Swag' (*Overland*), 325
'Swan-Men, The' (Roland Robinson), 330
swans, *see also Wild Swan, The*, 123, 342n-3
'Sweethearts' (Mary Gilmore), 184
Swinburne, A. C., 151, 331, 400
Sydney, 12n, 45, 54, 65, 73, 144, 153, 188, 219, 223, 251, 260, 266, 284, 340, 369, 382, 388, 392-3, 395
Sydney at Sunset and Other Verses (Ruth Bedford), 374
Sydney Harbour, 60, 71, 157, 376, 388
Sydney Mail, 71, 76, 381, 400
Sydney Morning Herald, 63, 65, 70n, 85n, 87, 99, 112, 124, 141n, 150n, 173n, 180-1, 184-5, 190, 192-3, 200n, 209, 219-21, 226n, 235n, 240, 247n, 252, 267,

292, 301-2, 313, 315-16, 330, 335, 368n, 379, 383, 386, 389, 396, 400
Sydney Opera House, 382
Sydney or the Bush (H. Drake-Brockman), 381
Sydney Teachers' College, 196
Sydney Theatre Magazine (Lala Fisher, ed.), 382
'Symphony' (D. G. Campbell), 235n
syringa, 273n

Tabare, An Indian Legend of Uruguay (J. Z. de San Martin), 246
Taboo (W. E. Harney), 191, 385
Tabulam, N.S.W., 236n
Tahiti, 375
Tale of Tiddley Winks, The (Mary Gilmore), 400
Talking Clothes, The (W. Hart-Smith), 385
Talking It Over (Nettie Palmer), 97n, 394
Tasmania, 373
Taylor, H. S. (Paraguay), 88, 158
Taylor, J. R. W., 181, 400
Taylor Square, Sydney, 249
'T.B.' (Mary Gilmore), 91
Tears and Triumph (Dowell O'Reilly), 394
Tea With The Devil (H. E. Boote), 375
Telegraph (Brisbane), 336, 347, 390
Tell The People (J. K. Ewers), 381
Temby, H. S., 236, 289, 302, 400
Temora Independent, 184
Ten Creeks Run ('Brent of Bin Bin'), 376, 383
Tennant, Kylie, 258, 400
Tennyson, Alfred, 73, 196-7
Territory, The (Ernestine Hill), 272
Thackeray, W. M., 249n
Thamyris, 43n
Thiele, Colin, 347n
Think of Stephen (Ruth Bedford), 374
Think—Or Be Damned (Brian Penton), 395
Thirty Poems (John Thompson), 400
Thirty Years in Australia (Ada Cambridge), 377
This Night's Orbit (R. D. FitzGerald), 226n, 398n-300, 303, 382
'This Understanding' (R. D. FitzGerald), 248
Thomas, Daniel, 363, 400
Thomas, William Kyffin, 158
Thompson, Francis, 50, 214, 331, 400
Thompson, John, 297, 347n, 400
Thomson, Miss C. Hay, 36
Thorndike, Dame Sybil, 369, 400
Those Golden Years (Dorothy Catts), 317n
Three Australian Three-Act Plays (Dymphna Cusack), 379
Three Dawns Ago (John Thompson), 400

Three Goats on a Bender (Winifred Birkett), 165, 375
Three Poems (Winifred Hamilton), 385
Three Radicals (W. H. Wilde), 42n-3n, 99n, 233n, 268n, 350n, 359n, 374, 380, 383, 394, 402
'Thunderbolt' (Frederick Ward), 329, 401
Thursday Island, 364
Thynne, Matthew, 175
Tiburon (Kylie Tennant), 400
Tiger Bay (David Martin), 391
Tilted Cart, The (Mary Gilmore), 63-4, 87, 94, 148, 400
Time of Conflict (Judah Waten), 401
Time of the Peacock, The (Mena Abdullah & Ray Mathew), 373, 392
'Time The Eternal Now' (Mary Gilmore), 325
Timor, 375
Titillah, Billy (Paraguay), 6
'To A Miniature' (May Brahe), 376
'To Hugh McCrae' (Mary Gilmore), 198
'Tollgate Islands, The' (Nan McDonald), 227
Tolpuddle Martyrs, 302, 389
'To Mary Gilmore' (Hugh McCrae), 123n, 244n, 283n
Toowoomba, Queensland, 347
Torrnunga, *see* Namatjira, Albert
Town and Country Journal, 183
'Town Under the Sea, The' (James Baxter), 332n
Townsville, Queensland, 221
Tracks We Travel, The (Jack Beazley, ed.), 366n
Trade Union Movement (Australia), 154, 222
'Trap Dams, The' (Mary Gilmore), 120
Tregear, Edward, 43, 400
Triad, 65, 393, 401
Tribune (Sydney), 275, 280, 288, 291, 313n-14, 325-6, 335, 346, 353, 393
'Trouble Belongit Mine' (Henry Lawson), 219, 352
True Patriots All (G. C. Ingleton), 280n, 387
Truth (Sydney), 170, 325, 381, 397
Turnbull, Clive, 252, 400
Turnbull, G. M., 112, 400
Turner, Ethel, 218, 321, 344, 400
Turner, Ian, 326, 336, 340, 400
'Twa Heads' (Hugh McCrae), 244, 308
Twelve Sonnets (Bartlett Adamson), 373
20 Australian Novelists (Colin Roderick), 258n
Twenty-six (J. A. R. McKellar), 391
Twenty-three (John Morrison), 393
2CH, Sydney, 177
2FC, Sydney, 200, 209

2KY, 109
Tyrrell, J. R., 281, 285, 401
Tyson, James, 323, 401

Uncivilized (Charles Chauvel), 127
Uncle Remus, 320n
'Under Which King?' (Vance Palmer), 61
Under the Wilgas (Mary Gilmore), 86n, 88n-90n, 92n, 94-5, 171n, 298n, 389, 401
University of Adelaide, 374
University of London, 398
University of Melbourne, 398
University of Sydney, 374, 376, 378, 381, 384, 398-9
University of Tasmania, 392
University Studies in English, 401
Unpublished Poems (Shaw Neilson), 380
Unspoken Thoughts (Ada Cambridge), 296n, 377
Up the Country ('Brent of Bin Bin'), 376, 383
Uralla, N.S.W., 401
U.S.A. (United States of America), 257, 261
'Us Fellers' (J. C. Bancks), 374

Van Doren, Mark, 224
Vanity Under the Sun (Dale Collins), 378
Vatican, the, 125
Victoria, 49, 176, 193, 244, 292
Victoria, Queen, 124-5, 342
Victorian Education Gazette, 183
Vietnam, 344, 383
Viking of Van Diemen's Land, The (Frank Clune & P. R. Stephensen), 307
Village Hamden, The (Eric Otto Schlunke), 397
Villarica *also* Villa Rica (Paraguay), 4n, 8n, 11, 18-19, 157, 354
Villon, François, 200-1, 401
Vincent, Alf, 106, 401
Vinci, Leonardo da, 339
Voice of the Forest (Hugh McCrae), 203n
Vosper, F. C. B., 95, 401
V.R., *see* Villarica

Wagga Wagga, N.S.W., 14-15, 138, 153, 200, 211n, 224-5, 227, 262n, 296, 303, 340-1, 344, 352
'Wagga Wagga' (Colin Simpson), 224n
Wakehurst, Lord, 267, 389, 401
'Walkabout' (A.B.C. radio programme), 224n
Walker, Alfred (Paraguay), 158, 161
'Walking Up Castle Street' (James Baxter), 332n
Wall, Arnold, 267, 401
Walsh, Adela Pankhurst, 401

Walsh, Dr Clement, 367
Wanderers in Australia (Colin Roderick, ed.), 247n-8n
Wandering Islands, The (A. D. Hope), 386
Wannon (Victorian Electorate), 177n
'War in Spain, The' (Sir Lionel Lindsay), 124n
waratah, 68
Ward, E. J., 249, 256, 401
Ward, Frederick, *see* 'Thunderbolt'
Wardens of the Seas (E. J. Brady), 376
Wast, Hugo, *see* Martinez, Zuviria Gustavo
Waten, Judah, 276-7, 280, 401
Water into Gold (Ernestine Hill), 386
Waterhouse, Professor E. G., 361
Watermen (Eric Lambert), 333, 388
Watt, E. A. S., 201n, 401
Watts, Reverend G. Stuart, 77n, 328n
Waverley Cemetery, Sydney, 67
Ways of Many Waters, The (E. J. Brady), 376
Webb, Francis, 347n
Webb, Joan, 83, 174
Webb, Mary, 109, 401
Webb, Yvonne, 83, 174, 402
Wee Waa, N.S.W., 12n
'Weldon, John' in *Earth's Quality*, (Winifred Birkett), 109
Wells of Beersheba, The (F. D. Davison), 129
Wentworth, N.S.W., 240
Wentworth Magazine, 65
'We're the Boomeranglanders' (Mary Gilmore), 173n
West Wind, The (Hubert Church), 378
Western Track and Other Verses, The (A. A. Bayldon), 374
Westminster Review, 389
Westwood, Thomas (Paraguay), 157, 162
What Bird is That? (N. W. Cayley), 377
'What Our Poets are writing About' (N. Bartlett), 254n
When Valmond Came to Pontiac (Sir Gilbert Parker), 240n, 395
'Where Old Friends Meet' (A.B.C. radio programme), 256n
Where the Dead Men Lie and Other Poems (Barcroft Boake), 375
Where the Pelican Builds and Other Poems (Mary Hannay Foott), 383
Where the Wind Goes (James Devaney), 380
White, Charles, 23, 402
White, Fred (Paraguay), 162
White, Myrtle Rose, 265, 292, 366, 402
White, Patrick, 387
White, Sir Harold, 236-8, 302, 402
'White Australia' (racial attitudes), 156

White Thorntree, The (F. D. Davison), 380
White Topee, The (Eve Langley), 388
Whitman, Walt, 291, 300, 402
Who Wrote the Ballads? (John Manifold), 391
Whyse, Imogen, 334
Whyte, William Farmer, 145, 173, 258, 402
Wicked and the Fair, The (H. Drake-Brockman), 381
Wide Brown Land, The (George & Joan Mackaness, eds), 98, 390
'Wife's Protest, A' (Ada Cambridge), 296n
Wilcannia Desert, the, 161
Wilcox, Dora, 63, 393, 402
Wild Colonial Boy, The (Frank Clune), 378
Wild Swan, The (Mary Gilmore), 66n, 72n, 84-5, 89, 94-5, 99n, 117, 171n, 342n, 402
Wilde, W. H., 12n, 42n-3n, 99n, 193n, 233n, 268n, 350n, 357n, 359n, 373-7, 379-80, 382-4, 387, 390, 394-6, 402
Wilkes, G. A., 376
Wilkinson, Kenneth, 237
Williams, Thomas Tudor- (Paraguay), 158
Willis, Henry, 49, 402
Wilmot, Frank ('Furnley Maurice'), 69n, 149n, 384, 398
Winds Are Still, The (John Hetherington), 386
'Windy Hill', Strathdownie, Victoria, 25
Wine and Roses (V. J. Daley), 379
Wisdom of a Vagabond, The (Michael Sawtell), 397
Witch Maid, The (Dorothea Mackellar), 391
With Cypress Pine (Ray Mathew), 393
W. M. Hughes (W. Farmer Whyte), 402
'Wollongong' (station), N.S.W., 37n
Woman, 108, 292n, 322, 324, 397
Woman to Man (Judith Wright), 257
Woman's Page, *see* Women's Page
Women's Budget, 397
Women's Club, the, Sydney, 69
Women's College, the, University of Sydney, 274
women's franchise, 222
Women's Page (*Worker*), 42n-4n, 100, 114, 138, 211, 219, 354, 388
Women's Voice (Laura Bogue Luffman), 389
'Wonder' (R. D. FitzGerald), 298-9

Wonder and the Apple, The (Mary Fullerton, 'E'), 383
Woods, W. A., 3n, 12-13, 24n-6, 30, 42-3, 153, 184, 402
Woollahra, Sydney, 51, 375
Woolloomooloo, Sydney, 169
Worde, Wynken de, 72, 402
'Word-Held' (Mary Gilmore), 259n
Wordsworth, William, 151
Worker (Brisbane), 356
Worker (Sydney), 40, 42n-4n, 56, 60, 63, 65-6, 99, 114, 132, 138, 176, 183-4, 211, 216, 219, 222, 296, 352, 354, 375, 388, 393, 402
Worker Cook Book, The (Mary Gilmore), 85, 322
Working Bullocks (K. S. Prichard), 180, 396
Working Man's Paradise, The (William Lane), 82, 160
World of Men, The (Vance Palmer), 58n, 61
World Peace Prize, 318
Wragge, Clement, 257, 402
Wright, Judith, 243, 257, 259, 268, 273, 291, 310-11n, 348, 402
Writers of the Bulletin (Douglas Stewart), 281n
Writers' Association, N.S.W., 114n
Wuthering Heights (Emily Bronte), 109
Wyndham Diaries, *see Generations of Men, The*
Wynn, Mary (Mrs W. Hart-Smith), 169, 175, 269, 402
Wynne Prize (landscapes), 385
Wynyard Square, Sydney, 280

Yanco, N.S.W., 75
Yandy (Donald Stuart), 356, 399
Yaralie (Donald Stuart), 399
'Yarn of the Nancy Bell, The' (W. S. Gilbert), 27n
Yarns of Billy Borker, The (Frank Hardy), 385
yarran tree, 275n
'Yea and Nay' (Mary Gilmore), 330n
Yearling, The (Marjorie K. Rawlings), 195
Yeats, Jean, 218
Yerong Creek, N.S.W., 352
Yonge, Charlotte, 225, 402
'Yugilbar' (station), N.S.W., 236n-8
Yugilbar Aboriginal tribe, 236n

Zoe (police dog), 211, 213, 229

Tom Inglis Moore (1901–78) graduated from Sydney University and later took out an M.A. from Oxford. After teaching English in the United States for two years he became Associate Professor at the University of the Philippines and stayed from 1927 to 1930. He later became a leader-writer on the *Sydney Morning Herald,* served in the Second A.I.F. in the Artillery and later as Deputy Associate Director, Army Education Service. After the war he became Associate Professor of Australian Literature at the Australian National University. His publications include several books of poetry and numerous critical works on Australian literature.

W. H. Wilde graduated M.A. from Sydney University, and served in the Second A.I.F. in New Guinea, New Britain and the Solomon Islands. He joined the staff of the Royal Military College, Duntroon, in 1964, was appointed a Senior Lecturer in 1965 and Associate Professor in 1977. His publications include works on major figures in the history of Australian literature and he is the authorized biographer of Dame Mary Gilmore.

Wholly printed and bound in Australia

www.ingramcontent.com/pod-product-compliance
Lightning Source LLC
Chambersburg PA
CBHW071939220426
43662CB00009B/918